CHINA'S INTERNATIONAL
INVESTMENT STRATEGY

INTERNATIONAL ECONOMIC LAW

Andrew D Mitchell is Professor at Melbourne Law
School, The University of Melbourne
Tania Voon is Professor at Melbourne Law
School, The University of Melbourne

The *International Economic Law* series, established by the late Professor John H
Jackson, addresses a range of issues in international economic law, which includes
international trade law, international investment law, and the global financial
order. The Series aims to encourage interest in the broad contours of international
economic law, heightening awareness of its significance across the globe as well as
its continuous interactions with other areas. The Series Editors encourage quality
submissions from a wide range of perspectives, including doctrinal, theoretical,
empirical, and interdisciplinary. Novel and cutting-edge research is particularly
welcome, as are contributions from both emerging and established scholars from
around the world.

China's International Investment Strategy

Bilateral, Regional, and Global Law and Policy

Edited by
JULIEN CHAISSE

OXFORD
UNIVERSITY PRESS

Great Clarendon Street, Oxford, OX2 6DP,
United Kingdom

Oxford University Press is a department of the University of Oxford.
It furthers the University's objective of excellence in research, scholarship,
and education by publishing worldwide. Oxford is a registered trade mark of
Oxford University Press in the UK and in certain other countries

First Edition published in 2019

Impression: 1

Published in the United States of America by Oxford University Press
198 Madison Avenue, New York, NY 10016, United States of America

British Library Cataloguing in Publication Data
Data available

Library of Congress Control Number: 2018951931

ISBN 978–0–19–882745–0

Printed and bound by
CPI Group (UK) Ltd, Croydon, CR0 4YY

Series Editor's Preface

Over the last four decades, since 1978 when Deng Xiaoping initiated the 'Open Door' policy that sought to attract foreign investment and drive economic growth, China has become an increasingly important actor in international investment law and policy. China has pursued a gradual and deliberate path towards increasing both inbound and outbound investment, through reforms in domestic investment law, taxation policy, bilateral investment treaties (BITs), bilateral and regional trade agreements, multilateral forums (including the G20 and participation in the International Centre for Settlement of Investment Disputes) and other programs, such as the Belt and Road Initiative (BRI). This comprehensive volume includes consideration of each of these aspects, and in so doing makes an invaluable contribution to our understanding of China's international investment law and strategy across the domestic, bilateral, regional and global levels.

The chapters in this volume offer wide-ranging analysis, spanning topics such as the national security challenges posed by investment from foreign State-Owned Enterprises, the importance of Free Trade Zones in providing a testing ground for market liberalisation reforms, and the BRI, as well as in-depth investigations of particular bilateral, regional and global relationships. The majority of the volume is dedicated to examining China's domestic legal framework for foreign investment and relevant international treaties, but the final section complements this coverage by exploring China's (relative lack of) involvement in investor-State dispute settlement. As editor of this volume, Julien Chaisse has brought together a highly qualified and diverse group of authors including practitioners, promising early-career researchers, and well-established scholars. The authors present a range of perspectives, with many based in China and others from North America, Europe, and across the Asia-Pacific region.

At the time of writing, China has concluded 150 BITs or other treaties including investment provisions (128 of which are in force), making it the most prolific non-European participant in this treaty regime.[1] But as the contents of this edited volume shows, it is not merely the number of agreements that China has concluded that makes its role in international investment law so significant. China is involved in negotiations that are currently taking place for several notable new investment agreements, including bilateral treaties with the European Union and United States, and regional discussions for the *Regional Comprehensive Economic Partnership* (RCEP) among the ten members of the Association of Southeast Asian Nations and their six current partners in preferential trade agreements. In addition, China used its presidency of the G20 in 2016 to encourage movement towards a multilateral framework for international investment, through the conclusion of a non-binding declaration of shared 'Guiding Principles for Global Investment Policymaking'. As the insightful discussion of these and other developments in this volume shows, China is helping to shape the future of international investment law. Consequently, the themes discussed in this book are relevant not only to scholars and practitioners whose work is focussed on China, but also to those across the Asia-Pacific region and the globe.

Andrew D Mitchell
Tania Voon
July 2018

---

[1] See United Nations Committee on Trade and Development (UNCTAD), *International Investment Agreements Navigator*, <http://investmentpolicyhub.unctad.org/IIA>.

Foreword

By Zhao Hong

Investment is an economic activity that involves the input of capital, technology, movable or immovable assets and human resources for obtaining profit or benefit. It is generally regarded by macro-economists as one of the driving forces for economic growth, job creation, and welfare increase in modern times. The impact of investment has become more prominent in the twenty-first century as the global supply chain has dominated the world trade pattern over the last two decades, with the supply chain generating over 70 per cent of total global trade. Besides economic impacts, how to assess social, environmental and even cultural dimensions that investment activities bring about, and make investment contribute to sustainable development, has long been a high-profile issue for governments of hosting countries. As the objective of investment has been more and more multi-faceted, the forms of investment multiply, being more innovative while technology advances with each passing day, investment law has become one of the most challenging areas of domestic regulation as well as international rule making.

During the past several decades, the domestic regulation on investment had undergone a circular trajectory of regulation, deregulation, and reregulation in most sectors, yet the market is waiting for broader space for liberalizing and transparency in fast growing economic sectors. Negotiations in domestic regulation in the Trade in Services Council at the WTO seems to be lagging behind the requirement from private sectors. Similarly, international investment law has demonstrated its own feature of development trajectory since its inception.

International investment law has long been part of the family of international law. It has influenced the formation and development of international law and has become one of the most dynamic and growing parts of it. Historians believe fundamental non-discriminatory rules of international law, such as the national treatment and the most favoured nation treatment, derived from the original idea of equal protection to assets of foreigners by hosting countries.

One of the unique features of international investment law is that the bulk of the body of its rules is composed of nearly 3,000 Bilateral Investment Treaties (BITs) signed between host and home countries or economies and around 340 investment chapters within Free Trade Agreements or Regional Economic Integration Agreements or Treaties, approximately 80 per cent of them are concluded and in force. In general, these BITs are highly identical and fundamentally similar in subject matters and structures, and there is much duplication in main substance, only with differences in specifics and languages thereof. That is why investment law scholars usually describe them as a spaghetti bowl of rules. These bilateral treaty networks not only raise costs for government to negotiate and implement them, but also make investors inconvenient to enforce their rights, and it also leaves loopholes for treaty shopping. It seems that the major multi-lateral treaty in investment area is the Washington Convention of 1965 that established the International Centre of Settlement of Investment Dispute (ICSID) in 1966, which helps resolve disputes between a state and investors of a third state. Therefore, the lack of multi-lateral rules in international investment means an

area that demands unification of rules in order to achieve a level playing field and enhance global governance. Efforts in this regard had been made during the second half
in the 1990s when the OECD sponsored a negotiation for a multi-lateral agreement
on investment (MAI), but it turned out to be futile, as even the major proponents, the
European countries, failed to accept it. When will it be ripe for a multi-lateral investment treaty to come into play and under which international forum? This remains a
question to be answered.

Another element worth mentioning in this area is the overlap of subject matter
under various treaties, such as BITs, investment chapters of FTAs and RTAs, ICSID,
and even relevant covered agreements under the WTO, such as TRIPs, TRIMs, and
GATS. This renders multiple lawsuits and potential multiple remedies possible, which
now looms large as an issue to be concerned with under international investment law.

The BIT which forms the major part of international investment law has followed
a spiral way in its evolution. After the end of the Second World War, investment protection as well as international arbitration as a major means of Investor–State dispute
settlement (ISDS) had since become the essential themes of the BITs during the post-
war economic reconstruction, with transnational investment booming in the post-war
era. Coming into the 1990s, as economic integration and globalization deepened, investment liberalization and market accession under the so-called national treatment
at pre-establishment phase, together with investment protection, had become the
prevailing themes of BITs negotiations, while witnessing more and more BITs adopt
such a provision that used to be regarded as an intrusion into domestic investment
approval system of hosting countries. Yet at the dawn of the twenty-first century, developed countries as hosting State have become more sensitive to the right to regulate
in foreign investment, and raised the concerns of labour, environment, health, cultural,
and other social implications of the foreign investment in their countries. A reflection over ISDS at the international forum caused serious constitutional debates at the
parliament and social media and hence a recoil from its previous positions by these
countries. Some developing countries suffered from similar process with its developed
counterparts and some even withdrew from ICSID or revised its standard BITs. The
recent proposal of 'opt in and opt out' approach over ISDS under chapter 11 by United
States in the renegotiation of NAFTA provides just another such example. Whither
the international investment rules in the future? It is the right moment to have deeper
reflections upon the question.

The year of 2018 marks the fortieth anniversary of the reform and opening-up policy
taken by China since 1978. The past forty years has witnessed a remarkable history for
the Chinese economy to be integrated into the world and has benefited tremendously
from being part of the global supply chain. During the past forty years, China has been
the largest trading Member of the WTO and is also now the largest trading partner
of over 100 countries in the world. The share of China's trade volume in terms of the
world total has increased from 0.8 per cent in 1978 to 11.5 per cent in 2016. China
has also become an important recipient of foreign direct investment (FDI) for many
years and has been the top FDI recipient among all developing countries over the past
twenty-five years. FDI has made great contribution to Chinese economic and social
development. Accounting for 3 per cent of the total enterprises of China, foreign invested companies contributed roughly 10 per cent of urban employment, 20 per cent
of company tax revenue and nearly 50 per cent of total import and export of China.

Now China is not only a FDI recipient as a hosting country but also has become
an important home country of outbound investment. In 2016, China was the second

largest outbound investment supplier among the world and has become a net capital exporting country since then.

China also actively participated in multi-lateral trade system for the negotiations of Doha Round, Trade Facilitation Agreement, the expansion of the scope of Information Technology Agreement at the WTO since its accession. It has also concluded a number of FTAs and RTAs with members of the WTO. China signed over 130 BITs and is a contracting party to the Washington Convention establishing ICSID. China's three foreign investment Laws promulgated in 1979 had marked the starting point of economic legislation and establishment of rule of law for market economy.

To sum up, China's experience as both capital import and export country and its abundance and unique practice in formulating BITs as well as investment chapters in FTA and RTA it entered, provides a good angle for the study of its success in economic development in the past four decades.

The book '*China's International Investment Strategy: Bilateral, Regional, and Global Law and Policy*' edited by Professor Julien Chaisse is a marvellous work for people to understand the law and practice of China's investment regime. An overview of the outline of the book (let alone the content) impresses me deeply that the work covers really comprehensive issues. I am sure readers will benefit greatly from reading the magnum opus.

Professor Zhao Hong
Member
Appellate Body
World Trade Organization
Geneva, Switzerland
25 March 2018

Acknowledgements

This book has benefited immensely from contributions from many sources, both at the institutional as well as at the individual level. I am delighted with the final result and would sincerely like to express my gratitude to all who have contributed to this project in one way or the other. I also want to express my gratitude to the many members of the CUHK Law Faculty who have played an important role in bringing this volume to fruition, namely Professor Christopher Gane (Dean of CUHK Law), Professor Kun Fan, Professor Samuli Seppänen, Professor Lutz-Christian Wolff, Professor Chao Xi, and Professor Yuhong Zhao. Indeed, a special mention must be made of all those who shared their valuable time and their thought-provoking ideas with me on this research: Professor Luke Nottage (Sydney University School of Law), Professor Debashis Chakraborty (Indian Institute of Foreign Trade), Professor Chang-fa Lo (National Taiwan University College of Law), Mr Rahul Donde (Associate, Levy Kaufmann-Kohler), and Professor Jesús Seade (Lingnan University Department of Economics). I have made extensive use of many libraries and the precious suggestions of their staff. Therefore, I wish to sincerely thank and appreciate Mr John Bahrij, Ms Agnes Cheung, and the librarians of the Lee Quo Wei Law Library at CUHK. I am also sincerely thankful to Oxford University Press for processing this work with efficiency for publication.

Contents

Table of Cases

NATIONAL JURISDICTIONS

China

Hong Kong

Singapore

Sweden

United Kingdom

United States

Abbreviations

AALCO	Asia–Africa Legal Consultative Organization
AANZFTA	Association of Southeast Asian Nations–Australia–New Zealand Free Trade Agreement
ACIA	Association of Southeast Asian Nations Comprehensive Investment Agreement
ADR	alternative dispute resolution
AEC	Association of Southeast Asian Nations Economic Community
AIIB	Asian Infrastructure Investment Bank
AIR	ASEAN Investment Regime
APEC	Asia-Pacific Economic Cooperation
APPI	Association of Southeast Asian Nations Agreement for the Promotion and Protection of Investment
ASEAN	Association of Southeast Asian Nations
BEPS	base erosion and profit shifting
BIT	bilateral investment treaty
BOT	build–operate–transfer
BRI	Belt and Road Initiative
CAI	Comprehensive Agreement on Investment
CCG	Centre for China and Globalization
CCPIT	China Council for the Promotion of International Trade
CETA	Comprehensive Economic and Trade Agreement
ChAFTA	China--Australia Free Trade Agreement
CIN	capital import neutrality
CJEU	Court of Justice of the European Union
CPC	Communist Party of China
CSR	corporate social responsibility
DSU	dispute settlement understanding
ECJ	European Court of Justice
EPA	economic partnership agreement
EPC	engineering, procurement, and construction
EU	European Union
FDI	foreign direct investment
FET	fair and equitable treatment
FTA	free trade agreement
FTAAP	Free Trade Area of the Asia-Pacific
FTZ	free trade zone
GATS	General Agreement on Trade in Services
GATT	General Agreement on Tariffs and Trade
GDP	gross domestic product
HKIAC	Hong Kong International Arbitration Centre
ICC	International Chamber of Commerce
ICJ	International Court of Justice
ICSID	International Centre for Settlement of Investment Disputes
IFC	international financial corporation
IFDI	inward foreign direct investment
IIA	international investment agreements
ILO	International Labour Organization
IMF	International Monetary Fund

ISA	Investment state arbitration
ISDS	investor—state dispute settlement
LCIA	London Court of International Arbitration
LOBs	limitation on benefits
LSAs	location specific advantages
MAI	Multilateral Agreement on Investment
MAP	mutual agreement procedure
MFN	most favoured nation
MNE	multi-national enterprises
MOFCOM	Ministry of Commerce
MOTIE	Ministry of Trade, Industry, and Energy
NAFTA	North America Free Trade Agreement
NDRC	National Development and Reform Commission
NGOs	Non-governmental organizations
NPC	National People's Congress
NT	national treatment
OBOR	One Belt One Road
ODI	overseas direct investment
OECD	Organization for Economic Cooperation and Development
OFDI	outward foreign direct investment
OIA	Overseas Investment Act 2005
PPT	principal purpose test
PRC	People's Republic of China
PSC	production sharing contract
PTAs	preferential trade agreements
RCEP	Regional Comprehensive Economic Partnership
RTA	regional trade agreement
SARs	special administrative regions
SAT	State Administration of Taxation
SCC	Stockholm Chamber of Commerce
SMEs	small and medium-sized enterprises
SOEs	state-owned enterprises
TAI	Thai Arbitration Institute
TFEU	Treaty on the Functioning of the European Union
TiSA	trade in services agreement
TPP	Trans-Pacific Partnership
TRIMs	Agreement on Trade-related Investment Measures
TRIPs	Agreement on Trade-related Aspects of Intellectual Property Rights
TTIP	Transatlantic Trade and Investment Partnership
UN	United Nations
UNCITRAL	United Nations Commission on International Trade Law
UNCTAD	United Nations Conference on Trade and Development
VCST	Vienna Convention on State Succession in Treaties
VLCT	Vienna Convention on the Law of Treaties 1969
WTO	World Trade Organization

Biographical Information on Authors
(Alphabetical Order)

Manzoor Ahmad

Dr Manzoor Ahmad is a Senior Fellow at the International Centre for Trade and Sustainable Development (ICTSD) in Geneva. A Pakistani national, he has served in various senior positions for his government and in international organizations. He was the Ambassador and Permanent Representative of Pakistan to the World Trade Organization (WTO) from 2002 to 2008. During that period, he chaired the WTO Council for Trade-related Aspects of Intellectual Property Rights (TRIPs) from 2004 to 2008 and the Balance of Payments Restrictions Committee during 2003–2004. He also served as the Director, Liaison Office, Food and Agriculture Organization to the United Nations from 2008 to 2010. For the last two years, Dr Ahmad has been working as an independent consultant on international trade and food security issues from Geneva and Islamabad. He is also one of the regular panellists on the WTO dispute settlement system. He acts in various leading capacities in a number of global public policy institutions, think-tanks and as an adviser to the government of Pakistan. He has published several papers in international and local journals on issues relating to international trade and is frequently invited to make presentations at international conferences, academic institutes and other influential forums. Dr Ahmad received his BSc (Hons) and MSc from the University of Peshawar and his PhD from the University of Hull, UK.

Adam Bryan

Adam Bryan joined LALIVE in 2017. He specializes in international arbitration, both commercial and investor-State. He is experienced in a wide range of industries, with a particular focus on the energy sector. Adam Bryan has acted in numerous international arbitrations, including under both ad hoc and institutional rules. He is a member of several professional associations including Young International Arbitration Group, Young Arbitrators Forum, Young Arbitration Practitioners Group, and the Young International Council for Commercial Arbitration. He has spoken and published on international arbitration. Adam Bryan trained in London and Paris with Cleary Gottlieb Steen & Hamilton (2008–2010). After qualifying, he practised international arbitration in Cleary Gottlieb's London office (2010–2014). He subsequently worked as an Associate in Three Crowns' Paris office (2014–2016) and as a Senior Associate (Registered Foreign Lawyer) in Allen & Overy's Hong Kong office (2016–2017). Adam Bryan holds a Bachelor of Arts in Jurisprudence (Law with Law Studies in Europe) from the University of Oxford (Merton College) (2003–2007). He also received a diploma from the University of Paris II Panthéon-Assas (2005–2006). In 2013, Adam Bryan became a Solicitor-Advocate (Higher Courts, Civil Proceedings) of the Senior Courts of England & Wales.

Julien Chaisse

Julien Chaisse is Professor at The Chinese University of Hong Kong (CUHK), Faculty of Law. He is an award-winning scholar of international law with a special focus on the regulation and development of economic globalization. His teaching and research include international trade/investment law, international taxation, law of natural resources, and internet law. Prior to joining CUHK in 2009, Dr Chaisse was a senior research fellow at the World Trade Institute (Switzerland). He also held an appointment as lecturer at elite school Sciences Po Aix (France) and served as a diplomat at the Embassy of France in New Delhi (India). Dr Chaisse has published numerous well-regarded and widely cited books and articles, such as *International Investment Treaties and Arbitration Across Asia* (Brill-Nijhoff 2018); *The Regulation of Global Water Services Market* (Cambridge University Press 2017); *International*

Economic Law and Governance (Oxford University Press 2016); 'Navigating the Expanding Universe of International Treaties on Foreign Investment' Journal of International Economic Law (2015); 'Maintaining the WTO's Supremacy in the International Trade Order' Journal of International Economic Law (2013); and 'Promises and Pitfalls of the European Union Policy on Foreign Investment' Journal of International Economic Law (2012). In recognition of his outstanding academic performance, Dr. Chaisse received the University's Research Excellence Award 2012, Vice-Chancellor's Exemplary Teaching Award 2015, and the Vice-Chancellor's Young Researcher Award 2017. Dr Chaisse has held the appointment of Director of the Centre for Financial Regulation and Economic Development at CUHK Law since 2013, and has established forward-looking legal projects and events at CUHK, including the series of 'Asia FDI Forum', which has become the most prominent conference on foreign investment regulation in Asia. In addition to his professorship, Dr Chaisse is a well-experienced arbitrator and a leading consultant to international organizations, governments, multi-national law firms, and private investors. He is also a member of the World Economic Forum's International Trade and Investment Council since 2016.

Manjiao Chi

Manjiao Chi is Professor and Founding Director, Center for International Economic Law and Policy (CIELP), Law School, University of International Business and Economics (UIBE), Beijing, China; and Deputy Secretary-General, Administrative Council, Xiamen Academy of International Law. His research fields cover international trade and investment law and policy, international dispute settlement, natural resource governance and international development and cooperation law. He teaches and publishes extensively in leading journals, such as *Journal of International Economic Law, Journal of World Trade*, and *Journal of World Investment and Trade*, and a recent monograph entitled *Integrating Sustainable Development in International Investment Law* (Routledge, 2017). He frequently presents in major international law conferences, law schools and other occasions. Among his affiliations, he is Executive Council Member, Chinese Society of International Law; Council member, Chinese Society of International Economic Law; Member, American Society of International Law; Headquarter Member, the International Law Association and ILA Committee of Rule of Law and International Investment Law. He also sits on the advisory board of several academic institutions and journals in the field of international law and relations. He has held visiting professorships in major European, North American and Asian universities. Before joining UIBE, he was full professor and deputy director of the International Economic Law Institute, Law School, Xiamen University; Consultant, United Nations Economic and Social Commission for Asia and the Pacific; Senior Fellow, Centre for Global Cooperation Research, Germany; Visiting Fellow, UNIDROIT; Edwards Fellow, Columbia Law School; and Visiting Fellow, Max Planck Institute for Comparative Public Law and International Law, Germany.

Won-Mog Choi

Professor Won-Mog Choi is a professor of international trade law and director of the WTO Law Center, Ewha Womans University School of Law at Seoul. He is also a member of Editorial Board of many journals including the *Journal of International Economic Law* (Oxford), the *Law and Development Review and Indian Journal of International Economic Law*, and a member of the New York Bar. Professor Choi received his legal education in the United States (Georgetown Law, S.J.D. and LL.M.) and Korea (Seoul National University, M.P.A. and LL.B). Prior to joining faculty of Ewha, he worked for the Ministry of Foreign Affairs and Trade of Korea for 11 years as a diplomat and legal officer in charge of numerous trade issues, including WTO dispute settlements, trade remedy issues, and FTAs. Currently advising the Korean Government on trade law and policy issues and working as columnist of major newspapers in Seoul, Professor Choi has actively published books and articles.

Horia Ciurtin

Horia Ciurtin is Research Fellow at the European Federation for Investment Law and Arbitration (Brussels); Senior Expert & Founder of DAVA - Strategic Analysis; Managing Editor of the EFILA blog. Horia Ciurtin holds a Bachelor of Laws (2011), Babes-Bolyai University, Cluj-Napoca, Romania; a Master of Laws in 'European and National Business Law' (2012), Babes-Bolyai University, Cluj-Napoca, Romania, as valedictorian. Horia Ciurtin is the author of the constitutional law and legal philosophy volume *The Dilemmas of Constitutional Review: Inquiry in the Euro-American Paradigms* [original title: *Dilemele controlului de constitutionalitate: Incursiune în paradigmele spatiului euro-american*], Rosetti International, Bucharest, 2013. Horia Ciurtin also is the author of the study 'Anomia and Justice: Paradoxes of Legal Deconstruction' [original title 'Anomie și dreptate—paradoxurile deconstructiei dreptului'] in the collective volume coordinated by Gratian Cormos, *Dilemmatic Restructurings* [*Restructurari dilematice*] (Argonaut Publishing House 2013). In 2014, Horia Ciurtin was awarded with the Honorable Mention in the Nappert Prize in International Arbitration and International Commercial Law (organized by McGill University). Horia Ciurtin is the author of more than twenty articles in the cultural press, as well as of numerous studies in domestic and international academic journals, in the field of international law, constitutional law, and legal philosophy.

Zhen Dai

Zhen Dai is Professor at the China Institute for WTO Studies, University of International Business and Economics, Beijing, China. Zhen Dai current research focuses on the structural issues of global economic governance (trade, investment, and finance), the international legal implications of China's recent emergence as a global superpower and the development of Chinese Law in contemporary China.

Kyle Dylan Dickson-Smith

As an arbitrator practising in Australia and North America, Kyle Dickson-Smith has extensive experience in international commercial disputes and investment treaty arbitrations. Kyle conducts arbitrations under the UNCITRAL, ICDR/AAA, and ICSID arbitration rules, amongst others. He has acted in investor–state proceedings under the NAFTA and bilateral investment treaties (BITs). He is a Fellow of the Chartered Institute of Arbitrators (FCIArb) and a member of the ACICA panel of arbitrators.

Marcia Don Harpaz

Marcia Don Harpaz is an Adjunct Lecturer at the Department of International Relations and Faculty of Law, Hebrew University of Jerusalem, and an international trade consultant, specializing in trade agreements and policy analysis. She served as Director of the International Agreements Division at the Israeli Ministry of Industry and Trade, where she led trade negotiations and coordinated Israel's foreign trade policy on bilateral and multi-lateral issues. Earlier, she was a senior economist-investigator in the Ministries Trade Levies Unit. She has been a Halbert Exchange Fellow at the Munk Centre of Global Affairs, University of Toronto, a Fellow at the Salzburg Seminars, and is currently a Member of Israel Roster of Panelists for Dispute Settlement under the Free Trade Agreement between Israel and Mexico. She attended the University of Illinois in Champaign-Urbana (BA), the Hebrew University (MA), Manhattan College in New York (MBA), and the Hebrew University (PhD). Her current research interests include China and international norms/adjudication, China's foreign trade policy, and Israel's foreign trade relations. Her publications have appeared in *Journal of World Trade, Mediterranean Politics, International Law Forum, Israel Tax Quarterly*, and in various edited volumes.

Michael J Enright

Called 'one of the world's reigning strategy gurus' by the Academy of International Business, Michael Enright is a leading expert on competitiveness, regional economic development, and international business strategy. Enright joined the University of Hong Kong as Professor of Business Administration in 1996 after six years as a professor at the Harvard Business School. He also directs the Asia-Pacific Competitiveness Program at the Hong Kong Institute of Economics and Business Strategy and was a Founding Director and current Advisory Board Member of The Competitiveness Institute (a global professional body with members in forty nations). As a researcher, Professor Enright has directed major reviews of the competitiveness of twenty different economies on five continents and has co-authored eight books or monographs on related topics. Enright's work on competitiveness and on the economies of Hong Kong and China has appeared in the *Harvard Business Review, WorldLink*, the *Far Eastern Economic Review, Asian Business, Asia Inc*, the *South China Morning Post*, and the *Business Times*, among others. It also has been featured in *The Economist*, the *Financial Times*, the *Wall Street Journal*, the *Asian Wall Street Journal*, the *Washington Post, Newsweek, BusinessWeek*, the *Straits Times, Business Times*, and many others. Current research projects include multi-year studies of multi-national strategies in the Asia-Pacific region, China's international competitiveness, and regional development in Greater China. As an adviser, Professor Enright has consulted for companies, governments, and multi-lateral organizations on business strategy, international competitiveness, and economic development and has appeared in more than thirty countries as an invited speaker and executive educator. Professor Enright received his AB (with honours), his MBA (with distinction), and his PhD (in Business Economics, Dean's Doctoral Fellow) from Harvard University. He is a non-executive director of Shui On Construction and Materials, Shui On Land, and Johnson Electric.

Susan Finder

Susan Finder is a Distinguished Scholar in Residence at the School of Transnational Law of Peking University (Shenzhen) and in the fall of 2015 was an Adjunct Professor with the Faculty of Law of the University of Hong Kong and is affiliated with its Centre of Chinese Law. She speaks often on Chinese legal issues (in Hong Kong, mainland China, the United States, and Europe), and works on Chinese law-related consulting projects and arbitrations from time to time. Occasionally, she writes for *The Diplomat*, the *South China Morning Post*, the Global Military Justice Reform blog. She will have several articles published in academic journals, where she is often cited. Her writings have also been published in China, including in several prominent Wechat public accounts. Major media that have sought her comments on Chinese legal developments include: *New York Times, Wall Street Journal, The Economist, Financial Times*, and *Reuters*. Earlier in her career, she taught Chinese law and other subjects in the Law Department of the City University of Hong Kong, where she began focusing her research on the Supreme People's Court, leading her to write the first close analysis of its operations. She then put her knowledge of Chinese law to work in the China practice group of the international law firm Freshfields Bruckhaus Deringer and several other law firms and institutions. She had the good fortune to study with three of the early pioneers of Chinese legal studies (in the United States): Jerome Cohen, R Randle Edwards, and Stanley Lubman and to have many leading practitioners and legal academics among her classmates at Harvard Law School (J.D.) and Columbia Law School (LL.M).

Matthew Hodgson

Matthew specializes in international arbitration and public international law. Since joining Allen & Overy in 2005, he has acted as counsel and advocate in many disputes worldwide including under all major arbitral rules. He was promoted to the global partnership of Allen & Overy in May 2016. He has substantial experience of disputes arising out of major energy, mining, infrastructure and construction projects. He has also acted in disputes relating to joint ventures, distribution agreements, financial instruments, and post M&A matters. Matthew has extensive experience of representing investors and states in investment treaty disputes. Recent matters include: (1) representing Pakistan in parallel ICC and ICSID claims by Tethyan Copper Company in relation to the Reko Diq copper/gold mining project;

(2) representing Deutsche Bank in its successful ICSID claim against Sri Lanka arising out of Central Bank interference with a derivative contract; (3) representing an international bank in an ICC arbitration for breach of representations and warranties in an SPA; (4) representing a Belgian investor in its successful ICSID claim against the Philippines relating to a major dredging project. Recognized as a leading arbitration practitioner by Chambers & Partners and Legal 500 since being identified as a 'rising star' in 2012 (Chambers Global), Chambers 2014 states '[Matthew] continues to be highly regarded for his international arbitration work'. Clients say: 'He is an impressive arbitration lawyer with exceptionally solid insight into arbitrations involving investment treaties'. Legal 500 states 'Matthew Hodgson is outstanding' (2013), 'sets the bar for others' (2015), and is 'perfect for complex arbitrations' (2016). Who's Who—International Arbitration Future Leaders (2017) describes him as a 'talented advocate with a big future ahead'.

Jie (Jeanne) Huang

Dr Jeanne Huang is an associate professor at the University of Sydney Law School. She teaches and researches in the fields of private international law, e-commerce law, international investment law, international litigation and arbitration, and underwater cultural heritage protection. She has published four books and authored more than thirty articles in law journals, such as Journal of International Economic Law and Journal of Private International Law. Twelve of her articles are indexed by SSCI. As a chief investigator, she has received funding from China National Social Science Fund (equivalent to Australian ARC), China Ministry of Education, the China Law Society, Shanghai Philosophy and Social Science Fund, and Shanghai Government Development and Research Center Fund. She also serves as an Arbitrator at the Hong Kong International Arbitration Center, Shanghai International Economic and Trade Arbitration Commission (Shanghai International Arbitration Center).

Anna Joubin-Bret

Anna Joubin-Bret is the Secretary of the United Nations Commission on International Trade Law (UNCITRAL) and Director of the Division on International Trade Law in the Office of Legal Affairs of the United Nations. Based on her considerable experience in international investment law, Anna Joubin-Bret has developed a practice of international arbitration, mediation and conciliation in disputes involving sovereign States and State entities parties. She acted as counsel, arbitrator, and mediator in numerous investor-State disputes. A former Senior Legal Adviser of the United Nations Conference on Trade and Development (UNCTAD), she has authored seminal research and publications on international investment law and teaches in universities and diplomatic training institutes all over the world. She holds a post-graduate degree (DEA) in private international law from University Paris I – Panthéon Sorbonne. She graduated in international business law from University Paris I and also has a degree in Political Science from Institut d'Etudes Politiques (Lyon II)

Sungjin Kang

Sungjin Kang is a consultant with WTA's International Trade Law Advisory Group and is a member of the firm's International Trade & Economic Policy Group. Prior to joining the WTA, he worked as an in-house counsel for LG Display Co Ltd and LG Electronics Co Ltd, in 2012 and 2013. He spent four years in Belgium, working for international law firms, practising the European Union antitrust, European Union trade and World Trade Organization laws between 2008 and 2012. Sungjin is admitted to practice in the State of New York, USA. He brings in about seven years of experience advising and litigating on a wide range of EU and international legal and policy-related matters. He is specialized in international trade law, antitrust law, international investment arbitration, international dispute resolution, and other regulatory issues. Sungjin's practice focuses on: International trade law (multi-lateral and regional trade agreements negotiation, trade remedies, trade in services, etc), Antitrust law (cartel, abuse of dominance, merger control, sector-specific regulations), International arbitration (international commercial arbitration and investment treaty arbitration), Regulatory compliance (supply chain management, anti-corruption regulation, etc), Technical assistance and capacity building. As a local liaison in Seoul, Korea, he serves clients and prospective clients in South Korea and elsewhere in Asia and other parts of the world who are interested or engaged in cross-border trade, investment, and other international export and investment transactions worldwide. He published several legal articles on his areas of expertise. He was also a speaker at several conferences on international trade issues. Sungjin's native language is Korean. He is fluent in English. He speaks conversational German and Japanese. Sungjin is based in Seoul, and travels frequently to client and partner locations.

Amokura Kawharu

Amokura (Ngāpuhi, Ngāti Whātua) holds a BA/LLB(Hons) degree from Auckland University and an LLM with a major in international law from the University of Cambridge. She became member of the Law Faculty's academic staff in 2005 after working for several years in private commercial law practice in Auckland and in Sydney. Her research interests include international trade and investment law, arbitration, and international disputes resolution. She contributes reviews on disputes settlement for the New Zealand Law Review and co-authored the leading text on New Zealand arbitration law with David Williams QC, *Williams & Kawharu on Arbitration* (LexisNexis 2011). Amokura is a member of the LCIA, the Australian and New Zealand Society of International Law, and the Arbitrators' and Mediators' Institute of New Zealand.

Matthew Levine

Matthew Levine is a Canadian lawyer. Mr Levine's experience with the law of international trade, investment, and arbitration includes: advising on arbitral appointments and challenges, jurisdictional objections, and applications for expedited and emergency procedures; researching and analysing international investment law on behalf of a prominent arbitration, especially in relation to sectors such as mining, oil and gas, and bio-technology; providing international investment agreement-related technical assistance to regional and national organizations in Southeast Asia; participating in advising a sovereign on dispute settlement and compliance panels at the World Trade Organization; and participating in advising an industry group on the Canadian International Trade Tribunal's review of trade remedy orders. In addition to Transnational Dispute Management, Matthew has contributed to Investment Arbitration Reporter, Investor–State Law Guide, Investment Treaty News, and the Asian International Arbitration Journal. Matthew's native language is English, and he is proficient in Mandarin and Japanese. He is a graduate of McGill University (BA) and the University of British Columbia (JD & MA).

Na Li

Na Li holds an LL.M. degree from Boston University (USA), a Bachelor of Law degree from Fudan University (China), and successfully completed the Doctoral Program in International Business Taxation (DIBT) at the WU (Vienna University of Economics and Business) in June 2015. In her thesis she investigated the effect of tax sparing mechanisms on attracting Chinese direct investment into the EU countries. Currently, she works as a post-doctoral researcher at the East China University of Political Science and Law (ECUPL) in Shanghai, China.

Flavia Marisi

Dr Flavia Marisi is an Italian-qualified lawyer since 2014. She holds a doctoral degree from Ghent University, with a thesis on environmental interests in investment arbitration. She worked at the Chinese University of Hong Kong, the Court of Justice of the European Union, the European Commission, both national and international law firms, and an environmental NGO. She lectured at the Chinese University of Hong Kong, King's College London, the National Chiao Tung University in Taiwan, since 2011 at the University of Milan Bicocca, and since 2016 at the University of Milan, where she graduated with 110/110 Summa cum Laude. She specialized in EU law with an LL.M. at the College of Europe, Bruges, and was a visiting scholar at the University of California, Berkeley, University of Nice Sophia Antipolis, Sheffield Hallam University, Institute of European Studies of Macau, and Tsinghua University in Beijing. With forty publications, her research interests vary between international investment law, EU law, environmental law, theory of law, and international litigation.

Sophie Meunier

Sophie Meunier is Senior Research Scholar in the Woodrow Wilson School of Public and International Affairs at Princeton University and Co-Director of the EU Program at Princeton. She is the author of *Trading Voices: The European Union in International Commercial Negotiations* (Princeton University Press 2005) and *The French Challenge: Adapting to Globalization* (Brookings Institution Press 2001), winner of the 2002 France–Ameriques book award. She is also co-editor of several books on Europe and globalization, most recently *The Politics of Interest Representation in the Global Age* (Cambridge University Press 2014) and *Speaking with a Single Voice: The EU as an Effective Actor in Global Governance?* (Routledge 2015). Her current work deals with the politics of Foreign Direct Investment in Europe, notably Chinese investment. She was made Chevalier des Palmes Academiques by the French Government.

Lu Miao

Lu (Mabel) Miao, Co-founder of the Centre for China & Globalization (CCG), Vice President of CCG & Secretary General of CCG. Dr Miao received her PhD degree on Contemporary Chinese Studies from Beijing Normal University and had been a visiting scholar at New York University and Harvard University. She has participated in a number of the Chinese government's and Social Science Foundation's research projects and she has published many research papers and books. The latest new well-known Chinese Blue Books she has authored and edited are: The Chinese Enterprises Globalization Report 2014/2015; The Chinese Overseas Students Development Report 2013/2014; The Chinese Overseas Returnees Development Report 2013/2014/2015; Chinese Overseas Professionals Report 2014; Chinese Enterprises Globalization Report 2014/2015; Chinese International Migration Report 2015; all published by China Social Science Academy Press the most prestigious publishing house under China Social Science Academy. Her latest book also includes *Global Think Tanks*, which is the best seller on the subject in China. In another capacity, Dr Miao is a Deputy Director of International Writing Centre of Beijing Normal University, where she assists Mo Yan, the Centre Director and the Chinese Nobel Laureate in Literature.

Luke Nottage

Luke Nottage is Professor of Comparative and Transnational Business Law at the University of Sydney Law School, specializing in arbitration, contract law, consumer product safety law, and corporate governance, with a particular interest in Japan and the Asia-Pacific. He is founding Co-Director of the Australian Network for Japanese Law (ANJeL) and Associate Director of the Centre for Asian and Pacific Law at the University of Sydney. He is also Managing Director of Japanese Law Links Pty Ltd (www.japaneselawlinks.com). Luke has or has had executive roles in the Australia–Japan Society (NSW), the Law Council of Australia, the Australian Centre for International Commercial Arbitration (ACICA), and the Asia-Pacific Forum for International Arbitration. He has contributed to several looseleaf commentaries and made numerous media appearances and public submissions to the Australian government, especially regarding arbitration and consumer law reform. Luke was admitted as a barrister and solicitor in New Zealand in 1994 and in NSW in 2001. He has consulted for law firms worldwide as well as ASEAN, the European Commission, OECD, UNCTAD, UNDP, and the Japanese Government. Luke is also a Rules committee member of ACICA and on the Panel of Arbitrators for the BAC, JCAA, KCAB, KLRCA, and SCIA. Luke studied at Kyoto University (LLM) and Victoria University of Wellington (BCA, LLB, PhD), and first taught at the latter and then Kyushu University Law Faculty, before arriving at the University of Sydney in 2001. He has held fellowships at other leading institutions in Japan and Australia as well as Germany, Italy, and Canada. Luke's publications include *Product Safety and Liability Law in Japan* (Routledge 2004), *Corporate Governance in the 21st Century: Japan's Gradual Transformation* (Edward Elgar Publishing 2008; lead-edited with Leon Wolff and Kent Anderson), *International Arbitration in Australia* (Federation Press 2010; lead-edited with Richard Garnett), *Foreign Investment and Dispute Resolution Law and Practice in Asia* (Routledge 2011; edited with Vivienne Bath), *Consumer Law and Policy in Australia and New Zealand* (Federation Press 2013; edited with Justin Malbon), *Asia-Pacific Disaster Management: Comparative and Socio-Legal Perspectives* (Springer, 2014; edited with Simon Butt and Hitoshi Nasu), *Who Rules Japan? Popular Participation in the Japanese Legal Process* (Edward Elgar Publishing 2015: edited with Leon Wolff and Kent Anderson), *ASEAN Product Liability and Consumer Product Safety Law* (Winyuchon 2016; edited with Sakda Thanitcul), and several other books. Luke has also published over 200 chapters and refereed other articles, mainly in English and Japanese.

Hadas Peled

Hadas Peled is a PhD candidate at Tsinghua University School of Law, a teaching associate at Bar Ilan University, Israel, and a counsel at Lapidot, Melchior, Abramovich & Co, focusing on China–Israel economic and legal relations.

Cristian Rodríguez Chiffelle

Mr Rodríguez Chiffelle is currently Head of Trade and Investment Policy at the World Economic Forum. Prior to joining the Forum, he served as a trade diplomat in various positions for the Chilean Ministry of Foreign Affairs, including as head of the Energy, Trade and Sustainable Development department, and as legal advisor on Services and Investment. He was also briefly in private legal practice beforehand. In these roles, Mr Rodriguez Chiffelle was responsible for negotiating bilateral investment treaties and different chapters of several free trade agreements, including at the Trans Pacific Partnership negotiations, and has formally represented Chile before the OECD, WTO, APEC and several UN bodies on trade, investment and environment. He holds a Master of Laws (LL.M.) from Harvard Law School, an LL.B. from the University of Concepcion, Chile and a MPA from the Harvard Kennedy School of Government, where he was an Edward S. Mason Fellow in Public Policy and Management.

Karl P Sauvant

Karl P Sauvant is a resident senior fellow at the Columbia Centre on Sustainable Investment, an adjunct senior research scholar, and a lecturer in law at Columbia Law School. He is also a fellow at the Academy of International Business and an honorary fellow at the European International Business Academy. He is a guest professor at Nankai University in China and theme leader of the International Centre for Trade and Sustainable Development/World Economic Forum Task Force on Investment Policy. Sauvant was the founding executive director of the Vale Columbia Centre (VCC) on Sustainable International Investment, where he sought to make the VCC a leading forum for discussions by scholars, policy-makers, development advocates, students, and other stakeholders regarding issues related to foreign direct investment in the global economy and the regulatory framework governing it, focusing particularly on the contribution of FDI to sustainable development. He teaches a seminar on FDI and public policy, and has published widely in the international investment area. Sauvant was previously the co-director of the Millennium Cities Initiative at the Earth Institute, responsible for helping African cities attract investment. A German national, Sauvant has served as director of the United Nations Conference on Trade and Development's Investment Division, managing the division and promoting international consensus-building in the areas of FDI, technology, and enterprise development, providing intellectual leadership for policy-oriented research, and conceptualizing and supervising technical assistance activities. He joined the United Nations in 1973, where he created the prestigious annual World Investment Report, of which he was the lead author until 2004. Sauvant is founder of the journal Transnational Corporations and served as its editor until 2005. He provided intellectual leadership and

guidance to a series of twenty-five monographs on key issues related to international invest-
ment agreements, and he edited the 20-volume *Library on Transnational Corporations* (with
Dr John H Dunning, Routledge), 2004, 2005. Sauvant received a PhD degree from the
University of Pennsylvania.

Shu Shang
Shu Shang is ADR counsel, Hong Kong International Arbitration Centre (HKIAC) since
December 2016. She previously worked as an assistant professor of law at the Shanghai
University of Finance and Economics (SUFE). Shang led the University's Free Trade and
ADR Research and Development Centre. Qualified in New York, the People's Republic of
China, and before the US Patent and Trademark Office, she also acted as a policy adviser for
the Shanghai Municipal Commission of Commerce and the British Consulate General in
Shanghai.

Joel Slawotsky
Joel Slawotsky is a former law clerk to the Hon Charles H Tenney, United States District Judge
for the Southern District of New York and AV peer-review rated attorney at Sonnenschein
(now Dentons) where he represented large corporations. Joel litigated in both Federal and
state court at the trial and appellate levels. Among significant rulings and verdicts obtained: a
New Jersey appellate court ruling affirming a trial court decision exonerating his client based
upon a lack of alleged corporate successor liability; a New York trial decision remitting a
US$13 million jury trial verdict by nearly 60 per cent and obtaining a jury defence verdict on
behalf of a client after being called in to represent the client after the trial had already commenced. Joel teaches in law and business schools and has published extensively on corporate
governance, corporate liability for violations of international law, federal civil procedure, investment treaty law, shareholder activism, regulation of sovereign wealth funds, investment
treaty law, and other business and corporate law topics. He has published in dozens of venues
including: the international law journals of Boston, Duke, Emory, Georgetown, Qatar Univ.
and Virginia; the U Penn business law journal; Delaware Journal of Corporate Law, Review
of Banking and Finance Law and the Chinese Journal of Global Governance (forthcoming).

Na Sun
China Institute for WTO Studies, University of International Business and Economics,
Beijing, China.

Xinquan Tu
Xinquan Tu, Ph.D. in International Trade, Professor and Dean of China Institute for WTO
Studies, University of International Business and Economics. Dr Tu's research fields cover
World Trade Organization, US Trade Policy and Sino–US Trade Relations, Chinese Economy
and Foreign Trade Policy, and Internationalization of Government Procurement. Mr Tu published China's position, role and strategy in the WTO, and seventy papers, the latest published
papers includes 'China's Visions of Future East Asian Economic Integration', 'Implications of
China's possible participation in the TISA negotiations', 'The national security review system
of the United States and its impact on Chinese SOEs' investments in the US', 'Sino–US relations and China's market economy status', and 'The multilateral trading system should be
given more support'.

Heng Wang
Heng Wang is associate professor and co-director of UNSW Law's Herbert Smith Freehills
China International Business and Economic Law (CIBEL) Centre. Previously, as a professor
at Southwest University of Political Science and Law (SWUPL), China, he headed a WTO
law centre (established by the Department of Treaty and Law, the Ministry of Commerce and
SWUPL) and has been the recipient of top research awards and several major grants, including
the triennial China Outstanding Law Research Award, twice, (China Law Society) and the
Outstanding Research Award in Humanities and Social Science (the Ministry of Education).

Besides books, he published widely within and outside of China in journals including the *Journal of World Trade*, *Cornell International Law Journal*, *Columbia Journal of Asian Law*, and *Tsinghua China Law Review*. One of his recent papers will appear in the *Columbia Journal of Asian Law*. His research has been quoted by scholars such as those from Oxford University and the Max Planck Institute. Heng's research interest focuses on China's interaction with international economic law, particularly the China–US economic relationship, multilateral and preferential trade agreements, the Belt and Road Initiative, services trade and investment, and Chinese law. Heng was an Executive Council member of the Society of International Economic Law (2008–2015), and is a founding member of the Asian International Economic Law Network, a member of the Asian WTO Research Network, and an executive member of the governing council of all three Chinese societies of international economic law or WTO law.

Hui Yao (Henry) Wang

Hui Yao (Henry) Wang is the Founder and President of Centre for China and Globalization (CCG), a top independent global think tank in China. In February 2015, Chinese premier Li Keqiang appointed Dr Wang as Counsellor for China State Council. Dr Wang is a well-known Chinese expert on China and globalization issues, on global migration, global talent, overseas Chinese, students, returnees, and on Chinese firms going global and MNC in China; he is also a founder of several Chinese well-known overseas returnees' organizations; a social entrepreneur and a top adviser to the Chinese government at both central and provincial levels, as well as to international organizations and large enterprises. He has a work life span over both Chinese and foreign governments, multi-national executive and business entrepreneurs, and academic circles. He has taught at Peking University, Tsinghua University, University of Western Ontario and was a visiting fellow at Brookings Institution and a senior fellow at Harvard Kennedy School. He is currently the Dean of Institute of Development of Southwestern University of Finance and Economics. He is on the Migration Advisory Board of the International Organization of Migration (IOM), a member of Yale University Asia Development Council, an adviser for Laureate Education Group, a member of the advisory board of Richard Ivey School of Business in Asia, a Steering Committee Member of Metropolis International, a policy fellow of IZA and an advising member to the board of Association of Executive Search Consultants in New York. He is also a frequent speaker at different international forums and often interviewed by various influential global media.

Lu Wang

Dr Lu Wang is a Lecturer at the Faculty of Law of the University of New South Wales, and a member of the UNSW Law's Herbert Smith Freehills China International Business and Economic Law (CIBEL) Centre. Lu's primary research area is international and comparative economic law, with a particular focus on international investment treaties, international arbitration, State-owned enterprises (SOEs) and Chinese regulation of international business. In 2015, Lu was commissioned to act as a co-guest editor of the *ICSID Review* (published by Oxford University Press) for the specific focus issues on SOEs and international investment law. Prior to joining the UNSW Law, Lu worked as a legal intern at the International Centre for Settlement of Investment Disputes (ICSID) in Washington DC (in 2017) and the Ministry of Commerce of P.R. of China Department of Treaty and Law in Beijing (in 2012). She was also a Visiting Fellow at the Lauterpacht Centre for International Law, University of Cambridge, in 2014. Lu holds the degrees of PhD, LL.M. and LL.B. from Xi'an Jiaotong University, China and the degree of PhD from the University of Liverpool, UK.

Qian (Frances) Wang

Ms Wang is focusing on both investment treaty arbitration and international commercial arbitration. She holds an LL.M. degree in International Legal Studies from American University Washington College of Law and graduated from East China University of Political Science and Law with a major in International Economic Law.

Jane Willems
Jane Willems is Associate Professor, School of Law, Tsinghua University. Jane joined the faculty from a successful private practice career with a leading international law firm in France where she specialized in civil and commercial litigation. Prior to entering private practice, she was awarded as a law clerk a position with the Paris Court of Appeal, providing research assistance to three senior appellate justices on the Court of Appeal. Jane specializes in arbitration and dispute resolution generally, as well in the areas of business associations and company law.

Claire Wilson
Claire has worked as a consultant in the private sector advising on complex financial issues. She joined Hong Kong Shue Yan University in 2011. Claire holds an LL.B. (Hons) degree from the Nottingham Law School, United Kingdom; a Masters of International Economic Law degree with distinction; and a Doctor of Juridical Science (International Finance Law) degree from the City University of Hong Kong. Claire is currently an Associate of the Chartered Institute of Arbitrators, a Hong Kong accredited mediator (HKIAC) (HKMAAL), and an Honorary Fellow of the Asian Institute of International Financial Law. She was promoted to Assistant Professor in 2015.

Ka Zeng
Ka Zeng is Professor of Political Science and Director of Asian Studies at the University of Arkansas. Her research focuses on China's role in the international political economy. Dr Zeng is the author of *Trade Threats, Trade Wars: Bargaining, Retaliation, and American Coercive Diplomacy* (University of Michigan Press 2004), co-author of *Greening China: the Benefits of Trade and Foreign Direct Investment* (University of Michigan Press 2011), editor of *China's Foreign Trade Policy: the New Constituencies* (Routledge 2007), and co-editor of *China and Global Trade Governance: China's First Decade in the World Trade Organization* (Routledge 2013). She is a contributor to journals such as *International Studies Quarterly, Review of International Political Economy, World Development, Journal of World Trade, International Interactions, China Quarterly, Journal of Contemporary China, Social Science Quarterly*, and *International Relations of the Asia-Pacific*.

Hong Zhao
Ms Zhao is a Member of the World Trade Organization (WTO) Appellate Body. She received her Degrees of Bachelor, Masters and PhD in Law from the Law School of Peking University in China. She currently serves as Vice President of the Chinese Academy of International Trade and Economic Cooperation. Previously she served as Minister Counsellor in charge of legal affairs at China's mission to the WTO, during which time she served as Chair of the WTO's Committee on Trade-Related Investment Measures (TRIMs). Ms Zhao then served as Commissioner for Trade Negotiations at the Chinese Ministry of Commerce's Department for WTO Affairs, where she participated in a number of important negotiations on international trade, including the Trade Facilitation Agreement negotiations, and negotiations on expansion of the Information Technology Agreement. Domestically, Ms Zhao helped formulate many important Chinese legislative acts on economic and trade areas adopted since the 1990s and has experience in China's judiciary system, serving as Juror at the Economic Tribunal of the Second Intermediate Court of Beijing between 1999 and 2004. She has also taught and supervised law students on international economic law, WTO law and intellectual property rights (IPR) at various universities in China.

Introduction

China's International Investment Law and Policy Regime—Identifying the Three Tracks

Julien Chaisse

China is expected by the rest of the world to adopt globalization fully, to protect free trade, maintain a balanced economic growth, and so on, in view of the expanding economic nationalism and undoubted economic interdependence around the globe. This is a noticeable situation for China to be in when considering that, at the 1944 Bretton Woods Conference, which founded the post-war global economic governance architecture (the UN system), China had a very small function to perform.[1] But just in the past fifty years, China has metamorphosed itself across generations in international economic law jurisprudence by living up to the difficult obligations of the World Trade Organization (WTO), introducing bilateral and regional trade and investment agreements, and ultimately having a significant say in multi-lateral investment law-making and policy agenda-setting.[2]

In view of the Go Global strategy introduced in 1999, China's accession to the WTO in 2001 has further increased its incorporation into the global economy and invigorated the dynamics of its local economy, accelerating the complexity of its exports through 'bringing in' inward foreign direct investment (IFDI).[3] Two major tools of economic growth are international trade and investment. China's international trading activities are now regulated by a rule-founded multi-lateral trading regime and supplemented by bilateral and regional favourite trade agreements, popularly called free trade agreements (FTAs).[4] As the WTO negotiations are conducted under the 'single undertaking' doctrine, known as 'nothing is agreed until everything is agreed', it demands China to assume all obligations relating to the WTO agreements that encompasses goods, services, and intellectual property. To promote the local reform agenda, China agreed to more rigid conditions than other developing countries and adopted

---

[1] See Jin Zhongxia, 'The Chinese Delegation at the 1944 Bretton Woods Conference: Reflections for 2015' (Official Monetary and Financial Institutions Forum Paper, July 2015) https://www.omfif.org/media/1067515/chinese-reflections-on-bretton-woods-by-jin-zhongxia.pdf (last accessed 17 April 2018).

[2] See Congyan Cai, 'China-US BIT Negotiations and the Future of Investment Treaty Regime' (2009) 12 Journal of International Economic Law 457.

[3] See World Trade Organization, 'China and the WTO' https://www.wto.org/english/thewto_e/countries_e/china_e.htm (last accessed 17 April 2018).

[4] The words 'regime', 'system', or 'framework' in this book are loosely used in the sense of political science rather than international law, as defined by Robert Keohane, *After Hegemony: Cooperation and Discord in the World Political Economy* (first published 1984, Princeton University Press 2005) 57: 'international regimes as "sets of implicit or explicit principles, norms, rules and decision-making procedures around which actors" expectations converge in a given area of international relations'.

Introduction: China's International Investment Law and Policy Regime—Identifying the Three Tracks. Julien Chaisse. © Julien Chaisse, 2019. Published 2019 by Oxford University Press.

'inseparable packages' of the WTO agreement, after almost fifteen years of arduous negotiations to join the WTO.[5]

International investments are not regulated by a multi-lateral system like the WTO's trade rules, which are basically negotiated agreements of the Uruguay Round among 123 countries, ranging from 1986 to 1994. Rather they are governed by a 'fragmented' international investment system which is made up of bilateral investment treaties (BITs) and the investment chapters of FTAs (generally called international investment agreements or IIAs). In the same vein, China's dual investments, namely inward foreign direct investment (IFDI) in China and Chinese outward foreign direct investment (OFDI), are regulated by 129 BITs and twenty FTAs with investment chapters which have achieved worldwide geographical coverage.[6]

International trade law and international investment law are relatively interwoven, but their respective objectives and mode of negotiation are basically different due to previously contracted FTAs or IIAs. Most countries appreciate the contribution of free trade and foreign investment in developing their ultimate local economic development, and thus encourage the liberalization of trade and investment. The WTO system, from a legal perspective, offers its members and potential members 'a simple proposition: join the trading club, follow the rules, and everyone benefits'. Flowing from the above logic, countries contracted FTAs, thereby establishing trading clubs, with the purpose of subsequently recompensing trade liberalization. On the contrary, investment protection and investment promotion are the two major objectives of the nations that come to the negotiating table to contract IIAs. Their method of negotiation is basically determined by their role as capital importing nations, capital exporting nations, or both.[7] The basis of the contemporary international investment law is what Professor Reisman called 'the great compact',[8] whereby capital exporting states relinquish their ability to engage their superior power to protect their investors in exchange for capital importing nations agreeing to submit investment disputes to international arbitration.[9]

China being both a capital importing (the world's largest recipient of foreign direct investment (FDI)) and a capital exporting nation (the world's second largest supplier of FDI), China must maintain a balance of this dual role through its IIAs system, attracting IFDI and at the same time protecting OFDI. To accomplish this balanced objective not only demands strategic planning to maintain a balance between safeguarding its offensive stakes as a supplier of FDI and protecting its defensive stakes as a receiver of FDI, but also requires leadership to introduce IIA discussions that serve national interests, promote regional integration, and contribute to the growth and

[5] See Lee Branstetter and Nicholas Lardy, 'China's Embrace of Globalization' in Loren Brandt and Thomas Rawski (eds), *China's Great Economic Transformation* (Cambridge University Press 2008) 650.
[6] On the purpose and scope of IIAs see Jeswald W Salacuse, *The Three Laws of International Investment: National, Contractual, and International Frameworks for Foreign Capital* (Oxford University Press 2013) 393.
[7] See Tim Büthe and Helen Milner, 'The Politics of Foreign Direct Investment into Developing Countries: Increasing FDI through International Trade Agreements?' (2008) 52(4) American Journal of Political Science 741, 750.
[8] See W Michael Reisman, 'The Empire Strikes Back: The Struggle to Reshape ISDS', White & Case International Arbitration Lecture (The Lamm Lecture) for Delivery at University of Miami School of Law on 9 February 2017.
[9] See also Duncan Williams, 'Policy Perspectives on the Use of Capital Controls in Emerging Nations: Lessons from the Asian Financial Crisis and a Look at the International Legal Regime' (2001) 70 Fordham Law Review 561, 614.

development of the international investment system.[10] China's dual role vis-à-vis FDI, owing to its three-prong investment strategies (bilaterally, regionally, and globally), targets the 'subsequent opening up to the outside and facilitating local reforms' and is efficiently transforming into the global economy as a reliable rule-maker.[11] Subsequent reform measures on FDI are a basic element to Chinese economic growth because most service sectors maintain restrictions on private and foreign investors, withholding prospective economy-wide productivity gains. Above their direct influence on the level of rivalry in the restricted services sectors, a major risk is that low productivity in these sectors indirectly inhibits growth in downstream sectors. China would likely gain advantage from greater effort to enhance its FDI system in this regard. China's major motivating force in subsequently contracting IIAs has been to strike a balance between investor protection and the government's power to regulate, in accordance with the developments and growth in international investment law, in this period of transition.[12]

The remarkable story of China's position in moulding the international economic regime has been majorly said and scrutinized by political scientists and economists. Analysis of the available hypothetical and empirical studies shows that there are principally three types of analysis. First, literatures were premised on case studies to provide Chinese company Go Global strategies with a nation-oriented or a regional-oriented appraisal.[13] Secondly, scholars saw China's dealings with international economic law, particularly its active involvement in major negotiations.[14] Lastly, from China's point of view, scholars have adjudged Chinese characteristics encouraging and protecting its OFDI and accelerating its experience with the international investment disputes resolution system.[15]

This book provides a new breakdown and extensive reappraisal of China's more radical method to international standard-setting through its advanced IIAs programme, which is required in order to enhance China's global presence in the future. This introduction provides an explanation of the main notion and definitions in respect of China's tripartite international investment policy.

This book is designed around the emerging tripartite investment policy of China and strategy propelled by the local reforms that are presently restructuring the regulatory framework for FDI.

Part I highlights the local strategies that are being put in place to revive China's stalled economic reforms and developmental goals, as clearly illustrated in China's

[10] See David Collins, *The BRIC States and Outward Foreign Direct Investment* (Oxford University Press 2013) 111.

[11] See Matthias Busse, Jens Königer, and Peter Nunnenkamp, 'FDI Promotion through Bilateral Investment Treaties: More than a Bit?' (2010) 146(1) Review of World Economics 147.

[12] See Yongjie Li, 'Factors to be Considered for China's Future Investment Treaties' in Wenhua Shan and Jinyuan Shu (eds), *China and International Investment Law: Twenty Years of ICSID Membership* (Brill 2015) 176.

[13] See eg Philippe Le Corre and Alain Sepulchre, *China's Offensive in Europe (Geopolitics in the 21st Century)* (Brookings Institution Press 2016); Huiyao Wang and Miao Lu, *China Goes Global: The Impact of Chinese Overseas Investment on its Business Enterprises* (Palgrave Macmillan 2016); Kerry Brown, *China and the EU in Context: Insights for Business and Investors* (Palgrave Macmillan 2014).

[14] See eg Lisa Toohey, Colin B Picker, and Jonathan Greenacre (eds), *China in the International Economic Order: New Directions and Changing Paradigms* (Cambridge University Press 2015); Ilan Alon, Marc Fetscherin, and Philippe Gugler (eds), *Chinese International Investments* (Palgrave Macmillan 2012) 466.

[15] See eg Wang Guiguo, *International Investment Law: A Chinese Perspective* (Routledge 2014); An Chen, *The Voice from China: An CHEN on International Economic Law* (Springer 2013); Zhang Hong, *China's Outward Foreign Direct Investment: Theories and Strategies* (Enrich Professional Publishing 2014).

Thirteenth Five-year Plan (2016–2020). For China's local investors, there is a considerable opportunity in the country compared to its very high savings rate. For international investors, China has been seen as the strictest investment territory among the G20 countries. It is thus expedient for China to regulate its investment rules and policies with its major economic partners and within the Asia-Pacific region.

Part II deploys the analysis at the international level in respect to the 'bilateral prong'. China, a nation which has preferred to transact bilaterally with foreign nations in times past, has in modern times engaged in bilateral talks with its top high-income trading partners to promote its stakes and attain more dominance. China has contracted bilateral agreements with some particular strategic partners, such as the Association of Southeast Asian Nations (ASEAN) (2010), Canada (2014), and Australia (2015). Furthermore, there are two outstanding agreements under negotiation: the US–China BIT (re-engaged in 2008) which will regulate a more complicated economic relationship between the world's largest economies, and the European Union (EU)–China investment treaty (contracted in 2014) additionally to open up China's economy.

Part III examines the 'regional prong'. China has also been actively involved in adjusting the economic architecture of the Asia-Pacific region. Stimulated by regional economic integration in the West (the EU, North America Free Trade Area (NAFTA), the South American Trading Bloc (MERCOSUR), and the Pacific Alliance) and thwarted by the impasse of the WTO multi-lateral negotiations, the countries in the Asia-Pacific region are inclined towards coming together and modernizing their foreign investment rules. To achieve the 'Asia-Pacific dream' advocated by President Xi, since 2006 China has been advocating an Asia-Pacific trade accord, the Free Trade Area of the Asia-Pacific (FTAAP), the Regional Comprehensive Economic Partnership (RCEP), and the Trans-Pacific Partnership (TPP) as a panacea established by China and the United States towards coming together. Subsequently, in 2014, the 'Trilateral Investment Agreement' between China, Japan, and South Korea came into existence. The analysis must also encompass the potential coming into existence of the TPP with China not being a party; it could also have a complicated and very important effect on the region's investment regime.

Part IV identifies a 'global prong', to which international solicitors have given little attention. China's initiation of One Belt–One Road (OBOR) in 2013 resulted in it aiming to fortify its 'going global' policy by creating new markets and boosting the importance of cross-border business. In addition, China also took over the G20 presidency in 2016, resulting in the embracing of the 'Guiding Principle for Global Investment Policy-Making' (Guiding Principles) by the G20 countries. The Guiding Principles made reference in particular to an all-embracing growth and sustainable development as the purpose of investment policy-making, the execution of which will be crucial in reducing the disintegration of subsequent international investment laws advancing policy development.

Part V expands the analysis conducted in the book by tracking the evolution of China's approach to entering into investment treaties—both as a matter of the identity of the counterparty and the substantive provisions—and considers the impact of the (relatively few) arbitrations that have been brought under these treaties. In particular, Part V seeks to explain the relative limited engagement of China with investor–state dispute settlement (ISDS).

I. The Foundations of China's International Investment Law and Policy

Part I examines the local forces of China's international investment policy. Since the embrace of China's 'open door' policy in 1978, which modified its development technique from self-sufficient to full involvement in the world market and targeted to captivate foreign investments in order to boost its economic development, the basic policy for mustering IFDI remains unaltered; that is, to aid the regulation of China's economy, to harmonize its modernization programmes and to enhance its policy of life.[16] An outward concentration on foreign investment was included as part of the 1997 launch of the Go Global policy in the form of OFDI characterized to avoid trade barriers and to enhance the competitiveness of Chinese firms, which were typically state-owned enterprises (SOEs). Although this work concentrates on China's investment policy, it is pertinent to remember the causation between local reforms and international policies. In this regard, in 2004, FDI was proclaimed in the Decision of the State Council on Reform on Investment System. Furthermore, on 3 September 2016, the Decision of the Standing Committee of the National People's Congress on Amending Four Laws in addition to the Law of the People's Republic of China on Foreign-Funded Companies was embraced at the Twenty-second Session of the Standing Committee of the Twelfth National People's Congress and it came into force on 1 October 2016 to change 'three central laws' and the laws of the People's Republic of China on the safeguarding of the investment of Taiwan Compatriot. The Ministry of Commerce (MOFCON) also brought out the Foreign Investment Law of the People's Republic of China (Draft for comment) (Draft for foreign investment law) that same day. The local law of foreign investment has gone through transformations, both in quantity and quality. The most essential stage of China's reform of its foreign investment regime must be MOFCOM's publication of the Draft Foreign Investment Law for public remarks on the 19 January 2015, which was supported by an official clarification which highlighted the legislative backdrop, purpose, and fundamental principles behind the draft. China's foreign investment law will not have only changed the 'three central laws' that presently control foreign investment, once promulgated, but it will also offer a better and all-embracing re-enactment of the foreign investment legal system in China. These reforms ushered in the development of the international policy that Part II intends to examine.

China's inward investment is the focus of Michael J Enright in Chapter 1. The gradual shift of China's economy to IFDI and foreign invested enterprises (FIEs) is one the most significant elements in China's economic reform programme. Although China is very much open to IFDI, China remains more fully involved than most large enterprises. In just a few years, the obvious contradictory trends towards building a free legal environment for IFDI in addition to highly advertised examples of pushback against FIEs in China has been seen. For a comprehensive understanding of China's approach towards IFDI and FIEs, it is mandatory to comprehend the history of IFDI and FIEs in China, the role that China plays in IFDI and FIEs, and to be fully aware that the effect of IFDI and FIEs is most often not highly esteemed. These characteristics will affect any investment treaties that are likely to be concluded by China and

---

[16] For a detailed analysis on the economic implications of the 'open door' policy see Guocang Huan, 'China's Open Door Policy, 1978–1984' (1986) 39 Journal of International Affairs 1.

the way they will be executed. Moreover, Chapter 1 talks about a wide perspective on China's approach towards IFDI and FIEs and fully portrays the outcome of the novel method of calculating the economic importance that IFDI and FIEs have brought to China. In conclusion, this chapter provides different views for those interested in the potential for the negotiation and execution of investment agreements with China.

Hui Yao (Henry) Wang discusses China's outward investment and, most importantly, Chinese enterprise globalization's features, trends, and obstacles in Chapter 2. The world economy has persistently been experiencing a slow recovery from the steep downturn of 2008–2009 since 2013, but the growth was uneven. In respect to developed economies, the United States encountered a large increase while the Eurozone economies did not grow at all. Emerging economies also encountered headwinds as the force of growth for most of these countries was not enough to power a larger expansion. Not minding these ongoing growth problems, global investment has not only been stable but is also coming up. The United Nations Conference on Trade and Development (UNCTAD) proclaimed that, from 2012 to 2013, global FDI inflow increased from 1.33 trillion to 1.45 trillion on a yearly rate of 9 per cent. In respect of FDI inflow, 54 per cent went to developing countries, China with other Asian countries continuously taking in the transnational investment. The measure of global cross-border mergers and acquisitions business continued to experience growth in 2013 and 2014. Monetary services, resource extraction industries (particularly energy), in addition to transportation and IT communication, were marked by important M&A activity. Green-field investment grew gradually but its total size was bigger than the cross-border M&A. As a result of a slow global economic recovery, the economy of China expanded at an exponential pace. The endogenous momentum of China's economic has been increasing as a result of the economic structural adjustment and transformation and upgrading progress that has been achieved and this is also firmly supported OFDI by Chinese enterprises. Simultaneously, after the Chinese government brought into the limelight the execution of the Go Global strategy following the Communist Party of China (CPC)'s Eighteenth National Congress, China's enterprises have greatly increased their overseas direct investment (ODI).

Na Li expands the analysis by providing a comprehensive picture of the influence of tax factors on Chinese FDIs in Chapter 3. Na Li further elucidates that investment treaties are not the only factors in Chinese FDIs. Tax factors also influence FDI into China and Chinese investment to other countries (the 'Chinese outbound investment'). This chapter also discusses the following questions: What are the influences of tax factors on FDIs? Is the Chinese experience of using tax instruments consistent with these empirical findings? Will China's execution of an anti-tax avoidance strategy drive FDIs away from China? What are the tax competition concerns for China? The final section contains a conclusion. Furthermore, although debates are still ongoing about the influence of tax factors on FDI, the chapter demonstrates that tax factors are largely used by China both to attract FDIs into China and support Chinese outbound investment. Moreover, anti-tax avoidance measures in recent years have made it clear that tax clarity and sureness are necessary tax factors influencing business decisions. Therefore, the Chinese government must take more into consideration tax factors' influence on business before executing forceful anti-tax avoidance strategies which could drive away FDIs.

In Chapter 4, Lu Wang considers the crucial case of SOE investments and national security protection. The quick growth of SOEs and their cross-border investment activities in modern times has attracted notable attention, specifically with regard to the anticipated effect such investments may have on the national security of host nations.

SOE investments are commonly from emerging economies, particularly China, and are eminent in the very important or 'strategic' industries, such as energy, infrastructure, telecommunication sectors, and financial service. In this vein, some national security considerations with regard to SOE investment have been intensified in an increasing number of countries. The role of IIAs with regard to national security protection is a vital issue. China's IIAs are reappraised with regard to the treatment of SOEs with the purpose of discovering the extent to which state capitalism has promoted the concluding of international treaties.

Jie Huang examines China's free trade zones (FTZs) and international investment policy and, specifically, the case of the negative list of non-conforming measures in Chapter 4. Before carrying out recondite reforms of the trade and investment legal framework, China frequently executes the reform on a small scale, usually in a particular geographic area as an experimental ground. If these experiments produce the expected outcome, the reform may then be adopted nationwide. A basic example is the five unique economic zones created in the 1980s. The first set of Chinese regulatory reforms in trade and investment took place in 1978, after the Cultural Revolution. Pioneered by late Premier Deng Xiaoping, China adopted the opening-up policy. Deng created five unique economic zones to lure foreign investment by permitting a larger role for individual self-determination and Western style market forces. The morals learnt from the unique economic zones were adopted nationwide. For instance, the Sino-foreign joint venture was first experimented in the unique economic zones and was adopted nationwide after it proved to be successful. These zones are also used to initiate tax holidays in China to lure foreign investment and many areas in inland China followed their examples. Special economic areas slowly ended their mission as experimental grounds in the 1990s. 2018 will witness an important reform, adopting a negative list to control foreign investment's market access. It basically deviates from China's long-time local practice and is targeted at harmonizing China's investment law with high-standard international agreements, most importantly the China–US BIT under negotiation. This chapter also concentrates on the negative list implemented by China's FTZs to control foreign investment's market access and examines its importance, explaining it insufficiencies and proffering solutions for improvement.

In Chapter 6, Manjiao Chi analyses sustainable development concerns through IIAs and offers an assessment of Chinese IIAs. The international communities have been confronted with serious sustainable development difficulties in recent times. International investment law, chiefly comprising IIAs, national investment laws, and some minor rules, is frequently condemned for not being effective enough in tackling sustainable development difficulties related to transnational investment activities. This is attributable to the fact that IIAs are usually and basically established to protect and promote foreign investment, while non-investment aims such as sustainable development promotion have not been adequately tackled in IIAs. As transnational activities are expanding actively, it is usually perceived that although IIAs should not be seen as the basic legal discourse for tackling sustainable development difficulties, they could be used as helpful tools in advancing sustainable investment. As indicated in the survey carried out by the Organization for Economic Cooperation and Development (OECD), almost all OECD and non-OECD governments can be presumed to be dedicated to sustainable development aims, but the majority do not use IIAs as a tool for achieving these aims. The present legal structure for foreign investment should be worked on to make sure that it can actively foster sustainable development. Most recently, many governmental bodies, non-governmental organizations (NGOs), and international organizations have jumped knee-deep into projecting and promoting sustainable development compatible (inclusive) IIAs where its negotiation power remains a factor in the ability/power of the IIA provisions necessarily to promote sustainable investments and, in terms of sufficiency and efficiency, the degree to which these provisions can foster the achievement of sustainable development goals in the states without reducing the protection levels of foreign investments. From the standpoint of China, sustainable development-compatible IIA enforcement is a paramount step, being one of the most successful IIA negotiating tools in the past decades and also as a result of the fact that China faces many sustainable development challenges. Against the back-drop of the Chinese sustainable development challenges, this chapter reports the level of success achieved by the Chinese IIAs in handling sustainable development challenges from a traditional perspective. In a brief introduction, and as an opening remark, this chapter outlines the developmental principles of sustainable development, after which it projects the three major variations of the sustainable development provisions in the Chinese IIAs (environmental provision, labour rights provision, and transparency provision), and their levels of efficiency in managing sustainable development challenges. Furthermore, it proposes several measures to promote the sustainable development compatibility of the Chinese IIAs on the basis of the conclusions drawn from the empirical study of major sustainable development provisions in the Chinese IIAs. On a final note, the chapter stresses that, although China has made some progress in recent times, it faces an urgent need to finalize sustainable development compatible IIAs.

II. The Bilateral Prong

China's involvement in international investment emphasizes its contribution to join multi-lateral investment-related legal agreements and to contract IIAs. Owing to its unpleasant antecedent of contracting 'unequal treaties', unlike other countries, China's involvement in the international investment system did not begin with the signing of free commerce and navigation (FCN) treaties. But, it began carefully to contract BITs with advanced countries (major capital exporting states to China at that time), concluding its first BIT with Sweden in 1982.[17] In spite of not getting involved early enough, as time went on China's expertise and involvement with the international investment system enabled it to develop towards liberalizing its IIA system, striking an equilibrium between the duties and profits relating to IIAs. Investment promotion and protection agreements were signed in the 1970s in a very direct socio-economic context. They were the marketable policy documents of the originally capital exporting states. They were intended to safeguard the investors of the north from the ultimate risks to which they were subjected by investing in the countries of the south: arbitrariness, spoliation, and discrimination. The critical question that guided the development of these documents was how best to safeguard investments contracted by foreigners against certain contumelious attitudes of the host nation. The manner in which China has participated in BITs shows a significant evolution over the past twenty years.[18]

---

[17] See Qingjiang Kong, 'Bilateral Investment Treaties: The Chinese Approach and Practice' (1999) 9 Asian Yearbook of International Law 107.

[18] See also Leon E Trakman, 'Geopolitics, China and Investor-State Arbitration' in Lisa Toohey, Colin B Picker, and Jonathan Greenacre (eds), *China in the International Economic Order: New Directions and Changing Paradigms* (Cambridge University Press 2015) 271–8.

The lessons learnt from the Canada–China Foreign Investment Protection Agreement (FIPA) for the US–China BIT and beyond is highlighted by Kyle Dylan Dickson-Smith in Chapter 7. Major lessons can be drawn from reviewing a special and newly contracted BIT—the Canada–China FIPA—in order to foretell and pinpoint the chances and difficulties for prospective BIT contracting party states of China (such as the United States, the EU, India, and the Gulf Cooperation Council of Colombia). The Canada–China FIPA and the expected US–China BIT (as well as the EU–China BIT) jointly fall into a special class of investment agreements, depicting a combination of different ideologies of international investment norms/protections with two different (East and West) basic local legal and economic policies. The aim of this chapter is to understand and harness the legal content of the Canada–China FIPA in order to separate the chances and difficulties for investment agreements presently under negotiation (concentrating on the US–China BIT). This analysis is carried out from the point of view of China's original BIT procedure and political-economic objectives, relating to that of its contracting state party. This chapter summarily addresses the economic and wider diplomatic relationship between China and Canada in contrast to that of the United States. It further analyses a wide collection of substantive and procedural duties of the Canada–China FIPA, addressing their influence individually and collectively, to deduce the lessons that can be learnt by the United States and other contracting party states. This analysis distinguishes the level investment liberalization and legal protection that China and Canada have attained, and whether these standards are meeting the two countries' expectations. The analysis is not void of the relevant political economy and negotiating position between China and its contracting party states, the anticipated economic advantages of each party, in addition to any diplomatic sensitive hindrance between the parties. Although this chapter does not analyse each substantive and procedural right thoroughly, it offers a sufficient all-embracing basis to disclose the difficulties awaiting the negotiation of future bilateral agreements with China.

Hadas Peled and Marcia Don Harpaz examine innovation as a basic stimulant in the China–Israel investment relationship in Chapter 8. The authors further assert in this chapter that scientific and technological innovation has strengthened recent China–Israel relations. Recently, investment and trade between China and Israel have improved tremendously irrespective of the global economic decrease, underlying political economic situations, and geopolitical inhibitions. This chapter contributes to the current scholarly text by recognizing innovation as a new verifying variable in China's bilateral investment diplomacy, via an analysis of the China–Israel connection. In spite of the decrease in global investment, and in FDI in Israel, China's investment channel into Israel has not decreased, and is concentrated particularly on invention. However, in the long run, as evidenced by global invention statistics, China is improving tremendously, and may soon exceed Israel's inventive ability. In the same vein, Israel is diversifying its inventive strategies. Moreover, a huge portion of Israeli invention is connected to its defence industries. In line with the special law, they are subjugated to Israeli defence export control policies. The approval of defence-related businesses is influenced by US interests and by China's policies and interests in the Arab continent, together with the supplying arms and technology to Israel's competitors.

Chapter 9 outlines the views of Flavia Marisi and Qian Wang on the proponents and challenges of the China–EU Investment Agreement (CAI) negotiations. The chapter examines taxation and transparency with respect to the fair and equitable treatment (FET) provision, which is the principal focus of the EU–China investment agreement. The focus on the FET is based on the fact that it is the most commonly breached standard in investor–state cases, especially where investors assert that the host state policies are detrimental to their business. It is noteworthy that although the EU–China treaty currently under negotiation covers only bilateral investments, it is seen as the best avenue for successful FTAs. Therefore, the CAI is a rather conclusive treaty, serving as the bedrock of a better deliberate relationship between the EU and China, and not just part of the many bilateral and multilateral agreements connoting the 'fragmented patchwork' of international investment agreements. The general outcome of the CAI, as well as the liberalization it hopes to achieve, will have a greater effect than agreements that border around bilateral cooperation. In effect, the future of the EU–China BIT will critically follow one of two directions: both regions will either cooperate and harness the benefits of a mutual economic relationship, or they will stand against each other in competition for the largest share of the global market, relying on third states' preferential trade agreements (PTAs). From a political view, the EU strategy in this negotiation is obviously economic on the surface: to set aside any non-conforming geopolitical issues and deliberate on economic matters. Clearly, a collaboration of this sort will symbolize the outcome of the economic position of the EU and China as both capital importing and capital exporting countries. The EU and China have good reasons to conclude a bi-directional investment promoting CAI. However, both of them will have to exert more effort in this negotiation so that, in the interest of the parties, both as home states and host states and of their investors, a satisfactory treaty can be concluded that will serve as a model for the rest of the world.

Xinquan Tu, Na Sun, and Zhen Dai examine the issue of SOEs in China's BITs, specifically the complicated case of the US–China BIT negotiations, in Chapter 10. The issue of SOEs has never ceased to exist since China is always at the negotiating table specifically with the United States. During the period China was expecting to enter the multi-lateral trading system, there were special sections for state trading enterprises in its accession protocol in accordance with Article XVII of the General Agreement on Tariffs and Trade (GATT) 1994. In respect of the BIT negotiation with the United States, which was resumed in 2008 and has gone through twenty-nine rounds of talks, the issue of SOEs came up again and is likely to be the main point obstructing the conclusion of the agreement. However, there are many changes in the present situation compared with the one sixteen years ago: China's economic status has increased and trade and investment relationships with its partners have achieved new dimensions. Reproducing the answer in the commitment in the WTO may not be pleasing to both sides. To advance the BIT negotiation on the SOEs issue an advanced approach is required, which requires more patience and tolerance.

In Chapter 11, Matthew Levine analyses the fourth generation of Chinese treaty practice. If China is not a rule-maker, this implies that China is a rule-taker. Some facts seem to point in this direction: among them, the decisive influence of North American Treaty practice, mainly that of the United States, and Beijing's unwillingness to modernize its own model treaty. However, research into China's partnership in the WTO and negotiation of regional trade agreements (RTAs) points to an optional notion. On this approach, Beijing is neither a rule-maker nor a rule-taker, but basically acts as a 'rule-shaker'. Even though this term has been used by a group of scholars to take into consideration similarities and differences between Chinese, Japanese, and Korean dealings with international economic law, it does not appear to be clearly spelt out. This is crucial for explaining China's most recent IIAs, as discussed in this chapter. Specifically, it pays to make the best use of particular sections that other authors have referred to as 'puzzling' and enable us to depart from tagging Beijing's most current treaties as 'incoherent'. The first section assesses the categories that have been used by scholars to classify China's large investment treaty practice. This brought about the line of thought that IIAs contracted from 2008 onwards as part of a universal Fourth Generation. This embraces several alterations of substantive investment protection sections. Most of these new concepts are reflective of a wider trend whereby nations are striving to strike a balance between investment protection and non-investment aims. It is therefore necessary to distinguish two forms of balancing mechanisms: interpretative ones and substantive ones. A frontline reason for the growth of balancing mechanisms in China's Fourth Generation is the 'NAFTA-ization Thesis'. However, in reviewing the specific provisions in depth, it becomes manifest that this provides only an incomplete elucidation. Ongoing negotiations with the United States and the requirement to choose novel language in that nation's present method of IIAs drafting offers proof for the complementary explanation of selective adaptation.

III. The Regional Prong

China is also actively involved in the ASEAN-led RCEP negotiations, a large regional trade contract between ASEAN (Brunei, Cambodia, Indonesia, Laos, Malaysia, Myanmar, the Philippines, Singapore, Thailand, and Vietnam) and its six FTA partners (Australia, China, India, Japan, South Korea, and New Zealand). The 'regional prong' is discussed in Part III. More so, China has been fully involved in acclimatizing the economic framework of the Asia-Pacific region. Instigated by the regional economic integration in the West (EU, NAFTA MERCOSUR, Pacific Alliance) and thwarted by the halt of the WTO multi-lateral negotiations, the nations in the Asia-Pacific region depend on harmonization and modernization of their foreign investment rules. To actualize the 'Asia-Pacific dream' talked about by President Xi, China has been elevating an Asia-Pacific trade pact, the FTAAP, arguably with RCEP and the Transatlantic Trade Partnership (TTP) as gateways formed by China and the United States towards harmonization since 2006. Additionally, in 2014, the 'trilateral investment agreement' between China, Japan, and South Korea came into actualization in the Thirteenth Five-Year Plan (2016–20), promoting the OBOR initiative as the 'climax' of its Go Global policy.[19] The Chinese government encourages enterprises from all nations to invest in China, and admonishes Chinese companies to involve themselves in structural construction in other nations along the Belt and Road, and industrial investment there (Vision and Actions).

Won-Moi Chog discusses the substantive provisions of the East Asian trilateral investment agreement and their implications in Chapter 13. The Korea–China–Japan Investment Promotion Facilitation and Promotion Agreement is the first treaty in the economic area to join three Northeast Asian countries on a single legal instrument. The provision of dispute settlement procedure in the treaty will enhance the making of a profitable investment climate in the host nation. Although there have been fears concerning vexatious claims that could inhibit legitimate control actions by

---

[19] English version of the Thirteenth Five-year Plan, translated by Compilation and Translation Bureau, Central Committee of the Communist Party of China, in respect of foreign investment see Article 49 Section 4 (foreign capital and outbound investment), Chapter 50 Section 1 (robust business environment), and Section 2 (the regulation system for Chinese overseas investment), http://218.189.123.39/videoplayer/P020161207645765233498.pdf?ich_u_r_i=0fcfc6c4af81270b7e3d674322521be9&ich_s_t_a_r_t=0&ich_e_n_d=0&ich_k_e_y=1745048917752163062456&ich_t_y_p_e=1&ich_d_i_s_k_i_d=9&ich_s_e_q=212115804&ich_u_n_i_t=1 (last accessed 20 November 2017).

the government, the construction of an investment chapter in the Korea–China–Japan FTA under negotiation is required by all in the region. Any appropriate answers to such an examination need to thoroughly contrast advantages and drawbacks of any development of rules and governance. At the end, a quest for an improved international investment governance in Northeast Asia in the future needs a thorough evaluation of lessons from the past and present.

Heng Wang emphasizes the RCEP investment rules and China's contribution to the RCEP negotiation in Chapter 13. The chapter analyses China's FTA approach to investment in terms of flexibility and its results for the RCEP. The following questions are analysed: What is the trend of China's FTA approach to investment in respect to flexibility? Is China a rule-follower, rule-shaker, or rule-maker? How may China approach the RCEP negotiations with respect to investment? Within China's FTAs, the chapter centres on the China–Korea FTA and China–Australia Free Trade Agreement (ChAFTA) while China's other FTAs are referred to when needed. The chapter shows that China is ready to consider improved rules and embrace newer-style investment that will be done in the future. For example, the US–China BIT negotiations show China's new development of investment freedom. China's FTA includes innovative guidelines of regulatory autonomy and ISDS procedural characteristics, in addition to the roster of arbitration penalties, the general welfare notice, the code of conduct for offenders, and the combined explanation of the annex by treaty parties. What is more, China will likely be a rule-shaker in a short or medium period and likely becomes a rule-maker in the long run. Its pattern may vary from selective adoption to innovations that are on plan. The purpose is clear as China will be largely involved in the development of investment norms because of the need to protect its outbound investment and improve investment trust in inbound investment. Being a rule-shaker in the RCEP negotiations, China will often qualify proposals of partners rather than offer a new set of clauses. The flexibility of China's FTAs will likely continue in the RCEP. In conclusion, the chapter stresses that the RCEP investment rules may be low-level ones with an early harvest approach. This derives from a number of elements, among which there is the special nature of mega FTAs, the 'stockpile' of already existing investment agreements, and China's approach to the ASEAN. The totality of these factors means that China will most likely take a more malleable stand in the RCEP than in bilateral FTAs. In any event, the RCEP will affect China's FTA approach to investment.

In Chapter 14, Amokura Kawharu and Luke Nottage re-examine the models for investment treaties in the Asian region and options for China. Many parallelisms and sporadic distinctions are present in Asian investment with regard to their laws screening FDI and current ways towards investment treaties, in addition to the present politically delicate issue of ISDS. This chapter likens important areas of existing treaties already signed by key Asian nations/entities (China, ASEAN) plus evident positions set forth by Australia and New Zealand in an opened investment chapter for the RCEP or 'ASEAN+6' agreement. Owing to the concern about the US-style treaty drafting shown recently by Indonesia and India, major economies are still bargaining the RCEP with New Zealand and Australia in addition to bilateral agreements with Australia.

Horia Ciurtin asks whether there is a new era in cross-strait relations in Chapter 15. The author provides 'a post-sovereign enquiry' into Taiwan's investment treaty system. Going beyond the traditional legal divisions, Taiwan has shown that it can bypass such limitations, being a main trend-setter who is innovating the area of international economic law. Specifically, a close look at Taiwan's nexus of investment treaty is eye-opening; Taiwan concluded twenty-nine BITs (some of them with countries that do not recognize Taiwan as a sovereign country), and six ample economic cooperation agreements with related investment provisions. The number and the importance of these agreements reveal that the concept of international recognition (and ensuing diplomatic relations) does not directly influence the behaviour of states which are willing to interact legally and economically. In this regard, non-diplomatic (but formal) relations might be used as a step forward, as Taiwan is closer to concluding an agreement with another post-sovereign entity, the EU. This relevant global actor may open up the scene for a multi-tier dynamic where some of its component member states are in principle against any liaison with Taiwan but will be bound to it because of their membership of the EU. To solve such legal (and geopolitical) contradiction, the established instruments of international law cannot be applied, and a new theoretical framework shall be developed. Obviously, the right answers can only be obtained by asking the right questions. To this end, the starting point must be to discuss sovereignty thoroughly. The chapter assesses the polity's effort for the development of diplomatic structures by means of investment and trade agreements, in this way avoiding the problems related to recognition. These kinds of agreement can be considered as a litmus test, showing Taiwan's capacity to shift traditional categories of Westphalian international law and emerge as a self-standing actor. The chapter will also show the Taiwanese expedient approach to using (or not using) the newly finished legal instruments for enforcing obligations. Further, the chapter demonstrates that Taiwan can obtain relevant advantages from further dealing with the EU, being linked to economic partners through (non-)diplomatic relations.

Part III shows that China is in a good position to close the contrast in the RCEP group and to support the togetherness of rules on investments and liberalization in the Asia-Pacific region. Since 2007, the terrain of China's IIA network has added the RCEP group. That is, China is already an IIA partner with all the RCEP concession parties, namely India (Sino–India BIT 2007), New Zealand (Sino–New Zealand FTA 2008), ASEAN (Sino–ASEAN Agreement 2009), Japan and South Korea (Trilateral Investment Agreement 2012), and Australia (Sino–Australia FTA 2015). First, it again displays the success of China's malleable and practical way of meeting the interests and needs of both developing and developed parties. Secondly, albeit not professing 'gold standard' status, the coverage of China's IIAs with the RCEP-negotiating parties shows the trend and the movement rate of 'new generation' IIA rule-making, following a wider and more complicated development policy plan while growing a completely advantageous investment environment, which implies that investment rules under the RCEP will not fall below anticipation of 'building a free, facilitative and competitive investment environment in the region'. Careful thinking is needed about the interplay between RCEP negotiations on trade in goods, trade in services, and investment to ensure a standard and balanced outcome as required by the 'Guiding Principles and Objectives for Negotiating the RCEP', the countries involved have adjusted their positions to ensure concessions on one area that could earn them influence over others on the long run.

IV. The Global Prong

Since the initiation of the Go Global strategy in 1999 and accompanying the process of China's WTO entry, China has been strategically adopting globalization and has internally and externally liberalized its trade and FDI rules. The execution of the Go Global plan has been emphasized in successive Five-Year Plans. The Eleventh Five-Year Plan (2006–2010) called for a 'better execution' of the Go Global system. The Twelfth

Five-Year Plan (2011–2015) promised to speed up the execution of the Go Global plan. In the Thirteenth Five-Year Plan (2016–2020), the 'capstone' of its Go Global policy is moving the OBOR initiative forward.

The Chinese government welcomes enterprises from all nations to invest in China and urges Chinese companies to become involved in the infrastructure of other nations along the Belt and Road and to ensure industrial investments there. On the global scale, China has also laid the main work for multi-lateral investment policy-making under its G20 governance through the G20 Guiding Principles for Global Investment Policy-Making (G20 Guiding principles). Within the WTO structure, the Agreement on Trade Related Investment Measures (TRIMs) and the General Agreement on Trade in Services (GATS) become most necessary to China's FDI inflow and outflow. Upon obtainment, China conceded to comply with the TRIMs Agreement by removing and ceasing the application of performance conditions of any type such as local content, transfer of technology, and the requirement for export performance. Same as all WTO members, China made greater GATS 'commercial presence' (Mode 3) commitments than in the other modes (namely Mode 1, Mode 2, and Mode 4). Although while the agreement presents a number of provisions directly or indirectly pertaining to investment-related matters, its areas are not as complete as those provided by the large majority of BITs. At the same time, China's loyalty to the WTO has had a positive effect on its OFDI. Lowered trade obstacles have seen foreign goods and services flowing into China's market, resulting in Chinese firms pursuing markets abroad by increasing OFDI. Similarly, China's adherence to TRIMs and GATS has helped to increase investment.

Karl P Sauvant discusses the idea that China is moving the G20 towards an international investment framework and investment facilitation in Chapter 16. China, being the leader of the G20 in 2016, has had an avenue to increase the deliberation on these matters. The country has a special interest in international investment, judging from the decision to form the G20's Trade and Investment Working Group. This shows both the function of FDI in China's own development and especially its recent rise as a necessary outward investor, included in the rise of emerging markets as host countries of multi-national enterprises (MNEs). The chapter also includes an explanation of some policy issues associated with the rise of FDI from emerging markets. A short explanation of matters centred on the future of international investment law and policy rules follows, in addition to an examination of the adoption of non-binding rules showing the structure of a complete framework on international investment. Finally, the chapter centres on a strong proposal for a sustainable investment progressive programme that could be initiated as a backup for discussions proclaimed under China's leadership.

Anna Joubin-Bret and Cristian Rodríguez Chiffelle discuss the G20 Guiding Principles for Global Investment Policy-Making (G20 Guiding Principles), in whose growth China has had a necessary role, in Chapter 17. They view the G20 Guiding Principles as a stepping stone for multilateral rules on investment. One of the most necessary and strong outcomes of China's G20 governance was the formation of a Trade and Investment Working Group (TIWG), seeing that large and sustainable trade and investment encourages economic growth and calling for high G20 trade and investment cooperation. The Chinese governance reformed approach was not only to bring investment cases to the G20 table, but also to rekindle the conversation on investment and trade policy-making by getting them closer together again. This has opened the way for clear, integrated discussions on trade and investment for the first time in fifteen years in the global political arena. On the issue of investment, the TIWG upheld the G20 Guiding Principles, a major achievement of the Chinese government. These were approved by the G20 ministers of trade in Shanghai in July 2016 and later by the G20 heads of state at the Hangzhou Summit in September 2016, with the purpose of promoting an open, transparent and conducive global policy environment for investment; advancing cooperation in national and international investment policy-making; also advancing all-embracing economic growth and sustainable development. The G20 Guiding Principles are contained in this chapter. The chapter commences with an overview of their crafting and several attempts to formulate guiding principles on international investment, and outlines some of the guidelines that have prepared the way for the Principles. Further, it considers their prospective effect on policy-making at the national and international levels. Finally, this chapter examines the wider work of the G20 TIWG, with trade and investment linkage, addresses the general state of affairs of G20 countries' investment agreements, and draws some preliminary conclusions and looks at ways forward.

In Chapter 18, Sophie Meunier discusses the political challenges presented by China's direct investment in Europe and the United States. The rapid growth of Chinese direct investment has been met in some issues by controversy and even resistance, both in developed and in developing economies. In the wider world, critics have expressed worry and fear related to the possible dangers of this investment: among the most common concerns there are the reduction of local labour standards, the declining competitiveness of its industrial core through repatriation of assets, and acquisition of dual-use technology. Alarmist media headings have warned against Chinese takeover of national economies one controversial investment deal at a time. The resulting political backlash has often had significant media attention and expectations over later deals. What elucidates the political challenges posed by the explosion of Chinese direct investment over the past few years in the United States and the EU? How and why have attitudes and policies in the West been changed over the past ten years towards Chinese FDI? This chapter looks at two different explanations for the political challenges provoked by Chinese investment in Western nations. The first is that Chinese FDI results in political unease because of its newness. The second is the view that there is something really distinct about the nature of Chinese FDI and, therefore, it should not be handled politically like any other foreign investment. These two analyses lead to a distinct set of predictions for the future of Chinese FDI in Europe and the United States. Section I explains how the originality of Chinese FDI may pose political challenges to Western politicians and the general public, and makes a comparison between the present situation and past examples of politically problematic sources of FDI. Section II explains the argument that there is something deeply distinct about Chinese FDI, namely that it stems from an emerging economy, a unique political system and a non-ally in the security dimension. Section III analyses the domestic political context in which these obstacles are raised: in Europe, the euro crisis and the rise of populism; in the United States, the focus on geopolitical contest and the rise of economic nationalism. In the conclusion some considerations are given about if and how these kinds of political challenge may influence the future of Chinese outward investment.

Ka Zeng discusses the political economy of Chinese OFDI in OBOR countries in Chapter 19. The main function of the OBOR initiative in China's total economic development strategy demands for a thorough scholarly analysis of China's trade and investment relations with OBOR countries and the possibility of the initiative to improve the country's economic growth. This chapter discusses such a task and provides an explanation of Chinese OFDI in OBOR nations from 2005 to 2014. Empirical results yield some important findings. First, there is hard proof supporting the resource-seeking motivation behind Chinese OFDI in OBOR countries. Secondly, in comparison to previous studies—which either discover that host-country political risk has no impact on Chinese OFDI or that Chinese OFDI is often likely to be attracted to nations with a high risk in terms of their political environment—this study yields some initial proof that Chinese OFDI is likely to select countries with low political risks. This outcome points to likely changes in the behaviour of Chinese investors in the future, as they increase the scale of their business operation, collecting a wider experience, and thus becoming more qualified players in the worldwide marketplace. Thirdly, the analysis obtained proof that is in line with earlier findings: OFDI tends to go to countries having good political relations with China, or to countries selected according to their geopolitical importance for China's total foreign policy programme. However, the study goes beyond previous studies, which dwell on the host-country political interaction with China and the United States, and looks at some preliminary evidence suggesting that countries with good political relations with the United States are more likely to host Chinese OFDI. Adding these results together shows that as long as OBOR countries are involved, Chinese investment tends to flow to nations with rich natural resources. This may also improve Beijing's influence, not only countries which have been in the past and still are closer with Beijing's values, preferences, and agenda, but also vis-à-vis countries that shared common values with the United States. This could strengthen a China-centric pattern of trade and investment in the Asian region. These results therefore focus on the suggestion that the nature of Chinese OFDI investment in OBOR nations is politically driven, and that it is likely that China will have a central role in guiding Chinese investment in the region.

Manzoor Ahmad, in Chapter 20, further increases the Belt and Road Initiative (BRI) elucidation by focusing on China's role and interest in Central Asia and, specifically, the China–Pakistan economic corridor (CPEC). The chapter gives an encompassing explanation of the CPEC, which is the most developed and ambitious of the six economic corridors comprised in the OBOR initiative. It was announced in November 2014 but has been under consideration for many years. It focuses on the Karakoram Highway joining north-west China (Xinjiang Province) and Pakistan, built from 1959 to 1979, and Gwadar, a port on the Arabian Sea built from 2002 to 2006. The main focus of CPEC will be linking these two infrastructures and contributing to the development of industrial zones along the route. The time schedule envisages a number of phases covering about fifteen years. Although most of the power and Gwadar-development projects are expected to be finished by 2020, the rail and water projects are likely to be completed in the final stage of the project. CPEC will also help Pakistan to capitalize on its strategic location, at the intersection of South Asia, Central Asia, China, and the Middle East, to its economic advantage. By means of CPEC, the seaports of Pakistan can offer the shortest routes to connect China and Central Asian countries with the rest of the world, despite the fact that at present hardly any transport trade passes through them. This chapter revisits the Chinese investments made in the sectors of energy, transport, and water with the objective of checking the dangers related to them. The chapter further showcases the main obstacles that will have to be addressed by China in the OBOR project: if CPEC proves to be a success, it could be duplicated in the other five main corridors of the global project.

In Chapter 21, Susan Finder reviews the shortcoming of the international fraud and corruption sanctioning system in the context of Chinese SOEs. This chapter concentrates on an unexplored feature of Chinese SOEs carrying out business abroad, the relationship of these enterprises with the integrity scheme adopted by the multilateral development banks and development institutions, targeted at curtailing fraud, corruption, and other abuses in projects funded by those institutions. Recently, many Chinese companies have begun engaging in business overseas, being inspired by the 'Go Global policy' and the OBOR project and have been actively bidding for MDB projects. Owing to many reasons, some Chinese enterprises come into conflict with the MDBs' integrity systems. This chapter offers a short examination of the integrity systems developed by the MDBs, dwelling on the interactions between Chinese companies and MDBs, the efforts of the Asian Infrastructure Investment Bank (AIIB) to incorporate that system, and the view of the Chinese government towards this system. It focuses on the position of and viable trends in the incorporation of the Chinese anti-corruption regulatory system with the MDB system.

Joel Slawotsky discusses China as a global power in Chapter 22. The chapter re-examines the potential ramifications of the new international law architects. It explains the need for China to have an ever-greater impact on international investment law, which is the main focus of international economic law. By engaging the mechanics of the present structure to take on a leadership role, China may become the new mastermind of a global legal and monetary framework. New structures and development banks, a growing application of the Yuan, and other incentives usher the emergence of an era of new international law architects. As long as new institutions may first work in collaboration within the subsisting structure, it is likely that the new architects will achieve sufficient influence to achieve an independent role in the international economic and legal regimes. This metamorphosis will probably lead to re-enacting the rules and will act as a means to downgrade the institutions which have implemented the global government architecture over the past seventy years. At least, the substitution of the current architects will offer a precise implementation challenge with respect to international law. A separate code of conduct may interfere with current standards of international law and will require concentrating on the likely division between the former and the new norms and traditions. The failure to handle the imminent conflict of customs may lead to the breakdown of global cooperation and implementation of international law, reduced prosperity, and the promotion of economic and military conflict.

Part IV of this book shows that China is an increasing presence on the global stage. In addition to the force achieved under China's G20 presidency, the adoption of the G20 Guiding Principles might be further developed to accomplish an all embracing economic growth and sustainable development as a panacea for multi-lateral rules on investment. This 'soft law' method of global economic governance is often a more feasible and 'realistic' method in some situations, and it is specifically viable in an international regime which is undergoing a legitimate crisis. A 'soft law' method is non-binding by nature, thus deviating from conventional formal arrangements under public international law which are organized using a 'hard law' method, treaty-based (e.g. WTO, NAFTA) and/or institution-based (e.g. OECD, APEC) to regulate global economic issues.

Notwithstanding the disadvantages of 'soft law'—its non-enforceable nature which does not impose any formal duties on the state, risking a 'cheap exit' from their expectations—a major advantage of the 'soft law' method is its ability to accomplish and maintain political agreement that to a large extent can enable the negotiation of an agreement in which conflicting issues will be handled and controlled. Corporate social responsibility and the resolution of investment disputes, are major areas of impasse in negotiations, and might even lead to a total dissolution of such agreement. Without doubt, investment as a tool for sustainable economic development requires a global meeting of minds and is enshrined in the UN Charter. Although relating to top-down methods, since the 1990s several international organizations have made efforts to make multi-lateral binding rules on investment, both substantive and procedural, but they have failed to do so.

The bottom-up method, with states as conventional law-makers in collaboration with NGOs, technocrats, civil society, and so on need to be utilized as an optional approach to global economic governance. By using the hard and soft law method of global economic governance together will supplement and surmount integral structural mistakes and weaknesses. In maintaining this momentum, China can and should add to the establishing of multi-lateral rules on investment, taking good advantage of its consensus building capability. China could apply the G20 Guiding Principles to equip a new (comprehensive and balanced) Model BIT at home. Additionally, China could help to accelerate the conclusion of the RCEP, building on its largely coherent treaty practice with ASEAN abroad. China could advance further by building on the political meeting of minds reached under its G20 leadership together with the assembly among the G20 nations' IIA practice towards a multi-lateral agreement on investment. Increasingly, China's position in and between Brazil, Russia, India, China, and South Africa (BRICS) and the G20 would strengthen multi-lateral investment policy-making and rule-making by luring more participants from the global south to be in alliance not only in trade, finance, and development, but also in investment rule-making. China could also extend the scope of the negotiations to take into consideration the wide and sometimes conflicting interests of investment safeguard and liberalization and sustainable development.

V. The Challenges of Investor–State Dispute Settlement

Investment dispute resolution and China seem to reveal a paradox. Presently China has the second largest BIT programme worldwide after Germany and has undergone three generations of BITs. Domestically, China has made an important amendment in its Constitution, in which foreign investments were permitted and protected for the first time, under the 1982 Constitution of the People's Republic of China (PRC).[20] After the accession of China to the International Centre for the Settlement of Investment Disputes (ICSID) Convention, most BITs featured in the second generation of Chinese BITs (1990–1997) referred to ICSID as a venue to arbitrate investor–state disputes with regard to the amount of compensation for expropriation.[21] China has also completed ten FTAs, improving political dealings with Asian neighbours and constructing closer business ties with resource-rich countries in Asia, Latin America, and Africa, although the investment rules presented in China's FTAs 'do not exceed the boundaries' of China's new BITs in terms of the level of safeguard and liberalization of investment.

---

[20] Article 18 of the Constitution of the PRC states:

The People's Republic of China permits foreign enterprises, other foreign economic organizations and individual foreigners to invest in China and to enter into various forms of economic cooperation with Chinese enterprises and other Chinese economic organizations in accordance with the law of the People's Republic of China. All foreign enterprises, other foreign economic organizations as well as Chinese-foreign joint ventures within Chinese territory shall abide by the law of the People's Republic of China. Their lawful rights and interests are protected by the law of the People's Republic of China.

[21] See J R Weeramantry, 'Investor–State Dispute Settlement Provisions in China's Investment Treaties' (2012) 27(1) ICSID Review 192.

In addition to the change of Chinese BITs in the level of the breadth and depth of investment rules, China's involvement in international investment rules is also influenced by the critics of the present ISDS system and investment claims, even though only a small portion of investment claims was brought against China.[22] Flourishing, China has realized the necessity of the balance between the protection of investors and the right to control, and will therefore 'embody an improved dispute settlement mechanism' in its future BITs. China's attempt to involve itself in the international investment regime not only delivers greater safeguards to both Chinese investors abroad and foreign investors in China by enriching its domestic rule of law. In the end, China is able to better to take its place in the world economy. Notwithstanding the significant number of international treaties and domestic reforms on investment law combined with the considerable volume of foreign investments in China, it is noteworthy to see that China has not been involved (as home or host country) in so many investment disputes. Part IV explores the reasons that explain past experience and sheds light on what the near future could be.

The role of China in international investment arbitration is examined in Chapter 23 by Matthew Hodgson and Adam Bryan. This chapter carefully investigates China's approach to bilateral agreements and makes some observations about its potential future strategy. This chapter analyses the relation between the development and nature of China's inward and OFDI with the protections offered in the BITs, taking into consideration the identity of China's partners therein. As in the West, confidence in investment treaties is at a low point—in view of the public dissatisfaction in Europe towards the draft Transatlantic Trade and Investment Partnership (TTIP) and the opposition of the Trump administration to investment treaties in general, and in particular to NAFTA and TPP—there might be a chance for China to display leadership and cooperation with domestic and global economic partners. This chapter first outlines the development of the protections offered in China's investment treaties, from the elementary safeguards in the early generation investment treaties to the broad-scale coverage in the more current ones. This chapter also ponders the extent to which China has succeeded in safeguarding its outward investment, with the repercussions of these protections on inward investment. It analyses the (relatively few) cases that have been brought under Chinese investment treaties and carries out a statistical analysis of the protection accorded to Chinese investment stocks, making a comparison with competitor economies. Lastly, this chapter considers where it is likely that China will focus its attention next, in view of the orientation of Trump's administration in the United States and China's investment priorities.

Jane Willems highlights the investment disputes under China's BITs in Chapter 24. This chapter reviews and contrasts the decisions delivered by arbitral tribunals and state courts on the scope of the agreed clauses contained in first-generation Chinese BITs, with the judgments delivered under other BITs with analogous wordings. The judgments relating to Chinese BITs have added to the debate on the interpretation of treaties taking into consideration the following decisions: arbitral awards related to the determination of the arbitral jurisdiction, and the subsequent state courts judgments that have reviewed, and on most instances sanctioned, these awards. These decisions

---

[22] For commentary on the jurisdiction of ICSID to investment disputes relating to China see Jane Y Willems, 'The Settlement of Investor State Disputes and China: New Developments on ICSID Jurisdiction' (2011) 8(1) South Carolina Journal of International Law & Business 1 and Monika C E Heymann, 'International Law and the Settlement of Investment Disputes Relating to China' (2008) 11(3) Journal of International Economic Law 507.

bear more details relating to BITs concluded by socialist nations than features characteristic of China's BITs. The circumstance is different from other jurisdictional issues. The territorial jurisdiction of arbitral tribunals under the Chinese BITs—and whether they are applicable to Special Administrative Regions (SARs)—was analysed by interpreting the territorial scope of agreements and under the moving frontier rule and the exceptions to these principles, in particular the intention alleged by China. The question of the nation of origin of the investor requesting the protection offered by Chinese BITs permitted arbitral tribunals for the first time to adopt, at an international level, the nationality test for both corporations and individuals established in the SARs contained in domestic law.

In Chapter 25, Claire Wilson reviews the major case *Ping An v Belgium*, which marks an important improvement in ISDS jurisprudence. It is the first case in which a mainland Chinese company has brought a claim before the International Centre for the Settlement of Investment Disputes (ICSID), and the first ICSID case with Belgium as a respondent. The dispute is of great public significance and resulted from actions taken during the 2008 global financial crisis. The claim centres on the standard of protection granted to Chinese investments in host countries with which China concluded successive treaties. The claim also offers additional knowledge from a strategic point of view. According to the investor, Belgium's financial restructuring measures enacted in 2008 amounted to a breach of the 1986 China–Belgium BIT, which the investor invoked for the ground of his claim but relying upon a subsequent 2009 BIT attempting to establish jurisdiction. Until recent times, only a few BIT claims regarding measures taken during financial crises have been brought against member states of the EU; of these most were restricted to claims resulting from measures issued in Cyprus and Greece. However, circumstances in Europe were very different from those characterizing Argentina's crisis, a point made in order to highlight the contrast between the EU and Argentina, where emergency legislation had damaged foreign investors' interests. The recent Argentinian bond cases entail new types of BIT claims related to bail-outs and forceful restructurings undertaken in the period of the 2001 crisis. Unlike other claimants, Ping An was unable to obtain a favourable outcome against Belgium: on 30 April 2005 the ICSID tribunal dismissed Ping An's claim for lack of jurisdiction, a decision which generated heavy criticism.

Sungjin Kang examines the possible problem of China's competitive steps under IIAs in Chapter 26. Since 2008, when the Anti-Monopoly Law (AML) was adopted in China, many cases have been brought, in several sub-branches of competition law. It is noteworthy that the Chinese government has been very keen to sample the experience of other countries and upgrade China's competition law implementation system in a short time, although lawyers and scholars have observed some procedural issues relating to the implementation of AML, mostly against foreign companies.

In essence, AML made room for possible judicial review by a competent court of China, although, in actual practice, most foreign companies are still not comfortable with the independence of China's judiciary and are still hesitant to refer the decisions of the relevant Chinese competition authorities to the Chinese courts. Furthermore, there are some occasions where Chinese competition authorities engage AML to foster China's own industrial policy instead of ensuring fair competition in the markets in question. In view of this, foreign companies do not have absolute trust in the judgment of the Chinese competition authorities applying the AML honestly to protect fair competition between Chinese enterprises and foreign enterprises. Therefore, foreign investors looking for a way to ensure the enforcement of 'fair and equitable' treatment prefer, in the alternative, a 'national treatment' under the investment agreements between China and its main trading partners. Luckily, there is an increasing number of investor–state cases against the Chinese government. Furthermore, there is an increasing scholarly debate on whether it is possible to engage the ISDS, particularly to contest the judgments of competition authorities on procedural grounds. The chapter's author is of the opinion that it is time for foreign investors in China to regard ISDS as an alternative to contest procedural aspects of the implementation of Chinese competition law. The author concentrates on the cases where the National Development and Reform Commission (NDRC) and the State Administration for Industry and Commerce (SAIC) use AML against the international syndicates' misuse of dominance cases. Of course, as the history of AML implementation is essentially brief, there are various avenues for the Chinese competition authority to improve, by bracing up with other competition governments. But by instituting an AML case before an ISDS tribunal, foreign investors may lure Chinese competition authorities to respect the due process and fair implementation of the competition laws, thereby advancing openness and predictability of the competition law implementation in China.

Finally, in Chapter 27, Shu Shang explores the option of implementing investor–state mediation in China's next generation of investment treaties, an interesting proposal taking into consideration that China could act as the respondent. The chapter first discusses the rise of mediation in international commercial and business dispute settings, and mediation's potential applications in resolving investor–state claims. It then discusses the background of the recent rise of alternative dispute resolution (ADR) in China, which may lead to the adoption of an investor–state mechanism in the country's future BITs, and how such a mechanism should be devised. At the end, it wraps up the discussion by arguing that rather than returning to political means of settling investor–state disputes, the recent rise of interest-based investor–state mediation indicates that, as the parties become more experienced with investment treaty claims, they may consider the amicable interaction between parties as more desirable and effective.

VI. Concluding Remarks

With great strength comes enormous responsibility. China has been required to review its BIT and FTA method. Since 1982, the major objective of Chinese IIAs was to attract and maintain FDI in China even though, in this era, China's ODI gradually increased. In 2014 for the first time China's OFDI surpassed its IFDI.[23] In the conclusion of IIAs, obligations and rights must be balanced so as to attain similar commitments between China and foreign nations, and to attain common interests between China and foreign investors. In addition, modern international investment policy should maintain a certain degree independence to enable China to respond to its developing economy.

Internationally, without the efficiency and implementation of the international legal system, a realistic accomplishment of international affairs is that it is power and not law that triggers the formation, function, and transformation of the international rule of law, as Kenneth Waltz has elucidated. Non-compliance with the international rule of law will increase reputational costs, which in turn could reduce coordination

---

[23] See Ben Yunmo Wang, 'China "Going Out" 2.0: Dawn of a New Era for Chinese Investment Abroad', Huffington Post, 4 November 2015, http://www.huffingtonpost.com/china-hands/china-going-out-20-dawn-o_b_7046790.html (last accessed 20 November 2017).

and cooperation from others if one state tries to promote its national interest on the international stage. At the sixtieth anniversary ceremony of Five Principles of Peaceful Coexistence, President Xi Jinping revalidated the responsibility of international rule of law in global governance:

[we] should jointly promote the rule of law in international relations. We should encourage all parties to comply with international law and well-recognised basic principles regulating international relations and use broadly applicable rules to distinguish between right and wrong and embrace peace and development.

One of the most striking characteristics of investment agreements is that they have transformed little in form and in substance since the first agreements were concluded in the 1970s. The international investment exchanges have drastically transformed and investment flows have themselves become more complicated. Most investors from developing nations and nations in transition are now migrating overseas to improve their economic activities (in the context of south–south and south–north flow). In fact, over the last ten years or so, there have been plans to reform IIAs—originally introduced by a few states and then passed by certain international organizations such as UNCTAD and the OECD. This modern trend has not yet eradicated the imbalance contained in these documents.

FDI, as long as it enables the transfer of technology and generates remarkable task revenues, is considered to be one of the major tools for sustainable development. Nevertheless, international normative documents take little notice of this sustainable development obligation and this is likely where China's leadership will be assessed. The separation of rights and obligations is blatant in the clash between states and foreign investors. IIAs can result in a real brake on the enforcement of public policy in favour of sustainable development. This is not just the treaties themselves, but the manner in which they are applied by some investors. Establishing the dispute mechanism is at the centre of this current discussion on the desired and desirable development of the IIAs. The importance of accepted international standards needs to be recognized in describing responsible investment, thereby incorporating investment agreements into a broader set of informal and formal normative documents that can interact with one another. From a participatory point of view, which is centred on a normative process whereby each of the stakeholders has been associated with the applicable law, this needs the involvement of states, international institutions, investors, and some NGOs.

This book is the product of careful research and a real quest to comprehend the contemporary dynamics of China's approach towards international investment law and policy, which has been backed by the General Research Fund (GRF), Hong Kong SAR Research Grants Councils, 2016–2018. This effort resulted in the Asia FDI Forum II held in Hong Kong on 29–30 November 2016, an event jointly sponsored by the Chinese University of Hong Kong (CUHK) Law Faculty and the Columbia University Centre for Sustainable Investment. Launched by the CUHK Faculty of Law in 2015, the series of meetings of the Asia FDI Forum offers a multi-stakeholder platform anchored in Hong Kong for participants from academia, government, the private sector, and civil society to discuss regional investment trends, highlight specific characteristics of investment treaties and policies, analyse Asia's relationship with other nations of the world, and explore the several legal and policy implications of the emergence of new actors, issues, and norms which determine the future of Asian FDI. The Asia FDI Forum has been established to offer an avenue for expert discussion based on academic research and policy-based analysis, mostly related to legal development but also key economics and politics issues on FDI in Asia.

1

China's Inward Investment

Approach and Impact

Michael J Enright*

I. Introduction

One of the most important components in China's economic reform programme has been the economy's gradual opening to inward foreign direct investment (IFDI) and foreign invested enterprises (FIEs). While China has become more and more open to IFDI over time, it remains far more closed than most large economies. In recent years, we have seen the apparent contradictory trends toward developing what appears to be a more liberal legal environment for IFDI combined with highly publicized examples of pushback against FIEs in China.

In order to understand China's approach towards IFDI and FIEs, it is necessary to understand the historical background of IFDI and FIEs in China, the objective function that China applies to IFDI and FIEs, and the fact that the impact of IFDI and FIEs on China's economy is often underestimated. These features will influence any investment treaties that might be reached with China and how they will be implemented. In the rest of this chapter, we provide a broad-brush perspective on China's approach toward IFDI and FIEs. We then describe the results of our novel method of estimating the economic benefits that IFDI and FIEs have brought to China. Finally, we provide some perspectives for those interested in the potential for the negotiation and implementation of investment agreements with China. In particular, we note that China's gradual approach toward IFDI is completely consistent with its gradual approach in terms of the types and details of the international investment agreements (IIAs) it has negotiated; and the expanded focus from bilateral investment treaties (BITs) to regional and potentially global arrangements.

II. Historical Perspectives

In the 19th century, foreign investment was imposed on China by force. The Treaty of Nanking of 1842, which ended the Opium Wars, opened five treaty ports to trade with foreign powers. Foreign shipping companies, trading companies, and banks

* Sun Hung Kai Professor of Business, The University of Hong Kong. The author wishes to acknowledge the research support of Edith Scott, Ella Dong, David Sanderson, and Sophie Zhang of Enright, Scott & Associates (http://enrightscott.com/). The research behind this chapter was funded by the Hinrich Foundation (http://hinrichfoundation.com/). A more extensive version of these arguments may be found in Michael J Enright, *Developing China: The Remarkable Impact of Foreign Direct Investment* (Routledge 2017).

soon set up in foreign-controlled enclaves at the ports. Foreign merchants also began to manufacture in the enclaves, even though this was not allowed by the original treaties. The Treaty of Shimonoseki of 1895, which ended the Sino-Japanese War, gave Japanese companies the right to manufacture in the ports that had been opened by treaty or by decree of the Chinese Government.[1] Companies from other treaty countries obtained the same rights through 'most favoured nation' clauses in the relevant treaties.[2]

IFDI soon spread to other parts of China. The value of assets owned by foreign entities through direct investment in China were estimated at US$2,682 million in 1936,[3] or in the order of US$46 billion in 2016.[4] By the mid-1930s, foreign investors had financed and controlled railroads, ships and shipping, the mining and metals sector, and around 35 per cent of manufacturing output in China (50 per cent or more in 'modern' manufacturing). The influence of foreign investment was so extensive one analyst stated that foreign capital was 'largely responsible for the development of whatever economic modernization took place in China before 1937'.[5] On the other hand, extraterritoriality, economic spheres of influence, dominance of foreign enterprises, difficulty in collecting tax from foreign companies, and huge differences between the incomes and lifestyles of foreign executives and local workers led many in China to associate IFDI with exploitation.

Under the Treaty of San Francisco, which ended the Second World War in the Pacific, China was granted all previously Japanese-owned assets in the country.[6] After the establishment of the People's Republic of China in October 1949, remaining FIEs were initially told that their operations would be protected.[7] However, China's economy was eventually socialized, and the assets of FIEs were expropriated or abandoned due to laws and regulations that made them unviable. By 1957, virtually all Western companies had exited China.[8] Cooperation between China and the Soviet Union soured in the 1960s, and by the early 1970s virtually all Sino-Eastern bloc joint ventures had been closed, leaving essentially no foreign investment in China.[9] It would take the re-entry of China into the international community, the end of the Cultural Revolution, and Deng Xiaoping's rise to leadership for China to reassess its approach toward IFDI and FIEs.

---

[1] There were a total of 105 open ports established in China, mostly by force or threat of force, from 1842 to 1930. See Chi-ming Hou, *Foreign Investment in China 1840-1937* (Harvard University Press 1964) 106.

[2] 'Most favoured nation' clauses meant concessions given to one foreign country signatory must be given to all other foreign country signatories.

[3] Hou (n 1) 13.

[4] Estimated by Enright, Scott & Associates based on US Government historical inflation charts.

[5] Hou (n 1) 130.

[6] UK Secretary of State for Foreign Affairs, *Treaty of peace with Japan, San Francisco, 8th September, 1951* (HM Stationery Office 1952); Werner Levi, *Modern China's Foreign Policy* (University of Minnesota Press 1953). At the end of the 1930s, Japan was the largest foreign investor in China, with an estimated share of 40% of total inward investment, including direct investments and loans. See Hou (n 1) 16–17.

[7] *Liberation Daily* (6 August 1950) quoted in Thomas N Thompson, *China's Nationalization of Foreign Firms: The Politics of Hostage Capitalism, 1949-57* (School of Law University of Maryland 1979) 21.

[8] Thompson (n 7) 21; Aron Shai, 'Hostage Capitalism and French Companies in China: A Hidden Element in Sino-French Relations' (1993) XII (1) Études chinoises.

[9] Yingqi Wei and Xiaming Liu, *Foreign Investment in China: Determinants and Impact* (Edward Elgar Publishing 2001).

III. China's Opening

The Third Plenary Session of the Eleventh Central Committee of the Chinese Communist Party in 1978 marked the beginning of China's opening and reform process. The Plenum called for modernization of agriculture, industry, science and technology, and national defence to improve the economy, improve the people's standard of living, and to enhance national security.[10] China's leaders wished to industrialize China and modernize industrial sectors that often lagged behind best practice by two or three decades and IFDI was seen as a 'package deal' that would provide technology, management skills, and access to foreign markets.[11]

IV. Legal Regime

Three major laws, the Law of the People's Republic of China on Joint Ventures Using Chinese and Foreign Investment (1979), the Law of the People's Republic of China on Enterprises Operated Exclusively with Foreign Capital (1986), and the Law of the People's Republic of China on Contractual Joint Ventures Using Chinese and Foreign Investment (1988), formed the early legal basis for foreign investment in China. Other major initiatives in this period included implementation regulations for the three laws, the Regulations on Special Economic Zones in Guangdong Province (1980), and the Provisions of the State Council of the People's Republic of China for the Encouragement of Foreign Investment (1986). Under the Company Law (1994) FIEs would be subject to the same laws as Chinese companies except for provisions overridden by the special foreign investment laws.

China's entry into the World Trade Organization in 2001 was accompanied by a wide range of concessions regarding IFDI. Many additional industries were opened to FIEs, and rules concerning foreign exchange balances, foreign currency purchases, local content, and export performance of FIEs were removed. In addition, FIEs were no longer required to file production and business plans with government authorities.[12] China's Provisions on Mergers and Acquisitions of Domestic Enterprises by Foreign Investors (2006) and Anti-Monopoly Law (2007) further clarified the regime for FIEs. While the AML is supposed to be equally applied to foreign and domestic firms, it specifically exempts state-owned monopolies and oligopolies, aims to 'promote the healthy development of the socialist market economy', and requires enforcement agencies to 'take into account industrial policy considerations'.[13]

In January 2015, the Chinese Ministry of Commerce released a draft of a New Foreign Investment Law (DFIL) for public consultation. The DFIL would replace the previous laws concerning IFDI with a single statute.[14] FIEs would come under China's Company Law. IFDI would be made on the same terms as domestic investments, without approvals or sector restrictions unless otherwise required by law. Most IFDI, except that into industries on a 'negative list' or involving amounts exceeding levels set

---

[10] ibid.
[11] Chunlai Chen, *Foreign Direct Investment in China: Location Determinants, Investor Differences and Economic Impacts* (Edward Elgar Publishing 2011) 34.
[12] ibid 55–56.
[13] Colin Shek, 'Understanding China's Anti-Monopoly Law' (2015) 18 CKGSB Knowledge 36.
[14] Christopher W Betts and others, 'China's MOFCOM Aims to Fundamentally Change the Legal Landscape on Foreign Investments' (Skadden Insights February 2015).

by State Council, would no longer need pre-approval, but instead would require an information report to be submitted at the time of investment and annual follow-up reports to be submitted to local authorities. In theory, this would substantially reduce the administrative burden associated with foreign investment. However, the DFIL had not been enacted by the end of 2016.

V. Sector-Based Policies

China's policy toward IFDI has involved the targeting of favoured or high-priority industries, sectors, and activities, and the restriction or prohibition of IFDI into sensitive industries. The Interim Provisions on Guiding Foreign Investment and the Catalogue for the Guidance of Foreign Investment Industries (1995) provided the initial guidance. Since 2002, the Catalogue has divided sectors into 'encouraged', 'permitted', 'restricted', and 'prohibited' categories, pursuant to the Provisions on Guiding the Orientation of Foreign Investment adopted in connection with China's WTO accession.[15] There are also specific catalogues for specific sectors and for some geographic regions. The catalogues' restrictions are not comprehensive—additional restrictions often exist for investments within the 'encouraged' and 'permitted' categories, and regulators can restrict investment for unspecified reasons.[16]

The 2007 Catalogue added a wide range of high-technology, resource saving, alternative energy, service outsourcing, and modern logistics industries to the encouraged category. On the other hand, investments exporting 100 per cent of production were omitted from the encouraged category. Several industries associated with high consumption of resources or pollution were placed in the restricted or prohibited categories. Publishing and media remained prohibited, and a variety of Internet-based businesses were added to the prohibited category. The 2011 Catalogue added encouragement of environmentally-friendly investments and adjustments to match current industrial policy. The 2015 Catalogue removed restrictions on IFDI in several manufacturing sectors, with more limited revisions in services, agriculture, and infrastructure.[17] According to China's National Reform and Development Commission (NDRC), the 2015 Catalogue lowered the number of 'restricted' industries from 79 to 38; the number of sectors in which Chinese-controlled joint ventures are required from 44 to 35; and the number of industries requiring joint ventures with Chinese partners, but allowing foreign control, from 43 to 15. It exempted e-commerce from the foreign equity cap of 50 per cent applicable to value-added telecom services. Restrictions on IFDI remained in banking, telecommunications, and cultural industries.[18]

---

[15] The WTO agreement also extended the industries open to foreign investors. For example, a wide range of service sectors including financial services, distribution, business services, communications, travel and tourism, healthcare, environmental services, and education were progressively opened to foreign investors, with geographic, business scope, and ownership restrictions generally being phased out. See generally Julien Chaisse and Mitsuo Matsushita, 'China's "Belt and Road" Initiative: Mapping the World Trade Normative and Strategic Implications' (2018) 52(1) Journal of World Trade 163.

[16] US State Department, 'China Investment Climate Statement' (2015) 7.

[17] Ashwin Kaja and others, 'The Chinese Government Issues 2015 Foreign Investment Catalogue: Effective April 10, 2015' Covington & Burling Global Policy Watch (24 March 2015).

[18] US State Department (n 16) 7.

VI. Geography-Based Policies

China's opening also had a geographic component. IFDI was first allowed in Special Economic Zones in Shenzhen, Zhuhai, Xiamen, and Shantou in coastal Guangdong and Fujian Provinces. The SEZs operated under special regulatory regimes designed to offer FIEs preferred terms, including income tax reductions, duty exemptions on imports used in the production of exports, export duty exemptions, facilitated entry and exit formalities, and fiscal and foreign exchange privileges.[19]

In 1984, the Chinese government opened an additional fourteen coastal cities and Hainan Island to IFDI. The Yangtze River Delta (around Shanghai), Pearl River Delta (near Hong Kong), and Min Nan Delta (around Xiamen) were designated as coastal economic open areas in 1985 and were encouraged to set up Economic and Technological Development Zones (ETDZs). In 1988, open policies for IFDI were extended to coastal areas in general. In 1992, IFDI incentives were expanded and projects that fulfilled industrial policy objectives could receive the same preferential treatment as in open areas, no matter where they were located. Fifty-two cities were opened to foreign investors and fifteen 'open border cities' were created under a variety of schemes. By late 1992, there were nearly 2,000 ETDZs across the country, most encouraging IFDI.[20]

In 2000, the State Council's Policies and Measures for the Western Development Strategy provided preferential policies to promote economic growth across Western and Central China. FIEs already present in coastal areas were offered preferential treatment for investments in Central and Western China. Subsequently, China has continued to encourage foreign firms to set up operations in Western, Central, and Northeastern China, via the Catalogue of Priority Industries for Foreign Investment in the Central-Western Regions, and subsequent initiatives.[21]

In September 2013, the Shanghai Pilot Free Trade Zone was launched as a testing ground for IFDI and market access reforms. The 'negative list' for investment approvals in the FTZ superseded the prohibited, restricted, and encouraged categories for the first time in China.[22] In April 2015, new Pilot FTZs were declared in Tianjin, Fujian, and Guangdong.[23] A revised 'negative list' was introduced in all four FTZs in 2015, with IFDI not subject to the negative list proceeding via a streamlined filing system. The FTZs represent the continuation of geographic experiments concerning IFDI and FIEs.

VII. China's Approach to IFDI and FIEs

China's gradual approach toward IFDI and FIEs in terms of legal regime, ownership structures, sectors, and geographies is not surprising given China's previous experience with foreign investment and the resulting fear of foreign domination. It is also not

[19] Yongjun Wang, *Investment in China: A Question and Answer Guide on How to Do Business* (American Management Association 1997) 28–29.
[20] Chen, *Foreign Direct Investment in China* (n 11) 42.
[21] Nancy Huang and others, 'Economic Development Policies for Central and Western China' (2010) 37 China Business Review 24.
[22] Deloitte Touche Tohmatsu, 'Taxation and Investment in China 2015' (2015).
[23] Dezan Shira and Associates, 'The New Free Trade Zones Explained, Part III: Tianjin' *China Briefing News* (2015) 39; Dezan Shira and Associates, 'A Guide to China's Free Trade Zones' *China Briefing* (2016) 162.

surprising given the fact that prior to China's initial opening the economy was completely dominated by the state. The lack of an indigenous private sector meant that the legal, regulatory, and administrative regime to deal with non-state actors had to be developed virtually from scratch to cover FIEs. The gradual approach allowed the Chinese Government to experiment, to learn how to deal with FIEs, and to channel investment into desired sectors and locations. The Chinese Government found that foreign investors would only make certain types of investments if they had greater control, flexibility in operations, and certainty of legal and regulatory regime than was present initially.[24] Thus, China's approach to IFDI and FIEs has been influenced by the constant tension for the Chinese Government between the desire to gain the advantages of IFDI while limiting the perceived downsides in terms of potential loss of sovereignty and control, and the constant tension for FIEs between the desire to benefit from investments in China while limiting the risks associated with operating in the Chinese environment.

The gradual approach has also been influenced by China's objective function when it comes to IFDI and FIEs. While in the West, the primary considerations concerning IFDI after national security tend to be job creation, GDP growth, and consumer welfare, in China industrial policy and a desire to build strong indigenous companies carry far greater weight. IFDI and FIEs, it was hoped, would bring not just capital, but know-how, technology, management expertise, exports, and controlled competition that would stimulate the improvement Chinese firms. The goal has been a strong Chinese economy with stronger Chinese firms succeeding domestically and internationally, rather than a Chinese economy dominated by foreign firms.[25] China's economic goals and policies are highlighted in its Five Year Programmes and a series of major initiatives, such as the One Belt-One Road, Manufacturing 2025, Internet Plus, Go West, and Go Global initiatives. Our experience of decades of consulting to FIEs in China is that companies whose business plans contribute to China's achieving the goals outlined in the programmes and initiatives receive far better treatment in China than others regardless of investment treaties or agreements in place.

The Chinese objective function regarding IFDI and FIEs is also reflected in an asymmetry in the English and Chinese literature on IFDI and FIEs in China. In an analysis based on citations, we found that the English language literature tends to address the impact on China's economy as a whole, including the impact on GDP growth, productivity, incomes, and sophistication of the economy, but the bulk of the most cited Chinese language literature addresses the impact of IFDI and FIEs on Chinese firms, in particular whether IFDI and FIEs crowd out indigenous investment, enhance the competitiveness of indigenous firms, or enhance the technological capabilities of local firms.[26]

The asymmetry is further reflected in interviews of auto industry executives carried out by the author. A foreign manager of one joint venture claimed that China's auto policy had been extremely frustrating for the foreign companies, given the restrictions in the sector, and tremendously successful for China, given the fact that China now has by far the largest automotive sector in the world, employs more people in the sector than any other country, and that Chinese consumers have far better options than they

---

[24] Yongjun Wang (n 19) 3; Ashok Kundra, *India-China, A Comparative Analysis of FDI Policy and Performance* (Academic Foundation 2009) 187–8; US State Department, (n 16) 7.
[25] Michael J Enright, *Developing China: The Remarkable Impact of Foreign Direct Investment* (Routledge 2017).
[26] ibid.

would have had without the FIEs. A Chinese manager from another joint venture, on the other hand, claimed that the policy had been a failure because no Chinese auto company was competitive in world markets based on its own designs and technology.[27]

VIII. IFDI Results

IFDI grew dramatically as China opened its economy. Utilized foreign investment increased from US$4,104 million in the 1979 to 1984 period, to US$3,487 million in 1990, to US$40,715 million in 2000, to US$114,734 million in 2010. In 2014, China was the world's top destination for IFDI, reporting 23,778 IFDI projects and utilized IFDI of US$119,562 million. From 1979 to 2014, China recorded a total of 810,163 projects with a cumulative utilized FDI value of US$1,590,062 million[28] (see Figures 1.1 and 1.2). While these numbers seem extraordinary, what is even more extraordinary is the fact that the vast majority of China's IFDI has been greenfield investment, rather than the merger and acquisitions that dominates IFDI into OECD countries.[29]

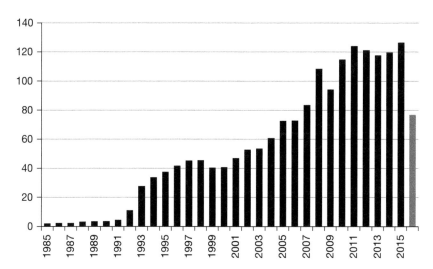

Figure 1.1 Annual IFDI flows into China, 1979 to 2016, US$ billion

Note: 2016—January to July.

Sources: CEIC; *China Statistical Yearbook 2016.*

[27] Author's interviews.

[28] The cumulative values in the Chinese statistics are the simple sums of the number of projects and investment flows from 1979 up to the year in question. The official statistics do not estimate a capital stock for foreign investment in China, nor do they adjust for inflation.

[29] Guoqiang Long, 'China's Policies on FDI: Review and Evaluation' in Theodore H Moran and others (eds), *Does FDI Promote Development?* (Institute for International Economics 2005); Wim Naudé and others, 'Industrialization and Technological Change in the BRICS: The Role of Foreign and Domestic Investment' in Wim Naudé and others (eds), *Structural Change and Industrial Development in the BRICs* (Oxford University Press 2015).

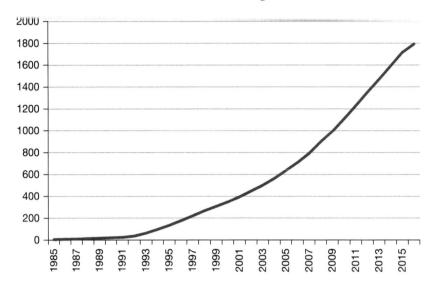

Figure 1.2 Cumulative IFDI flows into China, 1985 to 2016, US$ billion

Note: The cumulative figures are the sums of the relevant flows from 1979 up to the year in question.

Sources: CEIC; *China Statistical Yearbook 2016.*

While the IFDI amounts in China look large in absolute terms, they have become small in relative terms. IFDI's share in total investment in China grew significantly in the 1980s and 1990s, peaked at 14.3 per cent of gross capital formation and 11.8 per cent of fixed asset investment in the early to mid-1990s, and declined to under 3 per cent or under 1 per cent depending on the measure. These figures indicate that the importance of IFDI and FIEs has been diminishing in recent years in terms of the amount of capital invested (Figures 1.3 and 1.4).

Figure 1.3 IFDI as a % of gross capital formation in China, 1983 to 2013

Sources: CEIC; *China Statistical Yearbook 2014*; World Bank, *World Development Indicators.*

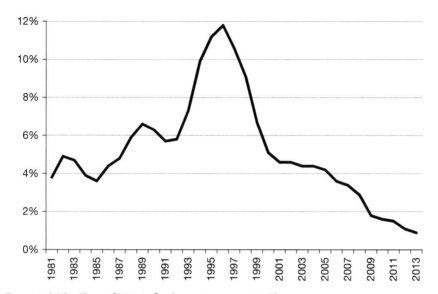

Figure 1.4 The Share of FIEs in fixed asset investment in China

Sources: CEIC; *China Statistical Yearbook 2014*; World Bank, *World Development Indicators*.

FIEs have helped China become the world's leading trading nation, its leading exporter, and its second leading importer.[30] The FIE contribution to China's trade peaked at 58 per cent of exports and 60 per cent of imports in 2006 (Table 1.1). By 2013, FIEs accounted for 47 per cent of China's exports and 45 per cent of China's imports. The net exports of FIEs actually made a negative contribution to GDP in the early 1990s. By 2007, FIE net exports exceeded US$100,000 million per year and in 2013 exceeded US$169,000 million. The FIE net export contribution peaked at 3.9 per cent of GDP in 2007 before falling below 2 per cent by 2011. FIEs also sell far more in China today than they export from China, with the 2013 ratio being 2.73 to 1 in favour of sales in China.

While the investment and even trade figures might indicate a limited influence of IFDI and FIEs, one gets a different picture when one examines the presence of FIEs in particular industries. There are several industries in China in which FIEs accounted for 20 per cent, 30 per cent, 40 per cent, or more of the assets, revenues, and/or profits. Overall, foreign invested industrial enterprises accounted for 22 per cent of total assets, 23 per cent of total revenue, and 23 per cent of total profit of all industrial enterprises (above scale) in China (Table 1.2).[31] FIEs have strong positions in some of the more advanced and more sophisticated industries with important spill-overs into the local economy (e.g. computers, communication and other electronic equipment; automobiles; and others).

---

[30] World Trade Organization (WTO), *International Trade Statistics 2015* (2015).
[31] 'Industrial Enterprises' (above scale) includes industrial enterprises of all types of ownership with revenue over RMB 20 million in 2013.

Table 1.1 Trade Performance of Foreign Invested Enterprises

Year	FIE Exports (USD mn)	FIE Imports (USD mn)	FIE Exports / FIE Imports	China's Exports by FIEs (%)	China's Imports by FIEs (%)	FIE Net Exports (USD mn)	FIE Net Exports as % of China GDP	FIE Domestic Revenue (USD mn)	FIE Domestic Rev / Exports
1993	25,237	41,833	60%	28%	40%	-16,596	-2.7%		
1994	34,713	52,934	66%	29%	46%	-18,221	-3.3%		
1995	46,876	62,943	74%	32%	48%	-16,067	-2.2%	74,257	158%
1996	61,506	75,604	81%	41%	54%	-14,098	-1.6%	68,639	112%
1997	74,900	77,721	96%	41%	55%	-2,821	-0.3%	82,155	110%
1998	80,962	76,717	106%	44%	55%	4,245	0.4%	NA	NA
1999	88,628	85,884	103%	45%	52%	2,744	0.3%	128,405	145%
2000	119,441	117,273	102%	48%	52%	2,168	0.2%	152,899	128%
2001	133,235	125,863	106%	50%	52%	7,372	0.6%	181,153	136%
2002	169,985	160,254	106%	52%	54%	9,731	0.7%	206,836	122%
2003	240,306	231,864	104%	55%	56%	8,442	0.5%	286,544	119%
2004	338,592	324,448	104%	57%	58%	14,144	0.7%	360,126	106%
2005	444,183	387,456	115%	58%	59%	56,727	2.5%	514,586	116%
2006	563,779	472,490	119%	58%	60%	91,289	3.4%	677,042	120%
2007	695,371	559,793	124%	57%	59%	135,578	3.9%	954,284	137%
2008	790,493	619,428	128%	55%	55%	171,065	3.8%	1,319,464	167%
2009	672,074	545,404	123%	56%	54%	126,670	2.5%	1,527,515	227%
2010	862,229	738,386	117%	55%	53%	123,843	2.1%	1,925,392	223%
2011	995,227	864,672	115%	52%	50%	130,555	1.8%	2,352,379	236%
2012	1,022,620	871,500	117%	50%	48%	151,120	1.8%	2,493,494	244%
2013	1,043,724	874,590	119%	47%	45%	169,134	1.8%	2,852,293	273%

Sources: China Statistical Yearbooks (several years); Enright, Scott & Associates analysis

Table 1.2 Importance of FIEs by Industry, Secondary Sector, 2013

Industry	FIE Assets % of Ind Ent	FIE Revenue % of Ind Ent	FIE Profits % Of Ind Ent
Manufacture of Computers, Communication and Other Electronic Equip	59%	72%	57%
Manufacture of Leather, Fur, Feather and Related Products and Footwear	44%	37%	33%
Manufacture of Paper and Paper Products	41%	26%	29%
Production and Supply of Gas	41%	38%	50%
Manufacture of Automobiles	40%	46%	55%
Manufacture of Textile, Wearing Apparel and Accessories	38%	32%	28%
Manufacture of Articles for Culture, Education, Arts/ Crafts, Sport, Entertainment Activities	37%	34%	28%
Manufacture of Foods	36%	30%	34%
Manufacture of Rubber and Plastic Products	35%	26%	22%
Manufacture of Furniture	33%	26%	22%
Manufacture of Chemical Fibers	31%	28%	38%
Manufacture of Measuring Instruments and Machinery	30%	30%	31%
Repair Service of Metal Products, Machinery and Equipment	30%	28%	14%
Manufacture of General Purpose Machinery	28%	25%	28%
Printing and Reproduction of Recording Media	27%	21%	26%
Manufacture of Electrical Machinery and Apparatus	26%	26%	24%
Manufacture of Liquor, Beverages and Refined Tea	26%	26%	20%
Manufacture of Raw Chemical Materials and Chemical Products	25%	23%	25%
Manufacture of Medicines	24%	22%	24%
Manufacture of Special Purpose Machinery	24%	20%	21%
Manufacture of Metal Products	23%	19%	18%
Processing of Food from Agricultural Products	23%	19%	16%
Manufacture of Textile	22%	17%	17%
Utilization of Waste Resources	22%	16%	1%
Other Manufacture	20%	22%	21%
Manufacture of Railway, Ship, Aerospace and Other Transport Equipment	19%	18%	25%
Manufacture of Non-metallic Mineral Products	15%	11%	11%
Production and Supply of Water	15%	16%	38%
Smelting and Pressing of Non-ferrous Metals	14%	11%	10%
Processing of Timber, Wood, Bamboo, Rattan, Palm, Straw Products	13%	9%	7%
Processing of Petroleum, Coking and Processing of Nuclear Fuel	12%	11%	21%
Smelting and Pressing of Ferrous Metals	10%	11%	9%
Production and Supply of Electric Power and Heat Power	7%	6%	15%
Mining and Processing of Non-Ferrous Metal Ores	5%	2%	4%

(continued)

Table 1.2 Continued

Industry	FIE Assets % of Ind Ent	FIE Revenue % of Ind Ent	FIE Profits % Of Ind Ent
Support Activities for Mining	5%	7%	223%
Extraction of Petroleum and Natural Gas	4%	6%	6%
Mining and Washing of Coal	4%	6%	9%
Mining and Processing of Non-metal Ores	3%	2%	2%
Mining and Processing of Ferrous Metal Ores	2%	3%	2%
Manufacture of Tobacco	0%	0%	0%
Mining of Other Ores	0%	0%	0%
All Industries	*22%*	*23%*	*23%*

Notes: 'Ind Ent' = industrial enterprises. 'Industrial Enterprises' includes industrial enterprises of all types of ownership with revenue over RMB 20 million in 2013. Information for foreign enterprises in the Manufacture of Tobacco was not reported in 2013. Some enterprises had losses, so the profit of foreign invested enterprises could be larger than total profit of enterprises of all types of ownership.
Sources: *China Statistical Yearbook 2014*; Enright, Scott & Associates analysis.

IX. Economic Impact Analysis

The conventional indicators of the importance of IFDI and FIEs do not nearly tell the complete story of the impact of FDI and FIEs on China's economy. We have undertaken a novel application of economic impact analysis tools usually used for individual investments to provide a more complete picture of the impact of IFDI and FIEs across the Chinese economy. Economic impact analyses of investments tend to estimate three or four types of impacts. 'Direct' impacts are generated by the construction of facilities and the operations of the FIEs. 'Indirect' impacts are generated by the supply chain for the 'direct' activities and the direct industry's suppliers. 'Induced' impacts are generated from the spending of the employees of the enterprises involved in the direct and indirect activities. Some analyses address 'Catalytic' impacts, which are impacts on downstream industries and other spill-overs into the local economy. Relatively few studies quantify catalytic impacts due to the substantial amounts of data required and the lack of standard estimation techniques.

There are two main methods for carrying out economic impact analyses. One uses multiplier models based on input-output tables. Multiplier models have the advantage of simplicity and availability. The disadvantages of multiplier models for forward-looking projections is that they do not take into account the potential impact an investment might have on labour and resource prices, and are not well-suited for answering counterfactual questions. The second uses detailed general equilibrium models based on macroeconomic models. These models have the advantage for forward-looking projections that take into account the potential for new investments to bid up prices of labour and other resources and are better for answering counterfactual questions. The disadvantage of general equilibrium models is the lack of availability of models or data to generate the models in many cases. Given model and data availability, and the fact that we are looking at historical impacts, rather than projecting forward-looking impacts, we have used multiplier models in our analysis.

We first compiled data for the IFDI inflows and the operations of FIEs in China by industry. We then generated the appropriate multipliers from the Chinese national input-output tables, taking particular care to remove the FIE portion of revenues in input industries (to eliminate the potential for double counting) and assuming that FIEs import a higher percentage of their inputs than indigenous companies (an assumption that makes the analysis more conservative). We assumed further that the investment amounts were spent on a combination of construction, support services, and plant and equipment (with half of the plant and equipment imported and therefore not having an impact on China's economy). For the service sector, where the official Chinese data is not as complete as in the industrial sector, we made the extremely conservative assumption that FIEs are no more productive than their indigenous counterparts.[32] We believe this latter assumption to be extremely conservative.

Table 1.3 shows that the estimated impacts of the investment phase associated with IFDI and the operations of FIEs, along with the ripple effects through the supply chains and employee expenditures, accounted for between 16 per cent and 34 per cent of China's GDP and 11 per cent to 29 per cent of China's employment from 1995 to 2013. The estimates for 2013 place the impact of the IFDI and FIEs at 33 per cent of GDP and 27 per cent of employment. The results suggest that China has benefited tremendously from foreign investment and that these benefits continue to be extremely important today.

X. Catalytic Impacts

The quantitative economic impact analysis shows that IFDI and FIEs continue to be enormously important to China's economy. The results are even more impressive when we recognize that they do not include non-quantified catalytic benefits such as spill-overs into the local economy, the impact on productivity in indigenous firms, the impact on technological and managerial capabilities in China, the social contributions by FIEs, or other impacts.[33]

FIEs have served to modernize companies and industries in China. Companies like P&G, Unilever, Coca-Cola, Kodak, Wal-Mart, and SGS helped modernize entire industries, in some cases introducing products that did not exist in China previously.[34] Chinese officials indicated that auto industry FIEs modernized the Chinese industry by '30 years'.[35] Firms from Hong Kong and Taiwan turned traditional industries like garments and footwear in China into export successes.[36] Thailand's CP Group and other FIEs

---

[32] The complete methodology may be found in Enright, *Developing China* (n 25).

[33] Enright, *Developing China* (n 25).

[34] Birgit Zinzius, *Doing Business in the New China* (Praeger 2004); Shuguang Wang, 'Foreign Retailers in Post-WTO China: Stories of Success and Setbacks' (2009) 15 Asia Pacific Business Review 59.

[35] Jianqin Deng, 'Foreign Capital Infusion Should Emphasize Direct Foreign Investment—On the Strategic Readjustment of China's Foreign Capital Structure' (1991) 2 Beijing International Trade Journal (in Chinese). Published in English as 'Shifting Emphasis to Direct Foreign Investment' (13 June 1991) JPRS-CAR-91-032 63; Eric Thun, *Changing Lanes: Foreign Direct Investment, Local Governments, and Auto Sector Development* (Cambridge University Press 2006).

[36] Michael J Enright and others, *Regional Powerhouse: The Greater Pearl River Delta and the Rise of China* (Wiley 2005).

Table 1.3 Combined Total Economic Impact of FDI and FIEs Operations and Comparison with China National Figures

Year	Value Added Impact (USD billion)					Employment Impact (persons)				
	Annual Investment	Secondary Industry	Tertiary Industry	Total	% China GDP	Annual Investment	Secondary Industry	Tertiary Industry	Total	% China Total Employment
1995	33	70	21	124	17%	20,955,392	35,003,000	16,488,198	72,446,590	11%
1996	36	75	22	134	16%	23,199,955	37,145,472	17,620,337	77,965,764	11%
1997	40	90	27	157	16%	25,089,495	43,999,735	20,590,080	89,679,310	13%
1998	39	106	36	181	18%	22,558,111	46,154,073	22,577,522	91,289,706	13%
1999	34	122	43	199	18%	17,687,248	47,499,028	23,524,449	88,710,725	12%
2000	34	152	52	238	20%	15,521,918	52,298,365	26,006,041	93,826,324	13%
2001	39	175	61	274	21%	15,175,087	53,520,566	25,638,860	94,334,514	13%
2002	43	209	72	324	22%	14,043,252	55,392,383	27,360,607	96,796,242	13%
2003	43	278	90	410	25%	12,713,903	68,484,648	33,379,751	114,578,302	16%
2004	48	353	103	504	26%	12,670,158	77,598,904	35,311,031	125,580,093	17%
2005	56	476	138	670	30%	12,927,285	92,947,943	41,470,297	147,345,526	20%
2006	57	608	180	845	31%	10,654,172	102,959,937	45,591,095	159,205,205	21%
2007	68	799	259	1,126	32%	9,507,822	114,770,660	50,902,111	175,180,592	23%
2008	89	1,045	360	1,494	33%	10,742,880	126,689,548	60,384,262	197,816,690	26%
2009	79	1,090	422	1,590	32%	8,729,079	121,154,548	61,219,748	191,103,375	25%
2010	99	1,377	566	2,042	34%	10,015,955	132,783,633	71,012,872	213,812,460	28%
2011	106	1,654	718	2,479	34%	9,492,409	134,554,419	75,971,728	220,018,557	29%
2012	104	1,770	806	2,680	33%	8,256,626	130,056,468	77,107,715	215,420,810	28%
2013	101	1,957	931	2,989	33%	7,109,175	125,333,060	77,573,984	210,016,218	27%
Total	1,148	12,406	4,907	18,460		267,049,922	1,598,346,390	809,730,688	2,675,127,003	

Note: China total employment includes both public and private sectors in both urban and rural areas. Employment figures are FTEs in job-years.

Sources: Enright, Scott & Associates; *China Statistical Yearbook 2014*; World Bank, *World Development Indicators*.

have been credited with bringing modern agribusiness to China and changing the nation's consumption patterns.[37]

FIEs also invested heavily in developing suppliers and distributors that have gone on to serve Chinese companies and consumers, and in some cases have become internationally successful themselves.[38] FIE trading firms, mostly from Hong Kong, and international retailers have helped develop thousands of Chinese suppliers.[39] Numerous FIE high-technology companies have developed world-class supplier bases in China as well.[40]

Foreign companies have been instrumental in expanding research and development capabilities in China.[41] According to a PwC study, FIEs accounted for 81 per cent of corporate R&D spending in China as of 2014.[42] The number of foreign-invested R&D centres in China grew from fewer than thirty in 1999, to 600 in 2004, to more than 1,300 in 2013, to more than 1,500 in 2015.[43] FIEs have shifted their R&D efforts in China from low-cost support to local operations, to adopting technologies to serve local demand, to fundamental research. Hundreds of foreign companies have set up research links with Chinese universities and research institutes. Siemens, for example, has research and technology relationships with more than two hundred universities in China.[44] Numerous Chinese high-tech spinoffs have come out of FIE-funded research centres and programmes.[45]

FIEs have been instrumental in improving business practices and standards in China. The accounting and management consulting sectors (and their standards) were introduced into China by FIEs.[46] Management tools and processes, such as ISO certifications, Six Sigma, and modern human resource practices were introduced to China by FIEs. FIEs such as BASF, BP, Corning, GM, Panasonic, Rio Tinto, Shell, Siemens, Sony, and Unilever, and environmental services firms such as ERM and CH2M HILL, introduced cutting edge sustainability practices to China.[47] FIEs were the first to

[37] St James Press, 'Charoen Pokphand Group History' in *International Directory of Company Histories Vol 62* (St James Press 2004).

[38] Peking University, Tsinghua University and University of South Carolina, Economic Impact of the Coca-Cola System on China (2000); Eric Thun, *Changing Lanes: Foreign Direct Investment, Local Governments, and Auto Sector Development* (Cambridge University Press 2006); Winfried Vahland, 'Volkswagen Strategy to 2018' (Volkswagen Group China—Investor Conference, Beijing 2010); Guangzhou Government, 'Fumiaki Matsumoto: Guangzhou is the Center of All Functions' (30 July 2013); Nissan, '2015 Social Responsibility Report of Nissan's Subsidiaries in China' (2015).

[39] Michael J Enright and others, *Regional Powerhouse* (n 36); Orville Schell, 'How Walmart Is Changing China' *The Atlantic* (December 2011).

[40] See eg Invest Guangzhou, 'Exclusive Interview of General Manager of LG Display: The 8.5th Generation of LCD Display: Making the Best LCD Panel' (9 December 2013).

[41] Sylvia Schwaag-Serger, *Foreign R&D Centers in China: Development, Drivers, Spillovers* (Swedish Institute for Growth Policy Studies and Research Policy Institute University of Lund 2008).

[42] Barry Jaruzelski, Kevin Schwartz, and Volker Staack, 'Innovation's New World Order' (Winter 2015), strategy+business.

[43] Regina M Abrami and others, 'Why China Can't Innovate' (2014) 92 Harvard Business Review 107; George Yip and Bruce McKern, 'Can Multinationals Innovate in China?' Forbes Asia (17 December 2014); Dominique Jolly and others, 'The Next Innovation Opportunity in China' (Autumn 2015), strategy+business.

[44] Siemens, 'Siemens signs memorandum with Ministry of Education of China to jointly promote engineering education' (16 February 2011); Siemens, 'Siemens R&D in China' (2015).

[45] Hongbin Cai and others, 'Do Multinationals' R&D Activities Stimulate Indigenous Entrepreneurship? Evidence from China's "Silicon Valley"' *National Bureau of Economic Research Working Paper 13618* (2007).

[46] Shuwen Deng and Richard H Macve, 'The Development of China's Auditing Profession: Globalizing Translation Meets Self-Determination in Identity Construction' (2015), http://dx.doi.org/10.2139/ssrn.2562226 accessed 9 September 2016; author's interviews.

[47] Michael M Gucovsky, 'Drivers of Environmental Industry in Asia: Bilateral and Multilateral Cooperation and Multinational Corporations' in Ryokichi Hirono (ed), *Environmental Industry*

develop and occupy LEED-certified green facilities, a practice increasingly adopted by Chinese companies.[48] FIEs brought the concept of CSR to China, introducing CSR practices, oversight boards, CSR reports, and extension of CSR efforts to supply chains, again practices increasingly adopted by Chinese companies.[49]

FIEs have contributed to significant improvements in China's financial sector. International accounting firms and investment banks have contributed to the development of Chinese capital markets through their auditing, advisory, and underwriting services.[50] Several studies have found that foreign bank entry has introduced competition and has improved the performance of Chinese banks.[51] FIEs have also been instrumental in the development of China's venture capital industry and many Chinese companies that have received investment from FIE venture capital companies have subsequently listed on international exchanges.[52]

Foreign entities have been crucial in bringing modern management training and education to China. The first MBA programmes in China were offered by European and American-sponsored institutions.[53] Today there are hundreds of MBA programmes in China, many with foreign participation. FIEs like Motorola (1993), Ericsson (1997), and Siemens (1997) were also pioneers in setting up corporate universities in China. By 2011, there were approximately 80 corporate universities founded by FIEs

---

Development in Selected Asian Developing Countries: China, India, Indonesia and Republic of Korea (Institute for Global Environmental Strategies 2004); General Motors China, '2013 Corporate Social Responsibility Report' (2013); Sam Yoonsuk Lee and others, *Green Leadership in China: Management Strategies from China's Most Responsible Companies* (Springer 2014); Eifion Rees, 'Unilever and the Case for Sustainable Business' *Chinadialogue* (16 April 2014); BP, 'Building a More Efficient PTA Plant' *BP Case Studies* (2015); CH2M HILL, 'CH2M HILL's Presence in China' (2015); Shell, 'Our Business in China' (2015); Sony, 'Corporate Information: Basic Philosophy of Supply Chain Management' (2015).

[48] Zheng Tan, Yufei Wang, and Edward Ng, '"LEED-Oriented" Projects in Mainland China and the Indication to Sustainable Practice in Developing Countries' (30th International PLEA Conference, CEPT University Ahmedabad 2014).

[49] CSR Asia and Embassy of Sweden in Beijing, *A Study on Corporate Social Responsibility Development and Trends in China* (2008); American Chamber of Commerce in Shanghai, *The China CSR Imperative: Integrating Social Responsibility into the China Supply Chain* (2012).

[50] Deloitte Touche Tohmatsu, 'Deloitte China Responsibility Report 2012' (n 22); Deng and Macve (n 46).

[51] Jian Lv, 'The Influence of Foreign Banks' Entry into China's Banking—Based on Panel Data Analysis]' (2006) 5 International Business (in Chinese); Nicholas C Hope and others, 'The Impact of Direct Investment by Foreign Banks of China's Banking Industry' *Stanford Center for International Development, Working Paper No. 362* (2008); Wei Li and Liyan Han, 'On the Market Competition of Foreign Banks in the Banking Industry in China: An Empirical Analysis Based on the Panzar-Rosse Model' (2008) 5 Journal of Financial Research (in Chinese); Xiongbing Chen and Zishan Chen, 'Whether the Entry of Foreign Banks Increased the Competition Intensity in the Banking Industry: Empirical Research from China' (2012) 5 Inquiry into Economic Issues (in Chinese); Xiangrui Zhang and Zhiwei Pei, 'The Competition Effect of Foreign Banks On Domestic Banks: Empirical Tests Based on China's Banking Industry during 2000 and 2013' (2015) 1 China Price (in Chinese).

[52] AVCJ, 'The Guide to Venture Capital in Asia' (2001) Asian Venture Capital Journal; S White, J Gao, and W Zhang, 'China's Venture Capital Industry: Institutional Trajectories and System Structure' (2002) Working Paper-INSEAD 1; Ernst & Young, '2014 Venture Capital Review' (2015); M Liu, J A Zhang, and B Hu, 'Domestic VCs versus Foreign VCs: A Close Look at the Chinese Venture Capital Industry' (2006) 34 International Journal of Technology Management 161; Feng Zeng, *Venture Capital Investments in China* (Rand 2004); Zero2IPO Research Center, *China Private Equity Market 2014 Annual Review* (2015) (in Chinese).

[53] Keith Goodall and Malcolm Warner, 'Management Training and Development in China: Laying the Foundation' in Malcolm Warner and Keith Goodall (eds), *Management Training and Development in China: Educating Managers in a Globalized Economy* (Routledge 2009).

and 320 by Chinese companies in China.[54] Many FIEs opened their programmes to local suppliers, customers, and government officials. Companies like Boeing, Maersk, and others have also provided special education and training programmes for Chinese managers and officials to help upgrade the standards in their industries.[55] In addition to formal training and education, FIEs have trained people that have founded leading Chinese firms in a variety of industries.

FIEs and foreign organizations have played a significant role in the evolution of China's legal, regulatory, and policy regimes. The need to establish a legal framework governing IFDI and FIEs influenced China's legal approach toward the economy.[56] Technical assistance from the US-China Business Council and foreign law firms helped introduce the international norms in commercial law. The rules for the China International Economic Trade and Arbitration Commission (CIETAC) were influenced by the UN's UNCITRAL Model Law.[57] China's Labour Laws were influenced by Hong Kong practice and by similar laws elsewhere.[58] China's Anti-Monopoly, Company Law, and Draft Foreign Investment Law were developed after reviewing similar legislation elsewhere and consulting with international experts. China's opening has involved policy advice from foreign experts since before Deng Xiaoping's 1983 exhortation, to 'beef up reform and opening-up with more help from foreign brains'.[59] National ministry officials meet frequently with representatives of FIEs for input on policies and high-level groups of FIE executives advise municipalities and provinces across China.[60]

XI. Implications

Our economic impact results show that IFDI and FIEs, and the ripple effects through their supply chains and the consumer spending of employees, accounted for in the order of 33 per cent of China's GDP and 27 per cent of China's employment in the most recent years for which data was available. There are also a wide range of unquantified catalytic impacts that might be equally important. These results suggest that the impact of IFDI and FIEs on China's economy has been much greater than most people realize.

There are several implications of these results for the potential for investment treaties with China. The first is that while foreign companies and governments might be frustrated with the slow pace and limited extent of China's opening, Chinese officials have every right to conclude that China's approach to IFDI and FIEs has been enormously

---

[54] Jie Liu, 'Novartis opens corporate campuses' *China Daily* (3 August 2009); Qianzhan Business Information Co, *China Corporate University Report, 2013-2017* (2015).

[55] Chunhang Liu, *Multinationals, Globalisation and Indigenous Firms in China* (Routledge 2009); Boeing Company, 'Boeing in China' (2015); Maersk, private communication.

[56] Deng (n 35) 67; J Fu, *Institutions and Investments: Foreign Direct Investment in China during an Era of Reforms* (University of Michigan Press 2000); Scott Wilson, *Remade in China: Foreign Investors and Institutional Change in China* (Oxford University Press 2009).

[57] Wilson, *Remade in China* (n 56).   [58] ibid.

[59] Junmian Zhang, 'Fortune Favour 500 as China Courts Foreign Advisors' *China.org.cn* (21 December 2011), China.org.cn (last accessed 9 September 2016).

[60] NEWSGD, '2013 Guangdong International Consultative Conference opens' *NEWSGD* (21 November 2013); Office of the Mayor of Shanghai, 'Yang Meets IBLAC Chairman' (22 November 2013); W Liao, 'Top Business Leaders Share Advice on Beijing's Sustainable Development' *China Daily* (29 May 2014); Shanghai Daily, 'IBLAC Conference to Focus on FTZ' *Shanghai Daily* (10 September 2014).

successful. The second is that foreign companies and governments generally do not use all of the tools at their disposal to 'make their case' when it comes to the value of IFDI to China. We would suggest that the analysis described in this chapter become the starting point for these discussions. The third is that even if foreign companies and governments highlight the full impact of IFDI and FIEs on China's economy that in order to receive favourable treatment in China it is also necessary to highlight the ability of IFDI and FIEs to contribute directly to China's industrial policy and major economic initiatives, as China's objective function regarding IFDI and FIEs is different from that generally found in the West. The fourth is that the economic impact tools described here can actually be used to estimate the impact of Chinese outward FDI (OFDI) on other economies, or in fact the impact of OFDI from any country to any other country for which the investment and operating data on FIEs, and current input-output tables are available. Thus, the tools described here can be used as analytical background not just for negotiations of investment agreements with China, but for negotiations with a wide range of countries and trading blocs.

China has clearly benefited from IFDI, perhaps more than any other nation in the last few decades. China now has well over thirty years of experience with IFDI. It also has become a net exporter of capital, with outward FDI (OFDI) significantly outstripping IFDI. It also has a much larger and stronger economy than it had in the early days of its reform process. As a latecomer to globalization, China had to accept the Breton Woods 'rules of the game' as they existed. Today, whether it is FTAs or IIAs, China increasingly is seeking to be a rule maker, rather than a rule taker. Thus, it is not surprising that China is expanding the scope of its IIA activities from BITs alone to BITs supplemented by regional and beyond regional discussions, particularly in the Asia-Pacific or areas covered by the One Belt-One Road initiative, as shown in other chapters of this volume. Given China's importance, how these discussions progress will have a substantial influence on regional and global economic governance.

We hope that the insights and results reported in this chapter are helpful to academics and analysts, as well as government officials and negotiators interested in the negotiation and implementation of investment agreements with China as well as with other nations around the world.

2

China's Outward Investment

Trends and Challenges in the Globalization of Chinese Enterprises

Hui Yao Wang and Lu Miao*

I. Introduction

After the steep downturn of 2008–2009, since 2013, the world economy has continued its slow recovery. However, this recovery has been uneven. Among developed countries, the US economy has grown relatively quickly while growth in the Eurozone has remained sluggish. Emerging economies have also suffered from weak growth momentum.

Despite these headwinds, global cross-border investment managed to stabilize and rebound, though flows have fallen again in recent years. According to the United Nations Conference on Trade and Development (UNCTAD), global FDI inflows rose steadily from US$1.33 trillion in 2012, reaching a high point of US$1.92 trillion in 2015. In 2016, this figure contracted to US$1.87 trillion and fell further to US$1.43 trillion in 2017, a year-on-year fall of 21.8 per cent.

Global cross-border M&A activity fell in 2017, down 21.8 per cent to US$694 billion. Cross-border M&A in primary industries saw a large contraction of 70 per cent year-on-year, while manufacturing also saw a decline. However, cross-border M&A in business services, machinery and equipment, information and communication saw increases of 43 per cent, 63 per cent and 66 per cent respectively.

2017 also saw a fall in global greenfield investment, down 13.6 per cent year-on-year to US$720 billion. Of this, greenfield investments in manufacturing were up 14 per cent to US$338 billion, while investments in primary and service industries were down 61 per cent and 25 per cent respectively.

Meanwhile, amidst a slow global economic recovery, the Chinese economy continued to grow strongly from 2012 to 2017. Economic restructuring and industrial upgrading contributed to China's endogenous growth momentum. This ongoing transformation also drove strong growth of overseas direct investment (ODI) by Chinese enterprises, supported by the government's Go Global strategy which was accelerated following the CPC's Eighteenth National Congress in 2012. 2015 was a landmark year as China became a net capital exporter for the first time as ODI exceeded FDI.

* Huiyao Wang, President, Center for China and Globalization; Lu Miao, PhD, Contemporary Chinese Studies, Beijing Normal University.

China's Outward Investment: Trends and Challenges in the Globalization of Chinese Enterprises. Hui Yao Wang and Lu Miao. © Hui Yao Wang and Lu Miao, 2019. Published 2019 by Oxford University Press.

II. History and Trends of Chinese Enterprise Globalization

This section traces the history of Chinese ODI and maps out key ODI trends in recent years, including overall quantity, state vs private ownership, regional distribution, and sectoral composition.

The globalization of Chinese enterprises began with the launch of the Reform and Opening Up Policy. In 1979, the State Council put forward a package of reforms explicitly allowing enterprises to 'go global' and made FDI development a national policy objective for the first time. From this point, foreign trade firms and international economic and technological cooperation companies in various cities began to open export abroad and overseas representative offices.[1] In November 1979, the Beijing Friendship Business Service Company and Tokyo Maruichishoji Co jointly established the first Chinese overseas enterprise of the reform era, marking the start of Chinese enterprise globalization.

Following this, successive CPC National Congresses called for greater overseas investment, leading up to the first unveiling of the Go Global strategy at the Fifth Plenum of the Fifteenth CPC National Congress in November 2000.[2] In 2001, the Go Global strategy was written into China's Tenth Five-Year Plan (2001–2005).

Since the launch of the Go Global policy, the Chinese government has continued to place more emphasis on strengthening the ability of firms to operate internationally, with the aim of nurturing a cohort of world-class multinational companies. By 2017, 25,500 Chinese investors had set up 39,200 ODI enterprises abroad, distributed across 189 countries and regions in the world. Accumulated ODI from Chinese enterprises has risen from less than $US 1 billion in 2000 to over US$1.8 trillion by the end of 2017.

The Go Global initiative has also had a significant impact on project contracting and labour cooperation, with a rapid rise in the number of international engineering contracts carried out by Chinese firms since the early 2000s. This includes diverse forms of cooperation, in particular engineering, procurement and construction (EPC) contracts and increasing use of the build–operate–transfer (BOT) model.

Regarding foreign labour cooperation, at the end of 2017, the total number of workers dispatched overseas reached 979,000, an increase of 10,000 compared to 2016. These workers were distributed across more than 180 countries and regions, covering a broad range of sectors including manufacturing, construction, shipbuilding, IT services, agriculture, food and beverages, and social services. (See the three modes of China enterprise globalization shown in Figure 2.1.)

Recent years have also seen innovations in the pathways to internationalization for Chinese enterprises, including the building of industrial and technology parks

---

[1] Pei Changhong, *Research on China's Systematic Support for Its Outbound Investment* (Social Science Academic Press 2012).

[2] See Julien Chaisse and Mitsuo Matsushita, 'China's "Belt and Road" Initiative: Mapping the World Trade Normative and Strategic Implications' (2018) 52(1) Journal of World Trade 163.

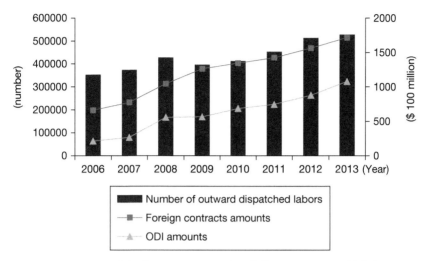

Figure 2.1 Comparison of the three operation modes of Chinese Enterprise Globalization, 2006–2013

Source: Figure created by CCG with data from China's Foreign Direct Investment Statistical Bulletin citation, 2004–2013

and overseas economic and trade cooperation zones. At present, the broad picture of Chinese enterprise globalization is marked by trends described below.

A. Trend 1: China's ODI has surpassed that of several major developed economies

Relative to the sluggish performance of worldwide FDI flows, China's ODI has grown strongly since the global financial crisis. In 2010, China's ODI flow surpassed that of traditional investment powerhouses such as Japan and Britain for the first time, rising to number three in the world. The total stock of Chinese ODI has grown from just US$44.9 billion in 2004 to US$1.81 trillion as of the end of 2017, ranking China second in the world in this regard.

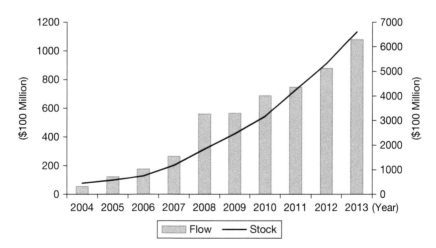

Figure 2.2 China's outward FDI flow and stock trend from 2002 to 2017

Source: Figure created by Center for China and Globalization (CCG) with data from China's Foreign Direct Investment Statistical Bulletin citation, 2004–2013

In 2015, China's ODI flows reached US$145.67 billion, exceeding inward FDI (US$135.6 billion) for the first time, marking the transition of China from being a net importer to a net exporter of capital.

B. Trend 2: Private firms play a larger role in ODI

Recent years have seen a diversification in the type of Chinese firms investing abroad, with private enterprises in particular becoming more active. According to CCG data, in 2017, private firms undertook 248 overseas investment projects, accounting for 73.8 per cent of the total that year. According to Ministry of Commerce, in 2017, the proportion of Chinese overseas investment accounted for by enterprises registered as state-owned fell to 49.1 per cent.

From this, it can be seen that private firms are playing a more active role in overseas activities, which also reflects the growing significance of the private sector in China's economy as a whole. In terms of policy, the Chinese government has sought to support private firms going global and improve resource allocation to help these enterprises find a competitive foothold in global value chains and overseas markets.

China's private enterprises have also become a driving force in overseas M&A. Notable cases include Lenovo's acquisition of Motorola's Smartphone business, Shuanghui's acquisition of Smithfield Foods, and Wanda's investment in the US.

C. Trend 3: Chinese ODI still focused towards Asia, with growing investment along the Belt and Road

According to the Ministry of Commerce, as of the end of 2017, Chinese firms had directly invested in 189 countries and regions.[3] Among these, Asia accounts for the highest cumulative amount of Chinese ODI of any region, amounting to 63 per cent of the global total or US$1.139 trillion. Of this, main recipients include Hong Kong, Singapore, and Indonesia. Next comes Latin America with a total of US$386.89 billion (21.4 per cent of total Chinese ODI), followed by Europe with US$110.86 billion (21.4 per cent), and North America with USD 86.91 billion (4.8 per cent), concentrated in the US and Canada.

In 2017, Chinese ODI flows into Europe reached US$18.46 billion, a record high and year-on-year increase of 72.7 per cent. Africa-bound ODI that year also jumped significantly by 70.8 per cent to reach US$4.1 billion. At the same time, 2017 saw considerable decline of Chinese ODI into North America and Latin America of 68.1 per cent and 48.3 per cent respectively. This follows many years of rapid growth of ODI into the US in particular.

For example, in 2015, Fosun International acquired US insurance firm Ironshore for nearly US$2.5 billion, and Anbang Insurance purchased the Waldorf Astoria Hotel in New York for US$1.95 billion. 2016 saw deals such as Alibaba investing in the US internet company Groupon and Haier's acquisition of GE Appliances for US$5.58 billion. In 2017, while US-bound Chinese ODI continued to diversify, the annual amount invested into the US fell by 62.1 per cent to US$6.43 billion due to the US–China trade dispute and increased scrutiny of foreign investments into the US.

---

[3] Ministry of Commerce and others (n 3).

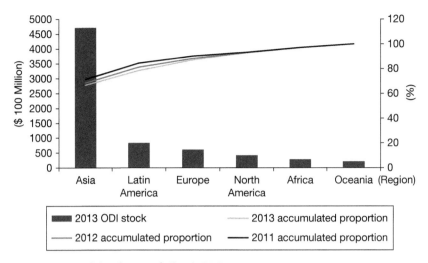

Figure 2.3 Regional distribution of China's ODI in 2017

Source: Figure created by Center for China and Globalization (CCG) with data from China's Foreign Direct Investment Statistical Bulletin citation, 2004–2013

Table 2.1 China's major ODI stock and flow contrast

Unit: US $100 million

Country and Region	ODI stock			ODI flow		
	2015	2016	2017	2015	2016	2017
Hong Kong	6568.55	7807.45	9812.66	897.90	1142.32	911.52
British Virgin Islands	516.72	887.66	1220.61	18.49	122.88	193.01
Cayman Islands	624.04	1042.09	2496.82	102.13	135.23	−66.06
US	408.02	605.80	673.81	80.29	169.81	64.25
Australia	283.74	333.51	361.75	34.01	41.87	42.42
Russia	140.20	129.80	138.72	29.61	12.93	15.48
France	57.23	51.16	57.03	3.28	15.00	9.52
South Africa	47.23	65.01	74.73	2.33	8.43	3.17
Germany	58.82	78.42	121.63	4.10	23.81	27.16
Indonesia	81.25	95.46	105.39	14.51	14.61	16.82
South Korea	36.98	42.37	59.83	13.24	11.48	6.61
Macao	57.39	67.83	96.80	10.80	8.21	−10.24
Thailand	34.40	45.33	53.58	4.07	11.21	10.58
Nigeria	23.77	25.41	28.61	0.51	1.09	1.38
Japan	30.38	31.84	31.97	2.40	3.44	4.44
Vietnam	33.73	49.83	49.65	5.60	12.79	7.64
Sudan	18.09	11.04	12.01	0.32	-6.90	2.55

Source: Ministry of Commerce, National Bureau of Statistics, State Administration of Foreign Exchange: The Statistical Bulletin of Chinese ODI (2011–2013).

D. Trend 4: ODI flowing to diversified sectors

By the end of 2017, Chinese direct investments overseas had covered virtually all sectors, with over six industries seeing cumulative ODI in excess of US$100 billion. The main recipient industries in order of cumulative ODI are leasing and business services (US$615.7 billion, accounting for 34.1 per cent of the total); wholesale and retail (US$226.4 billion, 12.5 per cent); information transfer, software and IT services

(US$218.9 billion, 12.1 per cent); and financial services (US$202.8 billion, 11.2 per cent) (see Figure 2.4).

In 2017, cross-border M&A by Chinese firms covered a broad range of industries, with 18 sectors including manufacturing, mining, power, and production and supply of heat, gas, and water. Notably, cross-border M&A in manufacturing doubled from the year before, with 163 M&A cases. Highlight investments include the acquisition of 12 per cent of Abu Dhabi National Oil Co (Adco) by China National Petroleum Corporation (CNPC) and CEFC China Energy, and the State Grid's major investment in Brazil's largest power distributor CPFL Energia SA.

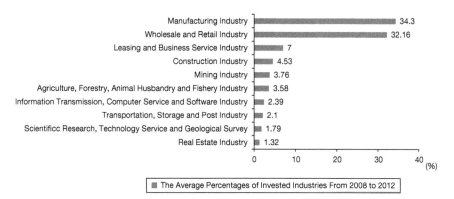

Figure 2.4 Industrial distribution of China's outward FDI stock by the end of 2017
Source: Figure created by CCG with data from the Heritage Foundation citation

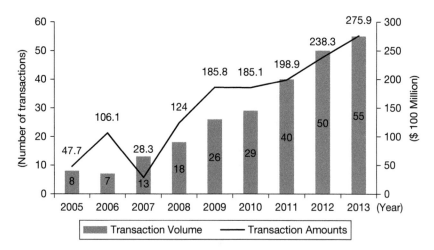

Figure 2.5 Investment in high-tech industry by Chinese enterprises from 2005 to 2013
Source: Figure created by CCG with data from the Heritage Foundation citation

III. New Features of Chinese Enterprises' Globalization

In addition to the key trends outlined in the previous section, in recent years, new features of Chinese ODI have emerged, notably increased attention to corporate social responsibility (CSR), alignment with the Belt and Road Initiative (BRI), and vertical integration through M&A.

A. Growing emphasis on CSR

Recent years have seen Chinese firms in many sectors pay increasing attention to CSR while investing abroad, seeing this as a way to ensure the success of ODI projects and cultivate a positive image in host countries. This is particularly so in European and North American countries, which attach relatively more importance to CSR compared to those in regions such as Latin America, the Middle East, and North Africa.

Research by CCG shows that Chinese firms' awareness of CSR is gradually increasing. Among surveyed companies, 23 per cent reported to have established effective channels of communication with relevant stakeholders for overseas projects; 20 per cent said they had assigned dedicated departments and persons responsible for overseas CSR; 19 per cent of enterprises had set overseas CSR targets and management plans; 15 per cent had built CSR into their overall overseas development strategies; 12 per cent have created CSR or sustainable development reports; and only 12 per cent reported having no overseas CSR activities.

B. Rising investment along the Belt and Road

In 2017, Chinese investment in countries participating in the Belt and Road Initiative (BRI) grew significantly across a broad range of sectors. According to the Ministry of Commerce, in 2017, nearly 300 companies undertook ODI projects in the 57 BRI countries, covering 17 sectors and amounting to a total of US$20.17 billion, a year-on-year increase of 31.5 per cent. This accounted for 12.7 per cent of Chinese total ODI in 2017. Top destinations for this investment included Singapore, Kazakhstan, Malaysia, Indonesia, Russia, Laos, Thailand, Vietnam, Cambodia, and the UAE.

In the five years since the BRI was launched, Chinese firms are deepening overseas cooperation in participating countries, with growing investment in sectors such as infrastructure, energy, transport. Over this period, the cumulative direct investment in BRI countries has reached US$80.73 billion.

C. Industrial chain integration through M&A

Rather than overseas sales, a firm's degree of globalization is better captured by its ability to effectively integrate the global industrial chain and thus achieve more complete control over production processes. In recent years, ODI data show a continued trend for Chinese enterprises to seek global industry chain integration through cross-border M&A.

In particular, Chinese companies have broadened their ODI activities to gain greater control over downstream and upstream parts of the industry chain. In so doing, such companies have begun participating in the vertical consolidation of certain industries on a global scale, while also moving from merely participating in these chains to occupying a dominant position in them.

IV. Challenges for the Globalization of Chinese Enterprises

While Chinese enterprises are expanding internationally at an unprecedented pace, they still face a number of challenges on their way to becoming global. The most significant of these relate to planning and strategy, risk management, financing channels, lack of cooperation, low level of enterprise internationalization, underutilization of intermediary services, challenges in dealing with complex host country environments, and cross-cultural differences. These issues are described in more detail in below.

A. Planning and strategy

At present, the globalization strategies of some enterprises lack clarity and thorough planning. For firms, globalization is a long-term, complex process that requires a carefully tailored approach for each developmental stage.

For Chinese companies, the first task before going global is to plan strategically by carefully exploring the global trends and changes likely to occur over the next few years in their respective industries. In particular, firms must investigate how they can benefit from these changes and trends through globalization.

At present, many Chinese firms investing abroad do so without first fully investigating conditions overseas or formulating clear strategies, often resulting in subsequent operational difficulties such as financial pressures brought on by making unsuitable project bids.

B. Risk management

Many Chinese companies have inadequate risk management mechanisms due to a lack of international experience. This is especially true for legal and political risks, which have been shown to be the greatest risks for the globalization of Chinese enterprises in recent years.

CCG analysis of 120 ODI investment failure cases[4] from Chinese ODI projects undertaken between 1 January 2005 and 30 June 2014 found that 25 per cent were due to political reasons. This included 8 per cent because of obstruction from political parties in host countries, and 17 per cent because of political unrest and changes in local governmental leadership.

Political and social unrest can lead to huge losses. For example, China had over fifty major ODI projects in 2011 in Libya with a total amount of over US$18.8 billion, only to have most of them aborted due to the subsequent civil war and chaos.[5] In May 2014, riots in Vietnam caused great losses for Chinese firms operating in Pingyang province. Subsequent events have highlighted how many otherwise attractive developing countries are subject to high levels of risk for international investors.

Legal risk is another major potential pitfall for ODI by Chinese firms. Policies and laws for FDI, regulations related to national security, anti-monopoly, environmental protection, labour, and taxation, along with trade restrictions in various countries differ and continuously change according to political and economic factors, resulting in legal risks for ODI projects. Moreover, most Chinese companies lack international experience and familiarity with the laws in foreign countries. This makes the legal risks associated with ODI for such firms especially high. According to the CCG's analysis of ODI failure cases, 16 per cent of them were directly or indirectly caused by legal factors, among which one-third stemmed from ignorance of or disobedience of the law, with another one-third being attributable to lack of familiarity with labour statutes. Chinese firms have also been relatively weak at using laws to safeguard their interests

---

[4] Listed Company Report, statistics of the CCG and the Heritage Foundation.
[5] Statistics Center of Ministry of Commerce.

and rights, instead all too often turning to the Chinese government and its foreign embassies for help. Fortunately, in 2015, Ralls, a company affiliated with the Sany Heavy Industry Group, won a lawsuit against the US government, providing a new lesson for Chinese enterprises investing abroad.

C. Financing channels

Many small and medium-sized enterprises (SMEs) face high ODI financing costs due to constrained access to financing. According to CCG research, 30 per cent of globalizing firms are unsatisfied with the current financing service for ODI. Some 68.4 per cent of them want government financial support for such activity. CCG's investigation also shows that since most major state-owned enterprises and private firms are listed companies, funds from capital markets constitute the major source of ODI financing. Moreover, most commercial bank loans, policy-based lending, and M&A loans currently flow to major state-owned enterprises. Combined, these factors makes it hard for SMEs to obtain the financing needed to go global.

The CCG investigation found that funding for SMEs mainly comes from three sources. The first source is the company's own savings, with 56.6 per cent of the investigated firms using their own funds for overseas investment. Since these funds were small and SMEs have lower risk tolerance, they have found it hard to operate globally over the long run. A second source of financing for overseas expansion by SMEs has been domestic financial institutions and their overseas branches. Since SMEs lack scale, reputation and well-established connections, only a few of them can obtain long-term loans from banks. Thus, just 17.4 per cent of the investigated enterprises acquired their ODI funding from domestic banks. Thirdly, SMEs obtained 14.3 per cent of their funds for ODI from capital markets. This research indicates that the high financing costs faced by SMEs in overseas expansion have impaired their competitiveness in going global.

D. Lack of cooperation

To date, there has been a lack of cooperation between Chinese firms when undertaking ODI. In recent years, growing numbers of Chinese companies have joint the increasingly fierce struggle to seize global business opportunities. Thus, some projects, notably construction of power plants, dams, roads, and railways in Africa, Latin America, and Southeast Asia, are subject to bids by several competing Chinese enterprises. These firms often undercut each other on price or resort to lowering construction quality in order to cut costs. These practices, along with the breaking of contracts by a few firms, have not only generated significant losses for Chinese companies, but also stained their image abroad.

E. Low level of internationalization

Many Chinese companies investing abroad remain at a relatively early stage of the internationalization process. Based on a large ODI data set, the CCG has formulated an evaluation system for assessing the globalization of Chinese enterprises. Among its criteria, this system considers investment efficiency, use of overseas talent, penetration of overseas markets, corporate social responsibility (CSR), and industry chain M&A.

This research indicates that the general level of internationalization among Chinese companies investing overseas is not high. According to the evaluation of the China

Enterprise Confederation and the China Enterprise Directors Association on overseas turnover, assets and the percentage of foreign employees, the average globalization index for the 100 Chinese multinational enterprises considered was 12.9 per cent, much lower than 62.3 per cent, the average level of the world's top 100 multinational enterprises, and also significantly below 39 per cent, the average level of the top 100 multinational enterprises from developing countries.

The globalization of talent is an important measure of a company's globalization. After analysing the employee structure and recruitment system of the overseas subsidiaries of Chinese enterprises conducting non-financial ODI, the CCG found that these firms score low on this crucial yardstick of business enterprise globalization. The share of foreign employees, managers, and members of the board of directors in such firms is relatively low. Most of their lower level staff and top management have instead been sent from Mainland China, with the small numbers of foreign employees coming mainly from developing countries.

F. Underutilization of intermediary services

Research shows that most Chinese firms do not make adequate use of intermediary agencies to assist their globalization process. Such intermediary agencies for ODI services can be broadly divided into two categories. The first is special services including accounting, law, and asset appraisal firms. The second category includes providers of general services such as investment and financial advisory services as well as investor relations and management consultancies.

These intermediary agencies have accumulated a wealth of knowledge and other resources to lower ODI risks, which makes them an important asset for Chinese firms seeking to go global. For example, due diligence investigations by qualified service providers can provide rigorous feasibility assessments and discern legal and financial risks to help businesses make the right decisions regarding overseas investment projects. However, since the fees charged by foreign agencies can be significant, some Chinese companies have eschewed the use of intermediary services to save costs. This has often resulted in expensive operational troubles caused by inexperience and failure to perform adequate due diligence.

G. Dealing with complex host country environments

Chinese firms need to improve their ability to deal with the complex political and social environments of many host countries. The CCG's analysis of cases of failed Chinese ODI cases found that Chinese companies investing abroad have faced many challenges stemming from the complex political and social environments in host countries.

For example, some Chinese ODI projects were halted because the company had failed to cultivate good relations with key political and social groups. These actors then opposed and blocked Chinese ODI efforts. According to the CCG's investigation and analysis, Chinese firms have made three major mistakes in managing relations within the host countries. The first is solely relying on the relationship with senior officials in a foreign government. Some foreign governments are highly unstable, so relying exclusively on such ties can arouse public opposition and even collective protests against Chinese companies and their ODI projects. The second is ignorance of opposition groups as well as the local media and NGOs, all of which play a key role in influencing public opinion, particularly during elections. The third is the failure of firms to fulfil their CSR commitments. While operating globally, Chinese firms should strive to help improve the overall economy and employment opportunities in the local overseas communities in which they do business through the investment projects. Hence, CSR is a key part of the CCG's system for evaluating the globalization of Chinese businesses.

H. Cross-cultural differences

CCG's analysis indicates there is much room for improvement in Chinese firms' understanding and management of cultural differences.

The languages, culture and customs, ideologies, value orientations, and religious beliefs in different host countries all influence ODI undertaken by Chinese companies. In addition, major differences in the business cultures of China versus other countries can create difficulties for investment and management. According to the CCG's analysis, in many of the ODI projects of many Chinese firms ODI failed not because of shortcomings in areas like technology or capital, but on account of cultural differences and their failure to effectively manage them. This also indicates that less culturally-inclusive host countries may pose greater investment risks for a company. Chinese enterprises going global should seek to undersand and respect the culture and customs of host countries and manage the related risks to safeguard their interests and investments.

V. Recommendations for Promoting the Globalization of Chinese Enterprise

Based on the challenges described in the previous section, this section sets out a range of proposed measures to support the continued globalization of Chinese firms. These cover ODI management, tax and financial support, legislation, international management practices, cooperation in overseas activities, risk management, international talent, and better use of external service providers.

A. ODI management

China's governmental approval mechanism for ODI has improved significantly in recent years. Nevertheless, the threshold for the examination and approval procedure was reduced in 2014, there is still room for improvement in this area.

It is suggested that for most investments, the recording and examination and approval system should not take effect until the investment has been made. Furthermore, efforts should be made to remove restrictions on the investment amount, destination countries, and industries and reduce government involvement in the ODI decision-making of companies.

Moreover, greater efforts should be made to standardize the management of state-owned enterprises in foreign countries, as opposed to simply supervising and regulating them. Steps also have to be taken to build scientific corporate governance structures in Chinese companies going global conforming to the laws in host countries and modern corporate management systems. In particular, the rights of recruitment, salary management, and performance assessment should be passed on to enterprise managers.

B. Tax and financial support

Despite significant improvements in recent years, there is still room for improvement regarding China's tax and financial policy for ODI. This could include refining relevant policies to support ODI in priority industries such as high-tech. It is also suggested that the ODI income tax system be optimized by further lowering taxes on priority ODI sectors and enhancing the transparency and execution of such policies.

In addition, China should accelerate its financial reform, building a multi-layered capital market to encourage ODI financing through the issuing of stocks and bonds to provide more funding for SMEs seeking to invest overseas. It should also promote the cooperation between banks and firms wishing to go global, build an ODI insurance system, especially for SMEs, and improve bank financing channels for such companies and other private companies seeking to invest abroad.

C. Legislation

As mentioned above, China's laws governing ODI have been improved significantly since the launch of the Going Global strategy in 2000. The State Council, National Development and Reform Commission, Ministry of Commerce, and the State Administration of Foreign Exchange have all formulated ODI policies and implementation suggestions which have greatly improved and standardized Chinese ODI.

However, as the international economic environment and Chinese globalization continue to develop rapidly, some policies and regulations can no longer accommodate new trends and imperatives in Chinese overseas investment. In addition, policies and measures need to evolve into legal statutes to better promote ODI by Chinese firms. It is therefore suggested that China should accelerate the formulation and implementation of the Outward Direct Investment Law as the basic law governing Chinese ODI. Doing so will provide the country with a single overarching legal framework for individuals and firms investing overseas, foreign investment patterns, examination and approval procedures, financing and taxation policies, management departments and their functions, intermediary agencies, and dispute settlement.

D. International management practices

While Chinese firms have acquired much successful ODI experience, many still face problems in the field of global management. These companies should strive to invest more in formulating effective strategies, improving management systems, operating ability, strengthen the sense of cooperation when expanding abroad, and work to fulfil CSR commitments.

For strategies, enterprises have to attach great importance to global operation strategies based on thorough investigation to ensure that such planning leads to appropriate decisions and sustainable globalization.

With respect to the management systems, companies ought to standardize their corporate management structures, implementing efficient decision-making systems to ensure compliance with the rules and laws of the global marketplace. These systems must be given reasonable financial and human resources to both empower Chinese companies investing overseas, but also to localize the management and operation of their foreign subsidiaries so as to ensure a smooth relationship between the parent and subsidiary firms.

It is also recommended that Chinese enterprises boost CSR activities to improve their global image, while respecting the laws and cultural practices of the host countries and behaving as good corporate citizens when it comes to protecting the environment. Companies must also strengthen communication with local communities and residents in host countries and actively participate in community and philanthropic events. In doing this, firms need to devise a systematic system for effectively carrying out CSR and develop close links with the local media to publicize their good work in this area.

E. Cooperation in overseas activities

Chinese companies should seek to improve cooperation with each other and with foreign firms in conducting ODI to achieve mutual benefits. First, Chinese enterprises can build up and operate joint ventures with host country companies when doing ODI. At the beginning of China's Reform and Opening up period, most foreign firms invested in the country by setting up joint ventures with Chinese enterprises. This experience provides a good model for Chinese companies currently investing abroad. Secondly, Chinese enterprises should strengthen international cooperation, share information with others, and act in ways that complement their strengths with those of other companies so as to avoid harmful competition. Thirdly, Chinese enterprises should strengthen cooperation with banks, venture capitalists, and other financial institutions to build consortia integrating such funding with industry-specific funding. Lastly, they should increase cooperation with local NGOs and industry associations in host countries to win their support.

F. Robust risk management

Experience indicates that Chinese enterprises need to increase efforts in building risk management systems. This calls for cooperation between the government, businesses, and third parties to manage risks and share relevant information.

The government should improve legislative safeguards for Chinese ODI. In particular, it needs to formulate an ODI Insurance Law and create insurance bodies and emergency funds for ODI, while signing bilateral agreements with more countries aimed at protecting Chinese overseas investments. The Chinese government should also build systems for evaluating and providing early warning about ODI risks and set up an emergency mechanism to deal with them. Another priority is devising information collection and release procedures to help overseas embassies and consulates to provide investment intelligence for Chinese firms investing abroad. The consular protection system of China to ensure the security and interest of Chinese people and enterprises needs to be enhanced as well. Finally, greater funding should be provided for research on companies going global by non-governmental think tanks and other research institutions.

At the firm level, companies ought to build a risk management system to forecast, prevent, and control risks. They should improve their internal management and supervision structures and learn from international experience to identify, control, and deal with risk in an effective and scientific manner.

Third-party organizations can play a role by helping to identify risks, while think tanks and other institutions conducting related research ought to promote and share their research on ODI risks. The latter should provide advice for companies going global regarding the choice of investment projects, partners, and multi-national operating strategies.

D. Build an international talent system

China has increased participation in the global competition for talent, as mapped out in the National Medium and Long-Term Talent Development Outline (2010–2020), which set a long-term development strategy for acquiring overseas talent and made it a top priority in the globalization of the Chinese economy.

Enterprise globalization has increased the need to recruit high-quality personnel. Generally speaking, China lacks an equivalent to the international elite managerial talent who are vital for ensuring the success of ODI projects undertaken by foreign companies.

Investigations carried out by international consulting firms such as McKinsey & Co and Accenture indicate that a major challenge for globalizing Chinese firms is the shortage of international talent with the requisite foreign language skills, business acumen, and experience, as well as legal and financial expertise. Since global talent is also a key factor influencing the success and failure of Chinese ODI, creating an international talent support system is an urgent priority.

E. Leveraging external service providers

Leading international agencies have accumulated great experience in providing ODI services. Chinese enterprises investing abroad should seek to make full use of this expertise to support successful overseas expansion. The Chinese government ought strongly to promote the development of such agencies in China by building a legal protection system for them and guiding and standardizing their formation. The government should also build supervision and management systems for ODI services providers, urge industry associations to standardize ODI services provision, and create a uniform set of industry-wide rules and management systems to ensure service quality. Finally, the government should enhance the education of practitioners to raise professional standards and build trust among their clients, while punishing practitioners who fail to follow legal regulations.

VI. Conclusion

Since China launched the 'Going Global' strategy, increasing numbers of Chinese firms have invested overseas. The Chinese government has established a clear policy and legal framework and roadmap for ODI, and the trends described in this chapter point to a growing level of globalization among Chinese firms in future.

While Chinese enterprises are investing all over the globe, some countries and regions stand out as top destinations. Developed nations in Europe and North America remain targets for Chinese investors, especially for private firms looking for higher value added targets. Meanwhile, Asia continues to be the overall favored destination for Chinese ODI and investments in BRI countries and regions such as Africa are growing fast.

In addition to mapping out key trends in recent Chinese ODI, this chapter also highlighted some of the main challenges that globalizing Chinese enterprises face and put forward recommendations for government and businesses to overcome these issues.

In particular, to fully capture the promise and benefits of globalization for both China and host countries, there is a need for Chinese firms to elevate their competencies in areas such as global management. There is also need for a more supportive, administrative, legal, financial, human resource environment and closer collaboration among Chinese enterprises, or between Chinese enterprises and foreign enterprises in the targeted countries.

The research and analysis presented in this chapter provide a reference for Chinese enterprises going global, policymaking agencies, and relevant research institutions. By increased cooperation, these groups can promote the globalization of Chinese enterprises, increase their worldwide influence, and contribute to the development of the world economy.

3

Impact of Tax Factors on Chinese FDIs

*Na Li**

I. Introduction

Investment treaties are not the only drivers of Chinese FDIs. Tax factors also play an important role in impacting foreign direct investment into China (FDIs into China) and Chinese investment to other countries (Chinese outbound investment). This chapter will examine the following questions: what are the impacts of tax factors on FDIs? Whether the Chinese experience on using tax instruments was consistent with these empirical findings? Whether China's implementation of anti-tax avoidance measures might drive FDIs away from China? What are the tax competition concerns for China? Answers to these questions are in fact a review of Chinese tax policies over the decades from the perspective of their effects on attracting FDIs into China. The last section contains a conclusion.

II. Impact of Tax Factors on FDIs

Tax factors refer to the general features of a jurisdiction's tax system, including tax base, tax rates, tax administrations, and international tax agreements and policies. There is a rich body of literatures examining the impacts of tax factors on FDIs.[1] One widely agreed finding is that both tax factors and non-tax factors play important roles in influencing FDIs, despite extravagantly different findings existing on the issue of the extent to which tax factors still influence FDIs.[2]

* Associate Professor, East China University of Political Science and Law, Shanghai, China and researcher, Tax Institute of Large Business, Jilin University of Finance and Economics, Changchun, China. The author can be contacted at na.li@wu.ac.at.

[1] See C M Tiebout, 'A Pure Theory of Local Expenditure' (1956) 64 Journal of Political Economy 416; W Steven Clark, 'Tax Incentives for Foreign Direct Investment: Empirical Evidence on Effects and Alternative Policy Options' (2000) 48 Canadian Tax Journal 1; Julien Chaisse, 'Investor-State Arbitration in International Tax Dispute Resolution: A Cut above Dedicated Tax Dispute Resolution?' (2016) 41(2) Virginia Tax Review 149; Enrique G Mendoza, Assaf Razin, and Linda L Tesar, 'Effective Tax Rates in Macroeconomics: Cross-Country Estimates of Tax Rates on Factor Incomes and Consumption' NBER Working Paper No 4864 (1994) 1; Alexander Klemm and Stefan Van Parys, 'Empirical Evidence on the Effects of Tax Incentives' IMF Working Paper WP/09/136; Samuel Tung and Stella Ho, 'The Impact of Tax Incentives on Foreign Direct Investment in China' (2000) 9 Journal of International Accounting, Auditing and Taxation 105.

[2] See Grubert Mutti, 'Empirical Asymmetries in Foreign Direct Investment and Taxation' (2004) 62 Journal of International Economics 337; Kenny W Lawrence and Winer L Stanley, 'Tax Systems in the World: An Empirical Investigation into the Importance of Tax Bases, Administration Costs, Scale and Political Regime' (2006) 13 International Tax and Public Finance 181; OECD, *Tax Effects on Foreign Direct Investment: Recent Evidence and Policy Analysis* (2007).

One view the author tends to agree with is that tax factors, although usually are not determinant to FDIs, but may be capable of influencing the investors' decision when non-tax factors are equal or similar.[3] The non-tax factors herein are too numerous to name, but include at least market circumstances, skill capability of workers, labour costs, availability of raw materials, infrastructures, legal framework, and macro-economic stability. When these non-tax factors are not going to change immediately, politicians frequently may choose to use tax instruments to stimulate the economy, especially to attract FDIs. For example, as far as in the United States, there were the Reagan tax cuts in the 1980s, the Bush tax cuts in the 2000s as well as the tax reform plans Trump brought out in 2016.[4]

In terms of tax factors' impact on investors' decisions, Devereux and Griffith in 2002 argued that the location of the FDI and its investment scale are affected by different tax factors.[5] Devereux and Griffith found that the location of the FDIs is usually affected by the effective average tax rate of the host country,[6] which measures the total tax burden on the total pre-tax profits of the investment, as investors normally prefer to invest at where the proportion of their pre-tax profit take in tax would be lowest.[7] In contrast, the investment scale of a FDI is usually affected by the effective marginal tax rate of the host country,[8] which measures the tax burden of the marginal unit of the capital invested. This tax rate could impact the investor making decisions on how much a new marginal investment should take place, as investors will invest less when they have to earn a higher than pre-tax return in order to meet their required after-tax return.

Then, according to Devereux and Griffith's findings above, the lower the effective average tax rates and the effective marginal tax rates are in the host country, the more attractive the host country could be to the investors. There are many tax factors determining these two effective tax rates; for example, the statutory tax rate and tax base in the host country, any tax incentives the host country may provide, the method in the home country to tax the profits derived from the host country, etc. Amongst these tax factors, China used to use tax incentives to reduce its effective tax rates for almost three decades in an attempt to attract FDIs.

[3] See James R Hines, *Lessons from Behavioral Responses to International Taxation* (Michigan Ross School of Business, Office of Tax Policy Research, Product Number WP 1999–91, 1999). See also Jacques Morisset and Nede Pirnia, 'How Tax Policy and Incentives Affect Foreign Direct Investment: A Review' World Bank Policy Research Working Paper No 2509 (1999); Michael P Devereux and Rachel Griffith, 'The Impact of Corporate Taxation on the Location of Capital: A Review' (2002) 9 Swedish Economic Policy Review 79; Michael P Devereux, 'The Impact of Taxation on the Location of Capital, Firms, and Profit: A Survey of Empirical Evidence' Working Paper 07/02 (Oxford University Centre for Business Taxation 2007); Georg Wamser, 'Foreign (In)Direct Investment and Corporate Taxation' (2011) 44 Canadian Journal of Economics/Revue canadienne d'économique 1497.
[4] See Jim Nunns and others, *An Analysis of Ronald Trump's Revised Tax Plan* (Tax Policy Center, Urban Institute & Brookings Institution 2016).
[5] See Devereux and Griffith (n 6) 79.
[6] See W Steven Clark, *Assessing the FDI Response to Tax Reform and Tax Planning* (OECD Global Forum on International Investment 2008) http://www.oecd.org/investment/globalforum/40315473.pdf.
[7] The effective average tax rate is the ratio of the present value of the taxes which will be paid in relation to a particular project to the present value of the pre-tax profit it will yield. In other words, the effective average tax rate relates total tax to total profit.
[8] The effective marginal tax rate is the proportionate difference between the expected pre-tax return on a project, that just yields the required after-tax rate of return and that required return itself.

III. Impact of Tax Factors on Chinese FDIs

A. Tax incentives for attracting FDIs into China

China opened its door to foreign investment in the late 1970s, but its economy and infrastructures at that time were of little attraction to investors. In order to compensate its disadvantages, China commenced using tax factors, in particular tax incentives, at the beginning of the 1980s to attract FDIs.

The first income tax laws respectively for foreign equity joint venture and foreign enterprise came into force in 1980 and 1981,[9] which provided generous tax incentives with a clear aim of attracting both foreign capital and technology. The tax incentives in forms of tax holidays, lower income tax rates, accelerated depreciation, and refunds of tax paid on reinvestment were obviously designed to attract foreign capital, while the tax incentives in forms of exempting withholding tax on royalties, lower income tax rates, and tax holidays for hi-tech foreign investment were designed to attract foreign technology. These FDI-specific incentives continued (even though China promulgated a new income tax law for foreign investment in 1991)[10] for almost three decades, until China's new income tax law came into force on 1 January 2008.[11]

The effectiveness of China's very generous tax incentives is an intensely debated issue. Although the United Nations Conference of Trade and Development[12] and the National Bureau of Statistics of China[13] both have statistics demonstrating a tremendous growth in the FDIs into China during the past three decades, these statistics still cannot lead to a conclusion that China's FDI-specific tax incentives were effective in attracting FDIs. One argument is that the FDIs would still have been poured into China even in the absence of tax incentives, because what attracted the investors were China's cheap labour, rich natural resources, and its huge domestic market.[14] Evidence supporting this argument is the fact that the investment from the United States, although it was one of the major sources of FDIs into China,[15] was that US investors could not actually benefit from China's tax incentives at all. This observation arises from analysis of the US tax system, which taxes its residents (the US investors) on their worldwide income and allows them to credit only taxes which have been paid in host countries. As China did not collect taxation from those US investors due to Chinese tax incentives,

[9] The Income Tax Law of the People's Republic of China Concerning Joint Ventures Using Chinese and Foreign Investment passed by the National People's Congress (NPC) on 10 September 1980 applied to equity joint ventures formed by a foreign investor and a Chinese partner. The Income Tax Law of the People's Republic of China Concerning Foreign Enterprises was promulgated by the NPC on 13 December 1981. It applied to foreign investment including contractual joint ventures, joint explorations, and wholly foreign-owned enterprises.

[10] Enterprise Income Tax Law for Foreign Invested Enterprises and Foreign Enterprises the People's Republic of China promulgated by the China NPC on 9 April 1991, which came into effect on 1 July 1991. This new income tax law abolished the former two income tax laws promulgated in 1980 and 1981 respectively applicable to foreign investments.

[11] Enterprise Income Tax Law of People's Republic of China, promulgated by the China NPC on 16 March 2007 and came into force on 1 January 2008.

[12] See United Nations Conference on Trade and Development: http://unctadstat.unctad.org/wds/TableViewer/tableView.aspx (last accessed 9 March 2017).

[13] See National Bureau of Statistics of China http://data.stats.gov.cn/easyquery.htm?cn=C01&zb=A060A&sj=2015> (last accessed 9 March 2017).

[14] Jinyan Li, 'The Rise and Fall of Chinese Tax Incentives' (2007) 8 Florida Tax Review 679.

[15] See Ministry of Commerce of People's Republic of China http://www.mofcom.gov.cn/article/i/dxfw/nbgz/201503/20150300911236.shtml> (last accessed 9 March 2017). See also Julien Chaisse and Mitsuo Matsushita, 'China's "Belt and Road" Initiative: Mapping the World Trade Normative and Strategic Implications' (2018) 52(1) Journal of World Trade 163.

these investors had to pay these China spared taxes to the US government when they fulfilled their US tax obligation. Consequently, the Chinese tax incentives were nullified by the foreign credit system of the United States; thus, it could be inferred that these US investors were not attracted to China by Chinese tax incentives.

This issue becomes more mysterious given the fact that the Chinese government has never published any tax expenditures illustrating its revenue losses and gains resulting from providing tax incentives. Thus, the public has been full of doubt regarding the effectiveness of China's FDI-specific tax incentives over the years. It is necessary for China to conduct a thorough analysis of the cost-benefit for using tax incentives to attract FDIs. This analysis should compare all relevant costs, such as tax revenue sacrifice, administrative costs,[16] market distortions,[17] opportunity costs,[18] social cost,[19] and with them benefits received in the form of revenue rises due to investment increases attracted by the tax incentives, employment, technology transfer, diversification, upgraded value chain, and spill-over effects. It is true that some costs and benefits are difficult to quantify, for example the administrative costs, market distortions, opportunity costs, social costs for implementing the tax incentives, and revenue derived from spill-over effects, etc. But China has to face these challenges, otherwise China, together with all the other countries using similar tax incentive instruments, would continue to use tax incentives based on its confidence that this instrument works.

B. Tax instruments for facilitating Chinese outbound investment

The recent concern of the Chinese government is tax disadvantage imposed on Chinese outbound investment. While Chinese residents are increasing their investments outside of China, China's tax system imposes taxes on Chinese investors' worldwide income. The foreign tax credit method China is using at present is similar to the US tax system allowing for crediting foreign taxes paid dollar for dollar up to the amount of the Chinese tax payable. It means that, in the same way as the US investors, the Chinese investors are now unable actually to benefit from the tax incentives provided in the host countries. This causes an increase of tax burden on Chinese investors when they compete with those non-Chinese investors who need not concern themselves with such a tax credit system in the home country, and these Chinese investors might then have to defer their profits remittance back to China for the purpose of deferring them to pay Chinese taxes.

China does not want to end up in the same situation as the US is facing at present, so China must resolve this problem as soon as possible. One remedy approach for China is to change its present 'credit' system into an 'exemption' system, whereby foreign income earned by a Chinese resident would be exempt from taxation in China. This exemption system is widely used in developed countries, in particular the OECD countries, as it is justified on the ground of capital import neutrality (CIN) in that

---

[16] The administrative cost means a country's cost for monitoring and administrating the tax incentives. See Mark Gallagher, 'Benchmarking Tax Systems' (2005) 25 Public Administration and Development 125.

[17] Market distortion means the costs between investments granted incentives and those without incentives, including the prices in relevant sectors or industries above international market rates, and the product quality in relevant sectors or industries below international market.

[18] The opportunity cost means a country's contrast costs for investments with other proposed or possible use of financial resources.

[19] The social cost means the costs of corruption and/or rent-seeking activities connected with abuse of tax incentive provisions.

the worldwide tax burden on the income is determined by the host country. Then the investors would not be concerned about their tax obligations in their home country. Thus, if China could convert to this exemption system, Chinese outbound investment would no longer suffer from the tax disadvantages imposed by the Chinese tax system. However, converting from a credit system to an exemption system requires amending the current Enterprise Income Tax Law[20] and the Individual Income Tax Law,[21] both of which can only be amended by the People's Congress in their annual meeting (which only takes place one week each year) and the amendment process is complex and time-consuming. Thus, this approach seems unlikely to be undertaken immediately.

Another remedy approach which could be used immediately is to include a tax sparing provision into the tax treaties which China concludes with other countries. As negotiating tax treaties is within the power of the State Administration of Taxation (SAT) of China, this approach could be immediately implemented without affecting any existing laws. A tax sparing provision in a tax treaty in general is to confirm that China will deem those taxes spared in the host countries as if they had been paid, and then allows Chinese residents to credit such spared foreign taxes against their Chinese taxes. In other words, Chinese investors would be able to keep the tax incentives provided by the host countries.

China was an advocate for using tax sparing mechanisms before 2008 when it provided generous FDI-specific incentives, in particular when China concluded tax treaties with those traditional capital exporting countries, such as the developed countries, namely the OECD member states.[22] Since 2008, when China abolished its FDI-specific tax incentives in its enterprise income tax law, China lost its motivation and thus suspended negotiating new treaties with tax sparing provisions after it signed the last tax sparing agreement with Ethiopia in 2009. However, in 2016 China resumed the use of this instrument in its tax treaty signed with Cambodia in 2016,[23] thereby recognizing the tax incentives provided by the Cambodian government as follows:

For the purposes of this Article, the term 'tax payable' shall be deemed to include the amount of tax which would have been paid if the tax had not been exempted or reduced in accordance with the relevant incentives designed to promote economic development in the domestic laws or connected regulations of either Contracting State. The provisions of this paragraph shall be effective for a period of 10 years starting from the entry into force of this Agreement. However, the period may be extended by mutual agreement of the Competent Authorities of the Contracting States.[24]

[20] Enterprise Income Tax Law of People's Republic of China, promulgated by the China NPC on 16 March 2007 and came into force on 1 January 2008.

[21] Individual Income Tax Law of People's Republic of China, promulgated by the China NPC on 10 September 1980 and last amended on 30 June 2011.

[22] Because of the United States insisting on no tax sparing policy, China was unable to include a tax sparing provision into the China–US tax treaty (1984). But what China and the US did was to sign an exchange of notes on 30 April 1984, providing that '(b)oth sides agree that a tax sparing credit shall not be provided in Article 22 of this Agreement at this time. However, the Agreement shall be promptly amended to incorporate a tax sparing credit provision if the United States hereafter amends its laws concerning the provision of tax sparing credits, or the United States reaches agreement on the provisions of a tax sparing credit with any other country'. Even with such an exchange of notes, the tax sparing credit has never been implemented, because the United States has so far not amended its laws concerning tax sparing credit nor agreed to a tax sparing credit with any other country.

[23] Agreement between the Government of the People's Republic of China and the Royal Government of Cambodia for the Avoidance of Double Taxation and the Prevention of Fiscal Evasion with Respect to Taxes on Income, signed on 13 October 2016.

[24] See Article 23(3) of the China–Cambodia tax treaty (2016).

Given that Chinese investment in Cambodia is rapidly increasing and the Cambodian government is providing generous tax incentives to foreign investment (a similar approach as China did before 2008), this tax sparing provision sends a clear signal to Chinese investors that the Chinese government will forgo its tax potential revenue for the purpose of relieving Chinese investors' concerns regarding their tax disadvantage.

IV. Two Unavoidable Issues

A. Tax planning versus tax avoidance

Since tax factors are deliberately designed to impact business behaviours,[25] it is unavoidable that business may respond with tax planning schemes to locate profits to those jurisdictions with low taxes or even no tax. Thus, a concern would arise for both tax policy-makers and tax administrative authorities on business tax avoidance activities.

One example is the round-trip investment scheme which was widely used by Chinese domestic investors before 2008 in order to benefit from those FDI-specific tax incentives. This round-trip investment scheme was a result of China implementing a dual income tax system before 2008. When the FDIs in China received generous tax incentives under their applicable income tax laws, a separate income tax law was running in parallel applicable only to Chinese domestic companies and did not provide any tax incentive.[26] Faced with such discrimination, Chinese domestic investors undertook a round-trip investment scheme by setting up a channelling company outside China and then using this channelling company to invest back into China. Consequently, those Chinese investments then became foreign investments and were eligible for all FDI-specific tax incentives under the income tax laws applicable to foreign investments. This scheme was an unexpected result of the actions of Chinese tax policy-makers, and resulted in the fact that a number of low tax or no tax jurisdictions, such as Hong Kong, the British Virgin Islands, and the Cayman Islands, etc were listed as those major jurisdictions where Chinese FDIs had originated.[27]

This round-trip investment scheme faded out following China's abolishing its FDI-specific tax incentives in 2008, but other tax avoidance schemes (or, as business would call them, 'tax planning schemes') still exist. For example, Hong Kong continues to function as a popular place for channelling FDIs into China as well as channelling Chinese outbound investment to other countries. Among many arguments given by business about Hong Kong being an ideal place for investment, such as having no foreign exchange control and Hong Kong's simple tax system being more convenient for business, one undeniable reason for using Hong Kong (besides other jurisdictions) as the channel place is that the Hong Kong–Mainland China tax arrangement provides a better chance for treaty shopping. As the Mainland China–Hong Kong tax arrangement provides more preferential tax treatment to income sourced by Hong Kong tax residents from Mainland China, business could take advantage of this tax

[25] Yoram Margalioth, 'Tax Competition, Foreign Direct Investments and Growth: Using the Tax System to Promote Developing Countries' (2003) 23 Virginia Tax Review 161.
[26] Provisional Regulation for the Corporate Income Tax of the People's Republic of China enacted by the Chinese State Council on 13 December 1993 and came into effect on 1 January 1994.
[27] Dongmei Qiu, 'Collecting Unpaid Tax Offshore: Caribbean Tax Havens and Foreign Direct Investment in China' (2014) 12 Bulletin of International Taxation 1.

arrangement, together with the separate treaty networks of Hong Kong and Mainland China, in order to reduce their global tax burdens.

The borderline between tax planning and tax avoidance, however, was never fixed, and this borderline has become even more blurred since the OECD initiated the Base Erosion and Profit Shifting (BEPS) project in 2013 to counterfeit tax avoidance activities.[28] Although not an OECD member state, China has been actively engaged in this BEPS project. Since 2013, China has been enforcing its existing anti-tax avoidance measures on the following three types of activities:(i) transfer pricing; (ii) treaty abuse; and (iii) offshore indirect share transfers.[29] The achievement of the Chinese government was significant; for example, the tax revenue collected in 2014 by applying anti-tax avoidance measures totaled US$7.8 billion, which was 113 times the related tax revenue collected in 2005.[30] In the meantime, however, a concern also arises: whether China's application of anti-tax avoidance measures would drive the FDI away from China. This is a valid concern. Business will lose certainty on the tax costs, as well as tax risk in China, when Chinese tax authorities implement their anti-tax avoidance measures aggressively in accordance with the 'spirit of law', rather than to the letter of the law.

1. *Transfer pricing*

China, as the largest state hosting inbound foreign investment, has suffered from profit shifting by multi-national companies for many years. This transfer pricing issue has become more serious since 2008, when China abolished its FDI-specific tax incentive policies, as multi-national companies tend more to shift their profits from China to those low tax or no tax jurisdictions. Consequently, transfer pricing was unavoidably listed as one of the key areas when China started to engage in the BEPS project. First, the SAT instructed its local branches to investigate whether excessive fees were being paid by the Chinese subsidiaries of multi-national companies to their foreign affiliates in respect of interest, service charges, management and technical fees, and royalties.[31] Secondly, following China introducing the concept of 'location specific advantages' (LSAs) in the UN Transfer Pricing Manual in 2013,[32] the Chinese tax authorities have put more effort into investigating whether multi-national companies have allocated 'reasonable profits' to China.[33] Chinese domestic law, however, only provides a general approach to the arm's length principle and does not contain any specific rule as to how to identify and calculate the comparative advantages derived from China attributable to LSA factors. Consequently, significant uncertainty remains for taxpayers as to how much profit should be allocated to China to demonstrate that they have satisfied the request of the Chinese tax authorities to allocate 'reasonable profits' to China.

[28] See OECD, *Addressing Base Erosion and Profit Shifting* (2013).

[29] SAT, Measures for the Administration of General Anti-Tax Avoidance (for Trial) (SAT Order 32), enacted by the SAT on 25 November 2014 with effect from 1 February 2015 www.chinatax.gov.cn/n810219/n810724/c1395143/content.html (last accessed 4 December 2017).

[30] See the SAT website at http://202.108.90.130/n810219/n810724/c1507274/content.html (last accessed 7 December 2016).

[31] SAT, *Notice on Conducting Anti-Tax Avoidance Investigation on Excessive Payment to Abroad* (Circular 146 [2014]), issued by the SAT on 29 July 2014 and SAT, *Announcement on Issues concerning Enterprise Income Tax on Expenses Paid by Enterprises to Their Overseas Affiliates* (Announcement No 16 [2015]), enacted by the SAT on 18 March 2015.

[32] UN, *Practical Manual on Transfer Pricing for Developing Countries*, ST/ESA/347 (UN 2013).

[33] SAT, Jiangsu Provincial Office, 2016–2018 Compliance Plan on International Tax Administration (Suguoshuifa [2016] No 125), published on 30 May 2016 with effect from the same day.

2. *Treaty abuse*

China has a large treaty network. As at the end of 2016, China had concluded tax treaties with 105 jurisdictions. Treaty abuse issues exist in respect of both inbound foreign investment into China and in relation to Chinese outbound investment abroad. In order to counter treaty abuse, in particular treaty shopping, China has enacted several circulars since 2009 to interpret the concept of 'beneficial ownership' with regard to the dividend, interest, and royalty provisions in all of the tax treaties that China has concluded.[34] These tax circulars have continuously narrowed the scope with regard to beneficial owners and expanded the documentation that taxpayers should provide, that is, all relevant transaction documents, including but not limited to contracts, resolutions of the boards of directors, or the meetings of shareholders, proof of payment, etc.[35]

In addition, following the suggestions contained in Action 6 of the BEPS project,[36] in 2015, for the first time, a principal purpose test (PPT) and a limitation on benefits (LOB) clause were included in the Chile–China tax treaty (2015).[37] It should be noted that the preamble to the Chile–China tax treaty (2015) expressly states that the purpose of the tax treaty includes the prevention of double non-taxation.[38] An LOB clause is then also included into the Chile–China tax treaty (2015) to limit the entitlement of treaty benefits solely to those 'qualified persons'.[39] In addition, a PPT provision is also included with the following wording to emphasize the fact that the burden of proof should lie with the taxpayer with regard to the principal purpose of given transactions:

Notwithstanding the other provisions of this Agreement, a benefit under this Agreement shall not be granted in respect of an item of income if it is reasonable to conclude, having regard to all relevant facts and circumstances, that obtaining that benefit was one of the principal purposes of any arrangement or transaction that resulted directly or indirectly in that benefit, unless it is established that granting that benefit in these circumstances would be in accordance with the object and purpose of the relevant provisions of this Agreement.[40]

3. *Offshore indirect share transfers*

Offshore indirect shares transfer is an important focus of the Chinese tax authorities. This form of shares transfer is often carried out by foreign investors selling the shares

---

[34] SAT, *Notice on Administration Method for Non-Residents to Benefit from Tax Treaties* (Circular 124 [2009]), with effect from 1 October 2009; SAT, *Notice of the State Administration of Taxation on How to Understand and Determine the 'Beneficial Owners' in Tax Treaties* (Circular 601 [2009]), with effect from 27 October 2009; SAT, *Bulletin on the Recognition of Beneficial Owners in Tax Treaties* (Notice [2012]), with effect from 29 June 2012; and SAT, *Supplementary Rules on 'Beneficial Owners'* (Notice 24 [2014]), with effect from 1 June 2014.

[35] SAT, *Administrative Method for Non-Tax Residents to Benefit from Tax Treaties* (Announcement No 60 [2015]), issued on 27 August 2015 with effect from the same date.

[36] OECD, *Action 6 Final Report 2015: Preventing the Granting of Treaty Benefits in Inappropriate Circumstances* (OECD 2015).

[37] *Agreement between the Government of the People's Republic of China and the Government of the Republic of Chile for the Elimination of Double Taxation and the Prevention of Tax Evasion and Avoidance with Respect to Taxes on Income* (25 May 2015).

[38] The preamble to the Chile–China Income Tax Treaty (2015) states that the tax treaty should not give rise to 'opportunities for non-taxation or reduced taxation through tax evasion or avoidance (including through treaty-shopping arrangements aimed at obtaining reliefs provided in this Agreement for the indirect benefit of residents of third States)'.

[39] See Article 26(2) of the Chile–China Income Tax Treaty (2015).

[40] See Article 26(5) of the Chile–China Income Tax Treaty (2015).

that they hold in a company located outside of China. Normally, the capital gains derived from such offshore shares transfers would not be taxed in China, unless the transaction can be proved to be effectively connected to China as specified in the capital gains provisions of a tax treaty that China has concluded with a particular contracting state. However, in the SAT's opinion, these capital gains should be taxed in China if the transfer of shares in respect of the foreign company has, in substance, a similar effect of selling an interest in its Chinese subsidiaries. While the test that the Chinese tax authorities apply to such shares transfer is the 'reasonable business purpose' test under the Chinese general anti-avoidance rule without providing any objective criteria and the burden of proof lies with the sellers in the offshore shares transfer.[41]

The *Children's Investment* case, which was ruled by the Higher Court of Zhejiang Province, China in December 2015,[42] could illustrate how Chinese tax authorities and Chinese courts apply this 'reasonable business purpose' test. TCI was a Cayman Island company and sold the shares it held in another Cayman Island in 2013. The whole share transfer transaction took place in the Cayman Islands and the only connection with China was the target company, which was also a Cayman Island company named Chinese Future Corporation, indirectly held 95 per cent of the shares in a Chinese company. The Chinese tax authorities argued that China should have taxing right on the Children's Investments capital gain derived from such shares sales in in Cayman Island, because this indirect share transfer had a similar effect as transferring the interest of the Chinese company. Then, the key issue of this case is whether the Children's Investment had a reasonable business purpose in carrying out this indirect share transfer transaction. In order to prove its reasonable business purpose, the Children's Investment argued that the intermediately companies, that is, Chinese Future Corporation and its subsidiary incorporated in Hong Kong, both have business activities. For example, Chinese Future Corporation has issued bonds, while its Hong Kong subsidiary leased out its immovable properties. However, the Higher Court of Zhejiang Province ruled that these were not sufficient evidence, as 'business substance' should be referring to active business activities such as being engaged in manufacturing industry, trading, or service activities, which neither the Chinese Future Corporation nor its Hong Kong subsidiary were ever carried out. Based on this logic, the court ruled that the Children's Investment did not prove the existence of its two intermediary companies having business substance, and consequently it failed in proving its having 'reasonable business purpose' in carrying out this indirect share transfer transaction. Thus, the court ruled in favour of the Chinese tax authorities to look through these two intermediary companies and then to tax the Children's Investment's capital gain.

[41] See Dongmei Qiu, 'Legal Interpretation of Tax Law: China' in R F van Brederode and R Krever (eds), *Legal Interpretation of Tax Law* (Kluwer Law International 2014) 77; J J P de Goede, 'Allocation of Taxing Rights on Income from Cross-Border (Indirect) Sale of Shares' (2012) 18 Asia-Pacific Tax Bulletin Journals 3; and Dongmei Qiu, 'China's Capital Gains Taxation of Nonresidents and the Legitimate Use of Tax Treaties' (2010) 60 Tax Notes International 8. The Chinese tax authorities have often published articles in newspapers sponsored by the Chinese government regarding their successfully investigating such indirect offshore share transfer transactions and having collected tax revenue from the foreign sellers. However, these articles are usually very brief with regard to the facts of the transactions and the information in respect of the relevant taxpayers is kept confidential. It is, therefore, difficult for readers to understand the investigation or to contact the taxpayers for the purposes of verification.

[42] Case: *Children's Investment Master Fund v Xihu District State Tax Bureau of Hangzhou City* (court judgment at the first instance zehangxingchuzi, 2015) 4, ruled by the Intermediate People's Court of Zhejiang Province on 9 July 2015; Case: *Children's Investment Master Fund v Xihu District State Tax Bureau of Hangzhou City* (court judgment at appeal zexingzhongzi, 2015) 441, ruled by the Higher Court of Zhejiang Province on 15 December 2015.

The vague and subjective criteria for this 'reasonable business purpose' test have caused huge concerns among the business world. In order to guide taxpayers on what circumstances would be deemed to have 'no reasonable business purpose', from 2009 onwards, Chinese tax authorities have issued several circulars to clarify whether the transaction is an artificial scheme with a primary purpose of obtaining tax benefits, for example, whether 75 per cent or more of the value of the shares in the foreign target company is derived, directly or indirectly, from Chinese taxable assets, whether 90 per cent or more of the income of the foreign target company is derived from investments in China at any time within one year prior to the indirect transfer, etc.[43] It is, however, not possible for the SAT to list all of the relevant circumstances, as a consequence, as long as the sole test with regard to such offshore indirect shares transfer is subjective, that is, the business purpose of the seller, uncertainty will remain in carrying out such transfers.

B. Tax competition

Another unavoidable issue is harmful tax competition. When tax incentives were booming in China from 1980 to 2007, the Chinese local governments actively engaged in tax competition through providing tax incentives in addition to those incentive measures already existing in the income tax laws. For example, numerous economic zones were set up by local government with a clear attempt to attract foreign investment, and the result was the local government losing tax revenue through racing to the bottom. This domestic competition was called off by the central government of China in 2008 through centralizing the power to enact tax incentives to central government. As a result, the local governments lost the capability of engaging in tax competition despite that they might still be willing to.

Concerns regarding tax competition with foreign countries, however, still exist. The 2008 enterprise income tax law adopted a universal tax rate of 25 per cent for all enterprises in China, and the tax incentives provided were limited in forms of a lower rate of 20 per cent for all 'small' enterprises and a lower tax rate of 15 per cent for all 'high-tech' enterprises, irrespective of them receiving FDIs or not. These tax rates were probably lower than many countries in the 2000s, but tax incentives booming in recent years led to a race for lower effective tax rates in many countries, especially in the neighbouring ASEAN countries. Thus, tax competition pressure comes back on China again, and calls for resuming use of tax incentives arise from both business and Chinese local governments.

There is no confirmed information on whether China will resume tax incentives. What China is doing at present is to seek a breakthrough in the BEPS project by arguing that jurisdictions should grant tax incentives on the basis of business having substantial activities within their territories, and China is also taking an active role

---

[43] SAT, *Notice on Issuing the Measures for the Implementation of Special Tax Adjustments (Trial)* (Guoshuifa [2009] No 2), issued by the SAT on 8 January 2009 but with retroactive effect from 1 January 2008; SAT, *Circular of the State Administration of Taxation on Strengthening the Administration of Enterprise Income Tax on Incomes from Non-resident Enterprises' Equity Transfers* (Guoshuihan [2009] No 698), enacted on 10 December 2009 but with retrospective effect from 1 January 2008; SAT, *Notice on Several Issues on Administration of Non-Residents Income Taxes* (Notice 24[2011]), enacted by the SAT on 28 March 2011 with effect from 1 April 2011; and SAT, *Announcement on Several Issues concerning the Enterprise Income Tax on Income from the Indirect Transfer of Assets by Non-Resident Enterprises* (Announcement No 7 [2015]), enacted by the SAT on 3 February 2015 with effect from the same date.

in joining the peer-review team to assess and review other jurisdictions' tax incentive schemes.

V. Conclusion

Significant changes have been made to Chinese tax laws and treaties in the past three decades, which clearly reflect the evolution of China's international investment policies. Despite ongoing debate regarding the impact of tax factors on FDI, Chinese experience demonstrates that tax factors are used extensively by the Chinese government in both attracting FDIs into China as well as relieving tax disadvantages of Chinese outbound investment. Although China's experience still cannot solve the mystery of whether tax incentives are effective on impacting FDIs, its implementing anti-tax avoidance measures in recent years disclosed that tax transparency and certainty are important tax factors impacting business decisions. Therefore, China should take further into account the impact of tax factors on business before FDIs are scared away when implementing aggressive anti-tax avoidance measures.

4

Chinese SOE Investments and the National Security Protection under IIAs

*Lu Wang**

I. Introduction

The rapid rise of state-owned enterprises (SOEs) and their cross-border investment activities in recent years has raised considerable concerns, particularly in relation to the potential detrimental impacts such investments may have on national security of host states.[1] For example, some argue that foreign SOE investments might pursue political objectives rather than purely economic goals, such as facilitating the home country's industrial planning or expanding foreign controls over critical industries,[2] or conduct commercial or even political espionage activities in host states by accessing sensitive technologies.[3] Meanwhile, SOE investments are mostly from emerging economies, especially China, and are prominent in the critical or 'strategic' industries, such as energy, infrastructure and telecommunication sectors and financial services.[4]

Whereas concerns related to SOE investments are mostly suspicions, fears have promoted a number of governments to strengthen the screening procedures on foreign investments and to bar certain deals due to national security considerations.[5] In

* Lecturer, University of New South Wales Faculty of Law; Member, Herbert Smith Freehills China International Business and Economic Law (CIBEL) Centre. Email: lu.wang10@unsw.edu.au.

The author would like to thank Dr Mavluda Sattorova, Professor Mark Feldman, and Professor Wenhua Shan for their very helpful comments and suggestions on an earlier draft of this chapter. Special thanks go to Professor Julien Chaisse for the invitation to present the paper at the Asian FDI Forum II. All errors remain the responsibility of the author herself.

1 Lu Wang and Norah Gallagher, 'Introduction to the Special Focus Issue on State-Owned Enterprises' (2016) 31 ICSID Review 1; Wouter P F Schmit Jongbloed and others, 'Sovereign Investment: An Introduction' in Karl P Sauvant and others (eds), *Sovereign Investment: Concerns and Policy Reactions* (OUP 2012) 11.

2 Przemyslaw Kowalski, Max Buge, Monika Sztajerowska, and Matias Egeland, *State-Owned Enterprises: Trade Effects and Policy Implications* (OECD Publishing 2013) 147, 12, and 15; Wouter P F Schmit Jongbloed, Lisa E Sachs, and Karl P Sauvant, 'Sovereign Investment: An Introduction' in Karl P Sauvant and others (eds), *Sovereign Investment: Concerns and Policy Reactions* (OUP 2012) 12.

3 OECD, *State-Owned Enterprises as Global Competitors: A Challenge or An Opportunity?* (OECD Publishing 2016) 62–3.

4 Przemyslaw Kowalski and Kateryna Perepechay, *International Trade and Investment by State Enterprises* (OECD Publishing 2015) 184, 8–9; UNCTAD, *World Investment Report 2014: Investing in the SDGs: An Action Plan* (UNCTAD 2014) 21. See also Julien Chaisse and Mitsuo Matsushita, 'China's "Belt and Road" Initiative: Mapping the World Trade Normative and Strategic Implications' (2018) 52 Journal of World Trade 163.

5 Since 2006 at least eight developed, developing, and transition economies have enacted legislation on foreign investment reviews on national security grounds (i.e. Canada (2009), China (2011 and 2015), Finland (2012), Germany (2009), Italy (2012), the Republic of Korea (2006), Poland (2015), and the Russian Federation (2008)); see UNCTAD, *World Investment Report 2016: Investor Nationality: Policy Challenges* (UNCTAD 2016) 95.

particular, some countries, including the US, Canada, and Australia have set stricter screenings for foreign SOEs. For example, under the Foreign Investment and National Security Act (FINSA) of 2007, the Committee on Foreign Investment in the US (CFIUS) shall conduct a forty-five-day national security investigation if the 'covered transaction' is controlled by a foreign government following the initial thirty-day review.[6] Under Australia's Foreign Investment Policy, 'all' foreign government investors must obtain approval before acquiring a direct interest in Australia, starting a new business or acquiring an interest in Australian land, regardless of the value of the investment.[7] In Canada, foreign investments are subject to the Investment Canada Act (ICA) 'net benefit' review where the review threshold for SOE investments is much lower than that for private investments.[8] In addition, the Canadian government explicitly stated that it will find the acquisition of control of a Canadian oil sands business by a foreign SOE to be of net benefit on 'an exceptional basis only' due to the inherent risks posed by foreign SOE acquisitions.[9]

Under this context, China's SOE investments, in particular, are receiving increasing concerns about their national security implications from the West. A famous case is the CNOOC–Unocal deal during 2005 which was eventually withdrawn by the Chinese SOE investor due to a strong negative response emphasizing national security concerns from the US.[10] More recently, Australia barred a Chinese SOE state grid corporation from purchasing a controlling stake in the country's biggest electricity company on national security grounds, warning that future bids by SOEs will face tougher scrutiny.[11] In 2016, the UK's new Prime Minister unexpectedly delayed a decision on the Hinkley Point nuclear deal citing national security implications of allowing a Chinese SOE, CGN, to purchase a 33.5 per cent stake in Hinkley Point and to build new plant stations at Sizewell and Bradwell.[12] Although the deal was approved eventually, the UK government has imposed 'significant new safeguards' for foreign investments to protect national security interests.[13] The delayed decision by Theresa May and the argument

---

[6] The term 'foreign government-controlled' transaction means any transaction that could result in the control of any person engaged in interstate commerce in the United States by a foreign government or an entity controlled by or acting on behalf of a foreign government. FINSA, 121 STAT. 246, PUBLIC LAW 110–49—JULY 26, 2007, SEC 2.

[7] 'Australia's Foreign Investment Policy' (last updated 1 July 2017) 5 https://cdn.tspace.gov.au/uploads/sites/82/2017/06/Australias-Foreign-Investment-Policy.pdf (last accessed 28 August 2017).

[8] To be specific, the review threshold for private sector investments is US$1 billion, while that for SOE investments is US$379 million; see https://www.ic.gc.ca/eic/site/ica-lic.nsf/eng/h_lk00050.html (last accessed 28 August 2017).

[9] Statement Regarding Investment by Foreign State-Owned Enterprises (modified July–December 2012) http://www.ic.gc.ca/eic/site/ica-lic.nsf/eng/lk81147.html (last accessed 6 March 2017).

[10] Ben White (Washington Post), 'Chinese Drop Bid to Buy U.S. Oil Firm' (3 August 2015) www.washingtonpost.com/wp-dyn/content/article/2005/08/02/AR2005080200404.html (last accessed 17 July 2016).

[11] Jamie Smyth (FT), 'Australia moves to block A$10bn power grid sale to Chinese: Recent election intensified unease over Chinese acquisitions' (11 August 2016) www.ft.com/content/918980ce-5f8f-11e6-ae3f-77baadeb1c93 (last accessed 1 January 2017); Jamie Smyth (FT), 'Australia defends moves to block Chinese bids: Future investments by state-owned companies will face tougher scrutiny' (19 October 2016) www.ft.com/content/94bb61c4-91ab-11e6-a72e-b428cb934b78 (last accessed 9 January 2017).

[12] Kiran Stacey and others (FT), 'UK decision to delay Hinkley Point plant catches China by surprise' (30 July 2016) www.ft.com/cms/s/0/acb715b2-55a0-11e6-befd-2fc0c26b3c60.html#axzz4HnDSkmdZ (last accessed 9 January 2017); BBC, 'Hinkley Point nuclear agreement reached' (21 October 2015) www.bbc.co.uk/news/business-34587650 (last accessed 9 January 2017).

[13] To be specific, 'the government will be able to prevent the sale of EDF's controlling stake prior to the completion of construction, without the prior notification and agreement of ministers; after Hinkley, the British government will take a special share in all future nuclear new build project and the Government will reform the approach to the ownership and control of critical infrastructure to ensure

by her advisor, Mr Nick Timothy, were criticized as 'China-phobia'.[14] Remarkably, immediately after the election of the new US presidency, the US–China Economic and Security Review Commission recommended the Congress 'authorising the CFIUS to bar Chinese SOEs from acquiring or otherwise gaining control of U.S. companies', particularly considering the 'high risk' of Chinese SOEs to the detriment of US national security.[15] In September 2017, President Trump blocked the Lattice Semiconductor deal backed by investors from China on the ground of national security considerations, which might signal 'more aggressive scrutiny of China's deal-making ambitions'.[16] In 2018, the US Congress passed the Foreign Investment Risk Review Modernisation Act (FIRRMA), which allows the CFIUS to review a wider range of transactions including any 'non-passive' investment in US firms involved in critical technology or other sensitive sectors.[17] Although that legislation does not target China by name, it has been said that 'China has weaponized investment in an attempt to vacuum up [US] advanced technologies'.[18]

It is, of course, a sovereign right of states to screen or to block foreign investments for national security considerations. However, recent developments in this respect have exposed some issues. For example, no country has provided an exhaustive and clear-cut definition of 'national security' in the context of foreign investments. As the scope of national security and relevant screening procedure varies among countries, foreign SOEs may face different admission conditions in different countries.[19] Meanwhile,

---

that the full implications of foreign ownership are scrutinized for the purposes of national security'; see UK Department for Business, Energy and Industrial Strategy, 'Government confirms Hinkley Point C project following new agreement in principle with EDF' (15 September 2016) www.gov.uk/government/news/government-confirms-hinkley-point-c-project-following-new-agreement-in-principle-with-edf (last accessed 9 January 2017).

[14] Mr Timothy claimed that the 'Chinese could use their role to build weaknesses into computer systems which will allow them to shut down Britain's energy production at will'; see Carrie Gracie (BBC), 'Is China the hitch for the Hinkley Point deal?' (29 July 2016) www.bbc.com/news/world-36922898 (last accessed 9 January 2017); Maria Ganga (The Guardian), 'Nuclear espionage charge for China firm with one-third stake in UK's Hinkley Point' (11 August 2016) www.theguardian.com/uk-news/2016/aug/11/nuclear-espionage-charge-for-china-firm-with-one-third-stake-in-hinkley-point (last accessed 9 January 2017).

[15] U.S.–China Economic and Security Review Commission, Executive Summary and Recommendations in *2016 Annual Report to Congress* (2016) 26. See also Jessica Dye (FT), 'US panel calls for ban on acquisitions by China state firms' (17 November 2016) www.ft.com/content/4393d61f-77ec-3bff-843c-cdf368664297 (last accessed 9 January 2017). See also Julien Chaisse, 'Demystifying Public Security Exception and Limitations on Capital Movement: Hard Law, Soft Law and Sovereign Investments in the EU Internal Market' (2015) 37(2) University of Pennsylvania Journal of International Law 583.

[16] Ana Swanson (The New York Times), 'Trump Blocks China-Backed Bid to Buy U.S. Chip Maker' (13 September 2017) https://www.nytimes.com/2017/09/13/business/trump-lattice-semiconductor-china.html (last accessed 11 November 2017).

[17] See Samuel Rubenfeld (WSJ), 'The Morning Risk Report: CFIUS Reform Becomes Law' (15 August 2018) https://blogs.wsj.com/riskandcompliance/2018/08/15/the-morning-risk-report-cfius-reform-becomes-law/ (last accessed 10 October 2018); Shawn Donnan (FT), 'Trump drops new restrictions on China investment' (28 June 2018) https://www.ft.com/content/a819ec8a-79f4-11e8-8e67-1e1a0846c475 (last accessed 10 October 2018). For the latest amendments see https://home.treasury.gov/system/files/206/FR-2018-22187_1786944.pdf (last accessed 10 October 2018).

[18] Jonathan Masters and James McBride (CFR), 'Foreign Investment and U.S. National Security' (28 August 2018) https://www.cfr.org/backgrounder/foreign-investment-and-us-national-security (last accessed 10 October 2018). See also Robert Delaney (South China Morning Post), 'China using "tentacles" to erode US security, senator warns, urging passage of bill boosting scrutiny of deals' (14 February 2018) https://www.scmp.com/news/china/policies-politics/article/2133263/china-using-tentacles-erode-us-security-senator-warns (last accessed 10 October 2018).

[19] UNCTAD, *World Investment Report 2016: Investor Nationality: Policy Challenges* (UNCTAD 2016) 94.

national security concerns have developed to encompass a wide range of interests such as energy safety, economic development, competition, food safety, and cyber security.[20] Accordingly, it is debatable whether such national policy responses related to foreign SOEs are designed to protect 'genuine' national security interests or constitute protectionist measures that favour local companies. Notably, the 2007 FINSA amended the previous section 721 and provided an non-exhaustive list of factors for consideration in the national security review, *inter alia*, whether the covered transaction is controlled by a foreign government.[21] Although the definition of national security is still openended, the provision suggests that SOE investments, or the broader state-controlled investments, may negatively impact on the national security of the US, and therefore ought to be subject to stricter conditions or blocked. Nevertheless, states should be aware that increasing scrutinies and bars against SOE investments or Chinese investments will erode the credibility of the host state as an open economy and discourage the needed international participation in certain key sectors.[22] There is, therefore, a tension between ensuring the market openness to foreign investments and investors and addressing national security concerns of host states.

As noted earlier, most current debates surrounding national security implications of SOE investments focus on domestic screening and review mechanisms in the pre-entry phase. However, it is noteworthy that in the post-entry phase host states may also impose restrictions (such as considerably change the legal regime, cancel the license or contract, divest the investment or benefit, restrict the capital transfer or travel of personnel, etc) on SOEs to protect certain national interests. In the second *Vattenfall* case, for example, the German parliament amended its Atomic Energy Act to phase out nuclear energy shortly after the Fukushima nuclear disaster in Japan, resulting in an immediate closure of a Swedish SOE Vattenfall's nuclear power plants.[23] Although such national regulations do not target SOE investments specifically, they may significantly affect any established foreign investments including those involving foreign SOEs, which are likely to be challenged in future investment arbitrations.

In fact, even if a host state has approved a transaction by foreign SOEs in a national security review, security-related concerns arising from SOE investments may resurface after its establishment, and the host state may then wish to take regulatory measures restricting or otherwise detrimentally affecting the SOE project. For example, the UK government in 1988 directed an SWF, Kuwait Investment Office (KIO), to divest its

---

[20] Frédéric Wehrlé, Joachim Pohl, *Investment Policies Related to National Security: A Survey of Country Practices* (OECD Publishing 2016) 2, 22–4.

[21] FINSA, 121 STAT. 246, PUBLIC LAW 110–49—JULY 26, 2007, Sec. 4.

[22] Lucio Blanco Pitlo III (China US Focus), 'National Security Review of Foreign Investments: Comparing China and the U.S.' (11 September 2015) www.chinausfocus.com/finance-economy/national-security-review-of-foreign-investments-comparing-china-and-the-u-s (last accessed 9 January 2017); Andy McSmith (Independent), 'Hinkley Point: China warns Theresa May over "suspicious" decision to delay nuclear power station' (1 August 2016) www.independent.co.uk/news/uk/politics/hinkley-point-china-theresa-may-nuclear-power-security-edf-a7166716.html (last accessed 9 January 2017).

[23] See Nathalie Bernasconi-Osterwalder and Rhea Tamara Hoffman, 'The German Nuclear Phase-Out Put to the Test in International Investment Arbitration? Background to the New Dispute Vattenfall v Germany (II)' (2012) IISD Briefing Note http://www.iisd.org/pdf/2012/german_nuclear_phase_out.pdf (last accessed 12 September 2017). In 2012, Vattenfall together with other energy companies also filed cases in the German court, and the Federal Constitutional Court made a judgment on 6 December 2016; see 'The Thirteenth Amendment to the Atomic Energy Act Is for the Most Part Compatible with the Basic Law' (Press Release No 88/2016, 6 December 2016) https://www.bundesverfassungsgericht.de/SharedDocs/Pressemitteilungen/EN/2016/bvg16-088.html (last accessed 12 September 2017).

21.6 per cent stake in British Petroleum (BP) to 9.9 per cent within a year for the protection of the 'public interest'.[24] While the KIO purchased the major stake in BP after its privatization on the open market, the British Monopolies and Mergers Commission investigated the holding and noted that 'unlike other shareholders, Kuwait is a sovereign state with wide strategic interests and could be expected to exercise its influence in support of its own national interest'.[25] This case provides a clear example that the host state may revoke an SOE investment on the basis of a vaguely defined public interest, even if it is a completely legal transaction.[26] Returning to the instance of the Hinkley Point case, whereas the deal was provisionally approved by Mrs May, it is possible for future British governments to take actions against the Chinese SOE investment in Hinkley and the other two nuclear power stations for national security interests. In such a hypothetical case, the host state may take various restrictive measures, such as shut down the facilities or force SOE investors to divest interests. Therefore, a question may arise of whether the host state's action is subject to international investment obligations. In other words, whether and to what extent international investment agreements (IIAs) allow the host state to take measures against SOE investments in order to protect national security interests.

II. Addressing National Security Concerns over SOE Investments in IIAs

While national security concerns have become an important part of foreign investment policies at the national level, most international treaties, especially the earlier BITs of European countries, do not seem to have adequately addressed this issue.[27] Recent treaties, however, have done a much better job, particularly by including national or essential security exceptions or other exception clauses in investment treaties. For example, the 2012 US Model BIT includes an essential security exception provision, stating that 'nothing in this Treaty shall be construed to preclude a Party from applying measures that it considers necessary for the fulfilment of its obligations with respect to the maintenance or restoration of international peace or security, or the protection of its essential security interests'.[28] The recent Comprehensive and Progressive Agreement for Trans-Pacific Partnership (CPTPP) provides a similar provision for security exceptions.[29] Accordingly, contracting states may take restrictive measures to expropriate or divest foreign SOE investments for essential security interests without violating international obligations under the treaty.

---

[24] From Reuters, 'British Tell Kuwait to Cut BP Stake: Arab Oil Producer Could Lose $593 Million in Selloff' *Los Angeles Times* (5 October 1988) http://articles.latimes.com/1988-10-05/business/fi-2758_1_arab-oil (last accessed 29 March 2017); Chester Brown and Audley Sheppard, 'United Kingdom' in Chester Brown (ed), *Commentaries on Selected Model Investment Treaties* (OUP 2013) 742.

[25] Chester Brown and Audley Sheppard, 'United Kingdom' in Chester Brown (ed), *Commentaries on Selected Model Investment Treaties* (OUP 2013) 742.

[26] Christopher Balding, *Sovereign Wealth Funds: The New Intersection of Money and Politics* (OUP 2012) 84.

[27] See Julien Chaisse, 'The Shifting Tectonics of International Investment Law: Structure and Dynamics of Rules and Arbitration on Foreign Investment in the Asia-Pacific Region' (2015) 47 George Washington International Law Review 563, 615–16.

[28] 2012 US Model BIT Article 18.

[29] Comprehensive and Progressive Agreement for Trans-Pacific Partnership (CPTPP) Article 29.2(b).

Nevertheless, given that language varies in respect of security exception clauses, a question arises of whether the state's restrictive measures on national security considerations fall within the scope of exceptions and therefore are exempted from treaty obligations such as non-discrimination treatment or expropriation. For instance, most treaties that include a security exception adopt the term 'essential security interests' or 'national security',[30] while some use other terms such as 'public order',[31] 'extreme emergency',[32] 'public moral',[33] and 'international peace and/or security'[34] that may describe a different kind of situation where the exception can be invoked.[35] Besides, most security exception clauses generally apply to the whole treaty, while some others only apply to specific provisions of the BIT such as the expropriation (e.g. Belgian–Luxembourger Economic Union–China BIT), non-discrimination (e.g. Japan–China BIT), dispute settlement (e.g. Austria–Mexico BIT), applicable laws (e.g. UK–India BIT).[36] As a result, certain domestic measures against foreign SOE investments might not fall within the scope of security exceptions but are subject to relevant treaty obligations.

Notably, some treaties adopt a self-judging security exception with the reference of 'it considers necessary', while others do not include such a qualification. Additionally, some treaties contain a WTO-like self-judging clause with a clarification of , or limitation on, essential security interests.[37] Norway's new Draft Model BIT, for instance, provides its essential security interests relating to 'investment in defence and security sector[s]' and 'fissionable and fusionable materials or the materials from which they are derived'.[38] Under a self-judging security exception clause, host states would retain more discretion and have more regulatory space in taking restrictive measures against foreign investments; but if the essential security is further defined, the conditions shall limit states' action to a certain extent.

---

[30] For example, the US treaties normally use the term 'essential security interests', while the Hungary–Russian Federation BIT (1995) adopted the term 'national security', see UNCTAD, *The Protection of National Security in IIAs* UNCTAD Series on International Investment Policies for Development (United Nations Publishing 2009) 72–3.

[31] See eg BLEU–Guatemala BIT (2005) Article 3(1).

[32] As noted, most BITs concluded by India adopt this approach; such as Article 11(2) of the Egypt–India BIT (1997). See UNCTAD, *The Protection of National Security in IIAs* (n 30) 76.

[33] See eg US–Egypt BIT (1986) Article X (1).

[34] See eg US–Uruguay BIT (2005) Article 18(2) adopts the term 'peace or security', while the Economic Partnership, Political Coordination and Cooperation Agreement concluded between the EU and Mexico (2000) used the term 'peace and international security'; UNCTAD, *The Protection of National Security in IIAs* (n 30) 78–9.

[35] For more discussions see UNCTAD, *The Protection of National Security in IIAs* (n 30) 72–80.

[36] Katia Yannaca-Small, 'Essential Security Interests under International Investment Law' in *International Investment Perspectives: Freedom of Investment in a Changing World* (OECD 2007) 99.

[37] For example, Article 2102(1) NAFTA provides that '(b) to prevent any Party from taking any actions that it considers necessary for the protection of its essential security interests: (i) relating to the traffic in arms, ammunition and implements of ward and to such traffic and transactions in other goods, materials, services, and technology undertaken directly or indirectly for the purpose of supplying a military or other security establishment, (ii) in time of war or other emergency in international relations, or (iii) relating to the implementation of national policies or international agreements respecting the non-proliferation of nuclear weapons or other nuclear explosive devices.

[38] 2015 Norway Model BIT (Draft version 130515), Article 26 (ii), http://investmentpolicyhub.unctad.org/Download/TreatyFile/28733350 (last accessed 9 January 2017).

Nonetheless, most treaties with essential security exceptions do not include any further clarifications in this respect.[39]

Although security exception clauses in IIAs are neither designed specifically against SOE investments nor draw any difference between private- and public-owned investments, it is possible for host states to use these security exceptions as a justification of restrictive measures against SOE investments to derogate from international obligations. However, the varied terms, scopes and contents of security exception clauses in treaty practice imply different degrees of flexibility and space of regulatory right of host governments in taking measures against SOE investments. Notably, the inclusion of national security exceptions has become much more frequent in recent investment treaties,[40] and many of them are self-judging, and some contracting states have provided 'essential security interests' with more details that might limit the invocation of security exceptions to certain circumstances.[41] Although a detailed security exception clause might set restrictions for host states to take restrictive measures against SOE investments, it could provide more guidance on invoking the exceptions. However, it is notable that some treaties, such as the 2015 Indian Model BIT, explicitly provide an open-ended 'essential security interests' by referring to the language of 'including but not limited to'.[42] Accordingly, even though the security exception has been clarified with certain conditions, the contracting states still retain considerable discretions in taking restrictive measures against SOE investments on national security grounds.

[39] Katia Yannaca-Small, 'Essential Security Interests under International Investment Law' in *International Investment Perspectives: Freedom of Investment in a Changing World* (OECD 2007) 98.

[40] UNCTAD, *World Investment Report 2015: Reforming International Investment Governance* (UN Publication 2015), 141; see e.g., Article 18 of China–Japan–Korea Trilateral Investment Agreement (2012), Article 17 of Japan–Kuwait BIT (2012), Article 5(2) of Pakistan–Turkey BIT (2012), Article 28.6 of Canada–EU CETA (2016), Article 13 of Argentina–Qatar BIT (2016) etc.

[41] For example, Article 274 of the EU–Kazakhstan EPCA (2015) provides '[... e]ssential security interests (i) connected with the production of or trade in arms, munitions or war material; (ii) relating to economic activities carried out directly or indirectly for the purpose of provisioning a military establishment; (iii) relating to fissionable and fusionable materials or the materials from which they are derived; (iv) relating to government procurement indispensable for national security or for defence purposes; or (v) taken in time of war or other emergency in international relations ...'. Similarly, Article 12.14 of the China–Republic of Korea FTA (2015) provides that measures for the protection of essential security interests can be taken '(i) in time of war, or armed conflict, or other emergency in that Party or in international relations; or (ii) relating to the implementation of national policies or international agreements respecting the non-proliferation of weapons'. Article 19.3 of the CETA provides that essential security interests is relating to the procurement: (a) of arms, ammunition or war material; (b) or to procurement indispensable for national security; or (c) for national defence purposes. In this context, the scope of essential security interests differs among investment treaties.

[42] Article 17.1 of the 2015 Indian Model BIT provides that a party can take any action which it considers necessary for the protection of its essential security interests including but not limited to: (a) action relating to fissionable and fusionable materials or the materials from which they are derived; (b) action taken in time of war or other emergency in domestic or international relations; (c) action relating to the traffic in arms, ammunition and implements of war and to such traffic in other goods and materials as is carried on directly or indirectly for the purpose of supplying a military establishment; (d) action taken so as to protect critical public infrastructure including communication, power and water infrastructures from deliberate attempts intended to disable or degrade such infrastructure. Similarly, Article 76(a) of the New Zealand and Singapore CEPA (2000) also includes the language of 'including but not limited to'.

III. Invocation of Security Exceptions to Justify Restrictive Measures Relating to SOE Investments

According to the 2016 report of UNCTAD, at least sixteen national security-related investment cases have been examined by international investment tribunals, and over one-third (277 cases) of all known investment arbitral cases involve investments in industries that may affect a country's national interests.[43] More importantly, national security arguments were used by the respondent states as a justification for measures against the investor (i.e. expropriations of investment through the adoption of legislative acts, cancellation of licenses or state contracts, or conduct of police investigations).[44] Therefore, it will be unsurprising if a host state invokes national security reasons to justify its actions against foreign SOE investments. However, while the security exception clauses discussed above may safeguard host states' ability to restrict foreign SOEs on the ground of national security considerations, it is still uncertain whether state actions against SOE investments would be found justifiable in investment arbitrations, especially considering that the security exception clause varies in treaties and the scenarios of SOE investments have not been discussed in a real case. Therefore, it is questionable whether, to what extent and under what circumstances the security exception clause can be invoked to justify a host state's action against an SOE investment.

A. Invoking the Security Exception Clause under Investment Treaties

If an SOE investor claims that the host state's action constitutes a violation of investment treaty obligations, whether and to what extent the action is justifiable under the security exception clause will be determined by the tribunal on a case-by-case basis. The key issue is to determine whether the SOE investment is a threat to national security or essential security interests, and if yes, whether the restrictive measure is a necessary action. However, the review approach of tribunals may vary under different security exception clauses.

1. Self-judging clauses

When applying the security exception clause, the tribunal is firstly faced with a problem of whether the security exception is self-judging or non-self-judging, because that will determine whether and to what extent the investment tribunal is competent to review a state's restrictive measure relating to SOE investments. Some investment treaties contain self-judging clauses that emulate Article XXI of the GATT, such as Article 18 of the US 2012 Model BIT, providing that nothing in the Agreement shall be construed to prevent any Party from taking any actions that 'it considers necessary' for the protection of its essential security interests. Accordingly, the contracting parties retain exclusive discretion to determine whether an SOE investment is a threat to its essential security and thus can take restrictive measures against the SOE

---

[43] UNCTAD, *World Investment Report 2016: Investor Nationality: Policy Challenges* (UNCTAD 2016) 97.
[44] UNCTAD, *World Investment Report 2016: Investor Nationality: Policy Challenges* (UNCTAD 2016) 97.

investment insofar as they consider such measures to be necessary.[45] To some extent, the necessity of taking a restrictive measure against SOE investments is mainly a political decision and a self-judging clause would allow political consideration to prevail over legal scrutiny.[46]

Nevertheless, some have argued that the self-judging nature does not entirely exempt contracting parties from international responsibility, and the invocation of the exception clause shall be made in good faith as a general obligation of the Vienna Convention on the Law of Treaties (Article 26).[47] According to the statement of Administrative Action in the U.S.' NAFTA Implementation Act of 1993, the national security exception is self-judging in nature, but 'each government would expect the provisions to be applied by the other in good faith'.[48] In the *LG&E* case, the tribunal stated that 'were the Tribunal to conclude that the provision is self-judging, Argentina's determination would be subject to a good faith review anyway'.[49] Accordingly, even when the investment treaty contains a self-judging exception clause, the tribunal may still need to consider whether the exception is applied in good faith. In this context, a good faith review may help to avoid the abuse of invoking the self-judging exception to justify the restrictive measure against SOE investment, and to limit the invocation for 'genuine' national security considerations rather than protectionist ends. In this regard, the responding state may bear the burden of proof for invoking the exception. However, no tribunal provides any detail on how to apply for the good faith review, and only the *LG&E* tribunal mentioned that the good faith review would 'not significantly differ from the substantive analysis [the Tribunal] presented' in the context of a non-self-judging clause in Article XI of the US–Argentina BIT.[50] Moreover, a good faith review may create uncertainty in investment arbitrations since the precise meaning of the good faith is unclear and the tribunal will face practical problems to decide the true purpose of the state in taking a restrictive measure. In addition, the *LG&E* approach to good faith reviews could mitigate the difference between self-judging clauses and non-self-judging clauses, elevating the lower standard of a good faith review to that of a higher full-bodied substantive review and so deprive the explicit self-judging character of its merits.

My view on the self-judging exception clause is, first, a self-judging clause indicates a declaration of discretion that contracting states would determine what constitutes 'security exception'. This would include whether a foreign SOE investment threatens its national security interests and what action against foreign SOE investment is necessary to protect national security. In this regard, tribunals are poorly placed to 'second-guess' the policy choice of a government.[51] Secondly, a self-judging clause does not bar

---

[45] The language of 'necessary' does not impair the self-judging nature of security exception under the self-judging exception clauses.

[46] UNCTAD, *The Protection of National Security in IIAs* (n 30) 93.

[47] Article 26 of the VCLT provides that '[e]very treaty in force is binding upon the parties to it and must be performed by them in good faith'. UNCTAD, *The Protection of National Security in IIAs* (n 30) 40.

[48] Reprinted in H.R. DOC. 103-159, 666. Stephan Schill and Robyn Briese, ' "If the State Considers": Self-Judging Clauses in International Dispute Settlement' (2009) 13 Max Planck Yearbook of United Nations Law 61, 111.

[49] *LG&E Energy Corp., LG&E Capital Corp., and LG&E International, Inc. v Argentine Republic* (*LG&E v Argentina*), ICSID Case No ARB/02/1, Decision on Liability, 3 October 2006, para 214.

[50] ibid; Stephan Schill and Robyn Briese, ' "If the State Considers": Self-Judging Clauses in International Dispute Settlement' (2009) 13 Max Planck Yearbook of United Nations Law 113.

[51] William W Burke-White and Andreas von Staden, 'Investment Protection in Extraordinary Times: The Interpretation and Application of Non-Precluded Measures Provisions in Bilateral Investment Treaties' (2008) 48 Virginia Journal of International Law 309, 381.

a tribunal from reviewing state action subject to a good faith review. But, a good faith review should not impair a state's discretion in taking action against SOE investments for the protection of national security interests. Thirdly, a good faith review under a self-judging clause is a review of whether the host state invokes the self-judging exception in good faith, both subjectively and objectively, rather than a 'substantive' review of national security per se. In this sense, tribunals' reviews are more like an oversight to prevent contracting states from abusing their discretion in self-judging or exercising the discretion improperly. Although it is uncertain whether the investment tribunal would be convinced in a particular case, the good faith test could constrain the freedom of states to invoke self-judging security exceptions, and then strike a balance between maintaining a host state's discretion in matters of national security and the protection of foreign SOEs from protectionism.

2. Non-self-judging clauses

Most treaties do not include the language of 'it considers' but adopt a non-self-judging security exception clause. For example, Article XI of the US–Argentina BIT provides that: 'This Treaty shall not preclude the application by either Party of measures necessary for the maintenance of public order, the fulfillment of its obligations with respect to the maintenance or restoration of international peace or security, or the Protection of its own essential security interests'.

Under this text, the first question is whether the security exception clause is inherently self-judging? In this regard, the ICJ held in the *Nicaragua* case that the essential security exception without a language of 'it considers' was not self-judging.[52] But Judge Schwebel in his dissenting opinion found that Article XXI of the US–Nicaragua FCN was self-judging, and the Court did not have jurisdiction over this matter.[53] Although the US insisted on the self-judging nature of the security exception clause, it is notable that its earlier treaty practice did not include a language of 'it considers' and its sole assertion on self-judging did not seem to be accepted by other contracting parties.[54] For instance, the State Department asserted that during the various BIT negotiations, the US made its view evident that the exception was self-judging.[55] But the history of NAFTA negotiations revealed that Canada did not agree with the US interpretation of a self-judging nature of the exception.[56]

---

[52] Article XXI of the US–Nicaragua FCN provides 'the present Treaty shall not preclude the application of measures: (d) necessary to fulfill the obligations of a Party for the maintenance or restoration of international peace and security, or necessary to protect its essential security interests'; see *Military and Paramilitary Activities in and against Nicaragua (Nicaragua v United States of America)*, Judgment of 27 June 1986 (Merits), para 222. See also James Mendenhall, 'The Evolution of the Essential Security Exception in U.S. Trade and Investment Agreements' in Karl P Sauvant and others (eds), *Sovereign Investment: Concerns and Policy Reactions* (OUP 2012) 323.

[53] *Military and Paramilitary Activities in and against Nicaragua (Nicaragua v United States of America)*, Dissenting opinion of Judge Schwebel on Judgment of 26 November 1984 (Jurisdiction of the Court and Admissibility of the Application), para 128; Mendenhall, 'The Evolution of the Essential Security Exception in U.S. Trade and Investment Agreements' (n 52) 324.

[54] Mendenhall, 'The Evolution of the Essential Security Exception in U.S. Trade and Investment Agreements' (n 52) 324–5.

[55] Burke-White and von Staden, 'Investment Protection in Extraordinary Times:' (n 51) 383–6; see also Mendenhall, 'The Evolution of the Essential Security Exception in U.S. Trade and Investment Agreements' (n 52) 325–8.

[56] Mendenhall, 'The Evolution of the Essential Security Exception in U.S. Trade and Investment Agreements' (n 52) 328.

In *Sempra*, the claimant did not accept the interpretation of a self-judging character of Article XI and maintained that 'a self-judging clause is an extraordinary exception that has to be clearly stated'.[57] In particular, the claimant and some scholars
argued that a self-judging interpretation 'would result in the creation of a broad and
sweeping exception to the obligations established under the Treaty and would eviscerate the very object and purpose of this kind of treaty'.[58] Also, the tribunal noted
that the GATT, the *Nicaragua* decision, and the *Oil Platform* case had confirmed
that 'the language of a provision has to be very precise for it to lead to a conclusion
about its self-judging nature' and a lack of such language turned out to be crucial to
the rejection of arguments favouring a self-judging interpretation.[59] As a result, the
tribunal concluded that Article XI of the US–Argentina BIT was not self-judging.[60]
Therefore, if an investment treaty does not include the language of 'it considers', the
tribunal may assess whether a SOE investment in dispute poses any threat to the
host state's security interests and whether state action is necessary for the protection
of national security.

Under a non-self-judging security exception clause, the second question is how
international tribunals interpret the notion of national security. To a certain extent,
even under a non-self-judging exception clause, arbitrators' analysis of the disputed
measure should be restricted by certain boundaries. In this regard, one may argue
that the concept of national security may lose its meaning and purpose if a third
party has the power to decide whether a threat to a state's national security exists
and what measures that state is allowed to take in response.[61] Therefore, at least
theoretically, it is doubtful whether any tribunal acting judicially can override the
assertion of a state that a foreign investment affects its security interests.[62] Given
that states may have different views on the threat required to trigger the security
exception, the tribunal's principal task would then be to determine the 'appropriate
boundaries of the margin of appreciation'.[63] In this regard, however, the boundaries
may be different from case to case, so the interpretation of a non-self-judging national security exception could be uncertain and inconsistent in investment arbitration practice.[64]

Nevertheless, arbitral tribunals have acknowledged that economic emergency or
crisis is covered by the essential security exception. For example, the *CMS* tribunal
stated that if the concept of essential security interests was understood and interpreted
'to exclude other interests, for example, major economic emergencies', it could well
result in an 'unbalanced understanding of Article XI'.[65] In *Enron*, the tribunal noted
that 'the object and purpose of the Treaty are, as a general proposition, to apply in

---

[57] *Sempra Energy International v Argentine Republic* (*Sempra v Argentina*), ICSID Case No ARB/02/
16, Award (28 September 2007), para 369.
[58] *Sempra Energy International v Argentine Republic* (*Sempra v Argentina*), ICSID Case No ARB/02/
16, Award (28 September 2007), para 372; Expert Opinion of Professor José E Álvarez (12 September
2005), para 64.
[59] *Sempra Energy International v Argentine Republic* (*Sempra v Argentina*), ICSID Case No ARB/02/
16, Award (28 September 2007), para 383.
[60] *Sempra Energy International v Argentine Republic* (*Sempra v Argentina*), ICSID Case No ARB/
02/16, Award (28 September 2007), para 388. Tribunals in the CMS, Enron, and LE&G reached the
same conclusion.
[61] UNCTAD, *The Protection of National Security in IIAs* (n 30) 41.   [62] ibid 42.
[63] Burke-White and von Staden, 'Investment Protection in Extraordinary Times:' (n 51) 374.
[64] UNCTAD, *The Protection of National Security in IIAs* (n 30) 42.
[65] *CMS Gas Transmission Company v Republic of Argentina* (*CMS v Argentina*), ICSID Case No
ARB/01/8, Award (12 May 2005), para 360.

the situation of economic difficulty and hardship that require the protection of the international guaranteed rights of its beneficiaries ... any interpretation resulting in an escape route from the obligations defined cannot be easily reconciled with that object and purpose ...'.[66] The *Sempra* Tribunal further considered that 'there is nothing that would prevent an interpretation allowing for the inclusion of economic emergency in the context of Article XI ... essential security interests can eventually encompass situation other than the traditional military threats for which the situation found its origins in customary law'.[67] In *LE&G*, the tribunal rejected the argument that 'Article XI is only applicable in the circumstances amounting to military action and war' and believed that 'when a state's economic foundation is under siege, the severity of the problem can equal that of any military invasion'.[68] Similarly, in the more recent *Continental Casualty Company* case, the tribunal pointed out that:

It is well known that the concept of international security of States in the Post-War II international order was intended to cover not only political and military security but also the economic security of States and their population ... States have invoked necessity to protect a wide variety of interests, including safeguarding the environment, preserving the very existence of the State and its people in time of public emergency, or ensuring the safety of a civilian population.[69]

However, tribunals disagreed on the degree of the severity of the economic crisis required to justify the restrictive measures, although their conclusions were made on the same facts. For example, the *CMS* and *Enron* tribunals considered that 'the Argentine crisis was severe but did not result in a total economic and social collapse',[70] and the argument of 'such a situation compromised the very existence of the state and its independence so as to qualified as involving an essential interest of the state is not convincing'.[71] In contrast, the *LG&E* tribunal considered that the crisis 'constituted the highest degree of public disorder' and threatened a 'total collapse' of the Argentina government, so Argentina was excused under Article XI from liability for any breaches of the Treaty.[72] In the *Continental Casualty* case, the tribunal adopted an objective assessment and considered that a crisis that brought about a series of threats[73] qualifies

---

[66] *Enron Corporation and Ponderosa Assets, L.P. v Argentine Republic (Enron v Argentina)*, ICSID Case No ARB/01/3, Award 22 May 2007, para 331.

[67] *Sempra Energy International v Argentine Republic (Sempra v Argentina)*, ICSID Case No ARB/02/16, Award (28 September 2007), para 374.

[68] *LG&E Energy Corp., LG&E Capital Corp., and LG&E International, Inc. v Argentine Republic (LG&E v Argentina)*, ICSID Case No ARB/02/1, Decision on Liability, 3 October 2006, para 238.

[69] *Continental Casualty Company v Argentine Republic (Continental Casualty v Argentina)*, ICSID Case No ARB/03/9, Award, 5 September 2008, para 175.

[70] *CMS Gas Transmission Company v The Republic of Argentina (CMS v Argentina)*, ICSID Case No ARB/01/8, Award, 12 May 2005, para 355.

[71] *Enron Corporation and Ponderosa Assets, L.P. v Argentine Republic (Enron v Argentina)*, ICSID Case No ARB/01/3, Award 22 May 2007, para 306.

[72] *LG&E Energy Corp., LG&E Capital Corp., and LG&E International, Inc. v Argentine Republic (LG&E v Argentina)*, ICSID Case No ARB/02/1, Decision on Liability, 3 October 2006, paras 229, 231.

[73] The threats include 'the sudden and chaotic abandonment of the cardinal tenet of the country's economic life, such as the fixed convertibility rate which had been steadfastly recommended and supported for more than a decade by the IMF and the international community; the near-collapse of the domestic economy; the soaring inflation; the leap in unemployment; the social hardships bringing down more than half of the population below the poverty line; the immediate threats to the health of young children, the sick and the most vulnerable members of the population, the widespread unrest and disorders; the real risk of insurrection and extreme political disturbances, the abrupt resignations of successive Presidents and the collapse of the Government, together with a partial breakdown of the political institutions and an extended vacuum of power; the resort to emergency legislation

as a situation where 'the maintenance of public order and the protection of essential security interest of Argentina as a state and as a country was vitally at stake'.[74]

In this context, economic crisis may pose a threat to national security, but arbitral awards seem to suggest that only a severe economic crisis can invoke essential security exception, although tribunals disagreed on the level of gravity of the economic crisis. Given that the concept of national security has expanded to cover not only political and military security but also the economic security,[75] it is possible that the state may invoke a security exception clause to justify their restrictive measures against foreign SOE investments for protecting political, military or economic security. Here the problem is it is uncertain whether the tribunal will accept the state's argument under a non-self-judging exception clause. For example, a state may argue that a foreign SOE investment distorts market competition that poses a threat to economic security, so it is necessary to take measures such as imposing taxes or restricting transactions to relevel the playing field. In this scenario, to invoke the security exception the tribunal may require the host state to prove that the economic security threat constitutes a total economic collapse of the state. In this regard, it may be hard for states to justify its restrictive measures under a non-self-judging exception clause because the market distortion or the anti-competitiveness by foreign SOEs does not normally imply to collapse the total economy of the host state. Thus, tribunals need to assess the facts on a case-by-case basis. Notably, the *Continental Casualty* tribunal considered that the protection of essential security interests 'does not require that total collapse of the country or that a catastrophic situation has already occurred before responsible national authorities may have recourse to its protection', and the invocation of the essential security exception clause 'does not require that the situation has already degenerated into one that calls for the suspension of constitutional guarantees and fundamental liberties'.[76] Such interpretations may expand the possibility of invoking the essential security exception against foreign SOE investments since the threat to national security by SOE investments is not required to have occurred already. In other words, any potential threats by SOE investments may invoke the security exception in arbitrations. Nevertheless, whether the future tribunal will adopt the same interpretation remains to be seen.

If the tribunal agrees with the respondent state's argument that SOE investment threatens essential security interests, in most cases it will then decide whether the state's action is a necessary response to the threat of essential security.[77] In arbitral practice, tribunals normally evaluate the necessity requirement against a 'proportionality test'.[78] In this sense, if a host state invokes a non-self-judging exception to justify its measures against foreign SOEs such as divestment, the tribunal may require the state to

granting extraordinary legislative powers to the executive branch ... '. See *Continental Casualty Company v Argentine Republic* (*Continental Casualty v Argentina*), ICSID Case No ARB/03/9, Award, 5 September 2008, para 180.

[74] *Continental Casualty Company v Argentine Republic* (*Continental Casualty v Argentina*), ICSID Case No ARB/03/9, Award, 5 September 2008, paras 180–1.

[75] *Continental Casualty Company v Argentine Republic* (*Continental Casualty v Argentina*), ICSID Case No ARB/03/9, Award, 5 September 2008, para 175.

[76] *Continental Casualty Company v Argentine Republic* (*Continental Casualty v Argentina*), ICSID Case No ARB/03/9, Award, 5 September 2008, para 175.

[77] As noted, most of security exception clauses have a nexus requirement and the typical language is 'necessary to'. For example, Article X (1) of the Bulgaria–US BIT (1992) provides that '[t]his Treaty shall not preclude the application by either Party of *measures necessary* for the maintenance of public order, the fulfilment of its obligations with respect to the maintenance or restoration of international peace or security, or the protection of its own essential security interests' (emphasis added).

[78] UNCTAD, *The Protection of National Security in IIAs* (n 30) 93.

prove that no less severe measures are available to protect its national security, except for divesting the foreign SOE investment. Also, the tribunal needs to assess whether the restrictive measure against foreign SOE investment is necessary to eliminate the threat to national security. In this regard, it is true that the regulatory discretion of the contracting parties will be restricted under a non-self-judging clause, but it is unclear whether it can enhance the legal clarity and predictability since arbitrators' interpretations are not always consistent. Nevertheless, some non-self-judging clauses do not include the requirement of necessity which merely provides that host states can take action for the protection of its essential security.[79] In this context, the contracting parties reserve some discretion on what measure is appropriate as long as it is directed towards the protection of national security.[80] Even though the tribunals do not expressly have the power to review the proportionality of the restrictive measure under such a treaty, it does not automatically preclude the review of the necessity by the tribunal under the customary international law.

B. Invoking the Necessity Defence under Customary International Law

As noted earlier, tribunals have referred to the necessity defence under the customary international law in assessing whether Argentina could invoke the security exception. However, most tribunals read the requirement set out in Article 25 of ILC Articles into Article XI of the BIT, thus conflating them into a single inseparable defence.[81] As stated by the *Sempra* tribunal, for example, 'the Treaty provision is inseparable from the customary law standard insofar as the definition of necessity and the conditions for its operation are concerned, given that it is under customary law that such elements have been defined'.[82] In the *CMS* and *Enron* cases, the tribunals assessed whether the Argentine crisis met the requirements of necessity defence of Article 25. The *CMS* tribunal was persuaded by the ILC's comment to the effect that the plea of necessity is 'excluded if there are other (otherwise lawful) means available, even if they may be more costly or less convenience' and concluded that the measures adopted by Argentina were

---

[79] For example, Article 12 (2) of the Hungary–India (2003) BIT provides that '... nothing in the Agreement precludes the host Contracting Party from taking action for the protection of its essential security interests or in circumstances of extreme emergency in accordance with its laws normally and reasonably applied on a non-discriminatory basis'. A similar approach is in Peru–Singapore BIT (2003), which provides that '[t]he provisions of this Agreement shall not in any way limit the right of either Contracting Party to apply prohibitions or restrictions of any kind or take any other action which is directed to the protection of its essential security interests, or to the protection of public health or the prevention of diseases and pests in animals or plants'. See UNCTAD, *The Protection of National Security in IIAs* (n 30) 94–95.

[80] ibid 94.

[81] ibid 47. Article 25 (1) of the ILC Articles provides:

    1. Necessity may not be invoked by the State as a ground for precluding the wrongfulness of an act not in conformity with an international obligation of that State unless the act: (a) is the only way for the State to safeguard an essential interest against a grave and imminent peril; (b) does not seriously impair an essential interest of the State or States towards which the obligation exists, or of the international community as a whole. 2. In any case, necessity may not be invoked by a State as a ground for precluding wrongfulness if: (a) the international obligation in question excludes the possibility of invoking necessity; or (b) the State has contributed to the situation of necessity.

[82] *Sempra Energy International v Argentine Republic* (*Sempra v Argentina*), ICSID Case No ARB/02/16, Award (28 September 2007), para 376.

not the 'only way' to safeguard its essential security interests.[83] Moreover, the tribunal observed that 'government policies and their shortcomings significantly contributed to the crisis and the emergency and while exogenous factors did fuel additional difficulties they do not exempt the Respondent from its responsibility in this matter'.[84]

However, the Annulment Committee of the *CMS* case considered that the tribunal made two errors and gave an erroneous interpretation to Article XI.[85] First, Article XI and Article 25 are substantively different:

[T]he first covers measures necessary for the maintenance of public order or the protection of each Party's own essential security interests, without qualifying such measures. The second subordinates the state of necessity to four conditions. It requires for instance that the action taken 'does not seriously impair an essential interest of the State or States towards which the obligation exists, or of the international community as a whole', a condition which is foreign to Article XI. In other terms, the requirements under Article XI are not the same as those under customary international law as codified by Article 25, as the Parties in fact recognized during the hearing before the Committee.[86]

On that point, the Committee criticized that the tribunal made a manifest error of law and did not enter into an analysis of the relationship between Article XI and Article 25, simply assuming that they are on the same footing.[87]

Secondly, the tribunal made another error of law because the excuse based on customary international law 'could only be subsidiary to the exclusion based on Article XI' and the tribunal should have 'applied Article XI as the *lex specialis* governing the matter and not Article 25'.[88] A similar interpretation approach in this regard was adopted in the *LG&E* case, where the tribunal considered that Article XI established the state of necessity as a ground for exclusion from wrongfulness of an act of the states.[89] In the *Continental* case, the tribunal addressed the differences between the two defences in Article XI and Article 25 and concluded that the 'invocation of Article XI under the BIT, as a specific provision limiting the general investment protection obligation (of a primary nature) bilaterally agreed by the contracting parties, is not necessarily subject to the same conditions of application as the plea of necessity under general international law'.[90]

---

[83] *CMS Gas Transmission Company v The Republic of Argentina* (*CMS v Argentina*), ICSID Case No ARB/01/8, Award, 12 May 2005, para 323.

[84] *CMS Gas Transmission Company v Republic of Argentina* (*CMS v Argentina*), ICSID Case No ARB/01/8, Award, 12 May 2005, para 329.

[85] The Committee considered that the Tribunal should have been more explicit in specifying that the very same reasons which disqualified Argentina from relying on the general law of necessity meant that the measure it took could not be considered 'necessary' for the purpose of Article XI, see *CMS Gas Transmission Company v The Republic of Argentina*, ICSID Case No ARB/01/8, Decision of the ad hoc Committee on the Application for Annulment of the Argentine Republic (25 September 2007), paras 124–5, 135.

[86] *CMS Gas Transmission Company v Republic of Argentina*, ICSID Case No ARB/01/8, Decision of the ad hoc Committee on the Application for Annulment of the Argentine Republic (25 September 2007), para 130.

[87] *CMS Gas Transmission Company v Republic of Argentina*, ICSID Case No ARB/01/8, Decision of the ad hoc Committee on the Application for Annulment of the Argentine Republic (25 September 2007), para 131.

[88] *CMS Gas Transmission Company v Republic of Argentina*, ICSID Case No ARB/01/8, Decision of the ad hoc Committee on the Application for Annulment of the Argentine Republic (25 September 2007), paras 132–3.

[89] *LG&E Energy Corp., LG&E Capital Corp., and LG&E International, Inc. v Argentine Republic* (*LG&E v Argentina*), ICSID Case No ARB/02/1, Decision on Liability, 3 October 2006, para 261.

[90] *Continental Casualty Company v Argentine Republic* (*Continental Casualty v Argentina*), ICSID Case No ARB/03/9, Award, 5 September 2008, paras 162–7.

However, the tribunal also pointed out there existed some connections between the two provisions. Thus, it would focus on the analysis of Article XI and conditions of its application, referring to 'the customary rule of the state of Necessity only insofar as the concept there used assist in the interpretation of Article XI itself'.[91]

Although it is not clear whether future tribunals will follow the interpretations by the *CMS* annulment committee and the *LG&E* and *Continental Casualty* tribunals, the arbitral practice has indicated that it is possible for the state to invoke the necessity defence under customary international law, regardless of whether an essential security exception clause is provided in the BIT. In this sense, even though a BIT does not include a security exception, the state may still take measures against foreign SOE investments by invoking the necessity defence. However, the ICJ case law has shown that to avoid the abuse, the invocation of necessity is restricted to strict conditions that may be hard to satisfy.[92] For example, it is doubtful whether the customary international law could provide an excuse for protecting strategic industries unless it occurred in the context of a severe crisis resulting in social upheavals or affecting the human rights of the population.[93] Also, it is uncertain to what extent the customary international law could justify the entry restrictions for foreign SOE investors even in the economic sectors that are directly linked to national security, since such restrictions could only be defended if there were no other means available to achieve the intended policy objective.[94] In general terms, host states' measures against foreign SOEs are easier to be challenged if the investment treaty does not provide a security exception clause. Also, it is notable that the invocation of essential security exception will exempt the state from obligations including compensation, while the state is still subject to compensation even if it has successfully invoked the necessity defence under customary international law.[95] Therefore, states that need to address national security concerns over SOE investments are strongly suggested to provide a self-judging security exception in their investment treaties.

IV. Conclusions: Implications for Chinese Investors and Policy-makers

In sum, the increasing national security concerns over SOE investments can be addressed at both national and international levels. At the national level, states can use

---

[91] *Continental Casualty Company v Argentine Republic* (*Continental Casualty v Argentina*), ICSID Case No ARB/03/9, Award, 5 September 2008, para 168.

[92] To be specific, the limitations of necessity defence include, firstly, the necessity under customary international law may only be invoked to safeguard 'an essential interest from a grave and imminent peril'; secondly, the conduct in question must not seriously impair an essential interest of the other state or states concerned, or of the international community as a whole; thirdly, necessity cannot be invoked to exclude wrongfulness of a non-conforming measure where the international obligation in question explicitly or implicitly excludes the plea of necessity; fourthly, necessity may not be used as an excuse if the responsible state has contributed to the situation of necessity, see Katia Yannaca-Small, 'Essential Security Interests under International Investment Law' in *International Investment Perspectives: Freedom of Investment in a Changing World* (OECD 2007) 100–1. See also José E Alvarez, 'Sovereign Concerns and the International Investment Regime' in Karl P Sauvant and others (eds), *Sovereign Investment: Concerns and Policy Reactions* (OUP 2012) 276; Sergey Ripinsky, 'Global Economic Crisis and the Danger of Protectionism: Does International Law Help?' (2009) 1 Amsterdam Law Forum 3, 11.

[93] UNCTAD, *The Protection of National Security in IIAs* (n 30) 36.   [94] ibid 37.

[95] Sergey Ripinsky, 'Global Economic Crisis and the Danger of Protectionism: Does International Law Help?' (2009) 1 Amsterdam Law Forum 3, 11.

the national security review mechanism to restrict and block foreign SOE investments on national security considerations. Considering the rapid growth of Chinese outward investments and their economic power, it is likely that Chinese investments, whether they are state-owned or privately-owned, will be more closely scrutinized. Notably, there are signs in recent years that both the US and the EU are taking a more aggressive stance, particularly toward deals involving China.[96] In this context, Chinese SOEs are more likely to be subject to a closer screening for national security reasons especially in critical or strategic industries.

At the international level, recent treaties tend to incorporate a self-judging security exception clause to safeguard host states' regulatory discretion. Thus, it is increasingly likely for host states to invoke such exceptions to justify their actions against SOE investments and even derogate from international investment obligations. Although the language varies in different treaties and the arbitral practice is not consistent, it is clear that a self-judging security exception clause would reserve more regulatory space for states in taking restrictive measures against SOEs.

It is important to address that the situation might be different in pre-establishment and post-establishment scenarios. If a host state restricts the admission of a foreign SOE for national security considerations, the SOE investor might not be able to challenge the state's action in international investment arbitrations under most investment treaties that merely provide protections for a post-establishment phase. Returning to the Hinkley point case, if the UK government had not approved the deal, the Chinese SOE investor could not bring a case in ICSID anyway because the UK–China BIT does not have a commitment to pre-establishment non-discriminatory treatment.[97] However, if the dispute was brought under a pre-establishment treaty, such as the US 2012 Model BIT, it might be possible for a SOE investor to challenge the CFIUS review decision in an investment tribunal, unless the contracting states have explicitly made reservation or exceptions. In such a case, one may argue that the security exception clause under the US BIT is 'broad enough' for CFIUS and the President to review investment transactions (because the review would be necessary for the protection of

---

[96] Jonathan Masters and James McBride (CFR), 'Foreign Investment and U.S. National Security' (28 August 2018) https://www.cfr.org/backgrounder/foreign-investment-and-us-national-security (last accessed 10 October 2018). In addition, President Trump, in a statement, said that 'upon enactment of FIRRMA legislation, I will direct my administration to implement it promptly and enforce it rigorously, with a view toward addressing the concerns regarding state-directed investment in critical technologies identified in the Section 301 investigation'. See Doug Palmer and Lorraine Woellert (POLITICO), 'White House softens plans to block Chinese investment' (27 June 2018) https://www. politico.com/story/2018/06/27/white-house-china-investment-restrictions-654337 (last accessed 10 October 2018). After US President Obama blocked a Chinese company's purchase of Aixtron on national security grounds, President Trump blocked the acquisition of Lattice Semiconductor Corp by a Chinese investor in 2017 and the acquisition of Qualcomm by Broadcom in 2018, which appeared to be related to China. See James K Jackson, 'The Committee on Foreign Investment in the United States (CFIUS)' Congressional Research Service (3 July 2018) https://fas.org/sgp/crs/natsec/RL33388.pdf (last accessed 10 October 2018); The Economist, 'CFIUS intervenes in Broadcom's attempt to buy Qualcomm' (8 March 2018) https://www.economist.com/business/2018/03/08/cfius-intervenes-in-broadcoms-attempt-to-buy-qualcomm (last accessed 10 October 2018). In September 2017, the European Commission proposed to establish a framework to screen foreign investments from third countries on grounds of security at the EU level, in order to address increasing concerns about strategic acquisitions of European companies with key technologies by foreign investors, especially SOEs. See European Commission, 'Communication from the Commission to the European Parliament, the European Council, the Council, the European Economic and Social Committee and the Committee of the Regions: Welcoming Foreign Direct Investment while Protecting Essential Interests', Brussels, 13.9.2017, COM(2017) 494 final.

[97] See UK–China BIT, Article 2, Article 3, and Article 5.

the US essential security interests).[98] However, no case to date has tested whether an adverse CFIUS review decision could be subject to an investment arbitration, leaving the issue unclear and unresolved.[99] It is notable that the China–Canada BIT explicitly provided that the national security review shall not be subject to the dispute settlement provisions of the agreement.[100] But most of the investment treaties do not include such a reservation and thus the impossibility of international arbitrations still exists.

In respect of Chinese SOE investments, whereas most debates relate to the national security review, the above discussions have shown that even after an SOE investment has been approved and established, the host government may still take restrictive measures against the SOE investment on national security considerations then invoke security exceptions under the applicable investment treaty to jusify its actions. Hence, it is of great practical significance for Chinese SOEs to understand the relevant investment treaty practice and its possible implications. In particular, under applicable Chinese investment treaties, can host states invoke national security exception clauses to justify their restrictive measures against Chinese SOE investments?

Although the earlier Chinese investment treaties sporadically allow contracting parties to apply prohibitions or restrictions in respect of essential security interests,[101] recent treaties tend to explicitly include a self-judging security exception clause to protect the essential security.[102] Moreover, many recent treaties include a WTO-like security exception clause which clarifies essential security interests with an exhaustive list. The China–Canada BIT, for example, provides that contracting parties can take any actions that 'it considers necessary for the protection of its essential security interests: (i) relating to the traffic in arms, ammunition and implements of war and to such traffic and transaction in other goods, materials, services, and technology undertaken directly or indirectly for the purpose of supplying a military or other security establishment, (ii) in time of war or other emergency in international relations, or (iii) relating to the implementation of national policies or international agreement respecting the non-proliferation of nuclear weapons or other nuclear explosive devices'. In this context, both the Chinese government and the other contracting party can take restrictive measures to protect their national security interests relating to certain circumstances. However, if a treaty does not include a security exception clause, such as the China–UK BIT, the state's action against foreign SOE investments are subject to investment commitments on non-discrimination treatment, fair and equitable treatment, and expropriation. Nevertheless, the limited arbitral practice also shows that although a self-judging security exception clause guarantees states' regulatory discretion to a large degree, the invocation of the exception may still be reviewed by the international tribunals, which could raise some uncertainties and might result in different interpretations even in the same situations.

Notably, China has committed to adopting pre-establishment national treatment obligations with a 'negative list' in the China–US BIT negotiation and is likely to adopt

[98] Daniel CK Chow, 'Why China Wants a Bilateral Investment Treaty with the United States' (2015) 33 Boston University International Law Journal 101, 120.

[99] Lauren Gloudeman and Nargiza Salidjanova, 'Policy Considerations for Negotiating a U.S.-China Bilateral Investment Treaty' (Economic and Security Review Commission Staff Research Report 2016) 25 https://www.uscc.gov/Research/policy-considerations-negotiating-us-china-bilateral-investment-treaty.

[100] Annex D 34 of the China–Canada BIT (2012).

[101] See eg Article 11 of China–Singapore BIT (1985).

[102] See eg Article 33 of China–Canada BIT (2012); Article 18 of China–Japan–Korea investment treaty (2012); Article 201 of China–New Zealand FTA (2008); Article 13 of China–Iceland FTA (2013); etc.

the same approach in the China–EU BIT.[103] In such a scenario, contracting states are not allowed to impose restrictions on the establishment of investment, in respect of market access, performance requirements, national treatment, senior management and boards of directors, unless such matters are explicitly excluded in the negative list or annexe.[104] In this context, the national security review by host government against foreign SOE investors and investments may constitute a violation of national treatment at a pre-establishment stage, if the treaty does not contain a reservation to the opposite effect. A good example is the CETA where Canada explicitly reserves its sovereignty of reviewing an acquisition under the Investment Canada Act.[105] Nevertheless, under most BITs that merely provides post-establishment protections, if a host state bars the transaction in the national security review or other foreign investment reviews, the Chinese SOE investor cannot challenge the decision in international investment tribunals, even if the decision is a manifest discrimination against China.

Nevertheless, national security is a 'double-edged sword'. On the one hand, it could be invoked by states to protect critical or strategic industries and to justify regulations against foreign investors without a violation of treaty obligations. On the other hand, the abuse of national security reasons may result in a discouraging and untrustworthy environment for foreign investments. In other words, the national security reviews and national security exceptions can be used by states to address national security concerns on SOE investments, but the abuse of restrictive measures against SOE investments on a national security ground may result in some negative impacts, including discouraging foreign SOEs to make more investments.[106] For example, after the delayed decision on the Hinkley nuclear project, the Chinese ambassador to Britain, Liu Xiaoming, stated that Hinkley Point is a test of mutual trust between the UK and China and the openness of the market is a condition for bilateral cooperation.[107] In this sense, blocking the investment by a specific Chinese SOE might discourage other Chinese SOEs and create an unwelcoming signal for all Chinese enterprises.

---

[103] In July 2013, China announced that it had agreed to engage in substantive negotiations with the US on an investment treaty based on the pre-establishment national treatment with a negative list approach. Later, in June 2015, the US and China had the initial swapping of 'negative lists' in Beijing. See Michael Martina, 'UPDATE1-China, U.S. swap investment treaty "negative lists"' (12 June 2015) https://www.reuters.com/article/china-usa-investment/update-1-china-u-s-swap-investment-treaty-negative-lists-idUSL3N0YY2R920150612 (last accessed 15 October 2017). See also Wenhua Shan and Lu Wang, 'The China-EU BIT and the Emerging "Global BIT 2.0"' (2015) 30 ICSID Review 260, 261. It is notable that the State Council of PRC in 2015 issued the Opinions on Implementing the Negative List System for Market Access as a significant part of the government's efforts to establish an open, competitive, and well-regulated modern market. See http://english.gov.cn/policies/latest_releases/2015/11/12/content_281475233639218.htm (last accessed 10 October 2018). In 2018, the NDRC and the MOFCOM jointly released the new national and free trade zone negative lists, which outlined prohibited and restricted industries for foreign investment. See Dorcas Wong (China Briefing), 'How to Read China's 2018 Negative List' (7 July 2018) http://www.china-briefing.com/news/how-to-read-chinas-2018-negative-list/ (last accessed 10 October 2018).
[104] For example, the CETA provides a separate section on the establishment of investments which provide detailed protections in respect of market access (Article 8.4) and performance requirements (Article 8.5). However, it also includes reservations and exceptions as well as annexes to exclude certain matters from the treaty obligations.
[105] See Annex I of the CETA, Reservation I-C-1, http://data.consilium.europa.eu/doc/document/ST-10973-2016-ADD-9/en/pdf#page=8 (last accessed 10 October 2018).
[106] UNCTAD, *World Investment Report 2016: Investor Nationality: Policy Challenges* (UNCTAD 2016) 17.
[107] Liu Xiaoming (FT), 'Hinkley Point is a test of mutual trust between UK and China' (9 August 2016) www.telegraph.co.uk/business/2016/07/29/theresa-may-delays-hinkley-nuclear-decision-amid-concerns-over-c/ (last accessed 15 August 2016).

Indeed, national security and security-related concerns in respect of foreign SOEs tend to reflect a mix of political and economic considerations. The real motive for taking measures on a national security basis against SOEs is often complicated and ambiguous. States have to face a dilemma that too open a market might result in a threat to national security, while too tight security regulations might discourage foreign investors. In the end, it is necessary for states to strike a proper balance between protecting foreign SOE investors and investments and addressing legitimate national security concerns in respect of SOE investments. The security exception clause should be invoked only as a last resort when other policies are not available to eliminate the national security concerns,[108] and the state should in principle provide an open and non-discriminatory environment to foreign investors and investments, regardless of their ownership structure.

---

[108] UNCTAD, *The Protection of National Security in IIAs* (n 30) 22.

5

Nationwide Regulatory Reform Starting from China's Free Trade Zones

The Case of the Negative List of Non-conforming Measures

Jie (Jeanne) Huang*

The year 2018 has witnessed the implementation of the first nationwide negative list of market access for both foreign and domestic investors in China.[1] This reform is important because it significantly departs from China's long-time practice of positive-list regulation, aims to bridge China's investment law with high-standard international agreements,[2] and will significantly reform China's market access regulation. This chapter explores China's historic evolution from positive-list to negative-list regulation of market access. It argues that, although the existing Chinese negative lists are laudable, they need further improvement in order to be adopted in future as China's high-standard free trade agreements (FTAs) or bilateral investment treaties (BITs). It also proposes suggestions for improvement.

I. Negative List versus Positive List

In international investment, having a 'positive list' means that a state only makes promises to open industrial sectors named in the list. Unlike the positive list, in a 'negative list' industries are principally open except for certain exceptions.[3] Foreign investors can automatically receive no less favourable treatment than domestic investors.[4] Non-confirming measures are the 'exceptions' to the negative list.[5] High-standard BITs

---

* Associate Professor, University of Sydney Law School, Australia. This contribution is made possible partly through the China National Social Science Fund (16BFX202). The author can be contacted at Jeanne.huang@sydney.edu.au. All comments are highly appreciated.

[1] See Report of the 19th National Congress of the Communist Party of China.

[2] Article 2.8 of the State Council's Advice on Implementing a Negative List for Market Access, Guofa [2015] No 55, a Chinese version is available at www.china.com.cn/legal/2015-10/19/content_36834934_2.htm (last accessed 23 January 2017).

[3] Patrick Low and Aaditya Mattoo, 'Is There a Better Way? Alternative Approaches to Liberalization under the GATS' 22 https://pdfs.semanticscholar.org/e8c8/68af3e3dc8d0427c9cfabc47478b6740 14b4.pdf (last accessed 1 January 2016, first published on 19 August 2008).

[4] Don Wallace, 'Book Review: NAFTA: The North American Free Trade Agreement: A New Frontier in International Trade and Investment in the Americas' (1995) 89 American Journal of International Law 668, 668. For a discussion of both negative list and positive list models in the context of investment treaties see Julien Chaisse and Christian Bellak, 'Navigating the Expanding Universe of International Treaties on Foreign Investment: Creation and Use of a Critical Index' (2015) 18(1) Journal of International Economic Law 79.

[5] Taylor, C O'Neal, 'Regional Trade Agreements: Current Issues and Controversies: The U.S. Approach to Regionalism: Recent Past and Future' (2009) 15 ILSA Journal of International & Comparative Law 424.

and FTAs generally have a negative list of non-confirming measures.[6] Typical examples are the US 2012 Model BIT and the Comprehensive and Progressive Agreement for Trans-Pacific Partnership (CPTPP).[7]

A negative list of non-conforming measures rarely appears in China's BITs. Only four BITs concluded by China mention non-conforming measures but none of them lists existing non-conforming measures.[8] Among all the FTAs concluded by China, the China–Australia FTA is the only one adopting a negative list of non-conforming measures to regulate investment and services. However, the negative list governs Australia only. China's commitment is still listed in a positive list.[9] The underlying reason for China's treaty practice can be traced back to China's domestic law where a negative list had never been legislated to regulate market access for foreign investment before 2013. For more than two decades, China has used the Foreign Investment Industry Guidance Catalogue (Catalogue for Foreign Investment) jointly published by the Ministry of Commerce and the National Development and Reform Commission, to regulate foreign investment.[10] Unlike the negative list, the Catalogue for Foreign Investment divides Chinese domestic industries into three categories: 'encouraged', 'restricted', and 'prohibited'. The 'encouraged' category covers industries in which foreign investment is eligible for such benefits as greater flexibility of foreign ownership, lower levels of governmental review, and tax and other investment incentives. The 'restricted' category covers industries in which foreign investment is subject to a higher level of government scrutiny and restrictions such as ceilings on foreign ownership and limitations on the choice of corporate forms (e.g. foreign investment is more likely to be limited to joint ventures instead of wholly foreign-owned enterprises). Industries listed under the 'prohibited' category are barred from foreign investment. In terms of the format, the Catalogue for Foreign Investment is only slightly unlike a typical negative list, as it has the 'encouraged' category. In substance, the Catalogue for Foreign Investment is fundamentally unlike a negative list, because industries not expressly listed in the Catalogue are not fully open to foreign investment. For example, the 2015 Catalogue for Foreign Investment clearly indicated that, apart from the Catalogue, foreign investment is also restricted or prohibited in industries according to other national laws and regulations.[11] Moreover, the 'encouraged' category also includes restrictions on and

---

[6] 'Measure' includes any law, regulation, procedure, requirement, or practice. See eg Article 1.4 of the US–Korea BIT.

[7] Trans-Pacific Partnership Ministerial Statement, http://dfat.gov.au/trade/agreements/tpp/news/Pages/trans-pacific-partnership-ministerial-statement.aspx (last accessed 10 December 2017). See also Julien Chaisse, 'The Shifting Tectonics of International Investment Law: Structure and Dynamics of Rules and Arbitration on Foreign Investment in the Asia-Pacific Region' (2015) 47 George Washington International Law Review 563, 615 and Julien Chaisse and Rahul Donde, 'The State of Investor-State Arbitration: A Reality Check of the Issues, Trends, and Directions in Asia-Pacific' (2018) 51(1) The International Lawyer 47.

[8] The four investment agreements are the China–Slovak BIT, the China–Swiss BIT, the China–Korea–Japan Investment Agreement, and the China–Canada BIT.

[9] Annex III: Investment and Services Schedules of Australia and China. Chapter 9 Investment of the China–Australia Free Trade Agreement http://dfat.gov.au/trade/agreements/chafta/official-documents/Pages/official-documents.aspx (last accessed 10 December 2017).

[10] China promulgated the Foreign Investment Industry Guidance Catalogue in 1995, and amended it in 1997, 2002, 2004, 2007, 2011, and 2015. In the 2015 Catalogue, there are 423 articles in total, including 349 articles for encouraged industries, 38 articles for restricted industries, and 36 articles regarding prohibited industries. The catalogue is a mandatory law. It amounts to a measure instead of a guideline.

[11] Article 14 of the restricted category and Article 12 of the prohibited category of the 2015 Catalogue for Foreign Investment.

prohibitions against foreign investment.[12] For example, the accounting and auditing service are in the 'encouraged' category but followed by a restriction: the principal partner must have Chinese nationality.[13]

For China, as a host state for foreign investment, the positive-list approach can help protect domestic industries. However, with economic development, China is not only a host state for foreign investment, but also the second capital exporting country in the world.[14] BITs and FTAs are reciprocal, so insisting on the 'positive list' means more restrictions on Chinese investors in foreign markets.

Because the Catalogue for Foreign Investment significantly differs from the negative-list approach, China needs a pilot to test whether its domestic governance can make a smooth shift from the former to the latter. This is one of the important reasons that the Standing Committee of the National People's Congress in China approved the Framework Plan of China (Shanghai) Pilot Free Trade Zone (Shanghai FTZ) in 2013.[15] Based on the successful experience of the Shanghai FTZ, in 2014, the Standing Committee of the National People's Congress decided to establish the China (Fujian) Free Trade Zone, the China (Guangdong) Free Trade Zone, and the China (Tianjin) Free Trade Zone.[16] In 2017, China established seven new FTZs and ultimately formed the '1+3+7' Geese Mode to prepare further opening up of its economy.[17] These FTZs shoulder the historic mission as testing grounds to restructure the trade and investment legal system.[18]

The negative list of special administrative measures for foreign investment market access was first published by the Shanghai FTZ in 2013 (2013 FTZ Negative List).[19]

---

[12] See the 'encouraged' category of the 1995, 2002, 2004, 2007, 2011, and 2015 Catalogue.

[13] Article 318 of the encouraged category of the 2015 Catalogue for Foreign Investment.

[14] See World Investment Report 2017, UNCTAD.

[15] http://www.china-shftz.gov.cn/NewsDetail.aspx?NID=6a441b33-45d8-45e1-956f-f1df348cc85c&CID=fb463223-5bcd-4907-ad64-2c7e294c767f&MenuType=3&navType=0 (last accessed 9 December 2017). Free trade zones (FTZs) are a type of special economic zones and can be broadly defined as 'demarcated geographic areas contained within a country's national boundaries where the rules of business are different from those that prevail in the national territory'. Farole, Thomas, 'Special Economic Zones in Africa: Comparing Performance and Learning from Global Experiences' *World Bank* (2011) (indicating these differential rules principally deal with investment conditions, international trade and customs, taxation, and the regulatory environment; whereby the zone is given a business environment that is intended to be more liberal from a policy perspective and more effective from an administrative perspective than that of the national territory).

[16] The Shanghai FTZ is 120.72 km², the Fujian FTZ is 118.04 km², the Guangdong FTZ is 116.2 km², and the Tianjin FTZ is 119.9 km². See Decision of the Twelfth Session of the Twelfth Meeting of the Standing Committee of the National People's Congress on 28 December 2014 http://news.china.com.cn/2014-12/29/content_34428633.htm (last accessed 1 December 2017).

[17] Update 1-China Approves 7 New Free Trade Zones in Bid to Open Economy https://www.reuters.com/article/china-trade-ftz/update-1-china-approves-7-new-free-trade-zones-in-bid-to-open-economy-idUSL3N1H83RM (last accessed 29 November 2017). The seven new FTZs are in Liaoning, Zhejiang, Henan, Hubei, Chongqing, Sichuan, and Shaanxi provinces.

[18] For China's FTZs see eg Jie Huang, 'Challenges and Solutions for the China-US BIT Negotiations: Insights from the Recent Development of FTZs in China' (2015) 18 Journal of International Economic Law 307; Shen, Wei, 'A Tale of Three Zones: Promises and Pitfalls of Three Financial Experimental Zones in China' (2014) 131 Banking Law Journal 399. Most of the scholarship is in Chinese, eg He, Li, 'On the Evolution of the Meaning of Trade and the Nature of China (Shanghai) Pilot FTZ' (2014) Haiguan Yu Jingmao Yanjiu [Study of Customs and Trade] 69; Yang, Feng, 'Reform and Improvement of Business Registration System in Shanghai FTZ' (2014) Fa Xue [Law] 104; Xiaoyong, He, 'Legal Safeguard for Financial Reforms in China (Shanghai) Pilot Free Trade Zone' (2013) 12 Fa Xue [Law] 114; Ding Wei, 'Exploration and Experiment of Legal Safeguard of China (Shanghai) Free Trade Zone' (2013) 11 Fa Xue [Law] 107.

[19] The full name of the negative list is Special Administrative Measures (Negative List) on Foreign Investment Access to the China (Shanghai) Pilot Free Trade Zone; see http://en.shftz.gov.cn/Government-affairs/Laws/General/213.shtml (last accessed 1 January 2017).

The 2013 FTZ Negative List was compiled in accordance with Classification and Codes of National Economic Industry (2011) and includes eighteen industries.[20] The list has 190 special measures, accounting for 17.8 per cent of all industries. Among these measures, thirty-eight ban foreign investment and seventy-four restrict foreign investment. The 2013 negative list deletes the 'encouraged' category of the Catalogue for Foreign Investment. However, in the substance of the 'restricted' and 'prohibited' categories, the Catalogue, and the 2013 negative list are relatively similar.[21]

Further investment liberalization took place for the Shanghai FTZ in 2014 through the amendment of the negative list.[22] The 2014 negative list for the Shanghai FTZ decreased the number of special measures from 190 to 139, 26.8 per cent less than the 2013 list. Among the fifty-one measures that have been eliminated, fourteen special measures are revoked and open to foreign investment.[23] Moreover, the 2014 list relaxes nineteen special measures.[24] For example, the requirement that the operating period for Chinese companies receiving foreign investments in aviation-supporting services must not exceed thirty years has been removed.[25] In addition, the 2014 list clarifies some measures in the 2013 list. For example, the 2013 list restricts foreign investment in direct selling, but without spelling out the details. The 2014 negative list specifies that foreign direct selling companies can invest in China only if they have more than three years of experience overseas and if their paid-up registered capital is no less than RMB 80 million.

With the establishment of the Tianjing FTZ, the Guangdong FTZ, and the Fujian FTZ, on 20 April 2015 China released the national Special Administrative Measures (Negative List) on Foreign Investment Access to China Free Trade Zones (2015 FTZ Negative List). As a uniform negative list for the four FTZs, it reduced seventeen non-conforming measures from the Shanghai 2014 negative list and also became more liberalized than the 2015 Catalogue for Foreign Investment.[26] The 2015 FTZ Negative

[20] '(S) Public management, social security and social organizations' and '(T) International organizations' are not subject to the negative list.
[21] Shang, Shu, 'Negative List for Foreign Investment's Access in China (Shanghai) Pilot Free Trade Zone' [2014] Fa Xue [Law] 31. The 2013 negative list also contains some entries that do not exist in the 'forbidden' category of the Catalogue. For example, foreign investors are not permitted to invest in auctions of antiques and the wholesale of salt.
[22] For a Chinese version see www.china-shftz.gov.cn/PublicInformation.aspx?GID=8f7d8298-3462-4c6f-8cc8-8c42a315143c&CID=953a259a-1544-4d72-be6a-264677089690&MenuType=1 (last accessed 10 December 2017).
[23] The other 37 eliminated measures are not meaningful, because 14 special measures are applied to both foreign and Chinese investments and thus do not have to be repeated on the list; and the remaining 23 were consolidated with similar items and are not essentially 'eliminated' from the list. For example, prohibitions on the pornography and gambling industries were removed from the 2014 list. But it does not mean they are open to foreign investors because conducting business in these industries is considered a crime for both foreigners and Chinese investors. Another example is the auction of cultural relics and the establishment of cultural relic shops. The 2013 list treats them as separate items. But the 2014 list combines them into one item.
[24] Zlto Matthew and others, 'Shanghai FTZ Revised Negative List Introduces Targeted FDI Reforms' www.china-briefing.com/news/2014/07/03/shanghai-ftz-revised-negative-list-introduces-targeted-fdi-reforms.html (last accessed 10 December 2017).
[25] For an English version of the major changes to the 2014 negative list see Hairong Yu, 'Shanghai FTZ Cuts "Negative List", but Critics Unimpressed' http://english.caixin.com/2014-07-02/100698595.html (last accessed 10 December 2017).
[26] 'Special Administrative Measures (Negative List) on Foreign Investment Access to China Free Trade Zones' www.china-shftz.gov.cn/PublicInformation.aspx?GID=f9bab6b4-34a6-414b-a080-383669ce93e0CID=953a259a-1544-4d72-be6a-264677089690MenuType=1 (last accessed 10 December 2017). It replaces the Shanghai 2014 negative list and applies to all China's FTZs from 8 May 2015. For comments see Jefferson Kiser, 'FTZ Update: State Council Releases 2015

List significantly differs from the Catalogue for Foreign investment, because all industries not listed are automatically open except for reasons such as protecting national security, public order and culture, financial prudence, government procurement and subsidy, and taxation.[27] This means that the Chinese government is making a landmark regulatory reform regarding the approach to regulate market access for foreign investment. Based upon the 2015 FTZ Negative List, the 2017 FTZ Negative List further reduces twenty-seven non-conforming measures, decreases restriction for foreign capital merger and acquisition, and increases transparency of foreign capital market access.[28]

Published on 28 July 2017, the most recent Catalogue for Foreign Investment also adopts a negative list of foreign capital market access (2017 Catalogue for Foreign Investment Negative List).[29] Four differences exist between the 2017 FTZ Negative List and the 2017 Catalogue for Foreign Investment Negative List. The first difference is their territorial scope of application. The 2017 FTZ Negative List only applies to the eleven FTZs, while the 2017 Catalogue for Foreign Investment Negative List applies to Chinese territory other than FTZs. Secondly, unlike the 2017 FTZ Negative List, the 2017 Catalogue for Foreign Investment Negative List divides special administrative measures to the 'restricted' and 'prohibited' categories. Thirdly, the 2017 FTZ Negative List generally imposes fewer restrictions than the 2017 Catalogue for Foreign Investment Negative List. For example, the 2017 FTZ Negative List provides that the performance brokers must be controlled by Chinese party except that the performance is conducted in the province/city where the FTZ is located. However, the 2017 Catalogue for Foreign Investment Negative List does not contain the exception. Another example is fishery activities in the waters of China. The 2017 Catalogue for Foreign Investment Negative List bans foreign capital from entering this industry while the 2017 FTZ Negative List allows foreign capital to enter this industry under the approval of the Chinese government. Fourthly, the 2017 FTZ Negative List explicitly provides that foreign investment has equal access as domestic Chinese investment in sectors not listed in the negative list. In contrast, the 2017 Catalogue for Foreign Investment Negative List contains no such provision. This gap may be filled by a negative list equally applicable to both domestic and foreign investments, which will be published in 2018. Notably, on 2 March 2016 the China National Development and Reform Commission and the Ministry of Commerce issued a trial negative list of market access (2016 Trial Negative List).[30] This list was piloted in Shanghai, Tianjin, Fujian Province, and Guangdong Province.[31] The 2016 Trial Negative List does not

---

FTZ Negative List' http://insight.amcham-shanghai.org/ftz-update-state-council-releases-2015-ftz-negative-list/ (last accessed 10 December 2017).

[27] See eg Article 3 of the 2015 FTZ Negative List.

[28] The 2017 FTZ Negative List; see http://www.china-shftz.gov.cn/PublicInformation.aspx?GID=0d64444b-b643-4927-a8be-b5cccae740c3&CID=953a259a-1544-4d72-be6a-264677089690&MenuType=1&navType=1 (last accessed 10 December 2017).

[29] 2017 Catalogue for Foreign Investment http://www.gov.cn/xinwen/2017-06/28/content_5206424.htm (last accessed 9 December 2017).

[30] The 2016 Trial Negative List was issued in accordance with the China State Council's Opinion on the Implementation of the Negative List Market-Entry System (Opinion) on 2 October 2015. A Chinese version is available at http://www.fdi.gov.cn/1800000121_23_72956_0_7.html (last accessed 17 May 2017). It was effective from 1 December 2015 to 31 December 2017.

[31] The 2016 Trial Negative List also applies to the four FTZs in the four provinces and municipalities, which meant that foreign investors in the FTZs were subject to both the 2016 Trial Negative List (up to 31 December 2017) and the FTZ Negative List.

apply to foreign investment only. It regulates market access measures applicable equally to both foreign and domestic investment. It does not create more market access to investors. Instead, it mainly consolidates non-conforming measures adopted by various laws, regulations, rules, and polices issued by the central government and applies these measures to both domestic and foreign investors on an equal footing.[32] It aims to facilitate Chinese central government to streamline regulation on investment and roll out a nationwide market access negative list in 2018.

In China, the special administrative measures that restrict or prohibit market access can be summarized as set out in the table below:

Table 5.1

Special Restriction or Prohibition Administrative Measures		
Provide national treatment for both domestic and foreign investment at market access	For foreign investment market access only	
	Applicable in China's territory except FTZs	Applicable only in FTZs
The 2016 Trial Negative List (it will be replaced by a formal list in 2018)	The 2017 Catalogue for Foreign Investment Negative List	The 2017 FTZ Negative List

As a conclusion, the Chinese regulatory framework for foreign investment is constituted by (1) the 2016 Trial Negative List providing pre-establishment national treatment for foreign investment and (2) the 2017 Catalogue for Foreign Investment Negative List as exceptions to the pre-establishment national treatment.

II. Insufficiencies of the Existing Chinese Negative List and Suggestions for Improvement

With the enactment of the 2017 Catalogue for Foreign Investment Negative List and the prospective 2018 Negative List for the market access of both foreign and domestic investment, China is moving towards adopting nationwide negative lists of special administrative measures. In FTAs or BITs, special administrative measures are also called non-conforming measures. A gap still exists between the existing Chinese negative lists

---

[32] The 2016 Trial Negative List includes 96 prohibited items in 17 sectors and 232 restricted items in 22 sectors. These items are from: (1) investment projects requiring administrative approvals as set out in the *Consolidated List of Administrative Approval Items by Departments under the State Council* (included in the list as restricted items); (2) project categories designated for elimination or closed for new investment under the *Catalogue for Guiding Industry Restructuring (2011 version)*, which make up 46 of the 96 prohibited items; (3) projects requiring approvals from the relevant development and reform departments under the *Catalogue of Investment Projects Subject to Government Verification and Approval (2014 version)* (included in the list as restricted items); and (4) projects restricted or prohibited under other national laws, administrative regulations, and State Council decisions. 12 of the 328 total items are (or include sub-items that are) entirely new and were not restricted or prohibited under previous laws and regulations. These new items include an approval requirement for collaborations between domestic media and foreign news agencies, and a content censorship requirement for gaming and entertainment equipment. See Ashwin Kaja, Timothy P Stratford, and Yan Luo, 'China Moves Forward with Negative List for Domestic and Foreign Market Access' https://www.globalpolicywatch.com/2016/04/china-moves-forward-with-negative-list-for-domestic-and-foreign-market-access/ (last accessed 17 May 2016).

and the negative lists of non-conforming measures in high-standard FTAs, especially those concluded by the US. Although the negative-list approach is new for China, it has been adopted by the US widely in its BITs and FTAs since the 1980s. In January 1983, the US designed the first template of a treaty between the government of the US and the government of [the country] concerning the encouragement and reciprocal protection of investment (Model BIT). Since then, the 1983 Model BIT has been revised three times, in 1994, 2004, and 2012, respectively.[33] All these Model BITs contain a negative list. This chapter compares the existing Chinese negative lists with that in the 2012 US Model BIT, the US–Korea FTA,[34] and the Australian negative lists in the China–Australian FTA. It argues that China may consider the following improvements when formulating its negative list of special administrative measures for future FTAs or BITs.

A. Format

The US–Korea FTA has three annexes for non-conforming special administrative measures. Annex I and Annex II contain non-conforming measures for services and investment. Annex III covers non-conforming measures in financial services. The difference between them is that Annex I specifies the parties' existing non-conforming measures that can be continued or amended and that the amendment should not decrease the conformity of the measure as it existed immediately before the amendment.[35] However, Annex II also states that with regard to the parties' existing non-conforming measures, the parties may maintain or adopt new or more restrictive non-conforming measures than the existing ones in the named industrial sectors.[36] Annex III is constituted by these two groups of non-conforming measures in financial services.[37]

Similarly, the Australian negative list in the China–Australia FTA contains two sections. Section A sets out Australia's existing non-conforming special administrative measures and Section B specifies the specific sectors, sub-sectors, or activities for which Australia may maintain existing, or adopt new or more restrictive, non-conforming measures.

Unlike the US–Korea FTA and the China–Australia FTA, none of the existing negative lists distinguish which special measure may be continued or amended in the future and become less or more restrictive for foreign investment, or vice versa. For two reasons, the current format of China's existing negative lists is inappropriate for FTAs or BITs that China may conclude in the future. First, it may send a misleading message to foreign investors: the negative list only contains non-conforming measures that

---

[33] The revision of Model BITs will not change the BITs that have already been ratified, but can lay a foundation for BIT negotiation in the future.

[34] The US–Korea FTA came into force on 15 March 2012. For the official text of the FTA see www. ustr.gov/trade-agreements/free-trade-agreements/korus-fta/final-text (last accessed 1 January 2016). See also New Opportunities for US Exporters Under the US–Korea Trade Agreement www.ustr.gov/ trade-agreements/free-trade-agreements/korus-fta (last accessed 1 January 2016).

[35] See eg Article 11.12.1(a) of the US–Korea FTA.

[36] Article 1 of Annex II Explanatory Notes.

[37] See eg Article 1.b and c of Annex III Schedule of Korea with respect to Financial Services, Introductory Note for the Schedule of Korea. Both Korea's and the US's schedules in Annex III are constituted by Section A and Section B. Section A stipulates the existing non-conforming measures that can be continued or amended and the amendment should not decrease the conformity of the measure as it existed immediately before the amendment. Section B provides the existing non-conforming measures that a party may maintain or adopt new or more restrictive measures do not conform to the obligations under the treaty.

may be removed sooner or later, and if the non-conforming measures are continued or amended and the amendment would not decrease the conformity of the measure as it existed immediately before the amendment. Consequently, this misleading message may create an improper expectation to the public that the list will only become shorter and all non-conforming measures may be eased in the long run. Secondly, there may be a certain new industry that does not exist currently but may develop in the future. Under the current format, all industries that are not named in the list are presumed to be open to foreign investment. Therefore, new industries will be automatically open to foreign investment. This is inappropriate.

The future negative list in China should also contain two sections: one section to contain the non-conforming measures that can be continued or amended and the amendment should not decrease the conformity of the measures as they existed immediately before the amendment; and the other section to specify the non-conforming measures, which the government may maintain, or adopt new or more restrictive ones than the existing ones in the named industries.

B. Substance

In terms of substance, China's existing negative lists should be improved from the following four aspects.

The first aspect is to identify the laws or regulations for each existing non-conforming measure. A critical difference between China's existing negative lists and those of the US–Korea FTA and the China–Australia FTA is that the latter two FTAs identify the laws or regulations for which each existing non-conforming measure is made but the former does not. In future FTA or BIT negotiations, the proposed negative list from the Chinese side should identify the laws or regulations for which each existing non-conforming measure is made. The benefits of this approach are demonstrated by the NAFTA case—the US *Trucking Services* case.[38] Mexico contends that the US violated the national treatment provision by taking measures that refused to allow Mexican firms to provide cross-border trucking services into the border states, because the United States had committed to phase out reservation of cross-border trucking services under Annex I of the NAFTA.[39] In fact, there were very few applications made by Mexican trucking firms approved by the US from 1995 to 2001. The US argued that Mexican trucking firms were not in like circumstances with US trucking firms in highway safety areas, considering the inadequacies of the Mexican regulation system.[40] However, the arbitral tribunal noted that the phase-out commitment was unconditional and the inadequacies of the Mexican regulation system did not provide a reason to make an exception to the phrase 'like circumstances', even though the parties were allowed to refuse applications from foreign investors if they failed to satisfy the market access requirements in a certain section ruled by the parties, and finally determined that the US refusal to approve Mexican investors' applications was and remained a breach of the national treatment provision.[41] As this case shows, identifying the laws or regulations for which each existing non-conforming measure is made can bring at

---

[38] Final Report, *In the Matter of Cross-Border Trucking Services*, No USA-Mex-98-2008-01.
[39] ibid paras 102–52.   [40] ibid paras 153–63.
[41] ibid para 295. For investors to be 'in like circumstances', three conditions must be met: the investor must be a foreign investor; the investor must be in the same economic or business sector; and the two investors must be treated differently. See Julien Chaisse, 'The Shifting Tectonics of International Investment Law: Structure and Dynamics of Rules and Arbitration on Foreign Investment in the Asia-Pacific Region' (2015) 47(3) George Washington International Law Review 563.

least two benefits. It provides clear guidance for foreign investors, because they can find detailed information about the non-conforming measures in the named laws and regulations. It also provides a clear framework for the host state so as to help avoid the government implementing non-conforming measures beyond the limit of the named laws and regulations.

The second aspect is to specify non-conforming measures at the central and regional/provincial level of governments. When China entered the WTO, it promised the uniform administration of the trade regime.[42] Regulations, rules, and other measures of both central, provincial, and local governments must conform to the obligations undertaken in the WTO Agreement and the China WTO Accession Protocol.[43] Therefore, some scholars argued that in the China–US BIT negotiation, the non-conforming measures proposed by China should also apply to measures adopted by local governments.[44] China's existing negative lists presumably cover measures adopted at central, provincial, and local level. However, the negative lists of the US–Korea FTA and the TPP contain non-conforming measures at the central and regional levels of governments.[45] Measures adopted by a local level of government are excluded from obligations of national treatment, most-favoured-nation treatment and the performance requirement.

Should China propose a negative list containing measures adopted by local governments for the China–US BIT negotiations? It is already a serious challenge for China to calculate how many existing central and regional non-conforming measures for foreign investment exist. It would be difficult, if not impossible, for China to list such measures clearly at the local level. BITs concern far more behind-the-border measures than the WTO. Compared with trade law, investment law is more difficult to implement uniformly throughout the country. Considering it is a standard practice in investment treaties to exempt non-conforming measures adopted by the local governments, arguably China should follow this.

The 'measures adopted or maintained by a Party' in the US–Korea FTA not only include measures of governments but also 'non-governmental bodies in the exercise of powers delegated by central, regional, or local governments or authorities'.[46] Delineating the administrative powers exercised by government-authorized non-governmental bodies is a serious challenge for China. China should calculate first how many non-governmental bodies are authorized by governments to regulate foreign investment at central, regional, or local levels; then, secondly, what non-conforming measures are implemented by these non-governmental bodies; and, finally, what measures should be included in the negative list for future FTA or BIT negotiations.

The third aspect is to clarify restrictions on foreign investment. Many entries in the Catalogue for Foreign Investment do not clearly indicate what the restrictions are on foreign investment. For example, Article 15 of the prohibited category of the 2017 Catalogue for Foreign Investment indicates that foreign investment in legal consultation concerning Chinese law is prohibited except that the consultation is about the impacts of the Chinese legal environment. The meaning of the impacts of the Chinese

---

[42] Article 2 of the China WTO Accession Protocol, WT/L/432, 23 November 2001.

[43] Article 2.A.3 of the China WTO Accession Protocol, WT/L/432, 23 November 2001. The Protocol does not differentiate regional and local levels. It uses a 'sub-national level' to include local and regional levels collectively.

[44] See eg Gong, Baihua, 'Legal Analysis on the "Negative Listings" of the National Treatment for FDI into China (Shanghai) Pilot Free Trade Zone' (2013) 6 World Trade Organization Focus 6, 27.

[45] Article 11.12 of the US–Korea BIT and Article 9.12 of the TPP.

[46] Article 11.1.3 of the US–Korea BIT.

legal environment is unclear. The 2017 FTZ Negative List provides that foreign law firms can provide legal services only by setting up representative offices, cannot provide legal services involving Chinese law, and cannot hire Chinese lawyers.[47] Compared with the 2017 Catalogue for Foreign Investment Negative List, the provisions of the 2017 FTZ Negative List better indicates what the restrictions are. If the contents of a non-conforming measure are unclear, the contour of the negative list is also ambiguous. The goal of investment liberalization may be hard to achieve. The proposed negative list by the Chinese side in the future FTA or BIT negotiations should clearly indicate each restriction to foreign investment.

C. Public participation in the making of a negative list

The Shanghai 2013 and 2014 FTZ Negative Lists were made by the Shanghai municipal government and the China 2015 and 2017 FTZ Negative List was issued by the State Council. The Regulation for Shanghai FTZ requires that the government should seek the general public, relevant industry associations, and enterprises' opinions on administrative issues.[48] Moreover, it also requires the government to respond to public opinions in the legislative process. Article 52 of the Regulation for Shanghai FTZ states that the Shanghai Municipal Government should disclose drafts of proposed policies, administrative provisions, procedures, and rules affecting the FTZ to the public, and should respond to public comments when publishing the final version. Articles 37 and 67 of the Chinese Legislation Law also requires legislators to seek public comments.[49] However, the drafting process of the negative list is not open to the public. Considering that the negative list of non-conforming measures is critical for investors' market access, Chinese government should increase public participation in the drafting process.

In contrast, both Singapore and US laws require public participation in administration and legislation of affairs concerning free trade zones. For example, the Singapore Free Trade Zones Act requires 'the [zone] authority shall present to the Minister annually and at such other times as the Minister may prescribe reports containing a full and correct statement of all operations, receipts and expenditure and such other information as the Minister may require'.[50] The Minister may give the annual report and other accounts of the zone authority to Parliament.[51] The US Foreign Trade Zones Board Regulations take a step further. It provides detailed rules for public participation in administration and legislation, and public access to official records. For example, § 400.52 of the US Foreign Trade Zones Board Regulations indicates that:

the Executive Secretary shall publish notice in the Federal Register inviting public comment on applications and notifications for Board Action ... An applicant ... shall give appropriate notice of its proposal in a local, general-circulation newspaper at least 15 days prior to the close of the public comment period for the proposal in question.[52]

---

[47] Articles 79, 80, and 81 of the 2015 FTZ Negative List.

[48] Article 52 of the Regulation for Shanghai FTZ. The Regulation for Shanghai FTZ, enacted by the Fourteenth Meeting of the Fourteenth Session of Shanghai People's Congress Standing Committee, effective since Aug 1, 2014. A Chinese version is www.shftz.gov.cn/WebViewPublic/item_page.aspx?newsid=635423280542723054&coltype=8 (last accessed 1 January 2016). The English translation of the Regulation for Shanghai FTZ in this contribution is made by the author.

[49] The Chinese Legislation Law, enacted by the 3rd Meeting of the 9th Session of National People's Congress on 15 March 2015 and amended by the 3rd Meeting of the 12th Session of National People's Congress on 15 March 2015.

[50] Article 14.1 of the Singapore Free Trade Zones Act.   [51] ibid Article 14.3.

[52] Article a of § 400.52 of the US Foreign Trade Zones Board Regulations, 15 CFR Pt 400.

Moreover, a party who may be materially affected by the zone activity in question and who shows good cause may request a hearing during a proceeding or review.[53] The Regulations also provide clear procedures for requesting a public hearing.[54] Furthermore, the foreign trade zone board must consider all information submitted in a proceeding to be public information, except as otherwise provided by law.[55] All official records of each proceeding within the foreign trade zone board's jurisdiction should be open to public access according to the Freedom of Information Act.[56] Public participation in administration and legislation is also consistent with the transparency requirement under the US 2012 Model BIT. Its Article 11 states that 'each party shall publish in advance administrative ruling of general application[57] that it proposes to adopt and provide interested persons and the other [p]arty a reasonable opportunity to comment on such proposed measures'.[58]

Compared with the US and Singapore laws, from two aspects, the Chinese government may take measures to increase public participation when drafting the negative list of non-conforming special administrative measures.

First, the current Chinese law (e.g. the Legislation Law and the Regulation for Shanghai FTZ) does not specify how a government should respond to public comments and what comment should be responded to. The draft of the Regulation for Shanghai FTZ was published for public comments from 23 April 23 to 8 May 2014 at the FTZ official website, but the Shanghai People's Congress and the municipal government neither addressed issues raised by public comments nor explained revisions in the final version. A good reference may be drawn from Article 11.3 of the US 2012 Model BIT, which indicates that when adopting final regulations, the central government should 'address significant, substantive comments received during the comment period and explain substantive revisions that it made to the proposed regulations in its official journal or in a prominent location on a government Internet site'.[59] Arguably, the Chinese government does not need to address all public comments, but it needs to respond to significant, substantive comments received during the comment period when finalizing a negative list of non-conforming measures.

Secondly, current Chinese law does not contain the procedure to seek public comments. For example, how much time in advance that a draft of negative list should be published for public comments, where the draft should be published, and whether the public can request an open hearing to address issues concerned. All these questions are unanswered.[60] In practice, the period for public comments on an act may range from fourteen days to thirty days. Notably, the US 2012 Model BIT suggests that in most cases the proposed regulations should be published not less than sixty days before the date public comments are due.[61] The Chinese government should specify the procedure to seek public comments of the proposed measures. In the case of enacting a negative list, the government may consider establishing a public participation system with a clear timetable in which natural persons, enterprises, representatives of relevant organizations, etc may take part.

---

[53] ibid Article b(1).   [54] ibid Article b(2), (3), and c.
[55] ibid § 400.53 and Article b, c of § 400.54.
[56] ibid Article d of § 400.54. See also Freedom of Information Act, 15 CFR part 4.
[57] For definition of 'administrative ruling of general application' see Article 10.2 of the US 2012 Model BIT.
[58] ibid Article 11.2.   [59] ibid Article 11.3.d.
[60] Article 52 of the Regulation for Shanghai FTZ.   [61] ibid Article 11.3.b.

D. Resolving disputes concerning a negative list

Currently, in China, it is unclear how to resolve disputes concerning a negative list. For example, whether a foreign investor can bring an action against the Chinese government if it alleges that the government has violated its obligations under the list.

Enhancing the current administrative dispute resolution mechanism is of significant importance for implementing a negative list in China. However, Chinese law fails fully to address administrative reviews and litigation concerning the existing negative lists. For example, although a negative list has been implemented in the Shanghai FTZ since 2013, the Shanghai FTZ law does not clarify how to resolve disputes about a negative list. Article 55 of the Regulation for Shanghai FTZ provides that if an investor disagrees with a concrete administrative behaviour[62] conducted by the FTZ board, the investor can request the Shanghai Municipal Government to conduct a review. However, it is unclear whether all concrete administrative behaviours conducted by the FTZ board are subject to administrative review. It is also unclear whether the administrative review is final or whether the investor can sue the FTZ board in court if it disagrees with the review result. A thorny case would be if the FTZ board determines that a proposed foreign investment falls in the negative list and so outlaws this investment, but the investor disagrees with the board's decision. Can the investor request the Shanghai Municipal Government to review the board's decision? The FTZ board's determination should be a concrete administrative behaviour, and the investor request for review should be allowed. A further question would be if the foreign investor is dissatisfied with the review result, whether it can litigate the case in court. The Regulation for Shanghai FTZ fails to provide an answer.

In contrast to Chinese law, the US Foreign Trade Zones Act and the Singapore Free Trade Zones Act specify the cases in which an investor should seek an administrative review and in which cases a court decision should be final.[63] Arguably, Chinese law should clarify which cases can be subject to administrative reviews and which can be submitted to court for a final decision.

In practice, if this hypothesized case were to occur in the real world, the government's review is final, and the foreign investor is not allowed to request judicial review. However, FTAs and BITs generally allow foreign investors to seek judicial review or bring an investment arbitration against the host government if the government acts against its obligation under the negative list. Therefore, the Chinese government needs seriously to consider how to resolve disputes concerning the negative list.

III. Conclusion and Looking Forward

The shift from the positive-list to the negative-list approach symbolizes that the Chinese government is conducting a fundamental regulatory reform regarding market access for foreign investment. Although its format, substance, drafting process, and the related dispute resolution system need further improvement, the existing negative lists are important steps towards improving Chinese foreign investment law according

[62] 'Concrete administrative behaviour' refers to when the government exercises administrative powers in administrative activities for specific citizens, legal persons, or other organizations on specific issues. See Article 2 of the Chinese Administrative Procedure Law.
[63] See eg Article 13 of the Singapore Free Trade Zones Act and § 81r of the US Foreign Trade Zones Act.

to high-standard FTAs and BITs. In 2018, China has ultimately adopted a national legal framework to regulate foreign investment by providing pre-establishment national treatment with the exceptions in a negative list. However, the practical functioning of this framework still needs to be tested. Therefore, future research needs to keep a close eye on the reform and development of a comprehensive negative list in China.

6

Addressing Sustainable Development Concerns through IIAs

A Preliminary Assessment of Chinese IIAs

*Manjiao Chi**

I. Introduction

The international community faces grave sustainable development challenges today. International investment law, mainly composed of international investment agreements (IIAs), including bilateral investment treaties (BITs), free trade agreements (FTAs) with investment chapters and a few multi-lateral treaties, national investment laws, and certain soft law rules, is often criticized for being ineffective and insufficient in addressing sustainable development challenges associated with transnational investment activities.[1] This is mainly because IIAs are traditionally and primarily designed to protect and promote foreign investment, while non-investment objectives, such as sustainable development promotion have not been sufficiently addressed in IIAs. As transnational investment activities are getting increasingly active, it is generally viewed that, although IIAs should not be deemed as the primary legal discourse for addressing sustainable development challenges, they could be employed as a helpful tool in promoting sustainable investment.

As suggested by a survey conducted by the OECD, nearly all OECD and non-OECD governments can be assumed to be committed to sustainable development objectives, but most do not use IIAs as a mechanism for achieving these objectives.[2] For this reason, it has been suggested that the current legal framework for foreign investment should be improved to ensure that it can actively promote sustainable development.[3] The inspiration for sustainable development-compatible (inclusive) IIAs is echoed by many governments, international organizations, and non-governmental organizations (NGOs) in recent years.[4] The key to negotiating sustainable development-compatible

---

* The author is Professor & Founding Director, Center of International Economic Law and Policy (CIELP), Law School, University of International Business and Economics, Beijing.

[1] See eg Julien Chaisse and Rahul Donde, 'The State of Investor-State Arbitration: A Reality Check of the Issues, Trends, and Directions in Asia-Pacific' (2018) 51(1) The International Lawyer 47.

[2] OECD, 'International Investment Law: Understanding Concepts and Taking Innovations' (2008) 138 www.oecd.org/daf/inv/investment-policy/40471550.pdf (last accessed 20 October 2015).

[3] M-C Segger and others (eds), *Sustainable Development in World Investment Law* (Kluwer Law International 2011) 10.

[4] See eg United Nations Conference on Trade and Development (UNCTAD), 'Investment Policy Framework for Sustainable Development' http://investmentpolicyhub.unctad.org/ipfsd; Organization for Economic Cooperation and Development (OECD), 'Investment Treaty Law, Sustainable Development and Responsible Business Conduct: A Fact Finding Survey' www.oecd.org/investment/investment-policy/WP-2014_01.pdf; International Institute for Sustainable Development (IISD), 'Model International Agreement on Investment for Sustainable Development' www.iisd.org/investment/capacity/model.aspx (last accessed 20 October 2015).

IIAs lies in whether IIAs contain necessary provisions to promote sustainable investment ('sustainable development provisions') and to what extent these sustainable development provisions could be effective and sufficient in helping states achieve sustainable development goals without necessarily lowering the level of protection of foreign investment.

To China, making sustainable development-compatible IIAs is particularly necessary and timely for a number of reasons. First and foremost, it is almost known to all that China faces unprecedented sustainable development challenges today. In the meantime, Chinese overseas investment has also been often reported to have raised profound sustainable development concerns, especially in African countries.[5] It is thus of paramount importance for China to ensure that foreign investments in China and Chinese overseas investments would contribute to the pursuit of sustainable development objectives in a positive way. Secondly, China has concluded a large amount of IIAs over the past decades,[6] and is still engaged in intense and active IIA-making at bilateral and regional levels, especially the negotiation of a BIT with the US and the European Union (EU). It thus becomes practically feasible for China and its partner states to make IIAs a helpful policy tool in addressing the mounting sustainable development concerns pertaining to transnational investment activities.

It can be reasonably expected that China will try to make sustainable development-compatible IIAs at bilateral, regional, and global/multi-lateral levels in the future. While most of China's existing IIAs are BITs, China has accelerated its negotiation and update of some regional FTAs, such as the Regional Comprehensive Economic Partnership (RCEP), a regional FTA joined mainly by the Asia-Pacific states. China's recent Belt and Road Initiative (BRI) also clearly shows that China seeks to play a more important and central role in regional economic governance among the vast number of BRI countries, among China's other objectives.[7] In addition, even at global and multi-lateral levels, China has also demonstrated its intention to make more sustainable development-compatible IIAs in the future. During the G20 meeting under China's auspices in 2016, the trade ministers of the world's largest economies agreed on a set of non-binding Guiding Principles for Global Investment and Policymaking, with the purpose to 'promote investment for inclusive economic growth and sustainable development'.[8]

It appears clear that China is determined to make its trade and investment treaties more sustainable development-compatible in the future, at bilateral, regional, and global levels. Against such background, this chapter aims at presenting an exclusive study on how (successfully or unsuccessfully) Chinese IIAs address sustainable

---

[5] See eg D Shinn, 'The Environmental Impact of Chinese Investment in Africa' https://intpolicydigest.org/2015/04/08/the-environmental-impact-of-china-s-investment-in-africa/ (last accessed 29 November 2017).

[6] For practical reasons, this chapter investigates 116 IIAs, including 104 BITs that are currently in force, the TIT and 11 FTAs, excluding the Closer Economic Partnership Arrangement between Mainland China and the Hong Kong Special Administrative Region, the Closer Economic Partnership Arrangement between Mainland China and the Macao Special Administrative Region and the Cross-Strait Economic Cooperation Framework Agreement between Mainland China and Taiwan as they should not be deemed as typical international treaties. All the remaining 11 FTAs include investment chapters.

[7] See Tu Yongqian, 'Enhancing the Belt and Road Initiative: Innovating New Ways for Global Governance' http://cpc.people.com.cn/xuexi/n1/2017/0510/c385474-29266613.html (last accessed 29 November 2017). See also Julien Chaisse and Mitsuo Matsushita, 'China's "Belt and Road" Initiative: Mapping the World Trade Normative and Strategic Implications' (2018) 52(1) Journal of World Trade 163.

[8] See G20 Guiding Principles for Global Investment and Policy-making http://investmentpolicyhub.unctad.org/News/Hub/Home/508 (last accessed 29 November 2017).

development concerns, mainly from a normative perspective. In addition to the Introduction, this chapter first briefly reviews the evolution of the principle of sustainable
development to set the scene for the study. The chapter then identifies three major
types of sustainable development provisions of Chinese IIAs, namely environment provisions, labour rights provisions, and transparency provisions, and then examines how
these different types of provisions can effectively and sufficiently address sustainable
development concerns. Based on the empirical study of the major sustainable development provisions in Chinese IIAs, this chapter puts forwards several proposals to enhance the sustainable development-compatibility of Chinese IIAs. Finally, this chapter
concludes that China faces an urgent need to conclude sustainable development-
compatible IIAs, despite the progress it has made in recent years.

II. A Skeleton Review of the Principle of Sustainable Development

The international community began to recognize the close relationship between development and environment over a century ago, but it is generally agreed that sustainable development was firstly incorporated into the global development agenda in
the Brundtland Report (1987).[9] This landmark report contains a commonly accepted
definition for sustainable development, providing that sustainable development refers
to 'development that meets the needs of the present without compromising the ability
of future generations to meet their own needs'.[10] Essentially, this definition reveals that
sustainable development requires a proper balance to be drawn between environmental
protection and economic and social development.

Normatively, the principle of sustainable development has been promoted and developed mainly through a number of documents, including various international organization resolutions, declarations, conventions, and judicial decisions.[11] Typically,
such documents include, to list a few, the Rio Declaration on Environment and
Development, the UN Convention on Biological Diversity, the UN Framework
Convention on Climate Change (1992), and the Johannesburg Declaration on
Sustainable Development (2002).[12]

Despite the global recognition of the principle of sustainable development, the legal
nature of this principle in international law remains unsettled.[13] Some commentators
have asserted that the principle of sustainable development has acquired customary
international law status, especially from a case law perspective.[14] Other commentators
have opined that, unlike many other customary law rules, the principle of sustainable

---

[9] N Schrijver, 'The Evolution of Sustainable Development in International Law: Inception,
Meaning and Status' (2007) 329 Recueil des cours 238.
[10] World Commission on Environment and Development, *Our Common Future* para 1 www.un-
documents.net/ocf-02.htm#I (last accessed 10 October 2015).
[11] V Barral, 'Sustainable Development in International Law: Nature and Operation of an Evolutive
Legal Norm' (2012) 23 European J Int'l L 377.
[12] Available at UN Documents www.un-documents.net/k-001303.htm (last accessed 10 October
2015).
[13] See eg D Tladi, *Sustainable Development in International Law: An Analysis of Key Enviro-economic
Instruments* (PULP 2007) 95.
[14] See eg Barral (n 11) 386; P Sands, 'International Courts and the Application of the Concept
of Sustainable Development' (1999) 3 Max Planck UNYB 389; Schrijver (n 9) 317; E Kentin,
'Sustainable Development in International Investment Dispute Settlement: The ICSID and NAFTA
Experience' in N Schrijver and F Weiss (eds), *International Law and Sustainable Development: Principles
and Practice* (Brill 2004) 309.

development is not created by the traditional combination of state practice and *opinio juris* or some variation thereon, but as a result of a few decades of UN-led promotional activities, which fails to enable it as a status of customary law rule.[15] In addition, it has also been suggested that, although sustainable development has widely penetrated treaty law, the softness of such treaty provisions appears incapable of giving rise to valid rules of international law.[16]

There is no need for this chapter to examine the legal status of the principle of sustainable development in detail. Suffice it to say that the principle of sustainable development is evolutive and multi-faceted in nature. Although sustainable development has been originally developed in the environmental discourse, it is no longer intended only to 'serve the needs of the environment'.[17] Over time, sustainable development has evolved from the original meaning of sustainable use of natural resources to a concept with more anthropocentric and also socioeconomic substance.[18] Today, it can hardly be denied that sustainable development has become an unavoidable paradigm underpinning almost all human actions and pervading the environmental, social, political, economic, and cultural discourses from the local through to the 'global' level by both the public and private sectors.[19] The evolution and comprehensiveness of sustainable development can be clearly sensed from the Johannesburg Declaration on Sustainable Development, which not only recalls the evolution of sustainable development from Stockholm to Rio de Janeiro to Johannesburg, but also recognizes the various pillars of sustainable development, that is, 'economic development, social development and environmental protection'.[20] Since the principle of sustainable development needs to be adaptive to the circumstances according to the time, the area or the subjects concerned, it has to be 'intrinsically evolutive' in nature and vary *ratione temporis, rationae personae*, and *rationae materiae*.[21] Such variability also makes it quite difficult to strictly identify the contents of sustainable development.

For the purpose of this study, it is neither possible nor necessary to produce an exhaustive list of all elements of the principle of sustainable development. On this issue, the Resolution adopted by the International Law Association (ILA) may be of guidance. The ILA New Delhi Declaration of Principles of International Law Relating to Sustainable Development (2002) identifies seven major sustainable development-related principles:

(1) The duty of States to ensure sustainable use of natural resources.
(2) The principle of equity and the eradication of poverty.
(3) The principle of common but differentiated responsibilities.
(4) The principle of the precautionary approach to human health, natural resources and ecosystems.
(5) The principle of public participation and access to information and justice.
(6) The principle of good governance.
(7) The principle of integration and interrelationship, in particular in relation to human rights and social, economic and environmental objectives.[22]

---

[15] See V Lowe, 'Sustainable Development and Unsustainable Arguments' in A Boyle and D Freestone (eds), *International Law and Sustainable Development* (Oxford University Press 1999) 34.

[16] Barral (n 11) 384.

[17] See P Birnie and A Boyle, *International Law and the Environment* (2nd edn, Oxford University Press 2002) 45.

[18] See Schrijver (n 9) 373.   [19] Barral (n 11) 377.

[20] See Johannesburg Declaration on Sustainable Development http://www.un-documents.net/jburgdec.htm (last accessed 10 May 2016).

[21] Barral (n 11) 382.

[22] ILA, 'New Delhi Declaration of Principles of International Law Relating to Sustainable Development' reprinted in (2002) 2 Int'l Env Agreements 211.

The above list is not an exhaustive list of all elements of the principle of sustainable development, but it clearly demonstrates that the coverage and meaning of the principle of sustainable development have been substantively expanded over time. Today, the principle of sustainable development not only touches upon environmental sustainability, but also includes a much broader range of issues, such as human rights, access to justice, and good governance. In addition, one may also sense that various aspects of the principle of sustainable development may have close ties with international investment law, and could be addressed through the discourse of IIA. For instance, the aspects relating to sustainable use of natural resources and protection of human health and human rights may be addressed through IIAs. As discussed below, these aspects have already been incorporated into a number of IIAs.

For the purpose of the present study, while recognizing the vagueness and the flexibility of the principle of sustainable development, this chapter focuses on three major types of sustainable development provisions in Chinese IIAs, that is, environmental, transparency (of law and regulation as well as dispute settlement procedures), and labour rights provisions. Although these three types do not constitute an exhaustive list of sustainable development provisions, they can be quite indicative in assessing the overall sustainable development-compatibility of Chinese IIAs.

III. The Major Types of Sustainable Development Provisions in Chinese IIAs

Up to the end of 2017, China has concluded 132 BITs, 104 of which are currently in force, including one trilateral investment treaty (TIT), that is, the China–Japan–Korea TIT;[23] and fifteen FTAs (including a preferential trade agreement), almost all of which incorporate an investment chapter or incorporate an existing BIT by reference.[24] Despite the huge number of IIAs China has concluded, no Chinese IIA contains a sustainable development clause titled as such. However, this does not mean that Chinese IIAs are completely delinked from sustainable development or have no role to play in addressing sustainable development challenges. To the contrary, like their international counterparts, an increasing number of Chinese IIAs begin to incorporate provisions relating to environmental protection, labour rights protection, and transparency of laws, regulations, and dispute settlement procedures, especially in the recent decade. These provisions are closely related with sustainable development and may play a helpful role in making these IIAs sustainable development-compatible.

A. Clear mentioning of sustainable development in the preambles

A few Chinese IIAs have taken note of the need of making international investment sustainable development-compatible. They either clearly mention the term sustainable development or use the alternative terms such as 'environment, health or safety' in their preambles. Typical examples can be found in some recent Chinese IIAs. For instance, the China–Canada BIT provides that it recognizes 'the need to promote investment based on the principles of sustainable development'.[25] Similarly, the

---

[23] A list of Chinese BITs and TITs is available at http://tfs.mofcom.gov.cn/article/Nocategory/201111/20111107819474.shtml (last accessed 6 October 2018).
[24] A list of Chinese FTAs is available at http://fta.mofcom.gov.cn/ (last accessed 22 October 2018).
[25] China–Canada BIT preamble.

China–Japan–Korea TIT recognizes 'that these objectives can be achieved without relaxing health, safety and environmental measures of general application'.[26]

There is no denying that clear mention of sustainable development in the preamble of the IIAs shows the strong and shared aspiration of the contracting states to make IIAs sustainable development-compatible. It also involves an obligation to seek a balance between sometimes conflicting economic, environmental, and social priorities in the development process, in the interests of future generations. Such balance can be achieved through procedures and substantive obligations of IIAs, depending on their wordings.[27]

However, as treaty preambles are often 'non-operational' thus their actual legal effectiveness is limited.[28] From treaty law perspective, preambles generally do not confer rights or obligations on the contracting states. They can only reflect rules of customary law[29] and play an assistive role in ascertaining the objects and purpose of the treaty.[30] Such assisting role of preambles has been confirmed clearly in arbitration practice. For instance, the ICSID tribunals in *Siemens v Argentina* and *Vivendi v Argentina* both held that the preambles of the underlying BITs set forth the objectives and purposes of these BITs and thus the tribunals shall be mindful thereof in arbitration.[31]

B. Environmental provisions in Chinese IIAs

Probably the gravest sustainable development challenge to the international community is environmental pollution. It is not infrequently seen that states need to take measures for environmental protection purposes that may frustrate foreign investors' expectations or are otherwise inconsistent with the states' obligations under the applicable IIAs. International arbitration practice suggests that foreign investors may claim such measures constitute (indirect) expropriation or violate fair and equitable treatment according to the IIAs. As a matter of fact, quite a few environmentally sensitive ISA cases have been initiated over the past decades.[32] For such reason, the environmental issue stands at the forefront of the thorny problem of balancing the preservation of states' regulatory power and policy space and the protection of foreign investment.

China faces grave environmental challenge nowadays, given its serious environmental situation and the fact that many Chinese overseas investors are reported to have caused serious environmental damages in host states, especially in environmentally vulnerable regions.[33] Against such factual background, enhancing the environmental provisions in Chinese IIAs seems both necessary and timely.

---

[26] China–Japan–Korea TIT preamble. [27] Segger (n 3) 142.
[28] See M Chi, 'The "Greenization" of Chinese BITs: An Empirical Study of the Environmental Provisions in Chinese BITs and Its Implications for China's Future BIT-Making' (2015) 18 J Int'l Econ L 511.
[29] See G Fitzmaurice, 'The Law and Procedure of the International Court of Justice 1951-1954' (1957) 33 Brit YB Int'l L 229.
[30] M E Villiger, *Commentary on the 1969 Convention on the Law of Treaties* (Martinus Nijhoff Publishers 2009) 44.
[31] See Decision on Jurisdiction (3 August 2004), *Siemens AG v Argentine Republic* (ICSID Case No ARB/02/8) para 81 www.italaw.com/cases/1026 (last accessed 20 September 2015); see also Award (20 August 2007), *Compania de Aguas del Aconquija SA and Vivendi Universal v Argentine Republic* (ICSID Case No ARB/97/3) para 7.4.4 www.italaw.com/cases/309 (last accessed 20 September 2015).
[32] See eg N Bernasconi-Osterwalder and L Johnson (eds), *International Investment Law and Sustainable Development: Key Cases from 2000 to 2010* (International Institute for Sustainable Development publication 2010) www.iisd.org/publications/international-investment-law-and-sustainable-development-key-cases-2000-2010 (last accessed 20 October 2015).
[33] See eg X Rice, 'Chinese Investment: The Money Is Welcome, But More Controls Are Needed' *Financial Times* (2012) www.ft.com/cms/s/0/d8f41dd6-b4a6-11e1-bb2e-00144feabdc0.html#axzz3MCLqR1ZN (last accessed 20 October 2015).

Table 6.1 below lists the environmental provisions in Chinese IIAs. As this author has done an empirical study of all of the environmental provisions in Chinese BITs and discussed their implications,[34] a few observations will be highlighted to avoid unnecessary repetition. First, despite the large number of IIAs China has concluded, only a fraction of them contain environmental provisions. For such reason, one may say that Chinese IIAs in general are insufficiently sustainable development-compatible. Secondly, despite the general scarcity of environmental provisions in Chinese IIAs, there is a clear trend that recent IIAs appear more sustainable development-compatible as they incorporate larger number of environmental provisions. It is for such reason that the author has mentioned that Chinese IIAs are becoming 'greener'.[35] Thirdly, there are two major types of environmental provisions in China, namely consultation clause and exception clause. The latter type can be further divided into three subcategories, that is, the stand-alone environmental exception, the expropriation exception, and the FET exception. The common feature of these exceptions is that host states will be exempted from their state liability for treaty violation by taking certain environmental measures that are otherwise inconsistent with their IIA obligations. In this sense, the exceptions may help the host states in preserving more regulatory power and policy space to take environmental measures that are necessary.

Table 6.1 Environmental provisions in Chinese IIAs

IIA	Article	Brief description
1. 2013 China–Tanzania BIT	Art.6	Exception to expropriation
	Art.10	Exception of Environmental Measures
2. 2012 China–Canada BIT	Art.18	Consultations of environmental disputes
	Art.33	General Exceptions[a]
	Annex B	Exception to expropriation
3. 2012 China–Japan–Korea TIT	Art.23	Exception of Environmental Measures
	Protocol 2C	Exception to expropriation
4. 2011 China–Uzbekistan BIT	Art.6	Exception to expropriation
5. 2008 China–Colombia BIT	Art.4.2.c	Exception to expropriation
6. 2006 China–India BIT	Protocol	Exception to expropriation
7. 2005 China–Madagascar BIT	Art.3	Exception to FET
8. 1996 China–Mauritius BIT	Art.11	Exception of Prohibitions and Restrictions

[a]For a detailed analysis of this specific type of general exceptions clause see Julien Chaisse, 'Exploring the Confines of International Investment and Domestic Health Protections: General Exceptions Clause as a Forced Perspective' (2013) 39(2/3) American Journal of Law & Medicine 332 (discussing the potential use of a WTO-inspired clause in the context of investment disputes).

C. Transparency provisions in Chinese IIAs

Transparency of investment laws and regulations and ISA proceedings is an important element of the principle of rule of law. This issue is specifically seen as necessary since in recent decades the global investment governance regime, ISA in particular, has been subject to criticism for lack of sufficient legitimacy, and enhancement of transparency

---

[34] Chi (n 28) 511.   [35] ibid.

of laws, regulations, and ISA proceedings is seen as an important and effective remedy to such a legitimacy crisis.[36]

With special regard to ISA, although confidentiality is often deemed as an inherent feature of international arbitration, there is a growing call for improving the transparency of ISA proceedings for good governance reasons. Transparency could be particularly needed in ISA because, on one hand, host states are often sued for their IIA-inconsistent regulatory measures and inappropriate administrative (or even judicial) practices; on the other hand, if host states 'lose the case', they will be obligated to compensate foreign investors out of their state revenues, which may give rise to the issue of accountability of the states to its taxpayers.

Table 6.2 below lists the transparency provisions of Chinese IIAs. Although China's level of rule of law appears lower than that in many developed countries, there is a clear trend that Chinese IIAs are becoming more transparent, given the growing number of transparency provisions. These provisions can be roughly divided into three types, each with a different stress and level of effectiveness.

The first type uses various declaratory phrases such as 'creating transparent investment conditions' or 'promoting greater transparency measures'. Although such phrases show the aspiration of the contracting states in creating and promoting a transparent investment environment, they do not create obligations on the contracting states.

The second type deals with transparency of investment-related domestic laws and regulations or ISA awards. It should be noted that such transparency requirement is not obligatory, but is subject to the disputing parties' consent. This type seems to represent the majority of the transparency provisions in Chinese IIAs. Practically speaking, they are not 'provocative' since China has already made profound transparency commitments to publish its trade regulations regularly upon its accession to the World Trade Organization (WTO).[37] In addition, as a matter of fact, the reports of panels and the Appellate Body of the Dispute Settlement Body (DSB) are routinely made public. Although there is still room for the improvement of the transparency of WTO dispute settlement on China's part, for instance, China may consider publication of its written submissions like some of its major trade partners, and China's accession to the WTO and especially its participation in WTO dispute settlement over the years have somehow prepared it to accept more and a higher level of transparency provisions in global investment governance.

The third type deals with the truly contentious issue of transparency of ISA proceedings. Out of China's IIAs, such provision can only be found in the 2012 China–Canada BIT, the most 'American style' BIT that China has ever concluded. It not only requires publication of relevant laws, regulations, and other relevant documents, but also permits conditional participation of non-disputing state and third parties in ISA proceedings. In a sense, the insertion of such provision in Chinese IIA represents a bold step in China's IIA-making with regard to transparency of ISA proceedings. It may also prelude an implied change of China's 'unfriendly' attitudes towards NGOs and other social movement organizations that are likely to become *amicus curie* in ISA proceedings.

Despite the improvement of Chinese IIAs, one should not overestimate the impacts of the transparency provisions. On one hand, transparency in ISA proceedings remains a heatedly debated issue at international level. Especially, the issue of *amicus curiae*

---

[36] See eg S D Franck, 'The Legitimacy Crisis in Investment Treaty Arbitration: Privatizing Public International Law through Inconsistent Decisions' (2005) 73 Fordham L Rev 1521. See also Chaisse and Donde (n 1) 47.

[37] See eg GATT 1994 art X.

participation in ISA proceedings is highly contentious and no uniform and clear rule in this regard has been established.[38] On the other, because China traditionally views the issue of NGOs (especially foreign ones), civil society movement, and probably all other organizations that are not controlled or supervised by the state as a 'sensitive' one, these organizations have not been sufficiently welcomed in China.[39]

To some extent, China's suspicious attitudes towards these organizations may help explain its reluctance in accepting third party participation in ISA proceedings. Owing to the fact that Chinese individuals and NGOs are unfamiliar with ISA and that the civil society and NGOs in China are not sufficiently developed, they have limited capability to participate in ISA proceedings as *amicus curiae*. As appeared in many cases, *amicus curiae* parties in ISA proceedings are foreign individuals and organizations. Thus, it is worried that if China allows *amicus curiae* in ISA proceedings through its IIA provisions, the *amicus curiae* do not really understand China and are not able to present their views truly impartially. Up to this point, no transparency provisions in Chinese IIAs have been applied in ISA practice, it remains to be seen what impacts these provisions may exert on China's future IIA-making, ISA practices, and investment governance at more general level.

Table 6.2 Transparency provisions in Chinese IIAs

IIA	Article	Brief description
1. 2012 China–Canada BIT	Art.17	Transparency of laws, regulations and policies
	Art.27	Non-disputing state's participation in ISA
	Art.28	Public access to hearings and documents
	Art.29	Submissions by a non-disputing party
2. 2012 China–Japan–Korea TIT	Art.9	Establish and maintain transparency IPR regimes
	Art.10	Transparency of laws and regulations
3. 2012 China–Chile FTA	Art.25	Transparency of laws and regulations
4. 2009 China–ASEAN FTA	Art.2	Improving the transparency of investment rules
	Art.19	Transparency of laws and regulations
5. 2008 China–NZ FTA	Art.146	Publish international investment-related agreements
	Art.147	Considering greater transparency of measures
	Art.157	Publishing arbitration-related information and documents

[38] See eg UNCTAD, *Transparency*, Series on Issues in International Investment Agreements II (2012) http://unctad.org/en/PublicationsLibrary/unctaddiaeia2011d6_en.pdf (last accessed 10 October 2015); OECD, *Transparency and Third Party Participation in Investor-State Dispute Settlement Procedures* (OECD Working Papers on International Investment, OECD Publishing 2005) http://dx.doi.org/10.1787/524613550768 (last accessed 10 October 2015); H Mann, 'Reconceptualizing International Investment Law: Its Role in Sustainable Development' (2013) 17 Lewis & Clark L Rev 521; E Levine, 'Amicus Curiae in International Investment Arbitration: The Implications of an Increase in Third-Party Participation' (2011) 29 Berkeley J Int'l Law 200; A Sabater, 'Towards Transparency in Arbitration (A Cautious Approach)' (2010) 5 Berkeley J Int'l L 47; B Choudhury, 'Recapturing Public Power: Is Investment Arbitration's Engagement of the Public Interest Contributing to the Democratic Deficit?' (2008) 41 Vand J Transnat'l L 775; A Newcombe and A Lemaire, 'Should Amici Curiae Participate in Investment Treaty Arbitrations?' (2001) 5 Vindobona J Int'l L & Arb 22.
[39] See A Panda, 'China to Regulate Foreign "NGOs"' http://thediplomat.com/2014/12/china-to-regulate-foreign-ngos/; S Lubman, 'China's Government's Ambivalence toward NGOs' www.law.berkeley.edu/article/chinas-governments-ambivalence-toward-ngos/ (last accessed 20 December 2015).

Table 6.2 Continued

IIA	Article	Brief description
6. 2008 China–Mexico BIT	Art.20	Awards will be publicly accessible unless otherwise agreed
7. 2007 China–Cuba BIT	Art.9	Awards shall not be made public unless otherwise agreed
8. 2007 China–Korea BIT	Art.11	Transparency of laws and regulations
9. 2004 China–Finland BIT	Art.12	Transparency of laws and regulations
10. 2002 China–B. & H. BIT	Art.2	Creating transparent investment conditions
11. 1988 China–Australia BIT	Art.6	Transparency of laws and regulations

D. Labour/human rights provisions in Chinese IIAs

It is often deemed that international investment law and human rights law develop along separate tracks as they have different regulatory focuses and approaches.[40] For such reason, IIAs often appear insufficient in addressing investment-related human rights concerns. It is particularly the case given that 'the legal protection of human rights has, since its inception, focused mostly on the obligations of states vis-à-vis individuals and/or communities, while investment treaties and international investment law have generally addressed corporate-state relations. The individual is rarely if ever considered in the contractual relationship'.[41]

In recent years, human rights issues seem to have penetrated international investment law, especially in ISA proceedings. Consideration of human rights in ISA and IIA-making may give rise to various fundamental and systematic issues, such as the hierarchical order of IIAs and human rights treaties and the scope of jurisdiction of ISA arbitrators on human rights claims based on IIA violation.[42] *Azurix Corp. v Argentina* is a good example to explain the link and conflict between human rights law and IIA.[43] The investor, Azurix, concluded a concession with Argentina for water and sewage services. Azurix claimed that Argentina failed to fulfil the infrastructure repair obligations, which led to Azurix's failure in providing satisfactory water services under the concession agreement and Argentina's refusal of payment. Azurix claimed that the refusal amounted to expropriation under the US–Argentina BIT, while Argentina raised the conflict between the BIT and human rights treaties that protect consumers' rights and claimed that this conflict was to be resolved in favour of human rights. Although the tribunal acknowledged the public purpose of Argentina's measure, it refused to discuss Argentina's human rights argument.[44]

---

[40] See A Khalfan, 'International Investment Law and Human Rights' in M C Segger and others (eds), *Sustainable Development in World Investment Law* (Kluwer Law International 2011) 53.

[41] See Segger (n 3) 59.

[42] See generally C Reiner and C Schreuer, 'Human Rights and International Investment Arbitration' www.univie.ac.at/intlaw/h_rights_int_invest_arbitr.pdf (last accessed 20 December 2015).

[43] *Azurix Corp v Argentine Republic* (ICSID Case No ARB/01/12) www.italaw.com/cases/118 (last accessed 20 December 2015). For a discussion see Julien Chaisse and Marine Polo, 'Globalization of Water Privatization: Ramifications of Investor-State Disputes in the "Blue Gold" Economy' (2015) 38(1) Boston College International & Comparative Law Review 1. See in particular at 16–23, 49–50, and 55–61.

[44] See generally T Meshel, 'Human Rights in Investor-State Arbitration: The Human Right to Water and Beyond' (2015) 6 J Int'l Disp Settlement 277.

Human rights are diverse in content and human rights treaties are numerous. Therefore, it is doubtful whether IIAs are truly helpful in addressing human rights concerns associated with transnational investment activities. At the international level, although developed countries tried to address human rights concerns in past IIA negotiations, as illustrated by the failed negotiation of the Multilateral Agreement on Investment (MAI), such efforts were not successful.[45] Even today, it remains largely true that IIAs seldom incorporate human rights provisions.

Human rights provisions are seldom found in IIAs, but recent IIAs begin to incorporate labour rights provisions, which may be helpful in addressing investment-associated human rights concerns. Although, strictly speaking, human rights and labour rights are separated, they bear close links.[46] By and large, labour rights provisions in IIAs seem evolutive. Traditionally, labour rights provisions are largely aspirational and do not create binding obligations on states from treaty law perspective.[47] Recently, as a response to the repeated calls of the international community for better human rights protection, some IIAs of developed countries begin to incorporate labour rights provisions that are more 'effective'. The 2012 US Model Bilateral Investment Treaty (US Model BIT) is a typical example. It contains a clause dealing with labour rights,[48] referring expressly to core labour standards (CLS) enshrined in the International Labor Organization Declaration on Fundamental Principles and Rights at Work and Its Follow-ups.[49] According to this declaration, CLS is composed of several major principles, including freedom of association, freedom from forced labour and child labour and non-discrimination in employment.[50] This provision also explicitly requires the contracting party to 'ensure that it does not waive or otherwise derogate from or offer to waive or otherwise derogate from its labour laws where the waiver or derogation would be inconsistent with the labour rights'.[51]

Table 6.3 below shows that there are only four Chinese IIAs with labour rights provisions. These provisions can be further divided into two types. The first type basically allows the contracting states to use measures for labour right protection as an exception to MFN treatment. The second type is a specific exception inserted in the transfer clause, which exempts the contracting states to withhold their treaty obligation of allowing free transfer of profits and benefits. As can be seen, all of these labour rights provisions are exception in nature. While recognizing their helpful role in preserving policy space for the host states in taking labour rights protective measures, none of them imposes an obligation on the contracting states to protect labour rights that might be violated in international investment activities. Consequently, such violations will be addressed by the national law of the host states mainly through local remedies.

It is not surprising to see China's unfriendly attitude towards labour rights provisions if one takes China's current social and political situation, especially its poor human rights situation, into account. Notably, no Chinese IIAs incorporates core labour standards. While China is negotiating BITs with the US and the EU, which are known for their high labour standards, it remains to be seen how the sensitive issue of labour rights will be dealt with in these BITs.

[45] See Segger (n 3) 57.
[46] See V Mantouvalou, 'Are Labour Rights Human Rights?' (2012) 3 European Labour LJ 151.
[47] A Sewlikar, 'Introduction of Labor Standards in Investment Arbitration' http://kluwerarbitrationblog.com/blog/2014/03/18/introduction-of-labour-standards-in-investment-arbitration/ (last accessed 20 October 2015).
[48] See 2012 US Model BIT art 13 (Investment and Labor).   [49] ibid art 13(1).
[50] P Alston, '"Core Labor Standards" and the Transformation of the International Labor Rights Regime' (2007) 15 European J Int'l L 457.
[51] See 2012 US Model BIT art 13(2).

Table 6.3 Labour/human rights provisions in Chinese IIAs

IIA	Article	Brief description
1. 2009 China–ASEAN FTA	Art.10	Exception to Transfer of worker's retrenchment benefits in relation to labour compensation
2. 1998 China–NZ BIT	Art.5	Exception to MFN Clause
3. 1985 China–Singapore BIT	Art.5	Exception to MFN Clause
4. 1985 China–Thailand BIT	Art.3	Exception to MFN Clause

E. Major observations

The above study discusses three major types of sustainable development provisions in Chinese IIAs. It has to be mentioned that these selected sustainable development provisions are not exhaustive. Other types of IIA provisions, such as some procedural IIA provisions, may also have profound sustainable development implications but are not reviewed in this chapter. That said, several observations can be drawn from the above empirical study.

First, despite the large number of Chinese IIAs, only a fraction of them have sustainable development provisions, which shows that insufficient attention has been put on sustainable development concerns in China's IIA-making, especially in the past years.

Secondly, there is a clear tendency that more recent IIAs contain larger number of sustainable development provisions. For instance, the China–Canada BIT, one of the most recent IIAs of China, contains several environmental provisions and transparency provisions. This seems to suggest that Chinese IIAs are getting increasingly sustainable development-compatible, which conforms to the general development of IIAs globally.

Thirdly, it appears that Chinese IIAs with developed countries appear more sustainable development-compatible, while those with developing countries are less so. This is probably caused by the fact that China adopts an implied 'dichotomic' strategy in IIA-making. This would mean that the attitudes of China's IIA partner countries towards sustainable development promotion may be a key factor in deciding whether and what types of sustainable development provisions are incorporated in IIAs.

Fourthly, it is of interest to note that with regard to different types of sustainable development provisions, China has different attitudes. While Chinese IIAs appear growingly accommodative to environmental protection and transparency enhancement, they remain reluctant towards labour rights protection mainly for social and political considerations. This seems to be the major hurdle to make China's future IIA truly sustainable development-compatible.

At more detailed level, one may also find the subtle but significant difference of the three types of sustainable development provisions in Chinese IIAs. Environmental and labour rights provisions in nature are exceptions for the contracting state to deviate from their IIA obligations to some extent, which help preserve regulatory power in taking certain measures that are otherwise inconsistent with its obligations under IIAs. In comparison, transparency provisions may directly impose obligations on the IIA contracting states to publish investment-related national laws, regulations, and to allow third party participation in ISA proceedings conditionally. Such provisions seem 'proactive', which may 'penetrate' China's investment governance regime at a more profound level.

IV. Enhancing Sustainable Development Compatibility
of Chinese IIAS

Chinese IIAs in general are not sufficiently sustainable development-compatible and are thus not constructive in helping China address investment-related sustainable development challenges. Today, it is self-evident that China faces probably the gravest sustainable development challenges in history. Although such challenges used to focus on environmental protection, they have begun to proliferate to other fields, such as human rights protection. For instance, due mainly to the shrinking labour force in the Chinese market, the 'blood and sweat factory' as an 'effective' form of utilization of investment has become unrealistic and unsustainable for China and foreign investors in China.[52] In addition, Chinese overseas investors are often reported to have caused serious labour rights concerns in the host states,[53] China's investment activities are criticized as 'neo-colonization'.[54] The issue of labour rights protection has become outstanding for both China and its investors and there is a growing call for China to seriously consider this issue in its IIA-making and national law-making.[55]

In addition, as China is negotiating BITs with both the US and the EU, which are widely known for their high sustainable development standards in general, it will not be surprising if future Chinese BITs contain high standard sustainable development provisions. In this regard, China may face increasing pressure to improve its IIAs from the perspective of regulatory competition. As mentioned, many sustainable development norms have penetrated IIAs, especially the recent ones concluded by some developed countries, such as the 2012 US Model BIT[56] and the Trans-Pacific Partnership Agreement (TPP).[57] Although China is not bound by these IIAs, it is not likely to be completely immune from their profound impacts. As China is determined to become a rule-maker in global economic governance,[58] it is reasonable to expect that in China's future IIA-making, the sustainable development issue is not likely to be neglected.

The question that naturally follows is how China can make its IIAs sustainable development-compatible. At the global level, some prominent institutions have put forward their suggestions or even model IIAs. For instance, the International Institute for Sustainable Development (IISD), a respected NGO, issued its 'Model International

---

[52] See eg Southern Weekend, 'Leaving the Blood and Sweat Factory' http://finance.sina.com.cn/g/20051027/10032070194.shtml (last accessed 20 October 2015) (original in Chinese).

[53] See eg Human Rights Watch, 'You Will Be Fired If You Refuse: Labor Abuses in Zambia's Chinese State-Owned Copper Mines' www.hrw.org/report/2011/11/04/youll-be-fired-if-you-refuse/labor-abuses-zambias-chinese-state-owned-copper-mines (last accessed 20 October 2015).

[54] K Caulderwood, 'China Is Africa's New Colonial Overlord, Says Famed Primate Researcher Jane Goodall' www.ibtimes.com/china-africas-new-colonial-overlord-says-famed-primate-researcher-jane-goodall-1556312 (last accessed 20 October 2015).

[55] See generally S Hang, 'Investing in Human Rights: Using Bilateral Investment Treaties to Hold Multinational Corporations Liable for Labor Rights Violations' (2014) 37 Fordham Int'l LJ 1215.

[56] The 2012 US Model BIT not only expressly mentions in the foreword 'to achieve these objectives in a manner consistent with the protection of health, safety, and the environment, and the promotion of internationally recognized labor rights', but also contains two separate clauses to deal with environmental issues (art 12) and labour issues (art 13).

[57] The TPP includes two separate chapters addressing environmental and labour issues. See Office of the United States Trade Representative, 'Summary of the Trans-Pacific Partnership Agreement' https://ustr.gov/about-us/policy-offices/press-office/press-releases/2015/october/summary-trans-pacific-partnership (last accessed 22 October 2015).

[58] See *People's Daily*, 'Making Efforts to Gain Its Say in International Investment Rule-Making' http://theory.people.com.cn/n/2014/0402/c40531-24801269.html (last accessed 20 October 2015) (original in Chinese).

Investment Agreement for the Promotion of Sustainable Development' in 2004.[59] Similarly, UNCTAD issued its 'Investment Policy Framework for Sustainable Development' in 2012, aiming to provide suggestions to facilitate making sustainable development-friendly investment policies and IIAs.[60] Despite the merits of these proposals, no uniform way has been identified to make sustainable development-compatible IIAs. Therefore, such IIAs will need to be negotiated by states with all attending circumstances taking into consideration. This would ultimately lead to the balancing of sustainable development promotion and investment protection in IIA-making.

In light of the social and economic situation in China, the following several proposals are raised to help China make sustainable development-compatible IIAs in the future. First and foremost, China should carefully reconsider its IIA-making strategy. Although Chinese IIAs have become increasingly accommodating of certain non-investment issues in recent years, such as the need to protect the environment, this should be deemed more a compromise to external pressure from China's partner countries than a result of China's spontaneous and willing response towards the sustainable development challenges. China needs to further enhance its sustainable development awareness in IIA-making and to accept that IIAs should not only be deemed as a forum for exchanging economic benefits, but may also be a possible discourse to address sustainable development concerns associated with investment activities.

Secondly, as can be found from the above study, China's attitudes towards the different types of sustainable development provisions are diverse. To be brief, while China becomes increasingly accommodating to the incorporation of transparency provisions and environmental provisions in IIAs, it remains reluctant to accept 'core labour standards' in its IIAs. In light of such background, it would be unrealistic to expect China's future IIAs to become sustainable development-compatible in a high-standard and full-range manner. Rather, it is advisable that 'differentiated' and 'creeping' strategy should be adopted when negotiating IIAs with China. The 'differentiated' strategy implies that partner countries may consider negotiating one or more types of sustainable development provisions with China, depending on their own needs and the 'sensitivity' of such provisions to China. It seems that China is more likely to compromise on some types of sustainable development provisions, such as environmental and transparency provisions, than on others, such as labour rights provisions. The 'creeping' strategy implies that it may take some time for China to shift its position on sustainable development provisions when negotiating IIAs; thus, partner countries may wish to negotiate sustainable development provisions with China in a gradual manner, depending on the 'sensitivity' of these provisions.

Thirdly, one of the most outstanding defects of China's existing IIAs is that they are often incapable of regulating the conduct of its overseas investors who are reported to have caused serious sustainable development damage in the host countries. In light of such situations, China may need to incorporate certain corporate social responsibility (CSR) provisions in its future IIAs.[61] Unlike IIA provisions that aim at protection of investors 'one-sidedly', CSR provisions help to address the sustainable development

---

[59] IISD, 'A Model International Investment Agreement for the Promotion of Sustainable Development' www.iisd.org/publications/model-international-investment-agreement-promotion-sustainable-development (last accessed 20 November 2015).

[60] UNCTAD, 'Investment Policy Framework for Sustainable Development' http://investmentpolicyhub.unctad.org/ipfsd (last accessed 30 November 2015).

[61] See Chi (n 28) 538.

challenges at the end of investors. It is particularly timely and necessary given the fact that transnational corporations have already become prominent and active in international investment activities and could be proper bearers of certain sustainable development obligations. For instance, it has been authoritatively suggested that 'the existing state-based human rights instruments and simply assert that many of their provisions now are binding on corporations as well'.[62] If this can be realized, CSR provisions incorporated in IIAs may impose certain sustainable development obligations on investors.[63] This is likely to make the existing IIAs more effective and applicable in addressing sustainable development challenges.[64] At this point, it is of interest to note that the recently signed TPP has included a CSR provision in its investment chapter, which encourages the incorporation of internationally recognized standards, guidelines, and principles of CSR by the contracting states.[65]

However, CSR provisions are often deemed as 'soft law' rules and the conduct of foreign investors is almost exclusively subject to the national laws of the host states.[66] Thus, as admitted by the special rapporteur Juggie, 'the assertion itself [making human rights norms binding on corporations] has little authoritative basis in international law'.[67] Therefore, it is suggested that the incorporation of CSR provisions in IIAs should aim at transforming the non-binding CSR norms into binding 'hard law' rules of treaties. Ideal as this may sound, it is no easy task. Ultimately, whether and to what extent this is accepted and achieved depends not only on the political willingness of the states, especially the developed countries that are often the host of multi-national corporations, but also on the improvement of the sustainable development awareness of these corporations.

V. Conclusion

This chapter, based on the broad understanding of the principle of sustainable development, examines the three major types of sustainable development provisions in Chinese IIAs, that is, environmental provisions, transparency provisions, and labour rights provisions. The overall assessment is that Chinese IIAs are insufficiently sustainable development-compatible, although progress has been made, especially in recent years. In addition, although up to the present no sustainable development-sensitive dispute relying on Chinese IIAs has been initiated against China, it would not be surprising that such cases may appear in the near future. It could be particularly the case given China's urgent need for taking sustainable development measures, especially

[62] See J Ruggie, 'Interim Report of the Special Representative of the Secretary-General on the Issue of Human Rights and Transnational Corporations and Other Business Enterprises' UN Doc E/CN4/2006/97 (2006), www1.umn.edu/humanrts/business/RuggieReport2006.html (last accessed 20 December 2015) para 60.
[63] See P Muchlinski, 'Regulating Multinationals: Foreign Investment, Development and the Balance of Corporate and Home Country Rights and Responsibilities in a Globalizing World' www.law.yale.edu/documents/pdf/Alumni_Affairs/Andrea_Bjorklund_readings.pdf (last accessed 20 October 2015) 10.
[64] See generally L Davarnejad, 'Strengthening the Social Dimension of International Investment Agreements by Integrating Codes of Conduct for Multinational Enterprises' www.oecd.org/investment/globalforum/40352144.pdf (last accessed 20 October 2015).
[65] See art 9.16 (Corporate Social Responsibility), TPP.   [66] See Segger (n 3) 7.
[67] See J Ruggie, 'Interim Report of the Special Representative of the Secretary-General on the Issue of Human Rights and Transnational Corporations and Other Business Enterprises' UN Doc E/CN4/2006/97 (2006) para 60 www1.umn.edu/humanrts/business/RuggieReport2006.html (last accessed 20 December 2015).

measures to upgrade environmental protection and to enhance China's current level of labour rights protection. It is thus necessary for China to make its future IIAs more inclusive to satisfy its increasing sustainable development needs.

Admittedly, negotiating sustainable development-compatible IIAs is difficult. Up to the present, the international community has not been successful in promoting a model sustainable development-compatible IIA that is suitable for all states because the needs of different states are diverse. In other words, there is neither a 'one size for all' model sustainable development-compatible IIA, nor is there a 'one size for all' formula of interpreting and applying IIA in settling sustainable development-sensitive disputes. Thus, despite the common aspiration for sustainable development-compatible IIAs, the way to conclude such IIAs should be based on the need of the individual state. When negotiating IIAs, negotiators should take all contending circumstances into consideration while bearing in mind the specific needs of their respective states. In the meantime, international arbitrators should also make their decisions on a case-by-case basis when adjudicating sustainable development-sensitive disputes.

It seems that China has determined to make more sustainable development-compatible IIAs in the future. However, more concerted and concrete efforts should be taken to address the serious sustainable development challenges in its future IIA-making. China needs to be aware that sustainable development is an evolutionary concept that may cover a broad range of issues beyond environmental protection and that IIAs are not merely instruments for investment protection and liberalization, but are also a possible discourse to accommodate certain non-investment values to ensure that its future economic development is made more sustainable. Making sustainable development-compatible IIAs would require China to incorporate a larger number and a higher standard of sustainable development provisions in future IIAs. Given China's economic size and its international influence, it is almost certain that more sustainable development-compatible IIAs of China will be helpful in fostering and developing an sustainable development-oriented investment governance regime at both national and global levels.

7

Lessons Learned from the Canada–China FIPA for the US–China BIT and beyond

Chinese Whispers or Chinese Chequers?

*Kyle Dylan Dickson-Smith**

I. Introduction

China, as the second largest recipient of foreign direct investment (FDI) and the sixth ranked outward investor, makes a powerful investment partner.[1] Similarly, the anticipated US–China bilateral investment agreement (BIT), which intends to regulate investment between the two largest economies, has the potential to establish a new archetypal wave of Chinese BITs within its evolving cycle.[2] Yet, China's bilateral investment strategy, particularly its intentions and aspirations, is not always forthcoming.[3] As China's practice often shifts throughout time and between counterparties, it is a frequent case of Chinese whispers, predicting outcomes through reading the tealeaves. This is particularly the case with China's slender history of BITs with capital exporting

* International Lawyer and Counsel, FCIArb., BSc, LLB, LLM (University of Melbourne). The author is very grateful for the thoughtful advice and comments provided by Professor Julien Chaisse, Lori Blahey, and Flavia Marisi. I welcome any comments and can be reached at info@kyledickson-smith.com. The views expressed (along with any errors) herein are exclusively the author's own and cannot be attributed to the author's employer.

[1] Leon Trakman, 'Enter the Dragon IV: China's Proliferating Investment Treaty Program' (2011) UNSW Faculty of Law 1. OECD, 'The Foreign Direct Investment: Flows by Partner Country' *OECD International Direct Investment Statistics* (2012) 1 www.oecd-ilibrary.org/finance-and-investment/data/oecd-international-direct-investment-statistics_idi-data-en (last accessed 28 January 2017).

[2] David Gantz, 'Challenges for the United States in Negotiating a BIT with China: Reconciling Reciprocal Investment Protection with Policy Concerns' (2015) Arizona Legal Studies Discussion Paper No 14-03, 248 https://papers.ssrn.com/sol3/papers.cfm?abstract_id=2383919 (last accessed 25 January 2017).

[3] Alex Berger, 'Investment Rules in Chinese Preferential Trade and Investment Agreements: Is China Following the Global Trend Towards Comprehensive Agreements?' *German Development Institute/Deutsches Institut für Entwicklungspolitik (DIE) Discussion Paper* (2003) 25 www.die-gdi.de/uploads/media/DP_7.2013.pdf (last accessed 25 January 2017). This is despite China developing model BITs, which too have changed over time and the executed BIT has often deviated from the model, depending on the practice of the relevant counterparty. The recent example is with respect to the US–China bilateral relations, whereby China's government has never formally articulated its goals, other than a probable generic interest in expanding bilateral investment. Lauren Gloudeman and Nargiza Salidjanova, 'Policy Considerations for Negotiating a U.S.-China Bilateral Investment Treaty' (2016) US-China Economic and Security Review Commission, Staff Research Report, 6 http://origin.www.uscc.gov/sites/default/files/Research/Staff%20Report_Policy%20Considerations%20for%20Negotiating%20a%20U.S.-China%20Bilateral%20Investment%20Treaty080116.pdf (last accessed 27 January 2017).

Lessons Learned from the Canada–China FIPA for the US–China BIT and Beyond: Chinese Whispers or Chinese Checkers? Kyle Dylan Dickson-Smith. © Kyle Dylan Dickson-Smith, 2019. Published 2019 by Oxford University Press.

or developed countries.[4] Nevertheless, certain lessons can be made from analysing a unique and recent BIT, the Canada–China Foreign Investment Protection Agreement (FIPA), in order the better to predict and identify the opportunities and challenges for potential BIT counterparties of China (such as the United States, the European Union (EU), India, the Gulf Cooperation Council, and Columbia).[5]

The Canada–China FIPA and the anticipated US–China BIT (and EU–China BIT) collectively fall into a unique class of investment agreements, in that they represent a convergence of diverse ideologies of international investment norms/protections with two distinct (East/West) underlying domestic legal and economic systems. The purpose of this chapter is to appreciate and utilize the legal content of the Canada–China FIPA in order to isolate the opportunities and challenges for investment agreements currently under negotiation (focusing on the US–China BIT). This analysis is conducted from the perspective of China's traditional BIT practice and political–economic goals, relative to that of its counterparty.

This chapter briefly addresses the economic and broader diplomatic relationship between China and Canada, comparing that with the United States. It then analyses a broad selection of key substantive and procedural obligations of the Canada–China FIPA, addressing their impact, individually and cumulatively, to extract what lessons can be learned for the United States (US) and other negotiating parties. This analysis identifies the degree of investment liberalization and legal protection that Canada and China achieved, and whether these standards are reciprocally applied. The analysis is not divorced from the relevant political economy and negotiating position between China and the counterparty,[6] the perceived economic benefits of each party as well as any diplomatic sensitive obstacles between the parties.[7] While this chapter does not exhaustively analyse each substantive and procedural right, it provides enough of a comprehensive basis to reveal those challenges that remain for future bilateral negotiations with China.

Approximately in 2005, China's focus shifted from a capital importer to a major capital exporter,[8] and generally altered its BIT strategy from attracting inward FDI

---

[4] These include China's BITs with Switzerland (2009) and Germany (2003). Yet China has entered into free trade agreements with New Zealand (2008), Switzerland (2013), and Korea and Japan (2012).

[5] The Ministry of Commerce of the Government of China (MOFCOM), China FTA Network http://fta.mofcom.gov.cn/english/ (last accessed 28 January 2017). See also John Whalley and Chunding Li, 'China's Regional and Bilateral Trade Agreements' (2014) 1 http://voxeu.org/article/china-s-regional-and-bilateral-trade-agreements (last accessed 28 January 2017).

[6] The current and anticipated FDI flows between the counterparties is an example. With respect to the US–China and Canada–China arrangements, as China is a net exporter of FDI (in relation to the US and Canada), it suggests that China is likely to seek further protections for its investors. In terms of the historical trends of FDI growth between the United States and China, over the last ten years, FDI flows from the US into China have been relatively stable, while the inverse shows that Chinese FDI has increased into the United States, especially in the last five years; David Dollar, 'United States-China Two-way Direct Investment: Opportunities and Challenges' (2015) Brookings Institution 11–12 www.brookings.edu/wp-content/uploads/2016/06/us-china-two-way-direct-investment-dollar.pdf (last accessed 27 January 2017). Gloudeman and Salidjanova (n 3) 6.

[7] Canada's recent discourse as to China's human rights concerns is an example of foreign policy issues affecting the bilateral relations between Canada and China. Justin Carter, 'The Protracted Bargain: Negotiating the Canada-China Foreign Investment Promotion and Protection Agreement' (2009) 47 The Canadian Yearbook of International Law 197, 215–16.

[8] 'From 2005 to 2010 the ratio of outward relative to inward FDI flows grew from 0.17 to 0.6'. United Nations, UNCTAD 'World Investment Report: Towards a New Generation of Investment Policies' (2012) Annex.

to promoting outward FDI.[9] This reflected a coordinated shift from a restrictive to a liberal/legalized BIT approach, resulting in enhanced legal protection of Chinese investors abroad (and, incidentally, foreign investors in China).[10] A relevant question for Canada, the US, and the EU is whether China adjusted this BIT strategy further as a result of entering into negotiations with other capital exporting states. It is reasonable to expect that China would maintain negotiating liberal/legalized BITs with developing states (such as India and Columbia),[11] enhancing legal protection of Chinese outward investors, but revert to a more restrictive approach when negotiating BITs with developed countries.[12] As such, between two duelling capital exporters, we anticipate the negotiation of agreements like the Canada–China FIPA and US–China BIT to comprise a challenging balancing exercise of reciprocal investment concessions. While China did enter into BITs with developed states contemporaneously with this FDI shift (namely, Germany (2003), Netherlands (2004), Finland (2006)), these progressive BITs do not reflect this reversion to a more restrictive BIT.[13] Given the timing of those BITs, however it would have been too early to tell.

II. Why, oh Canada?: Notable Similarities and Differences of Canada–China BIT Practice and Economy

Notwithstanding the Canada–China FIPA fits in unique class of BITs that China has concluded with a developed western power,[14] does it make a good case of comparison and what are the limitations of such an approach? There are various similarities between Canada and the United States (and other Western developed nations/unions) that can be explained by the party's respective treaty practice and political economy.

First, Canada and the United States have enjoyed a common heritage of treaty practice that derives from their mutual aspiration of investment liberalization. This common heritage can be traced back to 1994 with the NAFTA (and even further back to 1989, with the Canada–United States Free Trade Agreement (CUSFTA)).[15] The NAFTA text (augmented by the interpretations of tribunals and parties jointly, through the Free Trade Commission) formed a foundation on which each state adjusted the text of their model BITs accordingly. The substantive investor rights contained in these templates (national treatment, MFN, expropriation, and performance requirements), such as the US Model BITs of 2004 and 2012 and Canadian FIPPA (Foreign Investment

---

[9] Berger (n 3) (2003) 1. See also Julien Chaisse, 'The Shifting Tectonics of International Investment Law: Structure and Dynamics of Rules and Arbitration on Foreign Investment in the Asia-Pacific Region' (2015) 47 George Washington International Law Review 563, 615–16.

[10] ibid. See also C Cai, 'Outward Foreign Direct Investment Protection and the Effectiveness of Chinese BIT Practice' (2006) 7 Journal of World Investment and Trade 621.

[11] MOFCOM, China FTA Network http://fta.mofcom.gov.cn/english/ (last accessed 28 January 2017).

[12] Carter (n 7) 213.   [13] ibid.

[14] Note that China has entered into other bilateral arrangements, such as a free trade agreement with China; China–Australia FTA (ChAFTA). A complete list of Chinese BITs does not exist. For a list of Chinese BITs see MOFCOM, China FTA Network http://fta.mofcom.gov.cn/english/ (last accessed 28 January 2017) and UNCTAD, 'Investment Dispute Settlement Navigator' http://investmentpolicyhub.unctad.org/IIA/CountryBits/42#iiaInnerMenu (last accessed 20 January 2017).

[15] Canada–United States Free Trade Agreement (CUSFTA). Specifically, with respect to the investment chapter (Chapter 16). Meg Kinnear and Robin Hansen, 'The Influence of NAFTA Chapter 11 in the BIT Landscape' (2005) 12 University of California Davis Journal of International Law & Policy 101, 102 https://jilp.law.ucdavis.edu/issues/volume-12-1/kinnear1-27.pdf (last accessed 25 January 2017).

Promotion and Protection Agreement) since 2004, are very similar.[16] The Canadian and US BIT practice has established relatively high standards with extensive investor protections, market access opportunities and a robust investor–state dispute settlement (ISDS) mechanism.[17]

With counterparties like China, the United States and Canada are both on a trajectory shift, being encouraged to alter their BIT negotiation position, from that of capital exporting to capital importing states.[18] Historically, both North American nations entered into standard BITs with developing states that were, for the most part, formulated to protect its own investors in foreign jurisdictions with little focus on promoting inward investment.[19]

As such, in entering into bilateral arrangements with China, one can argue that there exists an intersection of two distinct, perhaps opposing, trajectories. BITs of Canada and the US have gradually become more restrictive, offering less favourable investment protections than those in earlier versions.[20] In contrast, since China's BIT programme was launched in 1982,[21] Chinese BITs have become gradually more abundant and, especially since 2005, more liberal, offering more favourable protections.[22] This collision course of opposing, evolving ideologies, however, is perhaps mitigated by other factors, such as the encroachment of Western BIT standards onto China's BITs. China's BIT approach in this regard, described as 'selective adaptation', is a flexible policy that selectively integrates the models adopted by its counterparts and doctrines from influential arbitration awards.[23] Along this line of argument, it is suggested that China's recent BITs and FTAs follow an 'Americanization' evolutionary path, inspired by those North American changes in investment treaties that respond to NAFTA jurisprudence.[24]

Another common feature of the China/Canada relationship and China's relationship with other developed states, concerns the perceived economic benefits. Chinese companies generally invest in developed markets like that of Canada, the United States, and the European Union to acquire new production technology and techniques from skilled workers.[25] In addition, relative to China, both the US and Canada are net

---

[16] Indeed, there has been some divergence in Canadian and US practice, with Canada's BITs providing public policy exceptions with broader application (explained below) and, recently, Canada's adoption of an 'investment court' with the European Union. Kyle Dickson-Smith, 'Does the European Union Have New Clothes?: Understanding the EU's New Investment Treaty Model' (2016) 17 Journal of World Investment & Trade 773, 784: 'The creation of an "Investment Court System" with a First-Instance Tribunal and second tier Appeal Tribunal, constituted by fixed-term members, drawn from a pre-determined state-selected roster of members, and including various procedural innovations (such as ethical prescriptions, increased transparency, and a summary procedure for unmeritorious claims)'.

[17] Peterson Institute for International Economics, 'Toward a US-China Investment Treaty' (2015) 4 https://piie.com/publications/piie-briefings/toward-us-china-investment-treaty (last accessed 25 January 2017).

[18] Gantz (n 2) 240. This has already occurred to an extent for Canada, through the Comprehensive Economic and Trade Agreement (CETA), yet Canada and the EU have similar legal standards in their respective investment agreements.

[19] Carter (n 7) 206.   [20] ibid 213.   [21] ibid 207.

[22] Peterson Institute for International Economics (n 17) 4 https://piie.com/publications/piie-briefings/toward-us-china-investment-treaty (last accessed 25 January 2017).

[23] Matthew Levine, 'Towards a Fourth Generation of Chinese Treaty Practice: Substantive Changes, Balancing Mechanisms, and Selective Adaption' (Chapter 11 in this volume) [8], citing Pitman B Potter, 'Legal Reform in China: Institutions, Culture, and Selective Adaptation' (2004) 29 Law & Social Inquiry 465. See also Berger (n 3) 2.

[24] Congyan Cai, 'China-US BIT Negotiation and the Future of Investment Treaties Regime: A Grand Bargain With Multilateral Implications' (2009) 12 Journal of International Economic Law 457.

[25] With respect to the US market, for example, Chinese firms invest in considerable research and development, to adapt their products to the American market. Gary Hufbauer and others,

importers of Chinese FDI (while the quantum of FDI is significantly greater for the US)[26] and both the US and Canada have indicated to increase market access for their prospective investors and investor protections for existing investors.[27] While more a concern of the United States, there are inherent security concerns and general diplomatic tensions involving China,[28] as well as concerns of China complying with its international obligations generally.[29]

Yet, the dynamic differences between the China/Canada and China/US relationships should equally be acknowledged. While Chinese interests in the US are concentrated on access to technology/know-how, a significant proportion of foreign investment in Canada is concentrated in the extractive sector, in light of Canada's vast mineral and petroleum resources.[30] The US also appears to have relatively heightened concerns regarding Chinese investment. The chief concerns of the US throughout the negotiations of the US–China BIT have been the impact of Chinese investment on local firms, manifesting as anxiety from loss of autonomy and security abatement over sensitive technologies.[31] A particular concern is the perceived preferences of SOEs that are accorded by the Chinese state, in the form of subsidies and discriminatory practices that restrict competition, impeding both its local firms in the US market and

'Committee on Foreign Investment in the United States and the US-China Bilateral Investment Treaty: Challenges In Meeting China's Demands' in *Toward a US-China Investment Treaty* (Peterson Institute for International Economics 2015) 36 https://piie.com/publications/piie-briefings/toward-us-china-investment-treaty (last accessed 25 January 2017).

[26] Of those Chinese outward FDI (OFDI) flows the US dominated flows to the region, accounting for over 75% of flows and stocks to North America. Alicia Garcia-Herrero, 'China's Outbound Foreign Direct Investment: How Much Goes Where after Round-tripping and Offshoring?' (2015) Banco Bilbao Vizcaya Argentaria 15/17 Working Paper 7 www.bbvaresearch.com/wp-content/uploads/2015/06/15_17_Working-Paper_ODI.pdf (last accessed 20 January 2017). Specifically, 'Chinese firms invested US$139.10 billion into North America between 2005 and 2015, with US$95.41 billion flowing into the United States and US$43.69 billion into Canada', Centre for Strategic and International Studies (CSIS), 'Does China dominate global investment?' http://chinapower.csis.org/china-foreign-direct-investment/ (last accessed 20 January 2017). Further, China FDI into the United States is in the range of US$38 to US$47 billion (in 2014–2015), whereas Chinese FDI stock in Canada was C$16.6 billion at the end of 2013. Global Affairs Canada (GAC), 'Canada-China Foreign Investment Promotion and Protection Agreement (FIPA) Negotiations' www.international.gc.ca/trade-agreements-accords-commerciaux/agr-acc/fipa-apie/china-chine.aspx?lang=eng (last accessed 20 January 2017). Diego Leis, 'The Sino-Canadian Foreign Investment Promotion and Protection Agreement: Presentation and Challenges', 2 https://papers.ssrn.com/sol3/papers.cfm?abstract_id=2194817 (last accessed 29 January 2017). Dollar (n 6) 11.

[27] Gus Van Harten, *Sold Down the Yangtze: Canada's Lopsided Investment Deal with China* (IIAPP 2015) 11 http://digitalcommons.osgoode.yorku.ca/faculty_books/270 (last accessed 20 January 2017).

[28] An example of such security concerns of both the United States' government and public is the operation of Chinese SOEs in the US' sensitive sectors, as to hacking, as well as territorial claims in the South and East China Seas. Gantz (n 2) 240.

[29] Namely, with the backdrop of various WTO disputes between the US and China, there are political concerns by the US government, manifesting as a level of distrust as to whether the Chinese would voluntarily comply with the provisions of a bilateral agreement. Carter (n 7) 217.

[30] Specifically, in the natural gas and mining (nickel, copper, iron ore, and potash) sector. Eric Girard, 'A Closer Look at the Canada-China Foreign Investment Promotion and Protection Agreement' (2012) 23, 35 http://ssrn.com/abstract=2230940 (last accessed 25 January 2017): 'In 2012, Chinese investment in Canada (about US$20 million), mostly in the energy sector, exceeded Chinese investment in the United States (about US$10 million)'. Gantz (n 2) 232.

[31] Peterson Institute for International Economics (n 17) 4, 34 https://piie.com/publications/piie-briefings/toward-us-china-investment-treaty (last accessed 25 January 2017). Sean Miner and Gary Hufbauer, 'State-owned Enterprises and Competition Policy: The US Perspective' in Peterson Institute for International Economics, *Toward a US-China Investment Treaty* (2015) 17 https://piie.com/publications/piie-briefings/toward-us-china-investment-treaty (last accessed 25 January 2017).

US investment in the Chinese market.[32] Reciprocally, China's concerns appear to be concentrated on the scope and practice of the Committee on Foreign Investment in the United States (CFIUS) in the investment screening review process, where China has sought equality and transparency for its investors.[33] Another consideration of the United States, that encourages it to maintain high investment legal standards, is the effect of establishing an undesired precedent in its future negotiations with other BRICS nations or Vietnam.[34]

III. Market Access, Admission of Investment, and Investment Protection

China has gradually expanded the operation of the national treatment obligation by removing those restrictions and qualifications that were implemented, particularly prior to 2000. This expansion can be explained by the deepening acceptance of national treatment in China's domestic law, particularly following China's accession to the WTO Agreement in 2001.[35]

China's commitments of national treatment have been traditionally restrictive, providing Chinese authorities with deference to discriminate against foreign investors under China's domestic laws.[36] Yet, there have been developments with respect to national treatment throughout the 2000s. China's national treatment obligation was more restricted, qualified by a best effort commitment, granted 'without prejudice to [the host state's] laws and regulations'.[37] With developed states, China's national treatment obligation was relatively less restricted (in the form of a grandfathering clause), allowing China to maintain those existing domestic laws that are incompatible with national treatment, but with an obligation not to escalate any discriminatory treatment, and to gradually remove such measures.[38] Yet, this grandfathering clause was often applied asymmetrically in Chinese BITs, such that the counterparty's national treatment obligation was absolute and unqualified.[39] These developments stopped short of including the pre-establishment phase of the foreign investor's interests, such that the host country maintained discretion to admit and deny entry of foreign investments.[40] These qualifications were likely made to protect infant and other sensitive industries, preserving the competitiveness of Chinese SOEs that dominated the domestic industrial landscape; where granting pre-establishment national treatment would likely erode the competitiveness of domestic industries by those foreign investors with more advanced levels of economic and technological development.[41]

---

[32] ibid. These practices are often focused on manufacturing firms and service providers.

[33] ibid. China seeks transparency in terms of both the decision criteria and the decision-making process. The CFIUS reviews those investment proposals that can impede the national security of the United States. These concerns are explained further below.

[34] Gantz (n 2) 213.

[35] Wei Wang, 'Historical Evolution of National Treatment in China' (2005) 39 The International Lawyer 759, 778 (Protocol on the Accession of the People's Republic of China http://unpan1.un.org/intradoc/groups/public/documents/APCITY/UNPAN002123.pdf (last accessed 23 January 2017).

[36] Berger (n 3) 10. [37] This was particularly so prior to 2008. Berger (n 3) 9.

[38] This practice commenced with the China–Netherlands BIT (2001). Berger (n 3) 9.

[39] See China's BITs with the Netherlands (2001), Germany (2003), Finland (2004), Czech Republic (2005), Korea (2007), and Switzerland (2009). Berger (n 3) 10.

[40] Wang (n 35) 337.

[41] ibid. 'The aim of protecting infant industries—and especially state-owned enterprises from foreign competition—may serve as an explanation in this regard'. Berger (n 3) 8. Carter (n 7) 210.

In contrast, Canada's practice,[42] like that of the United States,[43] was more expansive and included all phases of the investment to be accorded with national treatment (pre- and post-establishment protection).

In terms of the Canada–China FIPA agreement, the market access through the national treatment obligation is restricted along two planes. First, and conforming with Chinese practice, it excludes the establishment phase. The national treatment obligation extends only to the 'expansion, management, conduct, operation, and sale or other disposition' phase of the investment.[44] Secondly, the national treatment obligation follows the trend of incorporating the grandfathering qualification such that existing discriminatory measures (that would otherwise not conform with the national treatment obligation) are not precluded.[45]

On the basis of China's traditional approach, particularly the Canada–China FIPA, what can we predict about the scope of the national treatment obligation of the US–China BIT and future Chinese BITs? Given China's desire to obtain opportunities for its outward investors, it is reasonable to suggest that the United States would reciprocally obtain more favourable market access in some form. Indeed, based on the reporting of the treaty negotiations to date, the US–China BIT will diverge from China's traditional practice and contain a national treatment obligation that covers the establishment phase of the investment, yet is subject to a negative list.[46] A negative list allows foreign investors market access to all economic sectors and industries that are not specifically prohibited on the list.[47] As such, China's level market access will largely depend on the content and scope of the negative list. China has adopted a negative list in terms of its own policies, namely through its pilot Shanghai Free Trade Zone.[48] Whether it is not known how liberal the negative list of the US–China BIT will be,[49] it is likely that China's markets of financial services, telecommunications, media and broadcasting, agriculture, fishing, and transportation will be the target of the United States, where the existing barriers to foreign investment are high.[50] Other potential counterparties

---

[42] Canadian model FIPPA (2004) art 3(1). Céline Lévesque and Andrew Newcombe, 'Canada' in Chester Brown (ed), *Commentaries on Selected Model Investment Treaties* (OUP 2013) 16. Examples of Canadian BITs include the Canada–Mali BIT (signed 28 November 2014, entered into force 8 June 2016), Canada–Côte d'Ivoire BIT (signed 30 November 2014, entered into force 14 December 2015) and Canada–Republic of Korea FTA (signed 23 September 2014, entered into force 1 January 2015).

[43] US Model BIT (2004) art 3; US Model BIT (2012) art 3.

[44] Canada–China FIPA art 6. Namely, the terms 'establishment' and 'acquisition', which are included in various Canadian BITs, are omitted.

[45] ibid art 8(2)(a)(i). As such, the state is permitted to continue to discriminate in favour of domestic investors based on existing discriminatory measures, and only new discriminatory measures are precluded.

[46] US–China Strategic and Economic Dialogue (S&ED). US Department of Treasury, 'Joint U.S.-China Economic Track Fact Sheet of the Fifth Meeting of the U.S.-China Strategic and Economic Dialogue' (2013) 1 www.treasury.gov/press-center/press-releases/Pages/jl2010.aspx accessed on 16 January 2017. Miner and Hufbauer (n 31) 16.

[47] Miner and Hufbauer (n 31) 16.

[48] Jeffrey Schott and Cathleen Cimino, 'The China-Japan-Korea Trilateral Investment Agreement: Implications for US Policy and the US-China Bilateral Investment Treaty' in Peterson Institute for International Economics, *Toward a US-China Investment Treaty* (2015) 11 https://piie.com/publications/piie-briefings/toward-us-china-investment-treaty (last accessed 25 January 2017).

[49] As to the content of the typical/previous negative list of the United States BITs see US–China Business Council, 'Summary of US Negative Lists in Bilateral Investment Treaties' (2014) 1 www.uschina.org/sites/default/files/Negative%20list%20summary.pdf (last accessed 20 January 2017).

[50] Michael Martina, 'China, U.S. swap investment treaty "negative lists"' *Reuters* (2015) 1 www.reuters.com/article/china-usa-investment-idUSL3N0YY2R920150612 (last accessed 20 January 2017). Sara Hsu, 'The China-US Bilateral Investment Treaty: Next Week?' *The Diplomat* (2015) 1

of China that offer similar investment opportunities for China's outwards investors (particularly the European Union, ranked above the US and Canada combined as a destination of Chinese FDI)[51] are likely to obtain the same negative list approach.

The liberalization of investment screening rules is another area of resistance in China's BIT strategy. While it is not unusual for most nations to reserve an amount of discretion to regulate the admission of foreign investment according to their internal laws and regulations, China's regulatory framework is significantly less prescriptive and more ambiguous.[52] Every foreign investment must be approved by the responsible authority,[53] where China's legal framework operates through a list of prescribed industries where foreign investment is encouraged, permitted, restrictive, and prohibited.[54] While China established a series of mandatory security review laws in 2009, broad grounds denying which investments are admitted into China (or the expanding of existing investments) remain, which include the stability of the national economy, social order, and those key technologies related to national security.[55]

Similarly, Canada's BIT practice maintains its domestic apparatus to screen the establishment of an investment in its territory. Under the Investment Canada Act, the federal Canadian government may prevent a foreign takeover or investment if they believe that it will not provide a 'net benefit' to Canada, or that 'could be injurious to national security'.[56]

Yet, the approach taken in the Canada–China FIPA, which maintains discretion under each party's respective domestic laws to screen investment, gives rise to a non-reciprocal, or asymmetrical, application. That is, the Canada–China FIPA states that Canada may screen Chinese investments in accordance with the Investment Canada Act, while China retains the right to screen Canadian investment under any of its 'Laws, Regulations and Rules relating to the regulation of foreign investment'.[57] As such, in the absence of expressly referring to any particular domestic law of China, the discretion provided to China to screen investments are potentially broader than those circumscribed under Canada's Investment Canada Act. This effect is intensified by certain limitations of the Investment Canada Act itself as a framework for investment screening. For example, the legislation only allows the government to block an investment if it involves the takeover of a Canadian company,[58] and significantly, those

---

http://thediplomat.com/2015/09/the-china-us-bilateral-investment-treaty-next-week/ (last accessed 20 January 2017).

[51] The European Union is the second ranked destination of Chinese FDI (both in terms of stocks and flows), following Asia, after adjustments of OFDI have been made to account for stop-over destinations such as Hong Kong and offshore centres in the Caribbean. Alicia Garcia-Herrero, 'China's Outbound Foreign Direct Investment' (n 26) 7–8.

[52] Girard (n 30) 24.

[53] Cai Congyan, 'China' in Wenhua Shan (ed), *The Legal Protection of Foreign Investment: A Comparative Study* (Hart Publishing 2012) 259.

[54] The list of which industries fall within each category is set out in the Guidance Catalogue of Industries for Foreign Investment. Girard (n 30) 35.

[55] Circular of the General Office of the State Council on the Establishment of a Security Review System Regarding Mergers and Acquisition of Domestic Enterprises by Foreign Investors, published by China's State Council http://english.mofcom.gov.cn/article/policyrelease/aaa/201103/20110307430493.shtml (last accessed 25 January 2017) 2017. Vivian Bath, 'The Quandary for Chinese Regulators: Controlling the Flow of Investment into and out of China' in V Bath and L Nottage (eds), *Foreign Investment and Dispute Resolution Law and Practice in Asia* (Routledge 2011) 70.

[56] Girard (n 30) 26. Investment Canada Act, RSC 1985, c 28 (1st Supp) s 25.2(1).

[57] Canada–China FIPA Annex D.34 (Exclusions). Further, the footnote elaborates that for 'China, "national security review" may include a review of various forms of investments for national security purposes'.

[58] Such that greenfield investments are not covered. Investment Canada Act, RSC 1985 (1st Supp) c 28, s 14(1).

foreign takeovers of Canadian firms may proceed without any review where a foreign-owned company is expanding an existing business in Canada.[59] Further, under the Canada–China FIPA, as an 'expansion' of an investment is only covered by the national treatment obligation where prior approval is not required under existing laws (which applies to Canada only),[60] the asymmetrical relationship between Canada and China is intensified.[61] As such, an asymmetry of obligations between China and Canada arises with respect to these screening requirements, such that China has significantly more discretion and vagary to reject Canadian investments.

In the context of the US–China BIT negotiations, China criticized CFIUS (the Committee on Foreign Investment in the United States), which screens foreign investment, as unfairly obstructing investment on the basis of national security concerns, particularly those investments of Chinese SOEs.[62] Reciprocally, the US is concerned with China's broad concept of national security, which incorporates economic and social factors.[63] In light of these concerns, it has been reported that the United States and China have committed to limit scope of domestic national security review under equal standards.[64]

Conceptually, the United States BIT standard for admitting/refusing entry of an investment consists of whether the US 'essential security interests' are adequately protected.[65] CFIUS, operating under the Foreign Investment and National Security Act (FINSA)[66] has a mandate to investigate the effect of an investment transaction on national security 'if the transaction is a government-controlled transaction', 'the transaction threatens to impair national security', or 'results in the control of a critical piece of US infrastructure by a foreign person'.[67] These decisions made under FINSA are not subject to judicial review.[68] The particular criticism by the Chinese government with respect to the CFIUS process is that it is unfair to Chinese investment and not

---

[59] Investment Canada Act s 38; Industry Canada, 'Investment Canada Act: Related-Business Guidelines' www.ic.gc.ca/eic/site/ica-lic.nsf/eng/lk00064.html#p2 (last accessed 20 January 2017). See also Van Harten (n 27) 3, 23–4.

[60] China's mandatory security review laws cover both the admission and expansion of investments. See Bath (n 55) 70.

[61] Canada–China FIPA art 6(3), which states that: 'The concept of "expansion" in this Article applies only with respect to sectors not subject to a prior approval process under the relevant sectoral guidelines and applicable laws, regulations and rules in force at the time of expansion. The expansion may be subject to prescribed formalities and other information requirements'.

[62] China will likely seek transparent and politically stable operating environment for its SOEs operating in the US, especially at pre-establishment phase. See Gloudeman and Salidjanova (n 3) 13, 18.

[63] ibid 14.

[64] 'The United States and China commit to limit the scope of their respective national security reviews of foreign investments (for the United States, the CFIUS process) solely to issues that constitute national security concerns, and not to generalize the scope of such reviews to include other broader public interest or economic issues. The United States and China commit that their respective national security reviews apply the same rules and standards under the law to each investment reviewed, regardless of country of origin'. The White House, Office of the Press Secretary, 'FACT SHEET: U.S.-China Economic Relations' (2015) 1 www.whitehouse.gov/the-press-office/2015/09/25/fact-sheet-us-china-economic-relations (accessed 27 January 2017).

[65] US Model BIT (2012) art 18 contains an exception, which states 'Nothing in this Treaty shall be construed to preclude a Party from applying measures that it considers necessary for … the protection of its own essential security interests'. It has been argued that this security exception clause that is 'broad enough' for CFIUS and the president to review investment transactions considered necessary for the protection of its essential security interests. However, this principle has never been tested in practice, leaving the question 'unresolved'. Daniel Chow, 'Why China Wants a Bilateral Investment Treaty with the United States' (2014) Ohio State Public Law Working Paper No 268, 15 https://papers.ssrn.com/sol3/papers.cfm?abstract_id=2479893 (last accessed 31 January 2017).

[66] Foreign Investment and National Security Act of 2007, 50 USC app § 2170 [50 USC 401 ff].

[67] Chow (n 65) 11.   [68] ibid 11–12.

transparent.[69] Reciprocally, the US is exposed to the broader ambiguous, and perhaps asymmetrical, application of national security factors under China's domestic law. The principal issue surrounding the negotiations of the US–China BIT will be whether the parties utilize the opportunity to clearly circumscribe the level of discretion of each state to preclude or prevent the admission of an investment in its territory, with a transparent process, in order to prevent any potential unequal effect, as that contained in the Canada–China FIPA.[70]

Within a network of multiple BITs containing a variety of legal standards, the MFN obligation can form the thread that unifies and harmonizes such standards across BITs and between various signatory states over time.[71] MFN can thereby be the mortar as bilateral and regional investment arrangements evolve, perhaps towards a multilateral investment regime. However, the MFN obligation can also (if so, only transiently throughout this evolving process) create an asymmetry between the parties, depending on the scope of the obligation and BIT history between the signatories. The Canada–China FIPA is such an example; a fusion of two distinct ideologies of investment norms.

China's and Canada's BIT practice consistently applies both the pre- and post-establishment phases on the investment (full MFN).[72] As such, each state is obligated to provide investors of the counterparty the best treatment as to the admission of investments that each of them grants to investors of any third state.[73]

As such, it is no surprise that the Canada–China FIPA contains MFN for the pre-establishment and post-establishment phases of the investment.[74] Yet, the MFN treatment obligation is *de jure* asymmetrical. While the standard between each party appears to be facially neutral, the differences in each party's history of BIT standards generates an asymmetrical application, providing opportunities for each party to access better rights.

The Canada–China FIPA provides equally limiting MFN treatment extended through the parties' BITs entered into after 1 January 1994,[75] and preclude free trade agreements (or customs unions).[76] Yet the application of the standard of treatment largely depends on the extent of China's and Canada's key obligations (such as national treatment and fair and equitable treatment) granted to third party states (and ultimately to the investors of that third state), both prospectively and retrospectively (but after 1994). The consequence is that Chinese investors obtain broader market access

---

[69] Hufbauer and others (n 25) 34.

[70] Hufbauer and others (n 25) 34. Peterson Institute for International Economics (n 17) 4.

[71] Investment/trade law principles such as national treatment and MFN are designed to unify and harmonize the legal order of standards of treatment to foreign investors. Tony Cole, 'Boundaries of Most Favored Nation Treatment' (2012) 33 Michigan Journal of International Law 539.

[72] That is, such BITs include the term 'admission' or 'establishment' in the list of investment phases covered by the MFN clause. Berger (n 3) 11; Lévesque and Newcombe (n 42) 77. Recent Chinese IIAs include the China–Latvia BIT (2004), the China–Finland BIT (2004), the China–Korea BIT (2007), the China–New Zealand PTIA (2008), the China–Peru PTIA (2009), the China–ASEAN BIT (2009), and the China–Korea–Japan BIT (2012).

[73] Berger (n 3) 7, 11. Both Canada and China have followed the general practice of restricting MFN obligations to apply to treatment of ISDS procedures. For China, this has been the general practice since 2008.

[74] Canada–China FIPA art 5.

[75] ibid art 8(1)(b) states that the MFN provision does not apply to 'treatment accorded under any bilateral or multi-lateral international agreement in force prior to 1 January 1994'.

[76] ibid art 8(1)(a) states that the MFN provision does not apply to 'treatment by a Contracting Party pursuant to any existing or future bilateral or multi-lateral agreement ... establishing, strengthening or expanding a free trade area or customs union'.

rights through the formulation of the pre- and post-establishment national treatment obligation that has been included in previous Canadian BITs (such as the Canada–Mali BIT (2014) and Canada–Côte d'Ivoire BIT (2004)).[77] In light of China's tradition of not extending pre-establishment national treatment obligation, this benefits Chinese investors, not Canadian. Reciprocally however, Canadian investors could obtain better rights (relative to Chinese investors) through third party BITs containing a national treatment obligation not qualified by the 'like circumstances' language (such as the China–Switzerland BIT (2009), China–India BIT (2006), and the China–Portugal BIT (2009))[78] that has been included in various Canadian BITs with after 1994.[79] Similarly, Canadian investors could obtain, relative to Chinese investors, better fair and equitable treatment (FET) obligations offered under various Chinese BITs, such as those that provide an autonomous standard without a qualifying connection to the customary international law standard of treatment to aliens.[80]

Indeed, the US–China BIT could be exposed to a similar risk of asymmetry, particularly in light of the convergent US and Canadian practice following the NAFTA, and specifically with respect to the national treatment and FET obligation (discuss below).[81] The effects of the asymmetry can be aggravated or mitigated, depending on the legal and economic circumstances between the parties. It may be aggravated for counterparties like Canada and the United States, which import significantly more FDI from China (than the inverse), exposing that state to more ISDS claims.[82] The effects may be mitigated, where Canadian investors in China could benefit from obligations China provides in future BITs, including the US–China BIT itself, given that the MFN clause applies prospectively. Arguably, if the United States is provided with a national treatment obligation that includes the pre-establishment phase of the Chinese's investments (*albeit* restricted by a negative list), Canadian investors in China could equally access this broader obligation.[83] Indeed, this is the very purpose of the MFN obligation; to provide equal treatment between the counterparties of the various BITs entered into by a party.[84] Of course, these effects can be specifically circumscribed by the parties, by explicitly restricting such an application in the primary treaty.

Therefore, looking at the overall effect of nation treatment and MFN obligations, and investment screening discretion, if we were to assess China's level of divergence

---

[77] Canada–Mali BIT (signed 28 November 2014, entered into force 8 June 2016); Canada–Côte d'Ivoire BIT (signed 30 November 2014, entered into force 14 December 2015).

[78] China–Switzerland BIT (signed 27 January 2009, entered into force 13 April 2010), China–Portugal BIT (signed 9 December 2005, entered into force 26 July 2008). Both Switzerland and Portugal have generally negotiated on the basis of a 'European style' (which is to say 'old') model BIT. Similarly, the 'like circumstance' language is also not included in the China–India BIT (signed 21 November 2006, entered into force 1 August 2007).

[79] Lévesque and Newcombe (n 42) 77. For example, the Canada–Croatia BIT (signed 3 February 1997, entered into force 30 January 2001), the Canada–Czech Republic BIT (signed 6 May 2009, entered into force 22 January 2012), and the Canada–Nigeria Foreign Investment Promotion and Protection Agreement (FIPA) (signed 6 May 2014, yet to enter into force).

[80] This standard has been interpreted to be a measure 'sufficiently egregious and shocking – a gross denial of justice, manifest arbitrariness, blatant unfairness, a complete lack of due process, evident discrimination, or a manifest lack of reasons'. For example, *Waste Management., Inc. v United Mexican States*, ICSID Case No ARB(AF)/00/3, Award (30 April 2004) para 98 and *William Ralph Clayton, William Richard Clayton, Douglas Clayton, Daniel Clayton and Bilcon of Delaware Inc. v Government of Canada*, UNCITRAL, PCA Case No 2009-04, paras 442–3.

[81] Canadian model FIPPA (2004) arts 4, 5; Model BIT (2012) arts 3, 5.

[82] Van Harten (n 27) 4.

[83] The benefit of obtaining full MFN does not directly liberalize China's domestic policies, but it offers (to Canadian investors) the prospect of benefiting from any future concessions in this regard.

[84] Tony Cole, *The Structure of Investment Arbitration* (Routledge 2013) 124.

from traditional practice of market access liberalization for a capital exporting state like Canada, the Canada–China FIPA represents a modest change. That is, China has not further liberalized its investment regime (other than indirectly, and perhaps inadvertently, through MFN treatment afforded to third party states), nor provided market access to Canada's investors, through the national treatment obligation or investment screening exceptions. That stated, in light of bargaining power and investment opportunities for Chinese investors, we expect that US investors will be offered more market access than Canadian investors under the Canada–China FIPA.[85] However, the extent of that market access offered by China but will depend on the content on the negative list. Similarly, compared to the Canada–China FIPA, there is a greater prospect that each state's screening admission process prescribed in the US–China BIT will be transparent and equal. This is perhaps a result of the unique complaints of China arising against the United States, which fade in comparison to Canada's (and others, such as the European Union). Given this foreseeable progression of market access of China may be largely reflective of China's greater desire to increase investment flows of its investors into the United States, China's approach is unlikely to apply equally to all future counterparties, especially capital importing states.[86]

IV. Minimum Standard of Treatment and Expropriation

China's recent BIT practice (particularly since 2008) has been to include an obligation to accord a minimum standard of treatment that is referenced to be in accordance with the 'international law minimum standard of treatment of aliens' or expressly as that of 'customary international law'.[87] Specifically, that standard is stated to be no more than 'that which is required by the international law minimum standard of treatment of aliens as evidenced by general State practice accepted as law',[88] a formulation that is almost identical to that contained in Canada's model FIPPA (2004).[89] Yet in the Canada–China FIPA, there is no reference to 'customary' international law, nor state practice and *opinio juris*.[90] While this may due to the China's traditional position of rejecting customary international law as a Western legal norm, it is likely to be an anomaly that is inconsistent with China's recent BIT practice.[91]

As the United States has similarly taken to this formulation of the international law standard of treatment (but usually circumscribes in further detail the meaning and content of 'fair and equitable treatment')[92] the US–China BIT will likely include a minimum standard of treatment that is referenced to customary international law.

---

[85] That also accords with the status of the reported US–China BIT negotiations, above.

[86] Whether that relationship provides a long-term conversion of a more liberal investment regime and environment in China remains a live question.

[87] Recent BITs include the China–Seychelles BIT (2007), the China–Costa Rica BIT (2007), the China–New Zealand PTIA (2008), the China–Colombia BIT (2008), the China–Peru PTIA (2009), the China–Japan–Korea BIT (2012). The China–Mexico BIT (2008), for example, does not reference customary international law, as such, but does refer to 'international law minimum standard of treatment of aliens as evidence of State practice and *opinio juris*'. Berger (n 3) 10.

[88] Canada–China FIPA art 4(2).

[89] Canada model FIPPA art 5(2), which states: 'The concepts of "fair and equitable treatment" and "full protection and security" in paragraph 1 do not require treatment in addition to or beyond that which is required by the customary international law minimum standard of treatment of aliens'.

[90] Canada–China FIPA art 4.

[91] Cai, 'China-US BIT Negotiation and the Future of Investment Treaties Regime' (n 24) 468.

[92] These formulations, expressed in the Canadian model FIPPA (2004) and the US Model BIT (2004), are based on the 2001 NAFTA Free Trade Commission's Statement on NAFTA art 1105(1).

China's traditional expropriation obligation is generally phrased and did not expressly cater for indirect expropriation.[93] However, in the recent BIT with Japan and Korea, China has agreed to include indirect expropriation, restricted to apply only in 'rare circumstances', such as when the host state's measures are severe or disproportionate to their purpose and not where regulatory actions are non-discriminatory and for a 'legitimate public welfare' purpose.[94] This formulation, intended to provide states with space to adopt public welfare regulatory measures, is very similar to that contained in the Canada–China FIPA,[95] as well as the US Model BIT (2012).[96]

In light of the recent convergence of practice, the US–China BIT is likely to maintain obligations of both indirect and direct expropriation. Further, given the strict regulatory measures China is anticipated to invoke (such as pollution controls),[97] it is difficult to comprehend why China will not adopt similar parameters as the Protocol contained in the Japan and Korea trilateral agreement; excluding from indirect expropriation those regulatory measures invoked for 'legitimate public welfare objectives'.

V. Performances Requirements

China has rarely included any obligations precluding performance requirements in its investment agreements and specifically only in FTAs (not BITs).[98] Performance requirements are imposed requirements on investors as a condition to investing in the host state, and can usually take the form of requirements to export a percentage of their production or to source imports domestically (use local products, services, or labour).[99] China imposed these performance requirements (specifically, local content

Lee Caplan and Jeremy Sharpe, 'United States' in Chester Brown (ed), *Commentaries on Selected Model Investment Treaties* (OUP 2013) 775–7, 782; 2004 US Model BIT (2004) art 5 and US Model BIT (2012) art 5. See also CAFTA-DR Free Trade Agreement, Dominican Republic-Central America, (signed 5 August 2004) art 10.5, The Free Trade Agreement, United States-South Korea (KORUS) (signed 15 March 2012) art 11.5.

[93] See eg the China–Peru FTA art 133. Recent Chinese investment agreements have avoided the incorporation of the Hull Rule of 'prompt, adequate and effective compensation'. Carter (n 7) 239.

[94] China–Japan–Korea Trilateral Investment Agreement (2012) Protocol art 2(c).

[95] Canada–China FIPA, Annex B.10 art 3, which states: 'Except in rare circumstances, such as if a measure or series of measures is so severe in light of its purpose that it cannot be reasonably viewed as having been adopted and applied in good faith, a non-discriminatory measure or series of measures of a Contracting Party that is designed and applied to protect the legitimate public objectives for the well-being of citizens, such as health, safety and the environment, does not constitute indirect expropriation'.

[96] US Model BIT (2012), Annex B art 4(b), which states: 'Except in rare circumstances, non-discriminatory regulatory actions by a Party that are designed and applied to protect legitimate public welfare objectives, such as public health, safety, and the environment, do not constitute indirect expropriations'. See also CAFTA-DR, Annex 10-C art 4(b).

[97] Van Harten (n 27) 222.

[98] China has included performance requirements in the China–New Zealand FTA (2008) art 140 and the China–Korea–Japan FTA (2012) art 7. Wenhua Shan and Norah Gallagher, 'International Investment in China and the BIT Programme' in Norah Gallagher and Wenhua Shan (eds), *Chinese Investment Treaties: Policies and Practice* (OUP 2009), Wenhua Shan and Norah Gallagher, 'China' in Chester Brown (ed), *Commentaries on Selected Model Investment Treaties* (OUP 2013). Chester Brown, 'The Development by States of Model Bilateral Investment Treaties' in Wenhua Shan and Jinyuan Su (eds), *China and International Investment Law: Twenty Years of ICSID Membership* (Martinus Nijhoff 2014) 124.

[99] See Julien Chaisse, 'Renewables Re-energized? The Internationalization of Green Energy Investment Rules and Disputes' (2016) 10(1) Journal of World Energy Law & Business 269. See also Muthucumaraswamy Sornarajah, *The International Law on Foreign Investment* (3rd edn, Cambridge University Press 2010) 205.

requirements and technology transfer requirements) on foreign investors in order to advance its own economic interests.[100] The absence of obligations precluding performance requirements can also be explained by China's traditional approach of balancing the encouragement and promotion of investment with expressions of state sovereignty and national jurisdiction.[101] In those rare FTAs where China has adopted performance requirement restrictions, it incorporates into the Investment Chapter the WTO obligations of the Agreement on Trade-Related Investment Measures (TRIMs Agreement). In effect, investors are provided with a direct right to enforce certain performance requirements through investor–State arbitration, with the potential to award damages as compensation for retrospective loss.[102] This approach is an interesting extension of certain WTO obligations that were previously only enforceable by states under the Dispute Settlement Understanding.[103]

In contrast, Canada's (and the United States') practice[104] has been to provide a comprehensive list of restrictions on performance requirements, which encompasses both local content and technology transfer requirements.[105] Namely, it prohibits requirements 'to transfer a particular technology, a production process, or other proprietary knowledge to a person' in the other's territory.[106]

The Canada–China BIT adopts China's recent FTA practice of directly incorporating the norms expressed under the WTO TRIMs obligations. It is not clear what the effect will be. The Canada–China FIPA obligations cover Canada and China's existing obligations under the Article 2 and the Annex TRIMs Agreement,[107] which require states not to impose quantitative restrictions (Article XI of General Agreement on Tariffs and Trade, or GATT)[108] and not to discriminate between foreign and domestic investors in the case of performance requirements (through Article III of the

---

[100] Berger (n 3) 1. See Gloudeman and Salidjanova (n 3) 17.

[101] Gallagher and Shan (n 98) 37.

[102] For example, China–New Zealand FTA (2008) art 140 and the China–Korea–Japan FTA (2012) art 7.

[103] Understanding Governing the Settlement of Disputes, Marrakesh Agreement Establishing the World Trade Organization Annex 2, 1869 UNTS 401 (DSU).

[104] This is a departure from Canada's Model FIPPA (2004) and Canada's BITs that prohibit performance requirements. Van Harten (n 27) 3.

[105] 2012 US Model BIT art 8(1)(f); Canada Model FIPPA art 7(1)(f).

[106] 2012 US Model BIT art 8(1)(f); Canada Model FIPPA art 7(1)(f). The US Model BIT contains an additional requirement to ban requirements use technology supplied by the host country or its producers where the result is to afford protection to local suppliers. 2012 US Model BIT art 8(1)(h).

[107] Canada–China FIPA art 9. The Annex is an illustrative list of measures agreed to be inconsistent.

[108] 'The TRIMs agreement prohibits investment measures that violate GATT [General Agreement on Tariffs and Trade] Article III obligations to treat imports no less favorably than domestic products or the GATT Article XI obligation not to impose quantitative restrictions on imports.' Office of the US Trade Representative, '2014 USTR Report to Congress on China's WTO Compliance' (2014) 87 https://ustr.gov/sites/default/files/2014-Report-to-Congress-Final.pdf (last accessed 25 January 2017). US Department of State, 'China Investment Climate Statement 2015' (2015) 20 www.state.gov/documents/organization/241728.pdf (last accessed 25 January 2017). See also Directorate-General for External Policies of the Union, Investor–State Dispute Settlement (ISDS) provisions in the EU's international investment agreements (2014) 29 www.europarl.europa.eu/RegData/etudes/STUD/2014/534979/EXPO_STU(2014)534979(ANN01)_EN.pdf (last accessed 25 January 2017). '[I]t will be unclear whether to treat Performance requirements under the trade dispute settlement provisions on the basis of the national treatment principle and the prohibition of quantitative restriction or under the investment chapter ISDS or both'. Suzy Nikièma, 'IISD Best Practices Series: Performance Requirements in Investment Treaties' *International Institute for Sustainable Development*, 6–7, 11–12 www.iisd.org/sites/default/files/publications/best-practices-performance-requirements-investment-treaties-en.pdf (last accessed 25 January 2017).

GATT).[109] On the one hand, the Canada–China FIPA with the TRIMs standard is broader than the traditional Canadian/US approach, as the Canada–China FIPA does not prescribe certain reservations to the performance requirement obligation. These include reservations to exclude existing measures by sub-national (provincial and municipal) entities,[110] as well as those measures that protect the rights and preferences of aboriginal peoples or disadvantaged minorities, which are maintained in various Canadian BITs and FTAs.[111] On the other hand, the Canada–China FIPA, and TRIMs Agreement, does not expressly contain certain performance requirements (specifically, technology requirements) enumerated in Canadian and United States BITs.[112] The existence of that gap in technology requirements is likely to be a sensitive topic of the US–China BIT negotiations, in light of China's practice of requiring technology transfers in granting market access to US companies (directly or indirectly through encouragement).[113]

Similarly, there is uncertainty as to how the MFN clause will operate.[114] Will MFN in the Canada–China FIPA allow Chinese investors to access technology transfer requirement obligations contained in third party Canadian BITs? Can the GATT Article III:4 obligation be invoked through TRIMs Article 2 in order for Canadian investors to obtain pre-establishment national treatment obligations if only qualified by a remote connection to the TRIMs Agreement?[115] The successful outcome of these permutations will largely depend on what constitutes 'better treatment' and 'like circumstances' (as well as the language and scope of the MFN obligation in the primary treaty). A threshold issue is whether Article 2 of the TRIMs obligation (which, in turn,

[109] The TRIMs Agreement provides that no contracting party shall apply any trade-related investment measure inconsistent with Article III (national treatment) and Article XI (prohibition of quantitative restrictions) of the General Agreement on Tariffs and Trade (GATT). The Agreement on Trade-Related Investment Measures (15 April 1994) 1868 UNTS 186, which states: 'Without prejudice to other rights and obligations under GATT 1994, no Member shall apply any TRIM that is inconsistent with the provisions of Article III or Article XI of GATT 1994'.
[110] NAFTA art 1108(1)(a)(ii) and (iii), which states that the relevant obligations 'do not apply to … any existing non-conforming measure that is maintained by… a state or province … or … a local government'. NAFTA, Annex I and II (Schedule of Canada) states 'Canada reserves the right to adopt or maintain any measure denying investors of another Party and their investments, or service providers of another Party, any rights or preferences provided to aboriginal peoples'. Cited from Van Harten (n 59) 38–39. For a recent example of similar reservations see also Canada–Nigeria FIPA (signed 6 May 2014, yet to enter into force) Annex 1 art 17(2).
[111] Van Harten (n 27) 38.
[112] Canada FIPA (2004) art 7(1)(f); US Model BIT (2012) art 8(1)(f): 'When China joined the WTO in 2001, it committed to cease the enforcement of trade and foreign exchange balancing requirements, local content and export performance offsets, and technology transfer requirements under its TRIMs obligations. China also committed to enforce only those technology transfer rules that do not violate WTO standards on IP and TRIMs' US Department of State (May 2015), 'The Agreement on Trade-Related Investment Measures' (15 April 1994) 1868 UNTS 20. Gloudeman and Salidjanova (n 3) 16–17.
[113] While China has revised a number of investment measures to eliminate explicit requirements relating to local content and technology transfer, the revised measures are still criticized as encouraging such practices, particularly at the local, municipal, and provincial levels. These measures were revised in response to complaints from WTO members. Gantz (n 2) 237. US Department of State (n 112). Gloudeman and Salidjanova (n 3) 16–17.
[114] Nathalie Bernasconi-Osterwalder and others, 'Investment Treaties and Why They Matter to Sustainable Development: Questions and Answers' *International Institute for Sustainable Development* (2012) 25–32 www.iisd.org/pdf/2011/investment_treaties_why_they_matter_sd.pdf (last accessed 25 January 2017).
[115] Similarly, assuming the US–China BIT does provide any performance requirements, will the MFN obligation in the US–China BIT allow US investors in China to obtain this TRIMs obligation as better treatment?

incorporates other legal norms of trade from the GATT, constituting both relative standards (such as national treatment under GATT Article III) and absolute standards (such as quantitative restrictions, GATT Article XI)) constitutes a comparable class of treatment as that of any list provided in BITs of Canada and the United States.[116]

That stated, the inclusion of any performance requirements, regardless of the form (such as the TRIMs formula) and the practically reduced scope, is arguably a progressive step for China's BIT practice. As the practice of the United States is identical to that of Canada, the format of the performance requirement standard of the US–China BIT may mirror the Canada–China FIPA. The United States, however, may have more bargaining power to push to include restrictions on technology transfer requirements.

VI. Public Policy Exceptions

While China does not usually include express general exceptions for public policy regulations in their BITs, some (particularly the recent BITs) provide a framework to balance investment protection and the host state interests (public welfare effects).[117] Certain preambles, such as the China–New Zealand PTIA (2008), go as far as to expressly provide a 'right to regulate'.[118] China has also incorporated innovative provisions to maintain public welfare regulatory space. Namely, the China–Australia FTA (ChAFTA) contains a novel pre-emptory mechanism by which the states (China and Australia), after a claim has been initiated, may jointly determine that the measure alleged constitutes a 'legitimate public welfare objective' (as defined in the ChAFTA).[119] If the states jointly interpret the measure to accord with these welfare objectives, that interpretation is consequently binding on the tribunal when it renders its award.[120] This, however, is a novel approach of reserving regulatory space.

In contrast, Canada's practice (particularly since 2004)[121] is to include a general exception provision that expressly provides for enumerated categories of public welfare measures (namely, those that relate to the preservation of the environment, life, and health) with a '*chapeau*', or balancing test, that is very similar to that in GATT Article XX.[122] The text of the Canada–China FIPA adopts this Canadian

---

[116] MFN clauses are also subject to the *ejusdem generis* principle (whereby a MFN clause can only attract matters belonging to the same subject matter or the same category of subject as to which the clause relates), which has been used in their interpretation in several judicial and arbitral cases. Articles on Most-Favoured-Nation Clauses (ILC Draft), in *Yearbook of the International Law Commission* (1978) Vol II arts 9, 10 http://legal.un.org/ilc/texts/instruments/english/commentaries/1_3_1978.pdf (last accessed 29 January 2017). See also Van Harten (n 27) 39.

[117] For example, BITs with Trinidad and Tobago (2002) and Guyana (2003) contain a clause in the preamble, acknowledging that the promotion and protection of investment can be achieved without 'relaxing health, safety and environmental measures of general application'. Gallagher and Shan (n 98) 50.

[118] China–New Zealand PTIA (2008) preamble, which states: 'Upholding the rights of their governments to regulate in order to meet national policy objectives, and preserving their flexibility to safeguard the public welfare'.

[119] ChAFTA art 9.11(5)–(8). 'Measures of a Party that are non-discriminatory and for the legitimate public welfare objectives of public health, safety, the environment, public morals or public order shall not be the subject of a claim" by an investor'. See art 9.11(4). Anthea Roberts and Richard Braddock, 'Protecting Public Welfare Regulation Through Joint Treaty Party Control: a ChAFTA Innovation,' Columbia FDI Perspectives, No 176 (2016) 1.

[120] ChAFTA art 9.18(3).   [121] Canada Model FIPPA (2004) art 10.

[122] Canada Model FIPPA (2004) art 10; Canada Model FIPPA (2004) art 10(1)(a)–(c). A recent example is contained in the CETA art 28.3(1). 'In the WTO context, the approach taken

approach, thereby balancing the investment protections with public welfare objectives.[123]

The practice of the United States has somewhat diverged from that of Canada's in this respect, in that the United States' BITs usually limit the scope of specific substantive obligations for public welfare objectives, such as national treatment and MFN, rather than employ general exceptions that uniformly apply to all investment obligations.[124] As such, part of the textual and factual analysis in US BITs in determining whether foreign investments are treated discriminatively through national treatment and MFN, consists of a determination as to whether such measures are 'based on' legitimate public welfare objectives. A recent example is contained in the United States' Note of Interpretation the Trans-Pacific Partnership (TPP), which clarifies that 'like circumstances' depends on the totality of the circumstances, including whether the differential treatment was based on 'legitimate public welfare objectives'.[125] Given both the lack of consistent Chinese practice and the divergence of practice between China, Canada, and the United States, it is difficult to predict how public policy exceptions in the US–China BIT will be formulated. For other parties, it may depend on their respective practice.

For example, the EU will likely attempt to follow the Canadian approach of GATT Article XX-type exceptions for the China–EU FTA, especially in light of its recent practice in the CETA and the EU's proposed investment chapter of the Transatlantic Trade and Investment Partnership (TTIP) and EU–Vietnam FTA.[126]

in applying GATT Article XX is to achieve an effective balance between the obligation (eg not to discriminate between domestic and foreign products) and the policy justification'. Dickson-Smith (n 16) 791. This article also analyses the consequences of adopting this balancing test. See also Julien Chaisse, 'Exploring the Confines of International Investment and Domestic Health Protections: General Exceptions Clause as a Forced Perspective' (2013) 39(2–3) American Journal of Law & Medicine 332.

[123] Canada–China FIPA art 33. The *chapeau* states: 'Provided that such measures are not applied in an arbitrary or unjustifiable manner, or do not constitute a disguised restriction on international trade or investment'.

[124] Caplan and Sharpe (n 92) 775–7. Dickson-Smith (n 16) 786. However, for some obligations, such as indirect expropriation and performance requirements, the United States does incorporate a balancing mechanism somewhat similar to Article XX of GATT: see US Model (2012) BIT art 8(3)(c) Annex B art 4(b). However, particularly in the recent BITs of the United States, there are obligations not to 'waive or derogate' from or to fail to 'effectively enforce' domestic laws in order to encourage investment relating to environmental and labour standards. US Model (2012) BIT arts 12 and 13.

[125] Trans-Pacific Partnership (TPP) (signed 4 February 2016, yet to enter into force) ch 9 ('Investment') https://ustr.gov/sites/default/files/TPP-Final-Text-Investment.pdf (last accessed 19 January 2017); TPP, 'Drafters' Note on Interpretation of "In Like Circumstances" under Article 9.4 (National Treatment) and Article 9.5 (Most-Favoured-Nation Treatment)' para 2 www.tpp.mfat.govt.nz/assets/docs/Interpretation%20of%20In%20Like%20Circumstances.pdf (last accessed 18 January 2017).

[126] General exceptions designed on the basis of GATT Article XX arose from the Canadian treaty practice (in particular, the Canadian Model BIT (2004)) and have been included in recent investment treaties, such as the Australia–Korea FTA (signed 8 April 2014, entered into force 12 December 2014) art 22.1. The EU has also adopted the GATT Article XX-like clause in CETA. Dickson-Smith (n 16) 790. European Commission, 'Transatlantic Trade and Investment Partnership: Trade in Services, Investment and E-Commerce' (Proposal) (July 2015) ch 7 ('Exceptions') http://trade.ec.europa.eu/doclib/docs/2015/july/tradoc_153669.pdf (last accessed 19 January 2017). European Commission, EU–Vietnam Free Trade Agreement: Agreed text as of January 2016, 'Trade in Services, Investment and E-Commerce' ch 7 http://trade.ec.europa.eu/doclib/docs/2016/february/tradoc_154210.pdf (last accessed 19 January 2017).

VII. State-owned Enterprises (SOEs): A Sword That Cuts both Ways

The status of state-owned enterprises have become a vexed issue surrounding BIT practice, especially involving China, where its SOEs are highly integrated into the national economy.[127] China has a long history of SOEs, which exist in various forms (fully state-owned, joint enterprises, and shareholder limited corporations).[128] According to China's State Assets Supervision and Administration Commission (SASAC), control of SOEs was supposed to be limited to key sectors (defence, electricity, oil and petrochemicals, telecoms, coal, aviation, and shipping),[129] yet studies have indicated that SOEs have encroached into other non-strategic sectors (restaurants, retail, and low-end manufacturing).[130] A key issue surrounding SOEs is how a BIT can adequately and fairly address whether a SOE acts with commercial considerations and without state support, both at home and abroad, so as not gain an unfair competitive advantage.[131] The issue for BITs is thus twofold: whether the state is attributable for actions of SOEs and reciprocally, whether SOEs have standing to sue as an 'investor'. Restrictions on transparency makes the intentions of the SOE and the state difficult to measure; to adequately determine whether SOEs are accorded with special preferences (in the form of financial subsidy or granted monopolistic control) by their government and whether they are an instrument of the state, pursuing the policy goals of their government.[132]

China's BITs do not expressly state the relationship between the SOE and state responsibility.[133] Canada's practice on the other hand is somewhat more direct, expressly stating that the obligations under a BIT applies to 'any state enterprise' that is exercising government authority delegated to it.[134] China appears to have adopted

---

[127] In 2015, there were 150,000 SOEs in China, which dominate many sectors including aerospace, clean energy, biotechnology, oil, telecommunications, and railways. US–China Economic and Security Review Commission, Annual Report, Section 2: State–Owned Enterprises, Overcapacity, and China's Market Economy Status, 98–100 http://origin.www.uscc.gov/sites/default/files/Annual_Report/Chapters/Chapter%201,%20Section%202%20-%20State-Owned%20Enterprises,%20Overcapacity,%20and%20China's%20Market%20Economy%20Status.pdf (last accessed 19 January 2017): 'In 2014, there were 150,000 SOEs which accounted for 17 percent of urban employment'; Antonio Graceffo, 'State-owned Enterprises, Still a Major Force in the Chinese Economy and Abroad' https://brooklynmonk.wordpress.com/2015/10/13/state-owned-enterprises-still-a-major-force-in-the-chinese-economy-and-abroad/ (last accessed 19 January 2017). Further, '112 [of these 150,000 SOEs] are central SOEs directly under government control, while the municipal or provincial governments own the rest'. Chinese University of Hong Kong, 'China's State-Owned Enterprises Reform: Will It Work?' (2016) 1 https://cbkcuhk.wordpress.com/2016/01/05/china-state-owned-enterprises-reform-will-this-time-work/ (last accessed 27 January 2017).
[128] Miner and Hufbauer (n 31).
[129] Miner and Hufbauer (n 31) 17: 'Other sectors mentioned were equipment manufacturing, automobile manufacturing, electronics, constructions, steel, nonferrous metals, chemicals, surveying, and scientific research'.
[130] Miner and Hufbauer (n 31) 17. See also US Department of State, Investment Climate Statement (n 112).
[131] Paul Blyschak, 'State-owned Enterprises and International Investment Treaties When are State-Owned Entities and their Investments Protected?' 6 Journal of International Law and International Relations 1, 7–10. Miner and Hufbauer (n 31) 17. US Department of State, Investment Climate Statement (n 112) 24–6.
[132] Miner and Hufbauer (n 31) 20.
[133] Mark Feldman, 'The Standing of State-Owned Entities under Investment Treaties' in *Yearbook on International Investment Law & Policy 2010–2011* (OUP 2012) 631–4.
[134] Canada Model FIPPA (2004) art 8(4), which states: 'Each Party shall ensure, through regulatory control, administrative supervision or the application of other measures, that any state enterprise that it maintains or establishes acts in a manner that is not inconsistent with the Party's obligations

this approach in the text of the China–Canada FIPA, stating that the party's respective obligations applies to 'any entity' that exercises delegated governmental authority.[135]

Turning to whether, and how, SOEs are granted standing as investors, China does not typically expressly define a SOE as an investor and some of its BITs asymmetrically define SOEs, such that the Chinese SOEs are less likely to be granted standing.[136] Canada on the other hand usually defines 'enterprise' (which in turn, constitutes an 'investment') to encompass government-owned enterprises.[137] The Canada–China FIPA's definition of an investment is extensive enough to include a SOE, yet it does not contain an express reference to a state- or government-owned enterprise,[138] leaving that determination to be made by a tribunal.[139] However, there are not many determinations where a tribunal has examined the distinction between SOEs as states and SOEs as investors.[140]

The question as to whether the state is attributable for the acts of SOEs and whether SOEs can sue the host state is a very relevant and interesting issue surrounding the US–China BIT negotiations. It reveals the paradigm of a sword that cuts both ways for states, particularly China. On the one hand, China is likely to limit its exposure as the respondent for the acts (and omissions) of its SOEs.[141] On the other hand, it is part of China's national economic strategy to promote protections for outward investing Chinese SOEs,[142] it may be more likely to expressly provide its SOEs with the right to commence action against the United States for unfair and discriminatory measures.

---

under this Agreement *wherever such enterprise exercises any regulatory, administrative or other governmental authority that the Party has delegated to it …*' [emphasis added].

[135] Canada–China FIPA art 2.2. The provision states that: 'obligations … shall apply to *any entity* whenever that entity *exercises any regulatory, administrative or other governmental authority delegated* to it by that Contracting Party' [emphasis added]. Arguably, given the arrangement of this phrase, the 'regulatory' or 'administrative' authority need not be 'delegated', only 'other' governmental authority falling outside of these limits.

[136] Sometimes there is an asymmetrical definition of 'investor' between China and a counterparty (eg Qatar, Ghana) or silent (Uganda, Egypt). See China–Qatar BIT (signed April 1999) art 1(2)(b); China–Ghana BIT (signed 12 October 1989) art 1(b); China–Uganda BIT (signed 27 May 2004) art 1(2); China–Egypt BIT (signed 21 April 1994) art 1(2)(b): 'The BIT between China and Qatar, for example, defines "investor" in respect of Qatar to include "legal persons" including companies, general corporations, *public organizations, public and semi-public entities* constituted in accordance with the legislation of … Qatar and domiciled in its territory' [emphasis added]. However, the same article defines 'investor' in respect of China to include only 'economic entities established in accordance with the laws … of China and domiciled in the territory of … China'. A similar asymmetry exists in China's BIT with Ghana, where an identical definition of 'investor' in respect of China is provided while a Ghanaian 'investor' is defined to include 'state corporations and agencies and companies registered under the laws of Ghana which invest or trade abroad'. Therefore, while the definitions of Chinese investors under these treaties do nothing to expressly exclude the standing of Chinese SOEs, the express inclusion of SOEs within the definitions of Qatari and Ghanaian investors suggests that perhaps Chinese SOEs were not intended to be granted standing. Blyschak (n 131) 21–3.

[137] Canada–China FIPA art 1(1) and (10). Arguably, if the enterprise is not owned but it controlled, it may have standing to sue the host state.

[138] ibid art 1(1) and (10).

[139] Further, cases of SOEs as claimants in investment arbitration are not common. Blyschak (n 131) 19.

[140] Namely, in the *CSOB* case, the panel determined claims brought by SOEs constitute investor-state disputes as long as the activities of the SOE are commercial, 'even if the entity engages in activities that are "driven by" State governmental policies and is controlled by the State such that it is "required" to do the State's "bidding"'. Feldman (n 133) 616. *Československá Obchodní Banka, A.S. v Slovak Republic*, ICSID Case No ARB/97/4. Other cases that have provided some insight include *EDF (Services) Limited v Romania* (Award, 8 October 2009) ICSID Case No ARB/05/13 and *Bayindir Insaat Turizm Ticaret ve Sanayi A v Islamic Republic of Pakistan* (Award, 27 August 2009) ICSID Case No ARB/03/29.

[141] Gloudeman and Salidjanova (n 3) 18. Miner and Hufbauer (n 31) 17–19.   [142] ibid.

Given the inherent nature of the private/public dichotomy of investor–state rights and obligations,[143] China's approach towards labelling a SOE as a private investor may fuel its strategy of limiting its exposure to state responsibility for the acts of its own SOEs.

The US Model BIT (2012), like Canadian BITs, expressly extend state responsibility to those SOEs that have 'delegated' governmental authority,[144] and reciprocally, an 'enterprise' would arguably[145] extend to cover SOEs as an investor.[146] Indeed, negotiators of the United States intend that all obligations would effectively apply to SOEs, including coverage for Chinese government discrimination in favour of SOEs at the detriment of US companies.[147] Realistically however, the parties are likely to defer a determination of the factual circumstances, particularly the commercial nature of the SOE, its relationship of ownership and control between the entity and the state, to a tribunal.

As such, while there has been a marginal recent shift in the Canada–China FIPA towards expressly extending China's responsibility for discriminatory and unfair measures carried out by its SOEs, whether this shift will be adopted in the US–China BIT remains to be seen. Chinese SOEs, for example, comprise a significant proportion of investments in the United States (relative to, say, Canada).[148] Further, the question remains whether the definition provided in the Canada–China FIPA effectively does cover SOEs (namely, whether the SOEs in question have delegated government authority) and which disputing party (the investor or the respondent state) bears the burden of proof.

VIII. Investor–state Procedure: Extending the Theme of Asymmetry

In addition to using substantive obligations as markers of China's recent development of BITs, some aspects of the ISDS procedure deserve attention. These include requirements for an investor to commence a claim, the transparency of the process and the right of other stakeholders to obtain standing before a tribunal.[149] As with many ISDS provisions, China's BITs mandate a negotiation period of six months preceding the commencement of arbitration.[150] This process is complemented with a 'fork in the road' provision, requiring the investor to choose local court or arbitration.[151] Yet, when

---

[143] Larry Backer, 'Sovereign Investing in Times of Crisis: Global Regulation of Sovereign Wealth Funds, State-owned Enterprises, and the Chinese Experience' (2010) 19 Transnational Law & Contemporary Problems 3, 20, Micah Schwalb, 'International Law & State Corporatism' (2008) 73 http://papers.ssrn.com/sol3/papers.cfm?abstract_id=1350609 (last accessed 25 January 2017).

[144] US Model BIT (2012) art 2. The model BIT clarifies that delegated governmental authority includes 'a legislative grant, and a government order, directive, or other action transferring to the state enterprise or other person, or authorizing the exercise by the state enterprise or other person of, governmental authority'. US Model BIT (2012) art 2(2)(a), n 8.

[145] Blyschak (n 131) 20–6.

[146] US Model BIT (2012) art 1 ('enterprise), which includes 'privately or governmentally owned or controlled'.

[147] Gloudeman and Salidjanova (n 3) 18. Gantz (n 2) 221–2.

[148] It has been reported that, about 27 per cent of the total investments from China in the United States were by Chinese SOEs. Further, 'the SOE deals were generally larger than the deals of private Chinese investors, accounting for 42 percent, or over $18 billion, of total investments from China'. Miner and Hufbauer (n 31) 19.

[149] Julien Chaisse and Rahul Donde, 'The State of Investor-State Arbitration: A Reality Check of the Issues, Trends, and Directions in Asia-Pacific' (2018) 51(1) The International Lawyer 47.

[150] Gallagher and Shan (n 98) 46.   [151] ibid.

arbitration is chosen, the state respondent may require the Investor to undertake a domestic administrative review procedure first.[152]

The Canada–China FIPA is asymmetrical with respect to certain requirements preceding the arbitration process. Investors are equally required to waive or withdraw any domestic proceedings commenced in the host state.[153] However, if the measure alleged is Chinese, the Canadian investor must first undertake a Chinese 'domestic administrative reconsideration procedure' for at least four months, before proceeding to arbitration.[154]

There are two aspects of public interest and accountability pertaining to ISDS procedures: transparency in the process and the publication of materials (such as legal submissions and the underlying supporting witness and documentary evidence), and the right of audience of non-parties with an interest in the dispute (usually expressed as the right to submit *amicus curiae* briefs).[155] China's practice on both fronts has been, relative to the practice of most states, quite restrictive.[156] This approach may be a reflection of the lack of societal influence on the Chinese state.[157]

In stark contrast, Canada traditionally provides comprehensive ISDS procedures, which expressly allows for public access and disclosure of documents, as well as to provide 'a reasonable opportunity to comment' on the measures in dispute by 'interested persons'.[158]

The text of the Canada–China FIPA reflects both a general restriction on the transparency of the arbitral proceedings and yet a compromise by each party. Namely, China departed from its existing practice by providing some scope to publicly disclose documents and conduct hearings *in camera*, as well as to allow *amici* submissions by interested non-parties.[159] That stated, a state respondent holds a unilateral 'veto power' to ultimately determine whether documents as well as the arbitral hearings are made public.[160] If China maintains non-disclosure of those claims brought against it, and Canada maintains disclosure for claims brought against it, this is likely to exacerbate the asymmetrical operation of the BIT between the parties. Notably also, the text of the Canada–China FIPA contains a higher threshold than Canada (and the United States) BITs, in that the FIPA only allows those non-parties with a 'significant' interest in the arbitration to make written submissions.[161]

---

[152] ibid. Yet, the domestic administrative review process is usually time-restricted; see China–Germany BIT (2003) (with maximum a review process of three months), Protocol to the Agreement between the People's Republic of China and the Federal Republic of Germany on the Encouragement and Reciprocal Protection of Investments art 6.

[153] Canada–China FIPA Annex C.21. This is consistent with Canada's BIT practice: Canada FIPPA (2004) art 26(1)(e).

[154] Canada–China FIPA Annex C.21(1), (2).

[155] Magraw Barstow and Niranjali Amerasinghe, 'Transparency and Public Participation in Investor-State Arbitration' (2008) 15 ILSA Journal of International & Comparative Law 337; Anthony VanDuzer, 'Enhancing the Procedural Legitimacy of Investor-State Arbitration through Transparency and *Amicus Curiae* Participation' (2007) 52 McGill Law Journal 681. Katia Gómez, 'Rethinking the Role of *Amicus Curiae* in International Investment Arbitration: How to Draw the Line Favorably for the Public Interest' (2012) 35 Fordham International Law Journal 510.

[156] That is, China traditionally restricts public access without expressly providing interested non-parties standing or the right to submit *amicus curiae* briefs. Carter (n 7) 249.

[157] Gantz(n 2) 239.   [158] Canada–China FIPA 2004 arts 19, 38, and 39.

[159] ibid arts 28 and 29.   [160] ibid art 28(1), (2).

[161] ibid art 29(4), whereby 'significant interest' is one of an open list of circumstances a tribunal should consider when granting leave to file an *amicus* submission. US Model BIT (2012) art 28(3), US Model BIT (2004) art 28(3).

As the United States' traditional attitude as to disclosure and public access is consistent with Canada's,[162] it is interesting as to whether (and to what extent) the US will negotiate away these provisions. Depending on the resistant attitudes of the United States, the US–China BIT may lean towards China's practice of providing a presumption of maintaining confidentiality of the proceedings, but with scope for the US to maintain its practice of public disclosure, at least for those ISDS proceedings where it is the respondent. In the end, however, it appears that any BIT counterparty of China may be required to make concessions elsewhere in the BIT in order to obtain reciprocal public disclosure and scrutiny.

IX. Conclusion

The concluded Canada–China FIPA as well as the potential US–China BIT and EU–China BIT fall into a line of investment agreements with a unique dynamic, where each counterparty is both a capital importer and capital exporter. This dynamic is met with the challenge of balancing different interests and often conflicting positions, which is historically entrenched in divergent BIT practices. Beyond the legal framework, there are dimensional hurdles that complicate the bilateral relationship, in the nature of inherent security concerns, apprehensions as to compliance of BIT obligations, and general diplomatic tensions between the parties.

Can we conclude that China's BIT with Canada really amounts to a 'toothless tiger', such that it does not reciprocally offer investment protections and liberalized markets that were within its grasp? A lesson can be drawn that looks can be deceiving.

From the Canadian viewpoint, the BIT only marginally liberalized the Chinese investment market, and it failed to obtain coverage of various pre-establishment measures.[163] Canada also failed to rein in obligations concerning preferential treatment of SOEs, beyond that of a SOE exercising governmental authority delegated to it. The particulars of the relationship, such as the degree of control and influence between the SOE and state is left untended.[164] Significantly, there is a general lack of reciprocity between Canada and China's respective treaty obligations. While the MFN obligation is facially neutral, it has provided the investor of each state with the opportunity to expand the meaning of national treatment, *albeit* asymmetrically. Whether investors realize those benefits, however, is a different story. Further, a lack of reciprocity is not necessarily evidence of a 'bad BIT' or negotiated outcome, especially if mutually satisfactory concessions were made in other areas.

Conversely, certain compromises have been made by China, reflecting a potential evolutionary shift in its traditional practice. Notably, the Canada–China FIPA reflects a splicing of China's TRIMs obligations to the investor–state arbitration process, as well as a balancing formula for public welfare objectives with investment protections. In the context of China's general BIT practice, the Canada–China FIPA goes well beyond what China offered Switzerland some years ago,[165] exposing some negotiation

---

[162] US Model BIT (2012) art 29. US Model BIT (2004) art 29.

[163] Such that national treatment was restricted to investments admitted, and investments were obligated to be screened according to domestic laws, and measures that were imposed after the BIT was entered into force.

[164] In addition to the evidentiary issues, an ISDS arbitral tribunal is left with little guidance as to differentiating between those with commercial interests, and those nominally private enterprises that are pursuing foreign investment to further Chinese government goals.

[165] China–Switzerland BIT (2009). Gantz (n 2) 240.

opportunities for the US and other counterparties (such as the EU, India, the Gulf Cooperation Council, and Columbia).[166]

But where does this leave the prospect of achieving an adequate balance of investment liberalization and protection for the US–China BIT? The US–China Economic and Security Review Commission stated that the Canada–China FIPA 'falls short of US ambitions for market access reciprocity, pre-establishment national treatment, transparency, the scope of ISDS arbitration, performance requirements, and SOE treatment'.[167] The main battle line of the US and China will be drawn between SOE treatment and investment screening. Namely, the battle will be fought by the US to ensure that SOEs act at arm's length from the state and solely for commercial endeavours and fought by China through transparent screening rules by CFIUS, particularly where national security concerns are invoked.

As such, a significant gap remains between the legal standards of the US and China, whereby China has not recently demonstrated a significant elevation of its international commitments of investment liberalization and protection, consistent with Chinese FTAs with other developed states, such as New Zealand (2008) and Korea and Japan (2012). This gap remains, despite any influence of 'Americanization' of recent Chinese investment agreements.[168]

One would expect greater ease to liberalizing China's investment regime where the counterparty is similarly a capital exporter, as a strategy for China to gain reciprocal concessions for its outward investors. Yet, as China is more exposed to claims by foreign investors (relative to those from capital importing states, such as India[169] and Columbia), this requires a delicate balance between investment protections and liberalization. The China–Canada bilateral relationship, along with China's negotiations with the US and EU, fall into that category. Granted, where Canada may have 'failed', other counterparties may 'succeed', especially those wielding more negotiating power. While Canada is a significant destination of Chinese outward FDI,[170] China has yet to enter into bilateral agreements with those states and unions with more interest and influence on China's outward investments. These include the European Union (ranking second after the Asian region) and the United States,[171] which have a greater hope of achieving added concessions and maintaining their respective 'high standard' obligations contained their BITs.[172]

---

[166] The Ministry of Commerce of the Government of China (MOFCOM), China FTA Network http://fta.mofcom.gov.cn/english/ (last accessed 28 January 2017). Whalley and Li (n 5) 1 (last accessed 28 January 2017).
[167] Gloudeman and Salidjanova (n 3) 23. The main sticking points with respect to the US–China BIT negotiations have been described to be the scope of pre-establishment national treatment obligations, transparency of the investment screening process, treatment of SOEs, policies with respect to technology transfer requirements. Peterson Institute for International Economics (n 17) 10 https://piie.com/publications/piie-briefings/toward-us-china-investment-treaty (last accessed 25 January 2017).
[168] This effect is perhaps compounded by China's historical trend of 'selective adaptation'. Pitman Potter, 'Legal Reform in China: Institutions, Culture, and Selective Adaptation' (2004) 29 Law & Social Inquiry 465.
[169] Foreign direct investment (FDI)—FDI flows—OECD Data https://data.oecd.org/fdi/fdi-flows.htm (last accessed 20 January 2017). See also Supriya Chopra and Satvinder Kaur Sachdeva, 'Analysis of FDI Inflows and Outflows in India' (2014) 2 Journal of Advanced Management Science 331 www.joams.com/uploadfile/2014/0424/20140424052709217.pdf (last accessed 20 January 2017).
[170] Alicia Garcia-Herrero, 'China's Outbound Foreign Direct Investment' (n 26) 7–8. See also Alicia Garcia-Herrero, 'China's Outward Foreign Direct Investment' (2015) http://bruegel.org/2015/06/chinas-outward-foreign-direct-investment/ (last accessed 20 January 2017).
[171] ibid.   [172] Gantz (n 2) 213.

All told, if one were to use the Canada–China FIPA as a basis to predict the challenges and outcome of those obligations contained in the US–China BIT, and beyond, it would appear as follows, in accordance with Table 7.1:

Table 7.1 China BITs and Lessons Learned for Future Counterparties

Obligation	Canada–China FIPA	US–China BIT: Predicted Outcome	Lessons Learned for Future Counterparties
Market Access (National Treatment and Investment Screening)	No market access through national treatment (post-establishment NT only). Potential market access through MFN (China only). Apparent asymmetrical application of domestic investment screening standards as to deference.	Pre- and post-establishment national treatment restricted by negative list. Delineating scope and transparency of screening process likely to be a challenge, especially for SOEs. Investment screening at the discretion of the respective domestic authority, with a reference to be more transparent.	A capital exporter may have negotiating power to obtain pre-establishment national treatment with negative list (or a positive list) in exchange for viable sectors to liberalize. Clearly delineating China's investment screening criteria and transparency of process, on equal terms, is likely to be a significant hurdle.
MFN	Full MFN covering all phases of investment (pre-/post-establishment).	Full MFN, with potential same effect of asymmetrical application (unless expressly circumscribed).	Full MFN. If MFN obligation has retrospective application, foreign investors likely to obtain better obligations arising in earlier Chinese BITs (eg autonomous FET, national treatment not qualified by 'likeness'). Any asymmetrical effect aggravated by proportion of Chinese FDI into the counter-party's territory.
International Law Standard of Treatment	Restricted international law standard.	Restricted international law standard, content likely to be specifically circumscribed.	Restricted international law standard.
Expropriation	Indirect expropriation circumscribed and qualified respecting legitimate public welfare objectives.	Indirect expropriation circumscribed and qualified respecting legitimate public welfare objectives.	Indirect expropriation circumscribed and qualified respecting legitimate public welfare objectives.
Performance Requirements	Expressly incorporates TRIMs obligations to ISDS.	Likely expressly incorporate TRIMs obligations to ISDS, perhaps, in addition, precluding technology transfer requirements.	A capital exporter may have negotiating power able to incorporate TRIMs obligations. If potentially significant destination of Chinese OFDI, may preclude technology transfer requirements.

(continued)

Table 7.1 Continued

Obligation	Canada–China FIPA	US–China BIT: Predicted Outcome	Lessons Learned for Future Counterparties
Public Policy Exceptions	GATT Article XX-type general exceptions balancing public welfare objectives (environment, life and health).	No general exceptions, but scope for public welfare objectives applicable to key substantive obligations. Likely to be independent obligation to maintain acceptable environmental and labour standards.	Inclusion and scope of exceptions will depend on both traditional usage by counterparty and more likely included where counterparty. is a significant exporter of FDI to China (eg, EU)?
SOEs	State is attributable for conduct of SOEs with delegated public authority. SOE standing as investor not expressed.	State will likely be attributable for conduct of SOEs with delegated public authority. SOEs will likely have standing as investor.	Whether state (esp. China) is attributable for conduct of SOEs less likely for capital exporting counterparty (unless concession provided elsewhere). Challenge will be delineating whether state's attribution will be based on control and/or ownership of SOE in addition to exercise of delegated public authority. SOEs will likely have standing as investor.
ISDS Procedure (condition precedents, public access, transparency)	Asymmetrical condition of domestic review process. Transparency restricted. *Amici* submissions permitted.	Likely a condition of Chinese domestic review process. Degree of transparency somewhat limited, but dependent on need/concessions of US. *Amici* submissions expressly permitted.	Likely a condition of Chinese domestic review process. Transparency restricted. *Amici* submissions may be permitted.

China's BIT practice has thus evolved considerably, especially over the last fifteen years. The Canada–China FIPA forms the last instalment towards that evolutionary step. While China's BITs have not, thus far, demonstrated any strong signs of converging with US standards of comprehensive investor rights, the recent bilateral agreement with Canada demonstrates a proximal relationship. The final frontiers of investment liberalization and protection are comprehensive obligations precluding national discrimination and allowing market access, as well as coverage of SOEs.

Those novel and innovative treaty provisions of the Canada–China FIPA, such as TRIMs performance requirements and general exceptions for public policy objectives, appear on a case-by-case basis, leaving future counterparties to derive Chinese Whispers from a lack of coherent and proactive policy. Similarly, in the case of market access and pre-establishment rights of national non-discrimination, China's resistance to grant anything over-and-above its traditional BIT policy, bestows a negotiation strategy akin to Chinese chequers, whereby counterparties are left to play out their bargaining power in hand.

China's negotiations with the United States and the European Union are crucially important, not only as a measure of the economic relations between the world's largest economies, but also to identify the next, and perhaps final, evolutionary step of the bilateral international investment regime. As that regime evolves, patterns of convergence (or divergence) with the practice of developed countries will better crystallize and China's whispers will appear clearer and undistorted.

8

Innovation as a Catalyst in the China–Israel Investment Relationship

The China–Israel BIT (2009) and the Prospective FTA

Hadas Peled and Marcia Don Harpaz*

I. Introduction

In this chapter, we maintain that scientific and technological innovation has played an instrumental role in shaping contemporary China–Israel relations. Through an analysis of the China–Israel investment relationship, this chapter aims to contribute to the scholarly literature by identifying innovation as a key element in China's investment diplomacy. Nevertheless, given the speed with which China is catching up in developing its own innovation capacity, as well as the geopolitical constraints influencing the bilateral relationship, we conclude that the efficacy of innovation as a catalyst in China–Israel investment diplomacy is likely to decline in the future.

Our findings, pointing to scientific and technological innovation as an important explanatory variable in China's new investment approach, are not confined to the China–Israel relationship. China is pursuing innovation on three investment tracks: bilateral, regional, and global. This strategy has become an essential part of China's 'New Era' vision of a country of innovators, as articulated by Xi Jinping in his 2017 speech to the leadership of the Chinese Communist Party (CCP) at the Nineteenth Party Congress.[1] The China–Israel investment relationship, discussed in this chapter, is a good example of investment diplomacy led by innovation on the bilateral track. In addition, through many of the projects under the Belt and Road Initiative (BRI) China is promoting and investing in innovation both on regional and global tracks. A non-exhaustive list of examples includes large investments in industrial parks in China's neighbouring countries such as Vietnam, Thailand, and Russia. On a global level, under the banner of the BRI, China is pursuing and investing in innovation in less developed economies, such as in Africa,[2] as well as in advanced

* Hadas Peled, PhD Candidate, School of Law, Tsinghua University, Beijing, China and Dr Marcia Don Harpaz, Adjunct Lecturer, Department of International Relations and Faculty of Law, Hebrew University of Jerusalem

**We would like to thank Professor Tomer Broude and Professor Yizhak Shichor for their insightful comments. However, all mistakes are our own.

[1] Jinping Xi, Zai zhongguo gongchandang dishijiu ci quanguo daibiao dahui shang zuobaogao (Xi Jinping speech at the Nineteenth Party Congress) http://www.gov.cn/zhuanti/2017-10/27/content 5234876.htm (last accessed 7 December 2017). See also Laurence Brahm, 'In the New Era, Innovation Will Be the Key', *China Daily Europe* (29 October 29 2017) http://www.chinadaily.com.cn/kindle/2017-10/29/content_33852003.htm (last accessed 7 December 2017).

[2] Renmin University of China, *The Belt and Road Progress Report 2016* (Renmin University Press 2016). See also Julien Chaisse and Mitsuo Matsushita, 'China's "Belt and Road" Initiative: Mapping the World Trade Normative and Strategic Implications' (2018) 52(1) Journal of World Trade 163.

Innovation as a Catalyst in the China–Israel Investment Relationship: The China–Israel BIT (2009) and the Prospective FTA. Hadas Peled and Marcia Don Harpaz. © Hadas Peled and Marcia Don Harpaz, 2019. Published 2019 by Oxford University Press.

innovative economies, such as Switzerland[3] and Belgium.[4] The inclusion of Israel within the BRI framework should therefore be read in the context of China's pursuit of scientific and technological innovation on the global track.[5] The China–Israel investment and trade relationship, dominated by innovation over the past four decades, can therefore contribute to a better understanding of China's international investment diplomacy.

Scholars have analysed China's motivations in establishing international investment agreements (IIAs) and free trade agreements (FTAs).[6] Nevertheless, the existing literature does not provide much insight into the China–Israel case. The most commonly accepted motivation for China's pursuit of international economic agreements is to gain access to natural resources, raw materials, and foodstuff to support its rapidly growing economy.[7] This goal does not seem to explain the China–Israel case as neither country sources its energy or other natural resources from the other. Economic considerations such as trade promotion, access to new markets, and increasing exports are also common explanations of China's motivations in its economic diplomacy. However, market access through trade or investment is an unlikely explanation, given that the Israeli market is only equivalent to a mid-size Chinese provincial city.

Another broader goal motivating China has been to gain support for market economy status under World Trade Organization (WTO) anti-dumping rules. As a condition to starting negotiations, China is known to require its potential partners to renounce the use of non-market economy methodology in anti-dumping investigations of China.[8] However, the discriminatory non-market economy provision China agreed to upon acceding to the WTO, expired in December 2016, although China is pursuing WTO lawsuits against countries that still use the methodology (i.e. the US and the EU).[9] In fact, Israel cancelled the use of non-market economy methodology

---

[3] Baijie An, 'China and Switzerland to deepen innovative partnership during President Xi's visit' *China Daily* (12 January 2017) http://www.chinadaily.com.cn/business/2017wef/2017-01/12/content_27937350.htm (last accessed 31 August 2017).

[4] Ministry of Science and Technology of the People's Republic of China, 'The CTBC Science Park' (press release, 4 August 2016) http://www.most.gov.cn/eng/pressroom/201608/t20160804_127046.htm (last accessed 31 August 2017).

[5] Hadas Peled, 'Connectivity as an Engine for Innovation: the Israeli Perspective on BRI' *China Daily* (12 June 2017) http://www.chinadaily.com.cn/opinion/2017beltandroad/2017-06/12/content_29717111.htm (last accessed 31 August 2017).

[6] Peter Yu, 'Sinic Trade Agreements and China's Global Intellectual Property Strategy' in Christoph Antons and Reto M Hilty (eds), *Intellectual Property and Free Trade Agreements in the Asia-Pacific Region* (Springer 2014); Ka Zeng, 'China's Free Trade Area Agreement Diplomacy' (2016) 9 The Chinese Journal of International Politics 277; Julien Chaisse, 'The Shifting Tectonics of International Investment Law: Structure and Dynamics of Rules and Arbitration on Foreign Investment in the Asia-Pacific Region' (2015) 47 George Washington International Law Review 563, 615–16; Julien Chaisse and Christian Bellak, 'Navigating the Expanding Universe of Investment Treaties: Creation and Use of Critical Index' (2015) 18(1) Journal of International Economic Law 79.

[7] David Shambaugh, *China Goes Global: The Partial Power* (Oxford University Press 2013); Wei Liang and Junji Nakagawa, 'A Comparison of the FTA Strategies of Japan and China and Their Implications for Multilateralism' (October 2011) Indiana University Research Center for Chinese Politics and Business (RCCPB) Working Paper 11 http://dx.doi.org/10.2139/ssrn.2169361 (last accessed 31 August 2017). Nils Eliasson, 'The Chinese Investment Treaty Programme, Jurisdictional Challenges and Investment Planning: The Example of Chinese Outbound Investments in the Natural Resources Sector' in Wenhua Shan (ed), *China and International Investment Law: Twenty Years of ICSID Membership* (Brill Nijhoff 2014) 235–59.

[8] Henry Gao, 'China's Strategy for Free Trade Agreements: Political Battle in the Name of Trade' in Ross P Buckley, Richard Weixing Hu, and Douglas W Arner (eds), *East Asian Economic Integration: Law, Trade and Finance* (Edward Elgar Publishing 2011).

[9] WTO/DS515 United States—Measures Related to Price Comparison Methodologies—Request for consultations by China https://docs.wto.org/dol2fe/Pages/FE_Search/FE_S_S006.

in its anti-dumping investigations in 2005 (without receiving anything in return).[10] Given this reality, the elimination of non-market economy methodology cannot explain the ratification of the China–Israel BIT in 2008 or the later initiation of the China–Israel FTA negotiations.

Other oft-mentioned goals motivating China's economic statecraft focus on strengthening diplomatic and economic ties to promote China's leadership in East Asia, gain support for the One China Policy, and cultivate goodwill to combat the 'China threat'.[11] As further discussed below, US aid to Israel and its influence on Israel's foreign policy is no secret. Furthermore, Israel is not located in East Asia or closely linked with ASEAN economies nor does it have existential territorial concerns in East Asia. Thus, it is unlikely that China expects economic diplomacy to change Israel's policy towards Taiwan or anticipates greater Israeli involvement in the China dominated territory in the future. It is also difficult to link China–Israel economic diplomacy with the perception of the China threat.

We next consider attracting foreign direct investment (FDI) as a motivation. In the past, China, like other developing countries, signed bilateral investment treaties (BITs) in order to attract FDI, since BITS typically aim at protecting foreign investors from host state practices such as expropriation and nationalization. Indeed, attracting FDI to stimulate domestic growth was a central goal of the Chinese government and, in 2014, China even surpassed the US and became the largest global recipient of FDI.[12] Yet, studies have shown that there is no direct link between increased investment flows and BITs. In the case of Israel and China, bilateral investment was able to grow, first without a BIT in effect, and then, with a relatively outdated BIT in place.[13] We suggest that it is innovation that has served as the main catalyst in the China–Israel investment relationship.

This chapter opens with a discussion of the importance of innovation in the individual development strategies of China and Israel and their respective standing in the international innovation market. The chapter continues by demonstrating the instrumental role of innovation in China–Israel investment relationship since the launch of the reform era in China. We explain the role of innovation as a catalyst through analysis of investment patterns, and additional supporting indications from trade patterns. We further explain how innovation served as a main tool in the bilateral economic diplomacy, driving the political relations closer. We also show how, while innovation transfer was hindered owing to wider political concerns, this had serious implications on the relations. Then, we note the surprisingly positive repercussions of the 2008 global financial crisis (GFC) in bringing scientific and technological innovation to the forefront. We review the main steps taken by both governments to ensure that innovation drives their relationship, noting a new milestone in their relations when the

aspx?Query=(%20@Symbol=%20(wt/ds515/1%20))&Language=ENGLISH&Context=FomerScrip tedSearch&languageUIChanged=true# (last accessed 31 August 2017).

[10] Memorandum on Strengthening of Economic and Trade Cooperation (1 November 2005, Jerusalem), signed by Mr Raanan Dinur, Director General of the Israeli Ministry of Industry, Trade and Labor, and Wei Jianguo, Vice Minister of the Ministry of Commerce, People's Republic of China (on file with authors).

[11] See Yu (n 6); Gao (n 8); Liang and Nakagawa (n 7).

[12] UNCTAD, *World Investment Report 2015 Reforming International Investment Governance* (UN 2015) http//dx.doi.org/10.18356/e1ee3fa4-en.

[13] UNCTAD (2014) IIA Issue Note, 'The Impact of International Investment Agreements on Foreign Direct Investments, an Overview of Empirical Studies 1998:2014' (UN).

Comprehensive Innovative Partnership was established during the twenty-fifth anniversary of full diplomatic relations in 2017.

We then turn to the current FTA negotiations. In this context, we focus on three important aspects of innovation as a catalyst in China–Israel investment relations. First, we analyse the China–Israel BIT (2009),[14] its shortcomings, and the implications for the investment chapter in the FTA. Secondly, we examine the issue of intellectual property rights (IPR), which often arises in the context of investment and trade, in particular, in the context of innovation. Thirdly, we discuss the limits of innovation in China–Israel future investment relations. We conclude with remarks on the prospects of investment diplomacy based on innovation, their implications for the ongoing FTA negotiations, and the long-term diminishing impact of innovation as a catalyst in the China–Israel investment nexus.

II. Innovation as a Priority in China and Israel's Respective Development Strategies

China and Israel have both made innovation a top priority in their domestic development strategies. Historically, China was a source of innovation, the most well-known examples of which include inventions such as papermaking, the compass, gunpowder, and printing.[15] China's Century of Humiliation (1839–1949) is partially attributed to its failure to keep up with the scientific progress and technological change, taking place in the West at the end of the eighteenth century. Since its establishment in the early 1920s, CCP reforms stressed the need for modernization and scientific and technological innovation. The beginning of the reform era under the pragmatic result-oriented policies advocated by Deng Xiaoping further drove the Chinese quest for modernization through innovation. Chinese leaders have repeatedly declared innovation to be a top priority in China's development strategy. This strategy was gradually expanded, in China's 'Going Global' policies promoting investments in R&D abroad since the early 2000s. For example, in October 2004, as part of the 'Going Global' strategy, the promotion of overseas investment in R&D was one of four areas mentioned in a circular issued by the National Development and Reform Commission along with the Export-Import Bank of China. Innovation in various forms was included in all five-year plans (FYPs). The Twelfth and Thirteenth FYPs put innovation at the center with increased budgets devoted to the promotion of innovation. The pursuit of innovation is outlined in detailed programs such as Made in China 2025 [16] as well as longer-term roadmaps.[17]

---

[14] Agreement between the Government of People's Republic of China and the State of Israel for the Promotion and Reciprocal Protection of Investment (2009), http://investmentpolicyhub.unctad.org/IIA/country/42/treaty/915 (CIBIT).

[15] Joseph Needhams, *Science and Civilization in China, vol I* (Cambridge University Press 1954).

[16] Scott Kennedy, Made in China 2025, Center for Strategic and International Studies (1 June 2015) https://www.csis.org/analysis/made-china-2025 (last accessed 7 December 2017). In addition, see for example, Axel Berger, 'The Politics of China's Investment Treaty-Making Program' in T Broude, A Porges, and M Busch (eds), *The Politics of International Economic Law* (Cambridge University Press 2011); on Going Global, see Shambaugh (n 7) 174–82. Shambaugh also notes China's shift from outward foreign direct investment in developing countries to developed countries, particularly following the GFC.

[17] Yongxiang Lu (ed), *Science and Technology in China: A Roadmap to 2050: Strategic General Report of the Chinese Academy of Sciences* (Science Press Beijing and Springer 2010) (S&T in China Roadmap to 2050 Report).

The modern State of Israel regards scientific and technological innovation as essential to its survival. From ancient times, Judaism has valued knowledge and learning. Early Jewish thinkers worked to gain an understanding of the universe through the study of astronomy, cosmology, and medicine. With limited natural resources, geo-political isolation and a fast-growing population, from inception, modern day Israel needed to ensure food security and defence. Meeting these two basic needs led to government investment in the development of advanced agriculture and a domestic military industry and has contributed to Israel's status as a leading global source of solar energy, advanced agriculture, and defence innovation.[18]

The achievements of China and Israel's respective development strategies, vis-a-vis innovation, stand out in international studies. The World Intellectual Property Organization (WIPO) global innovation rankings is a neutral tool, providing insight into the parties' perceptions about their respective innovation capacity in the global competition for innovation.[19]

As shown in Figure 8.1 below, Israel's overall global innovation ranking is higher than China's. However, China's ranking is steadily improving, and it is closing the gap rapidly.

Global Innovation index

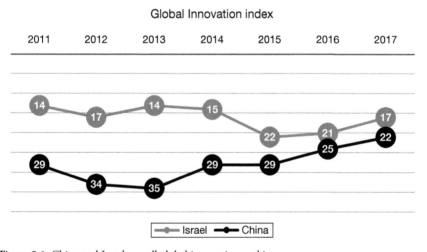

Figure 8.1 China and Israel overall global innovation ranking
Sources: Global Innovation Index Series 2011–2017

R&D and Human capital, which reflects level and quality of education, are important indicators since they are the basis for innovation. As Figure 8.2 shows, Israel is leading in these important areas, although China is steadily catching up.

---

[18] Dan Senor and Saul Singer, *Start-up Nation: The Story of Israel's Economic Miracle* (McClelland & Stewart 2009).

[19] Cornell University, INSEAD, and WIPO, *The Global Innovation Index 2011-2017* (2011–2017). (The Global Innovation Index published annually is a useful comparative benchmark of countries' achievements in innovation.)

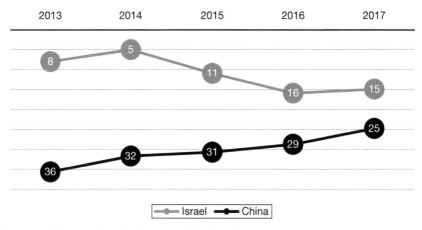

Figure 8.2 China and Israel education and R&D indicators
Source: Global Innovation Index Series 2013–2017

Knowledge and technology output such as registered IP (patents, PCTs, utility models) as well as scientific articles are all significant indicators of innovation. As Figure 8.3 shows, contrary to the overall ranking, China has already surpassed Israel.

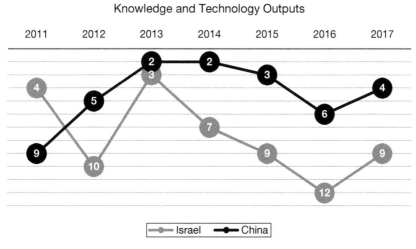

Figure 8.3 China and Israel knowledge and technology outputs indicators
Source: Global Innovation Index Series 2011–2017

In summary, while Israel's overall ranking in the global innovation index is presently slightly higher than China, China is quickly closing the gap.

III. Innovation as a Catalyst in China–Israel
Economic Relations

Innovation has taken a leading role in shaping recent investment relations between China and Israel. It is very difficult to assess the exact scope of cross-border China–Israel investments. However, there is a large body of evidence to be found in various media reports.[20] Israeli investors have been active players in China (relative to the size of the Israeli economy), investing in various projects related to scientific and technological innovation, with many notable examples. For example, in 2004, Netafim, a leading Israeli agri-tech company, invested in its first manufacturing facility in China.[21] One of the most interesting examples of successful Israeli investment in China is the Infinity group, which set foot in the door soon after the establishment of full diplomatic relations. In 2004, after receiving a number of requests from various foreign venture capital funds, China's first foreign-funded onshore RMB denominated licence was granted to Infinity. Furthermore, one of the group's companies, a leading global manufacturer in the chip industry, became the first company with a foreign co-founder to go public on the Shanghai Stock Exchange. Infinity, on its part, pledged to introduce, invest, and generate innovation in China.[22] Listing all such examples goes beyond the scope of this chapter.

In comparison, Chinese investments in Israel gained momentum only following the GFC, despite declines in Israel's overall FDI inflows. After a sharp decline in 2009–2010 following the global financial crisis, and in 2014 following the 2014 Gaza conflict, overall FDI flows to Israel dropped some 50 per cent from US$12.4 billion in 2013 to US$6.7 billion in 2014, in contrast to a global drop of 16 per cent, and a rise of 2 per cent into developing countries.[23] Since then, annual FDI in Israel has remained fairly steady reaching US$11.5 billion in 2015 and US$12.3 billion in 2016.[24] Yet, in 2015 and 2016, Chinese FDI in Israel mounted, accounting for roughly 40 per cent of the total FDI. Our analysis is based primarily on a Report of the Israeli Foreign Trade Administration at the Ministry of Economy and Industry. It is very difficult to determine the full scope of Chinese FDI in Israel, since in many cases, investments were carried out through off-shore Chinese companies. According to Israel's National Economic Council, Chinese-Israel tech deals amounted to US$50 million in 2013, by 2014 they had soared to US$300 million, and continued to rise in 2015 and 2016.[25] Many cases of Chinese FDI in Israeli hi-tech companies are reported in

[20]   China Deals Info Base chinadealsinfobase.com (last accessed 7 December 2017).
[21]   'Netafim Invested 14 Million USD in China' *Haaretz* (5.1.2004) https://www.themarker.com/misc/1.221408 (last accessed 31 August 2017) (in Hebrew).
[22]   Peter Stein, 'Israel R&D Goes to China: Infinity Group Exports Intellectual Property, Feeding Beijing's High Tech Hunger' *The Wall Street Journal* (21 September 2010) https://www.wsj.com/articles/SB10001424052748704190704575489503660213146 (last accessed 31 August 2017).
[23]   UNCTAD, *World Investment Report 2015: Reforming International Investment Governance* (UN 2015) ix http://dx.doi.org/10.18356/e1ee3fa4-en.
[24]   UNCTAD, *World Investment Report 2014: Investing in the SDGs—An Action Plan* (2014) 205 http://dx.doi.org/10.18356/3e74cde5-en; UNCTAD, *World Investment Report 2017: Investment and the Digital Economy* (UN 2017) 222 http://dx.doi.org/10.18356/e692e49c-en.
[25]   Israeli Foreign Trade Administration at the Ministry of Economy, China-Israel Economic Relations—A Report (March 2017) (China-Israel Economic Relations Report 2017) (file available with the authors) (in Hebrew).

the media. Leading hi-tech Chinese giants, such as Baidu and Alibaba, are investing in Israeli high-tech specialized venture funds such as Jerusalem Venture Partners and startups.[26] Since the purpose of this chapter is not to furnish a detailed business-intelligence list of examples, we believe this sample demonstrates to the reader this investment-innovation trend.

Since the fall of 2016, China has been increasing its scrutiny of outbound direct investments (ODI) companies. Despite China's new regulatory policy to restrict overseas investments, Israeli technology continues to be highly attractive to Chinese investment. Various Chinese declarations and reports have affirmed that despite the restrictions, investment in innovation will be supported.[27] Consistent with the trend to encourage investment in innovation, in August 2017, China formalized the regulatory path for ODI transaction approval with a priority catalogue. These regulations predominantly encourage outward investment in innovation.[28] It is therefore concluded that, as long as Israel can satisfy China's appetite for investment in innovation, the trend of substantial Chinese investment in Israel will continue.

China–Israel trade flows are also highly indicative of the central role of scientific and technological innovation in their bilateral economic relations. Since diplomatic relations were established in the early 1990s, trade has grown from US$50 million in 1992 to over US$9 billion in 2016.[29] Israel has historically been dependent on two main trading partners: the US and the EU. Israel signed its first trade agreement with the EC in 1964, a preferential agreement in 1970, an FTA in 1975, and an FTA with the US in 1985. This dependence made Israel highly vulnerable to developments in the EU and US economies, such as long-term stagnation in the EU and crises such as in the US housing market. In recent years, however, the trade pattern has changed significantly, and Israel has turned towards Asia, and above all, towards China. Since 2013, imports of goods from China have surpassed imports of goods from the US. In 2016, 13.5 per cent of Israel's imports originated in China as opposed to 3.2 per cent in 2002, while 12.3 per cent originated in the US as opposed to some 19 per cent in 2002. Israel's exports to China accounted for 1.7 per cent of its total exports in 2005 and accounted for 5.3 per cent in 2016. Since 2008, China has been Israel's largest trading partner in Asia, and third largest partner worldwide after the European Union and the United States (see Figure 8.4).[30]

---

[26] David Shamah, 'China's Baidu Makes Third Investment in Israel' *Times of Israel* (14 April 2015).

[27] Yifan Ding, 'Staying Power of China's Economy' *China-US Focus* (19 November 2015) https://www.chinausfocus.com/finance-economy/how-much-will-chinas-13th-five-year-plan-contribute-to-world-economy (last accessed 31 August 2017).

[28] Notice of the General Office of the State Council on Forwarding the Guiding Opinions of the National Development and Reform Commission, the Ministry of Commerce, the People's Bank of China, and the Ministry of Foreign Affairs on Further Directing and Regulating the Direction of Overseas Investments (国务院办公厅转发国家发展改革委商务部人民银行外交部关于进一步引导和规范境外投资方向指导意见的通知) (General Office of the State Council, 4 August 2017, Opinion no 74).

[29] Israel Export Institute, *Developments and Trends in Israel Export: 2016 Summary 2017 Forecast Report* (Israel Export Institute 2017) 26 (in Hebrew).

[30] Israel Export Institute, Sheng Enterprises, *Zoon In China: Development, Opportunities and Challenges* (2017) 54–5 (in Hebrew).

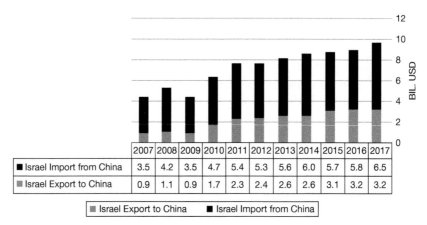

Figure 8.4 China-Israel trade balance
Source: Israel Export Institute 2010–2015

What is interesting, however, is not the absolute growth in trade but the trade patterns. An examination of Israel's exports to China shows that they are dominated by innovation. This pattern is anticipated to continue, as China increasingly stresses the development of innovation. As Figure 8.5 below demonstrates, in 2010, 40 per cent of Israeli exports to China consisted of electronics and components (the majority consisted of products from Intel Corporation in Israel, Orbotech, and Iscar Metalworking, all ranked as world leading innovative companies). As Figure 8.6 below shows, in 2015, five years later, not only had total Israeli exports to China grown in absolute terms despite the GFC, but 61.1 per cent of Israel's exports consisted of innovative electronics and components.[31]

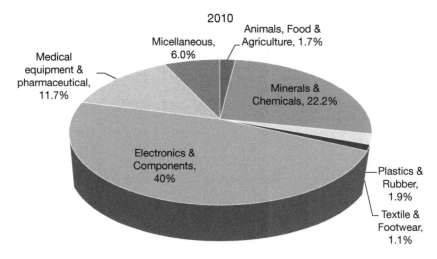

Figure 8.5 Israel export to China, 2010
Source: Israel Export Institute

---

[31] China–Israel Economic Relations Report 2017 (n 25) 5.

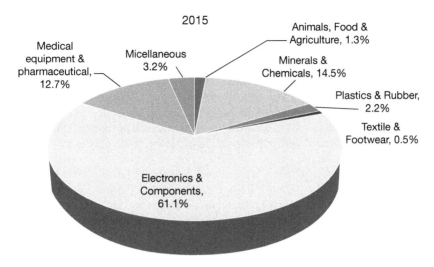

Figure 8.6 Israel export to China, 2015
Source: Israel Export Institute

These clear-cut innovation-centred investment and trade patterns have influenced Chinese and Israeli policy and political decision-makers.

IV. China–Israel Political Relations before the GFC and the Role of Innovation

While scientific and technological innovation has played an important role in the economic relations between China and Israel, it has also served as a catalyst in China and Israel contemporary political relations. China and Israel had much in common when established in 1948–1949: both were ancient civilizations, both suffered immensely prior to their establishment, and both states were influenced by Socialist ideology.[32] However, upon establishment, Israel was struggling and had little innovation to offer to China or any other third party. Although Israel was among the few countries that officially recognized the People's Republic of China in 1950, China did not recognize Israel. The Bandung Conference of 1955, which issued a declaration supporting the Palestinians and favouring Arab countries, ended any prospects of bilateral diplomatic relations in the near future. During the 1960s, as a result of China's growing international isolation, the relationship between the countries underwent a long period of stagnation. During that period, Israel improved its innovation capacity, while China became more isolated and fell further behind in technological development.

With the launch of the reform era in China, innovation proved to be vital to the renewal of their bilateral relations. Normalization between the two countries began with Israeli technical assistance and technology transfer to China even before formal

---

[32] Yoram Evron, 'Foreign Relations: China–Israel Relations in Retrospect: Obstacles, Success and Future Trends' (2008) 18 Yinuim Betkumut Israel 237, 243–6 (in Hebrew). For an historical overview of China–Israel relations see Aron Shai, *The Evolution of the Israeli-Chinese Friendship* (Tel Aviv University, S Daniel Abraham Center for International and Regional Studies, and the Confucius Institute, Research Paper 7, July 2014) www.tau.ac.il/~aashai/INSS-2014.pdf.

diplomatic relations were established. During the late 1970s and early 1980s, the two governments allowed initiatives promoting Israeli experts scientific and technological innovation support. Cooperation extended mainly to defense-related transactions aimed at modernizing China's army, and to a lesser extent, to civilian areas, such as agriculture. Israel was one of the few countries with experience in fighting Soviet weapons, and know-how in refurbishing them, making its experience invaluable to China since Soviet arms comprised the major part of Chinese arms at the time.[33]

The pace of building a bilateral institutional framework to support scientific and technological innovation transfer, however, moved slowly. It was only in 1987 that the sides opened representative offices. Ultimately, a ceremony marking the establishment of formal Sino–Israeli diplomatic relations was held on 24 January 1992 in Beijing. Subsequently, during the 1990s, China and Israel negotiated various supporting international agreements, including the bilateral investment treaty discussed in this chapter. However, due to broader geo-political constraints, neither government stressed the bilateral institutional framework.

The incident that most hindered high-level bilateral relations in the reform era, came to be known as the 'Phalcon Affair'. It is indicative of the greater geopolitical context and is linked with the US and innovation. In the late 1990s, Israel agreed to sell China an AWACS (airborne early warning and control system) system for some US$250 million per plane. After signing the sales agreement, China paid the required down payment, and Israel was to equip the first aircraft (a Russian aircraft) with the system. However, in 2000, after strong pressure by the US government, Israel backed out of the deal. The timing of the cancellation particularly aggravated the situation since it was announced shortly after personal reassurances by then Israeli Prime Minister Ehud Barak, to then President Jiang Zemin during a visit to Israel (the only visit of a Chinese president to date). Although Israel eventually provided monetary compensation of US$319 million to cover China's down payment and compensation for the cancelled deal, the process of establishing a comprehensive bilateral relationship was hurt significantly.[34]

The cancelled deal demonstrates the decisive role and crucial influence of an important third party, the US, on the transfer of innovation from Israel to China. In the late 1970s and early 1980s, the US viewed China as a counterweight to the Soviet Union, and even facilitated innovation transfer from Israel to China. However, with the collapse of the Soviet Union in 1991, and the aftermath of the Tiananmen Square incident, the US changed its stance, and started to view China as a strategic and economic threat. This was compounded when, after a 15-year negotiation process, China joined the World Trade Organization (**WTO**) in 2001, the Chinese economy took off, and China started to consolidate its position as a global economic power.[35] At the same time, to sustain its rapid economic growth, among other things, China required an enormous energy supply, leading to stronger relations between China and various Middle-East oil exporting countries, who were allies of Israel's historic enemies. The cancellation of the Phalcon deal demonstrated the limits of innovation as a driver of

---

[33] Joseph Shalhevet, *Science in the Service of Diplomacy* (Joseph Shalhevet 2009) (in Hebrew).

[34] Jonathan Goldstein, 'Quadrilateral Relationship: Israel, China, Taiwan and the US since 1992' in Jonathan Goldstein and Yitzhak Shichor (eds), *China and Israel: from Discord to Concord* (Magnes 2016) (in Hebrew).

[35] Marcia Don Harpaz, 'China's Coherence in International Economic Governance' (2016) 21 *Journal of Chinese Political Science* 123. See also Chaisse and Matsushita (n 2).

the Israel–China relationship and cast a heavy shadow over the development of the parties' formal bilateral cooperation.

The story of the China–Israel Bilateral Investment Treaty (CIBIT) discussed below reflects the sides' hesitancy in expanding their bilateral institutional framework resulting from Israel's cancellation of the Phalcon deal. CIBIT text negotiations started after the establishment of full diplomatic relations in 1992. However, even though the text of the CIBIT was finalized in 1995, Israel held up the ratification process by adding a stipulation in the Protocol to the text, calling on the parties to refrain from ratification until it completed an internal review and possible modification of its international investment treaties.[36] Stung from the Phalcon Affair, China did not 'push' Israel to complete the required ratification process. Thus, US intervention and the consequent cancellation of the Phalcon deal, led to a period of stagnation in China–Israel relations, and among other things, was responsible for hindering ratification of the CIBIT. It was only in 2008, during the GFC, when the Chinese and Israeli governments came to the realization that they both would benefit by strengthening bilateral economic cooperation through innovation, that the CIBIT was finally ratified.

An analysis of the pace of the expansion of the China–Israel Financial Protocol, demonstrates similar hesitancy in supporting investment in scientific and technological innovation. The Financial Protocol is a unique instrument that allows Israeli manufacturers to offer advanced innovation largely to local government-supported projects in China by granting long-term credit arrangements insured by the Israeli government, subject to advance approval by both governments. Over time, the Financial Protocol has facilitated notable projects in China aimed at advancing technologies in key industries such as communications, medicine and health care, water treatment, clean energy, agro-tech, and education (often in third-fourth tier localities). However, during the early period of the Financial Protocol, from its initiation in 1995 through the 2008 GFC, in the first and second financial protocols, only a modest sum of US$600 million was approved over a period of fifteen years.[37]

It was the GFC that provided new impetus to high-level bilateral cooperation. Both the Chinese and Israeli economies displayed strong resilience during the crisis. In fact, they were both surprised at the systemic failure of the Western liberal economic system, along with the ease at which it spread throughout the globe. As Israel decided to turn to Asia so as not to be completely dependent on the stagnating EU and US economies for trade and investment, China set innovation as a top priority, which Israel could provide. Indeed, the GFC was an important milestone in the bilateral relationship, motivating China and Israel to search for ways to expand economic relations.

V. A Comprehensive Innovative Partnership

Since the GFC in 2008, the governments of China and Israel have concentrated on strengthening their economic relationship and bilateral investments, with innovation as a central axis. As an important step, the parties sought the re-implementation of previously agreed upon accords. In line with this approach, the CIBIT that was negotiated and concluded in the mid-1990s was ratified in 2008 and put into force in

[36] CIBIT Protocol art 6.
[37] Hadas Peled, 'The China Israel Financial Protocol and the Belt and Road Initiative' *China-US Focus* (25 October 2016) https://www.chinausfocus.com/finance-economy/the-china-israel-financial-protocol-and-the-road-and-belt-initiative (last accessed 10 November 2017).

2009. Furthermore, previously existing tools to promote trade in innovation such as the above-mentioned China Israel Financial Protocol started to receive substantially larger financial commitments from the two governments.

Motivated by innovation, both governments deepened their cooperation by developing a multi-layered dialogue across different levels. It is beyond the scope of this discussion to refer to all the initiatives, so we will focus on several key indicative policies. In 2010, the parties signed a bilateral agreement to form the China–Israel Cooperation Program, with the primary aim of supporting joint industrial R&D projects. The Chinese Ministry of Science and Technology (MOST) and the Israel Innovation Authority on behalf of the Israeli government jointly manage this cooperation. The programme includes designated funds and industrial parks in Jiangsu, Shanghai, Shenzhen, Shandong, Guangdong, and Zhejiang. Projects approved by both sides are entitled to grants and subsidies. The approval process includes a clear IP allocation rights plan that allows both parties, Israeli and Chinese, to share IPR in these ventures.[38]

In May 2014, following Benjamin Netanyahu's first visit to China in 2013 and the 2014 visit of Vice Premier Liu Yandong to Israel, the two sides signed the Memorandum of Understanding between the Government of the People's Republic of China and the Government of the State of Israel on the Establishment of the China–Israel Joint Committee on Innovation Cooperation. The memorandum provided a three-year action plan for China–Israel scientific and technological innovation cooperation (2015–2017), and called for regular meetings between the parties, and between the different implementing ministries (e.g. health, environment, education, etc).[39]

Additionally, Israel opened trade and economic missions in four different locations: Beijing, Shanghai, Guangzhou, and Chengdu. These missions actively support cross-border investment and trade by engaging in direct economic diplomacy, actively organizing events and matchmaking between Chinese and Israeli companies. The investment in Israeli hi-tech venture funds discussed above, was promoted by events organized by these economic missions.[40] Promotion of investment and trade is further supported by joint semi-annual investment summits (that began in 2016), and held alternately in China and Israel. These investment summits, sponsored by both governments, attract thousands of participants from governmental and private sectors.[41] Equally important, in order to encourage people-to-people exchange and visits, China and Israel signed a Ten-Year Multiple Visa Agreement effective from November 2016.[42] The simplified visa arrangements have clearly encouraged Chinese business delegations to visit Israel.[43] These are all important examples of scientific and technological innovation serving as a catalyst in China–Israel economic diplomacy since the GFC.

---

[38] Israel Innovation Authority, China–Israel Industrial R&D Cooperation Framework http://www.matimop.org.il/china.html (last accessed 31 August 2017).

[39] Hagai Shagrir, *China-Israel Relations* (3rd Annual Israel-China Conference, INSS, June 2017).

[40] Ministry of Economy and Industry, Foreign Trade Administration, Mission to China, http://www.israeltrade.org.cn/ (last accessed 31 August 2017).

[41] David Shamah, 'Big Deals Expected at Biggest Ever Investment Event in China' *Times of Israel* (4 January 2016) http://www.timesofisrael.com/big-deals-expected-at-biggest-ever-israel-investment-event-in-china/ (last accessed 31 August 2017).

[42] Yunbi Zhang, 'Ten Years Multiple Entry Visa Pact Signed' *China Daily* (29 March 2016) http://www.chinadaily.com.cn/world/2016-03/29/content_24169906.htm (last accessed 10 November 2017).

[43] SIGNAL, China Israel Relations in 2016: Blue Book Essay 10 http://en.sino-israel.org/wp-content/uploads/2017/05/Israel-China-relations-2016-Blue-Book.pdf (last accessed 10 November 2017).

The establishment of the Comprehensive Innovative Partnership in 2017 captures the role of innovation as a catalyst in the economic diplomacy between China and Israel. In the decade following the GFC, China and Israel established various high and medium-level governmental exchanges to promote innovation. By adopting a practical approach, that is, without resolving all differences in the broader geopolitical context noted above, China and Israel have relied on economic diplomacy to strengthen their bilateral relationship. As shown above, such economic diplomacy has centred on innovation, and has been highly instrumental in strengthening trade and investment between China and Israel, despite the global economic slowdown. Furthermore, Israel joined the Chinese led Asian Infrastructure Investment Bank as a founding member.[44] As mentioned above, it is also party to the BRI. The initiation of FTA negotiations, is yet another milestone in the bilateral economic diplomacy, as we further discuss below.

VI. Investment Chapter in the FTA Negotiations—A Discussion

A prospective FTA between China and Israel was initially raised in May 2013. As a first step, the sides decided to prepare a feasibility study. Completed in November 2014, the study found that both sides would benefit substantially from an FTA.[45] Once officially launched, the FTA negotiations have been moving forward quickly. The second negotiating meeting was held in Beijing in July 2017, shortly after Israeli Prime Minister Netanyahu's visit to China in March 2017,[46] and the third negotiating round was held in Israel in November 2017.[47] Below we consider several factors highly relevant to the FTA negotiations in investment.

A. Legal analysis of the CIBIT

As explained above, there was a significant time gap of more than a decade between the negotiation and the ratification of the CIBIT. However, despite this significant time gap, the language of the text was not modified. Legal analysis of the CIBIT makes it clear that the new FTA should include a dedicated and up-to-date chapter on investment. The outdated BIT, drafted during the 1990s, does not meet current commonly-accepted standards, nor does it reflect the sides' recent IIA practices, and therefore requires considerable revision.

The existing text of the BIT is short and concise, in line with the conventional drafting patterns of the early 1990s. Interestingly, from a temporal perspective, it

---

[44] Ministry of Foreign Affairs, 'Israel Joins Asian Infrastructure Investment Bank' (15 April 2015) http://mfa.gov.il/MFA/PressRoom/2015/Pages/Israel-joins-Asian-Infrastructure-Investment-Bank-15-April-2015.aspx (last accessed 31 August 2017).

[45] Joint Feasibility Study on a China Israel Free Trade Agreement (November 2014) www.industry.org.il/GetFileCl.asp?File=China_Israel.pdf (last accessed 31 August 2017).

[46] MOFCOM, 'The 2nd Round of Negotiation of China-Israel Free Trade Area Held in Beijing' (15 July 2017) http://fta.mofcom.gov.cn/enarticle/enrelease/201707/35539_1.html (last accessed 7 December 2017).

[47] MOFCOM, 'The 3rd Round of Negotiation of China-Israel Free Trade Area Held in Israel' (7 December 2017) http://fta.mofcom.gov.cn/enarticle/chinaisraelen/chinaisraelennews/201712/36379_1.html (last accessed 7 December 2017).

applies to both pre-existing and post BIT Investments, without any limitation on submission of claims.[48]

The CIBIT predominantly focuses on investment promotion as its underlying-purpose without referring to state regulatory autonomy, policy space or the flexibility to introduce new regulations. Moreover, it does not refer to sustainable development goals or to social investment aspects such as human rights, labour, corporate social responsibility, or poverty reduction. Finally, it does not include any reference to environmental issues such as climate change, and plant or animal biodiversity. The only requirement included, prescribes that investment under the CIBIT should 'comply with the host country laws and regulations',[49] without specifying any narrative or guidelines for interpretation.[50] The substantive scope of the BIT is broad. It uses an open-ended definition of assets for investment.[51] Decisions concerning taxation, grants, and government procurement, typical in other BITS, are not excluded anywhere in the text.[52] Obviously, since it was adopted prior to *Salini*, the CIBIT does not incorporate any *Salini* controlling valves.[53] The text of the CIBIT includes an open and broad Most Favoured Nation (MFN) substantive guarantee on a post-establishment basis for both investors and investments.[54] The exceptions to the MFN provision are confined to taxation and FTAs or customs unions.[55] This analysis leads to an important query, about the link between the CIBIT and other BITs and instruments signed by China and Israel with other parties. In this context, it is worth mentioning that, to date, China has entered into 110 BITs and nineteen additional treaties with investment provisions, while Israel has entered into thirty-four BITs and four additional treaties with investment provisions.[56] What is referred to as the 'spaghetti' or 'noodle bowl' effect would lead to serious problems in interpretation of the short CIBIT in view of the numerous, and overlapping sources of obligation.[57]

In contrast with the MFN, the CIBIT does not contain a national treatment (NT) provision. This is consistent with China's approach to BITs at the time it negotiated the text.[58] In the twenty-year period between the start of CIBIT negotiations until its ratification, China's outward FDI has grown and recently even surpassed its inward FDI. Accordingly, its perspective has changed from an 'inward' orientation to both an

---

[48] CIBIT art 12.   [49] ibid arts 1, 2.

[50] Hadas Peled, 'Rethinking the China Israel BIT in light of the Fragmented International Investment Legal Order: A Commentary' (2016) 2 China and WTO Review 187.

[51] CIBIT art 1.

[52] Agreement between the Government of Canada and the Government of the People's Republic of China for the Promotion and Reciprocal Protection of Investments (2012) (1 October 2014) (China–Canada BIT) (art 8(5) for example excludes government procurement).

[53] *Salini Costruttori SpA and Italstrade SpA v Kingdom of Morocco* (ICSID Case No ARB/00/4) (https://icsid.worldbank.org/apps/ICSIDWEB/cases/Pages/casedetail.aspx?CaseNo=ARB/00/4) (this is clear from the drafting history, since the *Salini* case was only concluded after the conclusion of the text of the CIBIT in 1995). Emmanuel Gaillard, 'Identify or Define? Reflections on the Evolution of the Concept of Investment in ICSID Practice' in Christina Binder, Ursula Kriebaum, August Reinisch, and Stephan Wittich (eds), *International Investment Law for the 21st Century: Essays in Honour of Christoph Schreuer* (OUP 2009) 403–16.

[54] CIBIT art 3.   [55] ibid art 7.

[56] UNCTAD Database http://investmentpolicyhub.unctad.org/IIA/mappedContent (last accessed 31 August 2017).

[57] See Julien Chaisse, 'The Issue of Treaty Shopping in International Law of Foreign Investment: Structuring (and Restructuring) of Investments to Gain Access to Investment Agreements' (2015) 11(2) Hastings Business Law Review 225. See also Julien Chaisse and Shintaro Hamanaka, 'The "Noodle Bowl Effect" of Investment Treaties in Asia: The Phenomenon, the Problems, the Practical Solutions' (2019) 34(1) ICSID Review 44.

[58] Norah Gallagher and Wenhua Shan, *Chinese Investment Treaties: Policies and Practice* (OUP 2009).

'inward' and 'outward' orientation. Therefore, China's later generation BITs provide for NT.[59] Israel's BITs also grant NT.[60] The absence of a NT provision in the current CIBIT text may be read in the context of the existing most favoured nation (MFN) provision as discussed above. In the event of a dispute between China and Israel about the scope of application and the formula of the MFN provision, the absence of NT along with the existing MFN provision may lead to lengthy debate.

The CIBIT guarantees the protection of fair and equitable treatment (FET) through broad and general phrasing.[61] This text was common in many BITs written during the early 1990s, prior to the rise in investor–state litigation that often refers to the violation of such a broad and undefined formula.[62] The FET text does not provide for any qualifications, lists its elements (in an exhaustive or indicative list), and does not refer to international law in general and prohibits usage of unreasonable, arbitrary or discriminatory measures, without any exceptions. This leaves a very broad space for future claims concerning FET violations.

Finally, the expropriation provision in the CIBIT text allows for a very general set of circumstances.[63] It includes indirect expropriation without defining or limiting that term. It does not carve out any general regulatory measures such as compulsory licences in conformity with the WTO etc. The compensation formula for expropriation provides for a 'reasonable' compensation standard, without specifying relative rights to compensation as a comparator.

Another pertinent issue is the free transfer of fund commitment. This commitment does not exclude any exceptions to the transfer of funds obligation, due to balance of payment restrictions or any other specific exception such as protection of lawful creditors.[64] Although at the time of writing the Israeli Shekel and the RMB are stable strong currencies, circumstances can change quickly, and therefore such an exclusion may be desirable for both parties. This is consistent with international experience (e.g. Argentina).

In summary, the existing CIBIT provides for general substantive guarantees, without addressing regulation for public interest in areas such as health and environment, labour standards, corporate social responsibility, or exceptions in case of corruption. Furthermore, the text does not include an essential security exception, general public policy exceptions, or a prudential carve-out for financial measures. These are practices presently recommended by leading international experts, and found in recent BITs and IIAs of both parties.[65] The investment chapter in the new FTA in all likelihood will reflect these practices.

---

[59] Wenhua Shan, Norah Gallagher, and Sheng Zhang, 'National Treatment for Foreign Investment in China: A Changing Landscape' (2012) 27 ICSID Review 120.

[60] OECD, 'Accession of Israel to OECD: A Review of Investment Policies' (1 March 2012) http://www.oecd.org/israel/publicationsdocuments/reports/5/ (last accessed 31 August 2017).

[61] CIBIT art 2(2).

[62] UN, *Fair and Equitable Treatment—A Sequel: UNCTAD Series on Issues in International Investment Agreements II* (UN 2013) http://dx.doi.org/10.18356/c5d6a03e-en (last accessed 31 August 2017).

[63] CIBIT art 6.

[64] CIBIT art 5. See also Julien Chaisse, 'Exploring the Confines of International Investment and Domestic Health Protections: General Exceptions Clause as a Forced Perspective' (2013) 39(2–3) American Journal of Law & Medicine 332.

[65] A non-exhaustive list of IIAs or agreements and investment chapters includes: Free Trade Agreement between the Government of the People's Republic of China and the Government of Korea (2015); Agreement between the Government of Canada and the Government of the People's Republic

B. Dispute resolution in the investment chapter of the prospective FTA

Dispute settlement has become one of the most controversial topics in the negotiation of investment chapters in FTAs and IIAs in view of rising international disputes. Article 8 of the China–Israel BIT provides that any dispute 'with respect to the amount of compensation in the case of expropriation'[66] may be submitted to the International Center for Settlement of Investment Disputes (ICSID), and requires an investor to provide written notification, with a 'cooling off' period of six months, to allow an amicable resolution of the dispute. Although ICSID jurisdiction under the CIBIT may seem narrow, in fact, in view of the 'spaghetti/noodle bowl effect' created by the expansive MFN provision discussed above, it gives rise to complicated questions.[67] The MFN provision does not prescribe in detail the appropriate relationship between MFN and dispute resolution. In view of conflicting practices and approaches taken by different tribunals, it is necessary to clarify this focal gap presumptively. In addition, the ISDS does not contain a 'fork in road' provision, effectively allowing an investor to submit a dispute both to a national court and to international arbitration concurrently. This situation may potentially lead to conflicting decisions by different tribunals and courts, in different jurisdictions, at the same time.

The new investment chapter in the FTA should clarify dispute resolution provisions and specifically address adaptations and modifications of the existing BIT, including the transfer provisions. In this context, it should be noted that, to date, no investor–state dispute between China and Israel has arisen. The CIBIT was referred to once, in a claim by a Malaysian construction and development company against the PRC in 2011 on arts and culture facilities (regarding the revocation of a land lease by China).[68] Since the dispute was concluded at a preliminary stage, the claim supported by the BIT was never made public.

China has been observing Washington dominated ICSID investor–state arbitrations with caution. Criticism about expansive interpretation over jurisdiction was raised in China, even when the result of the arbitration favoured China.[69] Recently, China moved a step forward allowing its leading international arbitration institutions, such as the Shenzhen Court of International Arbitration, Beijing Arbitration Committee, Shanghai International Arbitration Committee and the biggest arbitration institution, China International Economic and Trade Arbitration Committee (CEITAC), to administer investor–state investment dispute arbitration as an alternative to ICSID. The press release from the China Council for the Promotion of International Trade (CCPIT), announcing CIETAC new investor–state arbitration rules, emphasized that in light of China's increased presence in international investment, and concerns over the lack of comprehensive investment legal systems in those countries covered by BRI. In another important development, in July 2018, China's Supreme People's court

---

of China for the Promotion and Reciprocal Protection of Investments (2012) (1 October 2014); Agreement between Japan and the State of Israel for the Liberalization, Promotion and Protection of Investment (2017).

[66] CIBIT art 8.

[67] Emmanuel Gaillard, 'Establishing Jurisdiction Through a Most Favored Nation Clause' (2005) 233 New York Law Journal 105.

[68] *Ekran Berhad v People's Republic of China* (ICSID Case No ARB/11/15) https://icsid.worldbank.org/en/Pages/cases/casedetail.aspx?CaseNo=ARB/11/15.

[69] An Chen, *The Voice from China: An Chen on International Economic Law* (Springer 2014). See also Julien Chaisse and Rahul Donde, 'The State of Investor-State Arbitration: A Reality Check of the Issues, Trends, and Directions in Asia-Pacific' (2018) 51(1) The International Lawyer 47.

officially launched international commercial courts, designed to deal with disputes related to BRI projects.[70]

Finally, sharp criticism of ICSID investor–state arbitration has led the European Commission to propose an alternative dispute settlement system to the Washington dominated ICSID Convention.[71] The EU–Vietnam FTA and the EU–Canada Comprehensive Economic Trade Agreement (CETA) incorporate a new mechanism for ISDS, through an investor–state permanent court (tribunal) (in contrast to the old ad hoc system) and an appellate body, that will enable the sides to challenge tribunal decisions. In addition, as of autumn 2018, the text of the 'New North American Free Trade Agreement', or USMCA (United States–Mexico–Canada Agreement), also limits investor–state arbitration. Although neither China nor Israel has established such a mechanism in their existing FTAs or IIAs, this new trend in ISDS may be considered by the sides in the present negotiations.

C. Intellectual property rights and innovation-driven investment

Protection of Intellectual Property Rights (IPR) is often raised as a particular concern when dealing with innovation, technology transfer, and R&D. China is frequently blamed by its trading and investment partners for its dubious IPR protection.[72] The US has been particularly active in attacking China over IPR, including suing China in the WTO over IP violations, and imposing tariffs on Chinese imports (without going through the WTO) based on Section 301 of the Trade Act of 1974.[73] Israeli investors and recipients of Chinese investment have also raised the issue of China's IPR protection.[74] However, it should be noted that since China's accession to the WTO China has made overall revisions of its IPR regime, considerably strengthening the protection of IPR.[75]

China and Israel have only a limited bilateral IPR protection framework. The most recent bilateral text related to IPR, signed during the twenty-five-year celebration of China–Israel relations (in March 2017) provides for limited, non-binding cooperation

[70] China Law Insight, CIETAC Rules Adds to Investment Treaty Practice (26 November 2017) https://www.chinalawinsight.com/2017/11/articles/global-network/cietac-rules-add-to-investment-treaty-practice/ (last accessed 7 December 2017). Wei Xun, International Commercial Court in China: Innovations, Misunderstandings and Clarifications, Kluwer Arbitration Blog (4 July, 2018) http://arbitrationblog.kluwerarbitration.com/2018/07/04/international-commercial-court-china-innovations-misunderstandings-clarifications/ (last accessed 10 October 2018).
[71] European Commission, MEMO/15/6060 http://europa.eu/rapid/press-release_MEMO-15-6060_en.htm (last accessed 7 December 2017).
[72] William P Alford, *To Steal a Book is an Elegant Offense: Intellectual Property Law in Chinese Civilization.* (Stanford University Press 1995).
[73] Peter Yu, 'The US-China Dispute over TRIPS Enforcement' in A Christoph (ed), *The Enforcement of Intellectual Property Rights Comparative Perspective form the Asia- Pacific Region* (Kluwer 2011); Tomer Broude, 'It's Easily Done: The China-Intellectual Property Rights Enforcement Dispute and Freedom of Expression' (2010) 10(5) Journal of World Intellectual Property 660. United States (2018), 'Presidential memorandum on the actions by the United States related to the Section 301 investigation', White House, at https://www.whitehouse.gov/presidential-actions/presidential-memorandum-actions-united-states-related-section-301-investigation/.
Request for Consultations, China—Certain Measures Concerning the Protection of Intellectual Property Rights, WT/DS542, submitted 23 March 2018.
[74] Niv Elis, 'Threat of IP Theft Lurks Beneath China-Israel Deals' *Jerusalem Post* (22 May 2014) http://www.jpost.com/Business/Business-Features/Threat-of-intellectual-property-theft-lurks-beneath-China-Israel-deals-353004 (last accessed 31 August 2017).
[75] Kirstie Thomas, *Assessing Intellectual Property Compliance in Contemporary China* (Springer 2017) 105–37.

in the field of IPR protection in which the sides are to provide one another with up-dates.[76] This MOU aims at enhancing and developing cooperation between the sides. Nevertheless, it does not constitute a binding agreement under international law, and is drafted with explicit intention not to create any legal rights or commitments between the parties.

In this context, it is important to emphasize that both China and Israel are WTO members, and thus, their legislation and enforcement are expected to meet TRIPs standards. Moreover, both China and Israel are signatories to the Madrid Protocol concerning the international registration of marks, the Patent Cooperation Treaty, and the Paris Convention for the Protection of Industrial Property. Therefore, although China and Israel have not made specific bilateral commitments in the field of IPR, they are certainly bound by a network of shared international obligations, already incorporated in their respective legislation.[77]

Here we arrive at another key point in our chapter. One would expect that economic diplomacy based on innovation would include a detailed mechanism and stronger undertakings to safeguard IPR. However, in view of the broader considerations discussed above, it seems more than plausible to assume that neither China nor Israel will suggest provisions that 'go beyond' formulas adopted previously in other similar economic agreements of the parties. If either of the sides were to suggest a new set of IPR obligations, it would require the other party to concede on other crucial issues which would be difficult for either side to achieve. Moreover, any concession by either of the countries would constitute a precedent for demands in future negotiations with other third parties. Since IPR is a particularly sensitive issue for China, it is not likely to agree to create an IPR scheme solely for Israel.

VII. Limits of Innovation as a Catalyst

While innovation is playing a vital role in expanding bilateral investment and trade relations, however, a number of factors limit its influence. From the Chinese perspective, following the GFC, the Chinese government prioritized innovation as a key source of development. This is a huge change from previous policies. The GFC made it evident to Chinese policy-makers that China's economy should no longer operate as the world's sweatshop, nor should it depend on trade and investment in low-tech industries.[78] China's long-term plan is to move to domestic scientific and technological innovation. To quote China's Science and Technology Roadmap (2050):

Efforts should be made to enhance international S&T exchanges and cooperation. We have to promote high level bilateral or multilateral collaborations … We should absorb various S&T innovation resources across the world, and selectively bring the professionals, intellectual resources, technologies and management so as to upgrade the national innovation capacity, and make China an active participant of international S&T cooperation, a leader and core player in regional S&T cooperation, and an influential member of international S&T organizations. We must be clearly aware that original innovation is the source of a country's international competitiveness. Key technologies of strategic significance can never be bought from the outside world.

---

[76] Memorandum of Understanding between the State Intellectual Property Office of the People's Republic of China and the Israel Ministry of Justice on Cooperation in the Field of Intellectual Property (on file with authors).

[77] Antons and Reto (n 6).

[78] Wing Thye Woo, 'China Meets the Middle-income Trap: The Large Potholes in the Road to Catching-up' (2012) 10 Journal of Chinese Economic and Business Studies 313.

In order to dramatically reduce the country's reliance on imported technologies, upgrade the innovation capacity and gradually gain the strategic initiative in this aspect.[79]

More generally, in making foreign investment deals China often requires technology transfer. China's demand for technology transfer is one of the huge points of contention between the US and China in their investment relations. Similar concerns have been echoed by Israeli experts, that Chinese investment in Israeli innovation could adversely affect Israel's economic growth and job creation.[80] Another constraint on China–Israel investment relations, is China's will to play a more influential role in global politics, and its desire to be viewed as a neutral player in the Middle East (unlike the US, which, under Trump, is increasingly being viewed as a biased broker). Further constraints include its interests in obtaining gas and oil from a number of Middle Eastern countries, as well as its concern in maintaining stability necessary for the advancement of the Belt and Road Initiative.

From the Israeli perspective, Israel monitors and restricts investment in defence-related innovation.[81] Eliminating such restrictions is inconceivable given Israel's fear that its technology might fall into the hands of its historical enemies.[82] In addition, since the US often co-develops such innovation with Israel, it has veto power over such innovation transfer. Thus, potential growth in investment in Israeli scientific and technological innovation must take into account the highly complicated geopolitical situation, and particularly, the US interests.

These concerns are not limited only to investment in defence-related innovation. Over the years, China has built a comprehensive regime governing foreign investment in China, which leaves very limited space to private forces, and unmonitored investment and trade. Although Israel does not have a comprehensive foreign investment review mechanism, strategic sectors such as finance, banking, insurance, telecommunication, defence-related and state-owned companies require pre-approval by the applicable regulator as part of the licensing terms. Some in Israel, opposed to Chinese investment, have proposed the establishment of a mechanism similar to that of the US, which would review potential foreign investment from all foreign sources. (Israeli officials have rejected the plan, claiming that it would have a chilling effect on FDI.)

In some cases, planned Chinese investments in Israel have led to serious public debate, particularly where national security concerns are considered to be involved. In fact, public debate over intended investments in these fields, has at times discouraged Chinese investments.[83] In the case of an economic crisis in China or globally, the Chinese companies may pull out, since their interests do not coincide with Israeli national interests. Here too we see that innovation as a driver of expanded China–Israel relations is constrained.

[79] S&T in China Roadmap 2050 Report (n 17) 117.

[80] European Business in China, Position Paper (2016/2017) http://www.europeanchamber.com.cn/en/publications-position-paper (last accessed 7 December 2017).

[81] The Israeli Defense Export Controls Agency http://www.exportctrl.mod.gov.il/ExportCtrl/ENGLISH/About+DECA/ (last accessed 31August 2017).

[82] Yitzhak Shichor, 'Israel's Military Transfers to China and Taiwan' (1998) 40 Survival 68; Yitzhak Shichor, 'Mountains out of Molehills: Arms Transfers in Sino-Middle Eastern Relations' (6 September 2000) http://www.rubincenter.org/2000/09/shichor-2000-09-06/ (last accessed 31 August 2017).

[83] Editorial, 'Israel for Sale' *Hamodia* (28 May 2014) http://hamodia.com/2014/05/27/israel-sale/ (last accessed 31 August 2017); David Wainer, 'Israeli Government Said to Oppose China Purchase of Insurer' *Bloomberg* (3 January 2017) https://www.bloomberg.com/news/articles/2017-01-03/israeli-government-said-to-oppose-china-purchase-of-insurers (last accessed 31 August 2017).

VIII. Conclusion

Our findings indicate that scientific and technological innovation served as a catalyst in expanding China–Israel investment and trade relations, from the late 1970s to the initiation of the recent FTA negotiations. This stands in contrast with the commonly accepted motivations for China's economic diplomacy before the GFC. Following the GFC, China's economic development policies have been undergoing a systemic shift. With regard to foreign investment policy, China started to change its focus from attracting FDI, to outward investment. In its outward investment shopping spree, innovation has become a priority. Indeed, innovation is central to China's global vision; under the BRI, China is seeking and marketing innovation on bilateral, regional, and global levels.

The China–Israel Comprehensive Innovative Partnership is the most striking example of this policy, encouraging investment in innovation. Despite downturns in global investment, and in FDI in Israel, China's investment flows into Israel have not waned, and are particularly focused on innovation. Specifically, Chinese investment in Israeli innovation is steadily rising. Given that Israel is uniquely situated as a leader in innovation, it has become a key target of Chinese investment. For its part, Israel is looking to China for help in scaling up. Thus, innovation has led to a mutually beneficial partnership. In the words of the Chinese Ambassador to Israel, His Excellency Zhan Yongxin: 'Israel is well known as the Start-Up Nation, strong in creation and innovation, or going from 0 to 1. China, with its strong manufacturing capacity and huge market, is good at going from 1 to 100'.[84]

In the longer run, however, as shown by global innovation indices, China is quickly catching up, and may soon surpass Israel's innovative capacity. If China is good in accelerating from one to 100, it will enhance its own capabilities to bridge the gap of zero to one. At the same time, geopolitical constraints affect Israel's policy, specifically US restrictions on sales of arms related technology. The Trump–Xi trade war may also cast a shadow on the China–Israel relations. Another constraint on Israel is related to China's policies and interests in the Middle East. China increasingly wants to be viewed as a neutral player in the Middle East, securing its long-term energy interests, and supplying arms and technology to Israel's rivals. Looking forward, innovation as a catalyst in the bilateral relationship is likely to decline.

In this context, the necessity of an FTA to reinforce the bilateral investment and trade relations becomes evident. The FTA, which is under negotiation at the time of the writing of this chapter is expected to include a chapter on investment to replace the outdated CIBIT, and will strengthen the political-economic relations between the countries.

[84] Yongxin Zhang, 'China's New Era of Development is Win-Win with Israel' *Jerusalem Post* (Israel, 26 October 2017) http://www.jpost.com/Opinion/Chinas-new-era-of-development-is-win-win-with-Israel-508572 (last accessed 7 December 2017).

9

Drivers and Issues of China–EU Negotiations for a Comprehensive Agreement on Investment

Flavia Marisi and Qian Wang*

I. Introduction

Since the time of the Roman Empire there have been regular communications and trade between China and Europe, which contributed to prosperity and progress of both regions.[1] Today, not only are China and the European Union (EU) among the largest traders in the world but they have also developed an intense network of direct economic relationships.[2] The EU is China's biggest trading partner, and China is the EU's second trading partner, behind the United States (USA).[3]

Over recent years the two regions have understood the importance of formalizing and regularizing their economic relationships through different types of agreements, which have tackled diverse matters to be resolved, one by one, on the economic, political, and legal levels. This route, which started in the 1970s, continues today with the stimulating challenge of the negotiations for a Comprehensive Agreement on Investment (CAI), currently ongoing.

The chapter is composed of six sections. Section II draws a panoramic picture on the economic, political, and social drivers between the EU and China, and analyses the economic agreements and policy papers issued in the time span from 1973 to 2013. Section III focuses on China–EU relations in the context of regional economic governance, analysing the general economic strategy conducted from the EU in Asia. Section IV proposes to examine the behaviour that the EU and its Member States, on the one hand, and China, on the other, have had throughout the time in the drafting and signing of their investment agreements, with the aim of highlighting the areas that modified their negotiation strategies in answer to different economic and political situations. Section V posits that certain issues deserve special attention in the drafting of the agreement between the EU and China and identifies them as fair and equitable treatment (FET), taxation provisions, and transparency. This selection derives from the hypothesis that, precisely on these issues, the EU and China will probably hold diverging positions. Section VI brings together the threads of our discussion. Notwithstanding time and space constraints, the chapter aims to provide a helpful tool to academics, legal counsels, and policy-makers, and contribute to both the knowledge

---

* Respectively, Dr Flavia Marisi is an Italian-qualified lawyer, and Ms Qian Wang is Senior Research Assistant, Faculty of Law, The Chinese University of Hong Kong.
[1] Susan Whitfield, *Life Along the Silk Road* (University of California Press 1999) 21.
[2] Eurostat, 'International Trade in Goods' http://ec.europa.eu/eurostat/statistics-explained/index.php/International_trade_in_goods (last accessed 12 February 2017).
[3] China http://ec.europa.eu/trade/policy/countries-and-regions/countries/china/ (last accessed 12 February 2017).

of certain aspects of investment treaties and the reflection on the possible implications
of provisions contained therein.

II. Economic, Political, and Legal Drivers towards a CAI

A wide range of tactical considerations surround and motivate the EU and China to seek
an 'ambitious and comprehensive' agreement on investment. One may argue an EU–
China CAI will deepen the EU–China comprehensive strategic partnership, better regulate Chinese investment flooding the EU, provide a level playing field for investors from
both sides, together (re)write investment rules for the Asia-Pacific region, or increase EU
and China competitiveness in global economy. Those reasons are certainly not exhaustive
but understandably float on the negotiation table. Both sides need to make conscious
efforts to strike a deal that reflects the state of the EU–China relations, meets domestic
demands, and paves the way for a high-level free trade agreement.

We consider the analysis of the dynamics of negotiating the EU–China CAI needs to be
factored in four dimensions: economic, political, legal, and regional governance aspects,
to paint a picture to see how far both sides have come together. It would be unwise not to
make a success story for leaders on both sides.

A. Economic drivers of the negotiation of a China–EU CAI

Foreign investment is one of the elements that contribute to economic development. Since
their inception, investment treaties were armed with two goals: (1) to create favourable
investment conditions for investors from one party in the territory of the other, and (2) to
contribute to the prosperity of both treaty parties.[4] The EU Member States and China are
no strangers in negotiating investment protection treaties and understanding what benefits it entailed.[5] In addition to delivering these two traditional goals, an EU–China CAI
will go further to promote, protect, facilitate, and liberalize investment along with their
economic policies.

More than 2,000 years ago, a silk road linked Chinese and Roman empires through
trade routes where, among other goods, the spice trade made its formal appearance.[6]
Evidently, China and Europe share a long history of trade. For navigating EU–China economic relations in the context of current EU–China CAI negotiations, this chapter will
primarily identify some landmark years which have progressively deepened the EU–China
relationship, especially on the economic front.

As early as December of 1973, in the first public statement—the Declaration of
European Identity—that intended to strengthen ties with China,[7] the nine Member
States of the European Communities pledged that: 'Conscious of the major role played

---

[4] Kenneth J Vandevelde, *Bilateral Investment Treaties: History, Policy, and Interpretation* (OUP 2010) 77–8.
[5] China maintains the world's second largest BIT network. According to the European Commission, Member States concluded more than 1,000 bilateral agreements relating to for-eign investment with third countries. See 'Proposal for a Regulation of the European Parliament and of the Council establishing transitional arrangements for bilateral investment agreements be-tween Member States and third countries' http://eur-lex.europa.eu/legal-content/EN/TXT/PDF/?uri=CELEX:52010PC0344&from=EN (last accessed 28 February 2017).
[6] James Innes Miller, *The Spice Trade of the Roman Empire, 29 B.C. to A.D. 641* (Clarendon Press 1969) 119.
[7] Marie Julie Chenard, 'The European Community's Opening to People's Republic of China, 1969-1979: Internal Decision-making on External Relations' (LSE PhD thesis 2012) 47 http://

by China in international affairs, the Nine intend to intensify their relations with the Chinese Government and to promote exchanges in various fields as well as contacts between European and Chinese leaders'.[8] Ever since, interactions and deliberations between the Community and China have developed substantially, which ultimately contributed to the establishment of the European Economic Community (EEC) and China diplomatic relations in 1975, after Sir Christopher Soames, the former Vice President of the European Commission who was responsible for external relations, made a historic visit to China.

Since the early 1970s, both sides have started to hold negotiations towards a free trade agreement, largely due to the expected expiration in 1974 of bilateral trade agreements between Member States and China that was a result of decisions made by the Community institutions in the formation of a joint trade policy at the Community level.[9] Finally, in 1978, the EEC–China Trade Agreement was signed, which, according to Article 1 of the agreement, aimed to 'promote and intensify trade'. Notably, the 1978 EEC–China Trade Agreement was a non-preferential agreement that was concluded for a period of five years and automatically renewable each year thereafter, and aimed at promoting the development of trade.[10] Apart from the fact that the volume of trade between the Community and China was very limited at the time, the signing of the 1978 Trade Agreement was coincidental with China's opening up, which indicated that both sides recognized the growing importance of bilateral relations and, hence, conclusion of a trade deal was based on the 1974 Outline Agreement[11] and, nevertheless, the 1978 EEC–China Trade Agreement had more political significance than economic motivations.

The subsequent 1979 Textile Agreement resulted from overly concentrated trade between the Community and China in which the textile trade accounted for one-third of China's exports to the Community. However, this significant and sensitive sector was omitted from the 1978 Trade Agreement. However, under the GATT Multi-Fiber Arrangement the 1979 Textile Agreement came out to standardize textile trade between two sides as far as tariff reduction was concerned, rather than as a symbolic 'political statement' as regards the 1978 EEC–China Trade Agreement. In 1985, economic links between the EEC and China were strengthened and broadened with the signing of a new agreement—the 1985 EEC–China Trade and Economic Cooperation Agreement.[12]

In the 1980s, a 'common narrative' in the literature of EEC–China relations was that economics come at first, until the relationship became comprehensive, when politics were included. In the 1990s, EU–China relations were on the trajectory with Europe's accelerated integration[13] and China's efforts to rejoin the world economy by

etheses.lse.ac.uk/641/1/Chenard_European_community%E2%80%99s_opening%20c.pdf (last accessed 18 October 2018).

[8] Bulletin of the European Communities (December 1973) No 12. Luxembourg: Office for official publications of the European Communities. 'Declaration on European Identity' 118–22 No 17.

[9] External Relations, European Information, 13/78, the Office for Official Publications in Luxembourg (1978) http://aei.pitt.edu/8243/1/31735055282234_1.pdf.

[10] Commission of the European Communities, Memorandum on the People's Republic of China and the European Community (1979) http://aei.pitt.edu/8242/1/31735055282226_1.pdf (last accessed 23 March 2017).

[11] Marie Julie Chenard, 'Seeking Détente and Driving Integration: The European Community's opening towards the People's Republic of China, 1975-1978' (2012) 18 ZGEI Zeitschrift für die Geschichte der Europäischen Integration 25.

[12] For a detailed discussion on the 1985 Agreement see 'legal drivers'.

[13] Enrico Spolaore, 'What Is European Integration Really About? A Political Guide for Economists' (2013) http://sites.tufts.edu/enricospolaore/files/2012/08/Euro-June-2013.pdf (last accessed 28 February 2017).

resuming its member status under the GATT and later joining the WTO. The EU and China were committed to the idea of pursuing greater prosperity and global presence through economic integration and expansion in a multi-lateral system.

The next milestone came in 1995 when the European Commission published its first Communication on China entitled 'A Long-term Policy for China-Europe Relations', which 'seeks to chart a long-run course for EU-China relations into the 21st century'. From 1995 to 2003, the European Commission published altogether four Communications and policy papers on China, all of which reinforced shared interests and challenges in a mutually beneficial partnership. In 2003, the Chinese government issued its first ever EU policy paper, 'China's EU Policy Paper',[14] that 'aims to highlight the objectives of China's EU policy and outline the areas and plans of co-operation'. Both sides had witnessed intensified economic relations and ever-greater shared interests.

In the 1980s and 1990s, when the deepening of European integration had reached a crucial point, economic reforms gained a central place in China's domestic agenda. Until the 2004 enlargement of the EU, the network of bilateral investment treaties (BITs) between the EU Member States and China has expanded since the EU embraced eight former communist countries.[15]

Since the launch of economic reform by Deng Xiaoping in 1978, although Chinese leadership and various relevant government agencies may have had different opinions on the breadth and depth of reforms and the way to achieve it, there has been a consensus of the necessity of reforms and continuingly opening up China's market to the world and liberalizing rules that regulate the market.

To manage future economic relations between an enlarging EU and gradually liberalizing China in a single set of comprehensive and precisely defined rules that will promote, protect, liberalize, and facilitate two-way investments with an effective implementation and enforcement mechanism to ensure a level playing field on both sides is politically and economically desirable.

B. China–EU economic relations: an overview of recent developments

There is no doubt that trade imbalance[16] shapes the EU's external policy in a way that strives to achieve the balance of imports and exports through trade agreements and, when necessary, to initiate safeguarding measures or adopt anti-dumping and anti-subsidy instruments to protect companies and workers in Europe, which are bearing the results of trade deficits with China. According to Euro Statistics, in the 1970s and 1980s, Europe enjoyed a trade surplus with China until the 1990s, when 'a small trade surplus in the 1980s turned into a deficit'[17] and, in 2002, China overtook Japan and

---

[14] China's policy paper on the EU, 2003/10/13, http://www.chinamission.be/eng/zywj/zywd/t1227623.htm (last accessed 28 February 2017).

[15] Wenhua Shan, 'EU Enlargement and the Legal Framework of EU-China Investment Relations' (2005) 6 Journal of World Investment & Trade 237.

[16] John Farnell and Paul Irwin Crookes, *The Politics of EU-China Economic Relations* (Palgrave Macmillan 2016) 220.

[17] Communication from the Commission to the Council and the European Parliament EU Strategy towards China: Implementation of the 1998 Communication and Future Steps for a More Effective EU Policy http://eur-lex.europa.eu/legal-content/EN/TXT/PDF/?uri=CELEX:52001DC0265&from=en (last accessed 28 February 2017).

became the EU's 'second-largest trading partner outside Europe'.[18] When the trade imbalance escalated, EU–China economic relations were not immune from tension and conflicts. As a result, trade frictions and disputes with China have been increasing and, eventually, led to high-profile trade disputes in certain sectors, such as the 'textile war'[19] in 2005 and the 'solar trade war'[20] around 2012.

While trade significantly contributes to the EU and China economies overall, another source of economic growth—investment—does not have the same pace as trade growth. Dating back to 1995, in its communication 'A Long-term Policy for China-EU Relations', the European Commission observed that two-way investment was less attractive than two-way trade. Recently, Chinese Premier Li Keqiang further expressed his concern at the World Economic Forum, saying that EU–China two-way investment, as two of the world's three largest economies, is 'hardly satisfactory'. Unlike trade, investment is not regulated on a rule-based multi-lateral system, and therefore a lack of consistency and predictability of investment rules considerably complicates cross-border business activities. As a consequence, the current fragmented framework cannot guarantee to maintain and attract foreign investment as a sustainable engineer for long-term economic growth.

Often, concerns about investment barriers and asymmetric market access are raised by investors from the other side. According to the OECD FDI Regulatory Restrictiveness Index, China maintains a relatively restrictive regime for foreign investors. Furthermore, increasing Chinese investment in the EU is to some extent considered as a challenge to Europe's economic security. All of those concerns are associated with the nature of China's economy and Beijing has promised to keep reforming and opening-up Chinese markets. An EU–China CAI is suitable to address and mitigate those concerns and will construct sustainable EU–China investment relations.

A. Future prospects for China–EU economic cooperation: untapped potential for China–EU comprehensive strategic partnership

Although there are ups and downs in EU–China economic relations, economic opportunities outweigh disagreements. In contrast with a share of two-way trade, China as the EU's second largest trading partner and the EU as China's largest trading partner, just 2-3 per cent of overall European outward investment reaches China, while the EU has hosted a surge in Chinese investment since 2008, which is increasingly growing and spreading throughout the EU.[21] Rhodium Group and China International Capital

---

[18] 'Commission Policy Paper for Transmission to the Council and the European Parliament: A Maturing Partnership—Shared Interests and Challenges in EU-China relations' http://eur-lex. europa.eu/legal-content/EN/TXT/PDF/?uri=CELEX:52003DC0533&from=en (accessed 20 February 2017).

[19] The Economist, 'Europe's Textile War with China—and Itself' (2005) http://www.economist. com/node/4314327 (accessed 20 February 2017). For more information on textile disputes between the EU and China see Qingjiang Kong, *China-EU Trade Disputes and Their Management* (World Scientific Publishing Company 2012) 20.

[20] Reuters, 'EU and China stumble towards solar trade war' (2013) http://www.reuters.com/article/us-eu-china-trade-idUSBRE91K0J920130221 (last accessed 28 February 2017).

[21] Thilo Hanemann and Mikko Huotari, 'Chinese FDI in Europe and Germany: preparing for a new era of Chinese capital, a report by the Mercator Institute for China Studies and Rhodium Group' (2015) 13 http://rhg.com/wp-content/uploads/2015/06/ChineseFDI_Europe_Full.pdf (last accessed 23 March 2017).

Corporation, a Chinese Investment bank, forecast China's outward FDI will reach between US$1 trillion to US$2 trillion by 2020 and the EU could be destined to receive between US$250 billion to US$500 billion of China's outward FDI. Therefore, concrete actions – not just declaratory talking points – are needed to tap the full potential of a recovering European economy and increased sophistication of the Chinese economy.

Cooperation has been a significant component in the EU's strategy towards China after first being identified in the 1995 policy paper, 'A Long-term Policy for China-Europe Relations' in which the European Commission suggested numerous cooperation areas that had economic significance to Europe.[22] At a macro level, the synergy of European and Chinese cooperation was fuelled by Mr Lu Zhongyuan's office of then Premier Wen Jiaobao's visit to Brussels in 2011. On this trip, he presented China's Twelfth Five-Year Plan (2011–2015). Common interests and goals in China's Five-Year Plan and Europe 2020 serve as a roadmap for both sides to unlock the full potential of the relationship and achieve 'faster growth'.[23] Two examples will put Europe and China cooperation into perspective: (1) EU–China cooperation in the renewable energy sector; and (2) both sides commit to each other's flagship initiatives, namely, OBOR and the Investment Plan for Europe.[24]

One of the overlapping objectives in both China's Twelfth Five-Year plan and Europe 2020, apart from research and development, environment, social development, and services industry, is energy, which is also highlighted in the EU–China 2020 Strategic Agenda for Cooperation. Over China's transformation to a sustainable economy, energy efficiency and energy security rank high in its development policies. A mutually beneficial energy partnership is reaffirmed in the EU–China Joint Declaration on Energy Security in 2012, and is guided by the EU–China Energy Roadmap, that looks to foster trade and investment in renewable energy and works to improve trade and investment conditions in the sector.

Furthermore, synergies of the OBOR and the Investment Plan for Europe will surely bring EU–China relations into a new area. To reap long-term geopolitical, economic, and geostrategic interests, the EU needs to respond to OBOR with one voice and coordinated policies.[25] Among other joint initiatives, the EU–China Connectivity Platform is to promote cooperation between China's Silk Road Fund and European Investment Bank in areas such as infrastructure, equipment, technologies, and standards.

To conclude 'economic drivers', undoubtedly the EC/EU has assisted to China's domestic reforms and development, in particular, in the area of sustainable development. Meanwhile, the significance of Chinese markets to Europe's economic security[26] and vice versa matters more than ever before on the domestic and global levels.

[22] See Julien Chaisse and Mitsuo Matsushita, 'China's "Belt and Road" Initiative: Mapping the World Trade Normative and Strategic Implications' (2018) 52(1) Journal of World Trade 163.

[23] Roderic Wye, 'The Chinese Five Year Programme (2011–2015) and Europe 2020' http://eeas.europa.eu/archives/docs/china/docs/division_ecran/is7_the_chinese_five_year_programme__2011-2015_and_europe_2020_rod_wye_en.pdf (last accessed 28 February 2017).

[24] European Commission, 'Investment Plan for Europe goes global: China announces its contribution to invest EU' http://trade.ec.europa.eu/doclib/docs/2015/october/tradoc_153844.PDF (last accessed 28 February 2017).

[25] Gisela Grieger, 'Briefing One Belt, One Road (OBOR): China's Regional Integration Initiative' *European Parliamentary Research Service* (2016) http://www.europarl.europa.eu/RegData/etudes/BRIE/2016/586608/EPRS_BRI(2016)586608_EN.pdf (last accessed 23 March 2017).

[26] Gustaaf Geeraets and Weiping Huang, 'The Economic Security Dimension of the EU-China Relationship: Puzzles and Prospects' in Emil J Kirchner and others (eds), *Security Relations between China and the European Union. From Convergence to Cooperation?* (Cambridge University Press 2016) 187–208.

B. Political drivers of EU–China Comprehensive Investment Agreement negotiation

Investment treaties, usually negotiated bilaterally between countries sharing diplomatic ties, are not just motivated by commercial interests. A BIT is a traditional vehicle to advance a broad foreign policy agenda. Friendship, commerce and navigation (FCN) agreements, the predecessors of modern day BITs, were used to regulate economic activities but also show the parties in *friendly* diplomatic terms.[27] Professor Salacuse speaks of the long-term goals of investment treaties more profoundly: 'Investment treaties are basically instruments of international relations, and the parties to them—sovereign states, not investors—undertake them in order to further certain long-term goals that may go well beyond the domain of investment'.[28]

C. China–EU political relations: from 'constructive engagement' to 'comprehensive strategic partnership'

Both political motivations and economic interests shape EU–China relations. However, for a long time after the EEC established diplomatic relations with China in 1975, a coherent and common policy on China was absent until 1995 when the Commission proposed 'constructive engagement' with China in its policy paper 'A Long-term Policy for China Europe Relations', saying 'it is in the interests of Europe, and of the international community as a whole, to engage China' (COM 1995). Afterwards, another three policy papers followed: 'Building a Comprehensive Partnership with China' (1998), 'EU Strategy towards China: Implementation of the 1998 Communication and Future Steps for a more Effective EU Policy' (2001), and 'A Maturing Partnership: Shared Interests and Challenges in EU-China Relations' (2003). These papers progressively articulated EU–China relations from 'constructive engagement' to 'comprehensive partnership' and, further, to 'comprehensive strategic partnership'.

The year 2013 marked the tenth anniversary of the EU–China comprehensive strategic partnership, and both sides jointly adopted the China–EU 2020 Strategic Agenda for Cooperation at the 16th EU–China Summit—'a comprehensive document setting out China and the EU's shared aims to promote cooperation in the areas of peace and security, prosperity, sustainable development and people-to-people exchanges, to take forward the China-EU Comprehensive Strategic Partnership over the coming years'.[29] While the EU–China Comprehensive Strategic Partnership has entered into its second decade, the Chinese government issued its second policy paper on the EU in 2014, 'Deepen the China-EU Comprehensive Strategic Partnership for Mutual Benefit and Win-win Cooperation' after President Xi's visit to the Netherlands, France, Germany, and Belgium and, as the first Chinese President, to the European institutions in Brussels. The 2014 policy paper 'defines its [China's] EU policy objectives in the new era, draw a blueprint for China-EU cooperation in the next 5 to 10 years and facilitate

---

[27] Lauge N Skovgaard Poulsen and Emma Aisbett, 'Diplomats Want Treaties: Diplomatic Agendas and Perks in the Investment Regime' (2016) 7 Journal of International Dispute Settlement 84.

[28] Jeswald W Salacuse, *The Three Laws of International Investment* (OUP 2013) 359.

[29] EU–China 2020 Strategic Agenda for Cooperation released at the Sixteenth China–EU Summit (2013) http://www.fmprc.gov.cn/mfa_eng/wjdt_665385/2649_665393/t1101804.shtml (last accessed 28 February 2017).

greater progress in China-EU relations' (*Xinhua News*)[30] and, among other items on the agenda, 'actively advance negotiations of an investment agreement'.

During Xi's visit to Europe in 2014, in addition to 'jointly forge four major China-EU partnerships for peace, growth, reform and civilization',[31] Xi's historical visit to the EU headquarters signalled 'a renewed focus on the EU'[32] that aims to liberalize and facilitate two-way trade and investment through direct engagement with the EU's machinery in Brussels. In the process of upgrading bilateral relations to the point of 'comprehensive strategic partnership', although initially centred on economic cooperation, the scope of 'win-win cooperation' has considerably expanded to develop 'all-dimensional, multi-tiered and wide-ranging cooperation'.[33] Meanwhile, economic and trade cooperation remains the cornerstone of the partnership.

D. EU's changing approach to China: from 'value-based linkage' strategy to 'interests-based engagement' approach

During the period of 1989–1991, Europe deployed economic sanctions as punishment for China's human rights situation at the time. However, the EU's linkage of bilateral economic relationship to human rights did not last long, and most sanctions were lifted around 1991. Zhang Xiaotong argued that 'linkages strategy underplays the partnership'. In fact, the Commission recognized that, reflecting on the effectiveness of its policy in reality in 1995, 'there is a danger that relying solely on frequent and strident declarations will dilute the message or lead to knee-jerk reactions from the Chinese government'.[34]

The deadlock of partnership and cooperation (PCA) negotiation evidently doubted the EU's linkage strategy since the EU insisted on the inclusion of a 'democracy and human rights clause', which partially brought the PCA negotiation to a halt.[35] Conversely, certain language in China's 2014 policy paper on the EU presumably responded to an 'ominous intent' regarding certain areas of cooperation in the EU's previous communication, 'EU China, Closer Partners, Growing Responsibilities'. For one of the EU's aspirations that 'The EU should continue support for China's internal political and economic reform process', China responded in a soft way using 'political guidance' and outlined areas that it is less enthusiastic about and repeatedly emphasized cooperation needs to be fulfilled 'in the spirit of equality and mutual respect'. In fact, the EU has achieved positive outcomes by applying the interests-based

---

[30] Xinhua carries 'full text' of China's policy paper on EU http://news.xinhuanet.com/english/china/2014-04/02/c_133230788.htm (last accessed 28 February 2017).

[31] Xi Jinping Holds Talks with President Herman Van Rompuy of European Council (2014) http://www.fmprc.gov.cn/mfa_eng/topics_665678/xjpzxcxdsjhaqhfbfwhlfgdgblshlhgjkezzzbomzb_666590/t1143124.shtml (last accessed 26 February 2017).

[32] David Scott, 'New Horizons in EU-China Relations? President Xi's Trip to Europe and the 2014 Policy Paper' *EU-China Observer* (2014) https://www.coleurope.eu/system/files_force/research-paper/eu-china_observer_issue_3_2014.pdf?download=1 (last accessed 26 March 2017).

[33] China's Policy Paper on the EU: Deepen the EU Comprehensive Strategic Partnership for Mutual Benefit and Win-win Cooperation http://www.fmprc.gov.cn/mfa_eng/wjdt_665385/wjzcs/t1143406.shtml (last accessed 28 February 2017).

[34] EU-China Trade Relations: A Concise History (1975-2014) http://www.whuced.com/show/?id=205&page=1&siteid=3 (last accessed 28 February 2017).

[35] Kim Van der Borght and Lei Zhang, 'The Current Legal Foundation and Prospective Legal Framework of the PCA' in Jing Men and Giuseppe Balducci (eds), *Prospects and Challenges for EU-China Relations in the 21st Century: The Partnership and Cooperation Agreement* (College of Europe Studies No 12, PIE Peter Lang 2010) 53–80, at 70.

engagement with China in its negotiations over China's accession to the WTO.[36] The Commission deployed a market access strategy in the EU–China WTO negotiations. Then Commissioner for Trade Pascal Lamy explained this strategy as:

The mandate I had this week was (having tested the depth of their resistance) to say to the Chinese: we need you to go as far as you can to the red line you have identified. But if you can't cross it, then we must have compensation, both inside and outside the particular sector concerned. We told the Chinese that we are not going to try to go into your political no-go-zone . . .

which led to the final breakthrough of the long EU–China WTO accession negotiations.

While Europe 'projects its model of society into a wider world'[37] and 'places universal norms and principles at the center of its relations with . . . the world',[38] 'value gaps' between those of that stipulated in the preamble of the Treaty of Lisbon—democracy, equality, the rule of law, and a respect for human rights, as core values of the EU, and China's core national interests—economic development over political pluralism, social stability, one-China policy, etc[39]can be adequately closed by addressing mutual interests and replacing values-based linkage to interests-based engagement. In other words, 'demand-driven cooperation'[40] could yield better results when it effectively avoids suspicion and even rejection from the other side.

To conclude 'political drivers', for the EU, an effective and coherent external policy on China is crucial for continuing 'all-round, broadened areas, and multi-dimensional cooperative framework, growing from economic cooperation to strategic interdependence'[41] with China. Despite challenges and sometimes obstacles, it is realistic and pragmatic to recognize that the foundation of EU–China relations has not been changed.

E. Legal drivers of EU–China Comprehensive Investment Agreement negotiation

In its 2010 communication, 'Toward a Comprehensive European International Investment Policy', the Commission set 'investment as a new frontier for the common commercial policy', and the EU should cover a life circle of inward foreign direct investment 'through both multilateral and bilateral agreements at EU level', including investment market access and investment protection and liberalization. A broad policy consensus has been reached by the Commission, the Council and the Parliament, that is, to provide a high level of protection for EU investors, to respect the right to regulate, to increase legal certainty, to include a state-of-the-art dispute settlement mechanism,

---

[36] Franco Algieri, 'It's the System that Matters: Institutionalization and Making of EU Policy Toward China' in David Shambaugh, Eberhard Sandschneider, and Zhou Hong (eds), *China-Europe Relations: Perceptions, Polices and Prospects* (Routledge 2008) 72.

[37] Romano Prodi, '2000–2005: Shaping the New Europe' speech/00/41 to the European Parliament (15 February 2000) http://europa.eu/rapid/press-release_SPEECH-00-41_en.htm (last accessed 27 September 2017).

[38] Ian Manners, 'Normative Power Europe: A Contradiction in Terms?' (2002) 40 JCMS 240.

[39] Paul Irwin Crookes, 'Resetting EU–China Relations from a Values-based to an Interests-based Engagement' (2013) 50 International Politics 639.

[40] Mikael Mattlin, 'Dead on Arrival: Normative EU Policy towards China' (2012) http://econpapers.repec.org/RePEc:kap:asiaeu:v:10:y:2012:i:2:p:181-198 (last accessed 28 February 2017).

[41] David Allen, 'Who Speaks for Europe? The Search for an Effective and Coherent External Policy' in John Peterson and Helen Sjursen (eds), *A Common Foreign Policy for Europe? Competing visions of the CFSP* (Routledge 1998) 41–58, at 51.

and to be consistent with the Union's external actions.[42] More importantly, action as a Union should be to deliver better results than those that Member States did or could have achieved individually.

F. Legal framework of EU–China relations

As Weiler commented[43] in 1992, '[t]he EC may not speak with one voice but increasingly speaks like a choir.' Unfortunately, this has not changed, especially regarding the EU's common commercial policy.[44] We are familiar with the rhetoric of 'speaking with one voice'[45] advocated by the European Commission in order for the EU to gain bargaining leverage in concluding a trade or investment deal with third countries. In the case of EU–China relations, the current legal framework governing EU–China trade and investment relations is composed of the 1985 EEC–China Trade and Cooperation Agreement and twenty-six BITs signed between twenty-seven EU Member States (except Ireland) and China. Notably, all of those BITs were signed in the period from 1982 (with Sweden) to 2007 (with France).

According to the communication of the European Commission in 2011—trade policy is a core component of the EU's 2020 strategy[46]—'to better address the need of investors from all Member States ... integrate investment protection together with investment liberalization into on-going trade negotiations. The Commission is also considering whether stand-alone investment agreements with other countries, such as China, would be worthwhile'. Although as early as 2006 the Commission claimed that: 'at the heart of [the EU's partnership with China] will be the new Partnership and Cooperation Agreement (PCA) with China',[47] the progress, or lack of progress, of the PCA negotiations eventually required the Commission to 'negotiate and conclude a comprehensive EU-China Investment Agreement that covers issues of interest to either side, including investment protection and market access',[48] starting with a stand-alone investment agreement with the option 'towards a deep and comprehensive FTA, as a longer term perspective'.[49]

---

[42] Frank Hoffmeister and Gabriela Alexandru, 'A First Glimpse of Light on the Emerging EU Model BIT' (2014) 15 Journal of World Investment & Trade 383.

[43] Joseph H H Weiler, 'The Evolution of Mechanisms and Institutions for a European Foreign Policy. Reflections on the Interaction of Law and Politics' *European University Institute Research Paper No 85/202* (1992).

[44] For the detailed examination of politics and origins of the EU's common commercial policy, particularly in the area of foreign investment, see Sophie Meunier and Kalypso Nicolaïdis, 'The European Union as a Trade Power' in C Hill, M Smith, and S Vanhoonacke (eds), *International Relations and the European Union* (OUP 2011) 276–98.

[45] José Manuel Durão Barroso, 'President of the European Commission, speech of Speaking with one voice: defining and defending the European interest, in Strasbourg' (2010) http://europa.eu/rapid/press-release_SPEECH-10-21_en.htm (last accessed 28 February 2017).

[46] European Economic and Social Committee, 'Trade, Growth and World Affairs: Trade Policy as a core component of the EU's 2020 strategy' http://www.eesc.europa.eu/?i=portal.en.rex-opinions.18523 (last accessed 28 February 2017).

[47] Accompanying COM(2006) 631 final: 'Closer Partners, Growing Responsibilities A Policy Paper on EU-China Trade and Investment: Competition and Partnership' http://trade.ec.europa.eu/doclib/docs/2006/october/tradoc_130791.pdf (last accessed 28 February 2017).

[48] EU–China 2020 Strategic Agenda for Cooperation (n 29).   [49] ibid.

G. The 1985 EEC–China Trade and Economic Cooperation Agreement

The 1985 Trade and Economic Cooperation Agreement, that was built upon and subsequently replaced the 1978 Trade Agreement signed between the EEC and China, aimed to 'introduce a new stage into their commercial and economic relations', as stated in its preamble.

Comparing the 1978 Trade Agreement and the 1985 Trade and Economic Cooperation Agreement, the terms of trade-related measures are the same, including 'to accord each other most-favored-nation treatment' (Article 2 of the 1978 Agreement; Article 3 of the 1985 Agreement). In the 1985 Agreement, the cooperation component was the highlight, with the establishment of a joint committee to 'review the various cooperation schemes' (Article 15), which was complemented in 1994 and 2002 by exchanges of letters establishing a broad EU–China political dialogue. Until this end, the legal framework of the EU–China includes both economic dimension and political implications.

However, if evaluating the 1985 Agreement from the perspective of promoting, protecting, liberalizing, and facilitating FDI, it falls short of ambitions. To be fair, the objectives of the 1985 Agreement are chiefly trade-related, and, indeed, mention 'investment' in its Article 12, stating 'to promote and encourage greater and mutually beneficial investment … based on the principles of equity and reciprocity'.

H. The BITs between EU Member States and China (except Ireland)

Apart from EU–China trade relations governed by the 1985 Trade and Economic Cooperation Agreement, the legal instrument of EU–China investment relations, at the bilateral level, is comprised of twenty-six BITs covering twenty-seven EU Member States except Ireland.

After examining the twenty-six BITs, we mainly reach two conclusions in the context of investment protection. Despite certain similarities, first, uneven protection, in breadth and depth, is spread across the twenty-six BITs. For example, the coverage of such a legal instrument does not cover *all* EU Member State and investment-related issues, such as environment and labour. As for the depth of investment protection, taking fair and equitable treatment (FET) as an example, none of the FET clauses is qualified, namely, the clauses are not linked to the minimum standard of treatment of aliens under customary international law.[50] Secondly, considering the signing date of those BITs, inherited features from an older generation of BITs are problematic and often invite criticism and law suits arising from the vague language used in older BITs in combination with broad and innovative interpretation by arbitral tribunals.[51]

From an institutional perspective, on the European side, on the one hand, the Commission acknowledged investment promotion and protection guaranteed under BITs between EU Member States and third countries; on the other hand, it also identified an uneven playing field for EU companies investing abroad.[52] On the Chinese

---

[50] Fair and Equitable Treatment, UNCTAD Series on Issues in International Investment Agreements II (2012) http://unctad.org/en/Docs/unctaddiaeia2011d5_en.pdf (last accessed 28 February 2017).

[51] See Julien Chaisse and Rahul Donde, 'The State of Investor-State Arbitration: A Reality Check of the Issues, Trends, and Directions in Asia-Pacific' (2018) 51(1) The International Lawyer 47.

[52] COM(2010) 'Toward a Comprehensive European International Investment Policy'. See Marc Bungenberg and Catharine Titi, 'The Evolution of EU Investment Law and the Future of EU-China

side, it is important to place the period of signing twenty-six BITs with EU Member States (mainly in the 1980s and 1990s) into the context of the level of China's development. Back then, foreign investments were 'desperately' needed to boost China's economic development. Therefore, rules were written in the European negotiating partner's terms, respecting European investors' interests.[53]

I. The 2007 launch of negotiations of the Partnership and Cooperation Agreement (PCA)

At the 9th EU–China Summit, 'in order to reflect the full breadth and depth of today's comprehensive strategic partnership between the EU and China … and also update the 1985 EEC-China Trade and Economic Co-operation Agreement',[54] both sides agreed to launch the PCA negotiation, 'which will encompass the full scope of their bilateral relationship, including enhanced cooperation in political matters'.

The objectives laid down in the PCA negotiation were in line with the traditional use of PCA for the EU 'to strengthen democracies and develop economies through cooperation in a wide range of areas and through political dialogue'.[55] However, concluding a PCA is not a usual practice in China's foreign policy.[56] With regard to the area of human rights and democratization, to which the European Parliament attaches 'considerable importance', the Commission is required to 'guarantee sustainable and fair socio-economic development in third countries'.[57] On this front, resistance from the other side is predictable.[58] As for a procedural issue—whether negotiating a new PCA and updating the 1985 Agreement is a single set of negotiations or two sets, which would result in two agreements if concluded,[59] the EU and China were not on the same page. Unsurprisingly, but sadly, the PCA negotiation is omitted from the EU–China 2020 strategic agenda for cooperation.

Investment Relations' in W Shan and J Su (eds), *China and International Investment Law: Twenty Years of ICSID Membership* (Brill Nijhoff 2014).

[53] M Xu, 'The Launch of China-EU Negotiations on the Investment Agreement Came at a Right Time' *People's Daily* (2013) http://world.people.com.cn/n/2013/1121/c157278-23609503.html (last accessed 28 February 2017).

[54] 9th EU–China Summit joint statement http://www.consilium.europa.eu/uedocs/cms_data/docs/pressdata/en/er/90951.pdf (last accessed 28 February 2017).

[55] Partnership and Cooperation Agreements (PCAs): Russia, Eastern Europe, the Southern Caucasus and Central Asia http://eur-lex.europa.eu/legal-content/EN/TXT/HTML/?uri=URISERV:r17002&from=EN (last accessed 28 February 2017).

[56] Jiao Zhang, 'The EU-China Relationship Arriving at a Bottleneck: A Look at the Ongoing Negotiation of the PCA' *EU-China Observer* (2011) 3.

[57] Promoting human rights and democratization in third countries http://eur-lex.europa.eu/legal-content/EN/TXT/HTML/?uri=URISERV:r10101&from=EN (last accessed 28 February 2017).

[58] For more Chinese perspectives on the PCA negotiations see Zeng Lingliang, 'A Preliminary Perspective of Negotiations of EU-China PCA: A New Bottle Carrying Old Wine or New Wine or Both?' (2009) 1 European Law Journal 121; Jing Men and Giuseppe Balducci (eds), *Prospects and Challenges for EU-China Relations in the 21st Century: The Partnership and Cooperation Agreement* (PIE Peter Lang 2010).

[59] Brian Colin, 'Obstacles in Upgrading the 1985 Trade and Economic Cooperation Agreement between the EU and China' (2010) 2 EU-China Observer 9.

J. The 2013 launch of negotiations of a Comprehensive EU–China Investment Agreement (CIA)

After identifying China as a potential partner with whom the EU could pursue negotiations for a stand-alone investment agreement at EU level in its Communication in 2010, the Commission accelerated the efforts in 'securing existing openness and delivering new liberalisation of the conditions for accessing each other's investment market'.[60] At the Sixteenth EU–China Summit in 2013, the EU and China announced the launch of negotiations of a China–EU CAI and held the first round of negotiations in January 2014.[61] To date, nineteen rounds of negotiations have taken place.[6263]

At the EU level, through accessing the EU–China investment relations, the Commission outlined two major problems:[64] (1) lack of level playing field for prospective and existing European investors in China; and (2) the lack of comprehensive framework to remedy shortcomings of the EU–China investment relationship. In order to address those concerns, the EU set the objectives of the CAI negotiation, which were to 'provide for progressive liberalisation of investment and the elimination of restrictions for investors to each other's market ... provide a simpler and more secure legal framework to investors of both sides by securing predictable long-term access to EU and Chinese markets respectively and providing for strong protection to investors and their investments'.[65] As for China, the significance of the CAI with the EU is two-fold: (1) harmonization of the twenty-six BITs into one set of comprehensive rules; and (2) active participation in global investment rule-making.

However, voices within EU do not share with what the Commission envisages. First, mounting criticism of international investment law, particularly true in respect of investor–state dispute settlement mechanisms in the TTIP and CETA has lead governments in Europe, notably Germany, to take an official position that would reserve their stance on international investment law and investor–state arbitration generally.[66] Secondly, the discrepancy between EU objectives and Member State practices is evident in documents[67] of the European Parliament on EU–China negotiations for a

---

[60] Commission press release, 'Commission proposes to open negotiations for an investment agreement with China' (2013) http://trade.ec.europa.eu/doclib/press/index.cfm?id=900 (last accessed 24 March 2017).

[61] Commission press release, 'EU and China begin investment talks' (2014) http://europa.eu/rapid/press-release_IP-14-33_en.htm (last accessed 24 March 2017).

[62] European Commission, note to the file, EU-China Investment Agreement: Report of the 12th Round of Negotiations (Brussels, 26–30 September 2016) http://trade.ec.europa.eu/doclib/docs/2016/october/tradoc_155061.pdf (last accessed 24 March 2017).

[63] European Commission, Report of the 18th Round of Negotiations for the EU-China Investment Agreement, 18 July 2018 http://trade.ec.europa.eu/doclib/docs/2018/july/tradoc_157143.pdf.

[64] Commission Staff Working Paper, 'Impact Assessment Report on the EU-China Investment Relations (Brussels, 23 May 2013) SWD(2013) 185 final http://ec.europa.eu/smart regulation/impact/ia_carried_out/docs/ia_2013/swd_2013_0185_en.pdf (last accessed 24 March 2017). See European Commission, 'Sustainability Impact Assessment (SIA) in Support of an Investment Agreement between the European Union and the People's Republic of China' final inception paper (2016) http://www.trade-sia.com/china/wp-content/uploads/sites/9/2014/12/SIA-EU-China-Final-inception-report-17-June-2016.pdf (last accessed 24 March 2017).

[65] European Commission 'Trade Policy on China' http://ec.europa.eu/trade/policy/countries-and-regions/countries/china/ (last accessed 24 March 2017).

[66] Schill, Editorial, 'The German Debate on International Investment Law' http://booksandjournals.brillonline.com/docserver/journals/22119000/16/1/22119000_016_01_S001_text.pdf?expires=1490569285&id=id&accname=guest&checksum=3C9A9E81FC589853D2DAE3DD1EEFDCBE (last accessed 28 February 2017).

[67] European Parliament Resolutions: 2013/2674(RSP), para 17; 2010/2203, paras 9, 18, 19; 2013/2674(RSP), para 17; 2010/2203, paras 9, 18, 19; 2010/2203, para 19;

bilateral investment agreement where the Parliament states that the EU–China treaty 'should be based on the best practices drawn from Member State experiences' and sets the standards that must be included in the CAI. Among other dissimilarities, one can note that elaboration of some of those 'best practice' and 'standards' are not similar to the *acquis* of Member State best practices, most obviously, in the formulation of the FET standard.[68]

On a positive note, in January 2016, the EU and China agreed on the 'ambitious and comprehensive' scope of the future CAI and, in particular, that the future investment deal 'should improve market access opportunities for their investors by establishing a genuine right to invest and by guaranteeing that they will not discriminate against their respective companies'.[69] Although both sides have made their political commitments early in the 2015 EU–China Summit by 'viewing the ongoing investment agreement negotiations as one of the most important issues in EU-China bilateral economic and trade relation' and 'aiming the expeditious conclusion',[70] the difficulties of progress on contingent issues including market access[71] and free trade zones[72] in the US–China BIT has presented one of the major challenges that will likely be encountered in the EU–China investment deal.

To conclude, since its first policy paper on the EU in 2003, China has clearly expressed that 'no fundamental conflict of interest' between both sides and laid out its vision that 'the common ground between China and the EU far outweighs their disagreements' will guide and develop EU–China relations 'in greater pragmatically-driven economic, financial and environmental directions'.[73] China's vision of building upon the common ground has been enhanced in its second position paper in 2014. Earlier in the same year, in President Xi's speech at the College of Europe, he stated that China and Europe 'need to build four bridges for peace, growth, reform and progress of civilization, so that the China-EU comprehensive strategic partnership will take on even greater global significance'.[74] Against the background of conflicting and shared interests, the EU and China should continue building upon the momentum achieved so far and, for the long-term prospects, collaborate on the 'common ground' for the interests of the Community, Member States, and, reciprocally, China itself.

2013/2674(RSP), para 17. See also European Parliament, 'Position of the European Parliament adopted at first reading on 16 April 2014 with a view to the adoption of Regulation (EU) No 912/2014 establishing a framework for managing financial responsibility linked to investor-to-state dispute settlement tribunals established by international agreements to which the European Union is party', Doc P7_TC1-COD(2012) 0163 (2014).

[68] Catharine Titi, 'International Investment Law and the European Union' (2015) 26 Eur J Int Law 639, 651.

[69] Commission news release, 'EU and China agree on scope of the future investment deal' (2016) http://trade.ec.europa.eu/doclib/press/index.cfm?id=1435 (last accessed 24 March 2017).

[70] Joint statement http://www.consilium.europa.eu/en/press/press-releases/2015/06/29-eu-china-statement/.

[71] Wenhua Shan and Lu Wang, 'The China–EU BIT and the Emerging "Global BIT 2.0"'.

[72] Jie Huang, 'Challenges and Solutions for the China-US BIT Negotiations: Insights from the Recent Development of FTZs in China' (2015) 18 Journal of International Economic Law 307.

[73] David Scott, 'New Horizons in EU-China Relations?' (n 32); and also T Zhang, 'Sino-European Relations: From the Height to the Width' (2009).

[74] Speech by H E Xi Jinping, President of the People's Republic of China at the College of Europe (1 April 2014) http://www.chinamission.be/eng/jd/t1143591.htm (last accessed 26 February 2017).

III. EU–China Relations in the Context of Regional Economic Governance

Developing the comprehensive strategic partnership at the beginning of the 21ˢᵗ century not only serves the mutual interests of China and the European Union but also contributes to peace, stability and development in our respective regions and the world at large.

Wen Jiabao, Premier of the State Council of the People's Republic of China,
6 May 2004

The EU and China are setting the stage in redefining economic architecture in the Asia-Pacific region. In the sense of global governance on economic agenda, the EU, China, and the transatlantic alliance is competing between and among themselves.[75] To execute its strategic pivot to Asia, in contrast with the US, even after rebranding its strategy as a 'rebalancing', the EU is performing a 'smart pivot'[76] by putting trade up-front in its engagement with Asian countries.

According to an overview[77] of FTAs and other trade negotiations undertaken at the EU level, published by the Commission in February 2017, in the Asia-Pacific, countries and regions that are negotiating FTAs with the EU include ASEAN, Japan, India, Malaysia, Thailand, Indonesia, the Philippines, and Myanmar. Vietnam and Singapore have already concluded (but not yet ratified) FTAs with the EU.

In respect of these ten FTA partners of the EU, China has either concluded a bilateral FTA with them (i.e. ASEAN and Singapore) or is engaging them in a trilateral (China–Japan–Korea FTA) and regional (RCEP) trade deal. After all, trade negotiations are organized under the auspices of the WTO. Efforts in writing the rules for twenty-first century trade in a world where intellectually shadow arguments for and against free trade agreements attract increasing support, are daunting if not frustrating.

On the bright side, the international investment regime in the Asia-Pacific region is moving towards harmonization.[78] Considering the economic and geopolitical significance, China is the heavyweight partner for the EU to have a stand-alone CAI for the present and a FTA for the future. Subsequently, the spill-over effects of an 'ambitious and comprehensive' investment agreement between the world's largest economies will shape the way of future investment agreement written with and among third countries in the Asia-Pacific region.

Any lack of political commitment or hesitation will result in a total loss of momentum, which is unaffordable for both parties to achieve greater prosperity and common interests within and for the EU and China, domestically as well as globally in

---

[75] Testimony before US–China Economic and Security Review Commission in 2005 https://csis-prod.s3.amazonaws.com/s3fs-public/legacy_files/files/attachments/ts050722niblett.pdf (last accessed 24 February 2017) and in 2012 http://origin.www.uscc.gov/sites/default/files/transcripts/4.19.12HearingTranscript.pdf (last accessed 24 February 2017).

[76] Javier Solana, 'Europe's Smart Asian Pivot' (2013) https://www.project-syndicate.org/commentary/the-eu-s-startegic-advantages-in-asia-by-javier-solana?barrier=accessreg (last accessed 24 February 2017).

[77] Overview Of FTA And Other Trade Negotiations http://trade.ec.europa.eu/doclib/docs/2006/december/tradoc_118238.pdf (last accessed 24 February 2017).

[78] Mark Feldman and others, 'The Role of Pacific Rim FTAs in the Harmonisation of International Investment Law: Towards a Free Trade Area of the Asia-Pacific' (2016) http://e15initiative.org/publications/the-role-of-pacific-rim-ftas-in-the-harmonisation-of-international-investment-law-towards-a-free-trade-area-of-the-asia-pacific/ (last accessed 28 February 2017).

the decades ahead. As long as both sides are determined to iron out their differences as discussed in sections III and IV, and to respond pragmatically to the current trends of the world economy, the CAI is fully achievable.

IV. Issues of China—EU Negotiations

In the framework of a constantly evolving economic relationship, the European Union and China are negotiating a CAI.

After having analysed the economic, political, and legal drivers that urge China and the EU to conclude an investment agreement, we will now focus on specific issues of China–EU negotiations. Negotiators have a delicate task of great responsibility, because both China and the EU are seeking the highest protection for their respective national investors in the territory of the other contracting party and, at the same time, their aim is to protect the internal market from competition represented by the goods and services provided by investors based in the prospective partners' territory.

Particularly regarding investment, according to official statistics issued by the State Administration of Foreign Exchange (SAFE), an administrative agency of the People's Republic of China, China's outward direct investment has increased exponentially in the last fifteen years, going from US$1.9 billion in 2004[79] to US$101.9 billion in 2017.[80]

A positive outcome from these negotiations could have a considerable impact, since the investment treaty may smooth the path for a potential free trade agreement between the EU and China.[81] In addition, the significance of the China–EU bilateral investment treaty may expand beyond the signatory regions and affect the liberalization of global economic relationships through future trade and investment agreements.[82] Considering the core issues under discussion, it is desirable that the parties find an opportune balance between protecting the rights of investors and the right of states to regulate in the public interest. In truth, on the one hand investment agreements aim at attracting foreign direct investment and, on the other hand, they seek to ensure that the achievement of that purpose does not obstruct the state's power to attain its objectives of public policy.[83] To this aim, the EU and China are currently discussing the inclusion of specific provisions and wordings, which ideally will favour the reaching of that equilibrium.

This section examines specific clauses in international investment agreements concluded by the EU and its Member States, on one hand, and China, on the other: the aim is to understand if, and highlight how, the prospective partners have responded to the evolution of the economic and political situation, with a parallel development in the way they draft international investment agreements.

---

[79] Duncan Freeman, 'China's Outward Direct Investment in the EU: Challenges of Rapid Change' (2015) 3(15) EU-China Observer 5 https://issuu.com/collegeofeurope/docs/eu-china_observer315 (last accessed 12 February 2017).

[80] World Bank, Foreign Direct Investment Net Outflows, October 2018

[81] Francesco Tenuta, 'The Motivations Behind the EU-China Bilateral Investment Treaty Negotiations' (2015) 3(15) EU-China Observer 20.

[82] Frank Bickenbach and others, *The EU-China Bilateral Investment Agreement in Negotiation: Motivation, Conflicts and Perspectives* (Kiel Policy Brief No 95, 2015) https://www.ifw-kiel.de/wirtschaftspolitik/zentrum-wirtschaftspolitik/kiel-policy-brief/kpb-2015/kiel-policy-brief-95 (last accessed 14 February 2017).

[83] ibid.

We will start with the analysis of the state of negotiations between China and the EU (sub-section IVA), to pass then to the research plan designed and the methodology applied (sub-section IVB), before we finally move to extract a pattern in the behaviour of the two global powers in the drafting of their international investment agreements (sub-section IVC).

A. The state of the negotiations

There is a wide range of issues that the parties will negotiate in an international investment agreement, ranging from the definition of investment, to standards of treatment such as most-favoured-nation, national treatment, full protection and security, fair and equitable treatment, direct and indirect expropriation, to the investor–state dispute settlement and state-to-state dispute settlement.

In the negotiations between the European Union and China, a number of these issues are already well advanced and do not give rise to major discrepancies in the respective positions; this is not surprising if we take into account that both parties pursue the goal of revitalizing their economies by boosting their still underdeveloped investment relations,[84] that they agree on the need to replace the old legal framework,[85] and that therefore they have a common interest in stipulating some provisions.

On other issues, there are currently some sources of disagreement,[86] in respect of which the parties will have to reach an agreement during negotiations.

In the present section, the focus will be on three particularly important provisions: transparency, fair and equitable treatment, and taxation. Space constraints do not allow a detailed description of all the provisions that are currently under negotiation, and several reasons have directed what must be included here. Among them are the following: (i) these provisons can be considered as deeply linked together, as stressed by research and by some investment arbitration awards, which considered regulatory transparency as forming 'part of the substantive standard of fair and equitable treatment';[87] (ii) they hold the power to shift the weight of the whole treaty; and (iii) it is our submission that these provisions are going to be among the most contentious issues, not only during the negotiations but very likely also in the subsequent arbitrations.

Consequently, we are convinced that an examination of these issues can indeed provide a good (although brief) overview of the top issues discussed during the negotiations.

B. Research plan and methodology

EU–China is not just one more treaty: it is greatly needed for legal, political, and economic reasons, as was highlighted in section I of the present chapter. In such a context,

---

[84] See Tenuta (n 81) 16.   [85] ibid 22.

[86] European Commission Directorate-General for Trade, Directorate B—Services and Investment, Intellectual Property and Public Procurement Investment, Note to the File http://trade.ec.europa.eu/doclib/docs/2016/october/tradoc_155061.pdf (last accessed 13 February 2017).

[87] Peter Malanczuk, 'China and the Emerging Standard of Transparency in Investor-State Dispute Settlement (ISDS)' in *Trade Development Through Harmonization of Commercial Law* (Hors Serie Volume XIX 2015) 65–109, 73 http://www.victoria.ac.nz/law/research/publications/about-nzacl/publications/special-issues/hors-serie-volume-xvi,-2013/Malanczuk.pdf (last accessed 12 February 2017).

considering that the negotiations have reached the Thirteenth round[88] and more will be needed to find an agreement, it would be prosaic to wait for the parties to deliver an outcome.

The methodology used for the present study encompasses a normative analysis of the existing treaties in a comparative way, while remaining informed by the ongoing negotiations. In more detail, it is our standing that the future China–EU BIT will build upon existing BITs and FTAs involving each party: the work conducted is based on the comparative analysis of international investment agreements: both those concluded, those signed but not yet ratified, and those still under negotiation.

Therefore, we have considered three aspects of the problem: (i) the EU's behaviour in the conclusion of its international investment agreements; (ii) relationships previously established through international investment treaties between the Member States of the European Union and China; and (iii) China's behaviour in the conclusion of its international investment agreements.

The purpose is to observe the behavioural constants and/or development trends in such a way as to forecast the future outcome of the China–EU negotiations aimed at concluding an investment agreement.

C. Behaviour in concluding international investment agreements

Comparing both China's and the EU's behaviour in concluding an international investment agreement can help to understand what the priorities of the two contracting parties are, how they evolved through time into their respective positions in various treaties, and where there can be similar or clashing stances in the negotiations with each other.

We decided to study the agreements, whose text is available, which have been previously signed between the European Union and other states: the bilateral agreements EU–Vietnam,[89] EU–Singapore,[90] the FTA EU–South Korea,[91] and the CETA.[92]

The EU has finalized but also not yet applied the following agreements: the Interim Economic Partnership Agreement with the East African Countries (EAC),[93] the Economic Partnership Agreement with West Africa,[94] and the trade agreement with Ecuador.[95]

---

[88] The Thirteenth round of negotiations was scheduled for the week of 5 December 2016 in Beijing. Note to the File http://trade.ec.europa.eu/doclib/docs/2016/october/tradoc_155061.pdf (last accessed 24 January 2017).
[89] EU–Vietnam Trade and Investment Agreements: Authenticated text as of August 2018 http://trade.ec.europa.eu/doclib/press/index.cfm?id=1437 (last accessed 6 December 2018).
[90] EU–Singapore Free Trade Agreement. Authentic text as of May 2015 http://trade.ec.europa.eu/doclib/press/index.cfm?id=961 (last accessed 24 January 2017).
[91] Free Trade Agreement between the European Union and its Member States, of the One Part, and the Republic of Korea, of the Other Part http://eur-lex.europa.eu/legal-content/EN/TXT/PDF/?uri=OJ:L:2011:127:FULL&from=EN (last accessed 24 January 2017).
[92] Comprehensive Economic and Trade Agreement (CETA) between Canada, of the One Part, and the European Union and Its Member States http://trade.ec.europa.eu/doclib/docs/2014/september/tradoc_152806.pdf (last accessed 24 January 2017).
[93] Economic Partnership Agreement between the East African Community Partner States, of the One Part, and the European Union and Its Member States of the Other Part http://trade.ec.europa.eu/doclib/idocs/2015/october/tradoc_153845.compressed.pdf (last accessed 24 January 2017).
[94] Economic Partnership Agreement between the West African States, the Economic Community of West African States (ECOWAS) and the West African Economic and Monetary Union (UEMOA), of the One Part, and the European Union and Its Member States, of the Other Part http://trade.ec.europa.eu/doclib/docs/2015/october/tradoc_153867.pdf (last accessed 24 January 2017).
[95] EU–Ecuador trade negotiations http://trade.ec.europa.eu/doclib/press/index.cfm?id=1261 (last accessed 24 January 2017).

However, for the purpose of the present chapter, they will not be analysed, because the trade agreement with Ecuador lacks an investment chapter, and although one of the aims of both the Interim Economic Partnership Agreement with the EAC and the Economic Partnership Agreement with West Africa is the promotion of investment, no mention is made of investment provisions in the text of these agreements.

Then we have examined the text proposed by the European Commission for the TTIP, still under discussion.[96] Although it is currently not possible to predict with absolute certainty whether the TTIP will be signed and ratified and, in this case, what wording the different treaty sections will have, it represents, together with CETA and the future China–EU Agreement, one of the most important international agreements negotiated, both in terms of turnover and magnitude of the markets involved, defined by the number of inhabitants.

We have conducted a thorough analysis of the BITs in force between each one of the Member States and China.

This meant analysing and comparing twenty-six BITs,[97] as it results from the fact that, on the one hand, no BIT was concluded between China and Ireland and, on the other hand, Belgium and Luxembourg signed in 2005 an agreement equivalent to a bilateral investment treaty, with the denomination of BLEU (Belgium–Luxembourg Economic Union)–China BIT.

Conversely, importance was given to the BITs that China has signed or is negotiating with third parties, as well as Chinese model BITs, with the aim of understanding China's position.

On this point, it should be mentioned, albeit briefly, the fact that in the distant past, China was mainly a capital importing state: therefore, the agreements signed in this epoch reflected China's intention to preserve the space to regulate.[98] Subsequently, starting from the 1990s, China undertook the going out policy, promoting investment abroad on behalf of state-owned enterprises.[99] This necessarily reflected on international agreements concluded in that period: in fact, for the first time, China was simultaneously a capital importing country (due to investments on the Chinese territory) and a capital exporting country (due to investments realized abroad by Chinese enterprises). Consequently, China's interest was no longer, as it had been previously, leaving maximum liberty to the host state to regulate, but, on the contrary, it became

[96] European Commission draft text TTIP—investment http://trade.ec.europa.eu/doclib/docs/2015/september/tradoc_153807.pdf (last accessed 24 January 2017).
[97] China–Sweden supplementary agreement (signed 29 March 1982), China–Denmark (signed 29 April 1985), China–United Kingdom exchange of no (signed 15 May 1986), China–Austria (signed 12 September 1985), China–Italy (signed 28 January 1985), China–Poland (signed 7 June 1988), China–Slovakia (signed 4 December 1991), China–Greece (signed 25 June 1992), China–Hungary supplementary agreement (signed 29 May 1991), China–Bulgaria (signed 27 June 1989), China–Croatia (signed 7 June 1993), China–Estonia (signed 2 September 1993), China–Lithuania (signed 8 November 1993), China–Slovenia (signed 13 September 1993, China–Romania additional protocol 4 (signed 12 July 1994), China–Cyprus (signed 17 January 2001), China–Netherlands protocol (signed 26 November 2001), China–Germany protocol (signed 1 December 2003), China–Latvia protocol (signed 15 April 2004), China–Finland (signed 15 November 2004), China–Belgium/Luxemburg protocol (signed 6 June 2005), China–Czech republic (signed 8 December 2005), China–Spain protocol (signed 24 November 2005), China–Portugal protocol (signed 9 December 2005), China–Malta (signed 22 February 2009), China–France (signed 26 November 2007).
[98] David Zweig, 'China's Political Economy' in William A Joseph (ed), *Politics in China: An Introduction* (Oxford University Press 2010) 192–221.
[99] Aravind Yelery, 'China's "Going Out" Policy: Sub-National Economic Trajectories' http://www.icsin.org/uploads/2015/04/12/e50f1e532774c4c354b24885fcb327c5.pdf (last accessed 24 January 2017).

finding the best balance between its interests as host state and its willingness to offer a fair legal protection to the interests of Chinese enterprises, be they state-owned or private.

V. The Core Elements of the Analysis

Based on a normative analysis, which compared the evolution of the treaties concluded by China to the more recent shaping of the EU's position, and finally, the twenty-six BITs of individual EU Member States with China, we have drawn hypotheses on both prospective parties' positions with respect to each treaty provision.

As a result of the comparative analysis, while certain clauses do not give rise to major disagreements between the two world powers, others may be a source of significant discordance. The provisions where the global actors are expected to hold diverging positions have been identified as fair and equitable treatment, taxation, and transparency.

A. Fair and equitable treatment

The fair and equitable treatment (FET) clause is often invoked by investors as having been breached by the state's behaviour,[100] and therefore lays the foundations for numerous disputes. Indeed, the FET provision has leapt to prominence in the last fifteen years as the principal ground of liability at issue in many if not most investment treaty arbitration claims. It is based on the notions of fairness and equity, which lack any fixed definition in international law.[101] Therefore, arbitrators have had a great opportunity to interpret the meaning of FET in a broad, all-embracing fashion. Consequently, this clause has been subject to different readings, leading to the unpredictability of the essence of FET.

In some instances, this problem has led states to negotiate an official treaty interpretation, as occurred in relation to the NAFTA.[102] In 2001, the three states parties to the NAFTA issued a Note of Interpretation,[103] to be applied to any case falling under the scope of the Treaty, future or pending. Specifically, the note links FET to customary international law and states that 'the breach of another provision of the NAFTA, for example, national treatment, does not in and of itself constitute a breach of fair and equitable treatment under Article 1105'.[104]

---

[100] The FET clause is the provision breached in the highest number of cases: according to the UNCTAD Investment Policy Hub (2016), breaches of the FET amount to 94 out of 142 breaches of IIAs. This renders it the undisputed 'queen' of treaty infringements.

[101] Rudolf Dolzer and Christoph Schreuer, *Principles of International Investment Law* (Oxford University Press 2012) 354.

[102] Omar E García-Bolívar, 'Defining an ICSID Investment: Why Economic Development Should be the Core Element' *Investment Treaty News* https://www.iisd.org/itn/2012/04/13/defining-an-icsid-investment-why-economic-development-should-be-the-core-element/ (last accessed 17 February 2017). See also Julien Chaisse and Christian Bellak, 'Navigating the Expanding Universe of Investment Treaties: Creation and Use of Critical Index' (2015) 18(1) Journal of International Economic Law 79.

[103] North American Free Trade Agreement Notes of Interpretation of Certain Chapter 11 Provisions NAFTA Free Trade Commission (2001) http://www.sice.oas.org/tpd/nafta/Commission/CH11understanding_e.asp (last accessed 24 January 2017).

[104] Gabrielle Kaufmann-Kohler, 'Interpretive Powers of the Free Trade Commission and the Rule of Law' in Emmanuel Gaillard and Frédéric Bachand (eds), *Fifteen Years of NAFTA Chapter 11 Arbitration* (JurisNet LLC 2011) 175–94, 181.

The importance of the note is based on the following elements: (1) taking inspiration from the note, many of the IIAs have concluded thereafter to adopt a qualified[105] FET, and (2) it provides a binding interpretation tool to the arbitrators.

It is interesting to note that qualified FET clauses were included in subsequent Canadian[106] and American[107] bilateral agreements, as well as in the recently negotiated CETA,[108] which confirms that the inclusion of specific wording is suitable for obtaining the effect that the parties desire.

On the other side, the American ISDS model is an example of how the concept of minimum standards of treatment in customary international law has been narrowed down.[109] However, little development can be observed in practice: since the arbitrators were particularly lenient in their proof requests towards the investors, the latter were relieved from the usual duty to provide evidence in their claim to define the applicable customary international law.[110]

Concerning the presence of a FET clause in IIAs signed with EU Member States, a chronological evolution can be observed, leading to the identification of three groups of BITs: (i) in the first group of BITs the FET clause is absent; (ii) in the second group only some elements of a FET clause appear, and (iii) in the third group, which constitutes the clear majority group, the BITs include an unqualified FET clause.

We will now briefly focus on some examples taken from each group.

(i) BITs in which the FET clause is absent. Neither the Austria–China BIT[111] nor the Slovakia–China BIT[112] have an FET clause at all. This is probably due to their belonging to the first-generation BITs, as they were signed in 1982 and 1991 respectively.

---

[105] The term 'qualified' attributed to a FET clause in some cases refers to international law; in other cases it makes a more precise reference to customary international law minimum standards.

[106] Canada–Côte d'Ivoire BIT art 6 http://investmentpolicyhub.unctad.org/Download/TreatyFile/ 3242 (last accessed 13 February 2017); Agreement between the Government of Canada and the Government of the People's Republic of China for the Promotion and Reciprocal Protection of Investments art 4 http://investmentpolicyhub.unctad.org/Download/TreatyFile/3476 (last accessed 24 January 2017).

[107] Dominican Republic–Central America–United States Free Trade Agreement art 10.5 https:// ustr.gov/sites/default/files/uploads/agreements/cafta/asset_upload_file148_3916.pdf (last accessed 13 February 2017); Agreement between the Government of the United States of America and the Government of the Sultanate of Oman on the Establishment of a Free Trade Area art 10.5 https://ustr. gov/sites/default/files/uploads/agreements/fta/oman/asset_upload_file976_8810.pdf (last accessed 13 February 2017).

[108] Comprehensive Economic and Trade Agreement (CETA) between Canada, of the One Part, and the European Union [and Its Member States http://trade.ec.europa.eu/doclib/docs/2014/september/tradoc_152806.pdf (last accessed 13 February 2017).

[109] Dominican Republic–Central America–United States Free Trade Agreement, 19 USCS S. 4011 (2005) (CAFTA) art 10.5(2).

[110] Matthew C Porterfield, 'A Distinction Without a Difference? The Interpretation of Fair and Equitable Treatment under Customary International Law by Investment Tribunals' *Investment Treaty News* (2013) https://www.iisd.org/itn/2013/03/22/a-distinction-without-a-difference-the-interpretation-of-fair-and-equitable-treatment-under-customary-international-law-by-investment-tribunals/ (last accessed 17 February 2017).

[111] Abkommen zwischen der Republik Österreich und der Volksrepublik China über die Förderung und den gegenseitigen Schutz von Investitionen samt Protokoll http://investmentpolicyhub.unctad. org/Download/TreatyFile/179 (last accessed 24 January 2017).

[112] Agreement between the Government of the Czech and Slovak Federal Republic and the Government of the People's Republic of China for the Promotion and Reciprocal Protection of Investments, http://investmentpolicyhub.unctad.org/Download/TreatyFile/777 (last accessed 24 January 2017).

(ii) BITS in which only some elements of a FET clause appear. Moving on to the group bearing only certain elements of the FET clause, it can be seen that two sets of treaties have a slightly different expression: Denmark–China[113] and Italy–China,[114] both signed in 1985, present a different wording and call for 'Equitable and reasonable treatment', instead of the traditional 'Fair and equitable treatment'. A few years later, the expression 'Equitable treatment' is used in both Poland–China,[115] signed in 1988, and Hungary–China,[116] signed in 1991, revealing an interesting lack of the adjective 'fair'.

(iii) BITS including an unqualified FET clause. In the largest part of BITs concluded between Member States of the European Union and China, the included FET clause can be characterized as 'unqualified',[117] because it lacks a precise definition. Indeed, in these BITs the most frequent phrasing used is the following:

'Investments and activities associated with investments of investors of either Contracting Party shall be accorded fair and equitable treatment in the territory of the other Contracting Party'.

In the BITs signed by the EU Member States with China, the FET wording evolved from being entirely absent, to being present only partly, and being present as unqualified FET, and has never reached the step of a qualified FET, not even in the last one, signed in 2007 between France and China.[118]

Only in 2009, when the EU acquired exclusive competence on foreign direct investment, it took the lead in the subsequent treaty negotiations and included an upgraded version of FET in the agreements signed. The constant evolution in this trend was confirmed by the agreements recently signed by the EU, such as EU–Vietnam, CETA, and EU–Singapore: in fact, in these agreements the FET is worded in such a way that it is considered as breached exclusively when the measures taken have certain implications or specific effects.

Compared to the first phases of this evolution, it is noticeable that the freshly baked FET formula applied both in the EU–Vietnam Investment Protection Agreement (IPA) and in the EU–Singapore FTA, is drafted in a very detailed fashion.

[113] China and Denmark Agreement concerning the encouragement and reciprocal protection of investments http://investmentpolicyhub.unctad.org/Download/TreatyFile/727 (last accessed 24 January 2017).

[114] Agreement between the Government of the People's Republic of China and the Government of Italy concerning the Encouragement and Reciprocal Protection of Investments http://investmentpolicyhub.unctad.org/Download/TreatyFile/3370(last accessed 24 January 2017).

[115] Agreement Between the Government of the People's Republic of China and the Government of the Polish People's Republic on the Reciprocal Encouragement and Protection of Investments, http://investmentpolicyhub.unctad.org/Download/TreatyFile/770 (last accessed 24 January 2017).

[116] Agreement between the Republic of Hungary and the People's Republic of China concerning the encouragement and reciprocal protection of investments http://investmentpolicyhub.unctad.org/Download/TreatyFile/740 (last accessed 24 January 2017).

[117] Sweden–China, United Kingdom–China, Greece–China, Bulgaria–China, Croatia–China, Estonia–China, Lithuania–China, Slovenia–China, Romania–China, Cyprus–China, Netherlands–China, Germany–China, Latvia–China, Finland–China, Belgium and Luxembourg–China, Czech–China, Spain–China, Portugal–China, Malta–China, and France–China.

[118] Accord entre le Gouvernement de la République Française et le Gouvernement de la République Populaire de Chine sur l'Encouragement et la Protection Réciproques des Investissements http://investmentpolicyhub.unctad.org/Download/TreatyFile/3342 (last accessed 24 January 2017).

In the EU–Vietnam IPA, the FET provision is included in Article 2.5:

"ARTICLE 2.5
Treatment of Investment

1. Each Party shall accord fair and equitable treatment and full protection and security to investors of the other Party and covered investments in accordance with paragraphs 2 to 7 and Annex 3 (Understanding on the Treatment of Investments).

2. A Party breaches the obligation of fair and equitable treatment referred to in paragraph 1 where a measure or series of measures constitutes:
   (a) a denial of justice in criminal, civil or administrative proceedings;
   (b) a fundamental breach of due process in judicial and administrative proceedings;
   (c) manifest arbitrariness;
   (d) targeted discrimination on manifestly wrongful grounds, such as gender, race or religious belief;
   (e) abusive treatment such as coercion, abuse of power or similar bad faith conduct; or
   (f) a breach of any further elements of the fair and equitable treatment obligation adopted by the Parties in accordance with paragraph 3.

3. Treatment not listed in paragraph 2 may constitute a breach of fair and equitable treatment where the Parties have so agreed in accordance with the procedures provided for in Article 4.3 (Amendments).

4. When applying paragraphs 1 to 3, a dispute settlement body under Chapter 3 (Dispute Settlement) may take into account whether a Party made a specific representation to an investor of the other Party to induce a covered investment that created a legitimate expectation, and upon which the investor relied in deciding to make or maintain that investment, but that the Party subsequently frustrated.

5. For greater certainty, the term "full protection and security" referred to in paragraph 1 refers to a Party's obligations to act as may be reasonably necessary to protect physical security of the investors and the covered investments.

6. Where a Party has entered into a written agreement with investors of the other Party or covered investments that satisfies all of the following conditions, that Party shall not breach that agreement through the exercise of governmental authority. The conditions are:
   (a) the written agreement is concluded and takes effect after the date of entry into force of this Agreement;
   (b) the investor relies on the written agreement in deciding to make or maintain the covered investment other than the written agreement itself and the breach causes actual damages to that investment;
   (c) the written agreement creates an exchange of rights and obligations in connection to the said investment, binding on both parties; and
   (d) the written agreement does not contain a clause on the settlement of disputes between the parties to that agreement by international arbitration.

7. A breach of another provision of this Agreement, or of a separate international agreement, does not establish that there has been a breach of this Article".[119]

The present enumeration narrows down the arbitrators' room for manoeuvre in their assessment of the case and restricts the scope of application of the rule concerning the FET, with a following significant impact on both the filing and the outcome of investment cases.

Maybe the most intriguing aspect related to the FET clause is how the negotiators drew up such a detailed clause, in other words what process has such phrasing undergone to be included in the draft. Indeed, the wording was chosen after a thorough analysis of

---

[119] EU–Vietnam Investment Protection Agreement, Chapter 2, Investment Protection, http://trade.ec.europa.eu/doclib/docs/2018/september/tradoc_157393.pdf (last accessed 18 October 2018).

several dozens of awards, which has been carried out examining in depth the decisions in which the tribunal found a breach of the FET. The present drafting scrupulously abides by the expressions used by the arbitrators, encompassing the reasons why an FET was found in past cases, to limit the application of the FET clause in future cases.

We will now analyse some of the FET qualifiers that appear in some of the treaties newly signed by the EU. What is particularly interesting is that, although few years divide the drafting of the EU–South Korea FTA (signed in 2011), from the 'new trend' EU–Singapore FTA (signed in 2015), EU–Vietnam IPA and CETA (both signed in 2016), the former can be considered as symptomatic of an already outdated view, in that it does not mention an FET clause, let alone explaining the requirements which shall be met to breach it. On the contrary, the latter agreements expressly specify the circumstances in which the FET provision is considered to be breached, by means of the inclusion of wording such as 'fundamental breach of due process', 'manifest arbitrariness', 'targeted discrimination on manifestly wrongful grounds, such as gender, race or religious belief'.

The expression 'Fundamental Breach of Due Process' can be found in the EU–Vietnam IPA, in the CETA, in the EU–Singapore FTA, and in the TTIP.

However, its wording is not entirely clear since, on the one hand, it could indicate a serious, not secondary breach, and on the other it could point to a breach of a fundamental rule of due process.[120] Even if the term 'fundamental' indicates a significant breach, however, the rule might be interpreted in different fashions by arbitral tribunals, putting emphasis on the one or the other interpretation, or even on an interpretation that requires the presence of both breaches.

The term 'manifest arbitrariness', also present in the EU–Vietnam IPA, in the CETA, in the EU–Singapore FTA, and in the TTIP proposal, applies a stricter criterion compared to the simple arbitrariness of a disputed measure. It does not refer to the gravity of arbitrariness, but rather to the degree of ease of its perception: according to this qualifier, the FET clause will be breached only when the arbitrariness of the public measure is evident and with no traces of ambiguity.[121]

Moving on along the list of qualifiers, the 'targeted discrimination on manifestly wrongful grounds, such as gender, race or religious belief' can be found in three of the most recent agreement concluded by the EU: the EU–Vietnam IPA, in the CETA, and in the TTIP proposal, while it is absent from the EU–Singapore FTA and the Korea FTA. In this provision, there is no mention of discrimination based on nationality, which is the most common in investment law,[122] probably because it is left to the national treatment provision to tackle this issue. Attention is, on the contrary, given to the grounds of gender, race, and religious beliefs, leaving outside sexual orientation, language, political, or other opinion, association with a national minority, property, birth, or other status.[123]

The abusive treatment of investors, such as coercion, duress, and harassment, appears as a qualifier in Article 8.10.2(e) of CETA, while in Article 2.5(e) of the EU–Vietnam IPA it has a slight language difference: 'abusive treatment such as coercion,

---

[120] Ursula Kriebaum, 'FET and Expropriation in the (Invisible) EU Model BIT' (2014) 15 Journal of World Investment & Trade 454, 474.

[121] Ursula Kriebaum, 'FET and Expropriation in the (Invisible) EU Model BIT' (2014) 15 Journal of World Investment & Trade 454, 474–7.

[122] ibid 477.

[123] See European Convention on Human Rights and its subsequent interpretations by the European Court of Human Rights art 14.

abuse of power or similar bad faith conduct', and does not appear in the other treaties signed by the EU.

Finally, and most importantly, CETA, EU–Vietnam and the TTIP provide for the possibility to update the list of qualifiers, with the agreement of the parties and under recommendation of a designated committee.[124]

As a conclusion, with the course of time and the massive proliferation of cases based on an alleged, and indeed often found, FET breach, countries have concluded that the current FET might be too broadly defined in its formula. Therefore, given the importance of FET, both in rule-making and in the case law, recent treaties by China and the EU promote the use of a FET featuring a detailed list of qualifiers. This is precisely why a similar choice in the China–EU BIT is to be expected, maybe with slight language differences from the provisions included in other IIAs.

B. Taxation

Tax law has an international dimension which is governed by treaties aimed at promoting economic growth and encouraging cooperation[125] through several measures directed to avoid double taxation, both on employment and investment, deter disproportionate taxation, prevent tax fraud, and exchange information between public administrations.[126]

As a method for dispute resolution, the mutual agreement procedure (MAP) is the chosen form of resolution for international tax disputes, 'provided for in Article 251 of the United Nations Model Double Taxation Convention between Developed and Developing Countries, that allows the representatives of the States that enter a bilateral tax treaty to resolve disputes, difficulties or doubts arising in relation to the interpretation or application of the treaty'.[127] In this kind of Convention there is no reference to arbitration.

After this general introduction, it is now necessary to take a step back in order to gain a broader perspective over the panorama of tax law throughout the world. In fact, the last thirty years have witnessed a tendency towards demolishing all barriers, apart from taxation, to encourage international trade and investment: institutions such as the World Bank, the World Trade Organization (WTO), the International Monetary Fund (IMF), and the OECD did not step back from putting in place various initiatives aimed at promoting liberalization policies. Their drives, together with the advancement and conclusion of an ever-increasing number of worldwide trade agreements, leave tax as 'the last trade and investment barrier',[128] as clearly illustrated by Professor Chaisse's studies.

---

[124] Examples thereof are CETA art 8.10.3, EU–Vietnam IPA art 14.3, and Chapter II of the TTIP art 3.3.

[125] Alexander Trepelkov and others, 'United Nations Handbook on Selected Issues in Administration of Double Tax Treaties for Developing Countries' (2013) 3 http://www.un.org/esa/ffd/documents/UN_Handbook_DTT_Admin.pdf (last accessed 17 February 2017).

[126] Ruth Mason, 'US Tax Treaty Policy and the European Court of Justice' (2005) 59 Tax L Rev 69.

[127] United Nations, 'Guide to the Mutual Agreement Procedure Under Tax Treaties' http://www.un.org/esa/ffd/tax/gmap/Guide_MAP.pdf (last accessed 16 February 2017).

[128] Julien Chaisse, 'International Investment Law and Taxation: From Coexistence to Cooperation, Strengthening the Global Trade and Investment System for Sustainable Development' *The E15 Initiative, International Centre for Trade and Sustainable Development (ICTSD) and World Economic Forum* (2016) 4 http://e15initiative.org/publications/international-investment-law-taxation-coexistence-cooperation/ (last accessed 17 February 2017). See also Julien Chaisse, 'Investor-State Arbitration in International Tax Dispute Resolution: A Cut Above Dedicated Tax Dispute Resolution?' (2016) 41(2) Virginia Tax Review 149.

The next step is to elucidate the two main ways in which a tax system can give rise to barriers to international exchanges. To start with, when enterprises decide if investing in a foreign country would be profitable, a key role is played by the presence of a double taxation treaty relieving the company from paying income taxes in both the host and the home country. In addition, further costs may derive from discrepancies within the tax regime applied to transfer pricing norms within cross-border enterprise groups.[129]

In recent years, there has been an important increase of tax issues ending up before investment tribunals.[130]

This is the reason why some treaties, like the China–Canada agreement, signed in 2012, and the China–Colombia bilateral agreement,[131] signed in 2008, carve out taxation, excluding it from the scope of the whole agreement: this is known as 'general exception to taxation'.

From the comparative analysis of a number of agreements we can observe that, in a different fashion, the old BITs of EU Member States with China always covered taxation including it in the scope of the treaty,[132] and some other treaties inserted it in a few specific exceptions to the MFN[133] or national treatment clause.

With regard to the future, it could be hypothesized that China will be more inclined to carve out taxation from the scope of the treaty;[134] in our opinion, however, it is very likely that EU Member States will ask the European Commission to have it covered, since it is already included in their BITs with China.

To gain a fuller picture, one additional element needs to be taken into consideration. It concerns the Base Erosion and Profit Shifting (BEPS) project, launched in 2013 by the Organization for Economic Cooperation and Development (OECD),[135] and finalized in October 2015 with the introduction of a packet of measures known as the BEPS Actions.[136]

Globalization has given multi-national enterprises the chance to avoid or significantly decrease the taxes they pay, by means of legal arrangements that dematerialize profits for tax purposes or give investors the opportunity to shift them to low or no-tax locations. The strategies that exploit gaps and mismatches in tax rules to this end are termed BEPS. The OECD initiative is aimed at avoiding BEPS, equipping government with international instruments which ensure that profits are taxed where the economic

---

[129] Chaisse, 'International Investment Law and Taxation' (n 128) 5.

[130] Chaisse, 'International Investment Law and Taxation' (n 128) 3 n 25.

[131] One example thereof is the Bilateral Agreement for the Promotion and Protection of Investments between the Government of the Republic of Colombia and the Government of the People's Republic of China http://investmentpolicyhub.unctad.org/Download/TreatyFile/720 (last accessed 24 January 2017).

[132] One example thereof is the Agreement between the Government of the People's Republic of China and the Belgian–Luxembourg Economic Union on the Reciprocal Promotion and Protection of Investments http://investmentpolicyhub.unctad.org/Download/TreatyFile/340 (last accessed 16 February 2017).

[133] One example thereof is the China–Greece BIT, signed in 1992 http://investmentpolicyhub.unctad.org/Download/TreatyFile/738.

[134] Chaisse, 'International Investment Law and Taxation' (n 128) 15.

[135] As described on the OECD site, BEPS refers to making use of 'tax planning strategies to exploit gaps and mismatches of tax rules to artificially shift income to low or zero tax locations where there is little or no economic activity, resulting little or no overall tax being paid'. See http://www.oecd.org/tax/beps/beps-about.htm (last accessed 24 January 2017).

[136] BEPS Actions of OECD http://www.oecd.org/tax/beps/beps-actions.htm (last accessed 23 January 2017).

activities that did generate the profits have been performed, promote a more coherent international tax framework and favour a more transparent normative tax system.[137]

A further instrument developed by the OECD is the Convention on Mutual Administrative Assistance in Tax Matters:[138] its purpose is to exchange information and enhance transparency in the tax sector.[139]

The BEPS actions have been endorsed by the G20, and already implemented by numerous countries.[140] Tax reforms are happening throughout the entire world, applying the BEPS actions, as an evident example of a shift from soft law to hard law. However, every tax reform, like the one promoted by the OECD, could lead to tax disputes: in fact, a change in the regulatory framework could increase the discrepancy between the profits expected by foreign investors and those actually made, with the consequent dissatisfaction of the investors. Therefore, the latter could consider such a regulatory change as a breach of the investment treaty; this increases the risks for any jurisdiction implementing the BEPS actions to become a respondent in an investment arbitration.

As a concluding remark, perhaps the way forward in the matter of taxation measures in the EU–China BIT lies in the drafting of specific exceptions. Unlike the radical carve-out option, having taxation covered under the scope of the treaty, except for the FET clause, seems a more reasonable, balanced, assertive, and far-sighted approach.

C. Transparency

Transparency in investment agreements is a heavily debated topic in academic circles, as well as among urban or court practitioners and among the general public.

Exactly for this reason, a reflection over transparency requires certain elucidations. First and foremost, the term 'transparency' indicates both regulatory transparency and transparency in ISDS. To start with, regulatory transparency demands that a state publishes its laws, administrative regulations, and orders that may somehow affect the investors' investment; not surprisingly, 'access to meaningful information is recurrently cited as a powerful incentive to invest'.[141] This type of transparency also presents a different side of the coin: reciprocally, the investor must also notify the host state on the impacts of his investment on the domestic system.[142]

Secondly, transparency in ISDS indicates features of publicity and openness in the arbitration proceedings.

Research has emphasized that there are diverse elements that can be distinguished within transparency in ISDS:

1. Publication of the notice of arbitration;
2. Publication of documents submitted during the course of the proceedings, with specific derogations for confidential information;

[137] OECD, *Action Plan on Base Erosion and Profit Shifting* (OECD Publishing 2013) 13 https://www.oecd.org/ctp/BEPSActionPlan.pdf (last accessed 17 February 2017).
[138] OECD, Tax Information Exchange Agreements (TIEAs) http://www.oecd.org/tax/exchange-of-tax-information/taxinformationexchangeagreementstieas.htm (last accessed 17 February 2017).
[139] OECD, Global Forum on Transparency and Exchange of Information for Tax Purposes Peer Review http://www.oecd.org/tax/transparency/ (last accessed 17 February 2017).
[140] OECD/G20 Base Erosion and Shifting Project. Executive Summaries http://www.oecd.org/ctp/beps-reports-2015-executive-summaries.pdf (last accessed 24 January 2017).
[141] OECD, 'Public Sector Transparency and the International Investor' (2003) 8 https://www.oecd.org/investment/investment-policy/18546790.pdf (last accessed 24 January 2017).
[142] Ivo Šperanda, Marija Vučković, and Damir Piplica, 'The Social Aspect of the Investment Effectiveness Analysis' hrcak.srce.hr/file/238263 (last accessed 24 January 2017).

3. Publication of the award;

4. *Amicus curiae*'s submissions;

5. Submissions of non-disputing party's submission, referring to the claimant's home state; and

6. Public access to hearings.[143]

Indeed, the extent of compulsoriness of these aspects of transparency varies according to the legal framework they belong to.

Now it is possible to take into consideration the various IIAs signed by China throughout the course of time. First and foremost, it is imperative to recall that the current investment law regime is widely fragmented, with the dream of a multi-lateral framework still far away. While for trade in goods and services and intellectual property rights the World Trade Organization sets a comprehensive system equipped with a dispute resolution body,[144] there is no equivalent for the investment sector.

In fact, several initiatives have failed, including the Multilateral Agreement on Investment (MAI) within the OECD framework, and the negotiations in the WTO Doha Round. However, investment is not unknown in the WTO agreements: touched lightly by the trade in services trade-related investment measures (TRIMs) and trade-related aspects of intellectual property rights.

Nevertheless, investment law lies upon a network of a multiplicity of international investment agreements.

After this preliminary reflection, we can examine: (a) the various investment agreements signed by China over the years, with the aim to consider under this historic profile China's position on transparency; and (b) the investment agreements signed by the EU since it acquired competence with the Lisbon Treaty in 2009.

On this subject, it is necessary to consider that, although China had already made great efforts to attract foreign direct investment since the end of the 1970s, it agreed to sign its first BIT only in 1982. For several years, China has shown an aversion to investor–state arbitration through widely used access-restrictive clauses: these clauses can also be found both in the first two versions of its Model BIT[145] and in the numerous BITs belonging to the first generation. In a nutshell, the early BITs contained a clause allowing state-to-state arbitration on matters regarding treaty interpretation, and investor–state arbitration only for disputes about expropriation; moreover, the clause was precisely aimed at establishing the amount of compensation due to expropriating acts.[146] Transparency was not even mentioned in the 1997 China Model BIT.

A particularly important role in the evolution of China's approach to IIAs is held by its growing interests as a capital exporting country, culminating in 1998, in which there was a crucial shift deviating from its historically conservative standing as a capital importing country.

---

[143] International Institute for Sustainable Development, *New UNCITRAL Arbitration Rules on Transparency: Application* (Content and Next Steps 2013) http://ccsi.columbia.edu/files/2014/04/UNCITRAL_Rules_on_Transparency_commentary_FINAL.pdf (last accessed 13 February 2017).

[144] Dispute settlement https://www.wto.org/english/tratop_e/dispu_e/dispu_e.htm (last accessed 13 February 2017).

[145] China Model BIT (1997) http://ebooks.narotama.ac.id/files/The%20International%20Law%20of%20Investment%20Claims/Appendix%205%20%20China%20Model%20BIT%20(1997).pdf (last accessed 13 February 2017); Chinese Model BIT Version I http://oxia.ouplaw.com/view/10.1093/law:iic/9780199230259.001.1/law-iic-9780199230259-appendix-011003 (last accessed 13 February 2017).

[146] An example thereof is Article 4.2 of the China Model BIT (1997).

Within the *travaux préparatoires* of the 2010 UNCITRAL Working Group, while taking stock of the situation at the time, China had confirmed that no other norm regarding *amici curiae*, publication of documents, or third party involvement had ever been included in any treaty signed by China up until that moment.[147] However, in the years that followed, China had second thoughts.

In fact, when in October 2013 the General Assembly of the United Nations was tackling the UNCITRAL work on the rules of transparency, the Chinese delegate Shang Zhen affirmed that: 'The Chinese Delegation believes that the implementation of the Rules on Transparency will be conducive to enhancing the transparency of international investment arbitration procedures'.[148]

Scrutinizing the BITs most recently signed by China, we will focus on the Canada–China FIPA signed in 2012.[149] The presence of various transparency provisions related to investor–state arbitration is remarkable, as well as the correspondence in their wording to the 2004 Canadian Model FIPA.[150]

Although on some points the two versions vary considerably, they align on the publicity of the award and the possibility for *amicus curiae* to file briefs with the tribunal. The other aspects of transparency, encompassing also the openness of hearings and the publication of written submissions and other documents to be filed with the tribunal, depend on the respondent state's consent.

Even though the recent China–Australia FTA (ChAFTA) of 2015 provides that 'With the agreement of the respondent, the tribunal shall conduct hearings open to the public',[151] it is also true that it highlights the host state's veto power in respect of certain transparency norms.

In 2013, the negotiations for the Regional Comprehensive Economic Partnership (RCEP) were officially launched,[152] with the underlying objective of reaching a broad free trade and investment agreement between the ten member states of ASEAN and Australia, China, India, Japan, South Korea, and New Zealand, each of which already have free trade agreements (FTAs) with ASEAN.

It is intriguing to note that all three of the EU–Vietnam, CETA, and TTIP treaties refer to the UNCITRAL Rules on Transparency in Treaty Based Investor State Arbitration.[153] The UNCITRAL Rules govern several aspects of transparency in ISDS: the publicity of the hearings, access to documents, the publication of the award, and third party participation.

---

[147] United Nations Commission on International Trade Law, *Yearbook Volume XLII: 2011* (United Nations 2014) 218 http://www.uncitral.org/pdf/english/yearbooks/yb-2011-e/UNCITRAL-Yearbook-2011-E.pdf (last accessed 13 February 2017).

[148] Statement by Mr Shang Zhen, 'Chinese Delegate at the 68th Session of the UN General Assembly on Agenda Item 79 Report of UNCITRAL on the Work of Its 46th Session' (2013) http://www.china-un.org/eng/hyyfy/t1091525.htm (last accessed 13 February 2017).

[149] Agreement between the Government of Canada and the Government of the People's Republic of China for the Promotion and Reciprocal Protection of Investments http://investmentpolicyhub.unctad.org/Download/TreatyFile/3476 (last accessed 13 February 2017).

[150] Agreement Between Canada and ... for the Promotion and Protection of Investments http://www.italaw.com/documents/Canadian2004-FIPA-model-en.pdf (last accessed 13 February 2017).

[151] Free Trade Agreement between the Government of Australia and the Government of the People's Republic of China 2015 art 9.17(3) http://investmentpolicyhub.unctad.org/Download/TreatyFile/34544 (last accessed 13 February 2017).

[152] Trade and Investment Regional Comprehensive Economic Partnership https://aric.adb.org/fta/regional-comprehensive-economic-partnership (last accessed 13 February 2017).

[153] UNICTRAL Rules on Transparency in Treaty Based Investor State Arbitration http://www.uncitral.org/uncitral/en/uncitral_texts/arbitration/2014Transparency.html (last accessed 13 February 2017).

Both the EU–Vietnam IPA and CETA have the greatest requirements for transparency, since they comprehend the UNCITRAL rules on transparency, the publication of laws, and the acceptance of third party funding if declared at an early stage.

Therefore, it is conceivable that, in its negotiations with China, the EU will put pressure to ensure at least a certain degree of transparency.

To conclude, it will be necessary to check the direction taken by the Chinese economy, taking into consideration some elements, such as whether China will develop as a capital importing or capital exporting state, whether there will be economic expansion or contraction, and how the political relations between China and other global powers will develop. All this may influence China's position in its negotiations of an international agreement with the EU.

Summing up, it can be inferred that the way the three issues discussed in sections VA, VB, and VC are agreed on will be the basis on which the whole treaty might be assessed. In the evaluation of whether it will strongly promote mutual investment while guarding public interest, or whether the two world protagonists in the global stage will choose a more protectionist approach, these three provisions will play a pivotal role.

Secondly, given the current trends, the China–EU BIT bears a systemic dimension. In fact, if the deal eventually sees the light of day, it will have significant impact on the negotiations of all other treaties in Asia: in this way, the China–EU investment treaty will not be far away from becoming a benchmark.

Conclusively, since the regions involved in the treaty have a great geopolitical and economic importance, the treaty and its provisions will have a large influence not only on the political and economic systems of the partner states, and consequently on their citizens, workers, and businesses, but also, it will serve as a benchmark that third countries can follow or distance themselves from in their respective future negotiations.

VI. Conclusion

The chapter has identified in the provisions of FET, taxation and transparency as the core issues of the investment agreement under discussion between the EU and China, and highlighted both their features and relevance. The latter can be inferred from the fact that these issues are the ones that are most frequently allegedly breached in investor–state cases, where investors claim to be harmed about the host state policies, and therefore it is on these issues that the legal discussion of the greater part of arbitration cases focuses. Also, it is exactly for this reason that it is essential that the EU and China carefully design all the clauses in their CAI.

Moreover, although the treaty under negotiation between the EU and China covers only bilateral investments, it can be deemed as the way to success for potential free trade agreements.

Furthermore, its relevance has aspects that go beyond the purely economic and legal ones, deriving from the central importance that these two regions have both economically and strategically in their 'wider neighbourhood'[154] and worldwide, often in competition with the interests of other world powers.

---

[154] Bertram Lang, 'The Prospective EU-China Bilateral Investment Treaty: Wider Regional Implications in East and Southeast Asia' (2015) 3(15) EU–China Observer 11.

Hence, the CAI is not simply one more of the numerous bi- and multi-lateral agreements forming the 'fragmented patchwork' of international investment law,[155] but it is a decisive treaty, and can be considered as a springboard for a closer strategic relationship between China and the EU.

Both the degree of liberalization that the CAI will achieve and its outcome will have a much broader impact than those of an agreement limited to bilateral cooperation. In fact, the destiny of the China–EU BIT will be crucial in taking one of the two following directions: either the two regions will increase their cooperation and enhance mutually beneficial economic relationships, or they will compete against each other for the largest share of the global market, relying on other PTAs with third states.[156]

This political perspective can be inferred from the EU strategy in this negotiation, which is purely economic on the surface, leaving aside any potentially discomforting geopolitical matters.[157]

Undoubtedly, the future of such cooperation will be significantly characterized by the economic conditions of both regions as capital importing and exporting countries.

In any case, currently both the EU and China have significant reasons to negotiate and conclude a CAI fostering investment in both directions. Therefore, although the negotiation of this agreement will not be effortless, a treaty that manages to satisfy the parties' interests, both as home states and as host states, will be welcome by the parties and their investors, and even serve as a role model for the rest of the world.[158]

---

[155] Stephan W Schill, 'Multilateralization: An Ordering Paradigm for International Investment Law' in Marc Bungenberg and others (eds), *International Investment Law* (Nomos/Hart Publishing 2015) 1866–87, 1866.
[156] See Lang (n 154) 15.   [157] ibid 15.   [158] Bickenbach and others (n 82) 1, 26.

10

Issues on SOEs in BITs

The (Complex) Case of the Sino–US BIT Negotiations

Xinquan Tu, Na Sun, and Zhen Dai*

China's performance in investment in the past decade will attract more attention than, if not the same as, what it has achieved in trade. Utilizing foreign direct investment (FDI) has always been one of the core tools in China's opening-up policy, as well as one of the largest contributors for China's economic development. Official statistics[1] show that China remains the top FDI destination among developing countries for the twenty-fifth consecutive year in 2016.

Another dramatic change happens in the other direction of capital flow, that is, China's outward foreign direct investment (OFDI). According to UNCTAD statistics,[2] China invested an amount of US\$55.9 billion abroad in 2008, ranking nineteenth globally, far less than the United States, which ranked first with an amount of US\$308.3 billion that year. While in 2016 China's OFDI surged to US\$183.1 billion, exceeding most of the industrialized countries and getting to the second largest OFDI country in the world, with a significantly narrowed gap with the front runner, which is the United States with US\$299 billion. In other words, China has transformed from a FDI net inflow country to a FDI net outflow country in less than a decade!

However, China's policy concerning FDI focused in the capital inflow for a long period of time, while shedding little light on the OFDI. There has been criticism that OFDI policy is left far behind its practice in the case of China.[3] The Chinese government has apparently accelerated its pace in protecting, managing, and enhancing OFDI by means of domestic policy design and international negotiations in recent years. At the multi-lateral level, China, along with others, has made a great effort to formulate the G20 Guiding Principles for Global Investment Policy-making, which is the first global framework of multi-lateral rules governing international investment[4] at the G20 Hangzhou Summit in 2016. It shows the great willingness of China in the infrastructure of international investment measures. At the regional and bilateral levels, China reached an agreement in investment with Japan and South Korea in 2012, and

---

* Authors are from the China Institute for WTO Studies, University of International Business and Economics, Beijing, China.

[1] Ministry of Commerce of the People's Republic of China, Report on Foreign Investment in China 2016 http://images.mofcom.gov.cn/wzs/201612/20161230131233768.pdf (last accessed 5 December 2017).

[2] UNCTAD data centre http://unctadstat.unctad.org/wds/ReportFolders/reportFolders.aspx?sCS_ChosenLang=en (last accessed 5 December 2017).

[3] Sibao Shen and Jing Peng, 'Research on the Supporting Legal System of China's Outward Foreign Direct Investment' (2012) 6 Social Science Journal 84.

[4] Xinhuanet, Graphically Understanding of President Xi Jinping's Closing Speech on G20 Leader's Summit in Hangzhou http://news.xinhuanet.com/world/2016-09/06/c_129271659.htm> (last accessed 6 December 2017).

has also added one single chapter on investment in its recently initiated free trade agreement negotiations, such as that with Australia.

The bilateral investment treaty (BIT) is still the main approach of China to upgrade its contribution to build international investment rules. The ongoing separate BIT negotiations with the United States and the European Union demonstrate the present concerns and the latest vision, although China has concluded BIT talks with over 130 countries, which concentrate mainly on investment protection and are a kind of old-fashioned BIT. Launched in 2008, Sino–US BIT negotiation unsurprisingly became the top priority for the Chinese government in a very long time, which also unsurprisingly turned out to be extremely tough. The Chinese government encountered great pressure facing the overwhelming advantage of the Unites States in investment rule-making. Of all the difficulties, state-owned enterprise is one of the central concerns.

I. Background

The issue of state-owned enterprises (SOEs) has never gone away once China began sitting around the negotiating table, especially with the United States. Sixteen years ago when China was expecting to enter the multi-lateral trading system, there were special sections for state trading enterprises in its accession protocol, in accordance with Article XVII of the GATT1994. While in bilateral investment treaty (BIT) negotiation with the US, which was reignited in 2008 and has undergone twenty-nine rounds of talks, the issue of SOEs was brought up to the table again and seemingly became a key point blocking the negotiation. However, with an ever-increasing economy of scale and front-ranking position in global trade and investment, it seems unsatisfying that China should be able to give the same commitments concerning SOEs as it did in the WTO negotiations, which was sixteen years ago. To put the BIT negotiation forward on the SOEs issue needs new solutions.

After more than three decades' of reform, SOEs in China are not only still dominant in the most important industries, but also aggressively expanding to the international markets. By the end of 2015, the total assets of Chinese SOEs was up to 120 trillion Yuan. The number of SOEs is still as large as 160,000. Among the 500 largest Chinese companies in 2015, 295 are SOEs. SOEs also accounted for half of Chinese overseas FDI stock by the end of 2015. In particular, China's large SOEs are becoming the most active acquirers of foreign companies in the world market.

The increasing influence of Chinese SOEs in both domestic and international markets has raised great concerns in the developed world, especially the US[5] and the EU.[6] They have taken some measures such as national security reviews of foreign investments and countervailing duty actions to restrain Chinese SOEs' expansions. They also intend to make some international rules on SOEs to balance the alleged unfair competitive advantages of SOEs who benefit from government support.

An important effort on this issue is that the US government is trying to introduce a chapter on SOEs into the Sino–US bilateral investment treaty under negotiation. The chapter is said to be following the TPP model, putting stricter regulations on SOEs' business behaviour and the relations between SOEs and government. While a formal

---

[5] *The Economist*, 'China's State Capitalism Not Just Tilting at Windmills' http://www.economist.com/comment/1682758 (last accessed 6 October 2012).

[6] Qi Jin, 'Chinese SOEs' M&A in Europe Cause Concerns' http://www.ftchinese.com/story/001066415#s=d (last accessed 2 March 2016).

institutional arrangement will surely be helpful to reduce uncertainties and conflicts regarding SOEs' commercial activities, such a new and extremely sensitive issue will also certainly complicate the already difficult negotiations.

II. Chinese SOEs' Investments in the US and Responses from the US

A. Chinese SOEs' investments in the US

Chinese FDI in the US is a relatively new phenomenon. Relevant statistics started from 2002. Since Lenovo's acquisition of the IBM PC department in 2005, Chinese investments in the US have been increasing fast. From 2009 to 2013, SOEs contributed to a large part of Chinese investments in the US. In 2011, SOEs accounted for more than half of the stock of China's FDI in the US. In 2012, the share of SOEs was still as high as 41 per cent.

However, with a long-time and strong tradition of a liberal market economy system, the United States is inherently suspicious of the role of the state in SOEs, especially from such an alleged authoritarian country like China. With the rapid growth of the international competitiveness of Chinese SOEs, the active roles of Chinese SOEs in the global market raised concerns in the US, and these SOEs are even labelled as 'state capitalism'. The United States not only strongly questioned the intentions of these Chinese SOEs based on public opinion, but also took various means to constrain their investment in the United States through policy tools.

As a result, the US government has taken some measures to restrict China's SOEs' investments in the US. The major tool is the National Security Review System, known as NSRS. In 2015, China's direct investment in the United States reached a record of US$15.7 billion, with an increase of 30 per cent compared with 2014. However, China's state-owned enterprises directly investing in the United States in that year accounted for only 16 per cent of the total investment, with a decrease of 3 percentage points compared with 2014. The share of SOEs in the FDI stock decreased to 32 per cent. Clearly, China's SOEs in the United States suffered from a more serious investment obstacle than in other regions. Given that mergers and acquisitions is the major form of foreign direct investment in the United States, the national security review of the US for foreign M&A transactions will undoubtedly become the most likely factor hindering the investment in the United States by Chinese SOEs.

B. National security review system of the US on SOEs

The national security review system for the state-owned enterprises is stricter than that for private enterprises. M&A transactions of Chinese SOEs in the US mainly focus on energy, the chemical industry, high technology, and other key industries, which poses a potential threat to national security, causing panic in the US. The US government strictly limits the M&A transactions of Chinese state-owned enterprises through the national security review system, and this leads to the low proportion of investment in the US.[7]

---

[7] Julien Chaisse, 'Demystifying Public Security Exception and Limitations on Capital Movement: Hard Law, Soft Law and Sovereign Investments in the EU Internal Market' (2015) 37(2) University of Pennsylvania Journal of International Law 583.

The national security review body in the US is the CFIUS (Committee on Foreign Investment in the United States). The focus of the review towards M&A transaction has two criteria, which are, in short, whether the transaction threatens national security and whether the enterprise is controlled by a foreign government.

In practice, CFIUS has never published the basic rules of its 'national security' review. Generally, the CFIUS has the right to terminate the transaction once the foreign direct investment involves any of the seven following behaviours:[8]

- Whether domestic production is able to meet the demands of national defence;
- Whether the ability of domestic industries could meet the needs of national defence, including human resources, products, technology, materials, and other supplies and services;
- Whether the domestic industries and businesses controlled by foreigners can meet the demands of national defence;
- Whether there is potential possibility that this transaction leads to sale of the military supplies, equipment, or technology to countries which support terrorism or the proliferation of missiles or biological weapons;
- Whether this transaction is manipulated by a foreign government or government controlled entities or individuals on behalf of the government;
- Whether this transaction is a potential threat to US leadership in technology and thus influences national security;
- Other issues which presidents or the CFIUS consider as threats to national security and need to be reviewed.

According to the provisions of the US Foreign Investment and National Security Law (2007), 'a deal controlled by a government' refers to any transactions that lead an American enterprise to be controlled by foreign governments or by individuals on behalf of the foreign government. The CFIUS will enter the stage of investigation if it finds that a M&A transaction is controlled by foreign governments. For SOEs, as long as the direct investment was made in the United States, there is a 100 per cent possibility of entering into an investigation phase of national security review. In the review of practice, to determine whether M&A transactions are controlled by foreign governments, the answer is mainly based on whether government subsidies are a part of the company's equity structure and whether the company's equity structure is transparent, etc. In addition, for Chinese SOEs, the CFIUS usually has special consideration of relevant risks, including the risk of the core technology transferred to third countries, the risk of espionage activities through the transaction by the Chinese government, the risk of strengthening China's military power, etc.

C. Results from the review system on China's SOEs investment in the US

According to the CFIUS' annual report, the manufacturing sector has been the centre of focus among all the industries involved under review. From 2009 to 2011, the

---

[8] Department of the Treasury, Office of Investment Security, Guidance Concerning the National Security Review Conducted by the Committee on Foreign Investment in the United States, https://www.treasury.gov/resource-center/international/foreign-investment/Pages/cfius-guidance.aspx (last accessed 8 December 2008).

number of reviews in manufacturing increased from seven in 2007 to twenty-four in 2009, with its proportion of all reviews rising from 54 per cent to 60 per cent. From 2012 to 2014, the number reached thirty-three, accounting for as high as 49 per cent of all review cases. Mining, construction and finance, and the information service industry also received extremely severe reviews.

On a country basis, among all M&A transactions, twenty-four Chinese companies were reviewed in the United States in 2014 (see Figure 10.1), accounting for 16.3 per cent of the reviews of the year, ranking first in the number of reviews for the third consecutive year. The number of Chinese enterprises under review shows a rapid growth trend. After the financial crisis in 2008, Chinese SOEs, with some strength, increased their efforts in M&A transactions in United States. These transactions surged in 2010, which caused the US to be concerned about its national security. Since the start of 2011, the CFIUS has delivered a series of requirements that are even more stringent.[9] Since 2011, the CFIUS has added the government's sensitive information, government contract information, and employee information into the review content. In addition, the CFIUS also stipulates that if foreign companies are located in the vicinity of certain types of US government facilities, the CFIUS will conduct a security review of the project.[10] This provision has led even more Chinese companies in M&A transactions to be reviewed in the US.

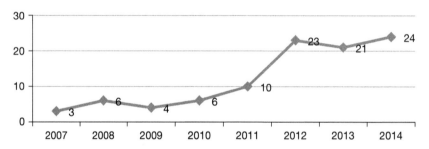

Figure 10.1 The number of cases under review of China's direct investments in the US (2007–2014)

Data source: Committee on Foreign Investment in the United States: Annual Report to Congress.

From 2007 to 2014, the number of the Chinese mining and construction companies under review grew rapidly, up from 7.7 per cent (2007–2009) to 28 per cent (2012–2014). The number of the reviews in finance and the information services sector increased from three (2007–2009) to thirteen in (2012–2014). As can be seen from the data above, the review towards Chinese enterprises (by the CFIUS) has focused on key industries related to national security. In China, many of these industries are capital intensive, of which the investors are mainly large state-owned enterprises.

The reason why the United States has stricter scrutiny on the direct investment of Chinese SOEs is twofold: on one hand, the large scale and the sensitivity of the investment poses a potential threat to national security; on the other hand, China's

---

[9] Committee on Foreign Investment in the United States: Annual Reports to Congress (2008–2014) http://www.treasury.gov/resource-center/international/foreign-investment/Pages/cfius-reports.aspx (last accessed 8 December 2015).

[10] Mei Wang, *China Investment Overseas: Question, Fact and Analysis* (1st edn, China CITIC Publishing House 2014) 34–44.

SOEs have a strong government background, and the government owns the shares and decision-making power of the enterprise. The United States is worried about the potential political intentions behind these transactions. For the above reasons, Chinese SOEs have become the enterprises which are most concerned and most likely to be rejected in all the direct investments to the United States.

From 1990 to 2015, fourteen major M&A transactions of Chinese enterprises have been investigated by the CFIUS on the grounds that they threaten national security. Among them, eight M&As in SOEs were obstructed for threatening national security, accounting for 57 per cent of the total transactions. Details are displayed in Table 10.1.

Table 10.1 M&A transactions of Chinese enterprises are intervened by the CFIUS on the grounds that they threaten national security (1990–2015)

Year	M&A project	Involved Areas	Reasons for the failure of M&A transactions
1990	CATIC's acquisition of Mamco	Aviation Technology	CFIUS believes that the transaction has large impacts on the US national security then implemented export control to China, the transaction was rejected by the US president.
2005	The CNOOC bid for Unocal oil company	Energy	CFIUS said CNOOC is under the control of the government, which threatens US energy security, moreover, the risks of oil mining technology leaks.
2009	West International's acquisition of the United States Excellent gold (First Gold) Company	Mining	CFIUS said the acquisition project was too close to the naval training base, military information and national security may be at risk.
2010	Tangshan Caofeidian Investment Group acquired 60% stake of the US fiber equipment manufacturer (Emcore)	Energy /Smelting	The US government is worried about the core technology leak.
2010	Anshan iron and steel's investment in US Steel Development Co.	Smelting	Anshan Steel as a SOE, will have access to the production technology and information of the new steel used in infrastructure for national defence.
2010	HUAWEI and ZHONGXING for the Sprint project	High-tech/ Telecommunication network	CFIUS said the two companies and the Chinese government is closely related, which is a threat to national security.
2015	The Thunis company's acquisition of Micron Technology	Semiconductor technology	CFIUS believes that the acquisition may lead to leakage of core technologies, which threatens national security.
2016	The Thunis company's acquisition of West Data	Storage technology	Acquisition involves core technology, which is a threat to US National security.

Data source: Based on relevant literatures.[a]
[a]Daniel H Rosen and Thilo Hanemann, 'An American Open Door? Maximizing the Benefits of Chinese Foreign Direct Investment' 64 http://asiasociety.org/files/pdf/AnAmericanOpenDoor_FINAL.pdf (last accessed 1 May 2011) Thilo Hanemann and Cassie Gao, 'Chinese FDI in the US: 2015 Recap' http://www.chinausfocus.com/finance-economy/public-vs-private-how-china-prefers-to-invest-in-the-us/ (last accessed 19 January 2016).

III. International Rules Regarding SOEs

While the US national security review system has significantly affected Chinese SOEs' investments, the existing international rules related to the SOEs investment cannot effectively constrain the restrictions or discrimination of other countries towards Chinese SOEs. On the contrary, since these rules are largely proposed by the US, relevant SOE rules are designed to regulate them rather than help their international commercial behaviours.

A. Relevant rules of SOEs under the WTO

Under the framework of the WTO, Article VI of GATT (anti-dumping and counter-vailing duties), Article XVII (subsidies), and Article XVII (state trading enterprise) and 'Agreement on Subsidies and Countervailing Measures' are all concerned with SOEs. But in the provisions of various organizations for the SOEs, the scope of applicability of the WTO rules is minimal, because the WTO does not consider the governance of SOEs as a top priority.

Generally, WTO rules only regulate the country rather than the company's behaviour. The WTO also did not mention the difference between SOEs and other enterprises, only that state trading enterprises are under the jurisdiction of the WTO. State trading enterprises are different from SOEs. The former are enterprises trading state monopolies of products which now cover very few products and are mainly minerals and agricultural sideline products. Thus, the provisions of the WTO for state trading enterprises cannot be applied to SOEs.

B. Relevant rules on SOEs in free trade agreements

Currently, there are few rules specially designated for SOEs in the free trade agreements (FTAs). One of the important examples in the United States is the Singapore Free Trade Agreement, which was signed in 2003 and entered into force on 1 January 2004. Compared with the WTO, the United States–Singapore FTA has more provisions in the governance of SOEs, and it has tighter requirements on information disclosure and transparency of the SOEs than that of the WTO on state trading enterprises. The requirements on SOEs in the United States–Singapore FTA are even higher than the standard of private enterprises: it requires disclosure to the extent to which the state controls the enterprise, from the visible controls, such as the control of shares, to in-visible ones, such as the number of government officials in the office of the board of directors in SOEs. However, the United States–Singapore FTA did not put forward more requirements on the operation of state-owned enterprises than the WTO, and it still focuses on commercial considerations and non-discrimination.

C. OECD and its rules of SOEs

The OECD features the most detailed rules of the corporate governance of SOEs among all international organizations. It not only covers all of the content of the WTO rules and the United States–Singapore agreement, but it also includes the details of corporate governance, such as the policy framework between the owner and the company and the rights of shareholders and stakeholders, etc. Unlike the vague requirement on 'commercial considerations' in the WTO and the United States–Singapore agreement, the OECD guidelines include detailed recommendations on, for example, the right of state-owned enterprises to enter capital competition, the freedom of the board of directors of state-owned enterprises, and the difference between the public functions and the commercial operation of the SOEs. Although the coverage of the OECD guidelines on SOEs and the requirement for the government is comprehensive and high-level, its enforcement is relatively weak, even though the OECD itself acknowledges that the guidelines in many countries have not been effectively implemented.[11] The main reason is that it is very difficult to implement detailed international rules at the national level, as the legal system of different countries may conflict with international rules. In order to maintain their national sovereignty, countries remain vigilant to the threats from international organizations.

D. Relevant rules of SOEs under the TPP

In the new development of relevant international rules of SOEs dominated by the United States, the influence of the TPP is particularly significant. Even not having entered into force, the TPP shows the US's great determination to tackle problems and would be the world's first multi-lateral rules on the behaviour of the special market for SOEs. The core principles of SOEs and state-designated monopoly in the TPP is Article 17.4—Non Discriminatory Treatment and Commercial Considerations, Article 17.6—Non Commercial Assistance, and Article 17.10—Transparency, as described below.

1. Broad and clear definition on SOEs

Article 17.1 gives a clear definition of SOEs that fall into the scope of the TPP, which is 'an enterprise that is principally engaged in commercial activities' and meets any of the three conditions, including a party 'directly owns more than 50 percent of the share capital', 'controls, through ownership interests, the exercise of more than 50 percent of the voting rights', and 'holds the power to appoint a majority of members of the board of directors or any other equivalent management body'.

By definition, the TPP regulates SOEs engaging in commercial activities, which corresponds to the non-commercial assistant regulation below and shows the slight transition of focus on SOE rules. Also, it clarifies that SOEs and the state can be related in stakeholder, voting, and appointment rights.

2. Regulation of non-commercial assistance

Non-commercial assistance is the innovative core provision for regulating SOEs in the TPP. Article 17.6 requires that parties must not cause adverse effects to the interests of another party through the use of non-commercial assistance, either directly or indirectly to any of its SOEs. There are three obligations for the contracting party, which are that the contracting party itself shall not provide non-commercial assistance, the contracting party shall make sure that there is no non-commercial assistance between SOEs, and the party shall not provide non-commercial assistance in the territory of

---

[11] Antonio Capobianco and Hans Christiansen, *Competitive Neutrality and State-Owned Enterprises: Challenges and Policy Options* (OECD 2011).

another party. Particularly, adverse effects must not be caused as the result of the above possible forms of non-commercial assistance.

The TPP's rules on non-commercial assistance are essentially disciplines on subsidy for SOEs. The concepts of adverse effects and injury in Article 17.8 are familiar and, indeed, they are *borrowed* from the WTO, from the Agreement on Subsidies and Countervailing Measures, to be accurate. The TPP uses related regulations in Article 5 and Article 15 of the SCM Agreement, but enlarged to cover trade in services and international investment.

3. Refinement on the requirement on transparency

Requirements on transparency are not rare in international rules, yet the TPP lays down very detailed rules for realization on transparency about SOEs. Mainly, a party must make a list of all its SOEs publicly available on an official website; a party must provide detailed information on SOEs such as terms of its designation, percentage of its share, and even annual revenue and total assets over the most recent three-year period; and a party must provide information regarding any policy OR programme it has adopted or maintains that provides for non-commercial assistance.

4. Jurisdiction of SOEs in commercial transactions

Last but not least, the TPP sets out rules on jurisdiction on SOEs operating in a foreign territory. According to Article 17.5, a party must provide its courts with jurisdiction over civil claims against SOEs of a foreign government based on a commercial activity carried on in its territory. Based on the explanation of Office of the United States Trade Representative (USTR) on this provision, SOEs in a foreign territory cannot claim state immunity against a civil claim for commercial activities,[12] which means SOEs have no absolute state immunity rights.

VI. The Ongoing Sino–US BIT Negotiation and the Issue of SOEs

A. Adding SOEs into Sino–US BIT negotiation

The negotiation of Sino–US BITs started in 2008 and can be called, in terms of economy and trade, the most important negotiations among all Sino–US negotiations so far. In July 2013, China and the US announced the 'pre-establishment national treatment (PENT) with a negative list' model to carry out substantive negotiations. In June 2015, the two sides exchanged a negative list price for the first time, and officially initiated the negative list negotiations. In September 2016, the two sides exchanged the third version of negative lists, indicating significant progress made in negotiations.

However, there are voices against BITs. Some from the political and business circle in the US believe that BITs will strengthen the unfair advantage of Chinese enterprises in competition, especially the SOEs, thus damaging US employment

---

[12] USTR https://medim.com/the-trans-pacific-partnership/state-owned-enterprises-and-designated-monoplies-bfddb20cb3b3#.bpf71vtiu (last accessed 24 November 2015).

and long-term economic benefits. In this sense, Chinese SOEs not only concern US national security, but also its economic competitiveness. Therefore, it is important to ensure SOEs' so-called competitive neutrality, whereby SOEs should not have additional competitive advantage thanks to their special linkages with the government.

In fact, the US BIT version 2012 had no single chapter for SOEs, which was brought up suddenly in July 2016, when the negotiation nearly came to a close following its relatively complete rules in the TPP. The notion dragged the negotiation down into its ninth year.

B. Possible solutions on the SOE issue

From the performance of China's SOEs in the US, which may seem somewhat aggressive according to the strong feedback from the US officials under the national security review system, there is little possibility that the US will give up this specific chapter regulating SOEs. Moreover, above all of the existing international rules on SOEs, the TPP's provisions and articles are closer to what the US intends to realize.

While the US may push its TPP model on SOE regulation, the Chinese side does not welcome this version, even if it is not totally against it. It cannot easily be accepted by China, for several reasons. SOEs in China are the important pillars of national economy development and security for the whole nation's benefit. Although, the direction of SOE reform is market-oriented, the path varies from stressing on cutting off the relationship and influence of government on SOEs. SOEs are assumed to have the responsibility from both political, economic, and social perspectives, meaning they are unlikely to make decisions based entirely on commercial considerations. In turn, the government must provide policy incentives and support to SOEs. In addition, the TPP version on SOEs also indicates great pressure on legislation and administration for China domestically. Even those SOEs listed outside the BIT may be affected by the possible changes and alternations, which adds more resistance to the negotiation.

One possible solution on the SOEs issue in BIT negotiation is that China may make a long list of exemptions and a long transition period which may also be used in other negotiations, for example, the GPA negotiation. Also, some details such as the definition on SOEs and the disclosure requirement on the SOEs information may also be amended or renegotiated.

V. Conclusion

Before coming to a conclusion based upon the above analysis, we may use a few paragraphs as to why the US is so concerned about China's investment, sometimes not even investment from SOEs, in its market. Usually, a destination country welcomes foreign direct investment (FDI) from other countries. This may be because of, although maybe not limited to, the following reasons. First, these are investments from developing countries to developed countries, quite contrary to the traditional theory of FDI. Secondly, developing countries like China buy the latest technology products, instead of those that are out of date, which is also contrary to the traditional technology transition theory. Thus, it can be explained why, even if it is not SOEs, transactions by Huawei and Zhongxing can also be vetoed by the CFIUS under the national security review system.

China is now following its own pace in SOEs reform, and it is unlikely to be changed by the Sino–US BIT negotiation. As far as the rules are concerned, China is not ready, and Chinese SOEs are not ready. But deep inside, China and Chinese SOEs need clear signals and policies which are headed in the right direction but have not yet appeared. If both sides want this great and important treaty to come to a conclusion, both sides need to be more constructive and make concessions, especially the US side, by introducing more tolerance and patience.

11

Towards a Fourth Generation of Chinese Treaty Practice

Substantive Changes, Balancing Mechanisms, and Selective Adaption

Matthew Levine*

For more than 1,000 years it has been said that 'all roads lead to Rome'.[1] In addition, the One Belt One Road initiative suggests that a similar turn of phrase may soon apply to Beijing. For readers of this volume it may largely go without saying that Beijing's place as a political and economic centre is increasingly transnational. We see this in the formulation of rules around project financing by the Asian Infrastructure Investment Bank and also in the negotiation of the Regional Comprehensive Economic Partnership. In addition, Beijing plays an increasingly central role in the Group of 20's trade and investment agenda. Drilling down to the level of international investment agreements (IIAs), however, it is much less clear whether Beijing can be considered as the centre or even a particularly important node in the IIA Universe.[2] Put slightly differently, although the People's Republic of China (China, or PRC) has actively negotiated IIAs since the early years of its opening up policy resulting in a voluminous treaty practice, very few observers, if any, would consider the PRC to be a IIA rule-maker. At the same time, the organizers of this Forum note that China is increasingly faced with novel questions about its overall approach to investment and that, in the context of a shrinking pool of desirable domestic investment opportunities and transition to the more market-orientated service economy contemplated in the Thirteenth Five-Year Plan (2016–2020), new foreign investment strategies are needed. This would appear to include new approaches to IIAs as China now has a strong interest in outward investment as well as the historical interest in inward investment.

If China is not a rule-maker, does it follow that it is a rule-taker? Certain facts appear to point in this direction, i.e. the acute influence of North American treaty practice, especially that of the United States, and Beijing's reluctance to update its own model treaty. However, research on China's participation at the World Trade Organization (WTO) and negotiation of regional trade agreements (RTAs), points to an alternative conceptualization. On this approach, Beijing is neither a rule-maker nor a rule-taker but rather increasingly acts a 'rule-shaker'.[3] Curiously, although this term has

* Research Fellow, Capital Markets Institute, University of Toronto. Barrister & Solicitor (Law Society of Ontario).

[1] Christine Ammer, *The American Heritage Dictionary of Idioms* (Houghton Mifflin Company 1997) 12.

[2] On the notion of an 'IIA Universe' see Wolfgang Alschner and Dmitriy Skougarevskiy, 'Mapping the Universe of International Investment Agreements' (2016) 19 Journal of International Economic Law 561.

[3] Henry S Gao, 'China's Ascent in Global Trade Governance: From Rule Taker to Rule Shaker, and Maybe Rule Maker?' in Carolyn Deere-Birkbeck (ed), *Making Global Trade Governance Work for Development* (Cambridge University Press 2011) 153.

Towards A Fourth Generation of Chinese Treaty Practice: Substantive Changes, Balancing Mechanisms, and Selective Adaption. Matthew Levine. © Matthew Levine, 2019. Published 2019 by Oxford University Press.

since been used by a group of scholars to consider similarities and differences between China, Japan, and Korea's interaction with international economic law, it does not appear to have been explicitly defined.[4] The key insight is in any case an invitation to move away from a dyadic analysis, which tends to focus on outcomes, and instead examine the process of 'shaking' or challenging existing rules to more completely suit the interests of new actors, such as China. This is important for understanding China's most recent IIAs, as I explore in the current chapter. In particular, it helps to makes sense of specific provisions that other commentators have described as 'puzzling' and allows us to move away from labelling Beijing's most recent treaties as 'incoherent'.[5]

I proceed as follows. The first section reviews the categories that have been devised by scholars for China's voluminous investment treaty practice. This leads to a framework for thinking about IIAs concluded from 2008 onwards as part of a protean Fourth Generation. This includes various changes to substantive investment protection provisions. And many of these novel formulations are indicative of a broader trend whereby states are seeking to balance investment protection against non-investment objectives. Here it is helpful to introduce the notion of interpretative balancing mechanisms and substantive balancing mechanisms. A leading explanation for the growth of balancing mechanisms in China's Fourth Generation is the 'NAFTA-ization thesis'. In examining the specific provisions in detail, however, it becomes clear that this offers only a partial explanation. Ongoing negotiations with the United States and the need to selectively adapt novel language in that country's current approach to IIAs provides evidence for the complementary explanation of selective adaptation.

I. Recent IIAs as a Fourth Generation

As of January 2017, China has concluded no less than 140 international investment agreements. The term international investment agreement or IIA includes either a stand-alone treaty on investment protection or an investment chapter in a broader treaty. The former are typically referred to as BITs. In this chapter the latter are referred to as preferential trade and investment agreements (PTIAs) as opposed to simply RTAs with investment chapters, which reflects the increasing importance of investment vis a vis trade.[6] In terms of the number of treaties, China's Ministry of Commerce (MOFCOM) currently provides a list of 104 BITs.[7] Alternatively, the United Nations Conference on Trade and Development's (UNCTAD) IIA database references 145 BITs that have been negotiated by China, although this includes treaties that have yet to enter into force or have already been terminated.[8] In reviewing UNCTAD's list of 'Treaties with Investment Provisions', at least eight include substantive and procedural investment protections thus qualifying as IIAs.[9] This includes two plurilateral treaties that are devoted exclusively to investment, i.e. the 2012 trilateral investment treaty

[4] Saadia Pekkanen, 'The Socialization of China, Japan, and Korea (CJK) in International Economic Law: Assessment and Implications' (2010) 104 American Society of International Law 529.
[5] Axel Berger, 'Hesitant Embrace: China's Recent Approach to International Investment Rule-Making' (2015) Journal of World Investment and Trade 843.
[6] See Julien Chaisse, 'The Shifting Tectonics of International Investment Law: Structure and Dynamics of Rules and Arbitration on Foreign Investment in the Asia-Pacific Region' (2015) 47 George Washington International Law Review 563, 615–16.
[7] MOFCOM's list of BITs that have entered into force is at http://english.mofcom.gov.cn/article/bilateralchanges/201309/20130900300306.shtml (last accessed 1 January 2017).
[8] United Nation's Conference on Trade and Development, Investment Treaties Online database: http://investmentpolicyhub.unctad.org/IIA/CountryBits/42 (last accessed 1 January 2017).
[9] China's 'Treaties with Investment Provisions' are listed by UNCTAD: http://investmentpolicyhub.unctad.org/IIA/CountryOtherIias/42#iiaInnerMenu.

'2012 Northeast Asia Trilateral IIA'[10] between China, Korea, and Japan and the 2009 ASEAN–China Investment Agreement[11] (2009 ASEAN IIA).

No matter what the exact number of IIAs, it is clear that the numbers involved—like so much involving China—are big. Indeed, China has concluded the second most IIAs of any state, behind only Germany, which has certain implications for treaty practice and analysis. Because the treaty practice is voluminous, it is useful and perhaps necessary to settle on a way of grouping it together and then analysing one part in detail.[12] There are various approaches to categorization and the following reviews what appears to be the leading approach, which is to group China's IIAs in to 'generations'.[13] In this light, the focus here is on introducing a 'Fourth Generation' of treaty practice. As of January 2017, this Fourth Generation compromises eight BITs, two plurilateral investment treaties, and three PTIAs. This includes BITs with the following partner states with year of entry into force: 2008 Mexico BIT,[14] 2008 Colombia BIT,[15] 2009 Mali BIT, 2009 Malta BIT,[16] 2010 Switzerland BIT,[17] 2011 Uzbekistan BIT,[18] 2013 Tanzania BIT,[19] and the 2014 Canada BIT.[20] There are also two plurilateral investment agreements, i.e. the 2012 Northeast Asia Trilateral IIA and the 2009 ASEAN IIA. Also, there are three broader agreements that include investment chapters, i.e. with New Zealand (2008), Peru (2009), and Australia (2015).[21] The following reviews three earlier generations by way of proposing that treaties from 2008 onwards may be viewed through the heuristic of a 'Fourth Generation'.

China's *First Generation* of IIAs begins in 1982 when a bilateral investment treaty was successfully negotiated with Sweden.[22] These were very much the early years of the open door policy.[23] Between the Sweden BIT and the 1989 Japan

---

[10] China–Japan–Korea Investment Agreement (entered into force 17 May 2014) http://investmentpolicyhub.unctad.org/Download/TreatyFile/2633 (last accessed 1 January 2017).

[11] ASEAN–China Investment Agreement (entered into force 1 January 2010) http://investmentpolicyhub.unctad.org/IIA/country/42/treaty/3272 (last accessed 1 January 2017).

[12] Wenhua Shan and Norah Gallagher, *Chinese Investment Treaties: Policies and Practice* (Oxford University Press 2009) 1.

[13] ibid.

[14] Agreement between the Government of the United Mexican States and the Government of the People's Republic of China on the Promotion and Reciprocal Protection of Investments (signed 11 July 2008, entered into force 6 June 2009) http://investmentpolicyhub.unctad.org/Download/TreatyFile/759 (last accessed 1 January 2017).

[15] Bilateral Agreement for the Promotion and Protection of Investments between the Government of the Republic of Colombia and the Government of the People's Republic of China (signed 22 November 2008, entered into force 2 July 2013) http://investmentpolicyhub.unctad.org/Download/TreatyFile/720 (last accessed 1 January 2017).

[16] China–Malta BIT (entered into force 1 April 2009) http://investmentpolicyhub.unctad.org/IIA/country/42/treaty/936 (last accessed 1 January 2017).

[17] China–Switzerland BIT (entered into force 12 April 2010) http://investmentpolicyhub.unctad.org/IIA/country/42/treaty/978 (last accessed 1 January 2017).

[18] China–Uzbekistan BIT (entered into force 1 September 2011) http://investmentpolicyhub.unctad.org/IIA/country/42/treaty/993 (last accessed 1 January 2017).

[19] China–Tanzania BIT (entered into force 17 April 2014) http://investmentpolicyhub.unctad.org/IIA/country/42/treaty/990 (last accessed 1 January 2017).

[20] China–Canada BIT (entered into force 1 October 2014) http://investmentpolicyhub.unctad.org/IIA/country/42/treaty/778 (last accessed 1 January 2017).

[21] http://dfat.gov.au/trade/agreements/chafta/pages/australia-china-fta.aspx. Not included are a number of trade agreements that either lack an investment chapter or contain an investment chapter without provision for investor–state dispute settlement.

[22] China–Sweden BIT (entered into force March 1982) http://investmentpolicyhub.unctad.org/IIA/country/42/treaty/976 (last accessed 11 November 2016).
It was also in 1982 that China was granted observer status at the General Agreement on Tariffs and Trade (GATT). Karen Halverson, 'China's WTO Accession: Economic, Legal, and Political Implications' (2004) 27 Boston College International and Comparative Law Review 319.

[23] For a general overview of the policy environment and debates surrounding FDI into China see ibid n12 pp 4–10. Between 1982 and 1989, foreign investment was almost exclusively limited to special economic zones, ie Shenzhen, Zhuhai, Shantou, and Xiamen.

BIT,[24] China concluded treaties with numerous Western European states including
Germany, France, and Italy. In this First Generation, China was clearly the capital
importing state. But, Beijing was consistently able to omit certain obligations with
which it was uncomfortable. In this regard, reference is made to investor-dispute
settlement and national treatment. Chi Manjiao and Xi Wang have usefully analysed the investor–state dispute settlement clauses in China's First Generation IIAs
as 'narrow'.[25] They note that '[s]uch ISA clauses are often incorporated in China's
first generation BITs. They may also be found in the BITs of other countries, especially "communist countries", such as the former USSR'.[26] This is the key point for
current purposes. Turning to substantive provisions, Norah Gallagher, for example,
finds First Generation IIAs omitted national treatment guarantees.[27] China's First
Generation treaties are thus characterized by at least three factors: they were negotiated with wealthy countries especially in Western Europe, they incorporated only
narrow consent to investor–state dispute settlement, and they omitted discipline
on discrimination between domestic and foreign nationals.[28]

China's Second Generation IIAs are defined in terms of continuity in the two doctrinal
factors noted above but broad shifts in Beijing's conduct of economic diplomacy.[29] Up
until the late 1980s, which is to say during the First Generation, the PRC negotiated IIAs
predominately with capital exporting states. Following certain events in the late 1980s
and early 1990s, Beijing appears to have taken the decision to shift its negotiating focus
towards developing countries. However, this did not entail a revision of treaty content.
The Second Generation treaties thus generally contain the particular characteristics described above, i.e. narrow consent to investor–state dispute settlement and no direct discipline on discrimination between domestic nationals and foreign nationals. The Second
Generation persisted until the late 1990s. Rather than a change in the formulation of
either substantive or procedural rules, the Second Generation category captures a shift
in policy. In particular, the Second Generation may be viewed, in retrospect, as an early
experiment whereby China played the role of capital exporting state in IIA negotiations.

China's Third Generation IIAs are defined in relationship to the period of history during
which the treaties were negotiated as well as certain key provisions therein. In terms of
time lines, the first Third Generation IIA is the 1998 China–Barbados BIT. The Barbados
BIT is important as the first Chinese IIA to include a 'broad' consent to investor–state arbitration.[30] In particular, the signatories consented to allow foreign investors to bring 'any
dispute concerning an investment' to international arbitration.[31] This notion of broad,
as opposed to narrow, dispute settlement provisions has been flagged as an important
characteristic of Chinese Third Generation IIAs.[32] Other important changes include the

[24] China–Japan BIT (entered into force May 1989) http://investmentpolicyhub.unctad.org/IIA/country/42/treaty/918 (last accessed 11 November 2016).
[25] Chi Manjiao and Xi Wang, 'The Evolution of ISA Clauses in Chinese IIAs and Its Practical Implications' (2015) Journal of World Investment and Trade 873.
[26] Chi, ISA Evolution, 873 In turn, Chi and Xi divide narrow dispute settlement clauses into gen-
eral and specific types. Narrow dispute settlement clauses of the general type provide that ' "disputes
concerning the amount of compensation for expropriation" can be submitted to ISA, without imposing other admissibility requirements'. Chi Manjiao and Xi Wang, 'The Evolution of ISA Clauses
in Chinese IIAs and Its Practical Implications' (2015) Journal of World Investment and Trade 875.
[27] Norah Gallagher and others, 'National Treatment for Foreign Investment in China: A Changing
Landscape' (2012) 27(1) ICSID Review 120.
[28] A third key point regarding substantive provisions is that First Generation IIAs subjected the
transfer of investment-related funds to national law. See eg Berger (n 5) 848.
[29] ibid 845.
[30] See Julien Chaisse and Rahul Donde, 'The State of Investor-State Arbitration: A Reality Check
of the Issues, Trends, and Directions in Asia-Pacific' (2018) 51(1) The International Lawyer 47.
[31] China–Barbados BIT 1998 art 9(1).
[32] For analysis focused on this shift in the dispute settlement provision as a defining characteristic
of the Third Generation see Stephan W Schill, 'Tearing Down the Great Wall: The New Generation

acceptance of national treatment.[33] It bears noting two important ways in which the Third Generation intersects with the Fourth Generation. First, in the late 1990s, which is to say at the beginning of the Third Generation, MOFCOM revised its model treaty (Third Model BIT), which was then used as a template in negotiation of the Third Generation treaties. The Third Model BIT is generally consistent with the key features noted above, i.e. broad dispute settlement provisions and the guarantee of national treatment. At least one treaty that chronologically falls under the Fourth Generation, i.e. the 2009 Mali BIT,[34] appears to have been negotiated on the basis of the Third Model BIT. However, one long-time commentator on China's investment treaties has observed that: 'China has not revised its Model BIT to reflect the type of treaties currently being negotiated'.[35] This has given rise to questions about whether the Fourth Generation reviewed below is 'incoherent' and reflects rule-taking vis-à-vis the NAFTA approach.[36] These questions are considered further in the following section in light of specific provisions in Fourth Generation treaties. Secondly, certain provisions that are otherwise only found in the Fourth Generation do appear in the later Third Generation treaties. For instance, both the China–Trinidad and Tobago BIT[37] and the China–Guyana BIT[38] entered into force in 2004, which is several years prior to the first Fourth Generation treaties. However, the preambles of both of these Third Generation IIAs contain aspirational language related to non-investment objectives. In fact, the relevant phrase is identical in the two treaties and states as follows: '[T]hese objectives can be achieved without relaxing health, safety and environmental measures of general application'.[39] As the 2009 Mali BIT manifests the extended shelf-life of the Third Model BIT, the 2004 Trinidad and Tobago BIT, and 2004 Guyana BIT manifest an inverse occurrence where Fourth Generation changes appeared prematurely. The key take-away from these exceptions is that the notion of generations is a heuristic device and not determinative in and of itself.

The Fourth Generation of Chinese IIAs can nevertheless be distinguished from previous treaty practice in a number of respects. The following paragraphs set out broad considerations while the next section dives in to specific treaty provisions. On a preliminary note, although this actually appears to be quite important in light of ongoing negotiations with the United States and the European Commission, the Fourth Generation remains an open-ended category as new treaties are still being negotiated.[40] It therefore does bear mentioning that we do not yet know as researchers what will prove to be the Fourth Generation's defining characteristic.[41] However, the following map illustrates the importance of regionalism.

Investment Treaties of the People's Republic of China' (2007) 15 Cardozo Journal of International & Comparative Law 73.

[33] Berger (n 5) 849; Gallagher and others (n 27) 120

[34] China–Mali BIT (entered into force 16 July 2009) http://investmentpolicyhub.unctad.org/IIA/country/42/treaty/935 (last accessed 11 November 2016).

[35] Norah Gallagher, 'Role of China in Investment: BITs, SOEs, Private Enterprises, and Evolution of Policy' (2016) 31(1) ICSID Review 88, 94

[36] Berger (n 5) 846.

[37] China–Trinidad and Tobago BIT (entered into force December 2004) http://investmentpolicyhub. unctad.org/Download/TreatyFile/787 (last accessed 11 November 2016).

[38] China–Guyana BIT (entered into force 26 October 2004) http://investmentpolicyhub.unctad. org/Download/TreatyFile/739 (last accessed 11 November 2016).

[39] China–Trinidad and Tobago BIT (entered into force December 2004) http:// investmentpolicyhub.unctad.org/Download/TreatyFile/787 (last accessed 11 November 2016) art xx; China–Guyana BIT (entered into force 26 October 2004) art xx http://investmentpolicyhub.unctad. org/Download/TreatyFile/739 (last accessed 11 November 2016).

[40] Between 2008 and 2016, China has signed BITs with the following partner states that have yet to enter into force: Turkey, Democratic Republic of Congo, Libya, Chad, and the Bahamas.

[41] For an earlier example of this delay, consider the fact that narrow investor–state arbitration clauses proved to be defining characteristic of First Generation IIAs only after a subsequent shift in practice made this pattern recognizable.

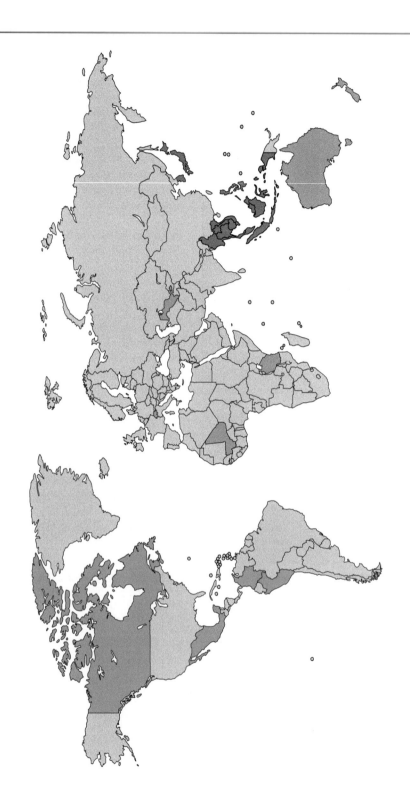

This map shows Fourth Generation treaty partners. States that have negotiated with China on a regional basis are in red, while those that have negotiated on a bilateral basis are in yellow. Regionalism is apparent in two senses of that word: negotiations are taking place with regional blocks and a significant number of the Fourth Generation partner states are China's immediate neighbours.

Secondly, as is not entirely surprising given that the PRC had already concluded such a large number of IIAs, a significant proportion of the Fourth Generation treaties re-flect the outcome of negotiations with the partner state to an existing treaty. This again takes two forms. Several of the Fourth Generation IIAs replace older treaties that have subsequently been terminated. For instance, the 2010 Switzerland BIT and the 2011 Uzbekistan BIT fit this pattern. The second pattern arises where a Fourth Generation IIA has been concluded and the older treaty has remained in force. For instance, the bilateral agreements that China had already concluded with Korea and Japan remain in force following the conclusion of the 2012 Northeast Asia Trilateral.[42] Wolfgang Alschner has usefully labelled this phenomenon as 'overlap' and notes that it appears to be a feature of the trend towards regionalization of international investment negotiations.

The third and fourth considerations transition from the political economy of negoti-ation towards the substance of the treaties. Third is the introduction of comprehensive investment chapters in to PTIAs.[43] As explored below, there are tentative signs that China's PTIAs—compared to BITs—are more likely to contemplate 'balancing' extra investment objectives.[44] The notion of balancing is examined further below. Fourth, there are signs that Chinese negotiators are monitoring the investor–state arbitration case law and there have been selective efforts at integrating doctrine from influential arbitration awards. An example appears in the 2012 Northeast Asia Trilateral, which includes in the definition of investment an approach that is commonly associated with the tribunal in *Salini*.[45] Article 1(1) thus provides that:

'investments' means every kind of asset that an investor owns or controls, directly or indirectly, which has the characteristics of an investment, such as the commitment of capital or other re-sources, the expectation of gain or profit, or the assumption of risk.[46]

An established arbitrator has noted that: '[t]he Salini test is routinely mentioned in order to refer to a certain number of criteria, be they 4, 5 or even 3'.[47] In the above passage, the PRC has declined to list explicitly either the duration of the economic relationship or the significance for the host state's development. Finally, the Fourth Generation IIAs demonstrate significant flux in the precise formulation of substantive investment protection rules. This is examined in the following section.

II. Evolution of Substantive Provisions in the Fourth Generation

In addition to the trends noted above—i.e. regionalization, renegotiation and overlap, PTIAs, and integration of case law—the evolution of substantive investment protection

---

[42] Wolfgang Alschner, 'Regionalism and Overlap in Investment Treaty Law: Towards Consolidation or Contradiction?' (2014) 17(2) Journal of International Economic Law 271.

[43] See Berger (n 5) 847, 852: 'Overall, non-economic objectives are more often included in Chinese PTIAs than in pure investment treaties'.

[44] ibid 847.

[45] *Salini Costruttori SpA and Italstrade SpA v Kingdom of Morocco*, ICSID Case No ARB/00/4 Decision on Jurisdiction (French Original: 129 Journal du droit international 196 (2002)) (English translation: 42 ILM 609 (2003), 6 ICSID Rep 400 (2004)).

[46] 2012 Northeast Asia Trilateral art 1(1).

[47] On the notion of the Salini Criteria generally see Brigitte Stern, 'The Contours of the Notion of Protected Investment' (2009) 24(2) ICSID Review 534, 536–7

provisions in Fourth Generation IIAs merits further consideration. Those commentators that have focused on the Fourth Generation find that substantive, as opposed to procedural or dispute-settlement orientated, provisions are changing in changing relatively rapidly.[48] The following reviews the specific provisions that have most often been 'in play' in negotiations. The result is a preliminary distinction between changes that have appeared in most of the Fourth Generation treaties and changes that appear to be the exception to the rule such as establishment stage non-discrimination and limits on performance requirements. The remainder of this section then turns to a longer list of changes that appear in most of the Fourth Generation treaties and can be conceptualized as investment protection 'balancing mechanisms'.[49] This discussion proposes a basic typology whereby interpretative balancing mechanisms are distinguished from substantive balancing mechanisms. It also uses these specific provisions to juxtapose the 'NAFTA-ization thesis' that China has acted as a rule-taker to a selective adaptation lens on China as a rule-shaker.

Establishment Stage Non-Discrimination disciplines are one of two major changes in Fourth Generation IIAs that do not relate to balancing. Instead, they suggest the expansion of negotiating objectives from investment protection to include investment liberalization. Relevant provisions have been included in certain Fourth Generation IIAs, i.e. the 2008 New Zealand PTIA, the 2009 Peru PTIA, the 2009 ASEAN PTIA, the 2012 Northeast Asia Trilateral, the 2012 Canada BIT, and the 2015 Australia PTIA. These six IIAs all offer establishment-stage most favoured nation treatment but not national treatment. On the one hand, this represents a departure from the PRC's pre-Fourth Generation practice of not using IIAs for investment liberalization. On the one other hand, for the time being at least, i.e. in the absence of more favourable treatment to investor's from a third country, the practical effect is limited. The 2012 Canada BIT provides an illustrative example: Canada is known to negotiate on the basis of establishment stage MFN and NT, subject to certain screening mechanisms.[50] And, Canada committed to both MFN and NT in relation to Chinese investors, but China only committed to MFN for Canadian investors. Establishment stage MFN can be seen as a consolation prize for Canadian negotiators in light of the contemporary expectation that Canadian investors would ultimately be able to free-ride on future concessions to a third country, such as the United States, on establishment stage non-discrimination. Although not a focus of the current chapter, this example points to two relevant themes: first, the Fourth Generation IIAs may be said to reflect the outcome of 'subsidiary games'– to use the language of game theory—that took place in the shadow of larger negotiations. Secondly, concerns about the 'asymmetrical' nature of establishment stage non-discrimination disciplines in, for example, the 2012 Canada BIT,[51] reflect at least in part the broader legitimacy challenges associated with China's transition from capital importer to capital exporter, and by extension rule-taker to rule-shaker.

---

[48] Elodie Dulac, 'The Emerging Third Generation of Chinese Investment Treaties' (2010) 4 Transnational Dispute Management 1; Berger (n 5) 843. Dulac uses the term 'Third Generation' for a category that is largely similar to the current Fourth Generation.

[49] Freya Baetens (ed), *Investment Law within International Law* (Cambridge University Press 2013); Steffen Hindelang and Markus Krajewski (eds), *Shifting Paradigms in International Investment Law: More Balanced, Less Isolated, Increasingly Diversified* (Oxford University Press 2016).

[50] See, Andrew Newcombe and Céline Lévesque, 'Canada' in C Brown (ed), *Commentaries on Selected Model Investment Treaties* (Oxford University Press 2013) 53. A particularly important screening mechanism is the application of Canadian competition law, which reviews potential acquisitions above a certain threshold.

[51] Gus Van Harten, 'The Canada-China FIPPA: Its Uniqueness and Non-Reciprocity' (2014) Canadian Yearbook of International Law/Annuaire Canadien de droit international 1.

China has international law obligations related to performance requirements as a member of the WTO.[52] With certain exceptions, China's IIAs prior to the Fourth Generation had not explicitly contemplated performance requirements.[53] In particular, the 2004 Finland BIT in its Article 3.3 states that: 'Further, neither Contracting Party shall impose unreasonable or discriminatory measures on investments by investors of the other Contracting Party concerning local content or export performance requirements'.[54] During the Fourth Generation, a larger albeit still limited number of IIAs have addressed the issue of performance requirements. Notably, all three of the treaties that address this issue have settled on the same approach. The 2008 New Zealand PTIA, the 2012 Northeast Asia Trilateral, and 2012 Canada BIT all provide that the WTO TRIMs agreement is incorporated into the relevant IIA.[55] This has the implication of ISDS being used to enforce the WTO obligations, but is not WTO-plus from a substantive perspective. Although the treaty text suggests that negotiations remain on-going,[56] reference to WTO TRIMs is perhaps most notably absent from the 2015 Australia PTIA. These two areas of rule-making, i.e. establishment stage non-discrimination and performance requirements, are both ways in which Fourth Generation IIAs are expanding the scope of investment protection. The following turns to five novel formulations in Fourth Generation IIAs that appear to cut in the opposite direction and therefore limit the scope of investment protection.

The following considers how an otherwise disparate array of drafting changes can be placed into two groups based on the type of mechanism that they activate for balancing investment protection. The first type of balancing mechanism found in China's Fourth Generation IIAs is interpretative balancing, which includes: addition of a 'like circumstances' criteria to limit the application of non-discrimination obligations; clarifying language aimed at restricting findings of indirect expropriation; and, qualification of the concept of fair and equitable treatment. Reviewing these provisions provides an opportunity to introduce the 'NAFTA-ization thesis', which argues that

> the NAFTA-ization of China's IIA practice was not a pro-active strategy pursued by the Chinese government. Quite the opposite: China's negotiating partners pushed China to accept novel IIA provisions such as qualified fair and equitable treatment and indirect expropriation. China's partner countries diffused innovative treaty language after reforming their IIA approach, whereas China, the economically stronger power, coherently defined only its defensive interest, in particular its rejection of pre-establishment national treatment.[57]

The NAFTA-ization thesis thus draws a strict line between rule-taking and rule-making. And it does so even while noting the incongruous nature of China acting as a rule-taker in negotiations with weaker partners. In fact, the NAFTA-ization thesis'

---

[52] In addition to the Agreement on Trade-Related Investment Measures, the particular terms of China's negotiated accession protocol are also relevant. See Julia Ya Qin, ' "WTO-Plus" Obligations and Their Implications for the World Trade Organization Legal System: An Appraisal of the China Accession Protocol' (2003) 37(3) Journal of World Trade 483.

[53] Two earlier exceptions are the 2004 Finland BIT and the 2007 Korea PTIA. NTD: Finland BIT art 3.3: 'Further, neither Contracting Party shall impose unreasonable or discriminatory measures on investments by investors of the other Contracting Party concerning local content or export performance requirements'.

[54] Two earlier exceptions are the 2004 Finland BIT and the 2007 Korea PTIA. NTD: Finland BIT art 3.3: 'Further, neither Contracting Party shall impose unreasonable or discriminatory measures on investments by investors of the other Contracting Party concerning local content or export performance requirements'.

[55] New Zealand PTIA art 140; 2012 Northeast Asia Trilateral art 7; Canada BIT art 9.

[56] 'Future Work Program' art 9.9.

[57] Berger (n 5) 866.

author does acknowledge that it offers only a partial explanation of the use of the interpretative balancing mechanisms (as well as the substantive balancing mechanisms that are introduced further below). He therefore notes that: 'Even more puzzling is the fact that China agreed to introduce environmental provisions in its BIT recently concluded with Tanzania'. Part of this 'puzzle' can be solved through adding a selective adaptation analysis, as considered on a provision by provision basis below. In this regard, leading legal scholars of China's economic reforms have used the analytical lens of 'selective adaptation'.[58] According to, for instance, Pitman Potter:

Selective adaptation offers insights to the process by which China has attempted to join on its own terms the international political economy, so as to balance international norms of economic regulation with local concerns over social welfare and balanced development.

Like the notion of rule-shaking, selective adaptation has to-date primarily been used by trade rather than investment researchers. By cross-applying these insights to the dynamic field of international investment law what becomes possible, I will argue below, is to more fully understand China's recent treaty practice.

In terms of a first interpretative balancing mechanism, a preponderance of Fourth Generation IIAs use the concept of 'like circumstances' to limit the application of non-discrimination obligations. The following illustrative example is taken from Article 3 on 'National Treatment' of the 2011 Uzbekistan BIT:

Without prejudice to its applicable laws and regulations, with respect to the management, conduct, maintenance, use, enjoyment, sale or disposal of the investments in its territory, each Contracting Party shall accord to investors of the other Contracting Party and associated investments treatment not less favorable than that accorded to its own investors and associated investments in like circumstances.[59]

The like circumstances criterion is also included in the non-discrimination provisions of the following treaties: 2008 New Zealand PTIA, 2008 Mexico BIT, 2008 Colombia BIT, 2009 Peru PTIA, 2009 ASEAN PTIA, 2011 Uzbekistan BIT, 2012 Northeast Asia Trilateral, 2012 Canada BIT, 2013 Tanzania BIT,[60] and 2015 Australia PTIA. This formulation is not used, however, in either the 2009 Switzerland BIT or the 2009 Malta BIT, which is consistent with the past treaty practice of these two West European states. It is also not included in the 2011 Mali BIT,[61] which appears to reflect the persistent influence of MOFCOM's Third Model BIT. The key point, however, is that after the 2011 Mali BIT, China's Fourth Generation treaties have consistently imposed a like circumstances criterion. The fact that it has been included in Chinese IIAs even with partners such Uzbekistan and Tanzania cannot be explained by the NAFTA-ization thesis, as these states have previously exhibited no such preference. Rather, what started off as a NAFTA-inspired change has triggered a process of selective adaptation, which now appears to be complete with regard to this particular interpretative balancing mechanism.

---

[58] Pitman B Potter, 'Globalization and Economic Regulation in China: Selective Adaptation of Globalized Norms and Practices' (2003) 2(1) Washington University Global Studies Law Review 119.

[59] 2011 Uzbekistan BIT art 3.

[60] Agreement between the Government of the People's Republic of China and the Government of the United Republic of Tanzania concerning the Promotion and Reciprocal Protection of Investments (signed 24 March 2013, entered into force 17 April 2014) (China–Tanzania BIT).

[61] Mali–China BIT http://investmentpolicyhub.unctad.org/Download/TreatyFile/4923. (This treaty is somewhat inaccessible by virtue of its having been made only in French and Chinese, with no English version.)

Secondly, the majority of Fourth Generation IIAs include novel language aimed at clarifying the notion of indirect expropriation. The most frequently used drafting technique is that of an interpretative annex, which is found in for instance, the 2012 Canada BIT. Proponents of the NAFTA-ization thesis would note that although an equivalent annex is not found in the actual text of NAFTA Chapter 11, the use of an annex to provide interpretative guidance can be traced back to the 2004 US Model BIT.[62] An alternative drafting technique is the inclusion of substantially similar text in a sub-article of expropriation provision. Article 6 of the 2011 Uzbekistan BIT provides an example:

2.   The determination of whether a measure or a series of measures of one Contracting Party constitutes indirect expropriation in Paragraph 1 requires a case-by-case, fact-based inquiry that considers, among other factors:
(a)   the economic influence of a measure or a series of measures, although the fact that a measure or a series of measures of the Contracting Party has an adverse effect on the economic value of investments, standing alone, does not establish that an indirect expropriation has occurred;
(b)   the extent to which the measure or the series of measures grant discrimination in scope or application over investors and associated investments of the other Contracting Party;
(c)   the extent to which the measure or the series of measures cause damage to reasonable investment expectation of investors of the other Contracting Party: such expectation arises from the specific commitments made by one Contracting Party to the investors of the other Contracting Party;
(d)   the character and purpose of a measure and a series of measures, whether it is adopted for the purpose of public interest in good faith, and whether it is in appropriation to the purpose of expropriation.[63]

Whether or not one views this incremental change as rule-shaking rather than pure rule-taking, it is clear that indirect expropriation is a case where the selective adaptation process remains ongoing. This is consistent with the relatively large number of Fourth Generation IIAs that do not make use of either of these drafting techniques and instead reserve to a prospective tribunal the exercise of interpreting the meaning of indirect expropriation. This includes Switzerland and Malta, which is in line with the above observation about European BIT practice. It also includes Mali—presumably due to the continued use of MOFCOM's Third Model BIT. More surprisingly, the 2009 Mexico BIT does not attempt to limit the scope of indirect expropriation, which is in direct contrast to the NAFTA-ization thesis.[64]

Thirdly, most of the Fourth Generation IIAs include a qualification of the obligation to provide fair and equitable treatment (FET). It is again useful to consider the 2009 Mexico BIT, which provides in Article 5 that:

2.   For greater certainty, this Article prescribes the international law minimum standard of treatment of aliens as the minimum standard of treatment to be afforded to investments of investors of the other Contracting Party. *The two concepts of 'fair and equitable treatment' and 'full protection and security' do not require treatment in addition to or beyond that which is required by the international law minimum standard of treatment of aliens as established by state practice and opinio juris.* A determination that there has been a breach of another provision

---

[62] Berger (n 5) 859.   [63] 2011 Uzbekistan BIT art 6.
[64] Also, the 2009 ASEAN IIA does not include this type of treaty language.

of this Agreement, or of a separate international agreement, does not establish that there has been a breach of this Article.[65]

The middle sentence associates the FET standard with a general norm rooted in international law. This is a departure from previous treaty practice and is cited as evidence for the NAFTA-ization thesis.[66] In terms of previous treaty practice, China's IIAs have contained various formulations regarding the FET standard and a limited number of older have even omitted it entirely.[67] However, with very limited exceptions, the pre-Fourth Generation provisions on FET have sought to contain this standard within the four corners of the IIA in question.[68] This is illustrated by the Third Model BIT, which in its Article 3 'Treatment of Investment' states as follows: '1. Investments of investors of each Contracting Party shall all the time be accorded fair and equitable treatment in the territory of the other Contracting Party'.[69] China's pre-Fourth Generation approach to FET was thus 'BIT by BIT' because it attempted to reserve the obligation to provide fair and equitable treatment as dependent on the existence of a binding treaty provision. This approach is in line with China's historical position that customary international law does not include an obligation to provide fair and equitable treatment to foreigners. This in turn needs to be contrasted to, inter alia, the American position that fair and equitable treatment is an element of customary international law. The result is, frankly, a fundamental question of contemporary economic diplomacy. Here, the focus is on whether the Fourth Generation demonstrates passive acceptance of the NAFTA approach or rule-shaking whereby MOFCOM is experimenting with various, novel formulations according to the core insight of selective adaptation.

Unlike in the case of like circumstances criterion but similar to the case of indirect expropriation, China's approach to qualifying FET has continued to evolve. This evolution, or selective adaptation, takes two forms: first the precise language used to reference international law norms has shifted over time. For instance, in the 2012 Canada BIT reference is made to the 'international law minimum standard of treatment of aliens as evidenced by general State practice accepted as law'.[70] This diverges from Canada's standard treaty practice, which references the 'customary international law minimum standard of treatment of aliens'.[71] Certainly this is a small change but considering Canada's relatively ample negotiating capital and the fact that negotiations are known to have taken place on the basis of Canada's model IIA it appears to indicate a noteworthy detail.

The second and perhaps more consequential change appears as early as the 2008 Colombia BIT. The relevant provision, Article 2.4.c, states that:

'Fair and equitable treatment' includes the prohibition against denial of justice in criminal, civil, or administrative proceedings in accordance with the general accepted principles of customary international law.[72]

---

[65] 2009 Mexico BIT (emphasis added). This text is based on the author's translation of the Chinese original, which is provided by MOFCOM. According to the final, unnumbered, paragraph of the main treaty text, the 2009 Mexico BIT was made 'in two originals in the Spanish, Chinese and English languages, all texts being equally authentic'. It further provides that '[i]n case of divergence of interpretation, the English text shall prevail'. In addition to the awkward wording of the above phrase—ie the claim of 'two originals' in three different languages—there appears to be a divergence between the Chinese and English texts as regards the italicized text in the quoted sub-article.

[66] Berger (n 5) 858.   [67] ASEAN–China Investment Agreement (n 11) 126–30.

[68] ibid 131.   [69] ibid 434.   [70] China–Canada BIT art 4.2.

[71] See eg Canada–Tanzania FIPA art 6.2.   [72] art 2.4.c.

Proponents of the NAFTA-ization thesis would and do cite this treaty's use of the specific words 'customary international law'.[73] However, this provision includes a second element, which cannot be clearly explained by the idea that China acted as a rule-taker, passively accepting the formulation proposed by NAFTA-friendly negotiating partners. That second element is the phrase 'prohibition against denial of justice in criminal, civil, or administrative proceedings'. In fact, most of the Fourth Generation IIAs qualify FET not by reference to a broad norm but in terms of this specific, narrow phrase. This is acknowledged by Berger, who writes that:

These treaties [i.e. with ASEAN, Uzbekistan, Korea and Japan, and Tanzania] omit references to international law and only include a similar clarification that fair and equitable treatment 'means that investors of one Contracting Party shall not be denied fair judicial proceedings by the other Contracting Party or be treated with obvious discriminatory or arbitrary measures.[74]

The consistent use of this phrase cannot be attributed to the preferences of ASEAN, Uzbekistan, Korea, Japan, and Tanzania. Indeed, the phrase is based on the 2004 US Model BIT but appears there as one of many examples of unfair and inequitable treatment contrary to customary international law. As a result, the Fourth Generation treaty practice does increasingly qualify FET through an interpretative balancing mechanism; but it is less accurate to say that the provision used reflects passive acceptance of the NAFTA position. Rather, China has selectively adapted US terminology on FET, which might serve as a starting point for negotiations with the US or simply as a new compromise as China moves closer towards the mainstream of international investment law. More generally, we can observe that the NAFTA-ization thesis has correctly identified the relevant starting point, i.e. on-going negotiations with the United States, but it has not accounted for the process that this has initiated.

A second type of balancing mechanism that emerges in China's Fourth Generation IIAs is that of substantive balancing. Substantive balancing entails the identification of non-investment objectives to be weighed—or 'balanced'—in the application of investment protection rules. A first example of substantive balancing is found the aspirational language of Fourth Generation preambles. The PTIAs concluded during the Fourth Generation are particularly likely to reference non-investment objectives. In this respect, the 2008 New Zealand PTIA provides an early example. The preamble of the entire PTIA makes reference, inter alia, to sustainable development through the following recital: '[m]indful that economic development, social development and environmental protection are interdependent and mutually reinforcing components of sustainable development and that closer economic partnership can play an important role in promoting sustainable development'.[75] Preambulatory recitals affirming non-investment objectives generally and sustainable development in particular have, subject to a time lag, also become common in Fourth Generation treaties that are concerned only with investment, i.e. the 2011 Northeast Asia Trilateral, 2011 Uzbekistan BIT, the 2012 Canada BIT, and the 2013 Tanzania BIT.

An additional and perhaps stronger example of substantive balancing is the gradual increase in General Exception provisions during the Fourth Generation.[76] For example, the earliest known use of a General Exception provision by China is found in the ASEAN IIA. [The Peru PTIA on the other hand has provision-specific carve-outs

---

[73] Berger (n 5) 858.   [74] ibid 859.   [75] ibid 4.
[76] On general exceptions clause see Julien Chaisse, 'Exploring the Confines of International Investment and Domestic Health Protections: General exceptions clause as a forced perspective' (2013) 39(2–3) American Journal of Law & Medicine 332.

In the National Treatment and MFN provisions.] The inclusion of a General Exception provision in both the 2011 Uzbekistan BIT and the 2013 Tanzania BIT suggest here that in terms of BITs as well as PTIAs a process of selective adaptation is underway. The 2012 Canada BIT is examined below as an illustration of China rule-shaking rather than rule-taking.

A close examination of the General Exception in the 2012 Canada BIT demonstrates two aspects of rule-shaking. Article 22.1 of the Canada–Korea FTA's investment chapter provides an example of Canada's standard formulation of a general exception provision.[77]

In contrast, Article 33 of the China–Canada BIT contains numerous 'general' exceptions. In particular, Article 33.2(c) is most directly comparable to Canada's standard formulation. It states as follows:

Provided that such measures are not applied in an arbitrary or unjustifiable manner, or do not constitute a disguised restriction on international trade or investment, nothing in this Agreement shall be construed to prevent a Contracting Party from adopting or maintaining measures, including environmental measures:
(a) necessary to ensure compliance with laws and regulations that are not inconsistent with the provisions of this Agreement;
(b) necessary to protect human, animal or plant life or health; or
(c) relating to the conservation of living or non-living exhaustible natural resources if such measures are made effective in conjunction with restrictions on domestic production or consumption.

Article 33.2(c) and the caveat that 'such measures are made effective in conjunction with restrictions on domestic production or consumption' is thus evidence of rule-shaking in relation to the Canada model. First, this reflects a continuation of the trend noted above whereby MOFCOM has started selectively to write international economic law case law into Fourth Generation IIAs. However, the case being invoked is not an investor state arbitration. Instead, this appears to be a reference to WTO dispute settlement involving China's export duties on certain raw materials, i.e. China—Raw Materials[78] and China—Rare Earths.[79] This orientation towards the WTO is further illustrated by 33.7, which states that:

7. Any measure adopted by a Contracting Party in conformity with a decision adopted by the World Trade Organization pursuant to Article IX:3 of the WTO Agreement shall be deemed to be also in conformity with this Agreement. An investor purporting to act pursuant to Article 20 of this Agreement may not claim that such a conforming measure is in breach of this Agreement.

---

[77] Canada–Republic of Korea FTA (signed 22 September 2014, entered into force 1 January 2015) http://investmentpolicyhub.unctad.org/Download/TreatyFile/3077 (last accessed 1 January 2017). It states in relevant part:

   3. For the purposes of Chapter Eight (Investment), subject to the requirement that those measures are not applied in a manner that would constitute arbitrary or unjustifiable discrimination between investments or between investors, or a disguised restriction on international trade or investment, this Agreement is not to be construed to prevent a Party from adopting or enforcing measures necessary:
   (a) to protect human, animal or plant life or health;
   (b) to ensure compliance with laws and regulations that are not inconsistent with this Agreement; or
   (c) for the conservation of living or non-living exhaustible natural resources.

[78] *China—Measures Related to the Exportation of Various Raw Materials* WT/DS394/AB/R; WT/DS395/AB/R; WT/DS398/AB/R.

[79] *China—Measures Relating to the Exportation of Rare Earths, Tungsten, and Molybdenum* WT/DS431/AB/R; WT/DS432/AB/R; WT/DS433/AB/R.

Secondly, the effect of Beijing's revision in Article 33.2(c) is quite distinct from, for instance, the addition of the Salini criteria. Integration of the *Salini* criteria narrowed the definition of 'investments' in the Northeast Asia Trilateral and therefore gave wider effect to the underlying doctrine. However, in the case of Article 33.2(c), the integration of the above cited caveat narrows without giving wider effect to the doctrine from the cases. Instead, the caveat supports the approach that MOFCOM had proposed, ultimately unsuccessfully, in those cases.

III. Conclusion

The Asia FDI Forum II explored recent developments related to China's policy towards foreign direct investment. Increasingly, Beijing occupies a central position in terms of capital flows and of related-financing frameworks such as the Asian Infrastructure Investment Bank and One Belt One Road.[80] However, in the field of international economic law, China's role is less obviously one of power and perhaps as a result harder to conceptualize. Nevertheless, the scholarship on China's role in WTO-era international trade law provides a useful starting point. Scholars of law and international relations have found that post-WTO ascension China is neither a rule-maker nor a rule-taker but, rather, a rule-shaker. Although there is still more work to be done in applying the rule-shaker category to specific case studies, the concept invites us to shift from an analysis that is focused solely on outcomes to instead integrate examination of the process of 'shaking' or challenging existing rules. As argued also by Professor Heng Wang at the Forum and in this volume,[81] the rule-shaker concept appears to be a promising approach to deeper understanding of China's most recent international investment treaties as well as its trade law activities.

That China may be viewed as a rule-shaker in negotiations of an IIA Universe[82] becomes especially clear when we delineate an emerging Fourth Generation of Chinese IIAs. To summarize briefly: China's First Generation of IIAs from 1982 to 1989 contained narrow treaties with developed, capital exporting states. Second Generation IIAs from 1989 until the late 1990s featured substantive continuity but were negotiated with developing states. In turn, this was followed by a Third Generation of treaties with both developed and developing states that included relatively broad dispute settlement clauses and guarantees of national treatment. Although the current chapter has argued that a Fourth Generation of IIAs begins in 2008, one complication needs to be acknowledged: the Third Model BIT, which was used as a template for Third Generation IIAs, has yet to be formally replaced and, as such, questions arise about whether the Fourth Generation is merely 'incoherent' rule-taking. The Fourth Generation of Chinese IIAs can nevertheless be distinguished from previous treaty practice on enough points to make it a useful heuristic category.[83]

As argued in section II above, an important tendency of Fourth Generation treaties is the increasing importance of regionalism: a significant number of Fourth Generation treaty negotiations have taken place within regional groupings and a significant

[80] See Julien Chaisse and Mitsuo Matsushita, 'China's "Belt and Road" Initiative: Mapping the World Trade Normative and Strategic Implications' (2018) 52(1) Journal of World Trade 163.
[81] See Heng Wang, 'RECEP: Learning from Past Chinese FTAs' in this volume.
[82] On 'IIA Universe' see n 2 above.
[83] The Fourth Generation is unavoidably an open-ended category as new treaties are still being negotiated: we cannot yet know as researchers what will prove to be the Fourth Generation's defining characteristic.

number of the Fourth Generation partner states are China's immediate neighbours. Another tendency is that a significant proportion of Fourth Generation treaties are the result of renewed negotiations with the partner state to an existing treaty. This includes cases where the older treaties have ultimately been terminated and other cases where the Fourth Generation IIA adds to an older treaty that remains in force. Alschner, for instance, has found this 'overlap' to be a feature of the trend towards regionalization of international investment law. In light of both regionalism and overlap, the overarching theme of this collection, i.e. that of 'tracks', appears to be fortuitous. In particular, it allows us to consider the various ways in which China's recent international investment law initiatives have bilateral, regional, and global dimensions.

In thinking about bilateral, regional, and global tracks, especially in the Fourth Generation, this chapter has argued that selective adaptation provides a valuable analytical frame. In particular, selective adaptation helps us to understand the increased appearance of both substantive balancing mechanisms and interpretative balancing mechanisms in China's Fourth Generation treaties. By way of conclusion, the selective adaptation of an interpretative balancing mechanism in the fair and equitable treatment (FET) provision of numerous Fourth Generation IIAs is instructive. Indeed, as Mark Feldman has argued in a policy report on the potential for harmonization of international investment law, the Pacific-Rim region has an important role to play.[84] In that report, Feldman and his co-authors cite FET provisions in recent Chinese IIAs as an indicia of potential and note especially that many recent Chinese IIAs—as examined above and elaborated on briefly below—have 'consistently placed limitations on the FET obligation'.[85] By way of conclusion, the following underlines that this selective adaptation has not only bilateral and regional dimensions but also global implications.

Prior to the Fourth Generation, although Beijing had begun to include FET provisions, it had resisted any acknowledgement of a link between FET and customary international law. Customary international law, of course, is a mechanism that potentially allows for the multi-faceted accretion of global investment protection norms.[86] Proponents of the NAFTA-ization thesis have cited the introduction of the specific words 'customary international law' into China's treaty practice as evidence that (a) China has been acting as a rule-taker; and (b) that it has passively accepted a NAFTA-friendly formulation of what is included in customary international law. The current chapter argued for a more complete analysis acknowledging a process of rule-shaking. As such, China has selectively adapted only some of the NAFTA-model FET norms while implicitly rejecting others. This is well demonstrated by the inclusion, in a significant number of Fourth Generation treaties, of one, and only one, of the NAFTA-model FET norms.[87] Specifically, the phrase 'prohibition against denial of justice in criminal, civil, or administrative proceedings' appears in Fourth Generation IIAs with diverse treaty partners such as ASEAN, Uzbekistan,

[84] Mark Feldman and others, 'The Role of Pacific Rim FTAs in the Harmonisation of International Investment Law: Towards a Free Trade Area of the Asia-Pacific' (International Centre for Trade and Sustainable Development and World Economic Forum2016).

[85] ibid 10.

[86] See generally Patrick Dumberry, *The Formation and Identification of Rules of Customary International Law in International Investment Law* (Cambridge University Press 2016).

[87] Indeed, the formulation in question is based on the 2004 US Model BIT but appears there as one of many examples of unfair and inequitable treatment contrary to customary international law. As a result, the Fourth Generation treaty practice does increasingly qualify FET through an interpretative balancing mechanism; but it is less accurate to say that the provision used reflects passive acceptance of the NAFTA position. Rather, China has selectively adapted US terminology on FET.

Korea, Japan, and Tanzania. As a result, China's selective adaptation of this interpretative balancing mechanism has had a direct impact on the bilateral track, i.e. in the Uzbekistan BIT and the Tanzania BIT, as well as on the regional track of negotiations with ASEAN and within the Northeast Asia Trilateral. Moreover, selective adaptation of this interpretative balancing mechanism has an indirect impact on the global track as it implicitly lays down a starting point for negotiation with the broader, global 'universe' of future IIA partners.[88]

---

[88] On ongoing negotiations see Mark Feldman, 'A U.S.-China BIT: A New Chapter for Investment Liberalization' in this volume.

12

Substantive Provisions of the East Asian Trilateral Investment Agreement and their Implications

Won-Mog Choi*

I. Introduction

The Korea–China–Japan Investment Promotion, Facilitation, and Protection Agreement (Trilateral Investment Agreement), signed on 13 May 2012 after five years of negotiation and ten years of discussions,[1] aims to enhance and protect investments made trilaterally, whilst also paving the way for a free trade agreement between Korea, China, and Japan. In the meantime, the bilateral investment treaty (BIT) between Korea and China was amended in 2007 after its entry into force in 1992. Also, there exist the China–Japan BIT (1988) and Korea–Japan BIT (2003). Given this existing system of BITs, the Trilateral Investment Agreement is not an innovative system of investment law in Northeast Asia. However, the agreement is the first legal framework between the three East Asian nations regarding investment and, indeed, the first treaty in the economic field that binds the three Northeast Asian countries together under a single legal instrument.

The Trilateral Investment Agreement is appraised to be a lower level of agreement than the Korea–Japan BIT in terms of investment liberalization and protection while being a higher level of agreement than the Korea–China BIT.[2] Owing to the Trilateral Agreement, the investment system will be put on a more stabilized basis in the midst of rapid increase of investment activities among the three Northeast Asian countries.

* Law School, Ewha Womans University, Seoul, Korea. Email: wmchoi@ewha.ac.kr. This work is a developed version of the author's previous publication entitled 'Composing an Investment Chapter of the Korea-China-Japan FTA: A Quest for Better International Investment Governance?' (2015) 13 Journal of International Logistics and Trade 71 and 'Composing an Investment Chapter of the Korea-China-Japan FTA' in Jiaxiang Hu and Matthias Vanhullebusch (eds), *Regional Cooperation and Free Trade Agreements in Asia* (Koninklijke Brill NV 2014). All of the analysis on the substantive provisions for investment protection under the Trilateral Investment Agreement made in the previous works is added to by new comparative analysis with equivalent provisions under the TPP and the TTIP.

[1] Agreement between the Government of Japan, the Government of the Republic of Korea and the Government of the People's Republic of China for the Promotion, Facilitation and Protection of Investment.

[2] According to the Trilateral Investment Agreement, an investor may selectively rely on a more favourable agreement among bilateral and trilateral agreements that are available. See Trilateral Investment Agreement art 25.

Substantive Provisions of the East Asian Trilateral Investment Agreement and their Implications. Won-Mog Choi. © Won-Mog Choi, 2019. Published 2019 by Oxford University Press.

The existence of effective dispute settlement procedures including the investor–state dispute settlement system (ISDS) will contribute to the creation of a favourable investment climate in the region.

Nevertheless, there have been fears about frivolous or vexatious claims that could inhibit legitimate regulatory actions by governments, as well as concerns with regard to balancing national and international methods of dispute settlement. In addition, the rather vague language of some treaty provisions and the increasing complexity of investment treaty provisions can make the outcome of arbitration less predictable.[3] How to harmonize with domestic judicial systems is also an issue of debate. These fears, concerns, and debate have already been raised globally and in Northeast Asia particularly during the process of negotiation and ratification of the Korea–US FTA,[4] the Trilateral Investment Agreement, the Trans-Pacific Partnership (TPP),[5] and the Transatlantic Trade and Investment Partnership (TTIP).[6]

In this light, how to compose an investment chapter of the Korea–China–Japan FTA[7] and the Regional Comprehensive Economic Partnership (RCEP)[8] that are being negotiated is a pressing demand for all in the region including China that is actively initiating these mega-regional legal frameworks departing from its formerly restrictive BIT policy towards a liberal approach. Any pertinent answers to such a quest require a thorough comparison of the benefits and drawbacks of any development of the governance. There have been many discussions on the issue of problems

---

[3] See note 1 above.

[4] Free Trade Agreement between the Republic of Korea and the United States of America, signed on 30 June 2007, entered into force on 15 March 2012.

[5] The TPP is a trade agreement pursuing a comprehensive and high-level of liberalization between Australia, Brunei, Canada, Chile, Japan, Malaysia, Mexico, New Zealand, Peru, Singapore, the United States (until 23 January 2017), and Vietnam. The finalized proposal was signed on 4 February 2016 in Auckland, New Zealand, concluding seven years of negotiations. It currently cannot be ratified owing to Donald Trump's Administration of the United States withdrawal from the agreement on 23 January 2017.

[6] The Transatlantic Trade and Investment Partnership (TTIP) is a proposed trade agreement between the European Union and the United States, with the aim of promoting trade and multilateral economic growth. Its main three broad areas are market access, specific regulation, and broader rules and principles and modes of cooperation. The negotiations were planned to be finalized by the end of 2014, but are going through a substantial delay subject to criticisms and oppositions by some unions, NGOs, and environmentalists, particularly in Europe, and the recent occurrence of Brexit.

[7] The Korea–China–Japan Free Trade Agreement is a proposed free trade agreement between China, Japan, and Korea. Negotiations on the agreement were launched in 2012. As of April 2017, 12 rounds of negotiation have been held. However, progress on negotiations has been hampered by many adverse factors, including territorial disputes among the participants and trade retaliations by China against THAAD (Terminal High Altitude Area Defense) deployment in the Korean territory by the United States.

[8] The RCEP is a proposed free trade agreement (FTA) between the ten member states of the Association of Southeast Asian Nations (ASEAN) (Brunei, Cambodia, Indonesia, Laos, Malaysia, Myanmar, the Philippines, Singapore, Thailand, and Vietnam) and the six states with which ASEAN has existing free trade agreements (Australia, China, India, Japan, Korea, and New Zealand). Scheduled to be finalized by the end of 2017, RCEP negotiations were formally launched in November 2012 at the ASEAN Summit in Cambodia. The RCEP is viewed as an alternative to the TPP that includes several Asian and American nations excluding China and India. It remains to be seen how this mega FTA endeavour will end up, given the weakening dynamics of the TPP initiative due to the US withdrawal from the TPP.

and possible improvement of procedural provisions for investment protection, such as the ISDS paradigm in investment treaties,[9] whereas substantive provisions for investment protection in the Asian context have been rarely discussed. In this chapter, focus will be given to the substantive provisions for investment protection of the Trilateral Investment Agreement. Luckily, investment protection clauses in the TPP and those drafted by the EU in the TTIP negotiation are available in order for us to make a comparative analysis.

II. Definition of Investment and Scope of Protection

The Trilateral Investment Agreement sets out a broad definition of investment and, thus, a comprehensive scope of protection for investors. As necessary characteristics of an 'investment', the agreement indicates 'commitment of capital or other resources, the expectation of gain or profit, or the assumption of risk',[10] and includes into the scope of investment such forms as 'an enterprise; equity participation; debt and loans; futures, options and other derivatives; intellectual property rights; rights conferred pursuant to laws or contracts such as concessions, revenue-sharing or turnkey; and any other tangible and intangible, movable and immovable property, and any related property rights such as leases, mortgages, liens and pledges'.[11]

This definition is based on the definition of investment under the model BIT of the United States[12] and is largely adopted by high-level BITs and FTAs including the TPP and TTIP as shown in Table 12.1.[13] The three characteristics, such as (i) commitment of capital or other resources, (ii) the expectation of gain or profit, or (iii) the assumption of risk, are widely indicated as the features of investment in many BITs and FTAs. Moreover, in such an investment case as *Salini v Morocco*,[14] the arbitral tribunal identified the following four elements as indicative of an investment for purposes of the ICSID Convention: (i) a contribution, (ii) a certain duration over which the project is implemented, (iii) a sharing of operational risks, and (iv) a contribution to the host state's development.[15]

---

[9] See eg Steffen Hindelang and Markus Krajewski, *Shifting Paradigms in International Investment Law: More Balanced, Less Isolated, Increasingly Diversified* (Oxford University Press 2016); Armand de Mestral, *Second Thoughts: Investor-State Arbitration between Developed Democracies* (Centre for International Governance Innovation 2017); Won-Mog Choi, 'The Present and Future of the Investor-State Dispute Settlement Paradigm' (2007) Journal of International Economic Law 1; William S Dodge, 'Investor-State Dispute Settlement Between Developed Countries: Reflections on the Australia-United States Free Trade Agreement' (2006) Vanderbilt Journal of Transnational Law 39; Kenneth J Vandevelde, 'The Bilateral Investment Treaty Program of the United States' (1988) 21 Cornell International Law Journal 201; Robert Renbert Wilson, *United States Commercial Treaties and International Law* (The Hauser Press 1960).
[10] Trilateral Investment Agreement art 1(1).   [11] ibid.
[12] 2004 Model BIT, Department of States, the United States Government.
[13] TPP art 9.1, Definition specific to investment protection, EU Commission draft TTIP-investment.
[14] *Salini Costruttori SpA v Morocco* (ICSID Case No ARB/00/4, 2001, 42 ILM, 2003).
[15] ibid para 130. This is the so-called '*Salini* test'.

Table 12.1 Definition of Investment in the Trilateral Agreement, TPP, and TTIP

Trilateral Investment Agreement[a]	TPP[b]	TTIP (EC)[c]
the term 'investments' means every kind of asset that an investor owns or controls, directly or indirectly, which has the characteristics of an investment, such as the commitment of capital or other resources, the expectation of gain or profit, or the assumption of risk. Forms that investments may take include:	**covered investment** means, with respect to a Party, an investment in its territory of an investor of another Party in existence as of the date of entry into force of this Agreement for those Parties or established, acquired, or expanded thereafter;	**'covered investment'** means an investment which is owned, directly or indirectly, or controlled, directly or indirectly, by investors of one Party in the territory1 of the other Party made in accordance with applicable laws, whether made before or after the entry into force of this Agreement.
	investment means every asset that an investor owns or controls, directly or indirectly, that has the characteristics of an investment, including such characteristics as the commitment of capital or other resources, the expectation of gain or profit, or the assumption of risk. Forms that an investment may take include:	**'investment'** means every kind of asset which has the characteristics of an investment, which includes a certain duration and other characteristics such as the commitment of capital or other resources, the expectation of gain or profit, or the assumption of risk. Forms that an investment may take include:
(a) an enterprise and a branch of an enterprise	(a) an enterprise;	(a) an enterprise;
(b) shares, stocks or other forms of equity participation in an enterprise, including rights derived therefrom;	(b) shares, stock and other forms of equity participation in an enterprise;	(b) shares, stocks and other forms of equity participation in an enterprise;
(c) bonds, debentures, loans and other forms of debt, including rights derived therefrom;	(c) bonds, debentures, other debt instruments and loans; (d) futures, options and other derivatives;	(c) bonds, debentures and other debt instruments of an enterprise; (d) a loan to an enterprise; (e) any other kinds of interest in an enterprise;
(d) rights under contracts, including turnkey, construction, management, production or revenue-sharing contracts;	(e) turnkey, construction, management, production, concession, revenue-sharing and other similar contracts;	(f) an interest arising from: (i) a concession conferred pursuant to domestic law or under a contract, including to search for, cultivate, extract or exploit natural resources, (ii) a turnkey, construction, production, or revenue-sharing contract, or (iii) other similar contracts;

(continued)

Table 12.1 Continued

Trilateral Investment Agreement[a]	TPP[b]	TTIP (EC)[c]
(e) claims to money and claims to any performance under contract having a financial value associated with investment;		(i) claims to money or claims to performance under a contract; For greater certainty, 'claims to money' does not include claims to money that arise solely from commercial contracts for the sale of goods or services by a natural person or enterprise in the territory of a Party to a natural person or enterprise in the territory of the other Party, domestic financing of such contracts, or any related order, judgment, or arbitral award. Returns that are invested shall be treated as investments and any alteration of the form in which assets are invested or reinvested shall not affect their qualification as investments.
(f) intellectual property rights, including copyrights and related rights, patent rights and rights relating to utility models, trademarks, industrial designs, layout-designs of integrated circuits, new varieties of plants, trade names, indications of source or geographical indications and undisclosed information;	(f) intellectual property rights;	(g) intellectual property rights;
(g) rights conferred pursuant to laws and regulations or contracts such as concessions, licences, authorizations and permits; and	(g) licences, authorisations, permits and similar rights conferred pursuant to the Party's law; and	
(h) any other tangible and intangible, movable and immovable property, and any related property rights, such as leases, mortgages, liens and pledges;	(h) other tangible or intangible, movable or immovable property, and related property rights, such as leases, mortgages, liens and pledges, but investment does not mean an order or judgment entered in a judicial or administrative action.	(h) any other moveable property, tangible or intangible, or immovable property and related rights;

Table 12.1 Continued

Trilateral Investment Agreement[a]	TPP[b]	TTIP (EC)[c]
Note: Investments also include the amounts yielded by investments, in particular, profit, interest, capital gains, dividends, royalties and fees. A change in the form in which assets are invested does not affect their character as investments.		

[a] Trilateral Investment Agreement art 1(1).
[b] TPP art 9,.
[c] Definition specific to investment protection, Commission draft TTIP-investment Http://trade.ec.europa.eu/doclib/html/153807.htm.

Note should be taken of the fact that an important difference exists. In the *Salini* test, the four elements were understood to be closely interrelated and thus, they need to be examined in their totality.[16] By contrast, in the above-mentioned agreements based on the US model BIT, the three elements are linked by the word 'or' (not 'and').[17] This means that one can even argue that those elements are respectively stated as independent and sufficient ones: if only any one of those three elements is met, there exists an investment. This also means that the scope of investment may reach too far, thereby subjecting overly broad areas into the coverage of treaty protection.

Concerning the form of 'rights under contracts', it is debatable whether *any* contractual right is eligible to be an investment.[18] Indeed, if a legal system adopts the strong principle of freedom of contract, there can arise various rights from contracts. Infringement of any of such rights by a host government can easily subject it to an investor–state dispute claim by the right holder under such a comprehensive definition of investment.

Whether a particular type of 'concessions, licenses, authorizations, and permits' has the characteristics of an investment must depend on such factors as the nature and extent of the rights that the holder has 'pursuant to laws and regulations'. In other words, among concessions, licences, authorizations, or permits that do not have the characteristics of an investment are those that do not create any rights protected under domestic law.

With respect to the category of 'any other tangible and intangible, movable and immovable property, and any related property rights', it needs to be noted that such

[16] Definition specific to investment protection, Commission draft TTIP-investment http://trade.ec.europa.eu/doclib/html/153807.htm. See also *LESI v Algeria*, Award of 27 December 2004, para 13(iv); http://www.worldbank.org/icsid/cases/lesi-sentence-fr.pdf.

[17] 'The term "investments" means every kind of asset that an investor owns or controls, directly or indirectly, which has the characteristics of an investment, such as the commitment of capital or other resources, the expectation of gain or profit, *or* the assumption of risk'. See Trilateral Investment Agreement art 1(1) (emphasis added).

[18] In *Siemens v Argentina*, a suspension of contract (a contract to establish a system of migration control and personal identification) by the new government of Argentina was challenged by Siemens. What was ruled as investment by the tribunal is not any contractual right, but 'claims to money that has been used to create economic value or claims to any performance under a contract having an economic value'. See para 150 of Decision on Jurisdiction, *Siemens A.G. v the Argentine Republic* (ICSID Case No ARB/02/8).

benefits as market share, market access, expected gains, and opportunities for profit-making should not be, by themselves, investments.

All of these points can be reflected into a definition clause of investment in the Korea–China–Japan FTA or RECP, according to which the three characteristics—(i) commitment of capital or other resources, (ii) the expectation of gain or profit, and (iii) the assumption of risk—are required to be considered in a cumulative manner for the purpose of determining any existence of investment. This will also make the definition of investment fully consistent with the *Salini* test.

Based on the broad notion of investment, the Trilateral Investment Agreement stipulates such comprehensive substantive obligations as the promotion and protection of investment, general treatment of investment, most-favoured-nation (MFN) treatment, transparency, expropriation and compensation, compensation for losses or damages, and freedom of transfers.

III. Non-discrimination Principle and General Treatment of Investment

A. Non-discrimination treatment

The Trilateral Investment Agreement does not protect the pre-investment stage by stating that the term 'investment activities' means 'management, conduct, operation, maintenance, use, enjoyment and sale of other disposition of investments'.[19] In contrast, TPP accords national treatment and MFN treatment to investments or investors of another Party with respect to such pre-establishment states as the 'establishment, acquisition' as well as to the post-establishment states of 'expansion, management, conduct, operation, and sale or other disposition' of investments.[20]

It seems that the Trilateral Agreement approach finds a balance between efforts to cover comprehensive activities of investment and to set out a cautious scope of protected stages of investment transactions by excluding the pre-investment stages. This balanced approach is also reflected in the national treatment principle, and the golden rule of trade does not apply to 'non-conforming measures, if any, existing at the date of entry into force of this Agreement'.[21] This blanket exemption of any existing non-conforming measures from the application of the golden rule helps signatory parties to preserve existing policy discretion.

On the other hand, the exemption is conditioned upon the so-called 'ratchet' and 'no less favourable than before' clause. That is, in order to claim this exemption, the amendment or modification of existing non-conforming measures must 'not decrease the conformity of the measures as it existed immediately before the amendment or modification' and the treatment granted to an investment once admitted shall 'in no case be less favourable than that granted at the time when the original investment was made'.[22] Such mechanisms exist similarly in the TPP.[23] These conditions are setting the limitation of the policy discretion. See Table 12.2 in this regard.

---

[19] Trilateral Investment Agreement art 1(5).
[20] TPP arts 9.4 and 9.5. It seems that the current draft of TTIP proposed by the EU does not include national treatment and MFN. See Julien Chaisse, 'The Shifting Tectonics of International Investment Law: Structure and Dynamics of Rules and Arbitration on Foreign Investment in the Asia-Pacific Region' (2015) 47 George Washington International Law Review 563, 615–16.
[21] Trilateral Investment Agreement art 3(2).   [22] ibid.   [23] See TPP art 9.11.

Table 12.2 National Treatment Provisions in the Trilateral Agreement and TPP

Trilateral Investment Agreement	TPP
Article 3	Article 9.4
National Treatment	National Treatment
1. Each Contracting Party shall in its territory accord to investors of another Contracting Party and to their investments treatment no less favorable than that it accords in like circumstances to its own investors and their investments with respect to investment activities.	1. Each Party shall accord to investors of another Party treatment no less favourable than that it accords, in like circumstances, to its own investors with respect to the establishment, acquisition, expansion, management, conduct, operation, and sale or other disposition of investments in its territory.
2. Paragraph 1 shall not apply to non-conforming measures, if any, existing at the date of entry into force of this Agreement maintained by each Contracting Party under its laws and regulations or any amendment or modification to such measures, provided that the amendment or modification does not decrease the conformity of the measure as it existed immediately before the amendment or modification. Treatment granted to investment once admitted shall in no case be less favorable than that granted at the time when the original investment was made.	2. Each Party shall accord to covered investments treatment no less favourable than that it accords, in like circumstances, to investments in its territory of its own investors with respect to the establishment, acquisition, expansion, management, conduct, operation, and sale or other disposition of investments.
3. Each Contracting Party shall take, where applicable, all appropriate steps to progressively remove all the non-conforming measures referred to in paragraph 2.	3. Each Contracting Party shall take, where applicable, all appropriate steps to progressively remove all the non-conforming measures referred to in paragraph 2.

The investment chapter of the Korea–China–Japan FTA or RCEP needs to adopt this negative listing approach combined with non-conforming measures so that it can achieve high-level protection of investment while preserving the necessary regulatory discretion for the signatory parties.

Application of the MFN principle in the Trilateral Investment Agreement is subject to significant exceptions: the principle does not apply to any preferential treatment resulting from regional trade agreements, any international arrangement for facilitating small scale trade in border areas, or aviation, fishery, and maritime agreements.[24] Also, the MFN principle does not apply with regard to provisions concerning the settlement of investment disputes,[25] and matters related to the acquisition of land property.[26] In comparison, TPP's MFN clause excepts only 'international dispute resolution procedures or mechanisms'[27] in the main text, but most member states have included as non-conforming measures any treaty preferences 'accorded prior to the date of entry into force of the TPP' and any preferential measures accorded in 'international agreements involving aviation, fisheries, or maritime matters'.[28]

The MFN guarantee exchanged among host states in Northeast Asia will facilitate the internal investment flow in the region. Therefore, any mega-FTA in the region will need to include this kind of guarantee. With respect to the scope of exception, excepting 'any preferential treatment resulting from regional trade agreements' from

---

[24] Trilateral Investment Agreement art 4(2).   [25] ibid art 4(3).
[26] ibid Protocol para 1.   [27] TPP art 9.5.
[28] See each member's non-conforming measures in Annex 2 of TPP.

the MFN principle needs to be avoided in such mega-FTAs. In this era of proliferating FTAs, where most of investment preferences are accorded through FTAs, the MFN principle may become meaningless if such preferences through FTAs are not subject to the principle. Having said this, one legislative option would be to provide, similarly to the TPP approach, that only excepted from the MFN principle are any preferences resulting from regional trade agreements that entered into force prior to the effectuation of the mega-FTA as shown by Table 12.3. This type of 'future MFN clause' in the Korea–China–Japan FTA or RCEP will make its MFN guarantee substantially meaningful. If any future preferences in particular fields are considered sensitive to particular member states, they may except any preferences accorded in those particular areas from the application of the MFN principle, similarly to the TPP approach.

Table 12.3 MFN Clauses in the Trilateral Investment Agreement and TPP

Trilateral Investment Agreement	TPP
Article 4	Article 9.5
Most-Favoured-Nation Treatment	Most-Favoured-Nation Treatment
1. Each Contracting Party shall in its territory accord to investors of another Contracting Party and to their investments treatment no less favorable than that it accords in like circumstances to investors of the third Contracting Party or of a non-Contracting Party and to their investments with respect to investment activities and the matters relating to the admission of investment in accordance with paragraph 2 of Article 2.	1. Each Party shall accord to investors of another Party treatment no less favourable than that it accords, in like circumstances, to investors of any other Party or of any non-Party with respect to the establishment, acquisition, expansion, management, conduct, operation, and sale or other disposition of investments in its territory.
2. Paragraph 1 shall not be construed so as to oblige a Contracting Party to extend to investors of another Contracting Party and to their investments any preferential treatment resulting from its membership of: (a) any customs union, free trade area, monetary union, similar international agreement leading to such union or free trade area, or other forms of regional economic cooperation; (b) any international agreement or arrangement for facilitating small scale trade in border areas; or (c) any bilateral and multilateral international agreements involving aviation, fishery and maritime matters including salvage.	2. Each Party shall accord to covered investments treatment no less favourable than that it accords, in like circumstances, to investments in its territory of investors of any other Party or of any non-Party with respect to the establishment, acquisition, expansion, management, conduct, operation, and sale or other disposition of investments. 3. For greater certainty, the treatment referred to in this Article does not encompass international dispute resolution procedures or mechanisms, such as those included in Section B (Investor-State Dispute Settlement).
3. It is understood that the treatment accorded to investors of the third Contracting Party or any non-Contracting Party and to their investments as referred to in paragraph 1 does not include treatment accorded to investors of the third Contracting Party or any non-Contracting Party and to their investments by provisions concerning the settlement of investment disputes between a Contracting Party and investors of the third	Annex II – Japan's Non-Conforming Measures Sector: All Obligations Concerned: Most-Favoured-Nation Treatment (Article 9.5 and Article 10.4) Description: Investment and Cross-Border Trade in Services 1. Japan reserves the right to adopt or maintain any measure that accords differential treatment to countries under any bilateral or multilateral agreement in force on, or signed prior to, the date of entry into force of this Agreement.

Table 12.3 Continued

Trilateral Investment Agreement	TPP
Contracting Party or between a Contracting Party and investors of any non-Contracting Party that are provided for in other international agreements. Note: For the purposes of this Article, the term "non-Contracting Parties" shall not include any separate customs territory within the meaning of the General Agreement on Tariffs and Trade or of the WTO Agreement that is a member of the World Trade Organization as of the date of entry into force of this Agreement.	2. Japan reserves the right to adopt or maintain any measure that accords differential treatment to countries under any bilateral or multilateral agreement, other than the agreement referred to in paragraph 1, involving: (a) aviation; (b) fisheries; or (c) maritime matters, including salvage.

B. General treatment of investment

The general treatment of investments clause in the Trilateral Investment Agreement requires a 'reasonable and appropriate standard of treatment accorded in accordance with generally accepted rules of international law'.[29] Separately from this clause, the agreement has an 'Access to the courts of justice' clause that requires each contracting party to accord the MFN and national treatment to the investors of another party with respect to access to the courts.[30]

This means that the Trilateral Investment Agreement does not require treatments pursuant to a minimum standard in customary international law when it comes to the matter of access to the courts, administrative tribunals, and agencies in all degrees of jurisdiction. As a consequence, each party to the Trilateral Investment Agreement may operate the justice system in accordance with its own standard in so far as it is non-discriminatory.

This approach contrasts with many BITs and FTAs including the TPP, in which the concept of 'fair and equitable treatment' and 'full protection and security' includes the element of access to the courts and a minimum standard of treatment is required. In the TPP, the 'fair and equitable treatment' and 'full protection and security' is defined as 'the obligation not to deny justice in criminal, civil or administrative adjudicatory proceedings in accordance with the principle of due process embodied in the principal legal systems of the world and to provide the level of police protection required under customary international law'.[31]

Interestingly, the EU's proposed text of the TTIP includes detailed provisions to elaborate what constitutes fair and equitable treatment and full protection and security. They include:

(a) denial of justice in criminal, civil or administrative proceedings; (b) fundamental breach of due process, including a fundamental breach of transparency and obstacles to effective access to justice, in judicial and administrative proceedings; (c) manifest arbitrariness; (d) targeted discrimination on manifestly wrongful grounds, such as gender, race or religious belief; (e) harassment, coercion, abuse of power or similar bad faith conduct; or (f) a breach of any further elements of the fair and equitable treatment obligation adopted by the Parties in accordance with paragraph 3 of this Article.[32]

---

[29] ibid art 5(1).   [30] Trilateral Investment Agreement art 6.   [31] TPP art 9.6.
[32] EU Commission draft text of TTIP Chapter II art 3.

According to this proposal, when applying the above fair and equitable treatment obligation, a tribunal may take into account 'whether a Party made a specific representation to an investor to induce a covered investment, that created a legitimate expectation, and upon which the investor relied in deciding to make or maintain the covered investment, but that the Party subsequently frustrated'.[33]

Given the differences in the system of access to the courts of justice between China on one hand, and several other countries in Asia on the other, it might be difficult for the Korea–China–Japan FTA or RCEP to require any minimum standard of treatment in terms of the access to the courts. Therefore, the non-discriminatory treatment obligations can form the basis of the access to the courts of justice clause in the Korea–China–Japan FTA or RCEP. Other aspects of the general treatment of investment may be dealt with by generally accepted standards of international law. Furthermore, it would be a good idea to elaborate what the general treatment of investment means similarly to the TTIP approach. Table 12.4 makes comparison of general treatment clauses and TTIP.

Table 12.4 General Treatment Clauses in the Trilateral Investment Agreement, TPP and TTIP

Trilateral Investment Agreement	TPP	TTIP (EC)
Article 5	Article 9.6	Article 3
General Treatment of Investments	Minimum Standard of Treatment	Treatment of Investors and of covered investments
1. Each Contracting Party shall accord to investments of investors of another Contracting Party fair and equitable treatment and full protection and security. The concepts of "fair and equitable treatment" and "full protection and security" do not require treatment in addition to or beyond any reasonable and appropriate standard of treatment accorded in accordance with generally accepted rules of international law. A determination that there has been a breach of another provision of this Agreement, or of a separate international agreement, does not ipso facto establish that there has been a breach of this paragraph. 2. Each Contracting Party shall observe any written commitments in the form of an agreement or contract it may have entered into with regard to investments of investors of another Contracting Party.	1. Each Party shall accord to covered investments treatment in accordance with applicable customary international law principles, including fair and equitable treatment and full protection and security. 2. For greater certainty, paragraph 1 prescribes the customary international law minimum standard of treatment of aliens as the standard of treatment to be afforded to covered investments. The concepts of "fair and equitable treatment" and "full protection and security" do not require treatment in addition to or beyond that which is required by that standard, and do not create additional substantive rights. The obligations in paragraph 1 to provide:	1. Each Party shall accord in its territory to covered investments of the other Party and investors with respect to their covered investments fair and equitable treatment and full protection and security in accordance with paragraphs 2 to 5. 2. A Party breaches the obligation of fair and equitable treatment referenced in paragraph 1 where a measure or a series of measures constitutes: (a) denial of justice in criminal, civil or administrative proceedings; or (b) fundamental breach of due process, including a fundamental breach of transparency and obstacles to effective access to justice, in judicial and administrative proceedings; or (c) manifest arbitrariness; or (d) targeted discrimination on manifestly wrongful grounds, such as gender, race or religious belief; or (e) harassment, coercion, abuse of power or similar bad faith conduct; or

[33] ibid.

Table 12.4 Continued

Trilateral Investment Agreement	TPP	TTIP (EC)
Article 6 **Access to the Courts of Justice** Each Contracting Party shall in its territory accord to investors of another Contracting Party treatment no less favorable than that it accords in like circumstances to its own investors, investors of the third Contracting Party or of a non-Contracting Party, with respect to access to the courts of justice and administrative tribunals and agencies in all degrees of jurisdiction, both in pursuit and in defense of such investors' rights.	(a) "fair and equitable treatment" includes the obligation not to deny justice in criminal, civil or administrative adjudicatory proceedings in accordance with the principle of due process embodied in the principal legal systems of the world; and (b) "full protection and security" requires each Party to provide the level of police protection required under customary international law. 3. A determination that there has been a breach of another provision of this Agreement, or of a separate international agreement, does not establish that there has been a breach of this Article. 4. For greater certainty, the mere fact that a Party takes or fails to take an action that may be inconsistent with an investor's expectations does not constitute a breach of this Article, even if there is loss or damage to the covered investment as a result. 5. For greater certainty, the mere fact that a subsidy or grant has not been issued, renewed or maintained, or has been modified or reduced, by a Party, does not constitute a breach of this Article, even if there is loss or damage to the covered investment as a result.	(f) a breach of any further elements of the fair and equitable treatment obligation adopted by the Parties in accordance with paragraph 3 of this Article. 3. The Parties shall, upon request of a Party, review the content of the obligation to provide fair and equitable treatment. The […] Committee (reference to article on Services and Investment Committee) may develop recommendations in this regard and submit them to the […] Committee (reference to article on Trade Committee). The […] Committee (reference to article on Trade Committee) shall consider whether to recommend that the Agreement is amended, in accordance with Article [relevant procedures for the amendment of the Agreement]. 4. When applying the above fair and equitable treatment obligation, a tribunal may take into account whether a Party made a specific representation to an investor to induce a covered investment, that created a legitimate expectation, and upon which the investor relied in deciding to make or maintain the covered investment, but that the Party subsequently frustrated. 5. For greater certainty, 'full protection and security' refers to the Party's obligations relating to physical security of investors and covered investments. 6. For greater certainty, a breach of another provision of this Agreement, or of any other international agreement, does not constitute a breach of this Article.

IV. Expropriation and Compensation

With respect to the obligation of expropriation and compensation, the Trilateral Investment Agreement obliges parties to compensate indirect expropriation as well as direct expropriation. Indirect expropriation is defined as 'an action or a series of actions by a contracting party' that has an 'effect equivalent to direct expropriation' and whether or not such effect has occurred requires a case-by-case, fact-based inquiry that considers economic impact on the investment, interference with distinct and reasonable expectations arising out of investment, and the character and objectives of such an action.[34] Except in rare circumstances, non-discriminatory regulatory actions adopted by a party for the purpose of legitimate public welfare do not constitute indirect expropriation (see Table 12.5 below).[35]

Table 12.5 Expropriation and Compensation Clauses in Trilateral Investment Agreement, TPP, and TTIP

Trilateral Investment Agreement	TPP	TTIP (EC)
Article 11	Article 9.8	Article 5
Expropriation and Compensation	Expropriation and Compensation	Expropriation
1. No Contracting Party shall expropriate or nationalize investments in its territory of investors of another Contracting Party or take any measure equivalent to expropriation or nationalization (hereinafter referred to in this Agreement as "expropriation") except: (a) for a public purpose; (b) on a non-discriminatory basis; (c) in accordance with its laws and international standard of due process of law; and (d) upon compensation pursuant to paragraphs 2, 3 and 4. 2. The compensation shall be equivalent to the fair market value of the expropriated investments at the time when the expropriation was publicly announced or when the expropriation occurred, whichever is the earlier. The fair market value shall	1. No Party shall expropriate or nationalise a covered investment either directly or indirectly through measures equivalent to expropriation or nationalisation (expropriation), except: (a) for a public purpose; (b) in a non-discriminatory manner; (c) on payment of prompt, adequate and effective compensation in accordance with paragraphs 2, 3 and 4; and (d) in accordance with due process of law. 2. Compensation shall: (a) be paid without delay; (b) be equivalent to the fair market value of the expropriated	1. Neither Party shall nationalize or expropriate a covered investment either directly or indirectly through measures having an effect equivalent to nationalisation or expropriation (hereinafter referred to as "expropriation") except: (a) for a public purpose; (b) under due process of law; (c) in a non-discriminatory manner; and (d) against payment of prompt, adequate and effective compensation. 2. For greater certainty, this paragraph shall be interpreted in accordance with Annex I [on expropriation]. 3. Such compensation shall amount to the fair market value of the investment at the time immediately before the expropriation or the impending expropriation became public knowledge, whichever is earlier, plus interest at a normal commercial rate, from the date of expropriation until the date of payment.

---

[34] Trilateral Investment Agreement Protocol para 2.   [35] ibid.

Table 12.5 Continued

Trilateral Investment Agreement	TPP	TTIP (EC)
not reflect any change in market value occurring because the expropriation had become publicly known earlier. 3. The compensation shall be paid without delay and shall include interest at a commercially reasonable rate, taking into account the length of time from the time of expropriation to the time of payment. It shall be effectively realizable and freely transferable and shall be freely convertible, at the market exchange rate prevailing on the date of expropriation, into the currency of the Contracting Party of the investors concerned, and into freely usable currencies. 4. Without prejudice to the provisions of Article 15, the investors affected by expropriation shall have a right of access to the courts of justice or the administrative tribunals or agencies of the Contracting Party making the expropriation to seek a prompt review of the investors' case and the amount of compensation in accordance with the principles set out in this Article.	investment immediately before the expropriation took place (the date of expropriation); (c) not reflect any change in value occurring because the intended expropriation had become known earlier; and (d) be fully realisable and freely transferable. 3. If the fair market value is denominated in a freely usable currency, the compensation paid shall be no less than the fair market value on the date of expropriation, plus interest at a commercially reasonable rate for that currency, accrued from the date of expropriation until the date of payment.	4. Such compensation shall be effectively realisable, freely transferable in accordance with Article 6 [Transfers] and made without delay. 5. The investor affected shall have a right, under the law of the expropriating Party, to prompt review of its claim and of the valuation of its investment, by a judicial or other independent authority of that Party, in accordance with the principles set out in this Article. 6. This Article does not apply to the issuance of compulsory licences granted in relation to intellectual property rights, to the extent that such issuance is consistent with the Agreement on Trade-Related Aspects of Intellectual Property Rights in Annex 1C to the WTO Agreements ("TRIPs Agreement").
Protocol 2. (a) The Contracting Parties confirm their shared understanding that paragraph 1 of Article 11 of the Agreement addresses the following two situations: (i) the first situation is direct expropriation, where investments are nationalized or	**ANNEX 9-B** **EXPROPRIATION** The Parties confirm their shared understanding that: 1. An action or a series of actions by a Party cannot constitute an expropriation unless it interferes with a tangible or intangible property right or property interest in an investment.	**ANNEX I:** Expropriation The Parties confirm their shared understanding that: 1. Expropriation may be either direct or indirect: (a) direct expropriation occurs when an investment is nationalised or otherwise directly expropriated through formal transfer of title or outright seizure.

(continued)

Table 12.5 Continued

Trilateral Investment Agreement	TPP	TTIP (EC)
otherwise directly expropriated through formal transfer of title or outright seizure; and (ii) the second situation is indirect expropriation, where an action or a series of actions by a Contracting Party has an effect equivalent to direct expropriation without formal transfer of title or outright seizure. (b) The determination of whether an action or a series of actions by a Contracting Party, in a specific fact situation, constitutes an indirect expropriation requires a case-by-case, fact-based inquiry that considers, among other factors: (i) the economic impact of the action or series of actions, although the fact that such action or series of actions has an adverse effect on the economic value of investments, standing alone, does not establish that an indirect expropriation has occurred; (ii) the extent to which the action or series of actions interferes with distinct and reasonable expectations arising out of investments; and (iii) the character and objectives of the action or series of actions, including whether	2. Article 9.8.1 (Expropriation and Compensation) addresses two situations. The first is direct expropriation, in which an investment is nationalised or otherwise directly expropriated through formal transfer of title or outright seizure. 3. The second situation addressed by Article 9.8.1 (Expropriation and Compensation) is indirect expropriation, in which an action or series of actions by a Party has an effect equivalent to direct expropriation without formal transfer of title or outright seizure. (a) The determination of whether an action or series of actions by a Party, in a specific fact situation, constitutes an indirect expropriation, requires a case-by-case, fact-based inquiry that considers, among other factors: (i) the economic impact of the government action, although the fact that an action or series of actions by a Party has an adverse effect on the economic value of an investment, standing alone, does not establish that an indirect expropriation has occurred;	(b) indirect expropriation occurs where a measure or series of measures by a Party has an effect equivalent to direct expropriation, in that it substantially deprives the investor of the fundamental attributes of property in its investment, including the right to use, enjoy and dispose of its investment, without formal transfer of title or outright seizure. 2. The determination of whether a measure or series of measures by a Party, in a specific fact situation, constitutes an indirect expropriation requires a case-by-case, fact-based inquiry that considers, among other factors: (a) the economic impact of the measure or series of measures, although the sole fact that a measure or series of measures of a Party has an adverse effect on the economic value of an investment does not establish that an indirect expropriation has occurred; (b) the duration of the measure or series of measures by a Party; (c) the character of the measure or series of measures, notably their object and content. 3. For greater certainty, except in the rare circumstance when the impact of a measure or series of measures is so severe in light of its purpose that it appears manifestly excessive, non-discriminatory measures of a Party that are designed and applied to protect legitimate public welfare objectives, such as the protection of public health, safety, environment or public morals, social or consumer protection or promotion and protection of cultural diversity do not constitute indirect expropriations.

Table 12.5 Continued

Trilateral Investment Agreement	TPP	TTIP (EC)
such action is proportionate to its objectives. (c) Except in rare circumstances, such as when an action or a series of actions by a Contracting Party is extremely severe or disproportionate in light of its purpose, non-discriminatory regulatory actions adopted by the Contracting Party for the purpose of legitimate public welfare do not constitute indirect expropriation.	(ii) the extent to which the government action interferes with distinct, reasonable investment-backed expectations; and (iii) the character of the government action. (b) Non-discriminatory regulatory actions by a Party that are designed and applied to protect legitimate public welfare objectives, such as public health, safety and the environment, do not constitute Indirect expropriations, except in rare circumstances.	

These provisions of indirect expropriation are an exact copy of the 2004 model BIT text of the United States. The similar rules of indirect expropriation have been spread worldwide through BITs and FTAs by the US initiative. It is no wonder that the TPP adopts very similar definitions and exception provisions to those provisions under the Trilateral Investment Agreement. Although the EC's draft provisions of TTIP expands the scope of public welfare exceptions by excepting from indirect expropriation such measures aimed for 'protection of public morals, social or consumer protection or promotion and protection of cultural diversity'[36] in addition to 'public health, safety and environment' under the TPP,[37] the basic definition and structure of the concept of expropriation remain very similar.

It can be argued that the term 'an action or a series of actions' is not clear and too inclusive and it might apply in an arbitrary manner to restrict many legitimate governmental regulations. Originally, the term 'an action or a series of actions' was drafted to catch a situation of the so-called 'creeping expropriation', where the host country government imposes the continual restriction of investment property rights gradually over time through various legislation and regulations in order to infringe upon investor's activities. This original intention notwithstanding, the current text is interpreted to catch as indirect expropriation any 'action or a series of action' that is even not directed towards the investment, as long as such an action causes an 'effect equivalent to direct

---

[36] EU's Draft Chapter of Investment of TTIP Annex I, para 2.
[37] TPP Annex 9-B, para 3.

expropriation'. It is because there are stated only two elements to constitute indirect expropriation, that is, action and effect.

Taking an example that shows the seriousness of this problem, the Ministry of Education (MOE) of the Korean Government recently considered developing an English testing service for the people who want to prove their English language proficiency. In the Korea–US FTA, Korea agreed to liberalize the sector of foreign language testing services. As the FTA has a similar definition clause of indirect expropriation to that of the Trilateral Agreement, the ETS (a US-based company who has made a substantial investment to Korea) might bring a complaint that this MOE project constitutes an indirect expropriation as an action that will cause a damaging effect on its existing English proficiency test service, that is, TOEFL.

This kind of scenario is always possible given the loose definition of indirect expropriation, no matter how legitimate purpose the regulating government has. The same problem may occur in the Trilateral Investment Agreement and the TPP, which copies the definition under the US model BIT.

In order to solve this problem, the Korea–China–Japan FTA or RCEP could use the term 'a measure or a series of measures directed toward a covered investment' instead of 'an action or a series of actions' as the definition of indirect expropriation. Otherwise, a possibility is always latent that an incidental action that is not intended to restrict investments might be caught as an indirect expropriation by the only reason that a damaging effect has occurred to the investment. In addition, a more comprehensive and exhaustive list of legitimate public welfare policies needs to be prescribed by including governmental actions aimed for public health, safety, environment protection, public morals, social or consumer protection or promotion, protection of cultural diversity and more if possible.

V. Exceptions

According to the Trilateral Investment Agreement, the agreement does not generally apply to taxation measures and in the event of any inconsistency between the agreement and any tax convention, the latter will prevail.[38] The caveat is that the expropriation and compensation provision in the Trilateral Investment Agreement applies to taxation measures and that any disputes concerning this matter are resolved by the investor–state dispute settlement (ISDS).

Therefore, it becomes a critical question whether a tax measure is an expropriation or not. According to the Trilateral Agreement, this question is not answered by objective criteria spelled out in the agreement. Instead, the determination is made by a joint decision-making process of tax authorities of both contracting parties involved. That is to say, the disputing investor must refer the issue, at the time of the submission of a written request for consultation, to the competent authorities of both countries to determine whether such measure is not an expropriation. If the competent authorities do not consider the issue or, having considered it, fail to determine that the measure is not an expropriation within six months, the investor may submit its claim to the ISDS arbitration.[39]

---

[38] Trilateral Investment Agreement art 21.

[39] ibid art 21. See generally Julien Chaisse and Rahul Donde, 'The State of Investor-State Arbitration: A Reality Check of the Issues, Trends, and Directions in Asia-Pacific' (2018) 51(1) The International Lawyer 47.

This joint decision process seems to reinforce the sovereign authority over taxation matters: unless competent authorities of both countries involved recognize the existence of expropriation regarding a tax measure, there is no way for the investor to move on to the ISDS arbitration. Indeed, a tax authority of the host country will seldom acknowledge any existence of expropriation created by its own tax measure.

It is true that the imposition of taxes does not generally constitute an expropriation. However, tax measures if taken in overly excessive and arbitrary manner may have an equivalent effect to the expropriation. In this light, the Korea–China–Japan FTA or RCEP should not adopt the joint decision process to exclude virtually all tax measures from the scope of expropriation. Instead, the FTA could prescribe the following criteria:

(a) The imposition of taxes does not generally constitute an expropriation. The mere introduction of a new taxation measure or the imposition of a taxation measure in more than one jurisdiction in respect of an investment generally does not in and of itself constitute an expropriation;

(b) A taxation measure that is consistent with internationally recognized tax policies, principles, and practices should not constitute an expropriation. In particular, a taxation measure aimed at preventing the avoidance or evasion of taxation measures generally does not constitute an expropriation;

(c) A taxation measure that is applied on a non-discriminatory basis, as opposed to a taxation measure that is targeted at investors of a particular nationality or at specific taxpayers, is less likely to constitute an expropriation; and

(d) A taxation measure generally does not constitute an expropriation if it was already in force when the investment was made and information about the measure was publicly available.[40]

The second exception where the Trilateral Agreement does not apply is 'the measures relating to financial services for prudential reasons, including measures for the protection of investors, depositors, policy holders or persons to whom a fiduciary duty is owed by an enterprise supplying financial services, or to ensure the integrity and stability of the financial system'.[41] Such a prudential measure exception in the Trilateral Agreement shows that the maintenance of a stable financial system is the common goal in priority in Northeast Asia. Note needs to be taken that such an exception should not be used as a means of avoiding the contracting party's obligations under the agreement.[42] This prudential measure exception needs to be copied in the Korea–China–Japan FTA or RCEP.

Other exceptions that need to be included are national security exceptions and temporary safeguard measures.[43] The security exception provision must not be used as a means of avoiding the contracting party's obligations.[44]

The problem is that there is no general exception clause in the Trilateral Investment Agreement.[45] According to Article XIV of GATS, several measures are generally excepted from the obligations under the agreement, which include (i) measures necessary to protect public morals or to maintain public order; (ii) measures necessary to protect

---

[40] See Korea–US FTA Annex 11-F (Taxation and Expropriation).
[41] Trilateral Investment Agreement art 20(1).
[42] ibid art 20(2).
[43] ibid arts 18, 19.
[44] ibid art 18(2).
[45] On general exceptions clause see Julien Chaisse, 'Exploring the Confines of International Investment and Domestic Health Protections: General Exceptions Clause as a Forced Perspective' (2013) 39(2–3) American Journal of Law & Medicine 332.

human, animal or plant life, or health; and (III) measures necessary to secure compliance with laws or regulations relating to the prevention of deceptive and fraudulent practices, the protection of the privacy of individuals, and safety.[46]

It can be reminded that the third mode of service supply under the GATS (the so-called 'commercial presence' mode) is related to the investment. This means that general exceptions equivalent to GATS Article XIV deserve to apply to any investment activities. Considering that many BITs and FTAs include a general exception clause in light of this spirit,[47] the investment chapter of the Korea–China–Japan FTA or RCEP needs to incorporate such exceptions. In this light, note should be taken that the TPP has incorporated several causes for such general exception, which include 'any measure to ensure that investment activity in undertaken in a manner sensitive to environmental, health or other regulatory objectives'.[48] TPP even has a provision that recognizes the importance of policies encouraging 'corporate social responsibility' within the territory of a party,[49] and the EU's draft TTIP includes a general exception clause on public debt, prescribing that 'no claim that a restructuring of debt issued by a Party breaches an obligation under Section 2 [Investment Protection] may be submitted'.[50] Table 12.6 shows these differences in the general exception clauses.

Table 12.6 Exception Clauses in Trilateral Investment Agreement, TPP and TTIP

Trilateral Investment Agreement	TPP	TTIP (EC)
Article 18 Security Exceptions 1. Notwithstanding any other provisions in this Agreement other than the provisions of Article 12, each Contracting Party may take any measure: (a) which it considers necessary for the protection of its essential security interests; (i) taken in time of war, or armed conflict, or other emergency in that Contracting Party or in international relations; or (ii) relating to the implementation of national policies or international agreements respecting the non-proliferation of weapons;	**Article 9.15: Investment and Environmental, Health and other Regulatory Objectives** Nothing in this Chapter shall be construed to prevent a Party from adopting, maintaining or enforcing any measure otherwise consistent with this Chapter that it considers appropriate to ensure that investment activity in its territory is undertaken in a manner sensitive to environmental, health or other regulatory objectives.	ANNEX II: Public debt 1. No claim that a restructuring of debt issued by a Party breaches an obligation under Section 2 [Investment Protection] may be submitted to, or if already submitted continue in, arbitration under Section 3 [Resolution of Investment Disputes and Investment Court System] if the restructuring is a negotiated restructuring at the time of submission, or becomes a negotiated restructuring after such submission. .....

[46] GATS art XIV.
[47] Korea–Singapore FTA art 21.2; Korea–India CEPA art 10.16 (Health, safety, and environmental measures), art 10.18 (Exceptions); Korea–EU FTA art 7.50 (Exceptions); Investment Agreement of the Korea–EFTA FTA art 20 (Exceptions); Korea–Peru FTA art 9.9 (Health, safety and environmental measures), art 24.1 (General exceptions). See also many BITs including art 16 of the Korea–Japan BIT.
[48] TPP art 9.15.
[49] ibid art 9.16.
[50] EU draft proposal of TTIP investment chapter Annex II.

Table 12.6 Continued

Trilateral Investment Agreement	TPP	TTIP (EC)
(b) in pursuance of its obligations under the United Nations Charter for the maintenance of international peace and security. 2. In cases where a Contracting Party takes any measure, pursuant to paragraph 1, that does not conform with the obligations of the provisions of this Agreement other than the provisions of Article 12, that Contracting Party shall not use such measure as a means of avoiding its obligations	**Article 9.16: Corporate Social Responsibility** The Parties reaffirm the importance of each Party encouraging enterprises operating within its territory or subject to its jurisdiction to voluntarily incorporate into their internal policies those internationally recognised standards, guidelines and principles of corporate social responsibility that have been endorsed or are supported by that Party.	

VI. Conclusion

It is uncertain whether the substantive provisions of investment protection under the Trilateral Investment Agreement model can play a pioneering role in the ongoing process of convergence of investment jurisprudence in Asia. Nonetheless, the implications of the investment treaty system in combination with equivalent provisions under TPP and TTIP are gaining more attention as foreign investors are increasingly making investment into Asia. International investment policy-making efforts to attract foreign direct investment (FDI) and benefit from it continue to intensify, and international investment agreements at the bilateral, subregional, regional, and inter-regional levels further proliferate.[51] Now, Asia is at the centre of this prevailing trend.

The existence of an effective investment protection system under a mega FTA will contribute to the creation of a favourable investment climate in the region. Stronger and more effective mechanisms for investment protection will generate common rules of the game that may help to engender a community spirit in the region. This basis will function as a stepping stone towards a system of Asian economic integration. Furthermore, it may eventually have a significant political importance and spill-over effect to other fields by building a leverage to resolve territorial disputes, to ease antagonistic national sentiments, and to prevent threats to national security in the region.[52] This benefit is particularly great for China which is initiating the process of

[51] UNCTAD, *Investor-State Disputes Arising from Investment Treaties: A Review* (United Nations 2005) 3.

[52] Indeed, signing of mega-scale integration agreements could be seen as an achievement for overcoming ongoing political tensions between China, Japan, and Korea. Economic relations between the three countries had largely proceeded without the baggage of political frictions dating back over a century. However, the firewall blocking political feuds from infecting commercial relations has shown signs of breaking down. Following Japan and Korea's diplomatic quarrels over the disputed Dokdo/Takeshima Islands, Japan announced its decision to roll back its emergency currency swap arrangement with Korea in 2015. In 2010, China issued a rare earth embargo against Japan following the Daiyo/Senkaku Islands fishing trawler collision. These incidents serve as a reminder that in the case of China, Japan, and Korea, the economics component in the emerging trilateral partnership must be

building mega-regional legal frameworks in Asia beyond the web of investment and trade agreements at the bilateral level.[53] As President Xi Jinping noted at a December 2014 Politburo session, China is now embarking on a 'new round of opening to the world as a leader', emphasizing that China would no longer take a passive role as 'a bystander in global economic governance'.[54]

Nevertheless, there have been fears about frivolous or vexatious claims that could inhibit legitimate regulatory actions by governments. How to compose an investment chapter of a mega FTA such as the Korea–China–Japan FTA and RCEP that are being negotiated is a pressing demand for all in the region. For China particularly, legitimacy of core regulatory measures reflecting socialistic or non-Western values needs to be preserved free from international legal challenges.[55] Any pertinent answers to such a quest require a thorough comparison of the benefits and drawbacks of any development of relevant rules and governance. In the end, a quest for better international investment governance in Northeast Asia in the future requires sound evaluation of lessons from the past and present. A successful governance needs a continuous process of revision and balancing. Lessons from the experiences under the Trilateral Investment Agreement, TPP, and TTIP and their coordinating efforts should be fully taken into account so that the newly emerging investment governance system will not lead to tension between nations in an area where precedent is scant, but the need is great.

---

even more substantial to overcome political frictions and wariness from historical experience. And as key competitors of each other both economically and politically in the region, the countries must now tread even more carefully in their bilateral relations. See PIIE, *Towards a US-China Investment Treaty* (PIIE Briefing 15–1, 2015).

[53] It is known that the growth of outward FDI has led the Chinese government to abandon its traditional restrictive approach that aimed at regulating inward FDI and to adopt a new liberal policy that—in line with the 'Going Global' strategy—provides Chinese investors with strong substantial and procedural investment protection. See, among others, Axel Berger, *China's New Bilateral Investment Treaty Programme: Substantive, Rational and Implications for International Investment Law Making* (German Development Institute 2008).

[54] See Tony Saich, *What Does General Secretary Xi Jingping Dream About?* (Ash Center for Democratic Governance and Innovation 2017).

[55] To China, it is obvious that utilitarianism or even mercantilism has been the driving force behind the investment legislation and that China's attitude towards FDI was rooted in mixed feelings of attraction and aversion. It is also known that China has a general tendency of lack of affinity for international arbitration and a preference for settling disputes informally through diplomatic consultations. Kong Qingjiang, 'Bilateral Investment Treaties: The Chinese Approach and Practice' (2003) 8 Asian Yearbook of International Law 110, 130.

13

The RCEP Investment Rules and China

Learning from the Malleability of Chinese FTAs

Heng Wang*

I. Introduction

The growth of China's outbound investment has been phenomenal in the past decade, and China's free trade agreements (FTAs)[1] are an effective channel for developing investment rules in China. China has actively worked towards facilitating investment. As a most recent example, the G20 Trade and Investment Working Group was set up in 2016, based on China's proposal.[2] Resulting from the discussions in this Working Group, the G20 Guiding Principles for Global Investment Policy-making[3] were issued under the Chinese G20 Presidency.[4] At the time of writing, China has concluded fourteen FTAs with twenty-two countries and regions,[5] nearly all of which contain investment provisions.[6] Investment rules of these FTAs not only involve investment protection, promotion, and facilitation, but also concern domestic reform such as the free trade zones (FTZs). Moreover, a few FTAs are being negotiated, with several FTAs to be upgraded. Among China's FTAs under negotiation, the Regional Comprehensive Economic Partnership (RCEP) is the only mega FTA to which China is a party. It has been actively promoted by China. The RCEP investment rules are likely to affect China's investment regime significantly, and deserve careful study.

For China's FTAs including their investment rules, malleability is their most noticeable and core characteristic. It is observed that '[a]fter a decade, the greatest defining

Associate professor and co-director of Herbert Smith Freehills China International Business and Economic Law (CIBEL) Centre, Faculty of Law, the University of New South Wales, Sydney; university visiting professional fellow, Southwest University of Political Science and Law. An early version of this chapter has been published under the title 'The RCEP and Its Investment Rules: Learning from Past Chinese FTAs' (2017) 3(2) Chinese Journal of Global Governance 160. The author is grateful to Markus Wagner, Jyh-An Lee, Cristián Rodríguez Chiffelle, Joel Slawotsky, and other participants of the Asian FDI Forum 2016 for their insightful comments. Special thanks go to Julien Chaisse for the invitation to speak at the Asian FDI Forum. Email: heng.wang1@unsw.edu.au.

[1] It is probably more accurate to use the term preferential trade agreements (PTAs), as these agreements are regulated rather than free trade. However, the term FTA is used in order to be consistent with the official titles of many of these trade pacts. Past Chinese FTAs refer to the FTAs that China has signed to date.

[2] Xinhua, 'G20 Trade Ministers to Meet in Shanghai in July' (2016) http://usa.chinadaily.com.cn/china/2016-02/17/content_23527532.htm.

[3] *G20 Guiding Principles for Global Investment Policy-making* (2016) 1.

[4] OECD, 'G20 agrees Guiding Principles for Global Investment Policy-making' (2016) http://www.oecd.org/investment/g20-agrees-principles-for-global-investment-policymaking.htm.

[5] China FTA Network, http://fta.mofcom.gov.cn.

[6] On the multiplication of FTAs to regulate investment see generally Julien Chaisse and Christian Bellak, 'Navigating the Expanding Universe of Investment Treaties: Creation and Use of Critical Index' (2015) 18(1) Journal of International Economic Law 79.

The RCEP Investment Rules and China: Learning from the Malleability of Chinese FTAs. Heng Wang.
© Heng Wang, 2019. Published 2019 by Oxford University Press.

feature of Chinese FTAs is their malleability'.[7] The malleability can be easily found in investment chapters of China's recent FTAs with Australia and Korea. Likely in order to finalize the treaty, the China–Australia FTA (ChAFTA) only contains an early harvest investment chapter. Unlike the China–Korea FTA, a number of key provisions (e.g. the minimum standard of treatment, performance requirements, expropriation, compensation, transfers, and services-investment linkage) are missing in the ChAFTA and need to be developed in future negotiations.

The chapter will analyse China's FTA approach to investment in terms of malleability, and its implications for the RCEP. The following questions will be discussed: what is the trend of China's FTA approach to investment concerning malleability? Is China a rule follower, shaker, or maker? How may China approach the RCEP regarding investment?

Within China's FTAs, the chapter will focus on the China–Korea FTA and ChAFTA, while other China FTAs will be referred to when needed. On the one hand, these two agreements are larger pacts that reflect China's latest treaty practice, and all three countries are RCEP parties. These agreements are likely to affect the RCEP. On the other hand, Australia and Korea appear to be affected by the US approach through the TPP or trade agreements with the US. Australia is a party to the Trans-Pacific Partnership (TPP) and concluded an FTA with the US. Korea concluded the US–Korea Trade Agreement (KORUS) and was interested in joining the TPP. Interestingly, the China–Korea FTA contains a few clauses that resemble those of the KORUS, and the KORUS is 'widely acknowledged as the baseline template for the TPP'.[8] The comparative study of China's trade agreements with Korea and Australia may help to observe the possible interaction between Chinese and American approaches.

To better understand China's approach in the context of world investment law recalibration, the chapter also strives to compare China's FTAs with two deep FTAs:[9] the Trans-Pacific Partnership (TPP) and the EU–Canada Comprehensive Economic and Trade Agreement (CETA). Notably, some RCEP parties (e.g. Australia, Japan, and New Zealand) negotiated the TPP and the TPP text may affect the RCEP talks. Although the US withdrew from the TPP, it is unlikely that the US will dramatically change its position on investment rules. The TPP is based on previous US practice and primarily reflects the US approach to investment. These deep FTAs could serve as a kind of 'benchmark'[10] for the comparison in this chapter. The comparative analysis helps to better understand the similarities and differences among the approaches of China, the US, and EU, which is important for exploring the future direction of investment law.

Section II will discuss the possible extension of China's investment rule malleability from investment protection to investment liberalization, and Section III will analyse China's increased malleability on regulatory autonomy and investor–state dispute settlement (ISDS). Section IV will assess China's role in investment rule-making,

---

[7] Jun Zhao and Timothy Webster, 'Taking Stock: China's First Decade of Free Trade' (2011) 33 University of Pennsylvania Journal of International Law 65, 99.

[8] Gary Clyde Hufbauer, 'Investor-State Dispute Settlement' in Kimberly Ann Elliott and others (eds), *Assessing the Trans-Pacific Partnership, Volume 1: Market Access and Sectoral Issues* (Peterson Institute for International Economics 2016) 117.

[9] 'Deep' FTAs are those agreements with stringent WTO-extra regulatory requirements that go substantially beyond the WTO norms. They contrast with traditional FTAs that largely copy the WTO rules with few novel regulatory disciplines.

[10] This chapter does not assess the substantive merits of these provisions. That is a complex subject that requires separate and extensive treatment.

followed by Section V, which will predict the impact of China's approach to the RCEP. Section VI concludes.

II. Extended Malleability of China's Investment Rules: From Investment Protection to Investment Liberalization

Up to now, the non-malleability of China's FTA investment rules exists regarding the avoidance of investment liberalization commitments. Deep FTAs highlight investment protection and liberalization. However, China's trade pacts focus on investment protection, but do not provide for investment liberalization.

In the future, China may progressively move towards investment liberalization at least to some extent. The progress regarding pre-establishment national treatment and negative list approach is likely to continue regardless of the difficulties of the TPP and the uncertainty of US–China bilateral investment treaty (BIT) negotiations under the new US administration. Such efforts have already been conducted widely in the FTZs and beyond (e.g. the domestic law change to promote negative list approach,[11] and the future work plan of China's FTAs with Australia and Korea).

Substantial malleability can be seen as the China–Korea FTA is very different from short form ChAFTA rules. On the one hand, the China–Korea FTA resembles deep FTAs and in particular the TPP in most aspects of investment protection, with some exceptions (e.g. performance requirements, the standard of compensation in expropriation, and the scope of MFN treatment). Highlighting investment protection, the China–Korea FTA seems to align with the TPP in a number of aspects, including the minimum standard of treatment, expropriation and compensation, special formalities and information requirements, the transfer of capital, and non-discriminatory treatment of investors and investments in cases of armed conflict or civil strife.

For the minimum standard of treatment, the China–Korea FTA adopts a nearly identical provision with the TPP,[12] but differs from the CETA that incorporates an unclear but exhaustive definition of the fair and equitable treatment (FET) obligation.[13] Both the TPP and China–Korea FTA contain a FET provision, but set its scope as limited to treatment available under customary international law.[14] Moreover, they provide that the breach of another provision of this pact or other agreement will not entail a violation of the FET rule.[15] Notably, the limitations placed on the FET obligation represent a consistent practice in China's recent investment agreements (e.g. China's BITs with Mexico and Canada BIT and the China–Korea–Japan Investment Agreement) and ASEAN investment treaties particularly those with Australia, New Zealand, and Korea.[16] Such practice continues in the China–Korea FTA,[17] which arguably provides stronger protection than China's other recent treaties. The China–Korea FTA is the same as the TPP in the sense of stronger protection by providing

---

[11] Xinhua, 'China Revises Inbound Investment Laws' (2016) http://news.xinhuanet.com/english/2016-09/03/c_135657360.htm.

[12] China–Korea FTA art 12.5 (2015); TPP arts 9.6 (Minimum Standard of Treatment), 9.7 (Treatment in Case of Armed Conflict or Civil Strife).

[13] CETA art 8.10.2.   [14] China–Korea FTA art 12.5.2 (2015); TPP art 9.6.2.

[15] China–Korea FTA art 12.5.3 (2015); TPP art 9.6.3.

[16] Mark Feldman and others, *The Role of Pacific Rim FTAs in the Harmonisation of International Investment Law: Towards a Free Trade Area of the Asia-Pacific* (2016) 10.

[17] China–Korea FTA arts 12.5.2 (FET obligations), 12.15 (denial of benefits) (2015).

for treatment 'including' FET and full protection and security (FPS).[18] As two recent investment treaties, the China–Canada BIT[19] and China–Japan–Korea Investment Agreement[20] only provide for FET and FPS.

Regarding expropriation and compensation, the China–Korea and China–New Zealand agreements[21] largely resemble deep FTAs,[22] including the criteria of the fair market value of the expropriated investments. For indirect expropriation, the China–Korea FTA has nearly identical wording with the TPP,[23] and is mostly similar to the CETA.[24] Concerning special formalities and information requirements, the China–Korea FTA also find parallels in the TPP.[25] The CETA has a concise provision on formal requirements,[26] but omits the provision on special formalities connected with a covered investment in the TPP and the China–Korea FTA.[27] In terms of subrogation, the positions of these three agreements are alike, but the China–Korea FTA sets out more detailed rules than the CETA and the TPP.[28]

On the other hand, the ChAFTA markedly differs from the China–Korea FTA regarding investment protection, and is unique concerning the heavy reliance on non-discrimination clauses, particularly the MFN treatment obligation. The ChAFTA incorporates only limited investment treatment provisions (mainly national treatment and MFN treatment), and contains the explicit plan to address most remaining issues in future negotiations (e.g. the minimum standard of treatment, expropriation, transfers, performance requirements, senior management, and board of directors[29]). On the one side, the ChAFTA MFN treatment provision covers pre-establishment and post-establishment phase, and enables investors to benefit from better treatment under future agreements.[30] This MFN provision does not exclude all the FTAs from its scope as does the China–Korea FTA.[31] Only the treatment to investors under 'bilateral or multilateral international agreement' in force before the effective date of the ChAFTA, including their subsequent review or amendment, are excluded from the MFN.[32] As with the China–New Zealand FTA,[33] it ensures that investors and investment in the free trade area will benefit from the treatment under future agreements concluded by the treaty parties. These agreements should include the US–China and China–EU BITs, if everything goes smoothly. On the other side, the ChAFTA lacks provisions such as FET obligation that is most commonly invoked by investors in the ISDS proceedings. The ChAFTA works with the China–Australia BIT regarding investment protection. Although the BIT entered into force in 1988 and is out-of-date, it provides for, among other things, FET,[34] expropriation,[35] transfers,[36] and the adherence to written undertakings given to investors.[37]

The ChAFTA rules will probably converge with deep FTAs concerning investment protection. The MFN treatment provision, which the ChAFTA depends crucially on, and Australian commitments on national treatment already bear close resemblance to

---

[18] ibid art 12.5.1;TPP art 9.6.1.   [19] China–Canada BIT art 4.1 (2014).
[20] China–Japan–Korea Investment Agreement art 5.1 (2012).
[21] China–Korea FTA art 12.9 (2015); China–New Zealand FTA art 145.
[22] TPP art 9.8; CETA art 8.12.
[23] China–Korea FTA Annex 12-B, para 3 (2015); TPP Annex 9-B, para 3.
[24] CETA Annex 8-A.   [25] China–Korea FTA art 12.13 (2015); TPP art 9.14.
[26] CETA art 8.17.   [27] China–Korea FTA art 12.13.1 (2015); TPP art 9.14.1.
[28] China–Korea FTA (2015); CETA art 8.14; TPP art 9.13.
[29] ChAFTA art 9.9.3(b) (2015).   [30] ibid art 9.4.1.
[31] China–Korea FTA art 12.4.2(a) (2015).   [32] ChAFTA art 9.4.3 (2015).
[33] China–New Zealand FTA art 139.1, 139.3.
[34] China–Australia BIT art III(a) (1988).   [35] ibid art VIII.   [36] ibid art X.
[37] ibid art XI.

the TPP counterpart.[38] Moreover, Australia is a TPP party, and China's another recent agreement with Korea is close to the TPP in investment protection. All these factors lay the foundation for the possible convergence.

China's FTAs rarely deal with investment liberalization on the part of China, which contrasts with the US approach. This finding also holds true for China's investment treaties. The 2012 China–Canada BIT, as one of the most recent of China's BITs, lacks a commitment to investment liberalization.[39] As with China's FTAs with Australia and Korea, the China–ASEAN FTA focuses on investment protection rather than investment protection and liberalization in Japan's EPAs with single ASEAN members.[40] Even though the ChAFTA contains basic market access provisions, most of them deal with the obligations of Australia. China's FTAs neither include investment schedules of China nor contain the provision on market access in FTAs as the case with the CETA.[41]

In China's FTAs, national treatment obligations only apply to the post-establishment stage of investment. In the ChAFTA, China's national treatment obligations do not extend to 'establishment, acquisition' or 'the establishment or acquisition of a new, separate investment'.[42] The absence of these terms avoids market access obligations, partially because investment liberalization involves challenging regulatory issues. In contrast, some of China's FTAs oblige parties to provide MFN treatment at pre-establishment and post-establishment stages, including China's FTAs with the ASEAN[43] and Australia.[44] However, these MFN treatment clauses do not impose stringent requirements regarding investment liberalization.

That said, China is progressively heading towards investment liberalization, possibly first in the US–China BIT and China's agreements with advanced economies and then in other FTAs. Overall, such plan focuses on a pre-establishment national treatment on the basis of a negative list. The move appears to be primarily driven by the US–China BIT negotiations, in which China recently offered more open negative list offer than in FTZs regarding several key sectors (e.g. banking, securities, insurance, telecommunications, culture, internet, and autos).[45] Moreover, China is moving towards investment liberalization by the amendment of the municipal law to promote the negative list approach,[46] and the development prospect of China's FTAs with Australia and Korea. For the latter, a key component of the ChAFTA forward work programme is China's commitments on market access, which may be connected with US–China BIT negotiations. In the future, national treatment obligations under China's FTA investment rules will extend from established investments to the pre-establishment stage. Meanwhile, the design of negative list needs to be addressed, which remains a crucial issue in the US–China BIT negotiations.

[38] ChAFTA arts 9.3, 9.4 (2015);TPP arts 9.4, 9.5.
[39] Axel Berger, 'Investment Rules in Chinese Preferential Trade and Investment Agreements: Is China following the global trend towards comprehensive agreements?' https://www.die-gdi.de/uploads/media/DP_7.2013.pdf.
[40] Julien Chaisse, 'The Shifting Tectonics of International Investment Law – Structure and Dynamics of Rules and Arbitration on Foreign Investment in the Asia-Pacific Region' (2015) 47 George Washington International Law Review 563, 615–16.
[41] CETA art 8.4.   [42] ChAFTA art 9.3.2, n 1 (2015).
[43] China–ASEAN Investment Agreement art 5.1 (2009).
[44] ChAFTA art 9.4.1 (2015).
[45] Yuanan Zhang, 'Wang Yang: Sino-US Cooperation is the Only Right Choice' *Caixin* (2016) http://international.caixin.com/2016-11-23/101010192.html.
[46] Xinhua, 'China revises inbound investment laws' (2016).

Why might China move towards investment liberalization? First, as probably the most important reason, investment liberalization will benefit Chinese overseas investment. As a major capital importer and exporter, China has balanced and neutral interests regarding outbound and inbound investment. In fact, China's businesses investing overseas have repeatedly called for the Chinese government to incorporate the pre-establishment national treatment into the investment treaty.[47] The FTAs of China may need to respond more efficiently to the needs of businesses participating in the global value chain. Secondly, investment liberalization helps to attract foreign investment and boost investor confidence in China, which is crucial for economic development. Last but not least, investment liberalization may facilitate domestic reform in China.

III. Increased Malleability of China's Investment Rules: Regulatory Autonomy and ISDS

Compared with other investment norms, more malleability of China's investment rules could be found in regulatory autonomy and ISDS. Relevant provisions are rather different between China's trade pacts with Australia and Korea, although overall they take a similar approach to investment and were signed on the same date.

More malleability can be seen concerning regulatory autonomy in China's recent FTAs, although they converge with the TPP and CETA regarding basic safeguards to retain policy space. The theme of investment rules remains the balance between the investment protection and the right to regulate.[48] The increased malleability is understandable in the sense that the deference to regulatory autonomy is easy to be accepted by governments as they provide regulators with more room. Like other trade agreements, the ChAFTA strives to protect regulatory space through provisions on general exceptions, non-conforming measures, and the denial of benefits.[49] Taking the provision on denial of benefits as an example, the ChAFTA has an identical provision with the TPP,[50] and the China–Korea FTA also takes a similar position. These FTAs are essentially alike by mainly targeting shell companies and the investor that is an enterprise owned or controlled by persons of a non-party or the denying party.[51] The denial of benefits provision is utilized to avoid forum shopping through establishing shell companies.[52] Moreover, these agreements explicitly address the circumvention of the measures adopted by the denying party.[53] The CETA adopts a similar approach to the denial of benefits but adds the consideration for the maintenance of international peace and security.[54] Despite these similarities, more malleability is evident regarding regulatory autonomy.

---

[47] Xiantao Wen, 'Review of China's Model Investment Protection Treaty (Draft): Part I' (2012) 18 Chinese Journal of International Economic Law 172.

[48] For the analysis of regulatory space see eg Markus Wagner, 'Regulatory Space in International Trade Law and International Investment Law' (2014) 36 University of Pennsylvania Journal of International Law 1.

[49] On the scope and meaning of general exceptions see Julien Chaisse, 'Exploring the Confines of International Investment and Domestic Health Protections: General exceptions clause as a forced perspective' (2013) 39(2–3) American Journal of Law & Medicine 332.

[50] ChAFTA art 9.6 (2015); TPP art 9.7.

[51] ChAFTA art 9.6.1 (2015); China–Korea FTA art 12.15.2 (2015); TPP art 9.15.1.

[52] China–Korea FTA art 12.15 (2015); ChAFTA art 9.6 (2015); TPP art 9.15.1(b).

[53] ChAFTA art 9.6 (2015); China–Korea FTA art 12.15.1(b) (2015); TPP art 9.15.2.

[54] CETA art 8.16(b)(i).

The China–Korea FTA provides a weaker safeguard for the right to regulate than the ChAFTA. The China–Korea FTA is more alike to the TPP, and both only recognize the right to regulate regarding narrow or isolated issues (indirect expropriation or few performance requirements). In contrast, the ChAFTA is closer to the CETA, and they defer more to regulatory autonomy than the China–Korea FTA and TPP. Compared with the China–Korea FTA, the CETA contains stronger safeguards for the right to regulate for legitimate policy objectives,[55] clarifies that regulatory change does not establish a breach of investment protection obligation,[56] and includes an exemption of changes of subsidies from the investment protection obligation.[57] As discussed below, the ChAFTA contains rules that are more advanced (e.g. the public welfare notice) or favourable (e.g. the broad exclusion of measures from ISDS) regarding regulatory space.

The ChAFTA is much stronger than other Chinese FTAs in preserving regulatory autonomy, some of which are innovative. To safeguard the right to regulate, it provides for the narrow scope of the ISDS mechanism and the related public welfare notice, as well as the governing law of the ISDS.

A wide range of claims are excluded from ISDS under the ChAFTA, which involves investment screening, regulatory measures, subsidies, and grants. Among them, claims related to foreign investment screening, such as the review by the Foreign Investment Review Board (FIRB), are exempted from the ISDS mechanism.[58] The ChAFTA further stipulates that subsidies or grants provided by treaty parties fall outside the scope of its investment chapter.[59] In the same context, the China–Korea FTA only excludes current measures concerning subsidies or grants from the application of treatment for the cases of civil strife,[60] and they should be subject to other investment rules.

As a carve-out for regulatory measures, non-discriminatory measures for legitimate public welfare objectives (i.e. health, safety, environment, public morals, or order) are not subject to the ISDS claims under the ChAFTA.[61] If the respondent deems that its disputed measure falls within such carve-out, it could deliver a notice elaborating the basis for its position to the claimant and non-disputing parties, which is referred to as the public welfare notice.[62] Significantly, the public welfare notice serves as an important safeguard for regulatory autonomy and is absent in China's previous FTAs. This notice will lead to ninety-day consultation between the respondent and the non-disputing party, during which the dispute resolution procedure will be suspended.[63] If the FTA parties decide that the challenged measure falls within the scope of the exception, the decision is binding on the ISDS tribunal regarding its decision or award.[64] Neither the non-issuance of a public welfare notice nor the absence of a joint decision by the treaty parties lends support to the tribunal for the adverse inference.[65] As an important and novel safeguard for regulatory space, the public welfare notice grants more control to governments and evokes more deference to public interests when warranted. Therefore, the support of the home country will be necessary for the claimant in such context as both governments may block the ISDS claims.

Relating to this, the ChAFTA goes beyond the China–Korea FTA, CETA, and TPP concerning regulatory autonomy in relation to expropriation and performance requirements. All of these other agreements exempt non-discriminatory regulatory measures for lawful public welfare objectives (e.g. public health, safety, and environment) from

[55] ibid art 8.9.1. [56] ibid art 8.9.2. [57] ibid art 8.9.3.
[58] ChAFTA Summary of Chapters and Annexes (2015). [59] ibid art 9.2.3(b) (2015).
[60] China–Korea FTA art 12.5.6 (2015). [61] ChAFTA art 9.11.4 (2015).
[62] ibid art 9.11.5. [63] ibid art 9.11.6. [64] ibid art 9.18.3.
[65] ibid art 9.11.8.

the indirect expropriation obligation.⁶⁶ The TPP also exempts these measures from
certain performance requirements with the conditions similar to the chapeau of the
GATT provision on general exceptions.⁶⁷ In contrast, the ChAFTA does not provide
for expropriation and performance requirements, and investors, therefore, cannot rely
on these provisions against regulatory measures under the FTA.

Regarding governing law, the ChAFTA requires the ISDS arbitration tribunal to
take into account the law of the respondent when 'relevant and appropriate'.⁶⁸ One
may argue that domestic law may be the governing law and carry more weight in
supporting regulatory autonomy. Under the TPP, the national law of the respondent,
including rules on the conflict of laws, could be the applicable law when conditions are
met.⁶⁹ The national law of the respondent may be considered as a factual matter in the
TPP and CETA.⁷⁰ However, the China–Korea FTA and CETA do not have explicit
provisions regarding the domestic law of the respondent.

Moreover, China appears to be more accommodating of ISDS rules than other investment provisions (e.g. the standard of compensation for expropriation). More malleability is revealed in China's agreements with Australia and Korea. For the structure,
the ChAFTA attaches a lot of importance to the ISDS stipulations and devotes one of
the two sections on investment to the ISDS, while the China–Korea FTA only contains one article on the ISDS. For specific obligations, the ChAFTA sets more detailed
rules for (e.g. the code of conduct for arbitrators) and stricter limits on (including a
public welfare notice) arbitration tribunals.⁷¹ The flexibility can be found in both technical (e.g. the consolidation of ISDS proceedings) and fundamental (such as treaty
parties' control on ISDS) provisions on investment dispute settlement.

Foremost, compared with the China–Korea FTA, the ChAFTA ensures that treaty
parties get more control over the ISDS through, inter alia, the scope of the claims, the
selection and disciplines of the arbitrators, as well as the interpretation and guidance
by treaty parties. Most of them are absent or less developed in the China–Korea FTA.

Arbitration claims under the ChAFTA are limited to the violation of national treat-
ment.⁷² It narrows the basis for the ISDS claim, and such limitation is absent in China's
FTAs with Korea and New Zealand,⁷³ the CETA,⁷⁴ and the TPP.⁷⁵ Concerning investment rule interpretation, the parties to the ChAFTA may take the initiative in
interpreting rules or interpret rules upon request. The ChAFTA parties could issue
a joint decision to declare their interpretation of the FTA provision, which will bind
the ISDS tribunals in ongoing and future cases.⁷⁶ On request of the respondent, the
tribunal shall seek the interpretation of annexes by the parties regarding whether a
challenged measure fits with the scope of an entry in Section A or B of its schedule of
non-conforming measures in Annex III.⁷⁷ The interpretation will be made in the form
of a joint decision within 90 days after the request from the tribunal.⁷⁸ Such interpretation is binding on the tribunal in current and future cases.⁷⁹ The China–Korea FTA
does not provide for such interpretation, under which the Joint Commission may 'seek

---

⁶⁶ China–Korea FTA Annex 12-B, para 3(b) (2015); TPP Annex 9-B, para 3(b); CETA Annex
8-A, para 3.
⁶⁷ TPP art 9.10.3(h).   ⁶⁸ ChAFTA art 9.18.1 (2015).   ⁶⁹ TPP art 9.25.2(b)(i).
⁷⁰ ibid art 9.25 n 34; CETA art 8.31.2.
⁷¹ See Julien Chaisse and Rahul Donde, 'The State of Investor-State Arbitration: A Reality Check
of the Issues, Trends, and Directions in Asia-Pacific' (2018) 51(1) The International Lawyer 47.
⁷² ChAFTA art 9.12.2 (2015).
⁷³ China–Korea FTA art 12.12.1, 12.12.3 (2015); China–New Zealand FTA arts 152, 153.
⁷⁴ CETA art 8.18.1.   ⁷⁵ TPP art 9.19.1.   ⁷⁶ ChAFTA art 9.18.2 (2015).
⁷⁷ ibid art 9.19.1.   ⁷⁸ ibid.   ⁷⁹ ibid art 9.19.2, 9.19.3.

to resolve differences that may arise regarding the interpretation or application of this Agreement'.[80] The interpretation of investment rules by the parties is possible under the TPP and CETA through a Trans-Pacific Partnership Commission[81] and the CETA Joint Committee.[82]

Notably, some of the ChAFTA stipulations are innovative, including the roster of arbitrators and the code of conduct for arbitrators.[83] Within two years after the effective date of the agreement, the ChAFTA Committee on Investment will establish a roster of ISDS arbitration panellists that consists of at least twenty individuals.[84] For such a panellist list, each country will select not less than five people and also jointly choose at least ten individuals as the tribunal chairperson who are not nationals of the ChAFTA countries.[85] The roster of arbitrators enables the treaty parties to choose ISDS adjudicators.

Secondly, the ChAFTA strives to rest the public concern over the ISDS process by providing more advanced stipulations than the China–Korea FTA. The focus seems to be transparency, the rules of interpretation, the consolidation of the ISDS arbitration proceedings, and the possible appeal system. The ChAFTA provides for the consolidation order for multiple claims with a common legal or factual issue or arising from the same events,[86] which seems to be absent in the China–Korea FTA. This rule helps to improve the efficiency, consistency, and predictability of the ISDS process.

As the ISDS procedure is criticized as being opaque, the ChAFTA emphasizes the transparency of the proceedings. Under the China–Canada BIT, the ISDS arbitration award must be publicly available.[87] The ChAFTA further requires the publicity of the consultation request, the notice of arbitration, as well as the orders, awards, and decisions of the ISDS tribunal.[88] Moreover, three categories of documents may be publicly available under the ChAFTA if certain conditions are met: (i) the disputing parties' pleadings, memorials, and briefs submitted to the tribunal, as well as written submissions presented in the consolidation of arbitration, (ii) minutes or transcripts of tribunal hearings, and (iii) written submissions by the non-disputing party.[89] More progress in this regard is envisaged. Both parties agree to, within one year of the entry into force of the FTA, consult on the application of the United Nations Commission on International Trade Law (UNCITRAL) Rules on Transparency in Treaty-based Investor–State Arbitration to ISDS arbitrations.[90]

For the rules of interpretation, the Vienna Convention on the Law of Treaties (Vienna Convention) will be utilized by the ChAFTA and CETA in ISDS[91] and the state-to-state dispute settlement (SSDS).[92] It helps to enhance the predictability of the interpretation. However, neither the TPP nor the China–Korea FTA refers to the Vienna Convention in its investment chapter. The interpretation rules in the Vienna Convention are only to be used by the panel to 'consider' the China–Korea FTA and the TPP in SSDS.[93]

The issue of the appeal system merits special attention on which the EU and US have significantly different positions. China may support the appeal system in ISDS. First, as a major economy, it is possible that a Chinese judge will serve in such an ISDS system, as is the case with the WTO dispute settlement system. Secondly, the appeal

[80] China–Korea FTA art 19.2.1(e) (2015). [81] TPP arts 9.25.3, 27.2.2(f).
[82] CETA art 8.31.3. [83] ChAFTA Annex 9-A (2015). [84] ibid art 9.15.5.
[85] ibid art 9.15.6. [86] ibid art 9.21. [87] China–Canada BIT art 28.1. 2014.
[88] ChAFTA art 9.17.2(a) (2015). [89] ibid art 9.17.2(b), 9.17.2(c).
[90] ibid Side Letter on Transparency Rules Applicable to Investor–State Dispute Settlement.
[91] ibid art 9.18.1; CETA art 8.31.1. [92] ChAFTA art 15.9.1 (2015); CETA art 29.17.
[93] China–Korea FTA art 20.11.3 (2015); TPP art 28.12.3.

system arguably helps to produce more predictable and consistent jurisprudence on investment law than is the case with ad hoc tribunals. Thirdly, the appeal system may be favoured by the governments as the appeal body judges are to be selected by treaty parties but not by the investors. Turning to the ChAFTA, it appears to lean towards the approach of the CETA on the possible ISDS appeal system. Within three years after the ChAFTA came into effect, the parties will commence negotiating the possible appellate review of legal issues in ISDS.[94] It may follow the path of the CETA on the ISDS appeal system. The China–Korea FTA does not mention the possibility of the ISDS appeal mechanism, and the TPP refers to the possible negotiations of such appeal arrangements if the appellate mechanism is developed elsewhere.[95]

Thirdly, the ChAFTA also strengthens investment protection through ISDS rules favouring investors in selected areas, which differs from the China–Korea FTA. It permits investors to seek interim injunctive relief in the judicial or administrative tribunal of the respondent.[96] The ChAFTA adopts nearly the same language as the TPP, except for subjecting it to domestic law by adding the condition of 'in accordance with the laws of the respondent'.[97] The CETA sets out interim measures of protection[98] with arguably similar effect. However, such provision is absent in the China–Korea FTA.

Furthermore, the ChAFTA does not allow for the domestic administrative review process that is permitted in China's FTAs with Korea and New Zealand. It enables the faster ISDS processes and favours investors. Under the China–Korea and China–New Zealand FTA, the responding party could require the investors to go through the domestic administrative review process before submitting to arbitration, and such review will take no longer than four months[99] or three months respectively.[100]

Last but not least, more malleability of ISDS rules in China's FTAs is attributable to various factors. For one thing, China's FTAs are exploring their model for the ISDS. China has limited disputes in the ISDS proceedings and has not encountered enormous challenges in this respect. Furthermore, China often relies on the proposals of FTA partners. It seems that the ISDS clauses are carefully drafted in the ChAFTA during the period when Australia became more cautious about the ISDS than before.

IV. China as a Rule Follower, Shaker, or Maker?

On the one hand, China has not been a dominant norm-maker concerning key investment clauses, and will probably remain as a rule shaker[101] in the short to medium term. China's FTAs are affected by FTA partners and seem to build on the partners' proposals. China's FTAs with Australia and Korea provide support for such argument. Regarding investment, the China–Korea FTA and ChAFTA appear to be affected, at least to some extent, by the KORUS and Australian approaches respectively. It is probably the reason why certain key investment rules in the ChAFTA substantially differ from the China–Korea FTA, including the lack of the FET obligation and the cautious attitude regarding investment protection enforceable through ISDS. Concerning ISDS, the ChAFTA is affected by the position of Australia, which has recently taken

[94] ChAFTA art 9.23 (2015).   [95] TPP art 9.23.11.
[96] ChAFTA art 9.14.4 (2015).   [97] TPP art 9.21.3.   [98] CETA art 8.34.
[99] China–Korea FTA art 12.12.7 (2015).   [100] China–New Zealand FTA art 153.2.
[101] The term 'rule shaker' has been used to describe the role of China in the world trade system. See Henry Gao, 'China's Ascent in Global Trade Governance: From Rule Taker to Rule Shaker, and Maybe Rule Maker?' Carolyn Deere-Birkbeck (ed), *Making Global Trade Governance Work for Development: Perspectives and Priorities from Developing Countries* (2011) 153–80.

a case-by-case approach.[102] In contrast, the China–Korea FTA resembles the TPP that is based on the KORUS. Furthermore, China's FTAs are not consistent in strong deference to regulatory space. Such deference could be seen in the ChAFTA (e.g. the public welfare notice, and domestic law possibly as governing law). It is probably attributable to the need for concluding the ChAFTA and to the concerns of Australia arising from investment disputes such as the tobacco plain package case. However, the China–Korea FTA is weaker in this respect and its investment rules are similar to those of the KORUS. In the same vein, China will probably be affected by the RCEP parties.

Its role as a rule shaker helps to explain why China has not formulated a consistent set of FTA investment clauses (e.g. ISDS, and regulatory autonomy). China's paradigm converges towards deep FTAs to a large extent, but detailed norms on investment protection (including the FET obligation) are affected by FTA partners. In spite of malleability, China's approaches to investment under FTAs with Korea and Australia are basically the same. Broadly speaking, investment stipulations of China's FTAs do not conflict with each other, and only differ in terms of their pace. The increasing level of investment protection in China's FTAs appears to be consistent. Investment liberalization is the major dissimilarity between China and developed economies (such as the US). However, such difference is to be narrowed through the US–China BIT negotiations if they go smoothly under the new US President. In any case, the negative list approach and the pre-establishment national treatment is expected to be explored in China's FTA upgrade with Australia and Korea.

On the other hand, China is not a rule follower. It has a cautious attitude about investment liberalization or 'intrusive' requirements, and modified or affected investment clauses when needed. These intrusive requirements involve, inter alia, state-owned enterprises (SOEs), labour, environment, and investments regarding cultural products. It seems that China prefers to progressively liberalize investment without unintended consequences.

China also demanded specific arrangements for investment issues in the FTAs. Under the ChAFTA, China demanded 'a more receptive investment environment'.[103] China secured specific arrangements in the ChAFTA to favour Chinese investment: the more liberal and higher FIRB screening threshold for non-SOE investment and the related labour mobility for Chinese workers. Regarding China's non-SOE investment in Australia, the investment screening threshold has been substantially lifted to 1.078 billion Australian dollars from 0.248 billion Australian dollars previously.[104] Moreover, the memorandum of understanding on an investment facilitation arrangement (IFA) is included in the ChAFTA. It facilitates the visa process under the IFAs,[105] which is the first one of this kind provided by a developed country to China.[106] This arrangement will help Chinese businesses to access the Australian market.

In the long run, China has the potential to be a major norm-maker in investment if properly managed. First, there is an increasingly strong need to shape investment rules to protect China's outbound investment and explore overseas markets. Investment clauses may take the lead in shaping China's possible FTA model. China is reported to

---

[102] Feldman and others (n 16) 6.

[103] Lingling He, 'Reassessing the China-Australia Free Trade Agreement Negotiation Process' (2015) 10 *Frontiers of Law in China* 714, 721.

[104] China FTA Network, *A Reading of the Free Trade Agreement between the Government of Australia and the Government of the People's Republic of China* (2016) http://fta.mofcom.gov.cn/article/chinaaustralia/chinaaustralianews/201506/22176_1.html.

[105] ChAFTA MOU on an Investment Facilitation Arrangement 2015, paras 8–11.

[106] China FTA Network (2016).

have become the globally top net capital exporter in 2015.[107] This fact illustrates why China's investment norms in international agreements evolve rapidly. It is in China's interests to call for high-level investment clauses. Therefore, China sometimes takes an approach to investment that differs from developing countries. Such approach involves key issues such as ISDS,[108] and is closer to that of developed economies.

Secondly, the potential role as a rule-maker is possible given that investment norms are the fastest developing area of China's FTAs, and that capacity building develops fast on the part of China. Taking the ChAFTA as an example, it arguably makes more innovations in investment than other areas if one compares it with China's older trade pacts. Moreover, China will probably develop a stronger capacity in investment than other areas of FTAs, owing to frequent participation in investment agreement talks. More importantly, some of the negotiations are high-level and deep (i.e. the BIT negotiations with the US and EU), qualities which are absent in other areas of FTAs. BIT negotiations with major economies (e.g. the US, EU, and Japan), and FTA negotiations with various partners under the framework of a bilateral or mega FTA help the capacity building of China.

Finally, challenges still exist for China, and open issues remain to be addressed. In the near future, China's role may not be as a rule-maker, but could change from selective adaption to selective innovation. Such targeted innovation may first occur in high-level investment agreements and particularly the US–China BIT.

For one thing, China will need the strong support of major economies, both developing and developed ones, to lead the shaping of new investment norms. It may be a challenging job to convince the partners. Furthermore, it remains to be seen whether China is prepared to accept stringent or sensitive investment stipulations (e.g. SOEs, and labour). Open questions in China's investment clauses include performance requirements, investment review by the host country, the appeal system in the ISDS, environment, labour, and SOEs. Regulatory uncertainty and barriers may exist in these aspects. For instance, the TPP chapter on SOEs and designated monopolies applies concerning the activities of these enterprises that affect 'investment between Parties within the free trade area'.[109] China's FTA investment rules have not dealt with SOE issues. Even when some of these matters are to be addressed, it may take a soft law approach such as hortatory language on the environmental issue in the China–Korea FTA.[110] However, the SOE and other thorny or 'intrusive' issues are not likely to be the major subject in the RCEP negotiations, owing to the different interests of RCEP parties.

V. China's FTA Approach to Investment and the RCEP

The RCEP is unique in several aspects. Firstly, the RCEP is special to China as the only mega FTA in which China is involved. For geopolitical considerations, China may strive to prioritize the conclusion of the RCEP rather than setting demanding requirements. China could have more incentives to compromise on the RCEP, since it enables market access to a larger number of countries than bilateral agreement and may bring

---

[107] 'China becomes world's top net capital exporter' (2016) www.atimes.com/article/china-becomes-worlds-top-net-capital-exporter/.
[108] Investment rules of China's recent FTA are dissimilar from India's recent BIT model. For instance, the exhaustion of remedies requirement in India's BIT model cannot be found in the ChAFTA.
[109] TPP art 17.2.1.   [110] China–Korea FTA art 12.16 (2015).

broader geopolitical effects. After the fall of the TPP, this could be the major incentive for China to move further with the RCEP, which will shape and mold the relationship with countries that otherwise would have been part of the TPP.

Secondly, the RCEP investment rules will probably be in a unique position given the existence of prior agreements. China has FTAs with the ASEAN, Australia, New Zealand and Korea, all of which contain investment clauses. Moreover, BITs often also exist between China and these RCEP parties (e.g. Australia and Korea), and China also concluded a FTA with Singapore, a founding country of the ASEAN. For the rest of the RCEP countries (i.e. Japan and India), there are China–Japan–Korea and China–India investment treaties, which entered into force in 2014 and 2007 respectively. From the perspective of China, a number of generally recent agreements[111] already exist between China and all other RCEP parties on a bilateral basis to deal with investment issues. The existing stockpile of investment rules could constitute 'Plan B', even if the RCEP does not contain detailed clauses on investment.

Thirdly, China appears to be more flexible in FTA negotiations with the ASEAN than other partners, and the ASEAN seems to lead the RCEP negotiations. Arguably it is basically because of geopolitical considerations. The ASEAN seems to lead the negotiations of the RCEP, which is supported by China.[112] China has been quite flexible with the ASEAN in the China–ASEAN FTA, which is one of China's earliest trade pacts. Besides Pakistan, China has only granted the ASEAN full post-establishment national treatment of investment in its old FTAs.[113] Additionally, the China–ASEAN FTA is the only FTA for which China used an 'enabling clause' of the WTO to ensure the WTO consistency of a lower standard FTA with developing countries.[114]

On the one hand, the RCEP may contain low-level or moderate investment norms. In the short term, China's approach to investment will probably remain the same concerning the malleability of investment protection, regulatory autonomy, and ISDS. However, China is unlikely to take strict investment liberalization obligations under the RCEP. Given the uniqueness of the mega FTA, China's flexibility for the ASEAN and the existence of 'back-up' agreements, China will probably facilitate the conclusion of the pact rather than demand stringent rules. Concerning investment, the RCEP will 'aim at creating a liberal, facilitative, and competitive investment environment in the region' and its investment negotiations are to cover 'the four pillars of promotion, protection, facilitation and liberalization'.[115] Owing to the different interests of the parties, the RCEP could eventually focus on investment protection rather than investment liberalization.

On the other hand, the RCEP could adopt an early harvest approach with future upgrades. China has common ground with other RCEP parties, and China's FTAs are mostly consistent with the general principles and objectives of the RCEP (including the facilitation of investment and the enhancement of transparency in investment relations[116]). Such efforts could be found in the ChAFTA in facilitating investment and

---

[111] The exception includes the China–Australia BIT, which came into force in 1988.

[112] Hucheng Gao, *Support the ASEAN to Lead RCEP Negotiations* (2016) http://fta.mofcom.gov.cn/article/fzdongtai/201608/32899_1.html.

[113] Nargiza Salidjanova, 'China's Trade Ambitions: Strategy and Objectives behind China's Pursuit of Free Trade Agreements' (2015) U.S.-China Economic and Security Review Commission Staff Research Report 18.

[114] ibid 21.

[115] 'Guiding Principles and Objectives for Negotiating the Regional Comprehensive Economic Partnership' http://dfat.gov.au/trade/agreements/rcep/Documents/guiding-principles-rcep.pdf.

[116] ibid.

increasing the transparency of ISDS. China could find common ground on investment with other RCEP parties based on existing agreements, since investment or trade agreements have been concluded between China and these parties. Among the parties, the ASEAN seems to lead the RCEP negotiations, and the viewpoints reflected in China's recent investment treaty practice are largely congruous with the ASEAN practice.[117]

Thorny issues could be addressed at a later stage (e.g. the market access obligations for developing countries), and a forward work programme may be provided in the RCEP. Such an arrangement will be useful in concluding the mega FTA at an early date, while leaves the possibility for its upgrade. In other words, there is a second chance to negotiate the FTAs. However, the upgrade of mega FTA will be much harder than bilateral ones given a large number of countries involved and their different positions. That said, the upgrades of FTAs also give China and other parties more flexibility to chart its course.

The early harvest approach and upgrade arrangement are not rare for China's FTAs. In contrast, the FTAs of the US and EU do not usually upgrade despite such possibilities. The China–ASEAN FTA is the first upgraded FTA of China, but it contains limited progress regarding rule development. The China–Korea FTA provides for the plan of subsequent investment negotiations. The ChAFTA investment clauses also adopt a two-stage approach: early harvest commitments and a future work programme (e.g. expropriation, performance requirements). The ChAFTA parties agree on 'a review of the investment legal framework between them' within three years after the pact enters into force,[118] and will eventually start negotiating on a 'comprehensive' investment chapter.[119] Therefore, the ChAFTA allows treaty parties to negotiate piecemeal for more investment liberalization. The ChAFTA model may be adopted for the RCEP as a work-in-progress type investment chapter. As the case with the ChAFTA, one possible arrangement under the RCEP could be that developed countries but not developing countries commit to market access provisions (e.g. pre-establishment national treatment obligations) at the very beginning.

VI. Conclusion

Primarily, the malleability of China's FTA will probably expand from investment protection to investment liberalization, and increased malleability of China's recent FTAs exists in regulatory autonomy and ISDS. This is because China's FTAs are largely adapted to the need of trading partners. China's recent agreements with Australia and Korea are seen as having a high degree of malleability. Overall, China's approach to investment protection is similar to deep FTAs with some exceptions (e.g. performance requirements, the standard of compensation in expropriation, the scope of MFN treatment, and the scope of ISDS claims).

Generally, China is willing substantially to improve rules and embrace newer style investment stipulations. As a typical example, the US–China BIT negotiations reflect China's new development of investment liberalization. The ChAFTA contains innovative safeguards of regulatory autonomy and ISDS procedural features (including the roster of arbitration panellists, the public welfare notice, the code of conduct for arbitrators, and the joint interpretation of the annex by treaty parties).

---

[117] Feldman and others (n 16) 9.   [118] ChAFTA art 9.9.1 (2015).
[119] ibid art 9.9.3.

Secondly, China will probably be a rule-shaker in the short to medium term, and possibly become a rule-maker in the long term. Its approach may evolve from selective adaption to targeted innovation. The reason is plain as China will be increasingly active in the development of investment norms owing to the need to protect its outbound investment and enhance investor confidence in inbound investment. As a rule-shaker in the RCEP negotiations, China will often modify proposals of partners rather than offer a new set of clauses. The malleability of China's FTAs will probably continue in the RCEP.

Finally, the RCEP investment rules will possibly be low-level ones with an early harvest approach. It is attributable to, among other things, the unique nature of mega FTA, the 'stockpile' of existing investment agreements, and China's approach to the ASEAN. All these factors mean that China will probably take a more flexible stance in the RCEP than in bilateral FTAs. In any event, the RCEP will affect the shaping of China's FTA approach to investment.

14

Towards an Asia-Pacific Regional Investment Regime

The Potential Influence of Australia and New Zealand as a Collective Middle Power

*Amokura Kawharu and Luke Nottage**

I. Introduction

China's approach towards investment rule-making at the regional level is influenced by a number of initiatives and actors that also contribute to the design of the investment regime in the broader Asia-Pacific region. In the regional track, China effectively competes with, and therefore has to be compared with, alternative models existing or emerging for investment treaties. This chapter instead considers one model embedded within a transnational regime for economic integration more broadly that adopts the following institutional features:

- Virtually free trade in goods and services, including a 'mutual recognition' system whereby compliance with regulatory requirements in one jurisdiction (such as qualifications to practice law or requirements when offering securities) basically means exemption from compliance with regulations in the other jurisdiction. Further, for some sensitive areas such as food safety, there is a trans-national regulator.
- Virtually free movement of capital, underpinned by private sector and governmental initiatives.
- Free movement of people, with permanent residence available to nationals from the other jurisdiction—not tied to securing employment.
- Treaties for regulatory cooperation, simple enforcement of judgments (a court ruling in one jurisdiction being treated virtually identically to a ruling of a local court), and to avoid double taxation (including a system for taxpayer-initiated arbitration among the member states).
- Inter-state commitments to harmonize business law more widely, for example for consumer and competition law.

* Respectively, Associate Professor, University of Auckland Faculty of Law; Professor, University of Sydney Law School. We thank Kirsten Gan for exceptional research and editorial assistance. Professor Nottage acknowledges support from an Australian Research Council Discovery Project (DP140102526).

No, we are not referring to the European Union (EU), or even aspects of the Association of Southeast Asian Nations (ASEAN) Economic Community—largely achieved by the end of 2015.[1] Instead, the aspects listed above characterize the Trans-Tasman framework built up between Australia and New Zealand, particularly over the last two decades. Much of this bilateral economic integration has been achieved by non-treaty means, including labour mobility and mutual recognition of goods (through parallel legislation in both countries) and business law harmonization (through loose memorandums of understanding). Occasionally it even involves unilateral abrogation of national sovereignty (as with New Zealand legislation recognizing video/game classifications from Australia).[2]

Yet the growing economic integration has also been underpinned by treaties binding at international law. Both countries, with comparatively small economies (and populations) historically dependent on agricultural product exports,[3] have long been supporters of multi-lateral trade liberalization initiatives. They were leaders of the 'Cairns Group', comprising mainly developing countries, during the Uruguay Round from 1986 that resulted in the creation of the World Trade Organization (WTO) in 1994.[4] Australia and New Zealand were also active users of the WTO's new and more effective inter-state dispute settlement system, as illustrated by Figure 14.1 below.[5] However, Australia did not bring a WTO claim for fifteen years, until proceedings initiated in 2018 against Canada over wine exports, and Australia did not join New Zealand in its 2013 claim that successfully established discrimination and other WTO violations by Indonesia concerning an array of agricultural products.[6]

---

[1] See generally Tham Siew Yean and Sanchita Basu Das, 'Introduction: Economic Interests and the ASEAN Economic Community' in Tham Siew Yean and Sanchita Basu Das (eds), *Moving the AEC Beyond 2015: Managing Domestic Consensus for Community-Building* (ISEAS Publishing 2016) 1–23.

[2] Luke Nottage, 'Asia-Pacific Regional Architecture and Consumer Product Regulation Beyond Free Trade Agreements' in Susy Frankel and Meredith Lewis (eds), *Trade Agreements at the Crossroads* (Routledge 2014) 114–39.

[3] See generally for Australia: www.dfat.gov.au/about-australia/land-its-people/Pages/economy.aspx and https://www.cia.gov/library/publications/the-world-factbook/geos/as.html; and for New Zealand: http://dfat.gov.au/trade/resources/Documents/nz.pdf and https://www.cia.gov/library/publications/the-world-factbook/geos/nz.html (all last accessed 9 December 2016).

[4] See generally Amrita Narlikar, *International Trade and Developing Countries: Bargaining and Coalitions in the GATT and WTO* (Routledge 2003) and eg Gabrielle Marceau, Interview with the former Secretary of Foreign Affairs for New Zealand www.wtocreation.org/en/videos?video=31933652 (last accessed 9 December 2016).

[5] Source: World Trade Organization, 'Disputes by Country/Territory' www.wto.org/english/tratop_e/dispu_e/dispu_by_country_e.htm (as of and last accessed 9 December 2016).

[6] *Request for Consultations, Australia: Measures Governing the Sale of Wine*, WT/D5337/1 (16 January 2018); *Request for Consultations, Indonesia - Importation of Horticultural Products, Animals and Animal Products*, WT/DS466/1 (30 August 2013); and *Request for Consultations, Indonesia-Importation of Horticultural Products, Animals and Animal Products*, WT/DS477/1 (8 May 2014). Australia probably did not join New Zealand's claim because of broader diplomatic tensions with Indonesia, and the possibility (as a larger exporter, eg for beef) of negotiating anyway some informal dispute resolution or free-riding on the outcomes from the WTO proceedings. New Zealand also eventually brought a successful WTO claim against Australia regarding its discriminatory measures concerning apple imports: *Panel Report, Australia-Measures Affecting the Importation of Applies from New Zealand*, WT/DS367/R (9 August 2010) and *Appellate Body Report, Australia-Measures Affecting the Importation of Apples from New Zealand*, WT/DS367/AB/R (29 November 2010).

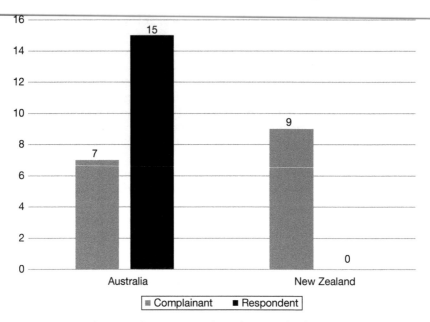

Figure 14.1 WTO dispute settlement—Australia and New Zealand

However, after it became clear from around 2000 that further liberalization was not going to be readily forthcoming through the WTO, both countries also started to expand their bilateral and regional free trade agreement (FTA) programmes. They had already the signed a Closer Economic Relations (CER) FTA in 1983 for trade in goods, when it was unclear what the future held for multilateral initiatives, and this was supplemented by a bilateral treaty for mutual recognition of services signed in 1988.[7] Australia and New Zealand added bilateral FTAs from the early 2000s, beginning with Singapore, as indicated in Figure 14.2 below:[8]

---

[7] Australia–New Zealand Closer Economic Relations Trade Agreement, Canberra, 28 March 1983, in force 1 January 1983, [1983] ATS 2; Protocol on Trade in Services to the Australia–New Zealand Closer Economic Relations Trade Agreement, Canberra, 18 August 1988, in force 1 January 1989, [1988] ATS 20.

[8] Source: Claudia Salomon and Sandra Friedrich, 'Investment Arbitration in East Asia and the Pacific: A Statistical Analysis of Bilateral Investment Treaties, Other International Investment Agreements and Investment Arbitrations in the Region' (2015) 16 JWIT 800; and UNCTAD, 'International Investment Agreements Navigator' *Investment Policy Hub* www.investmentpolicyhub.unctad.org/IIA (last accessed 9 December 2016). Years in which the first ISDS claims were filed are derived from: *Mobil Oil Corp v Her Majesty the Queen in Right of New Zealand*, Findings on Liability, Interpretation and Allied Issues, ICSID ARB/87/2, 4 May 1989; *Misima Mines Pty Ltd v Independent State of Papua New Guinea*, Discontinued, ICSID No ARB/96/2, 14 May 2001; *White Industries Australia Ltd v Republic of India*, Final Award, UNCITRAL, 30 November 2011; *Philip Morris Asia Ltd (Hong Kong) v The Commonwealth of Australia*, Award on Jurisdiction and Admissibility, PCA 2012-12, 17 December 2015.

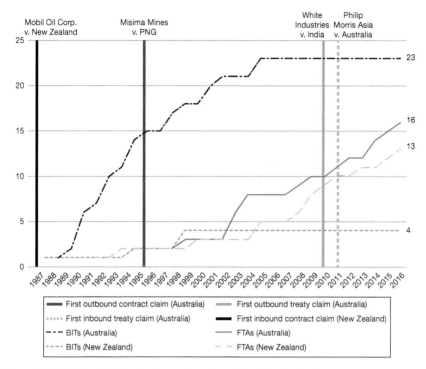

Figure 14.2 BITs and FTAs signed over time Australia v New Zealand

Yet this shared commitment to economic liberalization is quite recent. Over much of the 20th century, both countries were renowned for their strong welfare states, and high levels of tariffs and regulation. It was only from the mid-1980s, under the Lange Labour Government (1984–1990) and *laissez-faire* 'Rogernomics' in New Zealand, as well as the Hawke–Keating Labor Governments in Australia (1983–1996),[9] that both countries began deregulating and opening up their economies—typically unilaterally, as urged by neoclassical economists. Both countries promoted a similar approach in other economies in the region by actively supporting the Asia-Pacific Economic Forum (APEC) initiative from 1989.[10]

Inbound foreign direct investment (FDI) burgeoned as a result, especially from Australia into New Zealand (e.g. into the banking sector).[11] Yet national regulation

[9] See generally Shaun Goldfinch, *Remaking New Zealand and Australian Economic Policy: Ideas, Institutions and Policy Communities* (Georgetown University Press 2000); and Jane Kelsey, *The New Zealand Experiment: A World Model for Structural Adjustment?* (Pluto Press 1995).

[10] Rawdon Dalrymple, *Continental Drift: Australia's Search for a Regional Identity* (Ashgate 2003). The APEC legacy remains apparent in the policy advice in 2010 from the Productivity Commission and in the work of economists from the Australian National University: eg Shiro Armstrong and Peter Drysdale, 'The Influence of Economics and Politics on the Structure of World Trade and Investment Flows' in Shiro Armstrong (ed), *The Politics and the Economics of Integration in Asia and the Pacific* (Routledge 2011).

[11] Bill Rosenberg, 'Foreign Investment in New Zealand: The Current Position' in Peter Enderwick (ed), *Foreign Investment: The New Zealand Experience* (The Dunmore Press 1997) 24–32 and 40–1.

has remained relatively strict. According to the FDI Regulatory Restrictiveness Index compiled by the Organization for Economic Cooperation and Development (OECD), in 2015 Australia scored 0.14 overall (similar to Canada, Korea, and Russia), while New Zealand scored 0.24 (similar to India).[12]

New Zealand has also been more cautious about signing bilateral investment treaties (BITs, as evident in Figure 14.2 above). Australia's higher flows and stocks of outbound FDI[13] have been paralleled by a more active BIT programme, including many counterparties in the Asia region. Both countries have more similar programmes for FTAs, overwhelmingly concentrated on the Asia-Pacific region, where their main trade and investment relationships have existed for two decades.[14] Content-wise, their FTAs are also similar in balancing investment protections and liberalizations with substantive and procedural safeguards, influenced by the post-2002 US treaty practice,[15] which made it easier for both to join with ten other Asia-Pacific economies (including the US) in signing the Trans-Pacific Partnership (TPP) FTA on 4 February 2016, and then the renamed Comprehensive and Progressive Agreement for Trans-Pacific Partnership (CPTPP) on 8 March 2018 (excluding the US, under the Trump Administration). Australia and New Zealand also signed an FTA with ASEAN in 2009 (AANZFTA) and a bilateral investment protocol to CER in 2011 (CER Investment Protocol),[16] and have been negotiating the 'ASEAN+6' Regional Comprehensive Partnership (RCEP) FTA since late 2012.[17] Australia has also been negotiating bilateral FTAs with Indonesia and India, both of which have recently been reviewing their stances on investment treaties.[18]

---

[12] OECD, 'FDI Regulatory Restrictiveness Index' www.oecd.org/investment/fdiindex.htm (last accessed 9 December 2016).

[13] See Amokura Kawharu and Luke Nottage, 'Models for Investment Treaties in the Asian Region: An Underview' (2017) 34(3) *Arizona Journal of International and Comparative Law* 462, with a manuscript version at https://ssrn.com/abstract=2845088 (last accessed 9 December 2016). The present chapter adapts and updates the latter half of that work.

[14] For a listing of BITs in both countries see www.investmentpolicyhub.unctad.org/IIA/CountryBits/11 and www.investmentpolicyhub.unctad.org/IIA/CountryBits/150; for FTAs see www.dfat.gov.au/trade/agreements/pages/trade-agreements.aspx and www.mfat.govt.nz/en/trade/free-trade-agreements/ (all last accessed 9 December 2016).

[15] See generally Wolfgang Alschner and Dmitriy Skougarevskiy, 'Mapping the Universe of International Investment Agreements' (2016) 19 JIEL 561; Amokura Kawharu, 'Expert Paper #2: Chapter 9 on Investment' *TPP Legal Expert Papers* (2015) https://tpplegal.files.wordpress.com/2015/12/tpp-investment.pdf (last accessed 9 December 2016). Luke Nottage, 'The TPP Investment Chapter and Investor-State Arbitration in Asia and Oceania: Assessing Prospects for Ratification' (2016) 17 MJIL 313 (with a manuscript version at https://papers.ssrn.com/sol3/papers.cfm?abstract_id=2767996 (last accessed 9 December 2016).

[16] ASEAN–Australia–New Zealand Free Trade Agreement, Hua Hin, 27 February 2009, in force 1 January 2010, [2010] ATS 1; Australia–New Zealand Closer Economic Relations Agreement Protocol on Investment, Wellington, 16 February 2011, in force 1 March 2013, [2013] ATS 10.

[17] Department of Foreign Affairs and Trade, 'Regional Comprehensive Economic Partnership' www.dfat.gov.au/trade/agreements/rcep/pages/regional-comprehensive-economic-partnership.aspx (last accessed 9 December 2016). See generally eg Jeffrey D Wilson, 'Mega-Regional Trade Deals in the Asia-Pacific: Choosing Between the TPP and RCEP?' (2015) 45 JCA 345; Robert Scollay, 'APEC, TPP and RCEP: Towards an FTAAP' in Sanchita Basu Das and Masahiro Kawai (eds), *Trade Regionalism in the Asia-Pacific: Developments and Future Challenges* (ISEAS Publishing 2016) 297–322.

[18] Antony Crockett, 'Indonesia's Bilateral Investment Treaties: Between Generations?' (2015) 30 ICSID Rev 437; Prabhash Ranjan, 'India and Bilateral Investment Treaties: From Rejection to Embracement to Hesitance?' in R Rajesh Babu and Srinivas Burra (eds), *'Locating India' in the Contemporary International Legal Order* (Springer 2016).

Given their strong economic relations with the wider region, some ongoing commonalities in treaty (especially FTA) practice, and tight bilateral socio-economic and legal harmonization,[19] Australia and New Zealand might be viewed collectively as a 'middle power' potentially able to influence the ongoing 'regionalization' of international investment law especially in Asia, as posited generally by Schill (referring instead to Korea and ASEAN) and explored in other recent work.[20] Our earlier work has already therefore taken a closer look at the national FDI regulation and treaty practice of New Zealand and Australia, including a focus on the important and revealing issue of FDI screening.[21] From this largely common ground, Section II of this chapter compares key areas in key treaties (AANZFTA, the CER Investment Protocol, and TPP/CPTPP). Section III turns to both countries' negotiating positions as seemingly revealed in a leaked draft investment chapter for RCEP.[22] In light of this treaty practice, but also the current scepticism towards largely US-style treaty drafting exhibited now by Indonesia and India as negotiating partners, Section IV considers the scope to promote less pro-investor provisions in future treaties in the region. In particular, it looks at potential to include both substantive commitments and dispute resolution procedures closer to the contemporary European Union approach, found already in the latter's FTAs recently agreed with Singapore and especially Vietnam. Section V concludes that shifts in that direction are also likely given the domestic political situation now in New Zealand and Australia, including New Zealand's recent renunciation of ISDS for future treaties, as well as various policy arguments for generally winding back investment treaty commitments for foreign investors—but without eschewing them altogether.

---

[19] Both countries also share a history as British colonies and inherited the English variant of the common law tradition, which also made it easier to introduce a bilateral regime similar to that found within the EU regarding enforcement of judgments: Agreement between the Government of Australia and the Government of New Zealand on Trans-Tasman Court Proceedings and Regulatory Enforcement, Christchurch, July 24, 2008, in force 11 October 2013, [2013] ATS 32. For ongoing commonalities in recent investment treaty practice, but also some differences, see Amokura Kawharu and Luke Nottage, 'Renouncing Investor-State Dispute Settlement in Australia, Then New Zealand: Déjà Vu' Sydney Law School Research Paper No 18/03 (2018) https://ssrn.com/abstract=3116526 (last accessed 9 October 2018). A version of the first half, focusing on treaty developments, is forthcoming in the *Yearbook on International Investment Law and Policy*; a version of the second half, focusing on inbound and outbound ISDS cases related to New Zealand and (especially) Australia, is forthcoming in special issue 44(2) of the *University of Western Australia Law Review*.

[20] Stephan Schill, 'Can Asia Transform International Investment Law?' *East Asia Forum Blog* (2016) http://www.eastasiaforum.org/2016/07/27/can-asia-transform-international-investment-law/ (last accessed 9 December 2016), referring instead to Korea (and ASEAN) as potential regional leaders nowadays. See also generally eg Yoshifumi Fukunaga, 'ASEAN's Leadership in the Regional Comprehensive Economic Partnership' (2014) 2 APPS 103; Julien Chaisse and Luke Nottage (eds), *International Investment Treaties and Arbitration Across Asia* (Brill 2018), incorporating ASEAN (country) studies published in special issue 18(5–6) of the *Journal of World Investment and Trade* (2018); Luke Nottage and Ana Ubilava, 'Asia's Changing International Investment Regime: Sustainability, Regionalization and Arbitration: Review Essay' Sydney Law School Research Paper No 18/34 https://ssrn.com/abstract=3191718 (last accessed 9 October 2018).

[21] Kawharu and Nottage, 'Models for Investment Treaties in the Asian Region' (n 13).

[22] The leaked draft was available via Knowledge Ecology International, '2015 Oct 16 Version: RCEP Draft Text for Investment Chapter' (21 April 2016) http://keionline.org/node/2474 (last accessed 9 December 2016), which we used for the analysis in Section III below, but the link to it no longer functions; only a summary remains online.

II. Comparing Key Areas in Key Existing Treaties for Australia and New Zealand

A. CER Investment Protocol

The starting point for comparing New Zealand and Australia regarding the more technical aspects of investment treaties is the CER Investment Protocol, that is, the investment agreement between the two countries themselves. The principal CER treaty is regarded as one of the most liberalizing trade agreements globally, reflecting the long-standing strategy of both countries to integrate their economies and harmonize various business laws.[23] As explained in the Introduction above, however, it did not cover either services or investment, and while a services protocol was concluded in 1988, it was not until 2011 that the two countries agreed on commitments to address cross-border investment. Given that the CER was signed in 1983 (well before the practice of including investment in FTAs had become standard practice),[24] the initial omission of investment is perhaps not surprising. That said, another reason has been given for the long delay before the start of investment negotiations: it appears that Australia was reluctant to extend preferential treatment to New Zealand regarding investment as this would have required it to extend that treatment to its various other investment treaty partners.[25] The impetus for the protocol was Australia's FTA with the US, AUSFTA. Negotiations began in 2005, prompted by New Zealand's concern that the relative position of New Zealand investors in Australia would deteriorate as a result of Australia's AUSFTA concessions to the US.[26]

The Protocol is largely based on the 2004 US Model BIT, which marked a significant break with earlier US treaty practice partly in light of the US experience as respondent in NAFTA cases.[27] By the time it was signed, both New Zealand and Australia had already concluded FTAs with investment chapters that also broadly followed the US approach, including AUSFTA for Australia (albeit omitting ISDS altogether) and AANZFTA for Australia and New Zealand (albeit including more provisions deferential to host states, overlapping with some found in other ASEAN agreements[28]).

[23] Foreign Affairs Defence and Trade Committee, 'International Treaty Examination of the Protocol on Investment to the New Zealand-Australia Closer Economic Relations Trade Agreement Report' (8 April 2011) https://www.parliament.nz/en/pb/sc/reports/document/49DBSCH_SCR5090_1/international-treaty-examination-of-the-protocol-on-investment 2 (FADT Committee Report—CER Investment Protocol).
[24] It replaced the New Zealand Australia Free Trade Agreement (also abbreviated as 'NAFTA') which had entered into force in 1966, leading to the removal of tariffs and quantitative restrictions on 80 per cent of trans-Tasman trade by the late 1970s. The latter came to be seen as cumbersome and 'lacked an effective mechanism for removing remaining restrictions': see Department of Foreign Affairs and Trade, 'ANZCERTA: its Genesis and the Present' http://dfat.gov.au/trade/agreements/anzcerta/pages/anzcerta-its-genesis-and-the-present.aspx (last accessed 9 December 2016).
[25] FADT Committee Report—CER Investment Protocol, 2.   [26] ibid.
[27] Mark Kantor, 'The New Draft Model BIT: Noteworthy Developments' (2004) 21 JIA 383; Kenneth Vandervelde, 'A Comparison of the 2004 and 1994 US Model BITs: Rebalancing Investor and Host Country Interests' in Karl Sauvant (ed), *Yearbook on International Investment Law and Policy* (OUP 2009). The 2004 model was replaced in 2012 by a largely similar version: see Mark Kantor, 'Little Has Changed in the New US Model Bilateral BIT' (2012) 27 ICSID Rev 335.
[28] See generally Vivienne Bath and Luke Nottage, 'The ASEAN Comprehensive Investment Agreement and "ASEAN Plus": The Australia-New Zealand Free Trade Area (AANZFTA) and the PRC–ASEAN Investment Agreement' in Marc Bungenberg, Joern Griebel, Stephan Hobe, and August Reinisch (eds), *International Investment Law* (Nomos/Beck/Hart Publishing 2015) 283–303; Diane Desierto, 'Regulatory Freedom and Control in the New ASEAN Regional Investment Treaties' (2015) 16 JWIT 1018.

Apart from achieving consistency with this existing and expanding regional practice,[29] using the US model was a logical choice in the sense that a primary objective for New Zealand was to ensure a level of parity between New Zealand and US investors in Australia. Amongst the key (and often contentious) areas of investment treaties are their scope of application to defined investments,[30] the non-discrimination obligations of national and most favoured nation (MFN) treatment, and approaches to expropriation, the minimum standard of treatment, and ISDS. The Protocol more or less follows the US template on all these issues—apart from ISDS, which (as noted) is excluded altogether.

For instance, the definition of 'covered investment' in the Protocol is lifted directly from the US Model BIT of 2004:[31]

'covered investment' means, with respect to a Party, an investment in its territory of an investor of the other Party, in existence as of the date of entry into force of this Protocol or established, acquired, or expanded thereafter; ...

Then again, there are also efforts to integrate regional preferences, such as the inclusion of 'claims to money or ... contractual performance' in the definition of 'investment',[32] which also features in AANZFTA and other ASEAN, New Zealand, and Australian FTAs.[33]

Regarding investment liberalization, national treatment and MFN under the Protocol apply from the pre-establishment phase, subject to extensive exceptions listed in New Zealand's and Australia's annexes of non-conforming measures.[34] Both countries include their respective foreign investment screening regimes in their annexes, but they also agreed to raise the monetary thresholds for screening business investments. Australia raised its threshold for New Zealand investors to match the one it agreed under AUSFTA to apply to US investors. For Australian investors, New Zealand agreed to more than quadruple the standard threshold from NZD100 million to NZD477 million, indexed annually.[35] Particularly in view of the absence of a direct enforcement mechanism, the raised thresholds are probably the outcomes of greatest practical significance for trans-Tasman investors.

As for investor protections, the provisions on the minimum standard of treatment and expropriation generally follow the US model,[36] except that there is no annex to the Protocol setting out the parties' agreed understanding on what amounts to an indirect

---

[29] For a quantitative analysis showing the diffusion of contemporary US treaty drafting in individual countries such as Japan and in the TPP see Wolfgang Alschner and Dmitriy Skougarevskiy, 'Mapping the Universe of International Investment Agreements' (2016) 19 JIEL 561 Parts 5.B and 5.D.1.
[30] Definitions of terms like 'investment' and 'investor' have a material role in determining the normative content of investment agreements (and will often be the subject of negotiation). See eg UNCTAD, *Scope and Definition* (UNCTAD 1999).
[31] CER Investment Protocol art 1(a). The only differences are semantic, ie the addition of a comma, and 'Treaty' in the US version is replaced with 'Protocol': see US Model BIT (2004) art 1.
[32] CER Investment Protocol art 1(e)(vi). Cf eg Australia–Chile FTA art 10.1(j) fn 10-7, noting that: 'Some forms of debt, such as bonds, debentures, and long-term notes, are more likely to have the characteristics of an investment, while other forms of debt, such as claims to payment that are immediately due and result from the sale of goods or services, are less likely to have such characteristics'.
[33] See eg AANZFTA ch 11 art 2(c)(iv).
[34] CER Investment Protocol art 5 and art 9; Annexes I and II for New Zealand and Australia.
[35] CER Investment Protocol Annex I-NZ-2 (New Zealand) and Annex I-AUS-2 (Australia).
[36] CER Investment Protocol arts 12 and 14.

or regulatory expropriation. Instead, there is a footnote to the expropriation provision in the main text, along the lines of the final clause of the annex on expropriation in the US model, as follows:[37]

Except in rare circumstances, non-discriminatory regulatory actions by a Party to achieve legitimate public welfare objectives, such as protection of public health, safety, and the environment, do not constitute indirect expropriations.

B. AANZFTA

The positions taken on the above issues in the CER Investment Protocol could be explained by the lack of any enforcement mechanism in the form of ISDS, and consequently, the low risk of the agreement to both countries. Nevertheless, there is nothing in the Protocol on these issues that New Zealand and Australia have not been prepared to accept in other agreements, except, in the case of New Zealand, the lift in the screening threshold.[38] These other agreements include AANZFTA and the TPP/CPTPP, both of which also involve both New Zealand and Australia.

Like most of the ASEAN+ FTAs,[39] the AANZFTA has an investment chapter that provides for ISDS. The chapter, like the CER Investment Protocol, also follows the general format of and is clearly influenced by the 2004 US Model BIT. For instance, it includes a broad asset-based definition of 'investment' where an investment is defined to mean 'every kind of asset ...' (followed by an enumeration of examples), and tethers the minimum standard of treatment to customary international law.[40]

However, compared to the CER Protocol, the AANZFTA approach to investment is also more deferential to host states than the US template. For example, although the terms of the requirement to compensate for expropriation are generally the same, the interpretive annex defining what amounts to a regulatory taking does not have the 'rare circumstances' proviso (that allows public welfare regulation to be deemed expropriatory if the rare circumstances are present).[41] In some areas, AANZFTA is quite weak. As under the CER/US versions, national treatment applies from the establishment phase, but it remains conditional on further agreement being reached on reservations, and there is no MFN provision at all.[42] The AANZFTA investment chapter includes a provision on performance requirements, but this merely applies the parties' WTO obligations.[43] It does not have the more extensive and detailed prohibitions against the adoption of performance requirements as agreed in the CER Protocol,[44] which are a long-standing pro-investor feature of US investment treaties (even since

---

[37] CER Investment Protocol art 14(1) n 7. Compare US Model BIT (2004 and 2012 versions) Annex B.

[38] New Zealand has agreed to increase the screening threshold under the TPP, but only to NZD 200 million. Australia has agreed to lift the screening threshold under the TPP to the same higher level it applies to investors from the US, New Zealand and other FTA partners.

[39] The exception is ASEAN's FTA with Japan: see Shotaro Hamamoto and Luke Nottage, 'Japan' in Chester Brown (ed), *Commentaries on Selected Model Investment Treaties* (OUP 2013) 373.

[40] See AANZFTA ch 11 art 1(c) and art 6.

[41] See AANZFTA ch 11 Annex. In any event, however, the proviso has not been successfully relied on to date in claims brought under other treaties adding such wording.

[42] See AANZFTA ch 11 art 4. The negotiations on the reservations to national treatment (and MFN) are now taking place within the framework of the RCEP negotiations.

[43] See AANZFTA ch 11 art 5.   [44] See CER Investment Protocol art 7.

2004) and remain a concern particularly within Southeast Asia.[45] AANZFTA also follows typically ASEAN preferences on matters such as the definition of 'covered investment', which expressly requires that investments must be admitted in accordance with host state law in order to qualify for protection.[46] Such 'admission' requirements are aimed at ensuring compliance with screening and other foreign investment approval laws.[47] As above, the CER approach is to deal with admission regulations through non-conforming measures only.

In the event, the outcome under AANZFTA is overall less ambitious than New Zealand and Australia would have liked. This is evidenced by their efforts to expand the commitments on investment through the standing joint committee of the AANZFTA parties,[48] and by their interest in signing their respective FTAs with Malaysia shortly after AANZFTA was concluded, so as to build on the AANZFTA commitments (in 2010 for New Zealand, 2012 for Australia). That said, even in New Zealand's and Australia's respective FTAs with Malaysia, the more cautious approach of the AANZFTA is still evident. The same approach as under AANZFTA is taken to the definition of 'covered investment' (i.e. the admission requirement), national treatment (from establishment, but conditional on yet-to-be-agreed reservations), performance requirements (the application of the WTO commitments) and indirect expropriation (the lack of the 'rare circumstances' proviso).[49]

C. From the TPP to the CPTPP

The TPP signalled a move to even closer adherence to the 2004 US Model BIT than the CER Investment Protocol (and AANZFTA), albeit with several new provisions that were negotiated for the TPP to address concerns about its potential impact on the regulatory powers of host states. For these reasons, there is a mixture of 'firsts' as well as established practice for New Zealand and Australia in this agreement.[50] The TPP may have extended a few commitments beyond what New Zealand and Australia would ideally have wanted, as judged against some apparent resistance to certain US-led approaches prior to conclusion of the TPP.

---

[45] We are grateful to Professor Julien Chaisse for pointing out the significance of performance requirements (in particular, export requirements, local content requirements, technology transfer requirements, skills development requirements; trade balancing requirements) that are still retained in many Southeast Asian economies. On the use (and abuse) of performance requirements see Julien Chaisse, 'Renewables Re-Energized? The Internationalization of Green Energy Investment Rules and Disputes' (2016) 9(4) Journal of World Energy Law & Business 269. See also UNESCAP, Handbook on Policies, Promotion and Facilitation of Foreign Direct Investment for Sustainable Development in Asia and the Pacific (United Nations Economic and Social Commission for Asia and the Pacific 2017) 129–49.

[46] See AANZFTA ch 11 art 2(a). By virtue of a footnote, investments in Thailand and Vietnam also have to be approved in writing or, in the case of Vietnam, to be registered.

[47] Whether a given investment satisfies an admission requirement is a question of the domestic law of the host state. See Chester Brown, 'The Regulation of Foreign Direct Investment by Admission Requirements and the Duty on Investors to Comply with the Host State Law' (2015) 21 NZBLQ 301.

[48] See AANZFTA Joint Committee, 'Summary of Main Outcomes' (Seventh Meeting of the FTA Joint Committee, 29 June–3 July 2015) 1 http://aanzfta.asean.org/uploads/docs/FINAL_-_Summary_of_Outcomes_7th_FJC_for_Public_Release_20150818.pdf (last accessed 9 December 2016).

[49] NZ–Malaysia FTA arts 10.1, 10.4, 10.6, and Annex 7; Australia–Malaysia FTA arts 12.2(a), 12.4. 12.6, and annex on expropriation.

[50] See further Amokura Kawharu, 'Expert Paper #2: Chapter 9 on Investment' *TPP Legal Expert Papers* (2015) https://tpplegal.files.wordpress.com/2015/12/tpp-investment.pdf (last accessed 9 December 2016) and Nottage, 'The TPP Investment Chapter and Investor-State Arbitration in Asia and Oceania' (n 15).

In terms of coverage, a draft version of the TPP Investment chapter included an admission requirement in the definition of 'covered investment',[51] as under the AANZFTA, but in the final text it was omitted. Instead, the TPP definition is the same as that found in the US Model BIT and the CER Investment Protocol, as mentioned above.[52] This is intriguing given that, by the time the TPP was agreed in October 2015, the Australian government was well aware of the important practical significance of admission requirements. In a claim brought by Philip Morris, Australia had debated (in February 2015 hearings) whether or not those set out in Article 1(1)(e) of the Australia–Hong Kong BIT had been satisfied by Philip Morris in early 2011 when it applied and obtained Foreign Investment Review Board approval for its Hong Kong subsidiary to assume ownership of Australian interests (including trademarks, subsequently diluted by tobacco plain packaging legislation).[53] However, uniquely among all known investment treaties so far, the TPP allows member states to exclude applicability of ISDS altogether (but not inter-state arbitration) regarding a 'tobacco control measure', and both Australia and New Zealand appeared likely to do so.[54]

The TPP's obligations may extend to measures adopted or maintained by public enterprises, including potentially some activities of SOEs.[55] Each party's obligations under the investment chapter extend to 'measures' (defined widely in Chapter 1) adopted by a 'state enterprise' to the extent that it is exercising delegated governmental authority.[56] This was also a first for New Zealand and Australia, although again it is consistent with the United States' preferred practice. Such coverage is particularly notable, given the greater prevalence of government-linked companies in the economies of existing TPP signatories (e.g. Vietnam) and would-be prospective partners (e.g. Thailand).

In another first for New Zealand, although not Australia, the TPP enabled investors to bring proceedings for alleged breaches of certain investment contracts with host

---

[51] TPP draft art 12.2 Citizens Trade Campaign, 'Newly Leaked TPP Investment Chapter Contains Special Rights for Corporations' *citizenstrade.org* (13 June 2012) http://www.citizenstrade.org/ctc/blog/2012/06/13/newly-leaked-tpp-investment-chapter-contains-special-rights-for-corporations/ (last accessed 9 December 2016).
[52] TPP art 9.1, definition of 'covered investment'.
[53] The subsequent award rejected the Australian government's argument that the application was misleading, by not mentioning that the corporate restructuring could allow a BIT claim. The tribunal held that the government had not discharged its burden of proof that the admission was prima facie completed when a Treasury official had issued a 'no-objection' letter. See *Philip Morris Asia Limited (Hong Kong) v The Commonwealth of Australia*, Award on Jurisdiction and Admissibility, PCA 2012-12, 17 December 2015, paras 156–61 and 551–52 at http://www.pcacases.com/web/view/5 (last accessed 9 December 2016), and generally Jarrod Hepburn and Luke Nottage, 'A Procedural Win for Public Health Measures: *Philip Morris Asia v Australia*' (2017) 18 JWIT 307 (with a manuscript version at https://papers.ssrn.com/sol3/papers.cfm?abstract_id=2842065 (last accessed 9 December 2016).
[54] TPP, Exceptions and General Provisions art 29.5. See also generally Tania Voon and Andrew D Mitchell, 'Philip Morris vs Tobacco Control: Two Wins for Public Health, but Uncertainty Remains' *Columbia FDI Perspectives* No 182 (2016) http://ccsi.columbia.edu/files/2013/10/No-182-Voon-and-Mitchell-FINAL.pdf (last accessed 9 December 2016).
[55] The TPP is also noteworthy for including a separate chapter (17) on SOEs, defined as enterprises principally engaged in commercial activities and predominantly owned or controlled by the state party: see Department of Foreign Affairs and Trade, 'Chapter Summary: State-Owned Enterprises and Designated Monopolies' *Trans-Pacific Partnership Factsheet* (2015) http://dfat.gov.au/trade/agreements/tpp/summaries/Documents/state-owned-enterprises-and-designated-monopolies.PDF (last accessed 9 December 2016). Those commitments are enforceable under the (inter-state) dispute settlement chapter, unlike those under the broader competition law and policy chapter (16): see further Deborah Elms, 'TPP Impressions: Competition and State Owned Enterprises (SOEs)' *Asian Trade Centre Blog* (2015) http://www.asiantradecentre.org/talkingtrade/2015/11/17/tpp-impressions-competition-and-state-owned-enterprises-soes (last accessed 9 December 2016).
[56] TPP art 9.2(2)(b).

governments, as well as violations of substantive treaty commitments, or with respect to investment authorizations after granted by the applicable foreign investment authority (subject to ISDS carve-outs for certain countries, including New Zealand and Australia, regarding screening decisions as to whether or not admit investments under national laws).[57] That said, Australia has only once included these types of claims, in its FTA with Korea,[58] and initially (when the Gillard Government's Trade Policy Statement was in place) Australia sought a complete exemption from the TPP's ISDS provisions.[59] More generally, whether the ISDS provisions should enable investors to bring claims based on alleged breaches of their rights under contracts with TPP governments, as distinct from alleged breaches of the investment chapter, was one of the most contentious issues in the TPP investment negotiations. The US was reportedly alone in seeking the enforceability of contract claims in respect of contracts entered into before the TPP comes into effect, while most TPP countries opposed the inclusion of contract claims altogether.[60] This helps to explain why, when the TPP text was reviewed after the new Trump Administration withdrew the US signature in January 2017, the ISDS provisions on investment contracts and investment authorizations were suspended in the CPTPP (as discussed further below). However, the TPP was innovative (compared e.g. with the Australia–Korea FTA) by also facilitating consolidation of any ISDS claims based on substantive treaty commitments, with ISDS claims brought solely under contract law before specified arbitration institutions.[61]

The rest of the ISDS section of the TPP (and now CPTPP) investment chapter is reasonably standard. It reflects an approach to investment treaty arbitration that has become commonplace in investment agreements across the Asia-Pacific region,[62] and is also modelled on US practice. It includes a range of measures that have been developed in recent years in response to criticisms of the arbitral process. These include, for example, provisions that promote greater transparency, facilitate *amicus curiae* participation, limit the amount of recoverable damages, bind tribunals to accept joint interpretations by the TPP parties, and empower tribunals to expedite the hearing of preliminary objections.[63] Although these (or variants) are now quite familiar, not all are included in every recent agreement concluded by New Zealand and Australia, including AANZFTA (which lacks an express provision on amicus participation, for example). Unlike AANZFTA,[64] there is no express requirement that arbitrators be independent

---

[57] TPP art 9.19(1)(a)–(b) and Annex 9-H. On the carve-outs for initial screening decisions under the CER Protocol, see above Section 2.A.

[58] Korea–Australia FTA art 11.16(1)(a)–(b).

[59] This is based on a draft of the investment chapter that was leaked in 2012. Footnote 20 exempted Australia from the ISDS obligations. See Citizens Trade Campaign, 'Newly Leaked TPP Investment Chapter'.

[60] Lori Wallach and Ben Beachy, 'Analysis of Leaked Trans-Pacific Partnership Investment Text' *Public Citizen* (2015) http://citizen.org/documents/tpp-investment-leak-2015.pdf (last accessed 9 December 2016).

[61] TPP Annex 9-L. If the host state agreed in specified types of investment contracts to submit contract-based disputes to the Arbitration Rules of ICSID, UNCITRAL, ICC or London Court of International Arbitration, the investor cannot directly invoke the ISDS procedure in Section B of the investment chapter (paragraph 1). But it does not waive rights to initiate or proceed with arbitration under those agreed Rules (paragraph 2) 'with respect to any measure alleged to constitute a breach' under Art 9.18. Nonetheless, if such claims 'have a question of law or fact in common and raise out of the same events or circumstances' as a claim for breach of Section A substantive treaty commitments (or investment authorizations), the disputing parties can agree to consolidation of these sets of proceedings or otherwise be subjected to consolidated proceedings under art 9.27.

[62] See eg Nottage, 'The TPP Investment Chapter and Investor-State Arbitration in Asia and Oceania' (n 15).

[63] TPP arts 9.23(4)–(6), 9.24, 9.25(3), 9.29(1)–(6).   [64] AANZFTA ch 11 art 23.2.

of the parties. However, this would follow under the applicable Arbitration Rules and/
or background arbitration law, and could be elaborated in the code of conduct for arbitrators that must be agreed before the TPP may come into force.[65]

There are also variations to the standard format. For example, there is a requirement
that the tribunal provide its draft award to the parties for comment, modelling WTO
practice with respect to panel reports. This is not found in any of New Zealand's FTAs,
but it was provided already in the 2004 US Model BIT as well as in Australia's FTA
investment chapters with Chile (signed in 2008) and Korea (signed in 2014).[66] Finally,
the TPP parties agree to consider how an appeals facility might apply to their agreement.[67] The 2004 US Model BIT goes further, in that it obliges the parties to 'strive
to reach an agreement' on the application of the appeals facility. In the 2012 Model
BIT, this had been watered down to 'consider' its application, which is the approach
reflected in the TPP.[68] So far, this type of promise has paid lip service to the development of appellate review in ISDS. However, as discussed in Section IV below, appellate
review is now a feature of the EU's revised approach to investment treaties, including
as seen in its FTAs with Canada and Vietnam.

As to substantive investment liberalization and protection, the TPP includes clarificatory language across many provisions in the investment chapter to ensure public
welfare considerations may be taken into account in the assessment of a measure's compatibility with the agreement. For example, there is a footnote and a Drafters' Note
that together provide guidance on the interpretation of 'in like circumstances' for the
purpose of the national treatment and MFN treatment rules. The footnote clarifies
that whether treatment is accorded in like circumstances depends on the 'totality of circumstances, including whether the relevant treatment distinguishes between investors
or investments on the basis of legitimate public welfare objectives'.[69] There are also
provisions that address the relevance of investor expectations to a minimum standard
of treatment claim (not relevant, by themselves), and the meaning of such expectations in the context of an expropriation claim (including the requirements that the
expectations be reasonable and investment-backed, which may depend on the nature
and extent of regulation in the relevant sector).[70] Further exceptions deal with specific
matters such as public debt.[71]

At the same time, the TPP loads most of the safeguarding of regulatory space into the
investment provisions themselves. Unlike the approach taken in the CER Investment
Protocol and the AANZFTA, but otherwise consistent with US preferences, the general GATT/GATS-based exceptions in the TPP do not apply to the investment chapter
as an additional safeguard.[72] Negotiators may have taken comfort from the greater

[65] TPP art 9.22(6). Precedents for the code would be the Australia–China FTA (Annex 9-A) and
recent EU texts such as its FTA with Singapore (Annex 9-F), concluded before the former and which
therefore seems to have provided the template.
[66] Respectively arts 28.9, 10.20(9), and 10.20(11).   [67] TPP art 9.23(11).
[68] Compare art 28.10 of the 2004 US Model BIT with art 28.10 of the 2012 US Model BIT.
[69] TPP art 9.4, footnote 14 and associated Drafters' Note. For further discussion see Caroline
Henckels, 'Protecting Regulatory Autonomy through Greater Precision in Investment Treaties: The TPP,
CETA and TTIP' (2016) 19 JIEL 27, 45–46; and Richard Braddock, 'Striking a Balance: Protecting
Investors from Discrimination while Clarifying the Scope for Legitimate Government Regulation in
the TPP' *GELN Biennial Symposium: 'The Age of Mega-Regionals: TPP and Regulatory Autonomy in
IEL'* (University of Melbourne, 19 May 2016) (locating the Drafter's Note in the context particularly
of NAFTA case law, and arguing that the Note will have binding effect under the Vienna Convention
and general international law).
[70] TPP art 9.6(4), and Annex 9-B, and footnote 36.   [71] TPP Annex 9-G.
[72] See TPP art 29.1.

attention to the crafting of the various rules, or even determined that trade excep-tions are not apt to cover investment obligations.[73] Nevertheless, New Zealand had not taken the TPP approach in its previous treaties, whereas Australia had included a general exception specifically for investment in its FTA with Korea, and both had ex-tended GATS Article XIV exceptions to the investment chapter under AANZFTA.[74]

Apart from indicating levels of tolerance and ambition, the above agreements also say something else about New Zealand and Australian investment treaty practice. In general, both have been 'rule takers' rather than innovators. This is not evident from quantitative comparisons of the level of linguistic consistency in treaties concluded by Australia and New Zealand,[75] but rather by their recent reliance on the US Model BIT approaches to a range of key issues when crafting their CER Investment Protocol and recent FTAs. There are exceptions, but so far these have been limited in scope and/or to individual treaties. These include the express public health exception in New Zealand's BIT with Hong Kong,[76] missing from the Australia—Hong Kong BIT signed two years earlier; New Zealand's now standard exception relating to the interests of its in-digenous Maori (although it only benefits New Zealand); and interesting provisions in Australia's recent FTA with China on arbitrator ethics and 'public welfare notices'.[77] The latter allows a respondent state to issue a notice to the home state of the claimant investor, to trigger consultations on the applicability of the public welfare exception in the ISDS section of the investment chapter, with an inter-state decision potentially suspending proceedings at an early stage.

The reliance on the US-derived model has had its advantages in terms of its accept-ance within New Zealand's and Australia's spheres of interest across the Asia-Pacific, but it may also risk creating a 'status-quo' bias making it more difficult for either country to re-orient its treaty practice towards different approaches, such as the new model

---

[73] Cf generally Jurgen Kurtz, *The WTO and International Investment Law: Converging Systems* (CUP 2016).

[74] See, respectively, General Provisions and Exceptions art 22.1(3), and art 15.1.2. By contrast, per-haps reflecting the influence of NAFTA and subsequent US treaty practice, the earlier Chile–Australia FTA lacks such a general exception. For an early argument that such provisions are not a panacea for investment treaties, being mostly unsuited or unnecessary regarding public health measures such as tobacco regulation see Julien Chaisse, 'Exploring the Confines of International Investment and Domestic Health Protections – Is a General Exceptions Clause a Forced Perspective?' (2013) 39 AJLM 332, 359.

[75] Australia is actually ranked 3rd out of 133 countries, at 'Mapping BITs – Australia' http:// mappinginvestmenttreaties.com/country?iso=AUS (last accessed 9 December 2016), with departures in linguistic consistency with its other BITs mainly for the treaties concluded with Hong Kong (prob-ably due to the latter's tendency to follow the UK approach), Chile and Mexico (probably influenced by their strong reliance on the US approach), and India. New Zealand is not ranked, perhaps be-cause it has only 4 BITs to compare for internal consistency: 'Mapping BITs – New Zealand' http:// mappinginvestmenttreaties.com/country?iso=NZL (last accessed 9 December 2016).

[76] New Zealand–Hong Kong BIT art 8(3). It would have been interesting to see whether the lack of such an express requirement in the Australia–Hong Kong BIT (signed in 1993) would have made any difference to the tribunal (even psychologically) if the Philip Morris claim had proceeded to a decision on the merits. However, the omission in the Swiss BIT (signed in 1988) did not prevent the tribunal in the recent award in favour of Uruguay from interpreting that treaty in light of customary international law, noting (like many significant awards since 2000) that the latter had long recognized that the protection of public health is an essential manifestations of a state's 'policy power' (*lois de po-lice*). See generally Luke Eric Peterson, 'The Philip Morris v Uruguay Award on the Merits' *Investment Arbitration Reporter* (2016) https://www.iareporter.com/articles/the-philip-morris-v-uruguay-award-on-the-merits-part-one-of-our-three-part-analysis-focusing-on-the-expropriation-claim/ (last ac-cessed 9 December 2016).

[77] ChAFTA arts 9.11(4)–(8) and Annex 9-A.

being promoted by the EU.[78] Be that as it may, while the TPP may be the high water mark in terms of the breadth, depth and enforceability of obligations on investment, both countries have also been prepared to accept less ambitious approaches within the status-quo framework, as with AANZFTA, at least as an opening for further discussion and agreement. Furthermore, while there is some evidence that the TPP text has already influenced FTA negotiations in the Asia-Pacific,[79] the prospects that the TPP will enter into force are currently slim. Following the Trump Administration's decision to withdraw US signature from the TPP, New Zealand, Australia, and the other remaining parties reached an agreement in principle for a 'TPP11' agreement on the sidelines of an APEC meeting in November 2017, and then signed the renamed CPTPP in March 2018. The CPTPP suspends some TPP provisions, including those allowing ISDS in respect of investment contract and investment authorization claims.[80] This apparent retreat from some TPP principles allows greater space for alternative models, including RCEP and even possibly a wider FTA covering the Asia-Pacific, to flourish and take hold. Within this space, other regional powers such as China may step up. Yet, it would also provide New Zealand and Australia with a further opportunity to promote their preferences too. The development of alternatives through RCEP is explored next, and more broadly in Section IV below.

III. New Zealand and Australia in the RCEP Negotiations

The RCEP negotiations involve the ten members of ASEAN and the six countries with which ASEAN has existing FTAs (the 'ASEAN+' FTAs): Australia, China, India, Japan, Korea, and New Zealand.[81] Formal negotiations began in May 2013 following their agreement on a set of guiding principles and objectives that were announced at the margins of the East Asia Summit in Cambodia in late 2012.[82] As usual, and despite the recommendations of Australia's Senate inquiry majority report into treaty-making in 2015, RCEP negotiations are taking place behind closed doors. However, the Australian government invited various stakeholders for a forum on ISDS and investment chapter issues, hosted on 27 April 2016, on the side-lines of the negotiation round held in Perth.[83] In addition, some light was shed on the RCEP negotiations when an apparent draft of the investment chapter (dated October 2015) was leaked in April 2016.[84] There are inherent limitations in relying on documents where the authenticity

---

[78] Nottage, 'The TPP Investment Chapter and Investor-State Arbitration in Asia and Oceania' (n 15) (noting also a similar issue identified with Korea's treaty practice); Section IV below.

[79] For examples see Andrew D Mitchell and Tania Voon, 'Foreword: The Continuing Relevance of the Trans-Pacific Partnership' (2016) 17(2) MJIL i, v.

[80] CPTPP art 2, and Annex para 2(a)-(b).

[81] See generally Vivienne Bath and Luke Nottage, 'Asian Investment and the Growth of Regional Investment Agreements' in Christoph Antons (ed), *Routledge Handbook of Asian Law* (Routledge 2017) 182–99; Chaisse and Nottage (eds), *International Investment Treaties and Arbitration Across Asia* (n 20).

[82] Department of Foreign Affairs and Trade, 'Guiding Principles and Objectives for Negotiating the Regional Comprehensive Economic Partnership' (2012), http://dfat.gov.au/trade/agreements/rcep/Documents/guiding-principles-rcep.pdf (last accessed 9 December 2016).

[83] Department of Foreign Affairs and Trade, 'Twelfth Round of Negotiations - 17-29 April 2016, Perth, Australia' *RCEP News* (2016) http://dfat.gov.au/trade/agreements/rcep/news/Pages/twelfth-round-of-negotiations-17-29-april-2016-perth-australia.aspx (last accessed 9 December 2016).

[84] The leaked draft was available at http://keionline.org/node/2474 but the link no longer exists.

cannot be verified. Subject to this caveat, this RCEP investment chapter draft provides an interesting basis for analysis because it seemingly identifies the initial positions of each of the RCEP parties (except that the ASEAN countries are grouped together),[85] as well as new text that was been proposed by the RCEP investment working group. In some respects, for the purpose of analysis, this has more value than a final text. Taking the CER Investment Protocol for example, it is not entirely clear where New Zealand and Australia may have differed to begin with, if at all, compared to the final outcome.

Both former New Zealand Prime Minister John Key and former Australian Prime Minister Julia Gillard described the RCEP as complementary to the then TPP, in the sense that both agreements are part of each country's overall strategy to integrate economically into the Asia-Pacific.[86] At the same time, the two FTAs are competitive in terms of the economic as well as diplomatic and strategic interests involved.[87] The RCEP investment chapter draft and the TPP investment chapter are almost contemporaneous, given that the latter was finalized in November 2015. Our analysis suggests that negotiators from some RCEP countries had quite different ambitions for RCEP as compared with what was agreed for the TPP. Indeed, the RCEP provides an opportunity for the development of an alternative model in terms of legal text. The RCEP countries indicated some support for the idea that RCEP will be different and will reflect ASEAN preferences when they accepted that, as an ASEAN initiative, the RCEP negotiations would be ASEAN-led (through their recognition of 'ASEAN Centrality in the emerging regional economic architecture').[88] Their guiding principles for negotiation also prioritize respect for the heterogeneity amongst the RCEP economies, by directing that the agreement take into consideration the different levels of development of the participating countries.[89] At the same time, the guiding principles reflect the expectation that the RCEP will broaden and deepen the existing arrangements and have 'significant improvements' over the ASEAN+1 FTAs.[90]

Within the leaked investment chapter draft, New Zealand and Australia appeared to occupy the middle ground, at least to the extent that India's proposals (especially) present more radical pro-state options in line with its revised Model BIT (finalized in December 2015).[91] Within the middle ground, though, New Zealand tended to revert

[85] Each party has an identifier next to a clause, phrase, or word it supports. For instance 'Au' for Australia, 'NZ' for New Zealand, 'I' for India, and so on.

[86] John Key, Prime Minister of New Zealand, 'New Zealand Joins Launch of Asian FTA Negotiations' (Press Release, 21 November 2012) https://www.beehive.govt.nz/release/new-zealand-joins-launch-asian-fta-negotiations (last accessed 9 December 2016); Julia Gillard, Prime Minister of Australia and Craig Emerson, Trade and Competitiveness Minister, 'Australia Joins Launch of Massive Asian Regional Trade Agreement' (Joint Press Release, 20 November 2012) http://trademinister.gov.au/releases/2012/ce_mr_121120.html (last accessed 9 December 2016).

[87] See eg Jeffrey D Wilson, 'Mega-Regional Trade Deals in the Asia-Pacific: Choosing Between the TPP and RCEP?' (2015) 45 JCA 345.

[88] Department of Foreign Affairs and Trade, 'Guiding Principles and Objectives for Negotiating the Regional Comprehensive Economic Partnership' (2012) http://dfat.gov.au/trade/agreements/rcep/Documents/guiding-principles-rcep.pdf (last accessed 9 December 2016). The potential for ASEAN to take a lead role in the development of the RCEP is discussed in Yoshifumi Fukunaga, 'ASEAN's Leadership in the Regional Comprehensive Economic Partnership' (2014) 2 APPS 103.

[89] Department of Foreign Affairs and Trade, 'Guiding Principles and Objectives for Negotiating the Regional Comprehensive Economic Partnership' (2012) http://dfat.gov.au/trade/agreements/rcep/Documents/guiding-principles-rcep.pdf (last accessed 9 December 2016).

[90] Department of Foreign Affairs and Trade, 'Guiding Principles and Objectives for Negotiating the Regional Comprehensive Economic Partnership' (2012) http://dfat.gov.au/trade/agreements/rcep/Documents/guiding-principles-rcep.pdf (last accessed 9 December 2016).

[91] The revised text is available at http://finmin.nic.in/reports/ModelTextIndia_BIT.pdf (last accessed 9 December 2016); and is somewhat less pro-state than a consultation draft released earlier

to the more cautious AANZFTA approach, whereas Australia generally remained aligned with the US model and the TPP. This may reflect Australia's greater interests in promoting outbound investment as well as (anticipated) greater negotiating power vis-à-vis ASEAN and other major capital-importing countries engaged in the RCEP negotiations. That said, there is a mixture of convergence and divergence between both countries' positions. There is little evidence that either country proposed or supported novel approaches to the balancing of host government and investor interests, although both have put forward some clarificatory language derived from their other recent agreements. The date of the draft may partly explain this, as it pre-dates the tabling of the EU's proposed investment chapter for the Transatlantic Trade and Investment Partnership with the US (TTIP), the release of the TPP in November 2015, finalization of the revised Indian Model BIT and the subsequent discussions on these later texts.[92]

For example, in relation to investment coverage, the draft shows that New Zealand favoured the CER Investment Protocol / US Model BIT definition of 'covered investment' whereas Australia supported the inclusion of an AANZFTA-type admission requirement (along with ASEAN, China, and India).[93] On the other hand, New Zealand wanted to include the 'claims to money or ... contractual performance' element in the definition of 'investment' (as in the CER Protocol and AANZFTA), but Australia did not. Australia (supported only by Japan) was prepared to extend the chapter's protections to measures adopted by state enterprises exercising governmental authority, as under the TPP.

Regarding market access, as would be expected given their past practice, both New Zealand and Australia supported the application of national treatment from the pre-establishment phase.[94] Only India was an outlier on this. All the same, the key issue for both New Zealand and Australia concerns the scope of the exceptions to the obligation, rather than the in-principle acceptance of its application from the point of establishment. In this regard, the RCEP may yet provide an opportunity, in a way that the original TPP probably did not,[95] for both countries to reconsider their approaches to the scheduling (as non-conforming measures) of their respective screening regimes. For example, a revised reservation that allows the addition of new screening categories may relieve some of the domestic political pressure that the RCEP may otherwise attract.

---

in 2015, available still (quite confusingly) at https://www.mygov.in/sites/default/files/master_image/ Model%20Text%20for%20the%20Indian%20Bilateral%20Investment%20Treaty.pdf. Similar concepts can also be found in the 'Joint Interpretive Statement' reportedly proposed by India for (re) negotiations with existing BIT signatories, outlined by Sarthak Malhotra 'India's Joint Interpretive Statement for BITs: An Attempt to Slay the Ghosts of the Past' (12 December 2016) IISD Investment Treaty News www.iisd.org/itn/2016/12/12/indias-joint-interpretive-statement-for-bits-an-attempt-to-slay-the-ghosts-of-the-past-sarthak-malhotra/.

[92] The EU draft for the TTIP is available at http://trade.ec.europa.eu/doclib/press/index. cfm?id=1230 (last accessed 9 December 2016). The November 2015 TPP text, subject to legal check, was released by New Zealand in its capacity as the treaty's depository; see http://www.tpp.mfat.govt. nz/ (last accessed 9 December 2016).

[93] All of the provisions in the draft are numbered 'Article XX' and for this reason are not referenced.

[94] China also seems to have accepted, upfront, the application of national treatment from establishment. In contrast, it only agreed to national treatment post-establishment in its FTAs with New Zealand and Australia: New Zealand–China FTA art 138; and (for China) ChAFTA art 9.3(2) and (4).

[95] According to one observer, the US 'always demands less vetting of foreign investment' in its FTA negotiations: Jane Kelsey, *Hidden Agendas: What We Need to Know About the TPP* (BWB Texts 2013) 16. Australia faced pressure to exempt the US from its screening regime during the AUSFTA negotiations but instead agreed to significantly raise its screening threshold. See further L Crump, 'Global Trade Policy Development in a Two-Track System' (2006) 9 JIEL 487, 497.

India proposed language similar to that found in the TPP on the interpretation of 'like circumstances', although India's version is more elaborate and, by listing broad indicative factors for assessing the legitimacy of regulatory objectives, also more deferential to host governments. Neither New Zealand nor Australia supported it, at least they did not at the time of the 2015 draft. Australia, Japan, India, and Korea also provided text to clarify that national treatment refers, with respect to a regional level of government, to treatment of investors by that regional level of government. This is presumably to address the argument, raised in *Merrill & Ring Forestry Inc v Canada*,[96] that an investor can be discriminated against by one regional government if another investor receives more favourable treatment in a different region by a different regional government.[97]

New Zealand and Australia also supported the application of MFN from the pre-establishment phase, and again, India was the only country not to endorse it. Instead, it seems that India's position on MFN (which it eschews completely in the revised Model BIT finalized in December 2015) was to leave such treatment to individual negotiation. This is not entirely clear, however, given the way the draft text is presented. The ASEAN countries also sought an exception for future intra-ASEAN investment agreements.

On the investor protections, New Zealand generally backed language that closely tracks AANZFTA (and sometimes the CER Investment Protocol), while Australia favoured the language of the US model and the TPP. For the minimum standard of treatment, the differences are in the expression and ordering, rather than the substance. India proposed a list of proscribed behaviours, similar to that in the European Union—Canada Comprehensive Economic and Trade Agreement (CETA)[98] and the EU's TTIP draft,[99] but again neither New Zealand nor Australia indicated any support for this approach at the time. Australia (and Korea) proposed exceptions on health and environmental measures within the prohibitions on performance requirements. This perhaps suggests Australian acceptance of the TPP approach to incorporating policy space within substantive obligations rather than as stand-alone exceptions, although in its FTA with Korea, Australia had agreed to an overarching general exception (as mentioned in Section II.C).

New Zealand (aligned with India) proposed to exclude the 'rare circumstances' proviso to the policy safeguard for public welfare regulation in the annex on expropriation. Australia on the other hand accepted it, although it did not join Korea in seeking to clarify when such rare circumstances might arise (such as when a measure is extremely severe or disproportionate in light of its purpose).[100] New Zealand and Australia also differed on how to treat investor expectations as a factor relevant to the

---

[96] *Merrill & Ring Forestry LP v Government of Canada*, Award, UNCITRAL, 31 March 2010. The tribunal appeared to accept that regional variations could be justified by local conditions (at [225]).

[97] Similar language is also found in eg the Korea–Australia FTA art 11.3(3).

[98] CETA was concluded in mid-2014, then subjected to a 'legal scrub' which in fact significantly altered the text (see Wolfgang Alschner and Dmitriy Skougarevskiy, 'Mapping the Universe of International Investment Agreements' (2016) 19 JIEL 561), including shifting to the EU-preferred 'investment court' model. However, the agreed revised text has not yet been signed.

[99] According to UNCTAD, reaching agreement on an exhaustive list of specific obligations may be challenging but it may also lower the risk of unanticipated interpretations. See UNCTAD, *World Investment Report 2012: Towards a New Generation of Investment Policies* (UNCTAD 2012) 147.

[100] Australia (as well as Korea) proposed including proportionality as a relevant factor for the case-by-case analysis of a measure for its expropriatory effect. For arguments by Henckels and others for tribunals anyway to engage in more structured proportionality testing in investment treaty arbitration see Luke Nottage, 'Rebalancing Investment Treaties and Investor-State Arbitration: Two Approaches' (2016) 17 JWIT 1015 (with a manuscript version at https://papers.ssrn.com/sol3/papers.cfm?abstract_id=2795396 (last accessed 9 December 2016)).

case-by-case analysis of an allegedly expropriatory measure. The factor, as expressed by New Zealand (and India), was whether the measure breached a prior, binding, and written assurance by the host government. For Australia (and China, Japan, and Korea), investment-backed expectations have to be distinct and reasonable, indicating a lower threshold for proof. New Zealand sought to include, as a criterion for a finding of indirect expropriation, that the deprivation be so severe as to amount to a lack of good faith by the host government. Similar language is found in New Zealand's FTA with Korea,[101] as well as Korea's FTA with Canada.[102] According to the draft, however, Korea did not promote its inclusion in the RCEP.

China and Korea confirmed their acceptance of investment treaty arbitration as the primary mode of ISDS. So did Japan, which is interesting given that it gave up on seeking ISDS in its bilateral FTA with Australia (and earlier with the Philippines),[103] plus some concerns expressed particularly by some opposition party parliamentarians especially in the context of TPP negotiations.[104] Indeed, these three countries also proposed extending ISDS to the enforcement of investment agreements.[105] China appears to have promoted the idea of appellate review of awards, although there is no proposed clause on the matter in the draft. The New Zealand and Australian views on these potentially contentious issues cannot be discerned from the draft because in the version as leaked (seemingly October 2015) neither country had provided any text on ISDS. The 'suspension' of the TPP's ISDS coverage for investment contracts with host states, in the CPTPP signed in March 2018, is likely to impact on what ends up being signed in the RCEP investment chapter.

IV. Potential for Promoting More EU-style Treaties in the Asian Region

India finalized its distinctly more pro-state Model BIT in December 2015,[106] although this was dialled back from an earlier discussion draft.[107] Since mid-2016, India has

---

[101] New Zealand–Korea FTA Annex 10-C.

[102] Free Trade Agreement between Canada and the Republic of Korea, Ottawa, 23 September 2014, in force 1 January 2015 Annex 8-B.

[103] Luke Nottage, 'Investor-State Arbitration: Not in the Australia-Japan Free Trade Agreement, and Not Ever for Australia?' (2014) 38 JJL 37.

[104] Shotaro Hamamoto, 'Recent Anti-ISDS Discourse in the Japanese Diet: A Dressed-up but Glaring Hypocrisy' (2015) 16 JWIT 931.

[105] In recent BITs, by contrast, Japan has included a broader 'umbrella' or 'obligations observance' clause that elevates obligations assumed vis-à-vis investors on the part of the host state (even unilaterally) to substantive treaty commitments, which are usually (but not always) then subject also to possible enforcement via ISDS. See Shotaro Hamamoto, 'Debates in Japan over Investor-State Arbitration with Developed States' *CIGI Investor-State Arbitration Series Paper* (2016) 5–6 https://www.cigionline.org/sites/default/files/isa_paper_no.5.pdf (last accessed 9 December 2016).

[106] Prabhash Ranjan, 'India and Bilateral Investment Treaties: From Rejection to Embracement to Hesitance?' in R Rajesh Babu and Srinivas Burra (eds), *'Locating India' in the Contemporary International Legal Order* (Springer 2016).

[107] Joel Dahlquist and Luke Eric Peterson, 'Analysis: In Final Version of its New Model Investment Treaty, India Dials Back Ambition of Earlier Proposals – But Still Favors Some Big Changes' *Investment Arbitration Reporter* (2016) http://www.iareporter.com/articles/analysis-in-final-version-of-its-new-model-investment-treaty-india-dials-back-ambition-of-earlier-proposals-but-still-favors-some-big-changes/ (last accessed 9 December 2016). See also Prabhash Ranjan and Pushkar Anand, 'Investor-State Dispute Settlement in the 2016 Model Bilateral Investment Treaty: Does It Go Too Far?' in Julien Chaisse and Luke Nottage (eds), *International Investment Treaties and Arbitration across Asia* (Brill 2018) 579. Cf also Grant Hanessian and Kabir Duggal, 'The 2015 Indian Model BIT: Is This Change the World Wishes to See?' (2015) 30 ICSID Rev 729.

been approaching BIT partners (such as Australia) to inquire about renegotiating those early treaties according to this template.[108] India also can be expected to press for at least some of the features in its new Model BIT to be included also in FTAs, such as the bilateral treaty under negotiation with Australia since May 2011,[109] as well as RCEP. Some commentators welcome this possibility as a means to slow or reverse the expansion of US-style treaty drafting in the Asian region.[110]

However, pushback can be expected from countries such as Australia with significant outbound FDI stocks or potential, especially if its investors have already had adverse experiences in India (as evidenced by the first-ever and successful 'outbound' treaty claim by an Australian investor, filed on 27 July 2010).[111] Australia will also not want to agree to an Indian-style regime because it could encourage a similarly pro-state stance to be taken by Indonesia, which was also in FTA negotiations with Australia bilaterally since 2013 and through RCEP. Indeed, bilateral diplomatic relations have warmed recently and FTA negotiations were reactivated from 2016, resulting in Australia substantively concluding the bilateral agreement on 31 August 2018. The text remained unavailable as of December 2018, and there is no mention of ISDS (anyway available under AANZFTA and probably under an early BIT), but Australian government summaries of key outcomes mention that the treaty:

contains a set of high-quality, modern rules governing the treatment of services and investment, as well as modern rules on digital trade. Obligations are balanced with robust safeguards to preserve Australia's right to regulate in the public interest.[112]

This text may set a useful baseline for Australia with respect to India, bilaterally and in RCEP. Yet Indonesia had also been letting old BITs lapse since 2014, planning to replace them with 'new generation' treaties through FTAs and/or BITs based on its own new model.[113] The latter remains undecided or at least undisclosed, possibly allowing for more flexibility in negotiations, but countries may also need to be innovative in negotiating with Indonesia bilaterally as well as through RCEP.

In addition, the EU has been 'reorienting' towards Asia in recent years, concluding FTAs with Singapore on 17 October 2014,[114] and with Vietnam on 2 December

---

[108] Deepshikha Sikarwar, 'India Seeks Fresh Treaties With 47 Nations' *The Economic Times* (27 May 2016) http://economictimes.indiatimes.com/news/economy/foreign-trade/india-seeks-fresh-treaties-with-47-nations/articleshow/52458524.cms (last accessed 9 December 2016).

[109] Department of Foreign Affairs and Trade, 'Australia-India Comprehensive Economic Cooperation Agreement' http://dfat.gov.au/trade/agreements/aifta/pages/australia-india-comprehensive-economic-cooperation-agreement.aspx (last accessed 9 December 2016).

[110] Kyla Tienhaara and Belinda Townsend, 'Is India holding the line against another TPP?' *East Asia Forum* (2016) http://www.eastasiaforum.org/2016/05/20/is-india-holding-the-line-against-another-tpp/ (last accessed 9 December 2016).

[111] *White Industries Australia Limited v Republic of India, (Award)*, UNCITRAL (30 November 2011).

[112] Department of Foreign Affairs and Trade, 'Indonesia-Australia Comprehensive Economic Partnership Agreement: Outcomes' https://dfat.gov.au/trade/agreements/not-yet-in-force/iacepa/Pages/ia-cepa-key-outcomes-for-australia.aspx (last accessed 9 October 2018).

[113] Antony Crockett, 'Indonesia's Bilateral Investment Treaties: Between Generations?' (2015) 30 ICSID Rev 437; Antony Crockett, 'The Termination of Indonesia's BITs: Changing the Bathwater but Keeping the Baby?' in Julien Chaisse and Luke Nottage (eds), *International Investment Treaties and Arbitration across Asia* (Brill 2018) 159.

[114] See European Commission, 'Singapore' http://ec.europa.eu/trade/policy/countries-and-regions/countries/singapore/ (last accessed 9 December 2016), and Mahdev Mohan, 'The EU-Singapore Free Trade Agreement: Rationality "Unbound"?' (International Investment Arbitration and Dispute Resolution in Asia Conference, Bangkok, July 2016).

2015.[115] The latter, in particular, hopes to 'trigger a new wave of high quality invest-ment in both directions, supported by an updated investment dispute resolution system',[116] reflecting prominent features of the new EU approach towards investment treaty drafting—precipitated mainly by the TTIP negotiations with the US.[117] As part of the EU also now actively pursuing greater engagement with counterparts in the Asian region, FTA negotiations are also now underway (since June 2018) with Australia and New Zealand.[118] Although it is unclear if and how 'Brexit' will impact on the EU's negotiations in the region, in 2018 the EU also concluded a separate in-vestment agreement with Singapore that substituted its preferred 'investment court' mechanism for the more traditional TPP-like ISDS arbitration mechanism that had been included in their 2014 FTA.[119]

For all these reasons, a real possibility is emerging of contemporary EU-style drafting changing the trajectory of investment treaties in the Asia-Pacific region.[120] Drawing also on the analysis above of the main treaties recently concluded by Australia and New Zealand (section II) and their initial positions in RCEP negotiations (section III), section IV.A therefore examines some possibilities in terms of substantive commitments. Section IV.B focuses on various reform options for dispute resolution procedures, including the EU-style permanent 'investment court' alternative to ad hoc appointments of ISDS arbi-trators, as found in the recent EU–Vietnam FTA.[121]

---

[115] See European Commission, 'Vietnam' http://ec.europa.eu/trade/policy/countries-and-regions/countries/vietnam/ (last accessed 9 December 2016), and Nguyen Manh Dzung and Nguyen Thi Thu Trang, 'International Investment Dispute Resolution in Vietnam: Opportunities and Challenges' (International Investment Arbitration and Dispute Resolution in Asia Conference, Bangkok, July 2016).

[116] European Commission, 'The EU and Vietnam Finalise Landmark Trade Deal' *Trade News Archive* (2015) http://trade.ec.europa.eu/doclib/press/index.cfm?id=1409; Nguyen Manh Dzung and Nguyen Thi Thu Trang, 'International Investment Dispute Resolution in Vietnam: Opportunities and Challenges' in Julien Chaisse and Luke Nottage (eds), *International Investment Treaties and Arbitration across Asia* (Brill 2018) 243.

[117] August Reinisch, 'The European Union and Investor-State Dispute Settlement: From Investor-State Arbitration to a Permanent Investment Court' *CIGI Investor-State Arbitration Series Paper* (2016) 2 https://www.cigionline.org/publications/european (last accessed 9 December 2016).

[118] Department of Foreign Affairs and Trade, 'Australia-European Union Free Trade Agreement' http://dfat.gov.au/trade/agreements/aeufta/pages/aeufta.aspx (Australia); New Zealand Foreign Affairs and Trade, 'New Zealand-EU FTA' https://www.mfat.govt.nz/en/trade/free-trade-agreements/agreements-under-negotiation/eu-fta/ (last accessed 8 October 2018) (New Zealand).

[119] See Mahdev Mohan, 'The European Union's Free Trade Agreement with Singapore: One Step Forward, 28 Steps Back?' in Julien Chaisse and Luke Nottage (eds), *International Investment Treaties and Arbitration across Asia* (Brill 2018) 180; Tang See Kit, 'Brexit and the EU-Singapore FTA: Further Delays or a Slow-Death?' *Channel NewsAsia* (2016) http://www.channelnewsasia.com/news/busi-ness/singapore/brexit-and-the-eu/2929208.html (last accessed 9 December 2016); and European Commission, 'Key Elements of the EU-Singapore Trade and Investment Agreements' (18 April 2018) http://trade.ec.europa.eu/doclib/press/index.cfm?id=1827 (last accessed 9 October 2018). See also generally ; Sophie Nappert and Nikos Lavranos, 'BREXIT: Implications for the EU Reform of ISDS' *Practical Law* (2016) http://uk.practicallaw.com/5-625-7968?source=relatedcontent (last ac-cessed 9 December 2016).

[120] For some further preliminary views see also Luke Nottage, 'Towards a European Model for Investor-State Disputes?' *East Asia Forum* (2016) http://www.eastasiaforum.org/2016/07/01/towards-a-european-model-for-investor-state-disputes/ (last accessed 9 December 2016).

[121] See also Mark Mangan, 'The EU Succeeds in Establishing a Permanent Investment Court in its Trade Treaties with Canada and Vietnam' *Dechert LLP Client Briefing Publication* (2016) https://www.dechert.com/The_EU_Succeeds_in_Establishing_a_Permanent_Investment_Court_in_its_Trade_Treaties_with_Canada_and_Vietnam_03-23-2016/ (last accessed 9 December 2016); and gener-ally Stefanie Schacherer, 'TPP, CETA and TTIP Between Innovation and Consolidation: Resolving Investor-State Disputes under Mega-regionals' (2016) 7 JIDS 628.

A. Substantive provisions

The EU approach to investment coverage is to extend investor protections to a wide range of investment types. In common with US-style agreements, it follows the asset-based method for defining 'investment'. However, the EU's TTIP draft and CETA take a distinctly different approach to the definition of 'covered investment' as compared to the US Model BIT, by their incorporation of an express 'legality' requirement.[122] These types of provisions require investors to comply with the host state's foreign investment laws as well as other laws that may be applicable to the making of investments (including those aimed at preventing fraud and corruption). In this respect, a legality requirement arguably differs from an 'admission' requirement, which is only concerned with an investor's compliance with foreign investment laws. The wider scope of legality requirements is balanced against their less strict application, in the sense that tribunals have tended to require compliance with respect only to non-trivial provisions of the applicable laws.[123] The legality requirement in the EU's TTIP proposal is stated as follows (in italics):[124]

'covered investment' means an investment which is owned, directly or indirectly, or controlled, directly or indirectly, by investors of one Party in the territory of the other Party *made in accordance with applicable laws*, whether made before or after the entry into force of this Agreement.

By contrast, the Indian Model BIT adopts an enterprise-based definition of 'investment', where an investment is defined as an enterprise together with certain specified assets that it may possess. Enterprise-based definitions are normally (but not always) narrower in scope than asset-based ones.[125] In the case of the Indian Model BIT, portfolio investment (which is not itself defined) is expressly excluded from the list of qualifying assets. Expansive legality requirements covering not only the making of an investment, but also its operation, are included in the definitions of both 'investment' and 'enterprise'. The definition of 'investment' also requires that the enterprise be 'constituted, organised and operated in good faith'.[126] In common with most standard definitions of investment, the investment must have the characteristics of an investment, such as the commitment of capital and assumption of risk. In addition to this, the investment's contribution to the development of the host state is also a relevant factor. If the investor is a juridical person, the definition of 'investor' requires that it have 'substantial business activities' within the home state or be controlled by such an entity.[127] In the earlier draft, minority shareholder claims were excluded by a requirement that the investor own or control the investment (i.e. the enterprise). Interestingly, this has been removed from the final version.[128]

---

[122] EU TTIP draft art x1; CETA art 8.1. It may be possible to argue that at least some form of 'legality' requirement is implied anyway under background general international law.
[123] Reviewing 15 treaty arbitration cases, including five involving Southeast Asian states, it has been argued that admission requirements for the (initial) investment under host state law should be strictly observed, whereas any legality requirements under the relevant treaty should only preclude protection for 'non-trivial violations of a host State's legal order, violations of a host State's foreign investment regime, and violations of public policy, such as fraud or corruption'. See Chester Brown, 'The Regulation of Foreign Direct Investment by Admission Requirements and the Duty on Investors to Comply with the Host State Law' (2015) 21 NZBLQ 303, 315.
[124] EU TTIP draft art x1.   [125] UNCTAD, 'Scope and Definition' (n 30) 31.
[126] Separately, the Indian Model BIT (in art 11) has a substantive provision on investor obligations.
[127] Indian Model BIT art 1.3 (definition of 'enterprise'); art 1.4 ('investment'); and art 1.5 ('investor').
[128] There has also recently been some renewed interest as to whether and how minority shareholder claims can be brought under ISDS procedures, for example in the context of the TPP and

In some respects, the current Indian approach departs in such significant ways from New Zealand and Australian treaty practice that it is hard to see it gain much traction with either of them—in particular:

- the enterprise-based definition of investment and the exclusion from it of port-folio assets (depending on how those might be defined);
- the standing obligation to comply with host state law; and
- the express (but potentially vague) requirement of good faith as a condition to accessing the treaty protections.

Other aspects of the Indian Model BIT are dissimilar in terms of text or structure, but reflect common concepts. To this extent there is perhaps some scope for com-promise or finding common ground. For example, the potential for investment to contribute to development objectives is often spelt out in preambles. The Indian BIT differs in this respect because it is part of the definition of 'investment', but its status is only as a relevant characteristic of investments rather than a mandatory criterion. The requirement that an investor have substantial business activities within the home state (if a juridical person) is not totally foreign either, but is more commonly re-flected in 'denial of benefits' clauses that are aimed at addressing the problem of forum shopping. Including the requirement within the definition of 'investor' as under the Indian Model may be a more effective means of foreclosing on forum shopping. This is because, unlike denial of benefits clauses, the host state does not have to take the proactive step of denying benefits (and then potentially having to defend its right to do so). There has also been uncertainty about when the denial of benefits should take place, with some tribunals deciding that states must exercise the right to deny protec-tions before the commencement of any arbitral proceedings.[129] The Indian Model BIT clarifies this in a separate denial of benefits clause, which allows the respondent state to deny the treaty's benefits at any time, including after institution of legal proceedings. This seems arbitrary, and also unnecessary given the definitional requirement for sub-stantial business activities under which the investor must prove its presence within the home state as a threshold matter.

More generally, in their use of legality requirements, both the EU and Indian texts re-flect their concern about the need for investors to respect host state law when investing. New Zealand and Australia have also recognized this concern in their FTA practice, through their prior acceptance of both admission and legality requirements in agree-ments such as AANZFTA and their earlier BITs.[130] That said, so far, they have not been consistent, and in the CER Investment Protocol and TPP for instance, their screening regimes are only recognized as exempted non-conforming measures. Nonetheless, ad-mission and legality requirements align with their interests and values, specifically in

---

earlier given the first ever claim against Thailand (under a BIT with Germany): see Nottage, 'The TPP Investment Chapter and Investor-State Arbitration in Asia and Oceania' (n 15), Part III.B (with further references).

[129] See eg *Plama Consortium v Bulgaria*, Jurisdiction, ICSID Case No ARB/03/24, 8 February 2005; *Yukos Universal Limited (Isle of Man) v The Russian Federation*, Interim Award on Jurisdiction and Admissibility, PCA Case No 227, 30 November 2009; *Khan Resources Inc and others v Mongolia*, Jurisdiction, PCA Case No 2011-09, 25 July 2012. Contrast *Pac Rim Cayman LLC v El Salvador*, Jurisdiction, ICSID Case No ARB/09/12, 1 June 2012, paras [4.84]–[4.91].

[130] See eg Australia–Indonesia BIT (admission), Australia–Argentina BIT (legality), New Zealand–Hong Kong BIT (legality).

relation to their screening regimes, but also more broadly the respect for due process which is well established in both countries.[131] As noted earlier (section II.C), Australia's experience as respondent in the *Philip Morris* case should have raised its awareness of the practical significance of admission requirements as a 'gateway' through which investor claims need to pass.[132] For these reasons there is a clear possibility for the requirements to feature more consistently in their future FTA practice. In terms of form, the Indian Model BIT incorporates legality requirements into two definitions centred around its enterprise-based view of what constitutes an investment. The EU's approach of including a legality requirement in the definition of 'covered investment' is more consistent with the structure adopted by New Zealand and Australia to addressing investment coverage, and also their prior acceptance of admission requirements within that definition.

The national treatment and MFN treatment provisions in CETA do not have the clarificatory language regarding the meaning of 'in like circumstances' that is found in the TPP.[133] (The EU's TTIP draft has neither the national treatment nor most favoured nation treatment provisions at all, but references to them in the ISDS section of the draft suggest that they will be added eventually.) India's Model BIT does attempt to clarify what 'in like circumstances' means,[134] but the open-ended nature of the language it uses may leave too much room for states to discriminate against foreign investors. As noted above (Section III), India's proposal for national treatment in the RCEP negotiations (including similar language) was not agreed to by New Zealand and Australia in the 2015 leaked draft investment chapter. India's Model BIT does not include any MFN provision, as mentioned in section III above. Similarly, the EU has also been flexible with regard to MFN rights, excluding them from its recent FTA with Singapore. Accordingly, on national treatment and MFN, New Zealand and Australia may continue to prefer the TPP approach of including both while seeking to confine their scope to discrimination that cannot properly be justified on policy grounds.

In terms of the other substantive investor protections, one of the significant features of the EU's recent practice has been its development of a list of behaviours that it considers would breach the obligation of fair and equitable treatment. For example, for TTIP, the EU proposes a clause that states a party will be in breach of the obligation if a measure constitutes a denial of justice, fundamental breach of due process, manifest discrimination, targeted discrimination, harassment or similar bad faith conduct. The list may be added to by agreement of the standing joint committee of the parties,[135] as in CETA but in contrast with the Indian Model BIT's (completely closed) list.[136] Whether it is realistic to leave the development of the law to an FTA committee in this way may depend on how the committee structure is set up and supported, and may be particularly problematic in 'mini-lateral' agreements with multiple states party such as RCEP. To date, decision-making by FTA joint committees on matters concerning the scope of investment obligations has had minimal impact, apart from a

---

[131] For example, New Zealand and Australia rank fourth and 13th respectively in Transparency International's 2015 (anti-)Corruption Perceptions Index http://www.transparency.org/country/ (last accessed 9 December 2016).
[132] See Chester Brown, 'The Regulation of Foreign Direct Investment by Admission Requirements and the Duty on Investors to Comply with the Host State Law' (2015) 21 NZBLQ 301.
[133] CETA arts 8.6 and 8.7.   [134] Indian Model BIT art 4 footnote 2.
[135] EU TTIP draft art 3(2).
[136] Compare art 3.1 with CETA Investment Chapter art 8.10 available at European Commission, 'In Focus: EU-Canada Comprehensive Economic and Trade Agreement', http://ec.europa.eu/trade/policy/in-focus/ceta/ (last accessed 9 December 2016).

high-profile joint interpretation of fair and equitable treatment by the parties to the North American FTA.[137]

Unlike most contemporary investment treaties, the EU's proposed clause (and that already agreed in CETA) does not limit the obligations of fair and equitable treatment and full protection and security to the minimum standard of treatment under customary international law. This latter approach is intended to protect the regulatory powers of host states, but it has become contentious because of the discretion that is still available to tribunals to determine the content of the standard.[138] India too has developed a list of proscribed behaviours in its Model BIT,[139] but unlike the EU version (and that agreed in CETA), India's list seeks also seeks to tether it to customary international law. To date, New Zealand and Australia have seemingly preferred the flexibility of grounding their obligations in customary international law, but given the drawbacks of this they have also been receptive to efforts to make their views on that law clearer. A possible middle ground option would be a list of behaviours considered to breach the customary law standard that is provided on an illustrative but non-exhaustive basis.

In terms of expropriation, the EU approach is quite similar to that found in the US Model BIT in its use of an annex to determine the scope of indirect expropriation, and the EU's annex is also similarly worded compared to the US one (in turn strongly influenced by US domestic law standards). It differs in that it provides some explanation of when 'rare circumstances' might arise (for the proviso to the safeguard for public welfare regulation), and its TTIP draft (but not CETA) omits investor expectations altogether from the (non-exhaustive) list of assessment factors.[140] These features may be especially appealing to New Zealand, given its apparent retreat from the TPP/US text in the RCEP negotiations. Rather than using an annex, the Indian Model BIT explains the scope of indirect expropriation in the main body of the treaty.[141] The language it uses is fairly orthodox. It emphatically rejects the notion that public welfare regulation may be deemed expropriatory, and the 'rare circumstances' proviso is not included. This again may be appealing to New Zealand, although perhaps not for Australia, in view of its apparently different position in the RCEP negotiations (outlined in Section III).

Unlike the US, the EU favours applying general exceptions to the commitments on investment,[142] as does India. As explained in Part II, this seems to be another area of divergence between New Zealand and Australia, with New Zealand aligned more closely to the EU / India view. The EU also favours including a clause that affirms the parties' general right to regulate to achieve legitimate policy objectives.[143] A statement to similar effect is included in the preamble of the TPP (although not in the preamble of the US Model BIT). Preambles may be taken into account in the interpretation of treaty provisions, and the TPP statement may support more pro-state interpretations

---

[137] NAFTA Free Trade Commission, 'North American Free Trade Agreement Notes of Interpretation of Certain Chapter 11 Provisions' (31 July 2001) http://www.sice.oas.org/tpd/nafta/Commission/CH11understanding_e.asp (last accessed 9 December 2016).

[138] See Caroline Henckels, 'Protecting Regulatory Autonomy through Greater Precision in Investment Treaties: The TPP, CETA and TTIP' (2016) 19 JIEL 33.

[139] Indian Model BIT art 3.1.

[140] EU TTIP draft Annex 1.   [141] Indian Model BIT art 5.3.

[142] The FTA with Singapore incorporates exceptions within the national treatment rule, similar to Australia's proposal for the prohibitions on performance requirements under the RCEP.

[143] See eg EU TTIP draft art 2.1.

of that agreement.[144] Affirming the right to regulate in the main body of the treaty may give it greater interpretive weight, although at this stage the impact of this approach remains to be seen. That said, protecting the right to regulate underpins much of the controversy within New Zealand and Australia regarding FTAs. Both countries may be receptive to affirming the right to regulate in an operative provision as it would be an easily understood way of responding to public concerns.

B. Dispute settlement procedure

Controversy persists especially over ISDS, in several developed countries (such as Australia and more recently New Zealand), large developing countries (such as India and Indonesia) and in international society at large.[145] Already, Vietnam and even Singapore have agreed to treaties with the EU that accept at least some aspects of the latter's more cautious approach towards conventional ISDS.

Australia and New Zealand have also displayed some flexibility in their treaty practice with regard to ISDS, as explained above (sections II–III). They have excluded ISDS altogether vis-à-vis each other (in the CER Protocol, as well as within AANZFTA and TPP), and (for Australia) in bilateral FTAs with other developed countries (with the US and Japan, respectively, although ISDS will extend to them also if and when the TPP comes into force, and will at least extend to Japan if and when the CPTPP comes into force). Both have otherwise adopted contemporary US-style drafting of ISDS provisions, but displaying some flexibility with counterparties (e.g. in AANZFTA), and Australia has agreed to some innovative features in recent FTAs (notably the 'public welfare notice' procedure in its FTA with China, which is not found in any other Chinese agreements so therefore may derive from the Australian side). Following the election of a new Labour Party-led Government in New Zealand in late 2017, New Zealand renounced ISDS for future treaties.[146] Although the policy announcement refers to the rejection of 'ISDS', we assume the New Zealand policy opposes the traditional but controversial ad hoc arbitration mechanism for resolving investor claims, rather than investor state dispute resolution altogether.[147]

Accordingly, there seems significant scope for Australia, with New Zealand, to press for more EU-like features in treaties in future negotiations in the region, including RCEP (cf section III). In fact, there are at least five reform options. First, if the primary concern is inconsistency in decision-making by ISDS tribunals, an appellate review mechanism can be added to assess first-instance awards for errors of law (and possibly even some errors of fact) as well as the narrower grounds set out eg in the ICSID Convention.[148] This can be seen as a 'TPP+' approach, as it and earlier US-inspired

---

[144] A preamble can be taken as evidence of relevant intent and context for the interpretation of treaty commitments. See Vienna Convention on the Law of Treaties (in force 27 January 1980) art 31(1)–(2).

[145] See eg the Google news search and Twitter feed results reported in Luke Nottage, 'International Arbitration and Society at Large' in Andrea Bjorklund, Franco Ferrari, and Stefan Kroell (eds), *Cambridge Compendium on International Arbitration* (CUP 2019).

[146] Kawharu and Nottage, 'Renouncing Investor-State Dispute Settlement in Australia, Then New Zealand: Déjà Vu' (n 19).

[147] See Derek Cheng, 'Ban on Foreign House Buyers by Early 2018: But Aussie Buyers Exempt' *New Zealand Herald* (31 October 2017) http://www.nzherald.co.nz/business/news/article.cfm?c_id=3&objectid=11939067. Complete rejection of ISDS is unlikely to be sustainable for New Zealand, given that significant counterparties in RCEP and other agreements will continue to insist on some mechanism for directly resolving investor claims, in addition to traditional inter-state arbitration.

[148] Following the new EU approach, under art 29.1 of the EU–Vietnam FTA (at http://trade.ec.europa.eu/doclib/docs/2016/february/tradoc_154210.pdf), the grounds for appeal are: 'a) that the

treaty practice in fact envisaged or even required the state parties to consider adding some form of appellate review, even if that has never been implemented in the region. An appellate review body could be introduced under each treaty, as presently favoured by the EU, or through a proposed multi-lateral 'opt-in convention' extending a single appeal mechanism (or indeed a single permanent 'International Tribunal for Investment') to existing treaties.[149]

Secondly, in part perhaps to improve decision-making quality but primarily to address public perceptions (rightly or wrongly) about potential conflicts of interest or bias by arbitrators on ISDS tribunals, Australia and New Zealand may promote a code of conduct and/or predetermined panel for arbitrators. Australia already agreed to both in its FTA with China signed on 17 June 2015.[150] Because that was after conclusion of the EU–Singapore FTA on 17 October 2014, whereupon the EU issued a 'Factsheet' on investment provisions highlighting similar features in that earlier FTA,[151] it seems Australia and/or China followed this precedent.[152] The recent EU–Vietnam FTA also has extensive provisions on 'Ethics' for those deciding investor-state disputes. For example, they:

shall not participate in the consideration of any disputes that would create a direct or indirect conflict of interest.... In addition, upon appointment, they shall refrain from acting as counsel or as party-appointed expert or witness in any pending or new investment protection dispute under this or any other agreement or domestic law'.[153]

The additional words (not spelled out in the EU–Singapore or Australia–China FTAs) seek to avoid the increasingly criticized problem of 'double-hatting', whereby

---

Tribunal has erred in the interpretation or application of the applicable law; (b) that the Tribunal has manifestly erred in the appreciation of the facts, including the appreciation of relevant domestic law; or (c) those provided for in Article 52 of the ICSID Convention, in so far as they are not covered by (a) and (b)'.

[149] The latter was proposed by Gabrielle Kaufmann-Kohler and Michele Potesta for UNCITRAL: 'Can the Mauritius Convention serve as a model for the reform of investor-State arbitration in connection with the introduction of a permanent investment tribunal or an appeal mechanism? Analysis and Roadmap' *CIDS—Geneva Center for International Dispute Settlement Research Paper* (2016) http://www.uncitral.org/pdf/english/commissionsessions/unc/unc-49/CIDS_Research_Paper_-_Can_the_Mauritius_Convention_serve_as_a_model.pdf (last accessed 9 December 2016). UNCITRAL Working Group III has since initiated a work programme on ISDS reform, including consideration of a permanent multilateral investment court. See http://www.uncitral.org/uncitral/en/commission/working_groups/3Investor_State.html (last accessed 8 October 2018).

[150] See Annex 9-A and art 9.15(5)–(6). Under the latter, the states shall nominate at least 20 arbitrators for a list, within two years of it coming into force (20 December 2015), although so far it seems Australia has made no nominations. See generally Leon Trakman and David Musaleyan, 'Arguments for and against Standing Panels of Arbitrators in Investor-State Arbitration Evidence and Reality' (2016) (manuscript on file with the authors).

[151] See European Commission, 'Investment Provisions in the EU-Singapore Free Trade Agreement' (17 October 2014) http://trade.ec.europa.eu/doclib/docs/2014/october/tradoc_152845.pdf (last accessed 9 December 2016). For details see Annex 9-F and art 9.18(3)–(4) (providing for at least 15 arbitrators to be appointed within one year).

[152] It is unclear whether both features were promoted in their FTA negotiations primarily by Singapore or the EU, but the latter seems more likely to have provided the impetus. (On the shift in EU negotiating preferences in recent years see generally Reinisch, 'The European Union and Investor-State Dispute Settlement'). At least one other FTA concluded earlier by Japan provides for a list of arbitrators for ISDS tribunals, namely that with Mexico: Hamamoto and Nottage, 'Japan' (n 39) 395. However, that has never been created or at least publicized.

[153] Chapter 8 (Trade in Services, Investment and E-Commerce) art 14(1) European Commission, 'EU-Vietnam Free Trade Agreement: Agreed Text as of January 2016' *News Archive* (1 February 2016) http://trade.ec.europa.eu/doclib/press/index.cfm?id=1437 (last accessed 9 December 2016). Curiously, this refers to 'Annex II (Code of Conduct)', but that does not seem to be yet available.

an arbitrator may promote an interpretation or application of a similar treaty that advances his or her client's position in a pending or likely case under a similar treaty when serving as counsel.[154] In addition, however, the EU–Vietnam FTA provides that the dispute resolvers shall be nominated by the states on monthly retainers as members of a two-tier 'investment court'.

A third, more ambitious reform option (not yet found in the region) would be to combine appellate review with a code of conduct and/or predetermined panel of arbitrators. The fourth would be to add the EU's preference for a permanent investment court, as under its recent FTA with Vietnam.

A fifth conceivable option is based upon the revised Indian Model BIT. The latter provides quite extensive details aimed at preventing conflicts of interest among arbitrators, which may be supplanted by an agreed code of conduct, albeit no express prohibition of double-hatting. However, it has no predetermined list of arbitrators, and no commitment even to consult on an appeals facility.[155] The big difference is that the Indian Model BIT requires exhaustion of local administrative and judicial remedies, to be commenced within 'one (1) year from the date on which the investor first acquired, or should have first acquired, knowledge of the measure in question and knowledge that the investment, or the investor with respect to its investment, had incurred loss or damage as a result'. Then, but only after 'at least a period of five years from the date on which the investor first acquired knowledge of the measure in question', can the investor file a notice of dispute under the treaty, triggering at least six months of negotiations to take place at the capital city of the host state. The investor may then issue an claim to arbitration, but only if (i) preceded by a notice of arbitration at least ninety days before hand, (ii) no more than twelve months after exhausting local remedies, and (iii) no more than six years after the investor first acquired or should have first acquired knowledge of the measure and loss.

Essentially, therefore, the investor must proceed quickly to local courts or tribunals, then seek relief there for five years, and then file for arbitration under further tight conditions. This process is unlikely to be palatable for those familiar with the extensive delays in Indian courts, including those familiar with a BIT award in 2011 in favour of an Australian investor because India had not complied with a treaty commitment to provide 'effective means' for enforcing arbitral awards.[156] Indian investors have also started to take advantage of existing BITs to protect their outbound investments, namely in Indonesia.[157] Nonetheless, the Indian government is likely to begin treaty (re)negotiations, including for FTAs with Australia bilaterally and via RCEP, from the standpoint of its new Model BIT. If developed countries like Australia and New Zealand wish to avoid the revival of an exhaustion of local remedies requirement, which was a major impetus for moving away from customary international law to

[154] For an early and strong critique see Philippe Sands, 'Conflict and Conflicts in Investment Treaty Arbitration: Ethical Standards for Counsel' in Chester Brown and Kate Miles (eds), *Evolution in International Investment Arbitration* (CUP 2011).

[155] See especially art 19(10)–(11) and cf art 29 http://finmin.nic.in/reports/ModelTextIndia_BIT.pdf (last accessed 9 December 2016).

[156] *White Industries v Republic of India*, (Award), UNCITRAL (30 November 2011). However, this and subsequent BIT claims may have prompted some more general improvements in India's arbitration law and practice: see Harisankar K Sathyapalan, 'Indian Judiciary and International Arbitration: A BIT of a Control?' (2017) 33 AI 503.

[157] Jarrod Hepburn and Luke Eric Peterson, 'Indian Investor's BIT Claim Against Indonesia Moves Forward, With Tribunal Now Finalised' *Investment Arbitration Reporter* (2016) http://www.iareporter.com/articles/indian-investors-bit-claim-against-indonesia-moves-forward-with-tribunal-now-finalized/ (last accessed 9 December 2016).

investment treaties in the first place,[150] the compromise may well have to be at least option 1 or 2 above, or possibly even option 3 or 4.

V. Conclusions

The foregoing analysis has shown significant commonalities in Australian and New Zealand treaty practice, especially in their FTAs over the last decade inspired by contemporary US practice, yet also some significant flexibility depending on the issue (especially whether and how to incorporate ISDS) and on the counterparties (e.g. from Southeast Asia). This opens up considerable scope for both countries to influence the future trajectory of treaty negotiations in the Asian region, including moving it towards more contemporary EU-style drafting that is more deferential to host state interests. This seems particularly likely in relation to the procedure for direct claims by investors, where there exist various options short of a full-scale permanent investment court, some of which may prove an acceptable compromise in the face of the revised Indian Model BIT approach that is most unpalatable for investors. Australia and New Zealand also need to take into account the recent hesitancy displayed by Indonesia, in the face of some large treaty-based ISDS claims.

There are also other attractions for both countries to display more leadership now in reforming the traditional ISDS procedure, centred on ad hoc appointments of arbitrators and a single-tier dispute resolution mechanism. Most of the public concern, evident in media coverage and parliamentary inquiries recently in Australia and (more recently) New Zealand, has been fixated on this aspect of investment treaties rather than the scope of their substantive commitments, and the merits of the latter compared to domestic law standards of protection available to all investors through local courts and tribunals. This may be because it is easier to see that ISDS provides an 'extra' protection available only to foreign investors (even if that was precisely the point, especially in countries with less developed domestic law systems). But the critical commentary understandably has concentrated on the initial lack of attention regarding appointments of arbitrators, and current patterns (compare for example with appointments to WTO panels),[159] especially now that more and higher profile ISDS claims are being filed.

Those from the 'political left' argue that this encroaches too much on national sovereignty in matters of major public interest, and may concentrate on this issue in the hope of putting a brake on negotiating FTAs and economic liberalization in the wake of the Global Financial Crisis of 2008. Those from the 'economic right' also highlight the additional ISDS procedure as formally 'discriminatory', like FTAs, but in the hope of revitalizing multi-lateral or unilateral initiatives to promote instead greater economic liberalization. From this theoretical starting point, these economists are sceptical about whether ISDS-backed treaty commitments might still be worthwhile through promoting more cross-border FDI. Although a recent econometric analysis finds they do, it also finds (counterintuitively) that weaker-form ISDS provisions have an even stronger positive impact on FDI flows.[160]

[158] Rudolf Dolzer and Christoph Schreuer, *Principles of International Investment Law* (OUP 2009) 215.
[159] Joost Pauwelyn, 'The Rule of Law without the Rule of Lawyers? Why Investment Arbitrators Are from Mars, Trade Adjudicators Are from Venus' (2015) 109 AJIL 761.
[160] Shiro Armstrong and Luke Nottage, 'The Impact of Investment Treaties and ISDS Provisions on Foreign Direct Investment: A Baseline Econometric Analysis' (Sydney Law School Research Paper No

Apart from such principled policy considerations, and the current preferences of major counterparties to its pending and likely future investment treaty negotiations, the Australian Government in particular has pragmatic political reasons now for advancing more EU-like innovations. It has a razor-thin majority in the lower House of Representatives, and will most probably need the votes of the main Opposition Labor Party in the Senate, to pass tariff reduction legislation before being able to ratify the CPTPP or eventually the RCEP. Indeed, it could well lose power at (or even before) the next general election that must take place before April 2019. The opposition Labor Party, already emboldened by almost winning the general election held in July 2016, has reiterated its objections to ISDS provisions—in future as well as past treaties. More broadly, in January 2017 the Labor Opposition Leader criticized former Prime Minister Malcolm Turnbull for agreeing with his Japanese counterpart to proceed anyway to ratify the TPP, even if the incoming Trump Administration did not do so. Although Bill Shorten reportedly called such an initiative a 'waste of time', perhaps reflecting the fact that under its current wording the TPP required ratification by the US to come into effect, he went on to express concerns that were more protectionist than pragmatic.[161]

Nonetheless, the Turnbull Coalition Government joined the ten other TPP signatories in agreeing on the CPTPP in March 2018. During discussions in federal Parliament, Labor parliamentarians continued objecting in principle to the ISDS provisions.[162] However, as for past FTAs including ISDS and despite complaints from its Union backers, Labor voted with the Coalition Government for legislation introducing tariff reductions and other measures needed for Australia to ratify the CPTPP.[163]

Even if the CPTPP comes into force for Australia, with ISDS provisions retained, it seems likely that a future Labor-led Government may well revert to the policy of eschewing ISDS in future treaties that it enforced over 2011-3, and which subsequently remained the Labor Party's position in principle. A Labor-led Government may also seek to review old treaties, especially BITs. Even the current Coalition Government has started doing this, beginning with negotiations with Uruguay. If Labor remains in Opposition after the general election needed before April 2018, it will undoubtedly keep voicing criticisms of traditional ISDS. For these reasons, we wrote in late 2017 to the Minister and Opposition Spokesperson for Trade, urging a more bipartisan approach to treaty negotiations (including contemporary EU-style treaty innovations as a possible compromise way forward), working also more closely with the Labour-led Government in New Zealand that has renounced traditional ISDS in future treaties.[164] So far, this has not met with a positive response in Australia. However, a compromise

---

16/74, 15 August 2016) https://papers.ssrn.com/sol3/papers.cfm?abstract_id=2824090 (last accessed 9 December 2016).

[161] 'Trans-Pacific Partnership: Malcolm Turnbull Accuses Shorten of Populism Amid Dead Deal Comments' *The Australian* (16 January 2017) http://www.abc.net.au/news/2017-01-16/turnbull-accuses-shorten-of-populism-amid-tpp-deal-comments/8185132 (quoting Shorten as complaining that: 'In 2016, we lost 50,000 full-time jobs in Australia and I don't want to see a repeat of that this year').

[162] For evidence presented to one of the inquiries, with further references, see Luke Nottage and Ana Ubilava, 'Costs, Outcomes and Transparency in ISDS Arbitrations: Evidence for an Investment Treaty Parliamentary Inquiry' (2018) 21(4) International Arbitration Law Review 111–7, with a manuscript version at https://ssrn.com/abstract=3227401 (last accessed 9 October 2018).

[163] Ana Patty, 'Unions Accuse Labor of Selling Them Out Over TPP' *Sydney Morning Herald* (13 September 2018) https://www.smh.com.au/business/workplace/unions-accuse-labor-of-selling-them-out-over-tpp-20180912-p503bx.html (last accessed 9 October 2018).

[164] Our letters are available at http://blogs.usyd.edu.au/japaneselaw/2017KawharuNottage TurnbullGovt_Combined_LN01.pdf (last accessed 18 December 2017).

way forward for Australia and New Zealand to conclude treaties like RCEP may prove more attractive after Australia's upcoming general election.[165]

Meanwhile, as urged by one of us for Australia in parliamentary hearings to ratify the CPTPP,[166] both countries might seek or even commit in advance at least to a strict code of conduct for ISDS arbitrators (eg preventing 'double-hatting'), and to seek subsequent addition of an appellate review mechanism, as envisaged under the TPP/CPTPP. Even without agreement from counterparties to existing treaties, Australia and New Zealand could publish a predetermined list of arbitrators (as indeed required in Australia's FTA with China.

The Australian Government might also respond to calls from the Labor Opposition, through the 2015 Senate Inquiry, for greater consultation and openness about treaty-making generally. For example, it could commit to developing a model Investment chapter or at least negotiating parameters (perhaps listing and explaining several options in terms of investor–state dispute settlement), to frame future negotiations as well as a reassessment of its many early generation BITs. Such initiatives are important given the revival of broader concerns about inbound FDI in Australia, threatening bipartisan consensus since the 1980s.

As for New Zealand, there are now similar political pressures to make reform commitments, even though New Zealand has only one BIT in force that could benefit from a reassessment based on a new bipartisan template. Public media coverage of ISDS in New Zealand has been growing over recent years.[167] This coverage is likely to continue with ongoing discussion about the future of the TPP/CPTPP and RCEP negotiations underway. Political leaders cannot take for granted that interest in FTA negotiations, and their investment chapters in particular, will be positive. This was evident from select committee hearings on the FTA with Korea and the TPP, both of which exacerbated an emerging rift between the then National-led Government and the then Opposition Labour Party. Notably, Labour has started to adopt more critical stances on FTAs, which would have been inconceivable barely a decade ago. Indeed, Labour was elected into power in late 2017, albeit with only forty-six out of 120 seats in Parliament. It has formed a coalition with the populist New Zealand First party, and relies also on the Greens for votes on confidence and supply measures. New Zealand First and the Greens, as well as Labour since the 2017 election, are now all opposed to ISDS—but perhaps not to an EU-style investment court.[168] In other words, even in New Zealand, political factors tell in favour of New Zealand reassessing how it approaches its investment commitments. These same factors may also help to explain why New Zealand appears to have reverted to relatively more pro-state provisions for RCEP during negotiations in 2015, despite the former National Government's position that the TPP is at least tolerably safe. (Indeed, the National Government has remained ever hopeful that life remains in the TPP/CPTPP, despite the indications to the contrary following the 2016 US presidential election.[169])

---

[165] Kawharu and Nottage, 'Renouncing Investor-State Dispute Settlement in Australia, Then New Zealand: Déjà Vu' (n 19).

[166] Nottage Ubilava, 'Costs, Outcomes and Transparency in ISDS Arbitrations: Evidence for an Investment Treaty Parliamentary Inquiry' (n 162).

[167] Kawharu and Nottage, 'Models for Investment Treaties in the Asian Region' (n 13) (with a manuscript version at https://ssrn.com/abstract=2845088 (last accessed 9 December 2016)).

[168] See further Amokura Kawharu and Luke Nottage 'NZ Renounces ISDS: Deja Vu?' *Kluwer Arbitration Blog* (6 December 2017) http://arbitrationblog.kluwerarbitration.com/2017/12/06/booked-luke-nottage/ (last accessed 14 December 2017).

[169] The then Prime Minister John Key even joked that renaming the agreement the 'Trump Pacific Partnership' might be a way to save it: 'Trump Pacific Partnership? New Zealand PM's idea to save

However, the latter stance may also be anticipating the somewhat more cautious approach to investment treaty commitments evident in ASEAN+ agreements,[170] as well as now by influential individual counterparties such as Indonesia and India. More broadly, in current and foreseeable treaty negotiations, parts of Asia may demonstrate a (less acute) form of 'ideological hostility and collective memories of foreign intervention' identified for example in Argentina,[171] by commentary highlighting such 'social-constructivist' reasons behind that country's long-standing refusal to comply with adverse ISDS awards. Nonetheless, that study also emphasizes the importance of economic factors (stressed by 'realist' accounts of international relations) and manifestations of liberal-democratic values behind Argentina's recent move to paying out on some of those awards. Similar countervailing factors also appear to be operating in the Asian region.[172] If Australia and New Zealand wish indeed to project a collective 'middle power' influence on the future trajectory of international investment law in the region, and thus globally, both countries need to examine and reflect on their own historical experiences, values, and economic interests associated with foreign investment more generally.[173]

TPP' (*The Guardian*, 20 November 2016) https://www.theguardian.com/world/2016/nov/20/trump-pacific-partnership-new-zealand-pms-idea-to-save-tpp (last accessed 11 January 2017).

[170] See generally Sungjoon Cho and Jürgen Kurtz, 'The Limits of Isomorphism: Global Investment Law and the ASEAN Investment Regime' (2016) 17(2) CJIL 341; reproduced in Chaisse and Luke Nottage (eds), *International Investment Treaties and Arbitration Across Asia* (n 20).

[171] Moshe Hirsch, 'Explaining Compliance and Non-Compliance with ICSID Awards: The Argentine Case Study and a Multiple Theoretical Approach' (2016) 19 JIEL 681, 705.

[172] Cf eg Muthucumaraswamy Sornarajah, 'Review of Asian Views on Foreign Investment Law' in Vivienne Bath and Luke Nottage (eds), *Investment Law and Dispute Resolution Law and Practice in Asia* (Routledge 2011) 242–54.

[173] For a more detailed comparative analysis see Kawharu and Nottage, 'Models for Investment Treaties in the Asian Region' (n 13) (with a manuscript version at https://ssrn.com/abstract=2845088 (last accessed 9 December 2016)) Part II.

15

A New Era in Cross-strait Relations? A Post-sovereign Enquiry in Taiwan's Investment Treaty System

Horia Ciurtin *

I. Introduction

(Para)military and religious conflicts, civilizational divides, and post-sovereign deviations, economic breakdowns, and financial crises. The entire attention of the great 'global village'—so confidently proclaimed by the late modernity[1]—seems to be concentrated upon all these *centrifugal* dynamics, passing from one to another at a turbulent pace. None of the privileged subjects—be it the Syrian civil war, the secession of Donbas, or the seemingly unavoidable breakdown in the South China Sea—manages, however, to persist in more than a few subsequent issues of relevant publications.

In this emerging dynamic of international law, various phenomena can be observed. Among them is a repartition of international trade, which also appears a relocalization and internal cohesion-building of distinct spaces, governed by specific rules and predictable interactions. By comprehensive trade and investment treaties, the sovereignty of members is not blurred, but rather valorized in a distinct manner, new normative 'empires' arising through the cold letter of the law. The sovereignty of each retreats in order for a common goal of the signatories to be better projected in the race for global economic hegemony.[2]

Thus, even the Westphalian narrative appears to be eroded. A static order of exclusive—but exhaustive—sovereignties upon strictly defined territories no longer paints an accurate picture. Rather, the dynamics of shape-shifting polities allows new interaction modes to emerge, creating a new space for (post)sovereign relations. Legal macro-spaces (such as the EU, the Eurasian Union, or ASEAN), secessionist territories (such as Kosovo or Palestine), and non-state actors make their presence felt in the international scene, not only as passive objects, but also as rule-making actors.

On this complicated background, Taiwan and its shared claim to (legal) sovereignty upon a territory it no longer politically controls (mainland China) appear at the forefront of dismantling the rigid Westphalian arrangement. Moreover, the

* Research Fellow, *EFILA*; External PhD Researcher, *Amsterdam Center for International Law*, Associate Expert, *New Strategy Center*.

[1] For a clearer understanding of this notion and of the collective (global) imaginary in late modernity see Marshall McLuhan, *The Gutenberg Galaxy: The Making of Typographic Man* (University of Toronto Press 2011).

[2] Such a vision upon competing geopolitical (and legal) narratives was already presented in the context of TTIP negotiations for developing a transatlantic 'nomos' in Emanuela Matei, Horia Ciurtin, 'Turning Enemies into Adversaries: TTIP Negotiations and the Quest for a New Westphalia Momentum' (2016) 2 Turkish Commercial Law Review 27 http://the-tclr.org/wp-content/uploads/2016/07/3-matei_cuirtin-1.pdf (last accessed 15 June 2017).

internal-constitutional dimension is reflected by an increasing assertiveness in the international realm, showing—once more—that 'recognition' (and its artificial character) is not truly a *sine qua non* condition for emerging as an actor on the global arena.

However, Taiwan's international standing (and strategy) is closely dependent on China's own approach in the vicinity and far away across the oceans. Their bilateral interaction is defined by a non-Westphalian pattern which directly influences the regional *status quo* and the worldwide expansion (or retreat) of the two Sinic actors. Thus, a very assertive Chinese prong at a global level can often mean a voluntary withdrawal of Taiwanese representatives from international organizations or of its capital from (once) attractive FDI destinations. In the same manner, regional partners—such as those from ASEAN—play a very deferent attitude towards China's cross-strait sensibilities, largely constraining Taiwan's ability to sign trade and investment treaties at its own pace.

For these reasons, going beyond the traditional legal categories, Taiwan proved it can bypass such limitations and innovate this field as a major trend-setter. More precisely, a close look at Taiwan's nexus of investment treaty is revealing: twenty-nine signed BITs (some of them with countries that do not offer it international recognition), six signed ample economic cooperation agreements with related investment provisions. Such an expanding treaty presence bears witness that the concept of international recognition (and subsequent *diplomatic* relations) does not directly determine the capacity and willingness of states to legally and economically interact.

In this sense, non-diplomatic (but formal) relations might be taken even a step forward as Taiwan grows nearer to concluding agreements with another post-sovereign entity, the European Union. This major global actor could open up the scene for a multi-tier dynamics where some of its constituent member-states are rigidly against any connection with Taiwan, but will be bound to it by virtue of their membership of the EU.

Such legal (and geopolitical) paradoxes cannot be solved by using the established instruments of international law, but need to develop a new theoretical framework for arriving at the right solutions. Of course, as in any case, the right answers can only be found when asking the right questions. And the row of necessary interrogations cannot commence with anything else than a discussion about the nature and impasses of sovereignty.

For these purposes, our enquiry (sections II and III) will begin by depicting the network of investment (and trade) agreements which shall be assessed as a first step in the polity's efforts for developing diplomatic structures (and surpass its recognition dilemma), one that will prove to be a litmus test for its capacity to displace traditional categories of Westphalian international law and emerge as a self-standing actor. Briefly, it will also reveal the Taiwanese tactical approach to using (or not) the newly concluded legal instruments for enforcing obligations.

The final section (IV) will reveal a more coherent position that might emerge from this multi-tier dynamic and the possibility to further engage with other post-sovereign entity: the European Union. And, thus, the floating island could loosely be anchored in a different pattern of (non)diplomatic relations.

II. On the (Artificial) Fringes of International Law: Taiwan's Recognition Dilemma

As a starting point in our analysis, it must be first affirmed that the real dilemma of Taiwan's position within the international system stems from its troublesome interaction with mainland China and their—still—overlapping claims to territorial jurisdiction. This 'cross-strait' clash of sovereignties is not truly a Westphalian contradiction, but rather one rooted in a repressed vision of the Sinocentric order, well preserved under a thick layer of *imported* legal language-games. Once the European grasp upon the Far East was loosened, it only took an impulse for a lingering paradigm of sovereignty to re-emerge. Secularized and formally 'disenchanted', such a vision first became apparent in the relation between the two contenders for Chinese political hegemony: the Republic of China (ROC) and the People's Republic of China (PRC).

Among them—after surpassing an autistic phase of no-contact—both actors remained committed to a non-Westphalian view of territory and sovereignty upon it. On the other hand, when dealing with the 'outside' world, the ROC and the PRC rhetorically committed to the entrenched (Westphalian) rules of the game. And thus, the dual approach resembled an odd situation: within the realm, non-Westphalia; outside the realm, Westphalia.

They gradually arrived at an ambiguous status quo that used pre-Westphalian notions of Sinocentric order for accommodating a post-Westphalian insular entity that— informally—maintains relations in a system that could not allow it to. At this moment, given the existing Taiwanese *autonomy* and the desire to eventually maintain it, the cross-strait arrangement might not even be a dilemma of a unique authority. At least not in the terms of a single state-apparatus or exclusive rights for engaging the outside world, but a quest to ascertain that China as a polity is 'one'. As a community and not necessarily of a bureaucracy.

And this is the reason why Westphalia remains an uncomfortable constraint in negotiating arrangements that fit the present cross-strait dynamics. In many senses, the existing status quo is beyond any existing pattern of sovereignty: neither separatism, nor independence, neither autonomy within a federation, nor multi-speed union of multiple actors. Thus, the issue of cross-strait sovereignty appears as something that surpasses even Westphalian *dysfunctions*. It lies beyond any existing category of this narrative, making it of little use beside self-justificatory rhetoric.

Therefore, if our enquiry commences by acknowledging that Westphalia can only be a marginal explanatory discourse when analysing the 'internal' cross-strait dimension of sovereignty, the further step should be to see how far it can reach when dealing with the 'outside' world. In the realm of international relations (and law), both the ROC and the PRC made intensive use of the established rules of the game, fighting for recognition on multiple levels and blocking each other across the (now) flat surface of the globe.

A. To (diplomatic) hell and back: dealing with Resolution 2758

First of all, it must be said that (domestic) sovereignty's international corollary—that is, *recognition*—became subject to a much stricter Westphalian quest for the ROC and the PRC during the early phases of the Cold War. Both sides of the strait initially engaged in a race to the horizon for being admitted into the United Nations and to ensuring that they are formally recognized by the larger international community. Even though the cross-strait dilemma of territorial sovereignty over the greater China did not precisely fit into the 'classical' (Western-based) narrative their struggle for recognition in the global arena, to be admitted as 'a peer among peers' was from the beginning inscribed within the language-game of Westphalia.

While this approach initially favoured the ROC and its demand to be considered as the sole representative of 'China' at the international level, things gradually turned in the opposite direction, leaving the insular entity without 'external' recognition and with a limited 'internal' sovereignty upon a small portion of the claimed territory. Step by step—due to favourable geopolitical circumstances—the People's Republic of China came to be acknowledged as 'China' itself, ensuring that Taiwan and its government was left in an ambiguous situation that no longer fitted any Westphalian pattern. There were several subsequent phases in this history, one rather marked by external events and not by the ambiguous stalemate of the two actors across the strait.

A *first phase* in the recognition narrative lasted for more than two decades, spanning from the early '50s to the '70s. The strategic imperatives of the Cold War and the irruption of the Korean War largely held the ROC afloat by ensuring the support of the United States and most Western bloc states. The Chinese UN seat was occupied by the Taiwan-based authorities and it benefited from wide recognition. The ROC was in a (legally) comfortable and formal—although fictional—position of sovereignty over all of China. Most states preferred to turn a blind eye to the fact that its power only stretched so far into the strait. Not an inch beyond it.

In a *second phase*, beginning with 1971, things were gradually reversed in favour of the PRC. Such a metamorphosis of Taiwan's position within the international community was also generated by geopolitical causes, independent of the island's domestic situation or perspective. Once the Nixon-Kissinger rebalancing act moved towards the PRC in order to better 'contain' the Soviet threat, the basis for the ROC to plunge into (international) oblivion was laid.[3]

Soon after President Nixon's signs of a détente with continental China and his manifest intention to perform a visit, the United Nations General Assembly passed Resolution 2758. Its immediate consequence was the recognition of the PRC government as 'the only legitimate representative of China to the United Nations'[4] and the retreat of Taiwanese officials from the international forum. In a short period of time, most states followed this decision and switched their recognition from the ROC to the PRC, establishing diplomatic ties with the mainland. Similarly, the ROC membership in almost all international organizations was eviscerated, leaving it on the fringes of the multilateral post-War system.

Taipei gradually became isolated and—in a diplomatic *coup de grâce*—in 1978 its closest military ally, the United States, also went down the path of admitting that the only 'Chinese' government is that based in Beijing. It retreated its embassy and official representatives, although pledging still to protect Taiwan's uncertain position and maintain informal relations. After all, Taiwan remained one of its 'unsinkable aircraft carriers' (kept afloat by the unilateral promises comprised within US legislation, namely the TRA), but not a state and certainly not the 'true and only' China. Geopolitical interests moved the balance toward the PRC.

In the next decade, the mainland worked twofold: reaching out over the strait and offering a custom-made solution for Taiwan, while—at the same time—pressing the United States to stop (or reduce) the arms sales for the island. In a simultaneous tactic of cross-strait 'good cop' and trans-Pacific 'bad cop', the PRC government managed to isolate Taipei internationally even more during the 1980s.[5] Only a handful (varying at

---

[3] Kissinger himself admitted it, even if neither he, nor Nixon, desired such a (legal) outcome—see Henry Kissinger, *The White House Years* (George Weidenfeld & Nicolson 1979) 772.

[4] United Nations General Assembly, Session 26—Resolution 2758, *Restoration of the lawful rights of the People's Republic of China in the United Nations*, A/RES/2758 (XXVI).

[5] Richard C Bush, *Untying the Knot: Making Peace in the Taiwan Strait* (Brookings Institution Press 2005) 23–4.

a little over twenty) of impoverished Central American, African, and Insular states still maintained full diplomatic relations with Taiwan, recognizing it as the legitimate sovereign of China in exchange for generous aid. A notable exception from this rule came by the position of the Holy See, which never switched to the PRC.

A *third phase* began in 1988 when Chiang Ching-kuo died and KMT leadership went to the Taiwanese-born (rather than mainland *émigré*) Lee Teng-hui. The dismantling of authoritarian structures and the democratization of the society went hand in hand with a renewed international assertiveness. 'Pragmatic diplomacy', as it was later called, implied the wide deployment of informal diplomatic relations on the model already established with the United States, Japan, or other close partners.

Thus, former embassies were recommissioned as trade or cultural 'centres' with no publicly stated 'official affiliation, but [which] processed visa applications, conveyed messages back and forth, supervised commercial and cultural exchanges, and otherwise functioned like governmental agencies'.[6] The more flexible stance inaugurated by Lee Teng-hui helped to increase the level of informal interactions with cautious states across the world. First, East Asia, the Middle East and Central America, then European countries were engaged in the network of semi-official (often clandestine) relations, devised in this manner so as not to alter these states' ties with mainland China, but obtain a fair business connection with Taiwan.

Now it seemed that the ROC government was not any longer insisting on 'hard' legal recognition or on politically relevant declarations, but on going global and benefiting from all the opportunities of trading in the open liberal order. Gradually, the increasing informal support of numerous Western states (some of them true hegemons of this global arrangement) and mega-regional entities (such as the European Union) soon was translated into a renewed membership in international organizations. Neither as a sovereign 'state', nor as a dependent territory, Taiwan was eventually accepted into multilateral frameworks through creative language-games that remained beyond the strict borders of the statehood narrative.[7]

B. Apart, but not alone: creative diplomacy

Engaging in an analysis of Westphalia-as-discourse, it must be shown that the dilemma of (non)recognition altered the conceptual framework in which both China and Taiwan operated. While their bilateral position was one of gradual accommodation and tacit stalemate, the grand 'act' on the world scene appeared fairly different. Under more pressure, as it was placed outside the realm of classical international law, the territory controlled by Taipei was left with no other solution than to innovate and work at the extreme limits of the entrenched system. Stripped of its United Nations membership (this modern agora of solipsistic sovereignties) and of main allies' formal recognition, Taiwan started to deploy two parallel tactical lines, sometimes appearing as irreconcilable, but coherent when analysed on the long-term.

On the *first line*, Taiwan initially had to submit to a classic Westphalian discourse for the 'external' world in a quest for recognition and (re)establishment of diplomatic

[6] Robert Madsen, 'The Struggle for Sovereignty Between China and Taiwan' in Stephen Krasner (ed), *Problematic Sovereignty: Contested Rules and Political Possibilities* (Columbia University Press 2001) 176.
[7] For more details see the excellent account of Björn Alexander Lindemann, *Cross-Strait Relations and International Organizations: Taiwan's Participation in IGOs in the Context of Its Relationship with China* (Springer VS 2014) 74ff.

relations. As the ROC failed in obtaining such an 'integration' in the Westphalian community, the declaratory approach gradually softened, but still hesitated to renounce claiming the direct applicability of classical principles of international law. Even today, Taiwan maintains a costly network of more than twenty impoverished client-states that offer it *hard* Westphalian recognition.

As regards its *second line* of tactics, Taiwan practically needed to bypass the requirements of the system in one way or another, as it could not allow itself to be isolated from trade, investment and from seeking new alliances in the region to balance the perceived unbearable power of mainland China. It transformed its former diplomatic relations into non-formal representation and gradually took benefit from the erosion of the classical system of international law or from the emergence of post-sovereign actors with a claim in the global arena.

Thus, as regards its appearance on the world stage, Taiwan's recognition dilemma turned into one of *rhetorical allegiance* to the Westphalian principles of international law, while practically being able to bypass them through non-formal mechanisms. This uncertain status quo—although manageable on the medium-term—gained new momentum once the Cold War ended and no more stringent strategic imperatives dominated the region. The markets were unbound and mercantile activity was able to detach itself from Westphalia. In this sense, it is important to benefit from diplomatic recognition nowadays, but not impossible to survive—and prosper—without it.[8]

The prime vehicle for Taiwan's international assertiveness is—as mentioned above— informal bilateral diplomacy. Built as 'a device for minimizing the PRC-backed impediments to cooperation ... its nature is no different from diplomacy of any other sovereign state at any time in world history'.[9] From this perspective, it is different only in name from actual sovereign-driven diplomacy, fulfilling the same practical functions.[10] However, in the realm of international law language-games matter. And they matter greatly. Given that the entire system rests upon legal (and linguistic) fictions tacitly endorsed by every player—even by reluctant ones—dissidents are not allowed to challenge its basic tenets.

And this is the reason why Taiwan—in its precarious Westphalian position—never disputed the narrative per se, but only sought pragmatic manners to functionally overcome difficulties. As a first step, it acknowledged that informal diplomacy is not a 'creeping recognition' and has no ultimate consequences in arriving at a new status quo. It merely represents a *benign bypass* of classical international law, both limited in terms of political outcomes and very flexible in negotiating mercantile arrangements.

Using a worldwide network of trade and cultural centres—dealing with a large array of domains and not constrained by the protocol of traditional diplomacy—Taiwan's approach fosters an open-ended process of low-profile negotiation, only loosely binding for both parties. Thus, informal diplomacy often allowed decision-makers to 'control the resources and seal quiet bargains with their foreign counterparts without close scrutiny from the public'.[11] While bilateral agreements might be secret, so are failures to reach them. In such circumstances, the reduced level of public exposure can act as a catalyst to perform business without raising diplomatic 'walls'.

---

[8] This thesis was advanced by Madsen (n 6).
[9] Linjun Wu, 'How Far Can the ROC's Informal Diplomacy Go?' (1994) 30 Issues & Studies 82, 84.
[10] For a detailed account of the interaction between informal diplomacy and propaganda (as a subsequent language-game of diplomacy) see Gary D Rawnsley, *Taiwan's Informal Diplomacy and Propaganda* (Macmillan 2000) 22ff.
[11] ibid 93.

The second method of increased participation in the global community—also beyond a strict Westphalian understanding—takes the form of (re)gaining membership in international governmental organizations. While failing to join them as the Chinese sovereign or as a *sui generis* ambiguous entity, Taiwan resorted—with other major actors' consent—to an adaptive language-game. For WTO purposes, it is known as the 'Separate Customs Territory of Taiwan, Penghu, Kinmen and Matsu (Chinese Taipei)'. In APEC, it is listed as 'Chinese Taipei', while in the Asian Development Bank, it is called 'Taipei China'.

The most important membership is that within the WTO, a cornerstone of the globalized trade system. More tangible than other organizations, the WTO does not require its members to be actual 'states', but accommodates the possibility of 'separate customs territories' also to join. Thus, after acknowledging—together with most of its members—that there is only 'one China' and that Taiwan is a part of it, the WTO laid down the accession calendar in a direct reflection with that of the PRC. Only when the recognized 'sovereign' joined the organization could the 'separate customs territory' of Chinese Taipei follow it.[12]

However, once inside the WTO, the general rules apply for both entities in a two-fold manner: in cross-strait relations *and* with other entities around the world. The membership brings hard legal benefits for Taiwan, as it allows it to make use of the dispute settlement system with the PRC and with non-compliant states.[13] As long as WTO rules (and the custom-negotiated protocols) are concerned, no one can unilaterally and discriminatorily hinder Taiwan's rights to free trade without having access to an impartial forum. At the same time, no true progress in cross-strait relations has been noted due to the institutionalization of the two entities' relationship within the WTO,[14] but only a stabilization of their stalemate.

In parallel to informal diplomacy and accommodating positions within IGOs, Taiwan also pursued a hardline Westphalian game with a plethora of acquiescing (small) states. As inside observers within the ROC diplomatic corps noted, such a cash-for-recognition strategy aimed at pursuing a 'residual' claim to sovereignty on the fringes of the international system. In essence, this was an exercise in grand (geo) politics, rather than a direct engagement with the public of such client-states as a benevolent 'soft power'.[15]

More Westphalian than the PRC in its language, but using mercantile means to reach its goals, the Taiwanese approach proves very costly on the long-term. Thus, economically failed states regularly attempt to 'blackmail' it into granting generous aid in order to prevent switching their recognition to the PRC. At the same time, the ROC has almost no leverage in stopping such a phenomenon, neither bilaterally nor multilaterally (as the PRC has done within Africa, for example).[16]

---

[12] Lindemann (n 7) 98ff.

[13] Steve Charnowitz, 'Taiwan's WTO Membership and its International Implications' (2006) 1 Asian Journal of WTO and International Health Law and Policy 401, 419ff.

[14] For more details see the conclusions of Stephen Goldstein in his 'Postscript' in Julian Chang and Stephen M Goldstein (eds), *Economic Reform and Cross-Strait Relations: Taiwan and China in the WTO* (World Scientific 2007) 362.

[15] For a detailed account in this regard, mostly concerning Central America see Colin R Alexander, *China and Taiwan in Central America: Engaging Foreign Publics in Diplomacy* (Palgrave Macmillan 2014).

[16] Timothy S Rich, 'Status for Sale: Taiwan and the Competition for Diplomatic Recognition' (2009) 45 Issues & Studies 159, 178.

C. Preserving fragility: the art of Westphalian doublespeak

The most important factor, however, is to understand *how* and *why* Taiwan—or, rather, the ROC—claimed to be (and remain) recognized. At no point in time did it seek recognition as an independent 'Taiwanese' state, separated from mainland China. It either sought to be acknowledged as *the* Republic of China, the sole sovereign upon the entire Chinese territory (at the expense of the PRC),[17] or as a 'customs territory', which is self-administered but not completely distinct from an ambiguous and untold 'greater China'.

There are numerous reasons for which the insular authorities continue such a difficult great diplomatic game across the world's oceans, trying to outbid the unbearable mainland hegemony. First of all, it is a matter of internal politics. Success on the world scene is quickly reflected at home and is intended to boost the public morale. Second, the *desired* ambiguity of its status depends on liminal recognition. Although strictly limited—and largely insignificant—such an acknowledgement of its legitimacy as the representative of 'China' allows the ROC government to gain better negotiation positions with the mainland and be able to 'freeze' the existing stalemate.

Third, as a matter of self-preservation, unconventional (small) polities require international visibility in order to prevent their isolation, which—in Taiwan's case—'having no diplomatic space could allow it to be swallowed up by the PRC'.[18] Residual Westphalian recognition is not an attempted 'creeping statehood'—an offensive approach—but rather designed to stop the contender from absorbing it as a mere recalcitrant province. It is a defensive measure designed to enhance their political relevance, rather than extract direct legal effects within the international community.

Not least, failing to represent (or to claim representing) the Chinese *oikumene* even liminally would raise other doubts regarding the ROC title over the 'acquisition' of Formosa from Japan. The defeated belligerent ceded the territory to 'China' and not necessarily to the government of the ROC. If Taiwan's claim to being 'China' would be renounced retroactively, its pretension upon the island's territory itself would turn fragile. And—in such a case—the PRC (the only remaining 'China') would feel legally entitled to request dominion over the territory of Taiwan, voiding *ab initio* any possibility of a distinct 'Taiwanese' statehood.[19]

Therefore, independence (and recognition of such a reality) never really featured among the real options—or *manifested desires*—of the ROC authorities, despite episodic statements from some officials. And, in the end, as James Crawford pertinently argued '[s]tatehood is a claim of right [and] claims to statehood are not to be inferred from statements or actions short of explicit declaration'.[20] Such an explicit declaration never was made by Taiwan, as it did not seek international recognition as a *separate* 'statehood', but as a *continued* existence of the 1912 Republic of China.

The ROC never claimed to be a 'new' and 'distinct' state that needs a *novel* recognition—be it constitutive or declaratory in its effects[21]—but rather the *same* state

---

[17] In this sense, it can be emphasized that in 1979 Taiwan itself unilaterally cut ties with 44 states that recognized the PRC. It did not really accommodate the possibility of dual recognition, which would imply its 'separate' statehood—see Rich (n 16) 169.

[18] Jie Chen, *Foreign Policy of the New Taiwan: Pragmatic Diplomacy in Southeast Asia* (Edward Elgar Publishing 2002) 10.

[19] For a more ample discussion see the influential account of James Crawford, *The Creation of States in International Law* (2nd edn, Oxford University Press 2007) 207–11.

[20] ibid 211.

[21] For a (theoretical) starting point in this regard see the classical opinion of Hans Kelsen, 'Recognition in International Law: Theoretical Observations' (1941) 35 The American Journal of International Law 605.

as that established by Sun Yat-sen before the Great War. It is for these purposes that it demanded an exclusive Westphalian recognition as the 'true' China from its minor client-states, seeking to maintain (at least residually) the image of an undisturbed sovereign. Not necessarily for its legal effects, but rather as a means to manage the PRC's increasing power and to constrain its capacity to brutally incorporate it. The (hard) Westphalian language-game is one of preservation, a defence of the status quo meant to shield Taiwan from the mainland's irresistible grasp.

At the same time, the insular polity accommodated a post-Westphalian position within international organizations and with major actors across the globe. When interacting with the latter, it bypassed the need for recognition and no further inquired into the subject. Business as such was sufficient. And hard legal recognition no longer necessary. From a question of (geo)politics, the existing dynamic was reduced to a mercantile dimension. And thus, for Taiwan, the game arrived at a new momentum. As the ideological dialectics softened after the Cold War, so did the need to rhetorically emphasize Taiwan's stance in opposition with that of the PRC. It no longer tries to politically recoup *against* it, but to discreetly trade *aside* it.

Indeed, the ROC's recognition dilemma continues to be *legally* unsolved.[22] However, given the new postmodern context, it does not really need to be solved. It is a riddle of a past era. Taiwan now manages to utter two (apparently) conflicting tales, without getting lost in the labyrinth of positivist arguments. (Hard) Westphalia and post-Westphalia no longer exclude each other, but rather allow the insular authorities to maintain a margin of tactical manoeuvre. New narratives have emerged and new language-games are to be played, as the international environment itself is different. Old Westphalia tacitly coexists with another set of mercantile relations, while still allowing polities at the fringes of the system to preserve their prosperous fragility.

III. Beyond the Blockade: Bypassing Westphalia through Investment Treaties

From a Taiwanese perspective, after reaching a stalemate with the mainland, the present international world of eroded sovereignty appears beneficial. It allows the island to engage in *post*-Westphalian interactions with other countries (and non-countries), to become member in international organizations, without affecting its *non*-Westphalian arrangement with the PRC. While not exactly bright, the near future seems tolerable for the ROC in the international arena. Given that the global community no longer adheres to a rigid understanding of sovereignty, a 'flattened' earth seems open for Taiwan's informal diplomacy, allowing it to reap the benefits of postmodernity.

A. Eroding the system: Taiwan's network of investment agreements

The insular polity gradually overcame the error of thinking (and acting) as if there was an unbreakable bond between Westphalian (formal) recognition and the possibility to engage in international agreements. In this sense, a main vector for Taiwan's informal

---

[22] See eg the Crawford-Roth contradiction—Brad R Roth, 'The Entity That Dare Not Speak Its Name: Unrecognized Taiwan as a Right-Bearer in the International Legal Order' (2009) 4 East Asia Law Review 91.

relations with the outside world (and with the PRC) has taken the form of: (a) either 'pure' investment agreements, or (b) 'hybrid' trade-and-investment FTAs. All of them can be ascribed to the 'third phase' of conducting international relations, after the demise of the Cold War. The insistence upon soft forms of quasi-diplomatic engagement is reflected in the mainly economic quest to secure markets and footholds across the world. For these reasons, while Taiwan's network of investment agreements consists of twenty-nine 'genuine' BITs and six mixed-type FTAs, a few preliminary observations must be made.

First of all, a considerable part of these agreements relate to states that continue to offer the ROC formal recognition (or did so until very recently) (see Table 15.1 below). The mercantile value attached to them is severely limited, as the investment flux is unidirectional, only flowing from Taiwan to its impoverished 'client-states'. More precisely, eleven BITs have been concluded with Belize, Burkina Faso, the Dominican Republic, El Salvador, Guatemala, Honduras, Marshall Islands, Nicaragua (terminated), Paraguay, Saint Vincent and the Grenadines, Swaziland, *and* two mixed FTAs with Guatemala and Nicaragua.[23] Their significance is not economic, but strategic and (geo)political. Being rather classical treaties that pose no 'Westphalian' challenges, we shall no further address them here.

Secondly, a number of seven BITs (with Costa Rica, Gambia, Liberia, Macedonia, Malawi, Panama, and Senegal) and one mixed FTA (with Panama) date from the period when these states had official diplomatic relations with the ROC and afterwards switched it to the PRC (see Table 15.1 below). The main legal challenge in this regard is to establish what the effect of derecognition might have upon the international obligations (to promote and protect the investments of the other contracting party) voluntarily undertaken when signing the treaty. At a first glance, various objections can be raised.[24] Counter-examples can be offered.

Table 15.1 Taiwan's Network of Investment Agreements

Type of relations	BITs	FTAs
Full diplomatic relations with ROC	Belize	Guatemala
	Burkina Faso	Nicaragua
	Dominican Republic	
	El Salvador	
	Guatemala	
	Honduras	
	Marshall Islands	
	Nicaragua (terminated)	
	Paraguay	
	Saint Vincent-Grenadines	
	Swaziland	

[23] According to the Investment Policy Hub instrument offered by UNCTAD http://investmentpolicyhub.unctad.org/IIA/CountryBits/205 (last accessed 1 February 2017). Some additional treaties (not listed in the UNCTAD database) have been extracted from the official database of the Ministry of Foreign Affairs (ROC), available online at http://no06.mofa.gov.tw/mofatreatys/ (last accessed 1 February 2017). The situation regarding recognition is valid for mid-2017. Further political developments—and negotiations—might affect these numbers and should be treated accordingly.
[24] For example see the rather apologetic argument against the validity of such treaties presented by Baochun Zeng, 'Validity of a Treaty with a De-recognized Entity-Taiwan: An Issue That Remains Unsettled After *New York Chinese TV Programs v. U.E. Enterprises*' (1993) 15 Loyola of Los Angeles International and Comparative Law Review 885.

Table 15.1 Continued

Type of relations	BITs	FTAs
Switched formal diplomatic relations from ROC to PRC after signing the treaty	Costa Rica Gambia Liberia Macedonia Malawi Panama Senegal	Panama
Informal relations with both PRC and ROC at the conclusion of the treaty	Singapore	
Informal relations with ROC (full diplomatic relations with PRC)	Argentina India Indonesia Japan Malaysia Nigeria Philippines Saudi Arabia Thailand Vietnam	New Zealand PRC Singapore

The short conclusion would be to hint at the fact that recognition—unlike the actual commitment under a binding treaty—is also a political act: a political declaration. It might change the manner of conducing public diplomacy and the geopolitical rhetoric, but the simple process of switching recognition to another government does not void the initial legal obligation. Moreover, in the absence of a clear denunciation of the signed treaty, it cannot be assumed that its effects have automatically stopped for private individuals (and companies) that were assumed to be the beneficiaries of such an agreement. And, practically speaking, the signatory states have not denounced their BITs with Taiwan even after derecognition. The manner of enforcing such obligations, is an entirely different story.

Thirdly, the singular case of the 1990 Singapore BIT must be treated distinctly (see Table 15.1 below). At the time of concluding the treaty, Singapore maintained *informal* relations with both the ROC and the PRC. Shortly afterwards, it established full diplomatic relations only with the PRC, while the ROC itself silently changed its representation's operational model.[25] While it is an interesting case from a theoretical standpoint, in reality no effects can be ascribed to it as it was later replaced by the 2013 FTA, which embodied investment protection norms.

Finally, ten BITs and three comprehensive FTAs appear as illustrations of *informal* diplomatic assertiveness (see Table 15.1 below). All of them reflect relations with relevant economic partners from across the globe, mostly concentrated in South Asia, East Asia, and the Pacific Rim, but also three outliers from South America, Africa, and the Middle East.[26]

[25] J Chen (n 18) 81.
[26] The latter three BITs—with Argentina, Saudi Arabia, and Nigeria—are left aside for the purpose of this analysis, as they are outliers in some respects. The Argentina BIT was signed in 1993, but no additional information is available in relation to its validity, expiration, or denunciation. However, given the PRC's robust relations with Argentina (stretching even to the strategic level), make it

The BITs are quite uniform among themselves, containing similar provisions, as are the FTAs. As shall be shown, the true turning point in all this network of informal agreements is represented by the landmark Economic Cooperation Framework Agreement from 2010 with mainland China, which gave a new impetus to the signing of further investment-oriented treaties.

Therefore, when considering this last category of agreements (consisting of seven remaining BITs[27] and three FTAs from the Pacific Rim) (see Table 15.2 below) two general characteristics must be emphasized: (a) all of them are signed with states that do not recognize the ROC, but only the PRC as the legitimate representative of 'China'; (b) all of them are concluded in the name of informal representatives for both contracting parties.

Methodologically, they can be analysed and categorized in accordance with two criteria: (1) *temporal*—using the ECFA with mainland China as a 'turning point' in the investment agreement official programme and dividing them among pre-ECFA treaties and post-ECFA treaties; and (2) formal—relating to the actual form that the agreement takes, either 'pure' BIT or comprehensive FTA that encompasses an investment chapter. For the purposes of this limited assessment, the two taxonomies can be merged, as all the existing FTAs and only one BIT (with Japan) are temporally posterior to the ECFA. The remaining six BITs are pre-ECFA.

Table 15.2 Taiwan's Informal BITs and FTAs

	Pre-ECFA	Post-ECFA
BITs	India Indonesia Malaysia Philippines Thailand Vietnam	Japan
BIT Outliers *(excluded from analysis)*	Argentina Nigeria Saudi Arabia	
FTAs	ECFA—BIA (with PRC)	
		New Zealand Singapore

B. In the beginning, there was the (informal) BIT: before ECFA

In this sense, it can be argued that the six investment agreements which predate the ECFA are concentrated upon South-East Asian and South Asian maritime states, representing important business (and strategic) partners for Taiwan in an area increasingly

doubtful to assume that the agreement is considered fully operational by each side. In addition, we shall exclude it also on a geographical basis, as our selection of agreements rather concentrates upon South, South East Asia, and the Pacific Rim.

The Saudi Arabia BIT was signed, but it is not officially in force, whereas the Nigeria BIT was signed on behalf of the two governments, whereas they only maintain informal relations. Moreover, later geopolitical developments prompted Nigeria to sever even these loose unofficial connections, as it urged ROC representatives to close their office in Abuja.

[27] We have excluded the three mentioned BITs (Argentina, Saudi Arabia, and Nigeria—see n 26 above) from our analysis.

under the PRC hegemony. Thus, the BITs with India, Indonesia,[28] Malaysia, Philippines, Thailand, and Vietnam commence with limited-size preambles, which define the contracting parties not as 'sovereigns', but as informal representatives of the authorities that exercise jurisdiction upon each territory.

For most treaties, the non-state agent bears a title resembling a cultural centre, a foreign chamber of commerce or a bilateral friendship association. In this sense, Taiwan is often represented by a 'Taipei Cultural and Economic Office' (with Malaysia, the Philippines, and Vietnam), by the 'Taipei Economic and Cultural Center' (with India) or by the 'Taipei Economic and Trade Office' (with Indonesia and Thailand). Some of these agreements' preambles make reference to an additional 'authorization' that was already granted (Indonesia, the Philippines, and Vietnam) or will be granted (Malaysia) by the competent authorities of each party. In this manner, although informal and between non-governmental institutions, such treaties bear the mark of the 'shadow' polities that *indirectly* confirm their validity and effectiveness.

As regards the actual content of such preambles (see Table 15.3 below), it varies from agreement to agreement but maintaining some common features. It is important to highlight its central position when ascertaining the parties' intention and understanding of the nature and consequences of the signed agreement,[29] especially in uncertain cases. Therefore, all the six BITs underline that the parties 'desire' to *create favourable conditions* for economic cooperation (or to strengthen them), while also 'recognizing' that the (promotion and) protection of such investments will stimulate individual business initiatives and will increase prosperity in the territories.

Thus, such preambles are rather limited in scope when compared with the expansive United States Model BITs[30] (2004 and 2012) or with the medium-sized Netherlands Model BIT (2004), but very similar to the United Kingdom Model BITs (1991 and 2008). Swift and simple, their preambular provisions restrain from turning to issues such as public health, labour, or environmental concerns, reflecting a more classical approach that only concentrates upon 'promoting' and 'protecting' investment flows. The quest is mercantile and pragmatic, fit for the narrow margin of movement that an informal player has in the international arena.

When analysing the substantial protection offered by these BITs, it can be argued that it is far from the ordinary 'Dutch gold standard', which contains a fixed and broad set of standards. Fair and equitable treatment is offered in each of them, as is the protection against expropriation and the most-favoured-nation clause. However, the scope of the 'full protection and security' standard is limited to 'full' or 'adequate' protection, while in the Malaysia BIT it is entirely absent. Moreover, the national treatment standard is present only in the agreement with India, while the umbrella clause

[28] The fate of the Indonesia–Taiwan BIT also remains to be seen, as Indonesia notified the Netherlands in 2014 that it intends to terminate their existing investment agreement, along with 66 other such treaties—see the official release available at http://indonesia.nlembassy.org/organization/departments/economic-affairs/termination-bilateral-investment-treaty.html (last accessed 15 June 2017). For more details upon Indonesia's stance and this larger trend in international investment law see Horia Ciurtin, 'The Future of Investment Treaties: Metamorphosis or Deconstruction?' *EFILA Blog* (8 September 2015) https://efilablog.org/2015/09/08/10/ (last accessed 15 June 2017).

[29] For a more detailed argument in this regard see our previous study—Horia Ciurtin, 'Beyond the Norm: The Hermeneutic Function of Treaty Preambles in Investment Arbitration and International Law' (2015) 36 Revista Romana de Arbitraj 64 https://ssrn.com/abstract=2714355 (last accessed 15 June 2017).

[30] A thorough account of the evolution of Model US BITs preambles can be found in Kenneth J Vandevelde, *U.S. International Investment Agreements* (Oxford University Press 2009) 82–90.

Table 15.3 Taiwan Informal BITs Provisions

	India	Indonesia	Malaysia	Philippines	Thailand	Vietnam
Basic preamble	Yes	Yes	Yes	Yes	Yes	Yes
FET	Yes	Yes	Yes	Yes	Yes	Yes
Protection and Security	Full protection	Adequate protection	No	Adequate protection	Most constant protection and security	Protection
NT	Yes	No	No	No	No	No
MFN	Yes	Yes	Yes	Yes	Yes	Yes
Expropriation	Yes	Yes	Yes	Yes	Yes	Yes
Umbrella clause	No	No	No	No	No	No
ISDS forum	UNCITRAL ICC	Arbitration (unqualified)	Arbitration (unqualified)	Arbitration (unqualified)	Arbitration (unqualified)	ICC
Existing official authorization	No	Yes	No	Yes	Yes	Yes
Future official authorization	Yes	No	Yes	No	No	No

can be found nowhere. The reasons for this latter omission can be traced to the genesis of such treaties, given that they are not signed by official representatives and cannot automatically transform a contract into a treaty obligation undertook by the governing authorities.[31]

None of the treaties offer the possibility of ICSID arbitration as a method of dispute settlement, not even in the context of the Additional Facility. As Taiwan is not recognized as a state, it cannot become a party to the Washington Convention, nor gain access to its administrative apparatus. For this reason, one treaty offers the possibility of recourse to ad hoc arbitration under the UNCITRAL Rules or at the International Chamber of Commerce (ICC) (the India agreement), another permits litigation under the aegis of the ICC (the Vietnam agreement), while the remaining four BITs simply mention the possibility of 'arbitration', unqualified in any manner. Of course, if the parties agree, this vague provision allows for a generous number of possible arbitral venues and applicable procedural rules.

Most of the treaties in this category are designed to enter into force immediately upon their signing (Indonesia, the Philippines, Thailand, and Vietnam), as the informal agents have been 'duly authorized' by their respective authorities to enter into the agreement on their behalf. Only for the India and Malaysia BITs is a further confirmation or declaration from the governing bodies of each territory necessary in order to make their provisions effective.

Therefore, in many respects, these pre-ECFA agreements reflect a certain homogeneity of content, but being innovative for the period of their conclusion (mostly between 1990 and 1995) and a sign of Taiwan's newly found international assertiveness. In a certain sense, they represent the 'enthusiastic' and early phase of mercantile engagement with the (extended) neighbourhood and beyond, a groundwork preparation for the more ambitious FTAs signed afterwards.

C. The benefits of mercantile consensus: ECFA and beyond

ECFA-BIA. The next phase in developing Taiwan's network of investment (and trade) agreements is marked by the landmark consensus with the mainland. Until then a veritable 'elephant in the room', the lack of a legal agreement between the two sides of the strait represented an impediment for other major actors to engage with the insular polity. This 'gap' was all the more peculiar as the cross-strait exchanges and investments reached very high levels without being integrated in any normative arrangement.

From a geoeconomic perspective, the negotiation of such an ambitious framework was generated by the need to avoid marginalization within the ASEAN (plus three) neighbourhood. Even more, this appeared simultaneously with the mainland's expansion of its own network of investment-and-trade treaties.[32] In such a context, Taiwan risked being left behind capital and goods flows, while the PRC—and Japan or South Korea—would have integrated their complementary economies even more. Thus, the Ma Ying-jeou administration quickly moved to the negotiation of an ample agreement with the mainland, especially given the asymmetric mercantile relation between the two which needed to be preserved in Taiwan's favour. While much of the preparation

---

[31] Han-Wei Liu, 'A Missing Part in International Investment Law: The Effectiveness of Investment Protection of Taiwan's Bits Vis-à-Vis ASEAN States' (2010) 16 University of California Davis Journal of International Law & Policy 130, 141.

[32] See Zhao Hong and Sarah Tong, 'Implications of Taiwan-Mainland Economic Cooperation Framework Agreement' (2009) 1 East Asian Policy 69, 72ff.

phase continued during 2009, it was finally signed in June 2010 under the name of the Economic Cooperation Framework Agreement.

In its present form, the ECFA only represents an *'interim* free trade agreement',[33] which initially liberalized numerous sectors of economy and down-graded certain tariffs (for example the 'Early Harvest' category), it needed additional (specialized) agreements in order to become effective in all the envisioned areas. The ECFA itself was also informally concluded between quasi-diplomatic agents of the two sides, being negotiated and signed by the Straits Exchange Foundation (on behalf of Taiwan) and the Association for Relations Across the Taiwan Straits (on behalf of mainland China), two special purpose vehicles designed for the improvement of cross-strait relations.

As regards investments and their protection, Article 5 of the ECFA provided that the two parties undertake to 'expeditiously reach an agreement', which would—among others—relate to the 'establishing an investment protection mechanism', to 'gradually reducing restrictions on mutual investments between the two Parties' and to 'promoting investment facilitation'.[34] Thus, after a prolonged negotiation that failed to reach consensus for more than two years[35]—despite a six-month term in the original ECFA—the two parties finally signed the Cross-Strait Agreement on Investment Protection and Promotion (Bilateral Investment Agreement or BIA) in 2012. It came into force in early 2013.[36]

The agreement begins with a short preamble specifying the 'agents' that acted as signatories—the Straits Exchange Foundation and the Association for Relations Across the Taiwan Straits—while noting that its purpose is to 'to protect the rights and interests of investors across the Taiwan Straits, promote mutual investments, create an impartial investment environment, and enhance cross-strait economic prosperity'. It is not unspecific for the broader category of BITs concluded by either Taiwan or the PRC, being fairly limited to insisting on mercantile purposes and to the fostering of a fertile economic framework.

However, when analysing the substantive protection standards offered by this agreement, it does not only contain all the basic elements of the 'Dutch gold standard', but goes far beyond them. Unlike Taiwan's prior BITs, it refers not only to fair and equitable treatment, protection and security, most-favoured-nation clause, or protection against expropriation, but also a very broad version of national treatment, all of them nuanced and put into context, without leaving some of the 'classic' doubts that functioned in the benefit of the private investor.[37]

In addition, similar to the most innovative investment agreements—such as CETA or the EUSFTA—the BIA strictly circumscribes the understanding of fair and equitable as meaning that 'the measures adopted by a Party shall be in accordance with the principle of due process and shall not deny justice and fair trial to investors of

[33] Chi-An Chou, 'A Two-Edged Sword: The Economy Cooperation Framework Agreement Between the Republic of China and the People's Republic of China' (2010) 6 Brigham Young University International Law & Management Review 1, 3.

[34] For the text of the agreement see the UNCTAD database. The English version is available at http://investmentpolicyhub.unctad.org/Download/TreatyFile/2613 (last accessed 15 June 2017).

[35] Jie Huang, 'Negotiating the First Bilateral Investment Agreement between Mainland China and Taiwan: Difficulties and Solutions' (2012) 42 Hong Kong Law Journal 971, 972–3.

[36] Taiwan Affairs Office, 'Mainland-Taiwan investment protection pact effective from Fri' (31 January 2013) http://www.gwytb.gov.cn/en/CrossstraitTrade/201302/t20130201_3736343.htm (last accessed 15 June 2017).

[37] For a detailed analysis of the agreements' provisions and its historical background see Chi Chung, 'The Bilateral Investment Treaty between China and Taiwan and Its Historical Background' (2013) 5 George Mason Journal of International Commercial Law 107.

the other Party, and that obviously discriminatory or arbitrary measures may not be implemented' (Article 3.1). The full protection and security standard is limited to the concept of 'physical protection', stopping the hermeneutic trend that expanded this type of protection to the legal realm.

The expropriation standard is quite broad, attracting the responsibility of either party for actions that amount to 'indirect' expropriation. However, this latter understanding of the standard is placed within proportionality limits and a case-by-case analysis, not allowing any state act to easily qualify as such. In addition, there is a 'public policy' exception at Article 7.3, which emphasized that 'non-discriminatory regulatory measures adopted by either Party to protect the legitimate public welfare, such as public health, safety, and the environment, do not constitute indirect expropriation'.

At the same time, the BIA provides transparency requirements that would benefit the investor both pre-establishment and post-establishment, obliging each party to disclose in a public and timely manner all regulations and measures (and their further amendments) that pertain to the investment regime. A state of the art denial of benefits clause[38] is present in the agreement, designed to prevent nationals of third parties to benefit from such protection without conducting stable and relevant business within the territory of either signatory party. The possibility of using 'shell companies' as beneficiary proxies is thus blocked. However, the BIA—like all those of Taiwan, but unlike the Chinese BTs—contains no umbrella clause.

On the other hand, the Taiwan-mainland China BIA is rather uncommon with regard to its investor–state dispute settlement mechanism. While most existing BITs allow for a combination of negotiation, domestic litigation and—finally—international arbitration, the present agreement provides no possibility of resorting to arbitration. As it has been noted, perhaps that '[o]ne of the reasons for not including international arbitration as an option may be China's avoiding making the cross-strait matters to be referred to as «international»', as well as its general reluctance to consent to this type of international litigation even its 'regular' diplomatic relations.[39]

In Article 13, the BIA allows the pursuit of five different paths for the settlement of any dispute relating to investments that might arise with the other party: (a) amicable negotiation, (b) coordination, (c) resolution through the Article 15 ISDS mechanism (Cross-Strait Economic Cooperation Committee), (d) mediation, and (e) domestic litigation. Therefore, with the exception of the mediation procedure, there is no possibility to have a third-party national introduced in the settlement of the dispute, but only agents or experts from either Taiwan or mainland China. The ISDS part of the BIA is, in this sense, an intra-Chinese issue stretching only to the shores of the strait and reflecting the non-sovereign agreement of the two polities, which allows little (or none at all) space for 'external' presence.

After the ECFA. At the same time, besides laying a wide framework of cooperation with the mainland, the conclusion of the ECFA and BIA signaled to the larger world a relaxation of the tensions across the strait. In this sense, Taiwan quickly capitalized on its arrangement with the PRC and resumed the development of its BIT/FTA network. Given that the mainland's policy transformed into one of non-interference as long as such agreements did not pertain to matters of 'sovereignty' or 'official' governmental

---

[38] This provision from the BIA resembles the denial of benefits clause in the ECT and other recent treaties—see Loukas Mistelis and Crina Baltag, 'Denial of Benefits and Article 17 of the Energy Charter Treaty' (2009) 113 Penn State Law Review 1302.

[39] Tiffany Ting Sun, 'Investor-State Dispute Settlement Provision in the Cross-Strait BIT: Possible Enhancement in its Operation' (2014) 7 Contemporary Asia Arbitration Journal 195, footnote 73.

nature,[40] the insular polity signed in 2011 an additional informal BIT with Japan and in 2013 two comprehensive FTAs with New Zealand and Singapore.

The first agreement from this post-ECFA category is the BIT with Japan. It was signed between unofficial representative institutions, but whose mandate needed further 'consent' from their respective authorities in order to make the arrangement effective. When analysing its structure and provisions, it can be emphasized that it is a thorough reflection of the 'Dutch gold standard', rather modelled upon the Japanese practice than on the ROC one. In this sense, it contains all the classical standards—FET, full protection and security, national treatment, protection against expropriation—including the surprisingly broad 'umbrella clause' that had so far not featured in any Taiwan-based investment agreement.[41]

The BIT lacks any preambular provisions, but has an ample dispute settlement provision which allows for amicable negotiations and consultations, followed—if necessary—by international arbitration. However, the usual implicit consent to arbitrate is not present here (as it was not concluded by the authorities themselves), conditioning the commencement of arbitral proceedings upon the party's explicit agreement. As regards the actual arbitration, the agreement allows it to either take place under the UNCITRAL or ICC Rules or under any other rules agreed by the parties.

The other two post-ECFA agreements—with Singapore and New Zealand—were concluded in late 2013 and represent a new generation of wide-ranging and comprehensive FTAs, with a consistent investment chapter. As a deviation from the previous international agreements relating to a party that did not officially recognize Taiwan, these FTAs are signed by informal representatives[42] on behalf of Singapore and New Zealand as sovereign states with the 'Separate Customs Territory of Taiwan, Penghu, Kinmen and Matsu'. Thus, they resort to the WTO-accepted style and its shorthand of 'Chinese Taipei'.

From their structure, two main sources of normative influence appear evident: (a) the latest understanding of the WTO rules (including their constant hermeneutic construction within the case-law), and (b) the new wave of comprehensive FTAs that push economic cooperation closer to integration. As regards the latter, such a vision may be traced back to NAFTA, but it has also surged across the entire globe beyond limited regional frameworks. Thus, states from South East Asia—such as Singapore itself or Vietnam—have lately been involved in the conclusion of state of the art FTAs with the European Union, with China, with the United States.

The two analysed FTAs—Singapore–Taiwan and New Zealand–Taiwan—follow this trend and are homogeneous in regard to their content, especially in the investment chapter. Thus, they both offer fair and equitable treatment and full protection and security strictly circumscribed by detailed definitions and limited to the upper threshold of the minimum standard of treatment, according to customary international law. While both FTAs protect investors against expropriation and on the 'relative' lines of

---

[40] See Bonnie S Glaser, 'Taiwan's Quest for Greater Participation in the International Community' (November 2013) Center for Strategic and International Studies 34.

[41] For more details on the arrangement's provisions see Shotaro Hamamoto, 'The 2011 Japan-Taiwan Bilateral Investment Agreement or How to Establish International Law Relations with an Unrecognized Entity' (15–16 May 2013, Taipei) ILA-ASIL Asia-Pacific Research Forum: International Law and Dispute Resolution: Challenges in the Asia Pacific.

[42] For more details on the informal representation of New Zealand and Singapore in negotiating and signing the agreements see Jason Young, 'Space for Taiwan in regional economic integration: Cooperation and partnership with New Zealand and Singapore' (2014) 66 Political Science 3, 14ff.

national treatment or MFN, the latter standard is highly limited in the Singapore FTA
to certain types of conduct (for example, in cases of protection-compensation against
conflict and armed struggle).

Both agreements contain a denial of benefits clause and have no umbrella clause
that would allow contracts to be covered by the provisions of the respective FTA. On
the other hand, the dispute settlement mechanism allow for international arbitration
once the period of amicable negotiation has expired without any result. Thus, while
the New Zealand agreement grants access to ad hoc (or institutional) arbitration under
the UNCITRAL Rules, the Singapore FTA also allows it under the ICC Rules. In
most regards, both of them are fairly standard and in line with the general practice of
comprehensive FTAs.

When returning to the wide perspective of the entire Taiwan BIT network, it can be
considered as a successful quest to work besides the Westphalian framework. The ROC
diplomatic effort (formal and informal) managed to bypass the stumbling block of recognition and capitalized on the general erosion of the hardline sovereignty narrative.
The insular polity gradually developed a medium-sized investment treaty programme,
under-developed for an economy of its size, but definitely over-developed for a territory in a recognition limbo. More than thirty-five investment-related agreements represent a fair fundament for gaining increased international visibility and for achieving
a larger degree of participation within the global agora.

However, the existence of this treaty network at the fringes of the Westphalian
system poses a different type of problem when legally assessed: what is the actual effect
of such documents in case of an investment dispute? If the other party does not conform to the agreed terms and promised protection, would Taiwanese investors benefit
from commencing international litigation? All the answers lie in ascertaining the true
purpose of the BIT programme. The underlying rationale was not primarily to gain
an *enforceable* degree of protection for its own private investors, but rather to 'signal'
Taiwan's international assertiveness as a state and to construct a political leverage upon
the other party so as not to harass its investors in the respective territory.

Therefore, the relevance of such investment agreements is rather declaratory and
symbolic, but not without practical significance. For instance, when confronted
with the anti-Chinese riots in Vietnam—resulting in the destruction of Taiwanese
property—the authorities in Taipei publicly invoked the Vietnam-Taiwan informal
investment agreement, but no actual investor legally resorted to its dispute settlement
mechanism.[43] The Vietnamese government was well aware of the limited effects of
such an agreement and the further incapacity to enforce it, given Taiwan's lack of
access to the International Court of Justice (ICJ) if the arbitral award would not be
complied with.

However, politically, the rather rhetoric appeal to an investment treaty (although informal) is efficient in terms of dissuasion from further adverse action. More precisely,
in the context of an investment 'hungry' economy—such as Vietnam—a public signal
of unreliability would not send the right message for foreign investors. On the other
hand, for Taiwan the strategic limit of BITs was thus reached: in some cases it is pref-
erable to sustain economic losses and damage to its investors' property than to allow
others to see into the enforceability gap of the informal BIT network.

---

[43] See Julian Ku, 'Why Taiwanese Investors Should Think about Becoming Chinese (At Least
When Suing Vietnam)' *Opinio Juris* (19 May 2014) http://opiniojuris.org/2014/05/19/bits-rescue-
vietnam/ (last accessed 15 June 2017).

At the same time, the insular polity seems rather eager to give its consent to arbitration when the ISDS mechanism is put into motion *against* it. The recent legal claim of Singapore-based investors bears witness to this phenomenon. For Taiwan, it would be a political victory to show the effectiveness of its informal BITs or FTAs even if it should actually be defeated in the arbitration and ordered to pay damages. That would represent a small price for deploying its investment treaties into the ordinary practice of international litigation, without really being part of the Westphalian system.

A litigation bypass for an informal network.

IV. A (European) Path Forward: Anchoring in Post-sovereign Interaction

After the 'end of history' and beyond strict Westphalian constraints, Taiwan emerges as a *floating polity*. Neither truly grounded in territorial concepts of statehood, but nor unbound from any vision of sovereignty, it finds itself surrounded by a world order that has not yet completely crystallized. Hard power players, decaying normative empires, *realpolitik* grand games and postmodern entities form an ad hoc international environment which allows sufficient space for maneuver. The simultaneous existence of multiple forms of political existence permits Taiwan to follow a singular path that needs no longer to conform to a strict gridline of requirements.

In such a context, the island can 'anchor' itself in various partnerships and modes of interaction without adhering to another hegemon's paradigm. The multi-polar world tolerates the liminal—but significant—participation of unclassified polities, tacitly acknowledging that the uses—and abuses—of sovereignty at a global level proved to be a conceptual 'trap' for European and non-European actors alike. None got out of this experiment untarnished. And none really abides its tenets in an uncompromising manner any more.

For these reasons, the metamorphosis of the world scene may open another way out of the sovereignty impasse by resorting to a post-Westphalian understanding of international law and by addressing Taiwan's challenge to deal with another type of non-sovereign actor: the European Union. Such cooperation could prove to be an ultimate challenge to the classical system of state-to-state international relations, with structural implications (and disruptions) for the entire legal and geopolitical setting.

After the signing of the ECFA, the EU publicly manifested its goodwill toward Taiwan in negotiating an economic (with emphasis on this dimension) cooperation framework. In 2013, the European Parliament further mandated the Commission to commence discussions with the authorities in Taipei, arguing that 'the decision to start such negotiations with Taiwan should be based on *economic reasons*, and should not be interlinked with an assessment of relations between the EU and the People's Republic of China'.[44]

Thus, the bilateral 'prong' of China's investment policy had a direct consequence upon regional (i.e. Taiwan) and global (i.e. the European Union) players' international situation, allowing it to directly influence the mercantile interaction of (post-)state actors in its near abroad and far away from the mainland. Even though the cross-strait relation ended up in a legal *aporia* for several decades, China's intensive—and

---

[44] European Parliament, 'European Parliament resolution of 9 October 2013 on EU-Taiwan trade relations', 2013/2675(RSP), 9th October 2013, Strasbourg.

assertive—global stance allows it to indirectly model the limits of Taiwan's international standing even when dealing with post-Westphalian powers such as the European Union. Bilateral, regional, and global modes of interaction seem to be mere facets of the same strategic conundrum.

Nonetheless, despite being very mindful of the PRC's sensibilities, the EU signalled that its theory and practice of concluding international agreements (for economic purposes) does not overlap or contradict with any hard-power position on statehood, borders, or jurisdiction. This appears possible, as the EU is among the few actors 'able to speak a language very different from that of sovereignty. Therefore, the established relations neither need to conform to traditional diplomatic categories of sovereign-to-sovereign parlance, nor do they have to resort to informal surrogates of such institutions. A different, post-sovereign and non-statist mode of interaction can emerge'.[45]

The commencement of negotiations for a bilateral investment agreement between the EU and Taiwan may allow both actors to arrive at a win-win outcome with systemic implications. For the European colossus, such a treaty could mark the global expansion of its post-sovereign transformative grasp, signalling traditional Westphalian actors that international relations (and law) can be conducted differently. The actions to boost its presence in international organizations and mechanisms would well be supplemented by such an interaction with 'the floating island'. At the same time, by engaging an actor who lacks the insignia of classical sovereignty (not wishing any) and whose authority is horizontally dissipated into a bureaucratic self-referential network of rules, Taiwan could get into the position to demand a singular *locus* that transcends the need for diplomatic recognition.

In such a context, the formal or informal nature of interaction becomes largely irrelevant. Westphalia does not cease to exert influence, but it is no longer the only game in town. The erosion of its conceptual monopoly upon global dynamics may allow peripheral polities such as Taiwan to become fully integrated in the trade and investment flux, enhancing its already existing BIT network.

Without adhering to a strict Westphalian narrative and without allowing its international framework to degrade, Taiwan might find itself able to 'slip' between the Scylla of the PRC and the global Charybdis of classical international law. The insular polity is capable of avoiding isolation and dealing with another post-sovereign actor. Thus, the restructured international order offers a glimpse of a bearable future for Taiwan: anchored in mercantile agreements, but still floating upon the high seas of post-modern global dynamics. The earth may well be flat, but—at least—it is fluid.

---

[45] Horia Ciurtin, 'Not Just a Bridgehead: EU's (Possible) Vision for Taiwan' *DAVA | Strategic Analysis*, DAVA Mercantile Digest no 3 (24 October 2014) https://davastrat.files.wordpress.com/2017/10/dava-mercantile-digest-no-3-october-2017.pdf (last accessed 1 December 2017).

16

China Moves the G20 towards an International Investment Framework and Investment Facilitation

Karl P Sauvant*

I. Introduction

The world's investment needs are tremendous. Meeting the sustainable development goals alone will require trillions of additional dollars annually, not to speak about the implementation of the Paris climate change agreement and our desire to stimulate economic growth and sustainable development in general.[1] Domestic resource mobilization from the public and private sectors will have to finance a considerable share of these investment needs. However, foreign direct investment (FDI), too, can make an important contribution by bringing capital, skills, technology, access to markets, and other tangible and intangible assets to host countries. In fact, FDI flows will have to grow substantially if future investment needs are to be met. It is for this reason that all countries seek to attract such investment and maximize its development impact, and that the issues surrounding these efforts have become key global concerns.

At the same time, a broad discussion is underway about how the international investment regime, within which investment flows take place, needs to be reformed to reflect adequately the requirements of our time. In particular, all governments have subscribed to the sustainable development goals and committed to fight climate change. Against this background, there is a need to broaden the regime's purpose to encourage explicitly the flow of substantially higher amounts of sustainable FDI in the framework of a widely-accepted enabling framework that regulates the relationships between governments and international investors in a balanced manner: sustainable FDI for sustainable development.

China, as the President of the G20 in 2016, has had an opportunity to advance the discussion of these issues, as part of its global track of investment policy (which,

* Karl P Sauvant (karlsauvant@gmail.com), Resident Senior Fellow, Columbia Center on Sustainable Investment, a joint centre of Columbia Law School and the Earth Institute, Columbia University, USA. This is an updated version (in light of the results of the September 2016 summit of the G20) of Karl P Sauvant, 'China, the G20 and the international investment regime' in Andrea Goldstein and Alessia Amighini (eds), *Towards the 2016 G20: Global Analyses and Challenges for the Chinese Presidency* (2016) 24(4) Special issue of *China and the World Economy* 73.

[1] See most recently the following pronouncement of the G20: 'We are determined to foster an innovative, invigorated, interconnected, and inclusive world economy to usher in a new era of global growth and sustainable development, taking into account the 2030 Agenda for Sustainable Development, the Addis Ababa Action Agenda and the Paris Agreement'. See the 'G20 Leaders' Communique, Hangzhou Summit, 4–5 September 2016', para 5 www.consilium.europa.eu/press-releases-pdf/2016/9/47244646950_en.pdf. Electronic copy available at: https://ssrn.com/abstract=2901156.

of course, also influences, at least to a certain degree, its regional and bilateral international investment policy-making approaches). The country has taken a special interest in international investment, judging from the decision to create the G20's Trade and Investment Working Group. This reflects both the role of FDI in China's own development and especially its recent rise as an important outward investor.

This chapter discusses briefly, in section II, the emergence of China as an outward investor, embedded in the rise of emerging markets as home countries of multinational enterprises (MNEs). Section III contains an analysis of some policy issues related to the rise of FDI from emerging markets. A brief discussion of issues central to the future of the international investment law and policy regime follows in section IV, including the adoption of non-binding principles outlining the architecture of a comprehensive framework on international investment. Section V focuses on a concrete proposal for a sustainable investment facilitation programme that could be launched as a follow-up of the discussions initiated under China's leadership. Section VI concludes.

II. China's Rise as an Outward FDI Country

In the past, FDI originated overwhelmingly in developed countries. However, during the past decade or so, the rise of emerging markets,[2] and in particular China, as major MNE home countries, has fundamentally changed the FDI landscape. More specifically, over 120 emerging markets reported FDI outflows during at least one of the five years between 2009 and 2013, and there are now considerably more than 30,000 MNEs headquartered in these economies. FDI from emerging markets had reached 28 per cent of US$1.5tn world FDI outflows in 2014, compared to an average of 2 per cent of a rough annual average of US$50 billion world FDI outflows during 1980–1985.[3] In absolute amounts, FDI outflows from emerging markets have risen from approximately US$1 billion during 1980–1985, to US$409 billion in 2015 (US$378 billion from developing countries and US$31 billion from transition economies);[4] the 2015 figure for emerging markets outflows was eight times higher than *world* outflows were three decades ago. Since 2004, outward FDI (OFDI) flows from emerging markets have been over US$100 billion annually; in 2015, six of the top twenty home economies were emerging markets. MNEs from emerging markets have become important players in major global industries and in the word FDI market in general.

Among emerging markets, China is the star performer.[5] China's OFDI flows grew from US$7 billion in 2001 to US$146 billion in 2015, for an accumulated stock of US$1.1 trillion (MOFCOM, NBS, and SAFE, 2016). This made China the single most important home country among all emerging markets, and the second largest among all home economies in 2015.[6] In fact, China's OFDI flows have caught up with China's inward FDI flows: in 2001, OFDI flows were equal to 15 per cent of inward FDI flows; in 2015, the ratio had reached 107 per cent (MOFCOM, NBS, and SAFE, 2016).

---

[2] The emerging markets are defined here as all non-OECD countries.
[3] See UNCTAD (2016) and *UNCTAD Stat* https://unctad.org/en/Pages/DIAE/FDI%20Statistics/FDI-Statistics.aspx. All data in this article are from these sources, unless otherwise indicated.
[4] As defined in annex Table 1 of UNCTAD's *World Investment Reports* http://unctad.org/en/Pages/DIAE/World%20Investment%20Report/World_Investment_Report.aspx.
[5] In the following text, no adjustments are made for 'round-tripping' that leads to an overestimation of China's international investment position.
[6] This is not counting outflows from Hong Kong.

By the end of 2015, China's 20,200 MNEs had established 30,800 foreign affiliates in 188 countries and territories (MOFCOM, NBS, and SAFE, 2016). Chinese firms have invested substantially in both developed and developing countries, increasingly using mergers and acquisitions (M&As) as a mode of entry. Chinese's FDI distribution across sectors and geographic regions is difficult to ascertain; however, as more than two-thirds of China's non-financial sector outflows are channelled through financial centres, tax havens, and countries of convenience, consequently, the precise amounts, economies, and sectors in which funds are ultimately invested are unknown. It seems likely, however, that services and natural resources are the most important sectors.[7]

These figures should not disguise, however, that China's average shares in world FDI outflows and world FDI stock remain quite low: in terms of flows, China's share was 10 per cent in 2015, while the country's share in the world's OFDI stock was 4 per cent that year (MOFCOM, NBS, and SAFE, 2016).

A distinguishing characteristic of China's OFDI is the very important role played by state-owned enterprises (SOEs). By the end of 2015, these enterprises controlled over half of China's OFDI, a share that has been decreasing (MOFCOM, NBS, and SAFE, 2016). The role of SOEs is expected to remain particularly significant in the 'One Belt One Road Initiative',[8] where Chinese SOEs are operating in tandem with Chinese sovereign wealth funds and state-controlled banks, the first providing management skills and the second financing—not only for M&As but increasingly also for greenfield investments.

III. Policy Issues

Outward FDI from emerging markets faces a number of constraints, and the changing climate for FDI may stymie the outward expansion of firms headquartered in emerging markets. In particular, China's OFDI is attracting considerable attention and rising scepticism (Sauvant and Nolan, 2015). This scepticism stems from the speed with which this investment has grown; the leading role of SOEs in China's OFDI; the potential negative effects associated with FDI;[9] the fear that host countries do not benefit fully from this investment; and the suspicion that Chinese outward investors, when investing abroad, receive various benefits from their governments, giving Chinese SOEs an advantage over private companies investing abroad, thus resulting in unfair competition.

Moreover, a number of (especially developed) host countries are particularly concerned that China's OFDI might compromise their national security, given the central role of SOEs and the question of whether China's OFDI serves purposes other than commercial ones. Not surprisingly, therefore, these concerns have led to the creation or strengthening of regulatory review processes of incoming M&As, especially in critical infrastructure industries.

Regulatory attention has focused primarily on M&As by SOEs. This is reflected in the strengthening or creation of review mechanisms for inbound M&As in a number

---

[7] Judging from the data provided in MOFCOM, NBS, and SAFE (2015).
[8] See Julien Chaisse and Mitsuo Matsushita, 'China's "Belt and Road" Initiative: Mapping the World Trade Normative and Strategic Implications' (2018) 52 Journal of World Trade 163.
[9] Fears include that such investment can crowd out domestic firms; research-and-development capacities are being transferred out of the host country; transfer prices and taxes may be calculated to the disadvantage of the host country; local sourcing (and, hence, backward linkages) may be limited; and that restrictive business practices may be employed.

of countries, led by the United States (Sauvant, 2009).[10] For example, the Foreign Investment and National Security Act of the United States[11] establishes the presumption that a national security investigation needs to be undertaken by the Committee on Foreign Investment in the United States (CFIUS) if a merger or acquisition in the United States is undertaken by a foreign state-controlled entity. Not surprisingly, deals involving firms based in China accounted for the largest number of CFIUS filings during the period 2012–2014, nearly 20 per cent of all cases (Committee on Foreign Investment in the United States, 2016). Furthermore, fifty-two of the 147 notices received in 2014 by CFIUS proceeded to a second-stage investigation (following a thirty-day review).[12] While CFIUS does not identify the percentage of investigations by home country, 'it almost certainly is the case that a disproportionate percentage of those (second-stage) reviews have involved Chinese acquirers' (Covington & Burling LLP, 2016, 2). President Obama's September 2012 veto of a Chinese windmill project near a military base in Oregon, the first veto in twenty-two years, is emblematic of these concerns.[13] Such trends and occurrences underline the importance of the principle of non-discrimination for China.

With China having become a net outward investor, China's government is becoming more interested in protecting its outward investments than protecting its own firms from inward FDI in certain sectors. This is reflected in the changing orientation of China's 129 bilateral investment treaties (BITs) and nineteen other international investment agreements (IIAs).[14] Although these treaties were originally concluded with FDI in China in mind, they increasingly provide protection to the assets of Chinese investors abroad and seek to facilitate their operations. In line with this development, China and the United States reached a watershed accord in July 2013 (in the context of the US–China Strategic and Economic Dialogue) to continue their negotiations of a BIT on the basis of pre-establishment national treatment and the negative list approach to exceptions from such treatment.[15] Both changes had long been resisted by China and, hence, pinpoint the shift in emphasis in the country's investment perspective from a host country to a home country. They also have implications for China's broader approach to the international investment regime. In fact, at their 2015 Strategic and Economic Dialogue, the two governments used the even more ambitious expression 'high-standard bilateral investment treaty'.[16]

Furthermore, China's evolving approach to IIAs needs be viewed in the broader context of the changing global FDI landscape. With the number and size of MNEs

[10] For an analysis of the reforms of review mechanisms in the European Union see Julien Chaisse, 'Demystifying Public Security Exception and Limitations on Capital Movement: Hard Law, Soft Law and Sovereign Investments in the EU Internal Market' (2015a) 37 U Pa J. Int'l L 583 http://scholarship.law.upenn.edu/jil/vol37/iss2/3.
[11] See the Foreign Investment and National Security Act of 2007, Public Law No 110-49, 121 Stat 246 www.treasury.gov/resource-center/international/foreigninvestment/Documents/FINSA.pdf.
[12] See Committee on Foreign Investment in the United States, *Annual Report to Congress, Report Period: CY 2014* (Government Printing Office 2016) 2.
[13] See 'In rare move, Obama unwinds Chinese acquisition of U.S. wind farms' (2012) 12 Inside U.S. Trade 16.
[14] Data are as of November 2016 http://investmentpolicyhub.unctad.org/IIA.
[15] See J Li, 'China, US "pragmatic about pact"' *China Daily* (2014) 1 www.chinadailyasia.com/business/201401/16/content_15112679.html (last accessed 16 January 2014). This is reflected in the (shorter) negative list for the China (Shanghai) Pilot Free Trade Zone; see www.omm.com/resources/alerts-and-publications/publications/shanghai-ftz-unveils-2014-version-of-negative-list/Agreement. However, the China–US negotiations on the length and breadth of China's negative list continue to be difficult: see 'China Misses Deadline for "Negative List" Investment Offer to U.S.' *Reuters* (2016) http://uk.reuters.com/article/us-usa-china-trade-idUKKCN0WY5OU.
[16] See www.state.gov/r/pa/prs/ps/2015/06/244153.htm (last accessed 3 April 2016).

from emerging markets—as well as their volume of outward FDI—growing rapidly, the constellation of national interests of important emerging markets is changing profoundly, in a manner that favours a multi-lateral approach towards investment. When earlier efforts at the international level were undertaken, most notably the 1995–1998 OECD negotiations of a Multilateral Agreement on Investment and the subsequent discussions in the WTO, there was a clear distinction between home and host countries, typically along North–South lines.

Today, emerging markets (and particularly the biggest among them) define their policy interests no longer only defensively as host countries, but also offensively as home countries interested in protecting their investors abroad and facilitating their operations. This can be exemplified by China's change in approach to continue negotiating a BIT with the United States on the basis of pre-establishment national treatment and the negative list approach to exceptions from such treatment.

Similarly, traditional capital-exporting countries are recognizing their importance as host countries and their increasing role as respondents in international arbitrations. As a result, developed countries define their policy interest no longer only offensively as home countries, but also defensively as host countries interested in preserving adequate policy space and, therefore, the government's ability to regulate in the public interest. This is exemplified by the change of approach by the United States when, in its revised 2004 and 2012 model BITs, it narrowed protections afforded to foreign investors—a significant change for a country that had long led efforts to provide full protection to investors and facilitate their operations.

The convergence of policy interests between home and host countries, as well as between developed countries and a growing number of emerging markets, should facilitate reaching a multi-lateral agreement, if there is the political will to pursue this objective.

It is also significant that governments (including China's) continue to show a great willingness to make rules on international investment, as reflected in the proliferation of bilateral, regional and mega-regional IIAs (Chaisse, 2015b, 567). In particular, a number of important ongoing and concluded negotiations are likely significantly to advance a more harmonized approach to investment rule-making: 'recent treaty practice by the states negotiating the TPP [Trans-Pacific Partnership], the RCEP [Regional Comprehensive Economic Partnership], and the US–China BIT, as well as the recent Pacific Alliance Agreement, creates a significant opportunity for the harmonisation of the international investment law regime at a regional, Pacific Rim level' (Feldman and others, 2016, 12). The negotiations of a number of BITs between important countries (in addition to the United States–China BIT)[17] and the negotiations of the Transatlantic Trade and Investment Partnership (TTIP) between the European Union and the United States (should they continue), could lead to a more harmonized approach to investment rule-making and, de facto, to common rules on international investment.

These negotiations represent significant opportunities to shape the investment regime by narrowing the substantive and procedural international investment law and policy differences between and among the principal FDI host and home economies. They could set standards that might considerably influence future investment rulemaking and that would be also in the interest of China's growing outward FDI.

---

[17] These include the negotiations of BITs between China and the European Union, the European Union and India, the European Union and Japan, and India and the United States.

Should this occur, the result of these negotiations could form an important stepping-stone towards a subsequent universal investment instrument.

IV. China and the Reform of the International Investment Regime

Given these developments, China's presidency of the G20 provided that country an opportunity to lay the groundwork for a process that could eventually lead to a multi-lateral framework on investment, perhaps with an open pluri-lateral agreement as a first step.

In fact, broad discussions are underway, in academic circles, among governments and now increasingly also in the OECD, UNCTAD and since 2016 also in the G20, about how to improve the international investment regime. China has had an opportunity to advance this discussion through the G20's Trade and Investment Working Group, created in January 2016. The areas in which improvements can be made in the international investment regime are numerous, as outlined briefly in the following.[18]

Any discussion of the reform of the international investment regime needs to begin with the regime's very purpose. Given the origin of IIAs, it is not surprising that its principal purpose has been, and remains, to protect foreign investors and, more recently, to facilitate their operations, seeking to encourage in this manner additional FDI flows and the benefits associated with them, a concern China shares fully at all levels of its investment policy-making. But this purpose alone is no longer sufficient: it needs to be expanded. In particular, IIAs must recognize, in addition, the need to promote sustainable development and, in line with this objective, the encouragement of higher flows of *sustainable* FDI.[19] Broadening the purpose of the investment regime, moreover, has implications, among other things and most importantly, in terms of recognizing explicitly a carefully defined right to regulate, as well as a clearer definition of key concepts used in IIAs. It also raises the question of the responsibilities of investors and their recognition in IIAs.

Even if the investment regime's purpose is broadened and its key concepts are clarified more precisely, disputes between international investors and host countries can, and will, arise. Naturally, every effort needs to be made to prevent and manage such disputes at the national level. However, if they reach the international level, it is important that the investment regime's dispute-settlement mechanism is beyond reproach. A major reform would be the establishment of a world investment court as a standing tribunal with an appeals mechanism, as suggested by the European Commission (2015). While establishing such an investment court system faces many obstacles, it would institutionalize dispute settlement and represent a major step towards enhancing the legitimacy of the investment regime. It is, therefore, encouraging that this concept has already been incorporated in the Canada–European Comprehensive Economic and Trade Agreement and the European–Vietnam Free Trade Agreement. If broadly accepted, such a move would be comparable to the move from the ad hoc dispute-settlement process under the General Agreement on Tariffs and Trade to the much-strengthened dispute settlement understanding of the WTO.

---

[18] For a detailed discussion see K P Sauvant, 'The Evolving International Investment Law and Policy Regime: Ways Forward' (ICTSD and WEF 2016) https://papers.ssrn.com/sol3/papers.cfm?abstract_id=2721465.

[19] For a discussion of the concept of 'sustainable FDI' see below.

Even if a widely-accepted investment court system were to be established, it would not alleviate another shortcoming of the present regime, namely, that poor countries, especially the least developed among them, typically do not have the human and financial resources to defend themselves adequately as respondents in international investment disputes. And any dispute-settlement process that does not provide a level playing field for the disputing parties is compromised, undermining its legitimacy and, with that, the legitimacy of the international investment regime.

The solution to this problem is obvious, and it has been pioneered by the WTO: there is a need for establishing an advisory centre on international investment law. It could be patterned on the Advisory Center on WTO Law. Its main function should be to advise eligible countries as regards prospective disputes and, if need be, provide administrative and legal assistance to respondents facing investor claims that cannot defend themselves adequately. This is a straightforward proposal. The G20, any of its individual members or, for that matter, any other country could easily take the initiative to establish such an institution, in the interest of enhancing the legitimacy of the investment regime.

The discussion so far has dealt with individual aspects of the present investment regime. However, governments could also take a holistic approach to international investment governance, preferably by negotiating a multi-lateral framework on investment, perhaps beginning with an open pluri-lateral agreement. Obviously, this is not an easy road to take, given the experience of past efforts in this regard. However, as mentioned above, there are a few important developments since earlier efforts had taken place that augur well for a renewed initiative to take the multi-lateral path. Most importantly, as discussed earlier, the constellation of national interests of developed and developing countries has changed profoundly over the past decade, preparing, at least in principle, the way for a consensus approach. Moreover, governments have shown a great appetite to negotiate IIAs, not only bilaterally, but also regionally. In particular, the mega-regional agreements mentioned earlier could lead to a certain harmonization of the substantive and procedural aspects of international investment law. Finally, the investment court system could become the nucleus of a pluri-lateral/multi-lateral agreement.

China's evolving approach to IIAs reflects this changing interest constellation. Its leadership of the G20 in 2016 provided that country with the opportunity to initiate an inter-governmental discussion and process about how the international investment law and policy regime could be improved, and it seized this opportunity. Moreover, it could take the ideas that infused this process forward at the regional and bilateral levels.

The global process cannot be concluded during the year of China's leadership, but rather has to be continued in the G20's Trade and Investment Working Group (whose mandate was extended by the G20 Ministerial Meeting in July 2016, as confirmed by the subsequent G20 summit), or an inter-governmental organization, such as UNCTAD or the WTO. UNCTAD continues to examine the whole range of matters related to IIAs and has an established competence in this area. As to the WTO, it created a Working Group on the Relationship between Trade and Investment during its Singapore Ministerial Meeting in1996, but this Working Group was suspended during the WTO's Ministerial Meeting in Cancun in 2003. The WTO members are of course free to reactivate this working group if they choose to do so.[20] Alternatively, the WTO

---

[20] See in this context the following statement by the G20 Trade Ministers: 'We welcome further research and analytical work in UNCTAD, WTO, OECD and the World Bank, in consultation with the IMF, within their existing mandates and resources, to identify ways and means to enhance coherence and complementarity between trade and investment regimes. In this context, we take note

could establish a new working group (which would be free of the 'baggage' of the suspended working group), focusing on the coherence of trade and investment policies in the age of global value chains. In fact, regardless of what happens elsewhere, the WTO needs to have a discussion on the interface and overlap between trade and investment policies and regimes, including the various types of treaty instruments involved in both areas, and without any prejudice to what further joint action WTO members might want to take. In any event, the G20 could invite governments to do more work to explore the nexus of investment and trade.

The G20 chose a different approach. It agreed on a non-binding declaration on shared principles that would provide overall political guidance by laying out the principal elements that should guide international investment policy in general.[21] More specifically, the G20 Trade Ministers agreed on nine non-binding 'Guiding Principles for Global Investment Policymaking' (see annex) during their July 9–10, 2016 meeting in Shanghai, subsequently endorsed during the G20 Summit in Hangzhou, September 4–5, 2016.[22] They provide the following elements for investment policymaking: avoidance of FDI protectionism; openness, non-discrimination, transparency, and predictability; investment protection, including dispute settlement; transparency in investment rule-making, involving all stakeholders; coherence in investment rule-making, consistent with sustainable development; the right to regulate; investment promotion and facilitation; responsible business conduct; and international cooperation on investment matters. (Given the attention and rising scepticism that China's outward FDI is experiencing, the principles of avoidance of FDI protectionism and non-discrimination are of particular importance to China.) The Guiding Principles are meant to 'promote coherence in national and international policymaking and provide greater predictability and certainty for business to support their investment decisions'.[23]

Reaching this agreement presented a challenge, as the G20 members needed to muster the willingness to compromise in a very short period of time to find common ground, in spite of their disparate views on key principles. For example, if the text would have been very general, it would not have added much value in terms of being of use to policy-makers and IIA negotiators. On the other hand, if a declaration would have laid out a number of relatively detailed principles, governments seeking strong and clear principles (e.g., in order to protect their position in ongoing negotiations regarding the need for pre-establishment protection) would have clashed with governments that would have been less inclined to do that (e.g., regarding non-discrimination

of the B20's recommendation for the WTO Working Group on the Relationship between Trade and Investment to resume its work'. 'G20 Trade Ministers Meeting Statement' (2016) para 20 www.wto.org/english/news_e/news16_e/dgra_09jul16_e.pdf,.

[21] Something very similar was suggested, for the G20 in K P Sauvant and F Ortino, *Improving the International Investment Law and Policy Regime: Options for the Future* (Ministry for Foreign Affairs of Finland 2013); see also W H Shan, 'The Case for a Multilateral or Plurilateral Framework on Investment' *Columbia FDI Perspective* No 161 (Columbia Center on Sustainable Investment, a joint center of Columbia Law School and the Earth Institute, Columbia University, USA 2015). Such a declaration could be patterned on the 'Statement of the European Union and the United States on Shared Principles for International Investment' http://trade.ec.europa.eu/doclib/docs/2012/april/tradoc_149331.pdf.

[22] See the 'G20 Leaders' Communique (n 1) para 29. For an analysis and discussion of the Principles see A Joubin-Bret and C R Chiffelle, *G20 Guiding Principles for Global Investment Policy-Making: A Stepping Stone for Multilateral Rules on Investment* (International Centre for Trade and Sustainable Development and World Economic Forum, E15 Initiative 2017) and J Zhan, *G20 Guiding Principles for Global Investment Policymaking: A Facilitator's Perspective* (UNCTAD 2016).

[23] 'G20 Trade Ministers Meeting Statement' (n 20) para 19.

at the pre-establishment stage of an investment), or that would not have wanted to mention certain principles at all (e.g., investor–state dispute settlement). Finally, remaining silent on key (controversial) principles would have been a difficult option for some governments, as silence could be interpreted as meaning that these principles have lost importance for erstwhile proponents.

Obtaining compromise therefore required that the Guiding Principles needed to be formulated in general language, and certain issues could not be agreed, such as regarding specific protections. Other things could not be pushed further or clarified, for example, that investment promotion and facilitation should also include maximizing benefits for host countries; that investment, to contribute most to sustainable development, should have certain sustainability characteristics; and that responsible business conduct should include obligations, in such areas as contained, for instance, in the OECD Guidelines for Multinational Enterprises and the United Nations Guiding Principles on Business and Human Rights. More generally, the G20 Guiding Principles remain primarily focused— as is typical for the great majority of IIAs—on the obligations of host countries. They make only a modest reference to investor obligations. And they do not mention obligations of home countries at all.

Given China's interest in the subject matter and, also, in having a concrete deliverable in the investment area, it employed its diplomatic skills to bring about a compromise, aided by Canada as co-Chair of the Trade and Investment Working Group, helped by its links to the other members of the BRICS group and supported especially by the Secretariats of UNCTAD and the OECD.[24] Agreement was possible because the Guiding Principles are of a fairly general nature, are non-binding, retain the traditional focus on obligations of host countries, and perhaps allowed trade-offs in other subjects on the G20 agenda.[25] Overall, they are a desirable step towards outlining the architecture of a comprehensive framework on international investment and, in this manner, preparing the ground for a pluri-lateral/multi-lateral investment regime.

Finally, regardless of whether or not systematic inter-governmental efforts aimed at improving the international investment regime take place, it would be very desirable to initiate an informal, inclusive and result-oriented consensus-building process that takes place *outside* inter-governmental settings and, preferably, is led by a respected non-governmental organization. It would have to be informal and off-the-record, to make sure that all governmental and non-governmental participants feel free to speak up, and that they have the opportunity not only to make statements, but can actually discuss the issues. It would have to be inclusive to make sure that all stakeholders are being heard. In addition, it would have to be result-oriented to make sure not only that problems are identified, but also that solutions (or alternative solutions) are proposed. Such a process would also help to build bridges between various groups of stakeholders. There may be members of the G20 (or other countries) that might be interested in promoting such a process. After all, improving the international investment law and policy regime is a long-term process, and all stakeholders need to be on board to move this process forward.

---

[24] Apart from these two international organizations, the Working Group was also supported by the Secretariats of the WTO and the World Bank.
[25] Agreement was perhaps also facilitated by the fact that the International Chamber of Commerce (ICC) had adopted, in 2012, 'Guidelines for International Investment' www.iccwbo.org/Advocacy-Codes-and-Rules/Document-centre/2012/2012-ICCGuidelines-for-International-Investment/, suggesting that the climate for a pluri-lateral/multi-lateral approach is improving.

Despite the attractiveness of beginning a process of discussing, in an inter-governmental body, the desirability and feasibility of a pluri-lateral/multi-lateral investment framework and the systemic issues associated with such an endeavor, it is quite clear that key governments may not be interested in doing so at this point in time. This may be because key players involved in the negotiation of important bilateral and/or regional agreements with investment chapters may wish to wait until these negotiations are concluded before considering a pluri-lateral/multi-lateral approach. Therefore, dealing with this issue is a long-term challenge. It is also in China's interest to face the challenge of improving the international investment regime, given the rise of its own OFDI and the reception it receives in a number of host countries, and to meet this challenge in both inter-governmental and non-governmental settings.

V. A Concrete Proposal and Opportunity: An International Support Programme for Sustainable Investment Facilitation

Beyond the adoption of the Guiding Principles for Global Investment Policymaking and building on them towards a pluri-lateral/multi-lateral investment regime, there is one practical area in which it may be possible to make concrete progress in the near- or medium-term future, with a view towards eventually having an important deliverable initiated during China's G20 presidency.[26] It involves the development of a systematic international investment facilitation[27] programme to encourage higher flows of sustainable FDI to developing countries, and especially the least developed among them, in light of the need to mobilize substantially more resources to meet the investment needs of the future.

There is, of course, the issue of defining 'sustainable FDI', that is, to identify the sustainability characteristics of FDI,[28] a task that could perhaps be undertaken by a multi-stakeholder working group established for this purpose. It is a task not without challenges. While few (if any) governments are likely to object to an investment support programme as such, the proposal made in this chapter to focus on sustainable FDI may create the impression (especially in the private sector) that there is 'desirable' FDI and 'non-desirable' FDI. This is not the intention. Rather, the idea is that, when seeking to attract FDI and benefit from it as much as possible, investment that has

---

[26] For the original proposal and a discussion of the rationale for such a programme see K P Sauvant and K Hamdani, *An International Support Programme for Sustainable Investment Facilitation* (2015) available at https://works.bepress.com/karl_sauvant/397/ (last accessed 21 May 2016); for a further elaboration see Sauvant, 'The Evolving International Investment Law and Policy Regime' (n 18). UNCTAD has since then proposed a 'Global Action Menu for Investment Facilitation' http://investmentpolicyhub.unctad.org/Upload/Documents/GlobalActionMenuForInvestmentFacilitation.v4.16.09.2016.pdf.

[27] 'Investment facilitation', as used here, includes both investment promotion (ie, attracting FDI) and benefitting from FDI as much as possible. This is, admittedly, a broad definition, as it includes 'benefitting from FDI'. The reason for such a broad definition is that one needs to keep in mind that, for countries, FDI is just another tool to advance their growth and development; in other words, countries attract FDI not for its own sake, but with a particular purpose in mind, namely to advance their growth and sustainable development.

[28] For an analysis of sustainability characteristics as contained in 150 instruments relating to eight stakeholder groups and dealing with the relationships between foreign investors and host country governments see Karl P Sauvant and Howard Mann, 'Towards an Indicative List of FDI Sustainability Characteristics' (ICTSD and WEF 2017) https://papers.ssrn.com/sol3/papers.cfm?abstract_id=3055961.

certain sustainability attributes might benefit, for example, from various incentives. In this sense, the approach is not different from the approach taken towards, for example, encouraging renewable energies.

Discussions on investment facilitation (without, however, focusing on the 'sustainability' aspects of FDI) were initiated during China's presidency, but no concrete action programme was adopted, perhaps because of a lack of time. However, the trade ministers 'welcome[d] efforts to promote and facilitate international investment to boost economic growth and sustainable development, and agree[d] to take actions in this regard, including promoting investment in Low Income Countries (LICs)'.[29] Moreover, 'they encourage[d] UNCTAD, the World Bank, the OECD and the WTO to advance this work within their respective mandates and work programmes, which could be useful for future consideration by the G20'.[30] The G20 Summit in Hangzhou subsequently endorsed this approach.[31] This puts at least part of the responsibility of developing a coherent international effort for the promotion of higher FDI flows to developing countries, and especially the least developed among them, in the hands of the international organizations mentioned.

More specifically, these organizations could develop—preferably jointly—an international support programme for sustainable investment facilitation. Such an investment support programme is in the interest of host countries (i.e., all countries) seeking investment for growth and development, as well as of all home countries seeking to strengthen the international competitiveness of their firms by helping them to establish a portfolio of locational assets as an important source of such competitiveness.[32]

As mentioned earlier, all governments seek to attract FDI and benefit from it as much as possible. IIAs are meant to help these efforts in an indirect manner by protecting the investments made. However, evidence about the extent to which IIAs per se induce greater FDI flows in this manner is mixed.[33] This is not surprising given the importance of the economic FDI determinants, the role of the national FDI regulatory framework and the importance of investment facilitation and promotion to attract such investment. In any event, IIAs themselves typically do not require active and direct efforts to encourage FDI flows and to help host countries benefit from them as much as possible. This is crucial in particular for developing countries, and especially the least developed economies, since most of them simply do not have the capacity to

---

[29] 'G20 Trade Ministers Meeting Statement' (n 20) para 17.

[30] ibid para 18.

[31] See the 'G20 Leaders' Communique (n 1) para 29.

[32] China has a 'going out' strategy reflecting precisely these objectives; see K P Sauvant, and V Z Chen, 'China's Regulatory Framework for Outward Foreign Direct Investment' (2014) 7 China Economic Journal 141. Accordingly, an international support programme as suggested here, if adopted, would also embed China's own approach to outward FDI (and, for that matter, that of a number of other (especially developed) countries) in an international consensus.

[33] See K P Sauvant and L Sachs (eds), *The Effect of Treaties on Foreign Direct Investment: Bilateral Investment Treaties, Double Taxation Treaties and Investment Flows* (Oxford University Press 2009) 1 https://papers.ssrn.com/sol3/papers.cfm?abstract_id=2994235; for more recent studies see B Min, S Mujumdar, and J Rhim, 'Bilateral Investment Treaties and Foreign Direct Investment' (2011) Global Business and Finance Review 75; A Lejour and M Salfi, 'The Regional Impact of Bilateral Investment Treaties on Foreign Direct Investment' *Netherlands Bureau for Economic Policy Analysis, Discussion Paper* (2015) 298 www.cpb.nl/en/publication/the-regional-impact-of-bilateral-investment-treatieson-foreign-direct-investment (last accessed 21 May 2016); and L Gómez-Mera and others, *New Voices in Investment: A Survey of Investors From Emerging Countries* (World Bank 2015). The empirical evidence is particularly mixed in the case of BITs, but (logically) different in the case of investment chapters in preferential trade and investment agreements, as the latter enhance both protection and liberalization and link trade to investment.

compete successfully in the highly competitive world market for FDI (World Bank, 2012). They need assistance, not only to obtain more FDI, but *sustainable* FDI.[34]

Therefore, what is required is an international support programme for sustainable investment facilitation, focused on improving *national* FDI regulatory frameworks and strengthening investment promotion capabilities. Such a programme would concentrate on practical ways and means, the 'nuts and bolts', of encouraging the flow of sustainable FDI to developing countries, and, in particular, the least developed among them.[35] It would be situated in a context in which all countries seek to attract FDI in general, typically through national investment promotion agencies (but increasingly also through a growing number of sub-national agencies), but it would focus specifically on sustainable FDI.

Such a programme would complement the WTO-led Aid for Trade Initiative and the WTO Trade Facilitation Agreement (TFA, which focuses on practical issues related to trade and does not deal with such contentious issues as WTO-committed access conditions for agricultural and other products). In a world of global value chains, these two instruments address one side of the equation, namely, the trade dimension. An international support programme for sustainable investment facilitation would address the other side of the equation, namely, the international investment dimension.[36] In today's world economy, characterized by global value chains, trade facilitation alone cannot achieve the benefits that are being sought without investment facilitation. The interface of trade and investment requires close alignment of investment and trade policies.

Analogously to the WTO efforts and in support of them, an investment support programme would be entirely technical in nature, focusing on practical actions to encourage the flow of sustainable investment to developing countries and, in particular, the least developed among them.

An investment support programme could address a range of subjects:

- Host countries could commit to making comprehensive information promptly and easily available (online) to foreign investors on their laws, regulations and administrative practices directly bearing on inward FDI, beginning with issues relating to the establishment of businesses and including any limitations and incentives that might exist. Information about investment opportunities and help in project development would also be desirable. Host country governments, be they of OECD or non-OECD economies, could also provide an opportunity for comments to interested stakeholders when changing the policy and regulatory framework directly bearing on FDI, or when introducing new laws and regulations in this area; at the same time, they would of course retain ultimate decision-making power.

---

[34] See the 'G20 Leaders' Communique (n 1) para 29. For an analysis and discussion of the Principles see A Joubin-Bret and C R Chiffelle, *G20 Guiding Principles for Global Investment Policy-Making: A Stepping Stone for Multilateral Rules on Investment*, (International Centre for Trade and Sustainable Development and World Economic Forum, E15 Initiative 2017) 1 and Zhan (n 22) 1.

[35] See UN (United Nations), *Transforming Our World: The 2030 Agenda for Sustainable Development* (2015) https://sustainabledevelopment.un.org/post2015 (last accessed 21 May 2016) sustainable development goal 17: 'Strengthen the means of implementation and revitalize the global partnership for sustainable development' with target 17.5: 'Adopt and Implement investment promotion regimes for least developed countries'.

[36] However, it should be noted that an investment support programme as advocated here places special emphasis on the promotion of sustainable FDI and maximizing its benefits.

- Home countries, too, can increase transparency. From the perspective of investors, transparency is not only important as far as host countries are concerned, but also as regards support offered to outward investors by their home countries. Thus, home countries could commit to making comprehensive information available to their outward investors on the various measures they have in place, both to support and restrict OFDI. Supportive home country measures include information services, financial and fiscal incentives and political risk insurance.[37] Some of these measures are particularly important for small- and medium-sized enterprises.

- Multinational enterprises could make comprehensive information available on their corporate social responsibility programmes and any instruments they observe in the area of international investment, such as the Human Rights Council's Guiding Principles on Business and Human Rights, the ILO's Tripartite Declaration, the OECD's MNE Guidelines, the OECD's due diligence guidance in different sectors, and the United Nations Global Compact.

- Both host countries and MNEs could commit to making investor–state contracts publicly available.

Investment promotion agencies (IPAs), as one-stop shops, could be an investment support programme's focal points, possibly coordinating with the national committees on trade facilitation to be established under the WTO's Trade Facilitation Agreement. Within a country's long-term development strategy, IPAs could undertake various activities to attract sustainable FDI and benefit from it as much as possible (OECD, 2015).[38] They could improve the regulatory framework for investment; establish time-limited and simplified procedures for obtaining permits, licenses etc., when feasible and when these do not limit the ability of governments to ensure that the regulatory procedures can be fully complied with by investors and government officials; identify and eliminate unintended barriers to sustainable FDI flows; engage in policy advocacy (part of which could relate to promoting the coherence of the investment and trade regulatory frameworks); render after-investment services; facilitate private–public partnerships; identify opportunities for inserting a country in global value chains; promote backward and forward linkages between foreign investors and domestic firms; and, very importantly, find ways and means to increase the sustainable development impact of FDI in host countries.

Investment promotion agencies could also play a role in the development of investment risk-minimizing mechanisms badly needed to attract long-term investment in general and in various types of infrastructure in particular. They could, moreover, have a role in preventing and managing conflicts between investors and host countries, including by providing information and advice regarding the implementation of applicable IIAs and the preparation of impact assessments to avoid liability arising under these agreements. If conflicts occur, they could seek to resolve them before they reach the international arbitral level. Institutionalized regular interactions between host country authorities and foreign (as well as domestic) investors would be of particular help in this respect (e.g., through investor advisory councils in individual countries).

[37] For a detailed discussion of home country measures see K P Sauvant and others, 'Trends in FDI, Home Country Measures and Competitive Neutrality' in A K Bjorklund (ed), *Yearbook on International Investment Law & Policy 2012–2013* (Oxford University Press 2014) 3–107.

[38] See in this context also 'Investment promotion and facilitation' in *Policy Framework for Investment* (OECD 2015) 45–54.

Finally, as in the WTO's trade instruments mentioned above, donor countries could provide assistance and support for capacity building to developing countries (especially the least developed economies) in the implementation of the various elements of an investment support programme. This could begin with a holistic assessment of the various elements of the investment policy framework (economic determinants, the FDI policy framework, investment promotion and related policies) and how it is anchored within the broader context of countries' overall development strategies. The investment policy reviews undertaken by UNCTAD (or the WTO's trade reviews and the OECD's investment reviews) could provide a useful tool for more economies. Support could focus on strengthening the capacity of national IPAs as the country focal points for the implementation of an investment support programme.

An investment support programme could be advanced through:

- Extending the Aid-for-Trade Initiative to cover investment, and fully so,[39] creating in this manner an integrated platform for promoting sustainable FDI. This would be a logical and practical approach that recognizes the close interrelationship between investment and trade. Its initial emphasis could be on investment in services, given the WTO's General Agreement on Trade in Services: transactions falling under its Mode 3 ('commercial presence') account for nearly two-thirds of the world's FDI stock. The matter could be taken up at the next Global Review on Aid for Trade, as a first step in an exploratory examination of the desirability and feasibility of this approach: an Aid for Investment and Trade Initiative. Alternatively, the current Aid-for-Trade Initiative could be complemented with a separate Aid-for-Investment Initiative.

- Expanding the TFA to cover sustainable investment, to become an Investment and Trade Facilitation Agreement, either through an interpretation of the TFA or through amendment; in either case, member states would have to agree. A subsidiary body of the Committee on Trade Facilitation (to be established in the WTO when the TFA enters into force) could provide the platform to consult on any matters related to the operation of what would effectively be a sustainable investment module within the TFA.

- Launching—by all countries (or a group of interested) governments—a Sustainable Investment Facilitation Understanding that focuses entirely on practical ways to encourage the flow of sustainable FDI to developing countries. The WTO could work on such an understanding, as part of a post-Doha agenda. Work could also begin within another international organization with experience in international investment matters, especially UNCTAD, the World Bank, or the OECD. Or leading OFDI countries could launch such an initiative, with the G20 (or a number of its members) at its core.[40]

Every one of these options requires careful study, discussions and consultations, organized by any of the abovementioned international organizations, or by a credible non-governmental organization or by a group of experts and practitioners. IPAs and representatives of the business community should play a central role in this process, as they know best what would be needed to create an effective investment support programme.

---

[39] It has already been expanded to cover infrastructure and some elements of investment.

[40] The top ten outward FDI economies, which include four emerging markets, accounted for approximately four-fifths of world FDI outflows in 2014.

There are, of course, challenges to be addressed. In particular, there are financial implications of an investment support programme. At the present time, a number of bilateral, regional, and multi-lateral organizations undertake, on their own, various types of technical assistance meant to help countries attract FDI, and governments dedicate a substantial amount of financial resources to this objective. A basic characteristic of an investment support programme is that it goes beyond what individual countries or organizations are doing, by putting in place a systematic, well-organized international programme that is based on a comprehensive blueprint. Such a programme, internationally agreed upon, would still be financed by individual governments, as well as regional and multi-lateral organizations. This could be done if the Aid-for-Trade Initiative (which is already funded) were broadened to cover investment, or by following the TFA model: if a country fails to attract funding from other sources, it may approach the Trade Facilitation Agreement Facility (launched in July 2014)[41] as a last-resort source of finance. More generally, in the same manner as it is recognized that reaching the sustainable development goals will require additional finance, promoting higher flows of sustainable FDI would deserve support, as it directly strengthens the productive capacity of host countries.

The proposal's key premise is the importance and urgency of creating more favourable national conditions in host and home countries to encourage substantially higher sustainable FDI flows to meet the investment needs of the future. All countries should have an interest in this objective, as all countries seek to attract such investment, and many countries support their firms investing abroad. It is encouraging that the members of the G20, in their July 2016 Trade Ministers Meeting Statement and in their September 2016 Summit Communiqué, picked up the idea of investment facilitation, committing themselves to working towards this objective and encouraged international organizations to advance this subject within their respective mandates and work programmes. The G20 has given the impetus for initiating work to facilitate the flow of investment. It needs to keep this idea on its agenda, focusing especially on sustainable FDI, with a view towards launching an international support programme for sustainable investment facilitation.

VI. Conclusions

It is important that China has put the issue of the governance of international investment on the agenda of the G20, since it requires global attention. As inter-governmental discussions and negotiations, as well as the reaction of civil society, have shown, it is a very difficult subject. Hence, there was only so much that the G20 could have achieved during China's one-year presidency in 2016. As discussed earlier, a number of bilateral and regional negotiations are underway between and among important countries, and it must be expected that these countries would first want to resolve key issues among themselves before addressing the same issues in a more concrete and much wider context. China itself has an opportunity to advance these issues in the regional and bilateral contexts in which it pursues international investment matters.

Considering the difficulty of the subject matter and the shortness of time, the agreement reached by the G20 trade ministers (subsequently endorsed by the G20 heads of

[41] However, it is uncertain how the Trade Facilitation Agreement Facility (which is linked to the TFA) will function in its quest to act as a financing facility to support those developing countries that are unable to access funds from other funding agencies.

state and government at their summit in Hangzhou in September 2016) on 'Guiding Principles for Global Investment Policymaking' is an important accomplishment. Even though the Guiding Principles are fairly general, their adoption by such a diverse group of countries (accounting, as they do, for the lion's share of the world's FDI) is a desirable step towards outlining the architecture and key elements of a comprehensive framework on international investment.

Going forward, three things are particularly important.

The first is that governments need to build on the Guiding Principles. For example—and this would be the least that could be done—a review could be undertaken (in a mapping/gap analysis) of the extent to which existing international investment agreements reflect already the Guiding Principles and how new agreements take them into account; in the process, the various ways in which this was done could be identified. Another possibility would be for international organizations to monitor future treaty practice in this respect and regularly report on the results of such monitoring, or to invite countries to report about how they reflect the Guiding Principles in their investment policy-making. Finally, the Guiding Principles could be elaborated through the addition of annotations; in doing so, a number of the issues that were outlined earlier in this chapter relating to the reform of the international investment law and policy regime could be taken into account. The key is that governments work with the Guiding Principles. For that purpose, these need to be widely disseminated to anyone involved in the negotiation of international investment agreements.

Secondly, China's presidency has laid the groundwork for something concrete, relatively non-controversial and in the interest of everyone (including countries that are sceptical about IIAs), namely the facilitation of higher sustainable FDI flows to developing countries, and especially the least developed among them. The G20 explicitly encouraged work in this idea, and various international organizations have initiated such work. It is also encouraging that India has introduced the idea of an 'Agreement on Trade Facilitation in Services' in the WTO,[42] a proposal that explicitly covers Mode 3 (i.e., commercial presence) of the General Agreement on Trade in Services; FDI (akin to 'commercial presence') in services accounts for roughly two-thirds of total FDI. While there are several options to arrive at an international approach to the facilitation of higher amounts of sustainable FDI, an Agreement on Trade Facilitation in Services could become, in the longer run, a stepping-stone for a broader International Support Program for Sustainable Investment Facilitation. In the near future, however, one way to make progress in this area would be the preparation of G20 'Guiding Principles for Global Investment Facilitation', to draw on the precedence of the G20 'Guiding Principles for Global Investment Policymaking', adopted in Hangzhou, as a basis and stimulant for more concrete work.

Finally, the G20 decided to maintain its Trade and Investment Working Group, even if it may not meet at the ministerial level.[43] It could continue to be a valuable additional inter-governmental platform for the continued systematic inter-governmental discussion of the range of issues related to the governance of international investment and serve as an incubator for ideas in this respect.

---

[42] See 'Communication from India: Concept Note for an Initiative on Trade Facilitation in Services', document S/WPDR/W/55 of 27 September 2016, and 'Communication from India: Possible Elements of a Trade Facilitation in Services Agreement', document S/WPDR/W57 of 14 November 2016.

[43] For the terms of reference of the Working Group see www.wto.org/english/news_e/news16_e/dgra_09jul16_e.pdf.

Preferably, its work would be paralleled by an informal, inclusive and result-oriented consensus-building process that takes place outside inter-governmental settings, allowing in this manner for a free exchange of ideas. Germany, which holds the presidency of the G20 during 2017 and, in that capacity, will co-chair the Working Group, has an opportunity to move the G20's investment policy work forward. Argentina, which will hold the G20 presidency after Germany and which has a particular interest in facilitating FDI, could build on this work with a view towards additional concrete outcomes.

China's influence was limited when the international trade and financial regimes were created. The country, moreover, was not party to the Uruguay Round, as it joined the WTO only in December 2001. As the 2016 leader of the G20, China had the opportunity to initiate and help shape a process that could eventually lead to a pluri-lateral/multi-lateral investment agreement that encourages explicitly the flow of sub-stantially higher amounts of sustainable FDI in the framework of a widely accepted enabling investment framework that regulates the relationships between governments and international investors in a balanced manner. The process will take time, patience and the involvement of a wide range of stakeholders and, therefore, has to continue far beyond China's presidency of the G20. China will need to play an active role in moving this process forward in the multi-lateral, regional, and bilateral contexts—in its own interest and in the interest of improving the international investment law and policy regime.

VII. Annex

G20 Guiding Principles for Global Investment Policy-making

The following is a quote from the Guiding Principles:[44]

With the objective of (i) fostering an open, transparent and conducive global policy environment for investment, (ii) promoting coherence in national and international investment policy-making, and (iii) promoting inclusive economic growth and sustainable development, G20 members hereby propose the following non-binding principles to provide general guidance for investment policy-making.

    I. Recognizing the critical role of investment as an engine of economic growth in the global economy, Governments should avoid protectionism in relation to cross-border investment.

    II. Investment policies should establish open, non-discriminatory, transparent and predictable conditions for investment.

    III. Investment policies should provide legal certainty and strong protection to investors and investments, tangible and intangible, including access to effective mechanisms for the prevention and settlement of disputes, as well as to enforcement procedures. Dispute settlement procedures should be fair, open and transparent, with appropriate safeguards to prevent abuse.

    IV. Regulation relating to investment should be developed in a transparent manner with the opportunity for all stakeholders to participate, and embedded in an institutional framework based on the rule of law.

[44] 'G20 Trade Ministers Meeting Statement: Annex III' (n 20) 1.

V. Investment policies and other policies that impact on investment should be coherent at both the national and international levels and aimed at fostering investment, consistent with the objectives of sustainable development and inclusive growth.

VI. Governments reaffirm the right to regulate investment for legitimate public policy purposes.

VII. Policies for investment promotion should , to maximize economic benefit, be effective and efficient, aimed at attracting and retaining investment, and matched by facilitation efforts that promote transparency and are conducive for investors to establish, conduct and expand their businesses.

VIII. Investment policies should promote and facilitate the observance by investors of international best practices and applicable instruments of responsible business conduct and corporate governance.

IX. The international community should continue to cooperate and engage in dialogue with a view to maintaining an open and conducive policy environment for investment, and to address shared investment policy challenges.

These principles interact with each other and should be considered together. They can serve as a reference for national and international investment policy-making, in accordance with respective international commitments, and taking into account national, and broader, sustainable development objectives and priorities.

17

G20 Guiding Principles for Global Investment Policy-making

A Stepping Stone for Multi-lateral Rules on Investment

Anna Joubin-Bret and Cristian Rodriguez Chiffelle*

I. Introduction

Since its creation in 1999, but particularly since its first leaders' summit in November 2008 and its institutionalization in 2010, the G20 has gathered leading countries to diagnose, discuss, and work together towards a global recovery. Each G20 member, in turn assuming the presidency, has sought to shape the agenda and focus on concrete issues of international relevance to boost the economic recovery from the global financial crisis.

One of the most important and concrete outcomes of China's G20 presidency was the establishment of a Trade and Investment Working Group (TIWG), recognizing that robust and sustainable trade and investment reinforces economic growth and calling for enhanced G20 trade and investment cooperation.[1] The Chinese presidency's renewed approach was not only to bring stand-alone investment issues to the G20 table, but also to re-spark the conversation on investment and trade policy-making by bringing them closer together again, acknowledging the complementarity of trade and investment as the engines of economic growth. This has paved the way for coherent, integrated discussions on trade and investment for the first time in fifteen years in the global political arena.

On the investment side, the TIWG delivered the G20 Guiding Principles for Global Investment Policy-Making (G20 Guiding Principles), a key outcome of the Chinese presidency. These were endorsed by trade ministers in Shanghai in July 2016 and then by heads of state at the Hangzhou Summit in September 2016, with the objective of fostering an open, transparent, and conducive global policy environment for investment; promoting coherence in national and international investment policy-making; and promoting inclusive economic growth and sustainable development.[2]

* Anna Joubin-Bret, Secretary of the United Nations Commission on International Trade Law (UNCITRAL) and Director of the Division on International Trade Law in the Office of Legal Affairs of the United Nations. Cristian Rodriguez Chiffelle, Head, Trade and Investment Policy at the World Economic Forum, Geneva.

[1] G20 Leaders' Communiqué Hangzhou Summit (2016), http://europa.eu/rapid/press-release_STATEMENT-16-2967_en.htm.

[2] G20 Trade Ministers Meeting Statement (9–10 July 2016, Shanghai, People's Republic of China) Annex III: 'G20 Guiding Principles for Global Investment Policy-making' preamble http://www.oecd.org/daf/inv/investment-policy/G20-Trade-Ministers-Statement- July-2016.pdf.

The G20 Guiding Principles are introduced in Section I of this chapter. It begins with a background review of their crafting and various attempts at devising guiding principles on international investment, and identifies some of the guidelines that have paved the way for the Principles.

Section II focuses on the objectives, scope, and content of the G20 Guiding Principles and considers their potential impact on policy-making at the domestic and international levels.

Section III addresses the broader work of the G20 TIWG, including the trade and investment linkage, analyses the general state of play of G20 countries' investment agreements, and offers some preliminary conclusions and ways forward.

Understanding these new global principles on foreign direct investment (FDI) policy-making will be relevant for businesses and host and home countries alike, as they navigate the complex roles, rights, and obligations around FDI.

II. Building on Earlier Attempts—Taking a Realistic Approach

This section briefly reviews earlier attempts to establish international rules seeking either to regulate investment at the international level, or to address the role of international investment in broader policy initiatives. It suggests that the careful and circumscribed approach taken by the G20 Guiding Principles is the only realistic one which could have entailed delivery at this stage, and for that the effort has strong merit. The section also reviews several sets of rules and guidelines that have preceded the G20 Guiding Principles.

It is possible to take a strictly historical perspective and to show, over time, how various attempts have been made at negotiating multi-lateral rules on international investment, and on its key actors—multi-national enterprises—and how the issue of international investment has consistently resisted international consensus. In spite of multiple efforts in various fora over the years, no multi-lateral rules on international investment exist, as these negotiations have resulted in failures that have scared and scarred many institutions and champions.

Because of these failures, the outcomes of numerous discussions and negotiations on investment at the multi-lateral level have inevitably taken, at best, the form of non-binding guidelines, guiding principles or non-binding principles. Soft law has been the way to ensure that the results of negotiations that have not made it into an agreed set of hard rules are consolidated in instruments that, while not legally binding, would nevertheless contribute to the building of a corpus of rules disciplining FDI across nations.

This has typically been the fate of those instruments negotiated under the auspices of the World Bank (World Bank Guidelines on the Treatment of Foreign Investment),[3] the UN (Code of Conduct on Transnational Corporations),[4] and the OECD (OECD

---

[3] International Bank for Reconstruction/World Bank, 'The Legal Framework for the Treatment of Foreign Investment (Vol 2)' Report to the Development Committee and Guidelines on the Treatment of Foreign Investment 1992.

[4] Karl Sauvant, 'The Negotiations of the United Nations Code of Conduct on Transnational Corporations: Experience and Lessons' (2015) 16 Journal of World Investment & Trade 11.

Guidelines for Multinational Enterprises)[5] during the 1990s and the first decade of the current century.

At the multi-lateral level, while references to investment as an engine for sustainable economic growth can be found in the UN Charter,[6] the UN General Assembly Declaration on Social Progress and Development,[7] the UN Millennium Development Goals,[8] and the UN Global Compact[9]—and more recently—the UN Sustainable Development Goals (SDGs)[10] and the Addis Ababa Action Agenda[11]—no international consensus was found over the years on the need and the way to regulate the interaction and impact of international investment flows.

At the same time, however, international negotiations on investment even among 'like-minded' countries of mega-regional instruments such as the Trans-Pacific Partnership Agreement (TPP), the Trans-Atlantic Trade and Investment Partnership (TTIP), and Regional Comprehensive Economic Partnership Agreement (RCEP)—with the only recent exception of the Canada–EU Free Trade Agreement (CETA)—are yet to deliver concrete, enforceable results on which to build further.[12]

There is a general consensus over the need to ensure that the investment chapters of free trade agreements and mega-regionals clarify and streamline the content of the minimum standard of treatment, fair and equitable treatment, the operation of most favoured nations clauses and indirect expropriation, limit the reference to legitimate expectations of investors, and reaffirm the state's right to regulate for a public purpose.[13] However, there is no agreement over the way to go about it, let alone a possibility to consolidate the approaches between major international players. In addition, many civil society groups have been extremely vocal in opposing these treaties.

Entrenched negotiation positions have made it impossible to come to an agreement on core investment protection, liberalization, and promotion rules. For decades, the differences between the EU member countries' broad bilateral investment treaties (BITs) approach and the US model of pre-establishment protection and customary international law-based investment protection have been emphasized, if not artificially created to play one against the other in international investment disputes, and made

---

[5] OECD, *OECD Guidelines for Multinational Enterprises* (2011) http://dx.doi.org/10.1787/9789264115415-en.

[6] United Nations, Charter of the United Nations art 55 http://www.un.org/en/charter-united-nations/.

[7] United Nations General Assembly, Declaration on Social Progress and Development, General Assembly Resolution 2542 (XXIV) of 11 December 1969 art 16(a) http://www. ohchr.org/Documents/ProfessionalInterest/progress.pdf.

[8] United Nations Millennium Development Goals, Target 8.A, 'Develop Further an Open, Rule-based, Predictable, Non-discriminatory Trading and Financial System'http://www. un.org/millenniumgoals/global.shtml.

[9] United Nations Global Compact, *The Ten Principles of the UN Global Compact* https://www.unglobalcompact.org/ what-is-gc/mission/principles.

[10] United Nations General Assembly, Resolution adopted by the General Assembly on 25 September 2015, 70/1, *Transforming Our World: The 2030 Agenda for Sustainable Development* https://www.un.org/sustainabledevelopment/sustainable-development-goals/.

[11] United Nations, Addis Ababa Action Agenda of the Third International Conference on Financing for Development (2015) http://www.un.org/esa/ffd/wp-content/uploads/2015/08/AAAA_Outcome.pdf.

[12] See Julien Chaisse, 'The Shifting Tectonics of International Investment Law: Structure and Dynamics of Rules and Arbitration on Foreign Investment in the Asia-Pacific Region' (2015) 47 George Washington International Law Review 563, 615–16.

[13] More trade is conducted within the framework of bilateral and plurilateral trade agreements than outside: almost 55 per cent of goods exported took place within such frameworks in 2014, compared with 42 per cent in 1995 (source: ILO, *Translating the 2030 Agenda for Sustainable Development into Action: Integrating trade, investment and decent work policies* (2016) 7).

it harder to bridge the gap, if it is admitted that there is such a gap in international legal terms.

In this context, it is realistic to consider that agreement on substantive investment protection standards or approaches to investment liberalization is extremely difficult in the short to medium term, globally and even among members of the G20. Be it for lack of common understanding or for lack of appetite for global rules, it is to be expected that a top-down approach to investment regulation will not happen in a fortnight.

In this respect, the outcome of the G20 TIWG is an even greater achievement as it has taken realistic stock of the state of play and identified the need for a different approach to achieve consensus. It has focused on common aspirations, general non-contentious principles and effective policy-making, rather than on dividing approaches to substantive and binding legal commitments. The G20 Guiding Principles may actually represent the most elaborate achievement for many years to come.

III. Realistic Approaches that Preceded the G20 Guiding Principles

Institutions such as the OECD, UNCTAD, APEC, and ILO, as well as the World Economic Forum and International Chamber of Commerce (ICC), have made this pragmatic analysis and have come to the conclusion that mandatory rule-making is not a realistic option, even in the form of model agreements or core substantive principles. International organizations have therefore decided to tackle the international investment agenda from a different, less contentious angle.

The discussions within the TIWG, which resulted in the G20 Guiding Principles, drew first on UNCTAD's Investment Policy Framework for Sustainable Development (IPFSD) and its overarching core principles (the 'design criteria' for investment policies and for other IPFSD components). In fact, the first draft submitted to the members of the TIWG was based on UNCTAD's Core Principles of the IPFSD.

The UNCTAD IPFSD approach is based on identifying guidelines for investment policy-making at the national and international level, with a focus on improving the sustainable development dimension of investment rulemaking. In its 2015 version, a fourth building bloc of a comprehensive action plan for promoting the attainment of the SDGs was added. The architecture is based on an overarching set of core principles that translate the challenges of investment policy-making into a set of design criteria for investment policies and for the other IPFSD components. The UNCTAD IPFSD then develops two pillars for policy-making, centring on national investment policy guidelines. These are meant to provide guidance for policy-makers on how to formulate investment policies and regulations and how to ensure their effectiveness.

The OECD with its Policy Framework on Investment (PFI) has worked on the role and place of investment policies in global economic regulation and devised a toolkit to identify and implement policies that mobilize private investment that supports steady economic growth and sustainable development, contributing to the economic and social well-being of people around the world.[14] The PFI provides a framework by which to assess policies to improve investments and their impact, regularly updated to factor the various changes in the global investment landscape, examining twelve policy areas

---

[14] OECD, *Policy Framework for Investment* (2015) http://dx.doi.org/10.1787/9789264208667-en.

that matter for investment. It also aims to advance the implementation of the SDGs and to help mobilize financing for development in support of the post-2015 development agenda.

The PFI has been used to conduct OECD investment policy reviews by countries and for purposes of capacity building beyond the membership. It encourages policy-makers to ask appropriate questions about their economy, their institutions and their policy settings to identify priorities, develop an effective set of policies and evaluate progress. First developed in 2006, the PFI was updated in 2015 to take into account feedback from the numerous users of the framework at country and regional levels since its development, as well as changes in the global economic landscape.[15]

The PFI has been described as essentially a checklist which sets out the key elements in each policy area.[16]

With the PFI, the OECD has taken a pragmatic step to encourage countries to benchmark their investment policies against international good practices, to take a coherent approach to investment policies, focusing on an enabling framework for sustainable investment, and providing guidance and examples of good practice for domestic policy-making. The PFI has voluntarily downplayed the international top-down rule-setting on investment to favour the domestic policy approach to build consensus from the bottom up.

Indeed, what government could be opposed or take issue with good practices and practical recipes to improve the investment climate and thereby improve attractiveness for sustainable investment flows? The number of countries undergoing PFI reviews by the OECD or investment policy reviews by UNCTAD shows that this is not a contentious approach.

The Tripartite Declaration of Principles Concerning Multinational Enterprises and Social Policy (MNE Declaration) is an International Labour Organization (ILO) framework adopted and supported by business, unions, and governments to maximize positive social and employment impacts of multi-national enterprises and resolve possible negative impacts. It sets out roles and responsibilities for governments (home and host), multi-national enterprises, and workers' and employers' organizations, and brings these actors together to solve decent work challenges and identify opportunities for inclusive growth. Its principles cover areas of employment, training, conditions of work and life, and industrial relations.[17]

The MNE Declaration (v. 2006) states that 'where governments of host countries offer special incentives to attract foreign investment, these incentives should not include any limitation of workers' freedom of association or the right to organize and bargain collectively'.

Pursuant to the SDGs, ILO's Decent Work Agenda provides a crucial component of a comprehensive and integrated trade and investment approach. SDG 8, to 'promote sustained, inclusive and sustainable economic growth, full and productive employment and decent work for all', is reflected in full on the ILO's mandate of decent work for all and the complementarity of trade and investment policies with employment and decent work. This marks a significant policy shift, as until now trade and investment have often been pursued as ends in themselves, while employment and decent work have sometimes been relegated to outcomes that would come about semi-automatically by

---

[15] ibid.   [16] ibid.
[17] 'Translating the 2030 Agenda for Sustainable Development into Action: Integrating trade, investment and decent work policies' Background note of the International Labour Organization to the UN Conference on Trade and Development, 17–22 July 2016, Nairobi, Kenya.

simply going for growth.[18] This new policy imperative has been strongly picked up by
G20 Guiding Principle 5, prompting investment policies to be consistent with the
objectives of sustainable development and inclusive growth, and hence with goal 8 of
the SDGs.

The World Economic Forum and the International Centre for Trade and Sustainable
Development (ICTSD), through the E15 Initiative, also looked to assemble an ambitious number of policy recommendations for the investment regime, ranging from core
areas of investment protection and liberalization, to investment facilitation and constructive relationships with the trade regime, other international law regimes and other
areas subject to international regulation such as global taxation.[19] The E15 Initiative
took the interesting approach of looking ten to fifteen years ahead, identifying a vision
for 2030 and developing a coherent set of policies to achieve these priorities.

The recently released ICC Guidelines reaffirm fundamental principles for investment set out by the business community as essential for economic development. The
guidelines, following the same approach as the OECD PFI, include investment policies within a broader frame of economic governance and rule-making. They highlight
investment policies as a piece of a broader puzzle and take a global approach, addressing both states and business actors. Both the OECD PFI and the ICC Guidelines
insist on the necessary coherence between investment policies and other policy areas
relevant for economic governance. They have not taken a position on core elements of
investment protection or liberalization in international investment agreements beyond
general encouragement (ICC Guidelines 1.3.f).[20]

A special mention must be made here of the APEC non-binding principles on investment, whose original version dates back to 1994. Updated in 2011, they consolidate core investment protection and liberalization provisions, albeit in a non-binding
manner. In spite of repeated efforts and commitments, the APEC non-binding principles have so far not made it into a binding set of rules that would apply among APEC
member economies, although the question remains on the table through the Free Trade
Area of the Asia-Pacific (FTAAP) negotiations, in the absence of other mega-regional
investment agreements such as the TPP.

Whether the APEC non-binding principles are seen as a consolidation of a state of
play among APEC member economies on investment protection and liberalization,
or whether they are still aspirational and reflect mere objectives is debated. Detailed
studies of core investment protection and liberalization rules in FTAs among APEC
member economies FTAs show a high degree of convergence and the non-binding
principles may soon be considered obsolete in the region, representing an early stage
of investment regulation.

In light of this analysis, it is the pragmatic approach that has prevailed in the proposal to come up with G20 Guiding Principles. It was a risky endeavour, though, on
several grounds, including past experience. It required identifying acceptable building
blocks and carefully addressing domestic and international policy-making, as opposed
to rule-making, while not shying away from certain common principles where they
reflect consensus.

[18] ibid.   [19] E15 Initiative http://e15initiative.org/themes/investment- policy.
[20] International Chamber of Commerce, *ICC Guidelines for International Investment* (2016)
http://www.iccwbo.org/Advocacy-Codes-and-Rules/Document-centre/2016/ICC-Guidelines-
for-international-investment-2016.

IV. Objectives, Scope, and Content of the G20 Guiding Principles at the TIWG

The first immediate objective of the G20 Guiding Principles is to provide general guidance for investment policy-making. The nature and form of the text is clear: it is a set of design criteria, general in nature and non-binding. It is not specifically focused on domestic or international rule-making, but rather covers both.

The overall consensus that brings G20 members together on the Guiding Principles is the: role of international investment in the global economic recovery and an equally clear understanding of an overall desire for an open, transparent, and conducive investment framework; need for coherence between domestic and international investment policies; and role for investment to contribute and play its part in inclusive economic growth and sustainable development.

From these objectives follow three main drivers for the Guiding Principles:

Policy coherence: A key driver for the Guiding Principles was the desire to strengthen policy coherence between national and international policies, and consistency between investment policies and other policy areas, as well as sustainable development objectives.[21]

Sustainable development objectives and inclusive growth: The way sustainable development objectives should feature among the Guiding Principles was subject to discussion among the G20 members. As noted by James Zhan, Director of Investment and Enterprise at the United Nations Conference on Trade and Development (UNCTAD), two approaches were considered by the TIWG: to put sustainable development upfront as a fully-fledged, standalone guiding principle, or to focus on core investment policy issues and ensure the investment principles are in line with sustainable development objectives. The latter approach prevailed and language to this effect is included in the preamble of the Guiding Principles and finds its way again into the concluding paragraph. Sustainable development objectives are thereby reaffirmed in their role for investment policy-making, while avoiding characterizing their content and criteria and concrete translation into rules or principles. Inclusive economic growth and sustainable development objectives are further emphasized as common goals under principle 5.

Similarly, the objectives reaffirm the common understanding among G20 member economies on the role investment plays in the overall economic recovery and that it must be given full attention. This is in line with the broader approach taken by the G20 members to address international trade and investment as noted in the G20 Trade Ministers Statement.[22] Trade ministers endorsed the G20 Strategy for Global Trade Growth, committing to 'lead by example to lower trade costs, harness trade and investment policy coherence, boost trade in services, enhance trade finance, promote e-commerce development, and address trade and development'.

Non-binding character: While guiding principles for policy-making in and by themselves do not constitute mandatory rules and do not bind the members as to the content of rules or even over-arching principles, consensus could be achieved because of

---

[21] James Zhan, 'G20 Guiding Principles for Global Investment Policymaking: A Facilitator's Perspective' *E15 Initiative* (2016) http://e15initiative.org/publications/g20-guiding-principles-for-global-investment-policymaking-a- facilitators-perspective.

[22] G20 Trade Ministers Meeting Statement, 10 July 2016: '[r]esolv[ing] to step up efforts to better communicate the benefits of trade and investment openness and cooperation to a wider public, recognizing their important contribution to global prosperity and development'.

the way in which the non-binding character of these Guiding Principles was stressed. Member economies agreed upon the aspirational nature of the Guiding Principles, their role as a guiding instrument for the formulation of domestic investment policies and strategies. In his article, Zhan affirms that they may even go beyond and are also meant to serve as an important reference for drafting and negotiating international investment treaties.[23] This may be so when general principles are concerned to achieve effective investment policies. The Guiding Principles were ultimately agreed upon precisely because of their non-binding nature that would allow countries as far apart in their understanding of international investment protection and liberalization as India, South Africa, Brazil, China, the European Union, and the United States to find common ground.[24]

Both the preamble language and the concluding paragraph further highlights the role of these Guiding Principles to serve as a reference for policy-making in the domestic and international policy design process,[25] which can be looked at as a positive statement of agreement or the reiteration of an intentional vagueness in their focus.

The G20 Guiding Principles identify nine elements of investment policy-making that constitute a strong global statement around four key areas of investment policy-making (whether at the domestic or international levels): entry and establishment, treatment and protection, promotion and facilitation, and the settlement of disputes.

In addressing these four key areas, the Guiding Principles strike a delicate balance between substantive issues and the rule-making and design process itself. The way each of these key areas appear in the Guiding Principles is telling of the level of consensus or of the sensitivity of issues that are carefully avoided, such as for example competition for investment, through incentives, performance requirements and industrial policies, market access, core elements of investment protection, investors obligations and the role of home countries.

The main elements covered on different parts of the nine G20 Guiding Principles are as follows:

- avoiding investment protectionism
- openness, transparency, and non-discrimination
- investment protection
- transparency, coherence in investment rule-making, including consistency with the objectives of sustainable development and inclusive growth
- the right to regulate for public purpose
- investment promotion and facilitation
- responsible business conduct
- international cooperation on investment.

Discussing in further detail, the content of each of the nine Guiding Principles can be characterized as follows:

Avoiding investment protectionism is the first and most important guiding principle for G20 member economies and, as such, the first to be spelled out. It became

[23] Zhan (n 21).
[24] Comments to this effect were reiterated during the World Economic forum/ICTSD G20 Investment Principles Dialogue held in Geneva, Switzerland, on 7 November 2016.
[25] See UNCTAD Investment Policy Framework for Sustainable Development (IPFSD) Core Principles at http:// investmentpolicyhub.unctad.org/ipfsd.

apparent during the discussions of the Trade and Investment Working Group that it would need to be reflected first. Since its launch, the core concern for G20 members has been the temptation of investment protectionism that could result from the global financial and economic crisis, and that could drive countries to re-establish barriers to entry and operation of investment that have been systematically taken down over the last five decades. A mandate to monitor such potential protectionist trade and investment measures had been given in 2009 to the OECD, UNCTAD, and the WTO, the three organizations coming up with a quarterly report reviewing measures and identifying broader trends.

This first principle is both concrete and has broad-ranging implications on policy-making. Interestingly, the addressees of this first guiding principle are governments.

Directly linked to avoiding investment protectionism is the requirement to keep an open, stable, and predictable climate for investment. While the commitment to avoid protectionism is strong, the way to achieve policies that reflect this commitment are both precise and general. They are precise in so far as they rely on key concepts of international trade and investment frameworks: openness, non-discrimination, transparency, and predictability. Openness of an economy to investment is generally achieved through non-discrimination between foreign and domestic operators. Similarly, transparency regarding the conditions and procedures enabling investments is a basic feature of any investment policy framework at the domestic level. They are general however in so far as they announce an objective but do not go into the concrete means to achieve the ends themselves. For instance, whether these policies will apply at the pre-establishment stage or only once an investor has been admitted in accordance with the laws and regulations of the host state, however open and enabling they may be, is not addressed here. But there is logic to this, as doing so would most likely have constituted a major stumbling block within the negotiations.

The third guiding principle relates to investment protection and deals with strong protection and legal certainty.

It also addresses settlement of investment disputes that has become in recent years the fixation abscess of international investment negotiations. This guiding principle advocates for legal certainty and strong protection of investors and their investments, including both tangible and intangible investments. The scope of the principle goes beyond protecting traditional property rights and identifies tangible and intangible assets and rights as requiring strong protection. This is again the recognition that investment protection must go beyond the protection of property rights afforded by traditional investment rules and that they should encompass more recent forms of such rights (i.e. intellectual property rights, data, derived rights).

The interesting aspect of this principle is the emphasis on settlement of disputes, on dispute prevention policies and effective mechanisms to prevent, settle and then enforce the outcome of dispute settlement. The objective for rule-making or designing of mechanisms is to establish fair, open and transparent dispute settlement procedures.

The principle also explicitly identifies the risk of abuse by foreign investors of these procedures. While it is of course the main objective of this chapter to highlight the content of the Guiding Principles, it is also interesting in this regard to underline what is not there. There is no specific normative content, no standard or level of protection in this principle, beyond the affirmation that the protection must be strong and that disputes must be addressed. Similarly, there is no agreement on the type of mechanisms for dispute settlement beyond the principles of fairness, openness, and transparency. While fairness and transparency are clearly identified principles in dispute resolution, including in current investor–state dispute settlement mechanisms, particularly with the recent improvements on, the same cannot be said about openness. One wonders about the concrete implications, beyond public access to arbitration procedures and hearings. The two following principles address policy-making and design criteria to achieve the substantive objectives spelled out in the first three items.

Transparency and participation in the regulatory process is a core principle of the international trading system. It makes sense both to ensure that all players in the international trading system play by the rules and because the policies and rules at stake are limited and focused on the border/entry of investments. Although they are generally considered non-contentious also for investment policy-making, some transparency-related angles are highly controversial, such as the ones that relate to national security reviews; hence the need for a compromise. As discussed below, this is far from obvious however in the sense that investment policies address virtually all areas of domestic laws and regulations, and that any and all domestic laws and regulations are relevant for foreign investors. The scope of this aspiration for transparency and stakeholder participation in investment policy-making is therefore a double-edged sword and must be considered carefully to ensure that it matches domestic rule-making procedures and not become too burdensome and encroach on policy flexibility. Clearly, operationalizing this principle goes well beyond publication and access by investors to rules and measures and reaches well into domestic institutions.

Coherence between national and international investment policies is a very legitimate desire and objective; however, it is clearly more difficult to ensure in the absence of multi-lateral rules on investment and in a scattered landscape of rules and obligations. Although coherence does not mean harmonization, interestingly the overall objectives of sustainable development and inclusive growth are spelled out again, among the design or policy-making objectives, to emphasize that not only is coherence within investment policies desirable, but necessary.

The state's right to regulate investment for legitimate public purposes then follows the main design criteria. This principle is delinked from the investment protection principle, and the content has been cropped to achieve an agreement ad minima. This reflects the fact that, within and beyond the G20, there is no consensus on the best way to address legitimate concerns about a state's right to regulate. For some G20 member countries, the language of the principles is important to avoid implying that commitments by states at the national and international levels to protect foreign investors could clash with the state's right to regulate in the public interest, and that they would risk impinging on this right. Other member economies have made it a central feature of their international investment negotiations to protect the state's right to regulate, and it would therefore have been difficult to reach a consensus beyond reaffirming it. The difference in these approaches have dominated investment agendas of the last decade, including at the TTIP negotiations and in the new investment treaty models and policies of certain countries, such as Brazil or India. The European Union, for example, has put the issue of the right to regulate at the centre of 'trade for all', its new trade and investment strategy.[26]

The focus on investment promotion and facilitation, also picked up very strongly by the G20 and B20 in 2017 under the German presidency, is another important component of the Guiding Principles and shows the member countries' pragmatic approach to investment policies. The above principles and rules are of course meant to achieve a concrete objective: attracting and retaining investment that has a concrete

---

[26] European Commission, *Trade for All: Towards a More Responsible Trade and Investment Strategy* (2014) http://trade. ec.europa.eu/doclib/docs/2015/october/tradoc_153846.pdf.

and positive impact on the host state's economy. This can be achieved through co-herent and effective investment promotion and facilitation policies. Again, this prin-ciple refers to transparency, this time as a corollary to conduciveness. In practice, it refers to investment promotion measures and making the rules and regulations known to investors when entering but also when operating their business. As noted by Zhan in his paper,[27] and as was also apparent during the discussion of earlier drafts of the Guiding Principles, G20 members wanted to avoid the issue of investment incentives and their corollary: performance requirements linked to incentives.[28]

The issue of investment incentives that are consistently criticized for their lack of proven impact on investment decision-making also leads to competition for invest-ment among states and even within states. Some countries, however, are not yet ready to forego the possibility of providing these incentives. To avoid tackling the issue dir-ectly in the Guiding Principles, it was decided to focus on 'effective and efficient' investment promotion that reflects the positive and proactive role states can play in promoting investment. It is interesting to note in this regard that investment promo-tion and facilitation are at the core of the new treaty approach of Brazil and several countries that are looking into strengthening the promotion and facilitation role of investment cooperation.

The next principle on international best practices and applicable instruments of re-sponsible business conduct and corporate governance builds on the OECD Guidelines for multi-national enterprises and recognizes the role of best practices and soft law in-struments developed on these issues. The Guiding Principles incorporate by reference the OECD Guidelines and consolidate them as a desirable feature of policy-making at the domestic and international level. While it recognizes the importance of such instruments of responsible business practices, it is the closest the Guiding Principles come to spelling out obligations for investors, another issue often raised by civil society groups.

The last principle on cooperation could be seen as paying tribute to international institutions active in investment policy-making, such as the OECD, UNCTAD, the World Bank, and, where relevant, the WTO. The reference to cooperation and dia-logue is important in the absence of an international forum where investment issues are discussed. The term '[S]hared investment policy challenges' is more ambiguous and seems to represent a compromise to address the concerns voiced by some (typically developing) G20 member countries and the position of other members that beyond naming investment protectionism as the common concern, are not prepared to iden-tify downsides of investment policies, either at the national or international level.

The Guiding Principles conclude with an operational statement that they should not be considered in isolation and that, as indicated in the UN Guiding Principles, the OECD PFI or the UNCTAD IPFSD core principles for policy-making, they consti-tute a coherent set which needs to take into account national and broader sustainable development objectives and priorities.

The statement that the Guiding Principles 'interact with each other and should be considered together' warrants careful scrutiny. It reflects the overall aspiration to coher-ence and consistency in the policy-making process, to ensure that investment policies to avoid protectionism or on investment protection do not clash with other policies on investment promotion or on responsible business conduct. The concrete implication of

---

[27] Zhan (n 21).

[28] Gabriel Bottini, 'Extending Responsibilities in International Investment Law' *E15 Initiative* http://e15initiative.org/publications/extending-responsibilities-in-international- investment-law.

this statement does not go as far as the statement in an earlier draft suggesting that the principles should not be applied or interpreted in isolation. The fact that the Guiding Principles are non-binding does not make application or interpretation necessary beyond inspiration when drafting policies and aspiration for coherence.

V. Conclusions, State of Play, and the Way Forward

The Guiding Principles' opening and closing statements are indeed coherent on the role that is devolved to them, and closes the exercise. Before qualifying the Guiding Principles as non-binding, which leaves no doubt as to their legal nature, the preamble describes them as a proposal by the G20 members to provide general guidance for investment policy-making. The concluding paragraph states that they can serve as a reference for national and international investment policy-making and in so far emphasizes the role of the Guiding Principles as a policy-making checklist or a good practices manual.

Two interesting remarks come to mind with regard to the reference that is made in the concluding paragraph to international investment policy-making and to international commitments. This is the only place in the Guiding Principles, apart from the reference to necessary coherence between national and international policies, where international investment negotiations are addressed. Were it not for this reference, the exercise could be limited in its scope and application to domestic policy-making. It remains to be seen whether these Guiding Principles as they currently stand reflect an actual consensus on investment rule-making and it will be left to the implementation and the follow-up to show whether the focus is on setting a stepping stone for investment negotiations, or carefully circling around any kind of international investment rules.

As previously flagged, it may also be interesting to take a quick glance at what has made it into the G20 Guiding Principles and what has not. Four main issues do not feature prominently, as a result of a consensus approach, in the G20 Guiding Principles: a role for international rule-making, a clear focus on substantive investment rules, a balanced approach to investors' rights and obligations, and a strong and central reference to sustainable development as a Guiding Principle.

One could argue, however, that some of the elements are inherently contained within the principles. First, that liberalization, protection, regulation, and promotion are all covered here, and hence the role in international rule-making is more aspirational in nature. Second, the principles are supposed to aim at a higher level of consensus, and again by nature are not treaty provisions or the result of negotiations. Third, that investor's rights and obligations are covered strongly in principle 8 about responsible business conduct. And fourth, that the sustainable development dimension is emphasized in three critical places: the preamble, the last paragraph making it a common thread, and the overarching objective to be consistent with the objectives of sustainable development and inclusive growth. These arguments are again a witness to the constructive ambiguity under which the principles were built.

From the point of view of their scope of application, the G20 Guiding Principles offer answers and guidance, but also raise many questions. It could be argued that in this respect they miss their goal to set clear guiding principles for international rule-making. They remain too general and too vague, clearly on purpose. But they could also be seen as a crucial and very concrete first step in order to achieve further guidelines. Thus, they may be seen as a clever and non-contentious introductory stride that begins with common denominators that are less susceptible to disagreement and will build and flesh out where appropriate the commonly agreed principles.

In view of the large differences among investment policy-making processes around the globe, one should recognize the ground-breaking nature of the achievement in just agreeing a set of principles, no less because of the difference of views of the players within the G20 itself. Taking a more critical stance, as indicated at the outset, it is dangerous when discussing domestic or international rule-making on investment to use the term 'principle', as the reference to principles of international law comes immediately to mind. But it is obvious from the exercise that the TIWG members have sought to avoid any such reference in the Guiding Principles themselves and that the reference to investment policy-making is more about the process itself than about the substantive content and outcome.

Furthermore, a word of caution is needed in relation to transparency as a principle for policy-making. Transparency is a concept that comes up four times in the Guiding Principles and should be handled with care in the context of domestic and international rule-making, also because of contentious national security issues globally, but especially in key countries such as the United States which feature strong screening mechanisms on the matter.

In the realm of international investment rules, transparency is a means to an end and should not be seen as an end in itself that could be achieved once and for all and that should follow one model. While it is clear that transparency is an enabling characteristic for investment policies, to ensure that investors have a clear understanding of the rules and conditions that will apply to entry and operation of their investments in the host country, transparency in the domestic rule-setting and in the international investment negotiations process is another issue altogether. The fact that lack of transparency is one of the main grievances of civil society about investment arbitration, but also about international negotiations on investment, is telling of the need to deal carefully with legitimate aspirations to greater transparency in the policy-making process.[29] These comments do of course not apply to a greater level of transparency in investment dispute settlement where the Mauritius Convention on Transparency sets a standard.

The approach taken by the G20 Guiding Principles is also to carefully avoid any legal terminology and references to international law principles on investment protection or obligations relating to investment liberalization. None of the core investment treatment and protection standards and obligations are mentioned in the Guiding Principles, whether national treatment, most favoured nation treatment, fair and equitable treatment, protection against unlawful expropriation, and protection of free transfer of funds. The settlement of investment disputes is mentioned as a mechanism and, in so far as it is a contentious issue in international negotiations on investment, there is no position as to whether it should take one form or another. New features such as an international investment court, just sanctioned by CETA, were evidently off the table too. Only the overall objective of fairness, transparency and no abuse of the process are referred to.

This is where the Guiding Principles may be seen by some as a missed opportunity. A separate study prepared by Rodrigo Polanco from the World Trade Institute[30] on

---

[29] See Julien Chaisse and Rahul Donde, 'The State of Investor-State Arbitration: A Reality Check of the Issues, Trends, and Directions in Asia-Pacific' (2018) 51(1) The International Lawyer 47.

[30] Rodrigo Polanco, 'G20's International Investment Agreements and its Relationship with the Guiding Principles for Global Investment Policymaking' *E15 Initiative* (2017) http://e15initiative. org.

this subject shows that there is more convergence between a state's international investment agreements commitments than apparent, especially after China's shift to pre-establishment commitments based on a negative list.

Preliminary conclusions of Polanco's work are included below, outlining areas of convergence between G20 countries' international investment agreements already in force. Polanco studied common features between the Guiding Principles and traditional investment treaty practice of G20 countries, and he characterizes the common threads of their agreements, arguing that an average G20 country's international investment agreement would include the following features:[31]

Scope of application: Investment would be defined as every kind of asset, including a non-exhaustive list of covered assets, and would not require certain characteristics of the investment. Investors would be defined as natural persons who are nationals or citizens of the contracting party and judicial entities with their place of incorporation in the contracting party.[32]

Promotion and admission: The admission clause would merely require a non-binding establishment in accordance with contracting parties' domestic laws and regulations.[33]

Standards of treatment: The national treatment standard would cover only investments in the post-establishment phase and would be broadly defined without reference to 'in like circumstances'. The most favoured nation treatment standard would only stretch to investments in the post-establishment phase and would be limited to investments and investors 'in like circumstances' and certain sectors. Moreover, the investor–state dispute settlement mechanism (ISDS) would not be excluded from the scope of the most favoured nation treatment. An unqualified fair and equitable treatment standard would be included without reference to customary international law. The full protection and security standard would also be included without any further qualifications.[34]

Standards of protection: The free transfer of funds would be guaranteed without any further exceptions for financial difficulties and/or protection of creditors. A prompt, adequate, and effective compensation for expropriation would be provided (Hull formula), including compensation for indirect expropriation without any exceptions such as measures adopted for a public policy objective or compulsory licences under TRIPs. Depicting an evolution in BIT negotiations in G20 countries, an umbrella clause would not be included in the treaty. But there also would be no clause that prohibits performance requirements.[35]

Investor–state dispute settlement: The treaty would provide for ISDS without any exemptions for certain disputes or investors and inter-state dispute settlement mechanisms.[36]

With respect to the application of the Guiding Principles for global policy-making, the study concludes that there are clear differences between principles that correspond to a more traditional content of investment treaties (Principle 1: Performance requirements; Principle 2: NT, MFN, and transparency; and Principle 3: Prevention of disputes, 'enhanced' ISDS), which are largely followed, in comparison to more novel principles (Principle 4: Transparency; Principle 5: Sustainable development; Principle 6: Right to regulate; Principle 7: Investment promotion; Principle 8: Corporate social responsibility; and Principle 9: Technical cooperation/capacity building), that are largely pending of complete implementation, with important differences across G20 countries.

---

[31] ibid.   [32] ibid.   [33] ibid.   [34] ibid.   [35] ibid.   [36] ibid.

Foreign Direct Investment is a key component of the G20's ambition to raise global growth by at least 2 per cent above trajectory, over the next five years. With that goal, these non-binding principles are a very successful deliverable for the investment section of this year's G20 TIWG. These principles aim to foster an open, transparent, and conducive global policy for investment, providing coherence and broader predictability for businesses globally.

Highlighting investment as a key component to global value chains (GVCs), the general ideas established on the investment principles should be advanced globally and regionally to governments and policy-makers in order to achieve further coherence in newer treaties and regulations. The GVC component also highlights the link to trade, which has regained international momentum with G20 and B20, to name but a few, addressing these links as a central issue. As a matter of fact, the conversations at the new TIWG extended well beyond an investment-only focus.

On this specific issue, one of the other deliverables of the TIWG was a joint report between the WTO, OECD, UNCTAD, and the World Bank on the inter-relationship between trade and investment, and links beyond. The report identifies issues and areas where further analysis is needed on the interactions of both trade and investment measures and their regimes. A good query here is how this report and this—not new—issue should be taken forward at the G20 and beyond.

The institutionalization of the TIWG in itself is another major deliverable for China's G20 presidency. It creates a safe space for G20 trade and investment officials for discussing both topics together, having already started discussions on promotion and facilitation; the latter being taken forward vigorously by the G20 German presidency. There is a consensus also on continuing work on policy coherence, in particular between trade and investment policies. In this particular instance, UNCTAD coordinated the backstopping of the investment work of the TIWG and the Interagency Working Group (consisting of OECD, UNCTAD, World Bank, and WTO). It should be acknowledged that domestic reform is also of the essence, if international trade and investment reform is to have an impact.

Some of these topics were highlighted by the G20 Trade (and Investment) Ministers Statement, as they create a benchmark for future work on investment, and trade and investment matters, and to battle the increasing anti-trade rhetoric. Furthermore, the 2016 G20 TIWG ministerial communiqué highlights links with sustainable development, in which trade and investment ministers:[37]

Agreed to provide political leadership by acting with determination to promote inclusive, robust and sustainable trade and investment growth.

Resolved to step up efforts to better communicate the benefits of trade and investment openness and cooperation to a wider public.

Committed to lead by example in harnessing trade and investment policy coherence to contribute to global prosperity and sustainable development.

Valued discussion on investment promotion and facilitation, and endorsed the G20 Guiding Principles for Global Investment Policy-Making.

Called to work on investment promotion and facilitation and 'encouraged UNCTAD, the World Bank, the OECD and the WTO to advance this work within their respective mandates and work programmes, which could be useful for future consideration by the G20' (para 18).

---

[37] G20 Trade Ministers Meeting Statement (n 2).

Committed to ensuring that trade, Investment and other public policies, at both national and global levels, remain coherent, complementary, and mutually reinforcing.

The trade ministers also took note of the B20 recommendation for the WTO working group on the relationship between trade and investment to resume its work. Incorporating B20 recommendations is also a suggested angle, as the extensive work of the B20 task forces should have a more relevant say on policy issues. Further avenues for the B20 to input into the G20 would be much welcomed in future processes. Some of these principles were also recognized by leaders on the G20 Summit's communiqué, especially on avoiding protectionism and on investment promotion and facilitation, creating avenues for follow-up into the outputs of the G20 in the future.

It is important to stress that the mere fact of agreeing on a basic set of Guiding Principles itself constitutes a great achievement. It is now for policy-makers to decide if they will serve as a foundation to be taken further, or remain as a one-off. Either way, they are valuable in reflecting consensus in otherwise entrenched negotiations at the bilateral, regional, and multi-lateral levels. The principles could, for example, cross-fertilize with other regional policy discussions, such as APEC's work on investment and its non-binding investment principles.

It is important to read these Guiding Principles in the broader context of discontent and backlash against traditional investment treaty-making, where it is argued that investment treaties focus only on obligations for the state and rights for investors, and where the state's right to regulate for public purpose can be challenged without appropriate safeguards. This leads to the broader agenda of the reform of international investment policies. It remains to be seen whether the G20 Guiding Principle constitute a step towards new investment treaty-making or whether they remain more general and aspirational.

The key features of new essentials of investment policy instruments—such as the overarching achievement of sustainable development and inclusive growth, responsible business conduct on the part of investors and a retitling of the balance between the obligations taken by the state and the state's inherent right and duty to regulate for public purpose—are central in the Guiding Principles. The fact that they remain general, do not go into legal concepts and formulations to preserve consensus is illustrative of the current tension in investment treaty negotiations between different approaches to investment promotion and facilitation, investment protection and investment liberalization. A careful scrutiny of the way they will evolve and be reflected in operational investment policies will provide the test for their role as a building block in investment policy-making.

It will be particularly interesting to watch how they will be dealt with by the business community. There are clear signs for an appetite towards new approaches and new rules for investment, which reflect a changing economic landscape and a redistribution of roles. It may well be that it is the business community that can take these Guiding Principles one step further, following in the footsteps of the WTO Trade Facilitation Agreement, which is strongly supported by business. The trade and investment agenda of the International Chamber of Commerce, including the WTO Business Dialogues, and discussions at the World Economic Forum Annual Meeting in Davos, will provide a snapshot of business interest on the matter of further aligning investment policies, especially as the 2016 G20 Investment Guiding Principles are a good and commendable start, but they need to be taken forward in order to have further global policy-making impact.

18

Beware of Chinese Bearing Gifts

Why China's Direct Investment Poses Political Challenges in Europe and the United States

*Sophie Meunier**

From a non-existent player fifteen years ago, China has now become one of the largest senders of foreign direct investment (FDI) flows in the world. By and large, this new provenance of capital has been welcomed by host countries, especially given the drop in other sources of FDI in the wake of the American financial crisis in the late 2000s. This new investment has created jobs locally, has enabled it to keep some troubled firms afloat, and it has often opened up the Chinese market for local companies. FDI is indeed the backbone of economic globalization and a crucial source of transmission of capital, technology, and people across borders.

The exponential growth of Chinese direct investment, however, has also been accompanied in some cases by controversy and even resistance, both in developing and in developed economies. Around the world, critics have expressed fears and denounced some of the potential dangers of this investment, such as lowering of local labour standards, hollowing out of industrial core through repatriation of assets, and acquisition of dual use technology. Alarmist media headlines have warned against a Chinese takeover of national economies one controversial investment deal at a time. The ensuing political backlash has often received considerable media attention and increased scrutiny over subsequent deals.

What explains the political challenges posed by the recent explosion of Chinese direct investment in the United States (US) and the European Union (EU)? How and why have attitudes and policies in the West changed over the past decade towards Chinese FDI? This chapter considers two alternative explanations for the political challenges triggered by Chinese investment in Western countries. The first is that Chinese FDI causes political unease because of its novelty. The second is the perception that there is something inherently different about the nature of Chinese FDI and therefore it should not be treated politically like any other foreign investment. These two explanations lead to a different set of predictions for the future of Chinese FDI in Europe and the US.

The first section analyses how the novelty of Chinese FDI may pose political challenges to Western politicians and publics and compares the current phenomenon with past instances of politically problematic sources of FDI. Section II examines the argument that there is something inherently different about Chinese FDI, notably as

* Senior Research Scholar, Woodrow Wilson School of Public and International Affairs, Co-Director European Union Program at Princeton (EUPP), Princeton University.

Acknowledgements: Many thanks to Julien Chaisse and the participants to the Asia FDI Forum II at the Chinese University of Hong Kong Graduate Law Center, 29–30 November 2016.

stemming from an emerging economy, a unique political system, and a non-ally in the security dimension. The third section explores the domestic political context in which these challenges are raised: in Europe, the euro crisis and the rise of populism; in the US, the focus on geopolitical competition and the rise of economic nationalism. The conclusion raises some implications of these political challenges on the future of Chinese outward investment.

I. The Novelty of Chinese FDI as Political Challenge

From CNOOC's lease of the Greek port of Piraeus and Geely's acquisition of Swedish carmaker Volvo to Dalian Wanda's purchase of AMC Cinemas, Fosun's takeover of hotel chain ClubMed and Suning's investment in the InterMilan soccer club, foreign investment emanating from China has captured the attention of the European and American media. One explanation for this heightened public attention on instances of Chinese direct investment comes from its novelty. This section explores the novel phenomenon of Chinese direct investment in Europe and the US, compares it with past instances of politically controversial sources of foreign investment, and analyses the existence of a political threshold for FDI.

A. Chinese direct investment, a novel phenomenon

Chinese investment in Europe and the US barely existed a mere decade ago. This novelty has proven by itself a source of anxiety; initially people did not know what to make of this new phenomenon and expressed worries. This perception of a new source of investment as something to be feared is consistent with a long-held finding in the management literature on FDI about the 'liability of foreignness'[1] and the 'costs of doing business abroad'.[2] New and foreign is challenging, at least temporarily, especially if the institutional and cultural distance between host and home country is large.

It is not only the novelty but also the rapidity of the expansion that proved a cause of alarm. Indeed, Chinese investment in Western economies has risen almost exponentially over the past decade: from virtually non-existent in 2005, China is now one of the top three home countries for FDI in the world in flows. In the United States, the stock of Chinese investment grew from almost zero in 2005 to close to US$150 billion by the end of 2016.[3] In the European Union, the stock of Chinese investment had reached €50 billion by late 2015. Even more so than stock, flows contributed to shaping the impression of momentum, and therefore danger. Over half of all Chinese FDI flows in Europe and the US since 2000 have taken place in the past three years.[4] Chinese FDI rose 50 per cent between 2015 and 2016 and has doubled since 2012.[5] In the US, Chinese FDI flows surpassed US$50 billion in 2016. They tripled between

---

[1] Srilata Zaheer, 'Overcoming the Liability of Foreignness' (1995) 38 Academy of Management Journal 341, doi:10.2307/256683; Lorraine Eden and Stewart R Miller, 'Distance Matters: Liability of Foreignness, Institutional Distance and Ownership Strategy' in *Theories of the Multinational Enterprise: Diversity, Complexity and Relevance, Advances in International Management* (Emerald Group Publishing Limited 2004) 187–221, doi:10.1016/S0747-7929(04)16010-1.

[2] Steven Hymer, *The International Operations of National Firms* (Lexington Books 1976).

[3] Derek Scissors, 'Record Chinese Outward Investment in 2016: Don't Overreact' *AEI* (2017) www.aei.org/publication/record-chinese-outward-investment-in-2016-dont-overreact/.

[4] Baker McKenzie, 'Chinese Investment Tripled in US in 2016, Doubled in Europe' (2017) www.bakermckenzie.com/en/newsroom/2017/02/chinafdi.

[5] Scissors (n 3).

2015 and 2016.[6] In the EU, FDI from China rose 90 per cent in the past year.[7] In Germany, FDI deals from China were multi-plied by ten from US$1.3 billion in 2015 to US$12.1 billion in 2016.[8]

Moreover, it is not only the novelty but also the ubiquity of the expansion that fuels worries. China is investing everywhere in the world: Europe and the US are the latest destinations in a long list that started with resource-rich African countries and now includes the majority of countries in the world, from Australia to Canada by way of Central Asia. Chinese investment is also ubiquitous in every economic sector, including information technology, infrastructure, food products, tourism, industrial machinery, financial services, entertainment, and real estate.[9]

An additional source of worries has been the coupling of the novelty of Chinese direct investment with its rapidly expanding relative weight compared to other sources of FDI. Chinese investment was rising everywhere in absolute terms but it was also rising in relative terms. Indeed, the take-off of Chinese direct investment in Europe and the US coincided with the sharp decline of FDI worldwide until 2012 in the wake of the US financial crisis, especially in the EU. This relative growth has amplified the new phenomenon of Chinese investment to the public and made it seem scarier.

Finally, the nature of the investment deals initially made by Chinese companies increased the public spotlight. In general, greenfield investment is seen as more in-nocuous and less politically problematic than mergers and acquisitions. Yet the vast majority of Chinese investment in Europe and the US, at least in the early years, were takeovers. In 2016, acquisitions drove 97 per cent of the value of FDI activity in Europe and the US.[10] These are more likely to touch off opposition, no matter what the origin of the investment is.

B. Past instances of political challenges posed by novel sources of FDI

Chinese FDI startled the media and politicians at the beginning because it was a new phenomenon. It is not the first time, however, that foreign investment poses political challenges in the host country. This section explores briefly two prior instances of pol-itical controversy raised by foreign investment in Europe and the United States.

In Europe, one precedent is the 'coca-colonization' by American multi-nationals that occurred from the 1960s onwards. Massive investment by US companies cre-ated existential frictions in countries where the imported production processes and type of goods produced seemed to threaten the traditional way-of-life.[11] Nowhere was this fear more pronounced than in France, which resisted loudly this 'American chal-lenge', as coined in a 1968 bestselling book.[12] A later mobilization occurred with a new wave of American investment in France in the 1990s, which included the creation of the Disneyland Paris amusement park and a push by American fast food companies into France.[13] This second wave of hostility towards American FDI culminated with the opposition to the Multilateral Agreement on Investment (MAI) negotiated under the auspices of the OECD, which ultimately failed in 1998 after France withdrew its

---

[6] Baker McKenzie (n 4).   [7] ibid.   [8] ibid.   [9] ibid.   [10] ibid.

[11] Richard F Kuisel, *Seducing the French: The Dilemma of Americanization* (University of California Press 1997).

[12] Jean-Jacques Servan-Schreiber, *The American Challenge* (Avon Books 1968).

[13] Richard F Kuisel, *The French Way: How France Embraced and Rejected American Values and Power* (Princeton University Press 2011).

support.[14] Since then, opposition to American Investment has become mostly muted, even though the United States is still one of the top sources of inward FDI flows and stocks in France.

Another instance of political controversy raised by foreign investment in the host country happened in the late 1980s, which saw an explosion of Japanese FDI into the United States. American media and politicians became obsessed with the 'Japanese invasion' when acquisitions and greenfield investments from Japan experienced a rapid influx from less than US$1 billion of annual inflows in 1980 to US$18 billion by 1990.[15] A collective sense of panic swept the country as Japanese investors went for high-profile deals, such as the 1989 acquisition of New York City's Rockefeller Center by the Mitsubishi Group and of Columbia Pictures by Sony, fueling perceptions that Japan was taking over the US.

The fears raised by this Japanese investment 'invasion' prompted policy change to restrict the openness of the US to foreign investment. The proposed takeover in 1988 of the semiconductor firm Fairchild by the Japanese Fujitsu Ltd provoked intense backlash. This particular deal prompted Congressional action, which resulted in 1988 in the Exon-Florio amendment (50 USC App § 2170) authorizing the president to 'investigate foreign acquisitions, mergers, and takeovers of, or investments in, US companies from a national security perspective'. President Reagan in turn delegated this authority to CFIUS. Further restrictions were added by the Byrd Amendment of 1992 (Section 837(a) of P.L. 102-484), which required CFIUS to investigate proposed foreign investments when the acquirer is acting on behalf of a foreign government, and by the 2007 Foreign Investment and Security Act (FINSA) (P.L. 110-49), which expanded CFIUS' mandate to include a broader range of national security risks.

C. A FDI novelty curve?

Both historical examples suggest that foreign investments that provoked passionate opposition in the past have continued on without notice once they became normalized in the host country. In both cases, the more investment took place, the more the fears went away and the nationality of the investor became a non-issue. Novelty eventually wears off.

The controversies provoked by Japanese investment in the US in the 1980s provide probably the closest historical precedent to the current situation with Chinese investment. The context was eerily similar, marked by trade deficit, currency disputes, arguments over state subsidies and, above all, the rapid rise in relative power of an Asian country in an age presented as that of American decline.

This historical example may suggest the existence of a 'FDI novelty curve': the initial investments were met with no particular reaction at first. As more investments started pouring in, media and politicians started to put the spotlight on this new phenomenon and the fears snowballed into new legislation. Once a certain threshold of Japanese investments that continued to contribute positively to the American economy was met, interest in the issue plummeted. This was due to several reasons.

First, the economic effects of Japanese investment on the American domestic economy seemed overall positive. It contributed directly to the preservation and the creation of jobs, especially high-wage jobs, and R&D spill-overs flowed into the local

[14] Stephen J Kobrin, 'The MAI and the Clash of Globalizations' *Foreign Policy* (1998) 97–109.
[15] Curtis Milhaupt, 'Is the U.S. Ready for FDI from China? Lessons from Japan's Experience in the 1980s' in Karl Sauvant, *Investing in the U.S.* (Edward Elgar Publishing 2008).

economy. Secondly, the liability of foreignness seems to disappear with time. American people grew more familiar with what appeared so foreign at the outset, namely, Japanese owners and managers. Thirdly, the fears raised by critics of Japanese investment plainly failed to materialize. As a result, today Japan is the second largest source of FDI in the United States.

These two examples of American investment in France and Japanese investment in the US suggest, as historical precedents, that the growing familiarity with Chinese companies and potential of Chinese FDI to become a source of economic vitality in the host country will, over time, replace the initial worries raised by the new phenomenon. If novelty is indeed the explanation for the political challenges currently raised by FDI from China in Europe and the US, then these political concerns should decline as Chinese investment projects accumulate and become normalized in a few years.

II. The Distinctiveness of Chinese FDI as Political Challenge

By contrast, a second explanation for the political anxiety triggered by Chinese direct investment in Europe and the US is based on the argument that there is something inherently different and unique about Chinese FDI. It is not a matter of novelty but one of the intrinsic characteristics of FDI from China. This section explores how the case could be made for uniqueness on at least three counts –emerging economy, unique political system, and security non-ally.

A. An emerging economy

In spite of its spectacular growth over the past few decades, China is still, by all measures, an emerging economy. This characteristic poses its own set of political challenges when the United States and European countries host FDI from China.

First, the influx of direct investment from a developing to a developed economy, which has no historical precedent, shakes the traditional political dynamics of FDI and poses something of an existential problem for the host countries. They are more accustomed to investing in emerging, problematic economies than to being treated like one of them.[16] Historically, direct investment has flowed almost exclusively from developed to developing economies. Capital was a source and symbol of power. FDI was criticized in the host countries for being an instrument of neo-imperialist dependency.[17] Chinese investment into Europe and the US can be interpreted as an external sign that the tables have turned and as a precursor of what might be yet to come –a gradual slide of Western power relative to the rising power of China. As such a symbol, it is expected that some politicians and population in the host countries will put up a fight and resist what they see as evidence that the tables are turning.

Secondly, the usual benefits for the host economy that accompany inward foreign investment may not happen in a case where the investor is from a less advanced

[16] Sophie Meunier and others, 'The Politics of Hosting Chinese Investment in Europe' (2014) 12 Asia Europe Journal 109.
[17] Immanuel Wallerstein, 'The Rise and Future Demise of the World Capitalist System: Concepts for Comparative Analysis' (1974) 16 Comparative Studies in Society and History 387; Robert Gilpin and Jean Gilpin, *The Political Economy of International Relations* Princeton University Press 1987); Dani Rodrik, *Has Globalization Gone Too Far?* (Institute for International Economics 1997).

50 *Sophie Meunier*

economy that the target of the investment. FDI always has costs and benefits for the host country, but typically the benefits outweigh the costs, notably through technological and know-how spill-over. FDI fuels technological progress, a major driver of economic growth, because foreign firms usually bring with them superior management strategies and technologies developed in their home countries, as was the case of Japanese automobile producers in the US or American computer companies in Europe. These spill over into the local economy as workers and R&D move from the foreign-owned to national firms.

In the case of Chinese investment, however, some fear that the net positive economic impact may not happen because the technological and know-how flows do not appear to be going in the 'traditional' direction, from the home to the host country. With the exception of a few sectors, such as telecom equipment and port management, Chinese investors seem to be looking to invest precisely in Western firms whose main assets are their superior technology and know-how, from robot makers in the German Mittelstand to Hollywood production and distribution companies. An Italian analyst has called this the 'reverse Marco Polo effect':[18] this time it is the Chinese who are going to Europe to acquire technological innovation. This phenomenon is not limited to high-technology fields. It is also at play, for instance, in European football, where the fast-paced acquisition of foreign companies and players is seen as a fact-finding exercise in order to jumpstart Chinese soccer know-how and turn China into a 'soccer powerhouse', in the words of President Xi Jinping.[19]

Thirdly, the differentials in technology and wages between the emerging economy investor and the developed economy host country may potentially lead to asset-stripping. In that case, the Chinese investor could repatriate to China the assets of the company it took over and virtually close up shop in the host country—some critics even talk of a 'siphoning off'. The advantages for the investor are clear, such as legal acquisition of technology and know-how, as well as international cachet and reputation of brands which would manufacture everything in China. For the host country, in the short term such a scenario would bring only the costs of FDI, not the benefits, notably because the foreign investment would accelerate the loss of local employment. In the long term, the consequences could be even more damaging as the host country would see an erosion of its competitive lead.

B. A unique political system

A second feature making Chinese investment different from historical precedent is the uniqueness of China's political system and of 'capitalism with Chinese characteristics', which potentially pose several political problems for the host country. The most important problematic feature is undoubtedly the central role of the Chinese state in the economy. American and European democracies have little experience in what it means to have a foreign state manage (or not) companies' investment decisions, thereby fuelling several political concerns about the potential negative implications of the role of the Chinese state for host countries.

---

[18] Rebecca Valli, 'Italian Entrepreneurs Turn to Chinese for Help' *VOA* (2012) www.voanews.com/a/italian-entrepreneurs-turn-to-chinese-for-help/1507976.html.
[19] Owen Gibson, 'The Great Windfall of China: A Football Revolution That May Lead to World Cup' *The Guardian* (2016) www.theguardian.com/football/blog/2016/feb/06/china-football-revolution-world-cup.

For one, the injunction to Chinese firms to 'go out' has been the official policy of the Chinese government in successive five-year plans since 2000 for a variety of reasons, including the need to diversify the placement of foreign reserves, acquire resources and technologies, ease its access to foreign consumer markets, and further its international ambitions. For over a decade, Chinese firms and their managers received a series of carrots and sticks to internationalize their operations, such as financial incentives and individual career advancement. This 'going out' policy has been reinforced with the launch of the One Belt, One Road (OBOR) initiative in 2013, now known as Belt and Road Initiative (BRI), aiming to connect the Chinese economy with countries along the ancient silk and maritime roads, crossing Central Asia all the way to Western Europe.[20] Therefore, it is rational for host countries to interpret Chinese FDI as being directed centrally by China's government.

Moreover, the nature of the relations between Chinese investors and the Chinese government is often confusing. A majority of Chinese direct investment abroad is conducted by state-owned enterprises (SOEs)—although the proportion is smaller in Europe and especially in the US than in the rest of the world. Even in the case of transactions conducted by private investors, doubt persists as to the actual influence of the Chinese government and Communist Party. This has been an issue, for instance, with efforts to invest in the US by Huawei, a private company, whose owner is rumoured to entertain very close links with the Chinese government. Moreover, the lack of transparency of the governance structure of Chinese firms, whether state-owned or private, makes the investment transaction difficult to comprehend for the target company or the host country. In some cases, the deal by a Chinese company seems to have been spearheaded by someone who was either mysterious or not the actual person in charge—a public example of this happened in the case of the acquisition of a stake in the Toulouse-Blagnac airport in France by a Chinese investment consortium headed by Mike Poon, who later mysteriously disappeared temporarily (but has resurfaced since).

The opaque involvement of the Chinese government in the decisions of its companies to invest abroad also leaves some lingering doubt as to the ultimate rationale for the investment. Is it purely a commercial decision responding to market incentives or is there an ulterior motive to the deal? American and European politicians do suspect in some cases that these companies are acting to fulfil strategic goals, rather than market-developing and profit-maximizing goals.

The Chinese political economy model of state-led capitalism also leads Chinese companies to assume a different attitude towards risk than do market-driven capitalist companies. The Chinese state conducts explicit industrial policy whereby national champions are identified and backed with abundant subsidies and administrative help. They have access to cheap credit. This enables these companies to take more risks and be less concerned about immediate return and bottom-line. They can plan for the long instead of the short term and, therefore, offer bids which are higher than those of their privately-owned competitors.

Finally, the political economy of Chinese investment leads to fears that the government can manipulate the transaction by using its special leverage. This fear was illustrated by the case of Aixtron, a German technology company specializing in semiconductors. In 2015, Sanan Optoelectronics, a Chinese customer of Aixtron, cancelled a large order at the last minute, which provoked a crash of the price of Aixtron's shares. A few months later, the Chinese investment fund Fujian Grand Chip made a deal to

[20] See generally Julien Chaisse and Mitsuo Matsushita, 'China's "Belt and Road" Initiative: Mapping the World Trade Normative and Strategic Implications' (2018) 52(1) Journal of World Trade 163.

acquire Aixtron. According to the press, Sanan and Fujian had many connections, including a common investor, and were both linked to the Chinese government.[21]

C. Not a security ally

A third feature pleading for the distinctiveness of the political challenges posed by Chinese FDI comes from strategic security considerations. The United States and European countries are not used to receiving investment from countries which are not their security allies. The Soviet Union did not invest in the West during the Cold War. To be sure, China is not an enemy but rather a superpower with avowed geopolitical ambitions and foreign policy goals often at odds with those of the US and some European countries. This raises several causes for concern about the ultimate motive of investment, including issues of dual-use technology and strategic leverage.

One concern relates to the efforts by Chinese investors to acquire technology abroad, which is problematic from a security standpoint for at least two reasons. First, even though China itself is not a security enemy, it is on friendly terms with some countries considered pariahs or rogue states in the West, such as North Korea. Some of the technology acquired through Chinese FDI in Europe and the US could make its way into the hands of their leaders, with possible security implications.

Secondly, some Chinese investments that may seem innocuous at first glance may indeed have security implications. This could be, for instance, because of their strategic location, such as CASIL's investment in the Toulouse-Blagnac airport in France in 2015, which went through despite its location adjacent to the Airbus factory, and the Chinese-owned Ralls Corporation's investment in a wind farm in Oregon in 2012, which was blocked by presidential order because of its location overlooking a US military base. It could also be because of the dangers of dual-use technology, with technology peacefully employed in everyday consumer products having the potential to be adapted for military use. Two recent examples of concerns about this potential can be found in the 2016 attempts by the Chinese group Go Scale Capital to acquire Lumileds, a subsidiary of the Dutch company Philips making lighting components, and by the Chinese company Fujian Grand Chip to acquire Aixtron, a German company manufacturing silicon chip equipment, both of which were blocked by a review in the Committee on Foreign Investment in the United States (CFIUS) because of their potential implications for American national security.

Another security concern relates to the risks of political leverage and control arising from foreign ownership and, therefore, dependence. One potential risk is physical leverage. For instance, the Chinese owner could strip the assets of the company acquired in the host country, for instance machinery or intellectual property, provoking lay-offs in the short term and removing competitive advantages in the longer run. Countries worry particularly about specific physical risks (e.g. sabotage, espionage, control) associated with foreign ownership of sensitive critical infrastructure, such as nuclear power plants. This was the crux of the decision by British Prime Minister Theresa May to reexamine and delay final approval of the Hinkley Point deal in 2016, on the grounds that China could build weaknesses on purpose into some of the nuclear safety systems or could shut down British electricity production at will, thereby unleashing chaos in the country.

---

[21] Paul Mozur and Jack Ewing, 'Rush of Chinese Investment in Europe's High-Tech Firms Is Raising Eyebrows' *The New York Times* (2016) www.nytimes.com/2016/09/17/business/dealbook/china-germany-takeover-merger-technology.html.

Another potential risk, more subtle, is political leverage. China could potentially use its ownership of foreign assets to pressure and even coerce host governments into falling in line on the political issues that the Chinese government cares deeply about, such as the One-China Policy, the question of Tibet, and the issue of human rights.[22] The higher the dependence of a foreign country on Chinese investment, the larger we could expect the implicit or explicit leverage of China on controlling that host country's public policy towards meeting with the Dalai Lama or denouncing Taiwan, for instance.

Divergences between European countries and the United States exist on all three main perceptions of the unique dangers posed by Chinese investment—emerging economy, unique political system, and security non-ally. These divergences are particularly pronounced with respect to national security issues, which are the main lens through which the US has, up until now, been interpreting Chinese investment, whereas European countries have focused more on issues such as economic dependence and political leverage.

If the uniqueness of Chinese FDI, and not its novelty, is indeed the explanation for the political challenges encountered in Western democracies, then we should see political issues raised more in host countries as Chinese investment projects accumulate. This would manifest itself as increasingly negative articles in the media, changes towards more restrictive regulation and vetting of foreign investment, and an impact on negotiations of investment agreements.

III. The Domestic Political Context for Hosting Chinese FDI in Europe and the US

Whether the 'novelty' or the 'uniqueness' interpretation of the potential dangers posed by Chinese investment predominates depends in large part on the domestic political context in the host country. This section explores in turn the consequences for Chinese FDI of the evolving domestic political context in Europe and the United States.

A. Europe: the euro crisis versus the rise of national populism

Two related features of European politics in recent years frame two different responses to Chinese investment: on one hand, the euro crisis has made Chinese investment more valuable and has fostered a public rhetoric presenting Chinese acquisitions as salvation; on the other hand, a growing national populism in European countries is turning increasingly negative towards globalization and towards 'others', including foreign investment.

The surge of Chinese investment in Europe coincided with the outbreak of the euro crisis for several reasons.[23] For one, Chinese FDI started to arrive in Europe in the late 2000s as a result of official Chinese government injunctions to 'go out'—European countries, as well as the United States, were last on the list of the destinations for Chinese investors because there were more political and regulatory hurdles and the type of investment targets in these host countries were more complicated to manage

---

[22] Sophie Meunier, 'A Faustian Bargain or Just a Good Bargain? Chinese Foreign Direct Investment and Politics in Europe' (2014) 12 Asia Europe Journal 143 doi:10.1007/s10308-014-0382-x.

[23] Sophie Meunier, ' "Beggars Can't Be Choosers": The European Crisis and Chinese Direct Investment in the European Union' (2014) 36 Journal of European Integration 283.

than the resource-seeking investments made by Chinese companies in Africa, for instance. The simultaneity of this surge of investment and the euro crisis was therefore partly coincidental—the timing set forth by the Chinese government happened to coincide with the crisis.

Chinese investment also surged in Europe precisely as a result of the euro crisis, which created opportunities for bargain deals. On one hand, the supply of European companies for sale increased because of bankruptcies and the bursting of property bubbles. With so many countries burdened by debt, many European public assets were also put up for sale as part of privatization programmes. On the other hand, the demand for these assets dried up in Europe, where fewer local buyers were able to invest because of the crisis.

China was well placed to take advantage of these bargains, first because it possessed a gigantic accumulation of foreign exchange reserves. Also, the American financial crisis had convinced Chinese leaders of the need to diversify, both away from the US and away from sovereign debt. The SOE ownership of many Chinese investors enabled them to take higher risks, with the potential for higher returns.

As a result, Chinese investment was able to surge in Europe, both in the public and private sectors. For instance, in Portugal, Chinese investors acquired 45 per cent of the total assets put up for privatization under the Economic Adjustment Program and the IMF in sectors such as electrical infrastructure and financial services.[24] In Italy, Chinese companies invested in the power grid, deals that were made possible by a privatization programme by former Prime Minister Matteo Renzi in order to reduce Italy's national debt. In Greece, Chinese investors could take advantage of the many opportunities offered by the privatization programme designed to meet the bailout conditions, including COSCO's investment in the port of Piraeus in Athens.[25] In Germany, Chinese investors could acquire small and medium sized family companies that had been hurt by the global financial crisis, such as the Sany Group's acquisition of concrete pump-maker Putzmeister, whose revenue and staff had been cut by half since 2008 by the time of its takeover in 2012.[26]

It should be noted, however, that many Chinese acquisitions in the wake of the euro crisis were not economic bargains per se. In several cases, these acquisitions were the result of public battles where Chinese investors outbid other interested parties by paying a hefty premium—such as was the case with Fosun's acquisition of French resort chain ClubMed which happened in 2015 after an expensive, protracted two year takeover battle. Neither did Chinese investors jump at the opportunity to acquire all the European assets at bargain prices, many of which are still for sale at the time of writing.

The main political consequence of the euro crisis on Chinese FDI into Europe was to lessen political resistance and frame its public perception as a 'saviour' and 'white knight'. The crisis has transformed the time horizon of European politics: short-term concerns, above all employment, take precedence over long-term concerns, such as national security. If some European countries, such as France, had displayed an initial

[24] Anne-Claude Martin, 'Chinese Investments Soar in Crisis-Hit Europe' *EurActiv.com* (2014) www.euractiv.com/section/euro-finance/news/chinese-investments-soar-in-crisis-hit-europe/.
[25] Sophie Meunier, 'A Tale of Two Ports: The Epic Story of Chinese Direct Investment in the Greek Port of Piraeus | CritCom' *CritCom* (2015) http://councilforeuropeanstudies.org/critcom/a-tale-of-two-ports-the-epic-story-of-chinese-direct-investment-in-the-greek-port-of-piraeus/.
[26] Jack Ewing, 'European Companies Turn to Chinese Investors' *The New York Times* (2014) www.nytimes.com/2014/10/21/business/international/european-companies-turn-to-chinese-investors.html.

wariness about the unique characteristics of Chinese FDI, it dissipated as the impact of the crisis on the French economy became clear. This explains why deals such as the entry of Dongfeng into the capital of French auto maker Peugeot in 2014 were applauded by French politicians when a few years later they probably would have been blocked. Moreover, many European leaders started actively to court Chinese investment, both by stepping up their investment promotion efforts towards China, through state visits and a variety of incentives, and by lowering regulatory hurdles. In some cases, governments tried to encourage directly Chinese individual investors by offering them residency permits and even citizenship in exchange for certain amounts of investment.

Chinese investment has been seen as beneficial to many policy-makers in Europe in the context of the crisis not only because of its immediate impact, such as saving a company from bankruptcy or putting money in the state's coffers through privatization programmes, but also because of its long term economic implications. Most importantly, Chinese investment can be the key for European companies to penetrate the coveted Chinese market. For instance, in 2014 the Chinese company Sanpower Group acquired the venerable British retailer House of Fraser with the objective of launching the brand globally. It now has outlets in China and sells mostly British products there (but was sold back to a British investor in 2018).

In 2016, however, a combination of factors increased the political spotlight and negative perception of some Chinese investment deals in the two biggest destinations for Chinese FDI in Europe. In the UK, the 'Brexit' referendum ushered in a new Prime Minister, Theresa May, who questioned publicly the Hinkley Point deal, a project for France's EDF and China's CGN to construct a new nuclear power plant in Somerset, England. This provoked a lot of political debate and great media coverage about the soundness of this deal in particular and of Chinese investment in the UK in general. In the end the project was approved in September 2016, with some additional safeguards regarding national security.

In Germany, a series of Chinese investment attempts, some of which also involved the United States, increased the spotlight and the scrutiny on the soundness of accepting so much FDI from China. The proposed takeover of German robot-maker Kuka by Chinese home appliance maker Midea prompted Sigmar Gabriel, German minister of the economy, to propose an expansion of the 2009 Foreign Trade Law (*Aussenwirtschaftsgesetz*) in order to give the German government more opportunities to review and block certain foreign investments. In November 2016, several Chinese companies expressed interest in investing in Osram, a German company making lighting products and semiconductors. The IG Metall trade union said it would block any deal attempt because of the risks that a potential acquirer would 'siphon off Osram's technology' and shift production outside Germany.[27] In December 2016, the United States blocked the sale of German semiconductor company Aixtron to China's Fujian Grand Chip on the basis that it posed a risk to US security since it could make chips for the Chinese nuclear programme.

Overall, attitudes towards Chinese investment remain quite positive throughout Europe.[28] The main concerns are less about direct threats to national security than about the long-term implications for the economic competitiveness of the host country if China acquires technology. One policy response to the new challenge of Chinese

---

[27] Guy Chazan, 'German Labour Union Warns Chinese Suitors over Osram Bid' *Financial Times* (2016) www.ft.com/content/ed463896-aa74-11e6-9cb3-bb8207902122.

[28] See Julien Chaisse, 'Demystifying Public Security Exception and Limitations on Capital Movement: Hard Law, Soft Law and Sovereign Investments in the EU Internal Market' (2015) 37(2) University of Pennsylvania Journal of International Law 583.

investment in the EU would be the creation on a pan-European committee to vet foreign investment—along procedures similar to those used in the United States. The EU acquired institutional competence over foreign direct investment as a result of the 2009 Lisbon Treaty, which would make such a common review process logical, especially since goods and services can circulate freely throughout the single market.[29] Indeed, in February 2017, France, Germany, and Italy wrote to the EU Trade Commissioner in order to request a European debate over the conditions under which countries would be allowed to investigate and even block foreign investments, especially in the case of sensitive high-tech products or when the investor is state-owned.[30] A proposal is now about to be adopted for a warning and information mechanism at the EU level about inward investment, but it is far from the creation of a genuine pan-European committee, however, for many reasons. One is that the general political climate is not conducive to further European integration. Another is that the preferences of the various member states on the issue are too disparate—Chinese investment may be regarded by France as an issue of national security and by Germany as a threat to competitiveness, but for other EU countries it is only a welcome source of financing.

Since 2012, the EU and China have been negotiating a Bilateral Investment Treaty (BIT), the first standalone investment agreement with the EU as a party since the granting of the new FDI competence in the Lisbon Treaty. Some of the contentious issues such as market access and transparency of vetting procedures are part of the ongoing talks. Europe's main objective in the negotiations is to obtain reciprocity both on market access and investment protection—such as on access to the Chinese market with no obligation to form joint ventures with local partners, protection for European investments, elimination of state distortions, and increased transparency. As European Commission Vice-President Jyrki Katainen explained, 'as we don't have EU-owned companies we cannot [behave] the same [as China]'.[31] It remains to be seen what will be the impact, on one hand, of the national elections taking place in many EU countries in 2017—especially in France, Germany and Italy—and, on the other hand, of the US retreat from multi-lateralism and globalization under the Trump administration on the outcome of the EU–China BIT.

A big question mark also surrounds the consequences of Brexit on Chinese investment in Europe. The UK has been one of the top destinations for Chinese FDI in Europe in recent years. Some of the reasons that pushed Chinese investors towards Britain will still exist after Brexit, such as infrastructure and real estate. However, the attractiveness of the UK for Chinese investors has derived in large part from its participation in the EU Single Market. A 'hard Brexit', whereby the UK will sever its privileged ties to the Single Market, will likely reduce the willingness of Chinese investors to make acquisitions and greenfield investments there and redirect some of this investment, especially in manufacturing, towards EU countries on the continent.

---

[29] Sophie Meunier, 'Integration by Stealth: How the European Union Gained Competence over Foreign Direct Investment' (2017) 55(3) Journal of Common Market Studies http://onlinelibrary.wiley.com/doi/10.1111/jcms.12528/abstract.

[30] Guy Chazan, 'EU Capitals Seek Stronger Right of Veto on Chinese Takeovers' *Financial Times* (2017) www.ft.com/content/8c4a2f70-f2d1-11e6-95ee-f14e55513608.

[31] Janosch Delcker, 'Germany's Chinese Investment Problem' *Politico* (2016) www.politico.eu/article/germanys-chinese-investment-problem-sigmar-gabriel-eu/.

B. United States: geopolitical competition and renewed economic nationalism

Perceptions of Chinese investment in the United States are both similar and different to what they have been in Europe. On one hand, Chinese investment has been welcome, especially at the local level, for the same reasons it has been welcome in Europe: as a chance to create or save local jobs through greenfield and other acquisitions and an opportunity to tap into the coveted Chinese market. On the other hand, Chinese investment is viewed at the national level with much greater suspicion because of American concern about geo-politics and institutional procedures interpreting foreign investment exclusively through the lens of national security.

Investment from China, as is investment from everywhere, is welcome in the US, which is currently the first destination for both stock and flows of FDI in the world. Indeed, the US has long enjoyed a very liberal, 'open door' regime towards inward foreign direct investment based on the two guiding principles of absence of government intervention and national treatment for foreign investors.[32]

At the local level, politicians are not only accepting but also actively encouraging Chinese direct investment. Mayors, state representatives and governors are busy travelling to China and welcoming Chinese officials in the hope of attracting investment. They engage in all kinds of investment promotion and offer a variety of incentives to bring investment to their district. This explains why Chinese FDI in the US has reached record highs, with more than US$50 billion in investment deals in 2016 and 12 per cent of all M&A in the US that year[33]—major deals such as the purchase of General Electric's appliances unit by Haier (US$5.4 billion) and the acquisition of the Legendary Entertainment studio by Dalian Wanda (US$3.5 billion) but also a multitude of small deals. The number and volume of these deals plummeted in 2018.

At the national level, the picture is more complicated. Over several decades, foreign investments entering the US have become increasingly vetted and restrictive in response to successive episodes of backlash. The procedure in effect today requires the executive branch to screen incoming foreign investments and potentially to suspend or prohibit mergers and acquisitions. This is accomplished through a review process done by the Committee on Foreign Investment in the United States (CFIUS), an interagency committee including officials from the departments of Commerce, Defense, Homeland Security, State, and USTR, among others.[34] The review process applies to foreign investment in the US as well as to foreign investment in foreign companies that have affiliates in the US. According to the latest official CFIUS records for 2012–2014, China was the home country of the largest number of deals that went through the CFIUS process, followed by the United Kingdom, Canada, Japan, and France.[35] Chinese acquisitions are investigated more thoroughly because many of the potential investors are either SOEs or have close ties to the Chinese government. In 2016, CFIUS blocked, among others, the acquisition of Philips' Lumileds by Chinese private

---

[32] Daniel H Rosen and Thilo Hanemann, 'An American Open Door?' *Maximizing the Benefits of Chinese Foreign Direct Investment* (2011).

[33] Ellen Sheng, 'Chinese Investment In U.S. Hits Record High of $18.4 Billion in First Half Of 2016' *Forbes* (2016) www.forbes.com/sites/ellensheng/2016/07/25/chinese-investment-in-u-s-hits-record-high-of-18-4-billion-in-first-half-of-2016/ (last accessed 25 July 2016).

[34] James K Jackson, *The Committee on Foreign Investment in the United States (CFIUS)* (Congressional Research Service, 2014).

[35] CFIUS, 'Committee on Foreign Investment in the United States Annual Report to Congress CY2014' (2016).

equity investors and of German chip maker Aixtron by China's Fujian Grand Chip Investment on national security grounds.

If the Executive is the only branch responsible for the FDI approval process through CFIUS, Congress has been the locus of the heaviest politicization of investment deals over the years. Either out of genuine concern for American national security or to score political points by posturing, Congressional members may hold hearings and pass new legislation to restrict foreign investment.[36] They can also simply complain loudly and publicly about foreign investment in speeches, interviews, or campaign ads.

As a result of these procedures and practices governing the politics of foreign investment in the US, concerns for national security have been the principal lens through which Chinese FDI has been perceived at the national level in the US over the past decade. While it has captured the attention of the media and has drawn complaints by Chinese officials, it does not reflect the efforts that have been deployed at the local level to favour and expand Chinese investment.

The impact of the 2016 American election is still uncertain at the time of writing. On one hand, the tone of discourse emanating from President Trump has been initially more belligerent towards China in general and the Chinese economy in particular. He may direct his administration to review incoming foreign investments more broadly and thoroughly through the CFIUS process , which was reinforced by Congress through the 2018 Foreign Investment Risk Review Modernization Act (FIRRMA), and insist more forcefully on reciprocal access for American firms in China. Chinese investments are more likely to be scrutinized and decried in the political arena. Indeed, some bipartisan efforts are already underway in Congress to tighten scrutiny of Chinese investments into the US, for instance with special provisions for high-technology deals or with an expansion of the CFIUS mandate to include economic factors when assessing foreign takeovers.[37] On the other hand, getting more direct investment into the US will be crucial to Trump's objective of repatriating jobs and 'Make America great' again.

IV. Conclusion: Beware of Chinese Bearing Gifts?

Why do these political challenges matter? Because they are ultimately a central factor in determining the success of an investment—no matter how good the business plan is, the due diligence, or the financial backing, the foreign investment is not going to succeed in the end if the host government blocks the transaction or public opinion initiates backlash. Whether Chinese investments are interpreted as novel or unique do influence the type of political reception they receive in the host country—the more idiosyncratic they are perceived to be, the more likely they are to trigger political controversy and the creation of more stringent FDI vetting mechanisms.

Several recent developments will determine how much Chinese direct investment will continue to grow in Europe and the US over the next few years and whether they will be welcomed or treated as a potential Trojan Horse. For one, the Chinese government has imposed in late 2016 tighter controls on outbound investment, notably for Chinese companies undertaking major acquisitions of foreign firms unrelated to their

---

[36] Rosen and Hanemann (n 32).
[37] Kate O'Keeffe, 'Lawmakers Push for Tighter Scrutiny of Chinese Investment in U.S.' *Wall Street Journal* (2017) Politics www.wsj.com/articles/lawmakers-push-for-tighter-scrutiny-of-chinese-investment-in-u-s-1487678403.

core business, and established stricter approval requirements for cross-border deals over US$10 billion. Designed to curb capital flight, these new measures might transform the nature of the investment deals done in Europe and the US and increase the number of deals undertaken by private investors.

Another recent development has been the creation of the 'Made in China 2025' initiative by the Ministry of Industry and Information Technology. The objective is to upgrade Chinese industry and move it up the global value chain, notably by encouraging innovation, strengthening intellectual property rights, and nurturing human talent. Outbound Chinese FDI is likely to play a role in implementing this initiative. In the short term, this should increase Chinese efforts to invest in Europe and the US, especially in sectors with superior technology and know-how, which should have a positive impact on the host economies. In the long term, however, this will accelerate the competitiveness of Chinese industry.

On the host country side, one recent development related to the 'novel' vs. 'unique' dichotomy has been the publicization of some notable successes of Chinese investments. Initial media reports about new incoming Chinese investments in Europe and the US were most often focused on failures and mistakes, such as CNOOC's failed attempt to take over Unocal in 2005. Recently, however, now that Chinese FDI has been around for almost a decade, many articles are focusing on examples of successes, for instance in the case of big profile deals such as Geely's acquisition of Volvo and COSCO's management of Piraeus. Successful smaller acquisitions have also been featured in the media, such as Putzmeister, 'a German maker of pumps for concrete, [which] has seen its workers' jobs secured and its sales rise nearly a third since Chinese competitor Sany bought it in 2012'.[38] Indeed, Chinese investors have been careful not to provoke political backlash, which has happened thanks to a learning curve coupled with a clear Chinese strategy that has involved relying on Western public relations and legal firms to smooth out deals.

The simultaneous negotiations of bilateral investment treaties between China and the EU, on one hand, and the US, on the other, will also determine the nature and amount of future Chinese outbound FDI. Western countries are particularly concerned about hurdles to market access caused by a lack of reciprocity. China invested US$37 billion in the EU in 2016, while European countries invested only US$8.5 billion, dropping for a fourth successive year.[39] If no progress is made on making Western investments into China as easy as Chinese investments into Western countries, Europe and the US may tighten inbound investment regulations and make it more difficult for Chinese investors to make deals.

Finally, the politics of hosting Chinese investments will also depend on which other countries are trying to invest in local companies. As other potentially politically problematic countries, such as Russia and Qatar for instance, try to invest in Europe and the US, Chinese investment may become more politically desirable by comparison.

---

[38] Paul Carrel and others 'Don't Expect Trump-Style Protectionism from Germany' *Reuters* (2017) www.reuters.com/article/us-germany-china-m-a-analysis-idUSKBN14T1IO.

[39] Thilo Hanemann and Mikko Huotari, 'Record Flows and Growing Imbalances: Chinese Investment in Europe in 2016' MERICS Papers on China (2017) www.merics.org/fileadmin/user_upload/downloads/MPOC/COFDI_2017/MPOC_03_Update_COFDI_Web.pdf.

19

The Political Economy of Chinese Outward Foreign Direct Investment in 'One-Belt, One-Road (OBOR)' Countries

Ka Zeng*

I. Introduction

As China's export-oriented model of economic growth has come under increasing chal-lenge in the aftermath of the 2008 global financial crisis, the Chinese government has adopted a set of policies to respond to such shifting growth patterns. In addition to implementing a set of reform measures domestically to increase innovation and prod-uctivity growth and enhance consumption, Beijing unleashed a couple of ambitious external initiatives such as the Asian Investment Bank (AIIB), the BRICS Bank, and the 'One Belt, One Road' (OBOR) initiative[1] to redirect excess domestic capacity and capital for regional infrastructure development and to improve relations with partner countries. Promulgated by Chinese President Xi Jinping during his visit to Central Asia and Southeast Asia in September and October 2013, the OBOR initiative con-sists of the Silk Road Economic Belt, an economic land belt that links China with countries on the original Silk Road through Central Asia, West Asia, the Middle East, and Europe, and the so-called twenty-first century Maritime Silk Road extending from China through Southeast Asia, and on to South Asia, Africa, and Europe. The initiative represents not only an ambitious domestic investment drive, in which domestic firms are encouraged to go abroad in search of new markets and investment opportunities, but also a major push to enhance the country's international influence.[2] While impli-cating China's investment relations with both individual partner countries as well as with countries in the Asia-Pacific region, the initiative also has a clear global dimension to the extent that it seeks to enhance China's political and economic influence in other world regions through expanded trade and investment ties.

The prominent role of the OBOR initiative for China's overall economic development strategy and for its foreign economic policy thus calls for more scholarly analysis of the drivers of Chinese investment in OBOR countries. This chapter undertakes such a task and engages in an analysis of the political and economic factors that influence Chinese outward foreign direct investment (COFDI) in OBOR countries from 2005 to 2014. Empirical results yield a couple of important findings. First, there is strong evidence

* Professor, Department of Political Science, University of Arkansas, Fayetteville, AR 72701, Email: kzeng@uark.edu.

[1] The OBOR initiative has been renamed as the Belt and Road Initiative (BRI) by the Chinese government in 2016. Since this study covers the period before the BRI came into existence, it will use OBOR instead of BRI to refer to the initiative.

[2] See Julien Chaisse and Mitsuo Matsushita, 'China's "Belt and Road" Initiative: Mapping the World Trade Normative and Strategic Implications' (2018) 52(1) Journal of World Trade 163.

supporting the resource-seeking motivation behind COFDI to OBOR countries. Secondly, in contrast to previous studies which either find that host country political risk has no effect on COFDI or that COFDI tends to be attracted to countries with a more risky political environment, this study yields some preliminary evidence that COFDI has been more likely to seek out countries with low political risks. This result points to possible changes in recent Chinese investors' behaviour as they expand the scale of their operation to become more experienced players in the global marketplace. Thirdly, the analysis yields evidence consistent with previous findings which suggest that COFDI tends to go to countries with good political relations with Beijing either due to the role of good political relations in compensating for the risks of investing in the host country or the importance of geopolitical considerations for China's overall foreign policy agenda.[3]

Furthermore, the study goes beyond earlier analyses which focus on the host country's political relations with China to examine the host's political relations with the United States (US) and yields some preliminary evidence suggesting that COFDI has also been more likely to flow to countries with good political relations with the US.

Taken together, these findings indicate that, at least as far as OBOR countries are concerned, Chinese investment tends to be drawn to countries with rich natural resources and may be intended to enhance Beijing's influence vis-à-vis not only those countries that have historically aligned closer with Beijing's values, preferences, and agenda, but also those that have shared greater affinity with the US in order to cement a China-centric pattern of trade and investment in the Asian region. These findings thus point to the politically driven nature of COFDI in OBOR countries and the potentially central role of the state in guiding Chinese investment in the region.

II. Overview of Chinese Investment in OBOR Countries

COFDI stock in OBOR countries has steadily increased during the past decade to reach US$72 billion, or 10.9 per cent of total COFDI by the end of 2014 (see Figure 19.1).[4] Figure 19.2 presents the top ten recipients of COFDI among OBOR countries in 2013. As Figure 19.2 shows, Singapore, Russia, and Kazakhstan have the largest foreign direct investment (FDI) stock from China by the end of 2014.

Figure 19.3 shows average annual COFDI to OBOR countries by the host country's level of economic development, while Figures 19.4–7 present average annual COFDI to OBOR countries by the host country's level of political stability, regime type, political relations with China, and political risks, respectively.[5] A visual inspection of the data reveals a negative relationship between the host's regime type and COFDI and a positive relationship between the host's level of political stability or political relations with China, on the one hand, and COFDI on the other. In other words, COFDI seems to be more likely to be drawn to authoritarian countries as well as to countries with a higher level of political stability or those with better political relations, as measured

[3] Quan Li and Guoyong Liang, 'Political Relations and Chinese Outbound Direct Investment: Evidence from Firm- and Dyadic-Level Tests' (2012) RCCPB Working Paper 19 www.indiana.edu/~rccpb/wordpress/wp-content/uploads/2015/11/Li-Liang-RCCPB-19-Invest-Feb-2012.pdf (last accessed 8 December 2016).
[4] *Statistical Bulletin of Chinese Outward Foreign Direct Investment 2015* (Ministry of Commerce of the People's Republic of China 2016).
[5] Political relations is measured by the host country's United Nation's General Assembly (UNGA) voting affinity with China. For the method used to calculate the host country's political risks, see the discussion about political risks in the empirical analysis section below.

by United Nations General Assembly (UNGA) voting affinity with China. However, there does not seem to be any straightforward relationship between the host's level of economic development or political risks and COFDI. As the pattern that emerges from the above descriptive statistics is far from being definitive, the rest of the chapter will derive a set of hypotheses about the influence of a set of political and economic factors on COFDI to OBOR countries and then subject these hypotheses to empirical testing using available data.

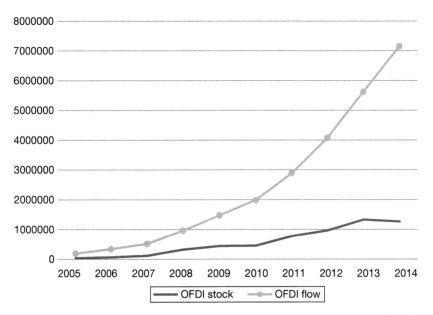

Figure 19.1 Chinese OFDI flow to and stock in OBOR countries, 2005—2014 (Million $)

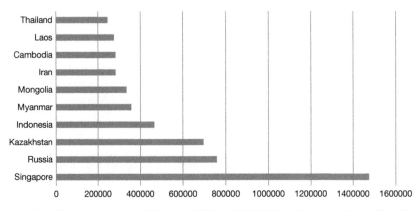

Figure 19.2 Top 10 recipients of Chinese OFDI in 2014 (FDI stock measured in million $)

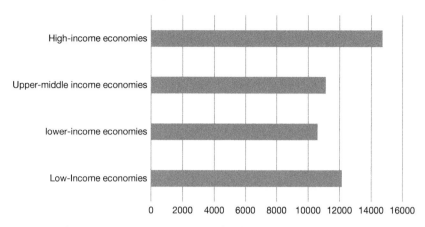

Figure 19.3 Chinese OFDI to OBOR countries by the host country's income level

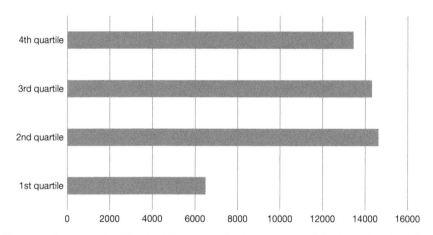

Figure 19.4 Chinese OFDI to OBOR countries by the host country's level of political stability

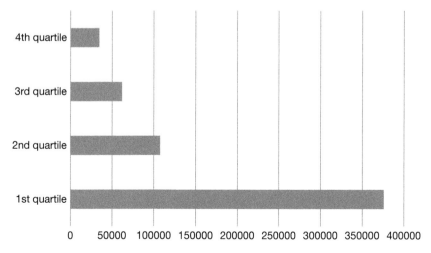

Figure 19.5 Chinese OFDI to OBOR countries by the host country's regime type

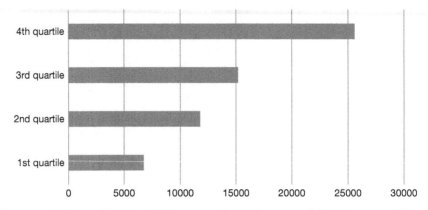

Figure 19.6 Chinese OFDI to OBOR countries by the host country's UNGA voting affinity with China

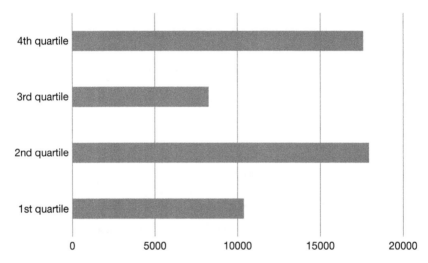

Figure 19.7 Chinese OFDI to OBOR countries by the host country's political risks

III. Literature Review and Hypotheses

Studies of the determinants of FDI tend to rely on Dunning's 'eclectic' theory which emphasizes the ownership, location, and internalization (OLI) advantages that firms may be able to capture by investing abroad.[6] Given that this study is most interested in analysing the cross-national variation in COFDI flows instead of their determinants at the firm level, it will focus on the economic and political environments of the host country that enhance its appeal to Chinese investors.

Previous studies have devoted some attention to the characteristics of the host country economic environment that attract foreign investment, including investment

---

[6] John H Dunning, *Explaining International Production* (Unwin Hyman 1988); John H Dunning, *Multinational Enterprises and the Global Economy* (Addison-Wesley 1993).

from China. One strand of the literature in particular emphasizes the resource-seeking motivation behind COFDI. For example, Broadman suggests that while COFDI in the earlier phases tends to be concentrated in infrastructure investment, the launching of the 'Going Global' strategy in 1998 has led a growing amount of COFDI to flow to countries with abundant oil and natural resource supplies.[7] Studies that survey the geographical distribution of COFDI in the developing world[8] or analyse COFDI in specific world regions such as Latin America or Africa[9] have generally yielded evidence in support of such a contention. Given that many OBOR countries are abundantly endowed in natural resources such as oil and gas, this should lead to the following hypothesis:

A. Hypothesis 1: COFDI should be more likely to be attracted to countries with an abundant supply of natural resources.

The political conditions in host countries that influence COFDI flows have also received some scholarly attention. While the mainstream FDI literature generally posits that political risk should be a major deterrent to FDI flows, studies of COFDI have yielded more mixed evidence on this issue, with some studies showing that Chinese firms are more likely to invest in countries with high political risks.[10] A couple of mechanisms underlie the argument that COFDI may be particularly likely to be attracted to countries with poor institutional environments.

First, it is possible that as Chinese investors operate from substantially different domestic institutional environments than investors from the developed world, they may be more likely to invest in those host countries with a similar institutional context. As Chinese companies are experienced in 'dealing with burdensome regulation' and 'navigating complex patron-client relationships ... in relatively opaque and difficult business environments',[11] this should have reduced the 'liability of foreignness' they face

---

[7] Harry G Broadman, *China's Silk Road: China and India's New Economic Frontier* (World Bank 2007).

[8] Hsiu-Ling Wu and Chien-Hsun Chen, 'An Assessment of Outward Foreign Direct Investment from China's Transitional Economy' (2012) 53 Europe-Asia Studies 1235; Mark Yaolin Wang, 'The Motivations behind China's Government-Initiated Industrial Investment Overseas' (2002) 75 Pacific Affairs 197.

[9] Anders Bastholm and Peter Kragelund, 'State Driven Investment in Zambia: Combining Strategic Interests and Profits' in Meine Pieter van Dijk (ed), *The New Presence of China in Africa* (University Press 2009); Ping Deng, 'Investing for Strategic Resources and Its Rationale: The Case of Outward FDI from Chinese Companies' (2007) 50 Business Horizons 71; Ping Deng, 'Why Do Chinese Firms Tend to Acquire Strategic Assets in International Expansion?' (2009) 44 Journal of World Business 74; Juan González García, 'The Relationship between Economic Growth and Energy in China: Medium- and Long-Term Challenges' (2013) 4 Latin American Policy 4; Ruben Gonzalez-Vicente, 'Mapping Chinese Mining Investment in Latin America: Politics or Market?' (2012) 209 The China Quarterly 35; Peter Kotschwar, Theodore Moran, and Julia Muir, 'Do Chinese Companies Exploit More?' *The Americas Quarterly* (2011) 5; Luisa Palacios, 'Latin America as Energy Supplier' in Rioradan Roett and Guadalupe Paz (eds), *China's Expansion Into the Western Hemisphere* (Brookings 2008).

[10] Peter J Buckley and others, 'The Determinants of Chinese Outward Foreign Direct Investment' (2007) 38 Journal of International Business Studies 499; Ivar Kolstad Ivar and Arne Wiig, 'What Determines Chinese Outward FDI?' (2012) 47 Journal of World Business 26.

[11] Henry Wai-Chung Yeung and Weidong Liu, 'Globalizing China: the Rise of Mainland Firms in the Global Economy' (2008) 49 Eurasian Geography and Economics 57; Randall Morck and others, 'Perspectives on China's Outward Foreign Direct Investment' (2008) 39 Journal of International Business Studies 337.

in the host market. Furthermore, the less stringent regulation in countries with poor institutions should also subject Chinese companies to less close scrutiny, thus reducing the moral and financial costs of engaging in ethically questionable practices such as corruption in the host country.

Secondly, another reason Chinese companies tend to invest in countries with poor institutions may have to do with the cushions provided by the political connections that many of these companies have developed with political elites.[12] Indeed, a large share of COFDI was conducted by state-owned enterprises (SOEs). The strong political connections of Chinese firms mean that instead of simply engaging in profit-maximization activities, the investment decisions of these firms may reflect political objectives such as promoting domestic development, ensuring regime survival, or assisting in the host country's economic development as a way of promoting China's overall foreign policy agenda. The achievement of the latter objective, in particular, may call for Chinese companies to invest in relatively poor countries with risky institutional environments.

Along similar lines, it has been argued that firms with patronage relations can be expected to be bailed out by the government when they are unable to achieve their expected returns on investment and are thus better able to socialize the risks associated with outward FDI. This helps to explain why they are more likely to invest in risky destinations abroad without having to concern themselves too much about seeking protection for their investment. Taken together, the above arguments suggest that firms with political connections with elites may be less risk averse in their investment behaviour. And even though COFDI has become more commercial in recent years, it is still reasonable to expect that Chinese firms may be more likely to be subject to political influence than firms from other countries.

B. Hypothesis 2: Chinese FDI should be more likely to flow to countries with weak institutions.

The effect of interstate relations on outbound FDI has also received some scholarly attention. Earlier studies of this issue emphasize the subjective perception of investors from the host country, arguing that out of concerns that host country officials and citizens may not be able to credibly distinguish their interests from those of the home country government, home investors may become particularly attentive to interstate relations that can help to signal the business environment in the host country.[13] A closely related argument focuses on the rational expectations of foreign investors about the uncertainty that interstate conflict may generate for their investment.[14] From this perspective, due to imperfect information and their inability to perfectly anticipate investment risks, investors who ideally would like to reduce investment in a host country *ex ante* can only make adjustments ex post when unexpected violence occurs. Thus, unanticipated interstate war may reduce a host country's ability to attract

[12] Weiyi Shi, 'The Political Economy of China's Outward Direct Investment' (DPhil thesis, University of California, San Diego 2015).
[13] Douglas Nigh, 'The Effect of Political Events on United States Direct Foreign Investment: A Pooled Time-Series Cross-Sectional Analysis' (1985) 1 Journal of International Business Studies 1.
[14] Quan Li, 'Political Violence and Foreign Direct Investment' in Michele Fratianni and Alan M Rugman (eds), *Research in Global Strategic Management, Vol 12, Regional Economic Integration* (Elsevier 2006); Quan Li, 'Foreign Direct Investment and Interstate Military Conflict' (2008) 62 Journal of International Affairs 53.

investment but may have relatively little impact on the volume of investment flows.[15] Building on the above argument, still other studies suggest that interstate cooperation should lower the productivity cutoff for firm entry, while interstate conflict should exert the opposite effect.[16]

While the mainstream literature on FDI emphasizes the positive effect of cooperative interstate political relations on outward FDI, recent studies of China's commercial diplomacy increasingly draw our attention to the influence of geopolitical considerations on the country's economic policy. For example, in a study of the decision of 37 central banks to add the Chinese currency renminbi (RMB) to their reserve portfolio since 2010, Liao and McDowell suggest that state preferences regarding international order play an important role in influencing their decision to invest in the RMB.[17] If every international monetary regime is built upon a particular political order, then the decision to invest in the RMB should reflect a state's interest in pursuing a new way of organizing political and economic interactions in international politics and in bringing about a revised international order away from the existing *status quo* dominated by the US. Thus, as a state's ideal point in United Nations General Assembly (UNGA) voting moves away from the US toward China, it should be more likely to adopt the RMB as a reserve currency. Research on China's free trade agreement (FTA) diplomacy similarly points to the strong influence of political and strategic calculations behind China's regional economic policy, suggesting that preferential trade and investment liberalization is mainly aimed at establishing China's leadership role in East Asia, counter-balancing Japanese or American influence in the region, and enhancing Chinese influence in other world regions. Driven by such political motivations, Chinese authorities have tended to negotiate agreements with those countries that enjoy good political relations with China or occupy a more prominent position on China's diplomatic agenda.[18]

The above arguments about the role of geopolitical considerations in shaping China's commercial diplomacy may be extended to COFDI as well. Indeed, geopolitical considerations have not been entirely absent in China's policy towards outward foreign direct investment. As a *China Daily* op-ed has suggested, 'For more than half a century, China has tended to see its outbound investment not as a pure economic activity but as a mixture blended with political significance, a gesture of friendship and humanitarian aid, to countries that were ignored by the traditional major powers of the world'.[19] McNally (2012) further developed the concept of Sino-capitalism and applied it to COFDI policy whereby the Chinese state is seen as playing 'a leading role in fostering and guiding capitalist accumulation'.[20] The promulgation of the *Going Out* strategy in 1998, for example,

[15] Quan Li, 'Political Violence and Foreign Direct Investment' (n 14).
[16] Quan Li and others 'Interstate Political Relations and Bilateral FDI Flows' (International Political Economy Society 2010 Meeting, Harvard University, 2010).
[17] Steven Liao and Daniel McDowell 'No Reservations: International Order and Demand for the Renminbi as a Reserve Currency' *International Studies Quarterly* (2016), DOI: http://dx.doi.org/10.1093/isq/sqv020 272-293.
[18] Henry Gao, 'China's Strategy for Free Trade Agreements: Political Battle in the Name of Trade' in Ross P Buckley and others (eds), *East Asian Economic Integration: Law, Trade and Finance* (Edward Elgar Publishing 2011); Razeen Sally, 'Chinese Trade Policy after (Almost) Ten Years in the WTO: A Post-Crisis Stocktake' *European Center for International Political Economy Occasional Paper No 2* (2011); Ka Zeng, 'China's Free Trade Agreement Diplomacy' (2016) 9 Chinese Journal of International Politics 277.
[19] Ed Zhang, 'Dark Side of China's Overseas Investment' *China Daily* (2015).
[20] Christopher A McNally, 'Sino-Capitalism: China's Reemergence and the International Political Economy' (2012) 64 World Politics 741.

can be considered as an example of the strategic use of FDI policy to enhance the global reach of Chinese firms and hence the influence of China in the global economy.[21]

The strategic purposes behind China's OBOR policy were even more apparent. Through the OBOR policy, the government has sought to enhance the country's energy security and improve relations with partner countries. The initiative highlights Beijing's strategic use of economic statecraft designed to incentivize governments in Asia to pursue greater cooperation with Beijing through the use of a major financial carrot to fill the existing infrastructure gap in the region. If successfully implemented, the initiative may help deepen regional economic integration and increase trade and investment flows between the region and the outside world. This may help to elevate the importance of Beijing as a major center of trade and investment activities and as an underwriter for infrastructure development for the regional economies, thus potentially increasing Beijing's diplomatic leverage in the region. If this is the case, then one would expect China to invest more heavily in countries with which it enjoys cooperative relations in order to build on the shared trust to further promote regional security and political confidence with its regional partners.

Applying the above insights to the Chinese case leads us to expect that COFDI should be more likely to flow to those countries with shared political goals or diplomatic agenda as the greater level of cooperation embodied in such relationships should both induce greater expectation of the stability of the host country investment environment for Chinese investors and enable the Chinese leadership to take advantage of shared political ties to facilitate the achievement of its major strategic objectives.

C. Hypothesis 3: COFDI should be more likely to flow to host countries with shared political goals or diplomatic agenda with Beijing.

Conversely, if the Chinese leadership has sought to use the OBOR initiative to cement its ties with states that are drawn to the Chinese model of order that increasingly represents a challenge to the ideas, values, and priorities that underlie the US-led *status quo*,[22] then it is possible that the likelihood that COFDI will flow to a partner country will decline as the latter's preferences move away from China and towards the US.

D. Hypothesis 4: COFDI should be less likely to be attracted to host countries with shared political goals or diplomatic agenda with the United States.

IV. Empirical Analysis

This chapter tests the above hypotheses using data on COFDI in OBOR countries from 2005 to 2014 available from the *Statistical Bulletin of Chinese Outward Foreign*

[21] Weiyi Shi, 'The Political Economy of China's Outward Direct Investment' (D Phil thesis, University of California, San Diego 2015).
[22] Naazeen Barma and others, 'A World without the West' *National Interest* (2007) 23; Stephan Halper, *The Beijing Consensus: How China's Authoritarian Model Will Dominate the Twenty-First Century* (Basic Books 2010); Martin Jacques, *When China Rules the World: The End of the Western World Order* (Penguin Press 2009).

Direct Investment (*Statistical Bulletin* thereafter). Since COFDI and export data are only available for 48 of the 63 OBOR countries, the following empirical analysis is necessarily limited to these 48 countries.[23]

COFDI. The dependent variable is the logged value of COFDI (in US$ million) in a host country in a given year.

Several measures are developed to test the above hypotheses regarding the influence of considerations about the host country's natural resources, political institutions, and interstate relations on COFDI flows.

Natural resource rents. To assess the resource-seeking motivations behind COFDI (hypothesis 1), the empirical analysis includes the share of natural resource rents in the partner country's gross domestic product (GDP). Total natural resource rents are the sum of oil, natural gas, coal, mineral, and forest rents and are calculated by taking the difference between the price of a commodity and the average cost of producing it and then multiplying it by the physical quantities extracted or harvested by a country. Data for this variable is taken from the World Bank's *World Development Indicators* (various years).

Political risk. This study draws on data from the Political Risk Service's International Country Risk Guide (ICRG) to examine how the host country institutional environment may affect COFDI flows. Specifically, this measure is a composite measure of the host country political institutions using data on corruption, law and order, bureaucratic quality, and investment profile.[24] All of these indicators should measure the latent level of property rights protection in the host country. Factor analysis suggests that there is only one underlying dimension among these four variables, with an eigenvalue of 2.59. Since the eigenvalue of all other factor loadings fall below the threshold value of one, we use the factor loading for this one underlying dimension as the measure of the institutional environment in the host country. It should be noted that all four of the variables used to measure political risks are measured on a scale of '0' to '4', with '4' indicating very low risk. Consequently, a negative relationship is expected between this variable and COFDI.

Ideal point distance_China and *Ideal point distance_US.* To test hypotheses 3 and 4 regarding the influence of the host country's political relations with China and the US, respectively, on COFDI, this study draws on the measure of ideal point distance, or the degree to which a state's ideal point in UNGA votes differs from that of China (or the US) in each of the years between 1946 and 2012. Developed by Bailey and Voeten,[25] dynamic national ideal point estimates represent an improvement over conventional dyadic similarity indicators such as the UNGA affinity score because they allow for better inter-temporal comparisons, are better able to distinguish shifts in UN agenda from changes in state preferences, and can more effectively separate signal from noise in identifying foreign policy shifts. Consequently, this measure should be well suited to measure the extent to which a state shares similar foreign policy goals and positions as Beijing.

In addition to the above main explanatory variables, a set of control variables are included in the analysis to take account of other potentially confounding factors on COFDI flows.

---

[23] The list of countries included in the analysis is available from the author upon request.

[24] Investment profile is in turn consisted of the following three sub-components: contract viability, repatriation, and payment delays.

[25] Michael A Bailey and others, 'Estimating Dynamic State Preferences from United Nations Voting' (2005) 61(2) Journal of Conflict Resolution 430.

GDP and *GDP per capita*. Previous studies generally suggest that host countries with a larger internal market or a higher level of economic development should be more likely to attract FDI due to the greater opportunities for the efficient utilization of scale and scope made possible by FDI.[26] Consequently, the following analysis controls for the influence of host country market size, measured by GDP, and its level of economic development, measured by GDP per capita.

Trade openness. The study further takes into account the host country's trade openness out of expectation that host economies more deeply integrated into the global market through international trade should be more appealing to foreign investors because of their greater ability to provide the scale economies that could help to expand the firms' global reach.[27] *Trade openness* is measured as the share of the host's total imports and exports in its GDP.

Political stability and rule of law are taken from the *World Governance Indicators* (various years).

Regime type. The regime type of the partner country is based on the country's POLITY score available from the POLITY IV database.[28]

Exchange rate. Previous studies suggest that a depreciation of the host country's currency should attract FDI by reducing the cost of production and the prices of assets for foreign investors.[29] Alternatively, an appreciation of the home country's currency should lead to greater FDI outflows by increasing firm wealth and reducing the costs of investment relative to firms in the host country that experience a devaluation of their currency. Consequently the tests use the real exchange rate between China and the partner country, expressed as the amount of RMB per partner country currency unit, to capture the effect of exchange rate fluctuations on FDI flows. A negative relationship is expected between the bilateral exchange rate and FDI. Data for the above control variables are taken from *World Development Indicators* published by the World Bank.[30]

Distance and *language*. The analysis further controls for geographical proximity and cultural affinity between the partners. While geographical distance is expected to deter foreign investment, cultural affinity should increase the attractiveness of a host country to foreign investors by reducing transportation costs or providing investing firms with better knowledge of the local market, customers, and business networks.[31] *Distance* is the logged value of the distance between the capital of China and the partner country.

---

[26] Avic Chakrabati, 'The Determinants of Foreign Direct Investment: Sensitivity Analyses of Cross-Country Regions' (2003) 54 *Kyklos* 89. Ping Deng, 'Outward Investment by Chinese MNCs: Motivations and Implications' (2004) 47 Business Horizons 8; Robert Taylor, 'Globalization Strategies of Chinese Companies: Current Developments and Future Prospects' (2002) 1 Asian Business and Management 209; Yongjin Zhang, *China's Emerging Global Business: Political Economy and Institutional Investigations* (Palgrave Macmillan 2003); UNCTAD, *World Investment Report 1998: Trends and Determinants* (UN 1998).

[27] UNCTAD, *World Investment Report 2009: Transnational Corporations, Agricultural Production and Development*. (United Nations Centre on Transnational Corporations 2009).

[28] Monty G Marshall and Ted Robert Gurr, 'Polity IV Project: Political Regime Characteristics and Transitions, 1800-2013' *Center for Systemic Peace* (2014) www.systemicpeace.org/polity/polity4.htm (last accessed 30 June 2016).

[29] Kenneth A Froot and Jeremy C Stein, 'Exchange Rates and Foreign Direct Investment: An Imperfect Capital Markets Approach' (1991) 106 Quarterly Journal of Economics 1191.

[30] Available online at http://data.worldbank.org/data-catalog/world-development-indicators (last accessed 10 October 2016).

[31] Bruce Kogut and Harbir Singh, 'The Effect of National Culture on the Choice of Entry Mode' (1988) 19 Journal of International Business Studies 411; Li and Liang (n 3).

Language, which is also a dummy variable, is coded '1' if the two countries share a common official language and '0' otherwise.[32]

FTA and BIT. Previous literature further suggests that the signing of international economic agreements such as FTAs or bilateral investment treaties (BITs) may enhance a country's prospects of attracting FDI by allowing the government to better signal its commitments to liberal economic policies than unilateral approaches to economic liberalization, providing foreign investors with access to a larger market, or raising the ex post costs of non-compliance.[33] To account for these possibilities, the study also includes dummy variables for *FTA* and *BIT*. These variables equal '1' if China and the partner country have a free trade agreement or a BIT in force in a given year, respectively, and '0' otherwise.[34]

Lagged COFDI. All of the estimation models below include the lagged level of the original dependent variable to control for the possible effect of path dependence as well as the impact of other unobserved variables not included in the models that may potentially affect FDI inflows.[35]

Table 19.1 presents estimation results using ordinary least squares (OLS) regression with Huber-White robust standard errors clustered over countries, an estimation strategy that can help account for both heteroscedasticity and serial correlation among the variables.[36] Table 19.2 adds host country fixed effects to control for the potentially confounding effect of other national structural variables and attributes on FDI. While fixed effects models can help address the omitted variable bias and ensure that the findings are not spurious, they also soak up variation in the dependent variable that may have been explained by other independent variables, thus increasing the difficulty of finding statistically significant results. Consequently, significant findings from fixed effect models also tend to be more robust and reliable.[37]

Both random- and fixed-effect model estimates corroborate the resource-seeking motivations behind COFDI. *Natural resource rents* has the expected positive sign and is statistically significant in most model specifications in Tables 1

[32] Data for both of these variables are from the CEPII database (2011) www.cepii.fr/CEPII/en/welcome.asp (last accessed 10 October 2016).

[33] Bruce A Blonigen and Jeremy Piger, 'Determinants of Foreign Direct Investment' *NBER Working Paper Series No 16704* (2011) (accessed 18 October 2016); Tim Büthe and Helen V Milner, 'The Politics of Foreign Direct Investment into Developing Countries: Increasing FDI through International Trade Agreements?' (2008) 52 American Journal of Political Science 741; Zachary Elkins and others, 'Competing for Capital: The Diffusion of Bilateral Investment Treaties, 1960-2000' (2008) 60 International Organization 811; Andrew Kerner, 'Why Should I Believe You? The Costs and Consequences of Bilateral Investment Treaties' (2009) 53 International Studies Quarterly 73. Eric Neumayer and Laura Spess, 'Do Bilateral Investment Treaties Increase Foreign Direct Investment to Developing Countries?' (2005) 33 World Development 1567; Susan Rose-Ackerman and Jennifer Tobin, 'Foreign Direct Investment and the Business Environment in Developing Countries: The Impact of Bilateral Investment Treaties' Yale Law & Economics Research Paper No 293 (2005).

[34] Data for *FTA* are drawn from the WTO's RTA database http://rtais.wto.org/UI/PublicMaintainRTAHome.aspx (last accessed 10 October 2016).

[35] COFDI is lagged by one year in the following analysis. Lagging COFDI by two or three years does not affect the main findings reported below.

[36] Rick L Williams, 'A Note on Robust Variance Estimation for Custer-Correlated Data' (2000) 56 Biometrics 645.

[37] Donald P Green and others, 'Dirty Pool' *International Organization* (2001) 441; Li and Liang (n 3).

Table 19.1 Ordinary-Least-Squares (OLS) Models of the Determinants of COFDI to OBOR Countries

Variable	(1)	(2)	(3)	(4)	(5)	(6)	(7)	(8)
Lagged COFDI	0.000004	0.000003	0.000003	0.000004	0.000005	0.000005	-0.0000004	0.000002
	(0.40)	(0.34)	(0.58)	(0.74)	(1.20)	(1.19)	(-0.05)	(0.30)
GDP	0.068	0.114	0.093	0.084	0.031	-0.107	-0.194	-0.191
	(0.48)	(0.84)	(0.46)	(0.48)	(0.18)	(-0.78)	(-1.13)	(-1.32)
GDP per Capita	0.00001	0.00003	0.0001	0.00004*	0.00004**	0.00004*	0.00003	0.00004
	(0.41)	(1.10)	(1.47)	(1.92)	(1.97)	(2.11)	(0.65)	(1.19)
Trade openness	-0.008	-0.011**	-0.010**	-0.012**	-0.005	-0.005	-0.008	-0.008
	(-1.50)	(-2.00)	(-2.28)	(-2.22)	(-1.42)	(-1.04)	(-1.57)	(-1.44)
Distance	-1.445	-3.246***	-1.905**	-4.126***	-1.407	-2.510***	-0.580	-2.728***
	(-1.59)	(-3.78)	(-2.05)	(-3.55)	(-1.51)	(-3.49)	(-0.58)	(-3.58)
Language	2.908	5.126**	1.804	4.664***	0.942	2.679**	0.891	3.015**
	(1.43)	(2.57)	(1.32)	(2.87)	(0.80)	(2.15)	(0.50)	(2.16)
Natural resource rents	0.018*	0.025**	0.010	0.040**	0.013	0.066***	0.029	0.046**
	(1.88)	(2.19)	(0.57)	(2.17)	(0.77)	(3.40)	(1.55)	(2.01)
Political Stability	0.713	0.497					0.668	0.226
	(1.44)	(0.91)					(0.89)	(0.35)
Rule of law	-0.334	-0.837					-0.852	-0.860
	(-0.48)	(-1.36)					(-0.60)	(-0.66)
Regime type	0.067	-0.033					0.053	-0.081
	(1.32)	(-0.58)					(1.36)	(-1.50)
Ideal point distance_China	-1.320*		-1.490**		-0.715		-1.437*	
	(-1.92)		(-2.19)		(-1.14)		(-1.70)	

Ideal point	−1.235***			−1.440***		−1.988***		−2.008***
	(−2.73)			(−3.13)		(−4.87)		(−3.48)
Distance_US								
Political risk			0.977	0.248	0.355	−0.221	1.297*	0.541
			(1.57)	(0.45)	(0.62)	(−0.48)	(1.67)	(0.83)
Exchange rate			−0.156**	−0.063			−0.111	−0.006
			(−2.39)	(−1.12)			(−1.62)	(−0.11)
FTA					1.829**	3.068***	1.914**	2.981***
					(2.40)	(5.33)	(2.17)	(3.48)
BIT					2.049***	2.053***	2.065***	2.563***
					(2.58)	(3.36)	(3.24)	(5.89)
Constant	18.90***	35.75***	22.66***	44.20***	16.14***	32.91***	15.48**	37.19***
	(2.82)	(4.31)	(4.42)	(3.78)	(2.59)	(5.57)	(2.10)	(5.57)
N	262	262	198	198	198	198	174	174

Note: t statistics in parentheses; * $p < .1$, ** $p < 0.05$, *** $p < 0.01$.

Table 19.2 Fixed Effect Models of the Determinants of COFDI to OBOR Countries

Variable	(1)	(2)	(3)	(4)	(5)	(6)	(7)	(8)
Lagged COFDI	0.000002	−0.000003	−0.000002	−0.000001	−0.000001	−0.0000003	−0.000003	−0.000002
	(0.02)	(−0.41)	(−0.38)	(−0.14)	(−0.37)	(−0.06)	(−0.51)	(−0.24)
GDP	−0.113	−0.0787	−0.0933	−0.242*	−0.107	−0.282**	−0.417***	−0.354**
	(−0.84)	(−0.64)	(−0.50)	(−1.77)	(−0.63)	(−2.45)	(−2.81)	(−2.36)
GDP per capita	0.0001	0.0001	0.0001*	0.0001*	0.0001*	0.00004	0.0002***	0.0001**
	(0.63)	(1.48)	(2.02)	(1.85)	(1.86)	(1.38)	(3.85)	(2.07)
Trade openness	−0.016*	−0.016**	−0.021**	−0.018**	−0.016**	−0.011*	−0.014*	−0.012
	(−1.86)	(−2.20)	(−2.68)	(−2.61)	(−2.54)	(−1.90)	(−2.02)	(−1.54)
Distance	0	0	0	0	0	0	0	0
	(.)	(.)	(.)	(.)	(.)	(.)	(.)	(.)
Language	0	0	0	0	0	0	0	0
	(.)	(.)	(.)	(.)	(.)	(.)	(.)	(.)
Political stability	0.647	0.726					1.344	0.820
	(0.78)	(0.89)					(1.16)	(0.77)
Rule of law	0.313	−0.363					−0.186	−0.503
	(0.16)	(−0.22)					(−0.06)	(−0.18)
Regime type	0.066	0.025					0.036	0.023
	(0.75)	(0.27)					(0.56)	(0.49)
Natural resource	0.025*	0.030***	0.025	0.048**	−0.006	0.033*	0.053	0.041
	(1.92)	(3.25)	(0.77)	(2.20)	(−0.17)	(1.82)	(1.55)	(1.65)
Rents								
Ideal point distance_China	−3.067***	−4.132***	−4.479***	−3.580***	−3.559***	−3.555***	−4.786***	
	(−3.05)	(−5.11)	(−4.08)	(−6.48)	(−3.23)	(−6.42)	(−4.42)	
Ideal point distance_US								−3.517***
								(−3.20)

	(1)	(2)	(3)	(4)	(5)	(6)	(7)	(8)
Political risk			1.809**	1.248**	0.972	0.570	1.498*	0.519
			(2.44)	(2.37)	(1.15)	(1.23)	(1.84)	(0.82)
Exchange rate			−0.985***	−0.353			−0.934***	−0.348
			(−3.47)	(−0.96)			(−2.98)	(−0.95)
FTA					2.138**	2.372***	2.106*	2.616**
					(2.29)	(3.22)	(1.80)	(2.68)
BIT					1.758**	1.955**	2.333***	2.695***
					(2.35)	(2.38)	(4.11)	(5.08)
Constant	13.40***	23.11***	16.06***	25.51***	11.11**	22.62***	19.99***	23.80***
	(3.74)	(5.90)	(3.44)	(6.85)	(2.66)	(7.05)	(5.01)	(5.91)
N	262	262	198	198	198	198	174	174
r2	0.120	0.224	0.268	0.339	0.267	0.400	0.373	0.362
F	2.038	5.851	7.966	15.90	8.309	14.20	28.26	48.15

Note: t statistics in parentheses; * $p < .1$, ** $p < 0.05$, *** $p < 0.01$.

and 2. Statistical tests yield no evidence that COFDI is more likely to be attracted to countries with weak institutions. Instead, the positive and statistically significant relationship between *political risk* and COFDI in model 7 in Table 19.1 and models 3, 4, and 7 in Table 19.2 points to the possibility that Chinese investors do indeed take into consideration property rights protection in making investment decisions in a way that is not unlike the pattern found in general studies of FDI. In addition, the results lend support to arguments emphasizing the politically driven nature of Chinese outward investment. COFDI has indeed been less likely to flow to countries with which it has a greater ideal point distance. *Ideal point distance_China* has the expected negative sign and is statistically significant in most model specifications in Tables 1 and 2. Somewhat counterintuitively, *ideal point distance_US* also shows up as having a negative and statistically significant relationship with COFDI across model specifications in Tables 1 and 2. This is in contrast to the expectation that COFDI should be more likely to flow to a host country whose values and priorities tend to align closer with Washington than with Beijing.

Consistent with expectations, test results point to a generally positive and statistically significant relationship between GDP per capita and COFDI, suggesting that COFDI has indeed been more likely to be drawn to countries with large internal markets. However, the results indicate that Chinese investors may be less concerned about the host country's market size in their siting decisions. Another puzzling result is that there is generally a negative and statistically significant relationship between the host country's trade openness and COFDI. Overall, the above results at best lend mixed support to arguments emphasizing the market-seeking motivation behind COFDI.

The results in Table 19.1 also suggest that distance tends to deter COFDI and that language affinity facilitates COFDI flows. They further suggest that a depreciation of the Chinese currency discourages COFDI flows. Also in line with expectations, international economic agreements such as FTAs and BITs boost outward FDI flows by signalling the partner country's commitment to liberal economic policies, increasing both the economic and reputational costs of noncompliance, or offering the prospect of impartial third-party dispute resolution. Finally, the results suggest that the host country's political stability, rule of law, and regime type do not play any role in influencing COFDI as these variables are broadly insignificant.

V. Robustness Checks

A couple of robustness checks are conducted in order to increase our confidence in the validity of the results. First, the study employs several alternative measures of political relations, including both conventional measures of voting similarly with China (voting affinity_China) and the United States (voting affinity_US) as well as the number of diplomatic meetings between Chinese leaders and their foreign counterparts in a given year (*diplomatic meeting*) to further assess the influence of political relations on COFDI. The use of *diplomatic meeting* as an alternative measure of political relations is warranted because it is reasonable to expect that Chinese leaders should be more likely to hold diplomatic meetings with leaders of those countries to which they attach greater strategic priority, whether political or economic. If Chinese FDI is intended to promote shared diplomatic understanding and strengthen China's relations with its strategic partners, then we should expect *diplomatic meeting* to take on a positive relationship with the main dependent variable. Data for *diplomatic meeting* is taken from *China Vitae*, which tracks the appearances and travel of up to 200 leading Chinese officials.[38]

Tables 19.3 to 19.5 present results using each of these alternative measures of political relations, with columns 1-4 in each of these Tables presenting results of random-effect models and columns 5-8 presenting results of fixed-effect models. Estimation results once again corroborate the main findings. While voting affinity_China did not achieve statistical significance in any of the model specifications, both diplomatic meeting and voting affinity_US show up as having the expected positive sign and are statistically significant across model specifications.

Secondly, previous studies of FDI emphasize the importance of running separate analyses for developed and developing countries in order to avoid spurious findings.[39] Following the lead of these earlier studies, the study divides the sample into two sub-samples, one for more developed countries with a GDP per capita of no less than US$12,000 a year, one for lower-income countries with a GDP per capita of less than US$12,000 a year. Estimation results, which are not shown here, are once again consistent with those reported above.[40] Both Ideal point distance_China and Ideal point distance_US have retained their negative and statistically significant effect on COFDI in most model specifications. Taken together, these results indicate that the finding regarding the importance of political relations in shaping COFDI flows is not driven by the particular sub-sample under consideration.

VI. Conclusion

The above analysis of the political economy of Chinese investment in OBOR countries reveals both similarities and differences with the general pattern of COFDI emphasized by previous research. Consistent with previous findings, this study yields substantial evidence suggesting that Chinese investors do indeed tend to seek out locales with rich natural resources. There is also no evidence that Chinese investment is more likely to be attracted to countries with weak institutions. Instead, there is some evidence, albeit limited, of a positive relationship between the host country's institutional environment and COFDI. In other words, Chinese investors may be increasingly averse to political risks in the host country in a way that is consistent with the pattern found in general studies of FDI. It is possible that property rights protection may be becoming an increasingly important concern of Chinese investors with the expansion of the scale of Chinese investment and this may be even more pronounced in a region known for its political and economic instability and thus the inherent risks posed to foreign investors.

Also consistent with previous findings about COFDI[41] (e.g. Li and Liang 2012), the above analysis yields considerable evidence pointing to the importance of political

---

[38] Data available at www.chinavitae.com/vip/ (last accessed 30 June 2015).
[39] Bruce A Blonigen and Miao Grace Wang, 'Inappropriate pooling of wealthy and poor countries in empirical FDI studies' *NBER Working Paper* 10378; Quan Li and Tatiana Vashchilko, 'Dyadic Military Conflict, Security Alliances, and Bilateral FDI Flows' (2010) 41 Journal of International Business Studies 765; Li and Liang (n 3).
[40] These results are available from the author upon request.
[41] Li and Liang (n 2).

Table 19.3 Regression Analysis Using Voting Affinity with China as an Alternative Measure of Political Relations

Variable	(1)	(2)	(3)	(4)	(5)	(6)	(7)	(8)
	Random-Effect Models				Fixed-Effect Models			
Lagged COFDI	0.00001	0.00001	0.00001*	0.000003	0.000001	0.000003	0.000003	0.000002
	(0.52)	(1.03)	(1.70)	(0.35)	(0.16)	(0.59)	(0.80)	(0.13)
GDP	0.107	0.137	0.003	-0.203	-0.053	-0.080	-0.117	-0.414**
	(0.78)	(0.73)	(0.02)	(-1.32)	(-0.36)	(-0.43)	(-0.72)	(-2.63)
GDP per capita	0.00002	0.00004*	0.00004**	0.00003	0.0001	0.0001**	0.0001**	0.0002***
	(0.82)	(1.71)	(2.14)	(0.89)	(0.87)	(2.62)	(2.42)	(3.51)
Trade Openness	-0.009	-0.009**	-0.00282	-0.005	-0.017*	-0.020**	-0.014**	-0.013*
	(-1.55)	(-1.99)	(-0.72)	(-1.11)	(-1.97)	(-2.45)	(-2.07)	(-1.73)
Distance	-2.648***	-2.993***	-1.937**	-1.866**	0	0	0	0
	(-3.38)	(-3.61)	(-2.55)	(-2.27)	(.)	(.)	(.)	(.)
Language	4.252**	3.178**	1.704	2.370	0	0	0	0
	(2.04)	(2.16)	(1.40)	(1.42)	(.)	(.)	(.)	(.)
Natural resource rents	0.020**	0.019	0.035**	0.036*	0.023*	0.010	-0.015	0.023
	(2.01)	(1.30)	(2.09)	(1.77)	(1.73)	(0.37)	(-0.54)	(0.68)
Political stability	0.605			0.468	0.762			0.941
	(1.16)			(0.67)	(0.87)			(0.82)
Rule of law	-0.823			-1.232	-0.601			-0.982
	(-1.28)			(-0.93)	(-0.31)			(-0.31)
Regime type	0.015			-0.025	0.066			0.038
	(0.31)			(-0.58)	(0.75)			(0.77)
Voting affinity China	-1.184	-0.415	-2.143	-2.740	-7.864	-8.701	-8.979	-6.683
	(-1.14)	(-0.30)	(-1.57)	(-1.79)	(-1.75)	(-1.58)	(-1.78)	(-1.20)

	(1)	(2)	(3)	(4)	(5)	(6)	(7)	(8)
Political risk	0.399	−0.175	0.788			1.271*	0.495	1.023
	(0.64)	(−0.30)	(1.04)			(1.77)	(0.67)	(1.39)
Exchange rate	−0.111*		−0.043			−0.759**		−0.675*
	(−1.95)		(−0.73)			(−2.19)		(−2.00)
FTA		2.449***	2.565***				2.512**	2.405**
		(3.43)	(2.92)				(2.67)	(2.15)
BIT		2.118***	2.454***				2.354*	3.142***
		(3.01)	(4.88)				(1.89)	(5.40)
Constant	27.94***	29.61***	21.65***	26.68***	16.52***	19.17***	15.31**	20.47***
	(3.87)	(4.06)	(3.60)	(3.99)	(3.24)	(2.86)	(2.51)	(3.29)
N	262	198	198	174	262	198	198	174
r2					0.093	0.203	0.255	0.298
F					1.714	5.019	5.377	132.4

Note: t statistics in parentheses; * $p < .1$, ** $p < 0.05$, *** $p < 0.01$.

Table 19.4 Regression Analysis Using Voting Affinity with the US as an Alternative Measure of Political Relations

Variable	(1)	(2)	(3)	(4)	(5)	(6)	(7)	(8)
	Random-effect Models				Fixed-effect models			
Lagged COFDI	0.000002	0.000002	0.000003	0.000001	-0.000004	-0.000003	-0.000002	-0.000003
	(0.26)	(0.42)	(0.73)	(0.13)	(-0.45)	(-0.48)	(-0.43)	(-0.44)
GDP	0.130	0.0560	-0.106	-0.164	-0.0401	-0.214	-0.248*	-0.341**
	(1.03)	(0.33)	(-0.79)	(-1.14)	(-0.32)	(-1.55)	(-2.01)	(-2.13)
GDP per capita	0.00003	0.00002	0.00001	0.00003	0.00005	0.00004	0.00003	0.0002**
	(1.05)	(1.17)	(0.90)	(0.83)	(1.08)	(1.27)	(0.93)	(2.42)
Trade openness	-0.009*	-0.009*	-0.003	-0.005	-0.016**	-0.017**	-0.011**	-0.013*
	(-1.71)	(-1.79)	(-0.64)	(-1.10)	(-2.08)	(-2.70)	(-2.07)	(-1.89)
Distance	-3.407***	-4.032***	-2.446***	-2.495***	0	0	0	0
	(-4.22)	(-3.75)	(-3.51)	(-3.13)	(.)	(.)	(.)	(.)
Language	5.148**	4.379**	2.348	2.805*	0	0	0	0
	(2.39)	(2.42)	(1.59)	(1.66)	(.)	(.)	(.)	(.)
Natural resource rents	0.025**	0.042***	0.059***	0.042**	0.029***	0.044**	0.029**	0.038*
	(2.51)	(2.67)	(3.63)	(2.14)	(3.11)	(2.52)	(2.14)	(1.82)
Political stability	0.480			0.253	0.716			0.694
	(0.92)			(0.41)	(0.90)			(0.72)
Rule of law	-1.027*			-1.081	-0.438			-0.679
	(-1.65)			(-0.87)	(-0.26)			(-0.24)
Regime type	-0.033			-0.062	0.033			0.016
	(-0.63)			(-1.39)	(0.35)			(0.32)
Voting affinity_US	3.225***	3.335***	3.872***	3.807***	5.344***	5.247***	5.056***	4.758**
	(3.01)	(3.80)	(4.96)	(2.98)	(3.57)	(5.63)	(5.48)	(2.72)
Political risk		0.385	0.0129	0.724		1.552**	0.936*	1.022
		(0.70)	(0.03)	(1.09)		(2.72)	(1.90)	(1.57)

Exchange rate	-0.070		-0.027		-0.280		-0.344
	(-1.50)		(-0.53)		(-0.80)		(-1.06)
FTA		2.692***	2.604***			2.120**	2.261**
		(4.37)	(3.16)			(2.34)	(2.08)
BIT		2.009***	2.314***			1.913*	2.589***
		(4.08)	(5.60)			(2.00)	(4.38)
Constant	34.59***	28.73***	30.87***	12.60***	16.90***	14.14***	15.74***
	(4.65)	(5.35)	(5.00)	(3.94)	(4.94)	(4.62)	(4.44)
N	262	198	174	262	198	198	174
r2				0.192	0.339	0.390	0.349
F				3.521	14.15	11.69	31.58

Note: t statistics in parentheses; * $p < .1$, ** $p < 0.05$, *** $p < 0.01$.

Table 19.5 Regression Analysis Using Diplomatic Meeting as an Alternative Measure of Political Relations

Variable	(1)	(2)	(3)	(4)	(5)	(6)	(7)	(8)
	Random-effect models				Fixed-effect models			
Lagged COFDI	0.00001 (-0.72)	0.000004 (-0.32)	0.00002 (-0.13)	0.00001 (-1.47)	0.00001 (-0.97)	0.00001 (-0.45)	0.00001 (-0.67)	0.00001 (-1.25)
GDP	0.102 (0.70)	0.140 (0.74)	0.019 (0.11)	-0.199 (-1.13)	-0.051 (-0.27)	-0.025 (-0.10)	-0.067 (-0.32)	-0.333** (-2.13)
GDP per capita	0.000002 (0.10)	0.00003 (1.46)	0.00004** (2.20)	0.00002 (0.60)	0.0002** (2.08)	0.0002** (2.56)	0.0001** (2.26)	0.0002* (1.98)
Trade openness	-0.011 (-1.32)	-0.011 (-1.62)	-0.005 (-0.90)	-0.007 (-0.84)	-0.023* (-2.02)	-0.023* (-1.93)	-0.015 (-1.52)	-0.008 (-1.05)
Distance	-1.673*** (-2.91)	-2.427*** (-3.12)	-1.612* (-1.69)	-0.800 (-0.83)	0 (.)	0 (.)	0 (.)	0 (.)
Language	2.076*** (2.73)	1.804*** (3.04)	0.460 (0.75)	0.407 (0.36)	0 (.)	0 (.)	0 (.)	0 (.)
Natural resource rents	0.038** (2.38)	0.029 (1.58)	0.017 (0.88)	0.051*** (3.03)	0.035 (1.32)	0.049* (1.79)	0.011 (0.37)	0.063** (2.82)
Political stability	0.351 (0.62)			0.526 (0.55)	0.675 (0.67)			2.163 (1.47)
Rule of law	-0.869 (-1.20)			-1.084 (-0.60)	-1.100 (-0.53)			-2.583 (-0.77)
Regime type	0.024 (0.50)			0.045 (1.30)	0.038 (0.39)			0.0671 (0.86)
Diplomatic meeting	0.092*** (4.06)	0.104*** (3.50)	0.086*** (2.91)	0.091*** (2.68)	0.085*** (3.20)	0.096*** (3.09)	0.085** (2.77)	0.075** (2.53)
Political risk		0.326 (0.55)	0.313 (0.58)	0.865 (1.06)		1.248 (1.51)	0.356 (0.41)	0.741 (0.83)

	(1)	(2)	(3)	(4)	(5)	(6)	(7)
Exchange rate	−0.098*		−0.071		−0.908**		−0.749*
	(−1.96)		(−1.48)		(−2.39)		(−1.82)
FTA		1.958**	2.319**			2.727**	3.014**
		(2.55)	(2.38)			(2.48)	(2.09)
BIT		2.160***	1.697**			1.997**	2.442***
		(3.27)	(2.41)			(2.25)	(3.34)
Constant	18.68***	17.04***	15.82***	8.829**	9.689*	5.779	12.74***
	(3.60)	(2.69)	(2.16)	(2.06)	(1.83)	(1.28)	(3.60)
N	211	168	148	211	168	168	148
r2				0.132	0.213	0.246	0.357
F				2.824	4.863	23.44	122.0

Note: t statistics in parentheses; * $p < .1$, ** $p < 0.05$, *** $p < 0.01$.

relations between China and the host country as an important determinant of COFDI. The finding that Chinese investment tends to be destined to countries with which it enjoys good political relations lends support to previous arguments that either emphasize the role of cooperative interstate relations in stabilizing investor expectations of the host country investment environment or the influence of geopolitical considerations on China's outward FDI policy.

Furthermore, not only has Chinese investment been more likely to flow to countries with shared diplomatic goals and agendas, it has also been drawn to countries with shared values and preferences with the US. This is in contrast to the expectation that Chinese investment to the host country should decline as its ideal point increasingly moves away from China and converges with the United States. While inconclusive, the preliminary evidence hints at the possibility that COFDI may be seeking out not only countries that traditionally are drawn to the China-centric international order, but also those whose policy stance has historically aligned closer to that of the US in order to expand the constellation of forces in favour of the Sino-centric pattern of trade, investment, and infrastructure development in the region.

Taken together, the above results are consistent with conventional interpretations of China's OBOR policy that emphasize the central role of the state in guiding foreign direct investment. They suggest that despite the growing importance of non-state-owned enterprises for COFDI (Shi 2015), the state may have retained its commanding heights over a strategic initiative such as OBOR and may have sought to achieve important objectives such as ensuring access to natural resources and promoting China's diplomatic relations with its regional partners. While the above conclusions are mostly based on a study of COFDI to OBOR countries before the formal launch of the initiatives, they should nevertheless have implications for understanding the trajectory of Chinese investment in OBOR countries in the future. As a study of the locational determinants of COFDI in OBOR countries, the research should also help to illuminate the host country characteristics that influence COFDI flows not only in China's immediate neighbourhood, but also in regions further away from home. As such, it shows how the bilateral, regional, and global tracks of China's investment policy may intersect one another in shaping Beijing's commercial interactions with its partner countries in the present era.

20

China's Role and Interest in Central Asia
China–Pakistan Economic Corridor

Manzoor Ahmad*

I. Introduction

Since the dissolution of the Soviet Union, China has assumed a greater role and influence in the Central Asian states, which include Kazakhstan, Kyrgyzstan, Tajikistan, Turkmenistan, and Uzbekistan. Over the last fifteen years, Chinese trade with the region jumped from US$1.5 billion to over US$50 billion and it has become the most important economic investor in the region. Most of these investments are for harnessing natural resources such as gas and oil through building of pipelines and development of transportation infrastructure such as roads, railways, and tunnels, but they also include agri-business and telecommunications networks.

China has also been making huge investments in other Central and Western Asian countries such as Azerbaijan, Georgia, Mongolia, Armenia, and Turkey but the scope of this chapter is limited to the above five Central Asian states and Pakistan.

With the announcement of the land-based 'Silk Road Economic Belt (SREB)' and the ocean-going 'Maritime Silk Road (MSR)' initiatives in Autumn 2013, previously known as 'One Belt, One Road (OBOR)' and now called the Belt and Road Initiative (BRI), this relationship has taken a much greater significance.[1] In fact, the 'Belt' originally targeted only Central Asia. However, now this concept includes not only the Central Asian countries on the original Silk Road but also extends to the Middle East and Europe. On the other hand, 'Road' links China's port facilities with the African coast, pushing up through the Suez Canal into the Mediterranean.

The Central Asian investments as well as the China –Pakistan Economic Corridor (CPEC) constitute important components of China's three-pronged investment strategy comprising bilateral, regional, and global tracks. These initiatives belong to all the three tracks by design and intention. They not only ensure supply of energy resources from and through the nearest bordering countries avoiding the bottlenecked chokepoint of the Strait of Malacca and the contentious South China Sea but also enable China to become connected to Europe, the Middle East, and Africa through alternative routes.

The BRI draws its inspiration from two historical routes: one of them being a network of trade routes, formally established during the Han Dynasty of China, which was used regularly from 130 BCE to 1453 CE, while the other related to the Chinese

---

* Senior Fellow, International Centre for Trade and Sustainable Development (ICTSD), Geneva.
[1] See Julien Chaisse and Mitsuo Matsushita, 'China's "Belt and Road" Initiative: Mapping the World Trade Normative and Strategic Implications' (2018) 52(1) Journal of World Trade 163.

China's Role and Interest in Central Asia: China–Pakistan Economic Corridor. Manzoor Ahmad.
© Manzoor Ahmad, 2019. Published 2019 by Oxford University Press.

admiral Zheng He's naval expeditions to the African east coast during the Ming Dynasty (1368–1644).

So far, sixty-five countries with potentially 4.4 billion people, or about 70 per cent of the global population, which generates roughly 55 per cent of global GNP and holds an estimated 75 per cent of known energy reserves, have shown their willingness to be partners in these initiatives.[2] The project envisages six economic corridors including China–Mongolia–Russia, New Eurasian Land Bridge, China–Central Asia–West Asia, China–Pakistan, Bangladesh–China–India–Myanmar and China–Indochina.[3]

BRI has been described by some as a modern day Marshall Plan since both programmes have many parallels in their scope and objectives. But there are important differences as well. The total amount of aid provided under the Marshall Plan was US$13 billion, which is equivalent to roughly US$100 billion today.[4] BRI is several times larger and more ambitious. Secondly, BRI is financed mostly through loans whereas the Marshal Plan was predominantly based on aid or even foreign direct investment. Thirdly, whereas the Marshall Plan spanned over a short period of four years, BRI's time frame is thirty-five years. Furthermore, unlike the Marshall Plan, which was intended to prevent spread of communism in Europe, BRI has no ideological underpinnings.

II. Notable Projects in Central Asia

There are a large number of projects in varying degrees of progress in almost all the Central Asian countries. In the last fifteen years, investment and trade of US$1 billion has swelled to US$50 billion in the region. Some of the more significant cross-border projects consist of gas pipelines, new railways, and highways.

Since 2006, China has been investing heavily in building gas transportation infrastructure. Three Central Asia–China Gas pipelines, known as A, B, and C have already been built. These start from Turkmenistan and go through Uzbekistan and Kazakhstan to the Xinjiang region of China. Each of each these three pipelines is more than 1,800 km in length. These currently allow for the export of around 55 billion cubic meters of gas annually—an amount equivalent to one-fifth of China's consumption. Lines A and B are able to carry 13 billion cubic meters of gas from the Chinese-run Amu Darya Project at Turkmenistan's Bagtyyarlyk field and another 17 billion cubic meters of gas sourced by Turkmengaz itself. Line C supplies a mix of gas from Turkmenistan (10 billion cubic meters), Uzbekistan (10 billion cubic meters), and Kazakhstan (5 billion cubic meters). China had started working on the 4th, or Line D, which would have been the longest and the most expensive of the China–Central Asia pipelines covering over 7,000 km. It was intended to go through Uzbekistan, Tajikistan, and Kyrgyzstan, thus diversifying the route and promising substantial royalties to these countries. However, currently further work on this has been delayed and the most recent reports suggest commissioning by the end of 2022.

The Silk Road high-speed railway, which will link Kazakhstan, the Kyrgyz Republic, Uzbekistan, Turkmenistan, and Iran with the Xinjiang region, is an enormous project.

---

[2] Gisela Grieger, 'One Belt, One Road (OBOR): China's Regional Integration Initiative' (2016) European Parliament Research Service PE586.608.

[3] See map, 'The Belt and Road Initiative: Six Economic Corridors Spanning Asia, Europe and Africa', HKTDC Research http://china-trade-research.hktdc.com/business-news/article/The-Belt-and-Road-Initiative/The-Belt-and-Road-Initiative/obor/en/1/1X000000/1X0A36B7.htm.

[4] Simon Shen, 'How China's "Belt and Road" Compares to the Marshall Plan: Should we think of "One Belt, One Road" as China's Marshall Plan?' *The Diplomat* (2016).

The network could eventually be extended further to Turkey and beyond into Europe. Already a 344 km long railway line for a high-speed bullet train connecting Tashkent and Samarkand in Uzbekistan has been built. This high-speed rail network links with northwest China's Gansu and Qinghai provinces, as well as the Xinjiang Uygur Autonomous Region.

Salient features of other Chinese involvement and its role in the economic development of various Central Asian countries are summarized below.

A. Kazakhstan

Amongst the Central Asian countries, Kazakhstan shares the longest border (1,533 km) with China. It was here in September 2013 where the Chinese president Xi Jingping announced the launch of the 'Silk Road Economic Belt' that Kazakhstan has emerged as China's most significant trade and investment partner in the region with bilateral trade exceeding US$25 billion, and investment now worth US$23.6 billion. Currently about 700 Chinese companies are working in Kazakhstan, which represents a 35 per cent increase over 2013.

Most of the investment is for harnessing Kazakhstan's major natural resources such as oil, natural gas, and minerals, including uranium, and is concentrated in the Western (Aktau, Atyrau, Aktobe) and southern regions of the country. In order to supply construction materials for all these activities, Chinese companies are also active in production and supply of construction materials. A railway line from Khorgos on the Chinese border to the Caspian Sea port of Aktau is being built with the support of China. In addition, an investment of US$2.7 billion is planned for modernizing locomotives, freight, and passenger cars and repairing 725 kilometres of railway track. Construction of a Western Europe–Western China motorway is another major undertaking. A dry port on the China–Kazakh border known as Khorgos Gateway was made operational in August 2015 and is expected to become a major cargo hub with an investment of US$600 million over five years. Through all these measures, Kazakhstan is aiming to become a key transit route between Europe and China and expects that 7 per cent of China's export goods to Europe will travel via Kazakhstan by 2020.

Other major investments are in the telecommunications market (supply of telecommunication solutions, installation of equipment, and various communication services). Another priority area is agriculture, where investments worth US$1.9 billion are envisaged.

Most of the investments are through 'tied loans' from Chinese banks but this investment is based on two key conditions—mandatory involvement of Chinese contractors in a project and state guarantees of return of financing.[5]

China and Kazakhstan are jointly implementing fifty-two industrial, logistical projects collectively worth around US$24 billion.

B. Kyrgyzstan

Although Kyrgyzstan has an 858 km common border with China, there were no transport links between the two countries till the independence of Kyrgyzstan in 1991. Since then Chinese investment in Kyrgyzstan has been growing rapidly and currently

---

[5] Yerzhan Yessimkhano, 'Kazakhstan: Activities of Chinese Companies in Kazakhstan, Central Asia Azerbaijan and Eastern Europe' *Grata International* www.gratanet.com/uploads/user_11/files/client_note_Yessimkhanov.pdf.

it amounts to about one third of the total investment made in the country. China has committed to investing US$3 billion in several energy projects including Kara-Balta oil refinery. Negotiations are underway for building two key hydropower projects which would generate around 4.6 billion kilowatt hours of power annually; which is equal to the current output of the country's biggest existing hydropower station at Toktogul. The high-voltage power lines from the south to north completed in 2015 have made Kyrgyzstan independent of its neighbours, as previously such supply lines passed through other countries.

China is also financing an US$850 million North–South route, which will connect Kyrgyzstan with Kazakhstan and Tajikistan. About 500 km of the railway line linking China with Uzbekistan will be passing though Kyrgyzstan and would involve Chinese investment of US$6 billion. This is expected to earn about US$200 million per year in royalties from the transit of goods through the Kyrgyz territory. China is also assisting in setting up several industrial units and relocating some of its own surplus manufacturing capacity. Construction of a new cardboard and paper mill is under way.

C. Tajikistan

Tajikistan shares over 400 km long borders with the Xinjiang region of China. In 2015, Chinese direct investment into Tajikistan was US$273 million or about 58 per cent of the total. The most notable projects already completed are the Dushanbe–Chanak highway, power lines, and hydropower plants. China is now setting up several industries at an estimated cost of US$500 million. Already a metal processing plant in the northern town of Istiqlol has been established at a cost US$200 million dollars. The Central Asia–China gas pipeline, when completed, will greatly benefit Tajikistan from transit revenue and improved energy security.

D. Turkmenistan

Turkmenistan used to be solely dependent on Russia for exports of its gas but since 2006, the situation has started changing. Now it is one of the main recipients of Chinese investment among the Central Asian republics. China financed the construction of the US$7.3 billion Turkmenistan–China gas pipeline. This is 3,666 km long and runs from the Turkmenistan/Uzbekistan border to Jingbian in China. Now China is the largest buyer of Turkmenistan gas.

E. Uzbekistan

China recently overtook Russia to become Uzbekistan's largest bilateral trading partner, with US$3 billion worth of trade. The most significant investment to date has been the aforementioned 344 km long railway line for the high-speed bullet train connecting Tashkent and Samarkand. The 19.2 km railway tunnel linking Ferghana Valley with the rest of the country is the largest of its kind anywhere in Central Asia and is also the biggest Chinese-led project ever completed in the region. China is also relocating some of its factories to Uzbekistan. Already telecoms companies Huawei and ZTE have established assembly plants there, while the Xuzhou Construction Machinery Group (XCMG) is also building a factory in the country.[6]

---

[6] Raffaello Pantucci, 'China's Place in Central Asia' *Eurasianet.org* (2016) www.eurasianet.org/node/79306.

III. Why Is China Undertaking this Huge Task?

There are many economic and political reasons and some of the more important ones are listed below.

First, when the 21st century mega-regional trade agreements were being negotiated from 2010 onwards, they included all major economies, that is, the United States, Europe, and Japan but excluding China. For example, the Transatlantic Trade and Investment Partnership (TTIP) was to be a free trade agreement between the EU and the US. Similarly, the Trans-Pacific Partnership was to involve three countries of North America with the nine richest economies of the Asia-Pacific region, excluding China. In response, China developed this plan so as to be at the centre of global trade.

Secondly, China's economic growth has recently been slowing down due to sluggish global demand. There is over-capacity in several industries such as iron and steel, electrolytic aluminium, cement, plate glasses, and vessels.[7] China's interest is in stimulating exports from such industries and to move some of them to other countries but as a part of China-centred production networks. Through this initiative, China is aiming at an annual trade worth US$2.5 trillion within ten years.

Thirdly, BRI will provide alternative routes to China for transportation of goods, energy products and communication, including information technology. Currently over 80 per cent of Chinese imports and energy supplies pass through the Strait of Malacca in the South China Sea. Establishing alternative trade routes mitigates risk for China.

Fourthly, China would be able to improve the prosperity of its lagging areas and promote equality within the country. Due to the prevailing inequality, there has been massive inter-regional migration from rural to urban areas and from North and Western China towards better-developed coastal areas.

Fifthly, it will promote the economic well-being of its close allies such as Pakistan and other countries, which already have active bilateral relationships with China.

Sixthly, it would be easier for China to move some of its domestic industrial production overcapacity to the neighbouring countries.

Seventhly, thanks to trade surpluses and capital inflows, China's reserves have multiplied almost twenty-fold from 2001 to peak at US$3.99 trillion in June 2014. Building regional infrastructure and industrial zones is a good investment.

Eighthly, this would enable China to make its currency more international to reflect its share of global trade, as is the case with the US dollar and the euro.

Finally, by bolstering the economic well-being of the region and having greater political influence, China hopes to stabilize its own restive western provinces and unstable neighbouring countries, such as Pakistan and Afghanistan.

A. Financing mechanism

There are two major funding mechanism for BRI: Silk Road Infrastructure Fund amounting to US$40 billion capitalized mainly by China's foreign exchange reserves and the Asian Infrastructure Investment Bank (AIIB), with registered capital of US$100 billion. This capital base makes it more than twice as large as the European

---

[7] World Trade Organization, 'Trade Policy Review: China' (Report by the Secretariat, WT/TPR/S/342, 2016) Trade Policy Review Body www.wto.org/english/tratop_e/tpr_e/s342_sum_e.pdf.

Bank for Reconstruction and Development. While the Silk Road Fund is exclusively being funded by China, the Bank has eighty-seven member states including nineteen prospective members. The AIIB, together with other China-led initiatives, such as the New Development Bank (NDB) and Contingent Reserve Arrangement (CRA), has a combined capital base of US$250 billion, which is roughly on a par with the World Bank.

IV. The China–Pakistan Economic Corridor

The China Pakistan Economic Corridor or CPEC is one of the six economic corridors included in the BRI initiative. It was formally announced in November 2014, but has been under consideration for several years. In fact, it builds on the Karakoram Highway linking northwest China (Xinjiang Province) and Pakistan, constructed from 1959 to 1979 and Gwadar, a port on the Arabian Sea constructed from 2002 to 2006. Linking these two infrastructures and developing industrial zones along the routes will be the cornerstone of CPEC. The overall time schedule is estimated at fifteen years in a phased manner. While most of energy and Gwadar development projects are expected to be completed on priority as 'early harvest' by 2020, the rail and water projects are expected in the last stage of the project.

Seen in the light of China's three-pronged investment strategy i.e., Bilateral, Regional, and Global Tracks, CPEC is more a part of the bilateral track, all projects within it being bilateral between China and Pakistan. However, at the same time it also promises to morph into an undertaking with regional importance, since China's declared intentions have been to involve other regional powers in it. The fact that the power project at Port Qasim near Karachi completed in November 2017 was jointly developed by the Power China Resources Limited and Qatar's Al-Mirqab Capital with a total investment of over US$2 billion shows the openness of this initiative to other countries. Furthermore, China has already invited all the countries of the region to join CPEC, and has received positive responses from Iran, Afghanistan, Russia, some Central Asian countries, Saudi Arabia, Gulf States, and Turkey. Several European countries including the UK and France have declared their intention to invest in the project. Thus, CPEC is a perfect embodiment of all the three tracks of China's investment strategies.

The project envisages construction of new roads, rail, ports, pipeline, and optical fibre networks through the 3,200 km long corridor (about 2,400 km in Pakistan and 800 km in China). The project also envisages building a number of new electricity generating facilities, which are expected to provide up to 16,400 MW and forty-one industrial estates. This promises to herald Pakistan into a brighter future. In addition, it will provide additional routes for China's energy imports from the Middle East—to reduce its dependence on sea routes.

CPEC would also enable Pakistan to capitalize on its strategic location, being at the junction of South Asia, Central Asia, China, and the Middle East, for its economic benefit. The seaports of Pakistan will provide the shortest routes to link China and Central Asian countries with the rest of the world although at present hardly any transit trade passes through them. CPEC could change all this.

The first phase consists of energy and infrastructure projects while industrial zones will form part of the second phase. The cost of the various projects is estimated to be US$62 billion. This amount far exceeds what Pakistan got from the US from 1948 to

2016. There is also an important difference. Whereas at least half of the US assistance was for security purposes,[8] CPEC funds are exclusively for economic projects.[9]

Pakistan has suffered colossal losses from terrorism since 9/11, and it has faced serious political instability over many years recently. In addition, chronic energy shortages have had a crippling effect on economy, estimated at 1.5 to 2 per cent of GDP annually. As a result, new foreign direct investment has been drying up (net FDI in 2015 was US$956 million). In such dire circumstances, CPEC has come as a great blessing. Not only it has eliminated or substantially reduced Pakistan's energy deficit, it is expected to give a big boost to the economic development of the country through massive CPEC-related infrastructure projects. The corridor promises to completely change the economic map of Pakistan.

The most significant impact will be in the area of energy, where US$35 billion is expected to be spent. Originally three-fourths, or US$27 billion, was earmarked for coal-based power projects[10] but this has now been changed in favour of gas-powered, hydro-electric, and other alternative energy projects. Several coal-powered projects such as the Muzaffargarh Coal Power Project (1,320 MW), Salt Range Mine Mouth Power Project (300 MW) including mining, Gaddani Power Park (1,320 MW), Sunnec Wind Farm (50 MW), and Chichoki Mallian Combined-cycle Power Plant (525 MW) have been dropped. Although Pakistan has a vast quantity of untouched indigenous lignite reserves—including nearly 200 billion tons alone in the Thar Desert region of Sindh Province, so far no serious effort has been made to exploit these reserves. This is due to huge funding requirements and low quality of these reserves. With the support of CPEC funding, a beginning has been made to exploit this resource. A local company, Sindh Engro Coal Mining Company (SECMC), has achieved financial close for a mine-mouth power plant of 2 x 330 (600 MW). Commercial operations for the first phase are expected to start by mid-2019. When fully operational, it would be mining 20.6 million tons annually and generating 3,960 MW of electricity. The cost for this project is estimated at US$2 billion.

Since the locally produced coal is likely to take several years to be fully operational and the government of Pakistan is keen to ameliorate the energy situation as soon as possible, most of the coal-run projects being set-up are based on imported coal. The first of such projects, Sahiwal 2 x 660 MW Coal-Fired Power Plant, with an estimated cost of US$1.6 billion has already become operational. Another one being built at Port Qasim at an estimated cost of about US$2 billion has become partially operational in November 2017 and is already generating 660 megawatt electricity. Its second unit will also be functional in February 2019.

Significant hydroelectric projects include 720 MW Karot Hydel Power station at a cost of US$1,420 million, 1100 MW Kohal Project costing US$2,397 million and 870 MW Suki-Kinari Hydro project costing US$1,800 million. These are expected to be completed by 2022/2023. CPEC is also covering other alternative sources of energy. For example, China's Zonergy company is constructing one of the world's largest solar power plants—the 6,500 acre Quaid-e-Azam Solar Park near the city of Bahawalpur with an estimated capacity of 1000 MW. Commercial operation of 3 x 100 MW was attained in August 2016. Several wind-power turbines have also been installed in

---

[8] 'Sixty Years of US Aid to Pakistan: Get the Data' *The Guardian* (2011) www.theguardian.com/global-development/poverty-matters/2011/jul/11/us-aid-to-pakistan#data.

[9] See map, 'Major Projects of the China-Pakistan Economic Corridor', Council on Foreign Relations https://www.cfr.org/expert-brief/behind-chinas-gambit-pakistan.

[10] Planning Commission of Pakistan 'CPEC Fact Book'.

Jhimpir (Sind) and some of these are already operational. These include the China–
Pakistan consortium United Energy wind-power plant at a cost of US$659 million and
the Dawood wind power project by HydroChina at a cost of US$115 million.

The energy projects are guaranteed a 17 per cent rate of return in dollar terms on
their equity. The financing would be provided by China Development Bank and China
Exim Bank, who would service the debt from their own earnings without any obligation on the part of the Pakistani government.[11]

After meeting the costs of energy projects, most of the remaining amount of US$16
billion is for building roads, railways, and ports. About US$6 billion has been appor-
tioned for new highways along three routes—eastern, central, and western— which
connect Northern parts of the country with the seaports in the South.[12]

The Eastern route is the main traffic conduit to connect Islamabad to Karachi passing
through populous cities such as Lahore, Faisalabad, Multan, Sukkur, and Hyderabad.
This will mostly involve upgrading existing routes. The Central route starts from
Islamabad and will end in Karachi/Gwadar passing through Darya Khan, Jacobabad
and Khuzdar. The Western route will connect Islamabad with Gwadar via Hasanabdal,
Attock, Dera Ismail Khan, Basima, and Hoshab. The Central as well as Western routes
will be going through less populated areas but have been added to respond to the concerns of smaller provinces of Khyber-Pakhtunkhwa and Baluchistan.

The major railway projects included in the first phase comprise up-gradation and
dualization of Pakistan Railway's 1,872 km main line track (ML1) from Karachi to
Torkham (a border town with Afghanistan). This is currently used for 75 per cent of
railway traffic. This phase would be completed over the next five years at a cost of US$8
billion, of which US$5.5 billion would be a concessional loan from China, while the
Asian Development Bank (ADB) would contribute the remaining US$2.5 billion. In
the next phase, 682 km of new rail tracks will be laid linking Havelian (the north-
ernmost rail station in Pakistan) with Khunjrab (in China). This will be an extremely
challenging and expensive undertaking, as it would require laying of track through a
high mountain pass at an elevation of 4,733 metres above sea level.

In addition, rail-based mass transit projects are to be built in all the four provinces including Lahore Orange Line Train Project (which is likely to be completed by March 2019),
Karachi Circular Railway (KCR), Greater Peshawar Mass Transit, and Quetta Mass Transit.

Besides energy projects, roads, and rails, development of an all-weather deep-water
Gwadar port near the Strait of Hormuz, costing US$793 million, is another major
project. The port was handed over to a Chinese state-owned enterprise in November
2015 until 2059. Although the first commercial cargo vessels started docking at the
port in 2008, the capacity of the port has been very limited with traffic of only half a
million tons in 2016. As the port is developed further, so will be the volume and, when
fully completed, it may process three hundred to four hundred million tons annually.
This port could potentially become even more significant than Dubai because it would
be able to handle larger cargo S-class ships and oil tankers. In addition to handling
transit trade, a number of other projects are also envisaged in the area. The China
Overseas Port Holding Company has already started construction of a US$2 billion
Gwadar Special Economic Zone. It is also planned to make Gwadar port into the Asian
Energy Hub for receipt, storage, processing, and transhipment of energy products.

Most of the infrastructure projects are to be financed through government-to-
government concessional loans at 2 per cent interest to be repaid over a period of

---

[11] Ishrat Husain, 'Financing Burden of CPEC' *The Dawn* (2017).
[12] See map, 'Proposed China-Pakistan Economic Corridor', Deloitte Consulting https://www2.
deloitte.com/content/dam/Deloitte/pk/Documents/risk/pak-china-eco-corridor-deloittepk-noexp.pdf.

twenty to twenty-five years. This debt servicing would be the Pakistan government's obligation. It is estimated that the additional burden on the external account would be US$3 to US$5 billion annually.

Water security is another area where CPEC is likely to be of major help. Of all the challenges Pakistan is facing, water is the most critical. The country is among the leading five that face extremely high water stress and low access to safe drinking water and sanitation. The Pakistani side has been pushing for inclusion of construction of the long-delayed Diamer-Bhasha dam on the Indus River as a part of CPEC. However, considering its high cost (estimated at about US$14 billion), and the Chinese terms and conditions for undertaking this project, as yet it has not been included in the CPEC projects. When, and if completed, the proposed dam has the potential to produce 4,500 MW of electricity in addition to serving as a huge water reservoir for the country.

With the near completion of several energy and infrastructure projects, CPEC is now entering the second phase where industrial development has been planned through setting up of nine special economic zones (SEZs) in Pakistan. These zones are a part of China's policy of promoting manufacturing cooperation in various areas such as petrochemical, steel, textile, leather processing, and construction machinery, etc, with specific reference to relocation of industries from China.

CPEC investments are already showing a positive impact on Pakistan's economy. After going through a serious energy crisis, Pakistan has finally become self-sufficient and there are no power outages as used to be the case for the last ten years. Its GDP growth in FY 2017/18 reached 5.8 per cent, or the highest in the last ten years. After stagnating or falling for several years, exports have finally started growing and in 2017–18, they increased by 12 percent compared to 2016–17.

Growth in imports (driven primarily by CPEC projects) was even stronger at 22.55 per cent to US$19.18 billion in the first four months of the current fiscal year as compared with US$15.65 billion in the same period of the last year.

CPEC will be beneficial to Pakistan but would also greatly benefit China. Trade and energy for China transiting through Pakistan from the Persian Gulf and East African states would reduce a distance of about 15,000 km to just 2,500 km and time taken from the existing six weeks to less than two weeks. Once a high-speed rail and road network across Pakistan is completed, oil tankers from eastern China would be able to reach Gwadar port within 48 hours.

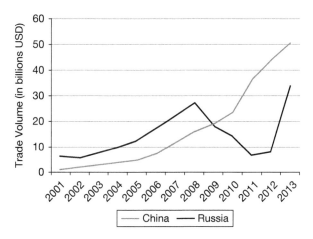

Figure 20.1 Pakistan Trade with China and Russia

Source: Elaborated by the Author from WITS TradeStat Database (as of October 1, 2018), available at https://wits.worldbank.org/countrystats.aspx

In November 2016, CPEC became partly operational when a caravan of fifty trucks carrying the first consignment of Chinese goods destined for the Middle East, Africa, and other markets transited through Gwadar port using the existing Karakoram Highway and other roads linking Gwadar with the upcountry and China.[13]

Furthermore, CPEC can also serve as a transit route for Russia and the five land-locked Central Asia countries discussed above.

CPEC is not without its challenges. The most obvious ones are securing the paths that pass through some restive areas of Pakistan. A Special Security Division, comprising nine army battalions and six civil wings having 13,700 personnel, has been established for protecting projects under the CPEC and the Chinese workers. The total cost of raising the force and providing it with necessary equipment is estimated at US$22 million. There are already plans for a second Special Security Division and the two divisions could raise the number of personnel to around 30,000. In addition, a Task Force 88 comprised of spy planes, drones, combat aircraft, and the latest weapons has been set-up by the Pakistan Navy to work jointly with the Special Security Division. China has donated two naval ships, which have already been inducted into the Pakistan Navy.

Another problem that has been hampering progress is the rivalry between various provinces within the country. The smaller provinces are worried that most of the benefits would go to Punjab, which is the largest and already the most affluent. Although some adjustments have been made to the infrastructure projects to cater to the needs of the smaller provinces, they are still not satisfied with the transparency of how projects are selected and implemented. They have voiced concerns that Pakistan would be burdened with huge loans and may become indebted to such an extent that it may compromise its independence.

The interprovincial rivalries are being fuelled by a lack of transparency. There is little clarity about the financing of the projects—whether they are loans or foreign direct investment. Another issue is the lack of clarity as to how the priorities are being determined. Other questions being asked are whether any toll will be collected for the maintenance of roads and their security.[14] Some commentators have raised the question of the legal basis under which transit through Pakistan will be allowed to Chinese companies.

Then there are regional rivalries. There is a widespread perception that India does not see the CPEC project favourably. There are repeated assertions in the Indian press that CPEC 'passes through disputed territory' and that Gwadar port is a Chinese military outpost designed to hamper New Delhi's interests. While there are serious concerns in Pakistan about the Indian opposition to the project, there have been some recent efforts to get India aboard and join the project.

Many, including the IMF and the World Bank, feel that import intensive CPEC investment projects may be partially responsible for the mounting debts and the balance of payment crisis, which Pakistan is now facing. They caution that Pakistan's capacity to repay CPEC debts will be under serious threat and that is likely to have significant implications for its economic stability and growth.

---

[13] See map, 'Highways network of CPEC, Government of Pakistan' http://cpec.gov.pk/map-single/1.

[14] 'Senior Economist Raises Several Questions Regarding CPEC' *The Express Tribune* (2017).

V. Making CPEC a Success

In order to make full use of this prospect, there are at least seven major areas where immediate attention is needed.

First, Pakistan's potential of hydropower capacity is estimated at 59,000 MW, as against installed capacity of 6,600 MW.[15] Hydropower is not only less costly (3 to 5 US cents per kilowatt-hour versus 8 to 10 cents for coal-powered plants) but is also the most sustainable and the cleanest source of energy. In the past it has been ignored for two reasons: initial construction cost of hydropower projects is high and their gestation period is long. Since enough funding is available and the time horizon of CPEC is sufficiently long, a forward looking and better approach would have been to spend more on hydropower projects rather than those based on imported coal. Besides making Pakistan energy secure, construction of hydropower projects would also be of tremendous help in increasing Pakistan's chronically low water storage capacity and in controlling frequent floods. It would be unfortunate if Pakistan were to burden itself with costly and environmentally hazardous fossil fuels. In particular, moving coal to the up-country power production sites without adequate rail infrastructure would be a logistical nightmare. China has the highest installed hydropower capacity in the world and Pakistan should benefit from the Chinese experience rather than rushing to coal-powered projects.

Secondly, there seems to be far more emphasis on constructing new roads versus laying new rail tracks. Currently, 96 per cent of the total freight tonnage (domestic, international, and transit trade) in Pakistan is handled by road transport. This is unlike most other countries where most freight is carried by railways. This is partly because of the neglect and the lack of investment in rail services over the past several decades. Greater spending on railways would not only be cost-effective but could make a significant contribution towards a cleaner environment. CPEC presents a brilliant opportunity to do so. Therefore, if one of the three routes (Eastern, Central, or Western) were devoted to building a new railway track instead of new highways, the dividends would be much better.

Thirdly, CPEC provides great opportunities to form partnerships between Pakistani and Chinese companies and attract other global companies. However, the government's only focus seems to be to facilitate Chinese investors. Thus, as the project is progressing, it is tilting the field in favour of the Chinese companies at the expense of locals and other investors. Through various statutory regulatory orders (SROs), specific exemptions from import and other taxes have been allowed for certain Chinese companies, which amounts to special subsidies for them. The government should provide a level playing field so that CPEC could become a magnet for investments from sources worldwide and also benefit local investors.

Fourthly, unlike other countries, Pakistan's experience of allowing transit trade has not been economically beneficial to the country so far. This is partly because Pakistan's taxes on international trade are extremely high. This gives an incentive for smuggling and diversion of transit goods in the country. Pakistan should reform its taxation regime so that it can become a facilitator of transit trade rather than a source of hindrance as has been noticed in the case of Afghanistan.

Fifthly, CPEC would only be a 'game-changer' if Pakistan's bureaucracy and workforce are fully trained in order to make full use of this opportunity. There is an urgent

[15] 'Water in Them Hills, South Asia's Hydro-politics' *The Economist* (2014).

need to work on the 'software' side, such as training the work force and simplifying regulations. Pakistan is ranked amongst the countries with the worst score on the World Bank's Doing Business 2018 ranking (147 out of 190). If Pakistan has the 'hardware' such as roads and railway networks but does not have adequate 'software,' the only beneficiaries will be the Chinese traders, who would have a shorter route connecting China's western border provinces with the Middle East.

Sixthly, there needs to be more transparency in the allocation of funding and projects within Pakistan. Serious efforts should be made to address the concerns of the smaller provinces and make them a part of the decision-making. Recent moves to include representatives of the smaller provinces as members of the Joint China–Pakistan Ministerial meetings where most of the decisions relating to the inclusion of the projects are taken are a welcome step and should be made a permanent arrangement.

Finally, instead of antagonizing its neighbours and fuelling regional rivalries, Pakistan should encourage them to become part of CPEC rather than become its detractors. That would reduce its security expenses and would also make the project cost-effective and durable. Pakistan has to realize that CPEC is a part of bigger BRI plans linking dozens of countries and not just limited to a transit corridor through Pakistan. CPEC can become a real game-changer if Pakistan can make use of its full potential by becoming a hub of regional trade for all neighbouring countries, including South, Central, and Western Asia. Already there is speculation that Russia may merge the Moscow-led Eurasian Economic Union (EAEU) with the CPEC. Since the Sino-Russian cooperation for a Eurasian partnership has been solidifying, there is a good chance that Russia may participate in the CPEC and use the Gwadar Port for its exports. It is expected that Russia's presence in the CPEC would help to ease tensions with India.[16]

---

[16] Li Xing, 'Russia Can Be a Welcoming Presence at CPEC' *Global Times* (2017).

21

The International Fraud and Corruption Sanctioning System

The Case of Chinese SOEs

Susan Finder*

This chapter focuses on a particular aspect of the Global Prong—the relationship between the 'going global' policy, in which Chinese companies, typically state-owned enterprises (SOEs), have shifted to an outward focus, particularly in international contracting, constructing, and investment, while company internal controls and related Chinese legislation have remained domestically focused and fail to synchronize with the international environment. In addition to Chinese government projects, Chinese companies are more actively bidding for multi-lateral development bank and development institutions (MDBs) projects.

This chapter focuses on an unexplored aspect of Chinese SOEs doing business overseas—the interaction of these companies with the integrity systems implemented by the MDBs, aimed at preventing fraud, corruption, and other abuses in projects undertaken by those institutions. For various reasons described below, some Chinese companies fall foul of the MDBs' integrity systems.

The chapter provides a brief overview of the integrity systems developed by the MDBs, focusing on Chinese company interactions with that system, the efforts of the Asian Infrastructure Investment Bank (AIIB) to integrate with that system, as well as the view of the Chinese government towards this system. It looks at the status of and possible trends in the integration of the Chinese anticorruption regulatory system with the MDB system.

I. MDBs' Integrity System

The evolution of the MDBs' integrity system dates back to World Bank President Wolfensohn's speech in 1996, in which he warned about the 'cancer of corruption'. It has evolved over the years, to become a sophisticated and relatively transparent system, with many crucial aspects harmonized across the MDBs.

As described below, the MDBs' integrity system is an administrative system, without criminal law enforcement powers. Each MDB has established its own investigation procedure harmonized with the other MDBs, followed by administrative sanctioning procedures. While some commentators have raised questions about the standard of

* Distinguished Scholar in Residence, School of Transnational Law, Peking University and Visiting Fellow, Centre of Chinese Law, University of Hong Kong.

The International Fraud and Corruption Sanctioning System: The Case of Chinese SOEs. Susan Finder.
© Susan Finder, 2019. Published 2019 by Oxford University Press.

proof and other issues,[1] the fact is that the principles and procedures represent a consensus across the MDBs and it is the system with which Chinese companies competing for MDB business must interact.

Although the list changes over time, significant numbers of Chinese companies, many of them SOEs, are found on lists of sanctioned entities made public by the MDBs.[2] Each MDB makes public the names of persons and companies that it has sanctioned, as well as those debarred by counterpart institutions under an agreement described below. The most well-known of these lists is the 'List of Ineligible Firms and Individuals'.[3] The question of why many of the Chinese companies are SOEs is explored later in this chapter.

Mutual debarment by the MDBs is enabled by the Agreement for Mutual Enforcement of Debarment Decisions (AMEDD), concluded by five of the MDBs in 2010. Under the AMEDD, individuals and entities debarred by one MDB (for a minimum of one year) are debarred by the other MDBs.[4] The MDBs that signed the AMEDD are:

1. The African Development Bank Group[5]
2. The Asian Development Bank
3. The European Bank for Redevelopment and Development
4. The Inter-American Development Bank Group;[6] and
5. The World Bank Group.[7]

The legal framework by which the MDBs are able to impose sanctions is through the contractual protections in funding and services agreements in MDB-financed projects. See, for example, the description of practices prohibited by the World Bank and the investigatory and sanctioning process in the World Bank's Consulting Services Manual.[8] Because the procedure is considered to be an administrative one, the burden of proof and evidentiary standards are lower than for criminal proceedings, although MDB sanctions can have significant commercial consequences for a company. Because

[1] M Diamant, C Sullivan, and J Smith, 'Sanctionable Practices at the World Bank: Interpretation and Enforcement' (2016) 18(4) U of Pennsylvania Journal of Business Law 985 http://scholarship.law.upenn.edu/cgi/viewcontent.cgi?article=1520&context=jbl; J Coogan and others, 'Combatting fraud and corruption in international development: The global impact of the multilateral development banks' sanctions regimes' (2015) 22(2) Journal of Financial Crime 228 https://doi.org/10.1108/JFC-10-2014-0045.
[2] A 2018 Chinese press report noted that about 75 SOEs had been sanctioned http://silkroad.news.cn/2018/0426/93136.shtml.
[3] World Bank Listing of Ineligible Firms & Individuals http://web.worldbank.org/external/default/main?theSitePK=84266&contentMDK=64069844&menuPK=116730&pagePK=64148989&piPK=64148984.
[4] The African Development Bank Group, the Asian Development Bank, the European Bank for Reconstruction and Development, the Inter-American Development Bank Group, and the World Bank Group, Agreement for Mutual Enforcement of Debarment Decision http://www.ebrd.com/downloads/integrity/Debar.pdf.
[5] The African Development Bank, The African Development Fund, and the Nigeria Trust Fund.
[6] The Inter-American Development Bank and the Inter-American Investment Corporation, Multilateral Investment Fund.
[7] The International Bank for Reconstruction and Development, the International Development Association, the International Finance Corporation, the Multilateral Investment Guarantee Agency, and the International Centre for Settlement of Investment Disputes.
[8] World Bank, *Consulting Services Manual: A Comprehensive Guide to Selection of Consultants* http://siteresources.worldbank.org/PROCUREMENT/Resources/csm-final-ev3.pdf.

the MDBs are international organizations, their decisions are usually not subject to judicial oversight.[9]

Although each MDB has its own investigation and sanctioning procedures, the MDBs have harmonized their definitions of sanctionable practices, general principles and guidelines for sanctions,[10] and principles for the treatment of corporate groups.[11]

A summary description of how the system currently works follows below.[12]

II. Sanctionable Practices

The MDBs penalize what are termed as 'sanctionable practices'. The definitions and interpretations are harmonized and are set out in the Uniform Framework for Preventing and Combating Fraud and Corruption.[13]

Sanctionable practices include:

- corruption
- fraud
- collusion and
- coercion.

Several MDBs also sanction the practice of obstruction, including the World Bank Group and ADB. The ADB also includes waste, conflict of interest, violations of ADB sanctions, and retaliation against whistle-blowers or witnesses among its integrity violations.[14]

The definition of each sanctionable practice is brief.

A corrupt practice is the offering, giving, receiving, or soliciting, directly or indirectly, anything of value to influence improperly the actions of another party.

A fraudulent practice is any act or omission, including a misrepresentation, that knowingly or recklessly misleads, or attempts to mislead, a party to obtain a financial or other benefit or to avoid an obligation.

A coercive practice is impairing or harming, or threatening to impair or harm, directly or indirectly, any party or the property of the party to influence improperly the actions of a party.

A collusive practice is an arrangement between two or more parties designed to achieve an improper purpose, including influencing improperly the actions of another party.[15]

---

[9] FINANCIER Worldwide, 'FORUM: Fraud and Corruption Investigations in Multilateral Development Banks' (February 2016) https://www.financierworldwide.com/forum-fraud-and-corruption-investigations-in-multilateral-development-banks/#.WKhXUhJ95Vo.

[10] Diamant, Sullivan, and Smith (n 1) 993.

[11] Asian Development Bank, 'MDB Harmonized Principles on Treatment of Corporate Groups' http://lnadbg4.adb.org/oai001p.nsf/0/A7912C61C52A85AD48257ACC002DB7EE/$FILE/MDB%20Harmonized%20Principles%20on%20Treatment%20of%20Corporate%20Groups.pdf.

[12] Diamant, Sullivan, and Smith (n 1) set out a more detailed description.

[13] ADB, 'Uniform Framework for Preventing and Combating Fraud and Corruption' (September 2006) https://www.adb.org/publications/uniform-framework-preventing-and-combating-fraud-and-corruption.

[14] ADB, 'Integrity Violation' https://www.adb.org/site/integrity/integrity-violations.

[15] ADB, 'Uniform Framework for Preventing and Combating Fraud and Corruption' (n 13).

Each MDB has further explanations and information on its website with further information. For example, the World Bank has examples of each sanctionable practice on its website.[16]

III. Sanctions and Procedures

Although each MDB has its own sanctioning procedures,[17] the type of sanctions and procedures have been harmonized across the MDBs in the 2006 agreement General Principles and Guidelines for Sanctions (General Principles for Sanctions).[18] Each MDB may impose sanctions additional to the ones that are harmonized. In addition to the MDBs mentioned above, the European Investment Bank (EIB) and the International Monetary Fund (IMF) are also signatories to that document. Sanctions that can be imposed (in order of increasing magnitude) include:

- letter of reprimand
- restitution or remedy
- conditional non-debarment
- debarment with conditional release
- debarment
- permanent or indefinite debarment.

The sanctions can be imposed singly or in combination. The base sanction set out in the General Principles for Sanctions is debarment for three years, which can be increased or decreased, depending on whether there are aggravating or mitigating factors. A letter of reprimand is issued where there is a lack of oversight, or for isolated or minor violations, while restitution or remedy can be imposed if a determination is made that a quantifiable amount can be restored.[19] Conditional non-debarment means that the sanctioned person or entity is required to comply with certain conditions, usually preventative or remedial, to avoid debarment. Debarment with conditional release or reinstatement means that the sanctioned person or entity can be reinstated or be debarred for a shorter period if it complies with the conditions imposed by the MDB, such as putting a voluntary compliance programme into operation. Debarment means that the sanctioned person or entity can be reinstated after the debarment period elapses. Finally, permanent or indefinite debarment is imposed on individuals and closely held companies where there are no reasonable grounds that the sanctioned person or entity can be rehabilitated through compliance or other conditions.

MDBs can also impose further sanctions. For example, the Enforcement Committee of the EBRD can direct the rejection of a procurement contract proposed to be awarded and cancellation of a portion of EBRD financing that had not been disbursed.[20] Other MDBs also have sanctions unique to their institutions.

---

[16] World Bank, 'What is Fraud and Corruption?' http://www.worldbank.org/en/about/unit/integrity-vice-presidency/what-is-fraud-and-corruption.

[17] World Bank Group procedures http://siteresources.worldbank.org/EXTOFFEVASUS/Resources/WBGSanctionsProceduresJan2011.pdf.

[18] World Bank, 'General Principles and Guidelines for Sanctions' http://pubdocs.worldbank.org/en/2213514491696 31786/Harmonized-Sanctions-Guidelines.pdf.

[19] ibid 3(f).

[20] R Schaap and C Divino, 'The AMMEDD Five Years On: Trends in Enforcement Actions and Challenges Facing the Enforcement Landscape' (2016) 57 Harvard International Law Journal 4 http://www.harvardilj.org/wp-content/uploads/January-2016_Vol-57_Schaap-Divino.pdf.

The MDBs have set out a framework for mitigating and aggravating circumstances, set out here:[21]

Increase in Base Sanction	Aggravating Circumstances
1–5 years	Severity
	• Repeated Pattern of sanctionable conduct
	• Sophisticated means
	• Central role in the sanctionable conduct
	• Management's role in the sanctionable conduct
	• Involvement of public official or IFI staff
	Harm Caused
	• Harm to Public Welfare
	• Harm to the Project
1–3 years	Interference with investigation, or obstruction of the investigative process
	• Intimidation/payment of a witness
	• Refusal to accept notice/failure to respond
Up to 10 years	• Past history of sanction by any institution
	• Violation of a Sanction or Temporary Suspension

Prior sanctions by another MDB or violation of a MDB sanction leads to the largest increase in the base sanction, with violations such as refusal to accept notice or failure to respond treated less seriously.

Under the sanctioning procedures of most MDBs, the matter may be settled by agreement.

IV. The Sanctioning Procedure

The MDB sanctioning procedure, generally follows the following format. A possibly sanctionable practice is brought to the attention of the MDB in question in the form of a complaint. For the World Bank Group in fiscal year 2016, for example, 34 per cent of the complaints were brought by World Bank Group staff, while 66 per cent were brought by non-bank sources, such as competitors, government officials, and NGOs.[22]

For the World Bank Group, an initial screening is done by the staff of the relevant institution and thereafter the complaint is forwarded to the Integrity Vice President (INT) in Washington, DC for further investigation. At the ADB, for example, the investigation function is carried out by the Office of Anti-corruption and Integrity.[23]

---

[21] World Bank, 'General Principles and Guidelines for Sanctions' (n 18).

[22] World Bank, 'Annual Update Integrity Vice Presidency' (fiscal year 2016) http://pubdocs. worldbank.org/en/118471475857477799/INT-FY16-Annual-Update-web.pdf, http://pubdocs. worldbank.org/en/703921507910218164/2017-INT-Annual-Update-FINAL-spreads.pdf.

[23] ADB, 'Process for Dealing with Allegations of Integrity Violations Involving Bidders, Consultants, Contractors, Suppliers, or Other Third Parties in ADB-related Activities' https://www. adb.org/sites/default/files/page/161290/process-for-dealing-with-allegations-external-parties.pdf. ADB has prepared a very useful flow chart describing the investigation and sanctioning process.

The ADB has issued International Financial Institutions Principles and Guidelines for Investigation in a format integrated with paragraphs specific to the ADB.[24]

For the World Bank Group, for example, in 2016, of the 279 preliminary inquiries forwarded to the INT, sixty-four new cases were opened, primarily fraud or collusion cases. Of that number, 62 per cent were substantiated.

A complaint is substantiated if the INT finds sufficient evidence to conclude that it is more likely than not that the alleged conduct, or other sanctionable conduct, occurred. The timeline for this is generally twelve to eighteen months. The World Bank describes the standard of proof as similar to the 'balance of probabilities'.[25] At this point, the INT considers how the matter should proceed—whether it should be referred to relevant national or international authorities, or whether the INT should initiate the formal sanctions process. If the INT decides to initiate the formal sanctions process, it prepares a statement of accusations and evidence (SAE) presented for review/issuance to a suspension or debarment officer (independent of the INT). The suspension/debarment officer will review the case to determine if there is sufficient evidence and what an appropriate sanction is. An appeal is available to the World Bank's Sanctions Board. The Sanctions Board invites persons from outside the bank to be a member of the panel, holding a hearing if needed.[26] Sanctions board decisions are made public, but without releasing the name of the party. This provides greater insight into the reasoning behind the sanctioning decision, while publicity serves to warn others.

A separate office monitors compliance with sanctions by sanctioned persons or entities. In 2010, the INT established the Integrity Compliance Office (ICO, which also decides whether conditions imposed under a sanction or negotiated resolution agreement have been satisfied.

As mentioned above, parties can settle through a negotiated resolution agreement.

In its Fiscal Year 2016 (FY16), four out of fifty-five persons and entities sanctioned were Chinese, and one letter of reprimand was issued. Debarment can be for an entire group or ring-fenced and sanctions can be referred to national/multi-national institutions for further proceedings.

V. Outreach Efforts

The ADB (and other MDBs) carry out educational activities to prevent the occurrence of sanctionable practices. The World Bank, the IFC, and the ADB all have offices in Beijing and carry out awareness building and capacity building efforts among Chinese companies and other institutions from time to time in an effort to mitigate and prevent incidences of fraud and corruption in activities financed, administered, and supported by the MDBs. In FY16, for example, the World Bank's Integrity Vice Presidency revealed that the institution had carried out outreach on contract management training, due diligence checks on document authenticity and identification of corruption red flags in China that year.[27] Similarly, the ADB held

---

[24] ADB, 'Integrity Principles and Guidlines' (2015) https://www.adb.org/sites/default/files/institutional-document/32131/integrity-principles-guidelines.pdf.

[25] http://www.worldbank.org/en/about/unit/integrity-vice-presidency/investigations.

[26] http://siteresources.worldbank.org/EXTOFFEVASUS/Resources/3601045-1377105390925/WBG_Policy_Statute_of_the_Sanctions_Board_(10.18.2016).pdf.

[27] http://pubdocs.worldbank.org/en/118471475857477799/INT-FY16-Annual-Update-web.pdf.

outreach activities in China in 2018, such as one co-sponsored by the Ministry of Finance.[28]

VI. Chinese Companies and the MDB Sanctioning Procedure

The February 2017 list of Chinese individuals and companies on the debarred list is set out below.

Debarred Firms and Individuals

Name: [ ]   Country: [China]   [GO] [Reset]

Firm Name	Address	Country	Ineligibility Period From	To	Grounds
FIRST BRANCH TIANJIN HUASHUI TAP WATER CONSTRUCTION CO. LTD. (天津市华水自来水建设有限公司第)	4 JINGJIANG ROAD, HEBEI DISTRICT,, TIANJIN CITY (天津市河北区靖江路4号)	China	18-JAN-2017	17-APR-2018	Fraudulent practice, 2011 Procurement Guidelines, para. 1.16(a)(ii).
FOURTH BRANCH TIANJIN HUASHUI TAP WATER CONSTRUCTION CO. LTD. (天津市华水自来水建设有限公司)	2 HAIYUAN ROAD, HONGQIAO DISTRICT, TIANJIN CITY (天津市红桥区海源道2号)	China	18-JAN-2017	17-APR-2018	Fraudulent practice, 2011 Procurement Guidelines, para. 1.16(a)(ii).
MECHANICAL AND ELECTRICAL EQUIPMENT INSTALLATION BRANCH TIANJIN HUASHUI TAP WATE	2 HAIYUAN ROAD, HONGQIAO DISTRICT, TIANJIN CITY (天津市红桥区海源道2号)	China	18-JAN-2017	17-APR-2018	Fraudulent practice, 2011 Procurement Guidelines, para. 1.16(a)(ii).
SECOND BRANCH TIANJIN HUASHUI TAP WATER CONSTRUCTION CO. LTD. (天津市华水自来水建设有限公司)	2 HAIYUAN ROAD, HONGQIAO DISTRICT,, TIANJIN CITY (天津市红桥区海源道2号)	China	18-JAN-2017	17-APR-2018	Fraudulent practice, 2011 Procurement Guidelines, para. 1.16(a)(ii).
SPECIAL CONSTRUCTION BRANCH TIANJIN HUASHUI TAP WATER CONSTRUCTION CO. LTD.	2 HAIYUAN ROAD, HONGQIAO DISTRICT, TIANJIN CITY (天津市红桥区海源道2号)	China	18-JAN-2017	17-APR-2018	Fraudulent practice, 2011 Procurement Guidelines, para. 1.16(a)(ii).
THIRD BRANCH TIANJIN HUASHUI TAP WATER CONSTRUCTION CO. LTD. (天津市华水自来水建设有限公司第)	2 HAIYUAN ROAD, HONGQIAO DISTRICT,, TIANJIN CITY (天津市红桥区海源道2号)	China	18-JAN-2017	17-APR-2018	Fraudulent practice, 2011 Procurement Guidelines, para. 1.16(a)(ii).
TIANJIN HUASHUI TAP WATER CONSTRUCTION CO., LTD. (天津华水自来水建设有限公司)	HUASHUI BUILDING 4TH FLOOR, 2 HAIYUAN ROAD, HONGQIAO DISTRICT, TIANJIN	China	18-JAN-2017	17-APR-2018	Fraudulent practice, 2011 Procurement Guidelines, para. 1.16(a)(ii).
URBAN ENGINEERING AND CONSTRUCTION BRANCH TIANJIN HUASHUI TAP WATER CONSTRUCTION	2 HAIYUAN ROAD, HONGQIAO DISTRICT, TIANJIN CITY (天津市红桥区海源道2号)	China	18-JAN-2017	17-APR-2018	Fraudulent practice, 2011 Procurement Guidelines, para. 1.16(a)(ii).
GOU XUEJUN	C/O CHINA FIRST METALLURGICAL COMPANY, NO. 3 INDUSTRY	China	21-OCT-2016	06-NOV-2017	Cross-Debarment: ADB

[28] Correspondence with ADB official in possession of author, see also Deputy Director Liu Weihua attended the Asian Development Bank's 'Procurement and Anti-Corruption Seminar to Improve Project Implementation Efficiency' http://gjs.mof.gov.cn/pindaoliebiao/gongzuodongtai/201807/t20180705_2949619.html.

	DISTRICT, WUHAN				
JIANGXI HENGJIAN ROAD AND BRIDGE ENGINEERING CO., LTD. (江西恒剑路桥工程有限公司)*334	MIAOPU, YINCHENG COUNTY, DEXING CITY, SHANGRAO, JIANGXI PROVINCE, ZIP CODE: 334200	China	05-AUG-2016	04-AUG-2018	Procurement Guidelines, 1.14(a)(ii)
HUNAN CONSTRUCTION GROUP CO., LTD. (湖南建设集团有限公司)*301	LAST KNOWN ADDRESS:23 CHENGNANZHONG ROAD, RONGAN BUILDING 5TH FLOOR, CHANGSHA, HUNAN	China	14-JAN-2016	13-JAN-2019	Procurement Guidelines, 1.14(a)(ii)
HUNAN CONSTRUCTION GROUP CO., LTD. (湖南建设集团有限公司)*301	LAST KNOWN ADDRESS: STATION ROAD NO. 70, WAN XIANG XIN TIAN BUSINESS MANSION 5, BUILDING NO. 31, 32F, FURONG DISTRICT, CHANGSHA, HUNAN	China	14-JAN-2016	13-JAN-2019	Procurement Guidelines, 1.14(a)(ii)
HUNAN CONSTRUCTION GROUP CO., LTD. (湖南建设集团有限公司)*301	LAST KNOWN ADDRESS: 70 NORTH CHEZHAN ROAD, WAN XIANG XIN TIAN BUILDING, FURONG DISTRICT, CHANGSHA, HUNAN 410007	China	14-JAN-2016	13-JAN-2019	Procurement Guidelines, 1.14(a)(ii)
XINJINZHU MUNICIPAL LANDSCAPING ENGINEERING CO., LTD. f/k/a Henan Xinjinzhu Landscaping Engineering Co., Ltd. *286	5TH FLOOR, JINZHU BUILDING, NORTH OF THE NEW BRIDGE, HUANGCHUAN, HENAN PROVINCE, 465150	China	14-JUL-2015	13-JUL-2018	Procurement Guidelines, 1.14(a)(ii)
XINJINZHU MUNICIPAL LANDSCAPING ENGINEERING CO., LTD. f/k/a Henan Xinjinzhu Landscaping Engineering Co., Ltd. *286	15TH FLOOR, TAIHONG YANGGUANG BUILDING, INTERSECTION OF ZHONGZHOU AVENUE AND XINYUAN ROAD, ZHENGZHOU, HENAN PROVINCE, 450002	China	14-JUL-2015	13-JUL-2018	Procurement Guidelines, 1.14(a)(ii)
HUBEI HENGDA STEEL STRUCTURE CO., LTD.*279	,	China	02-JUL-2015	01-JUL-2018	Procurement Guidelines, 1.14(a)(ii)
HUBEI SUNLIGHT ELECTRIC CO., LTD.*278	NO. 90 YONG AN AVENUE, XIANAN DISTRICT, XIANNING CITY, HUBEI PROVINCE, 437000	China	02-JUL-2015	01-JUL-2018	Procurement Guidelines,1.14(a)(ii)

HUBEI GEZHOUBA MUNICIPAL ENGINEERING COMPANY LTD.(湖北葛洲坝市政工程建设有限公司) Registration No.420500000006846 *263	4 GUANGMING ROAD, YICHANG, HUBEI PROVINCE, CHINA 443000	China	26-MAY-2015	Ongoing	2010 PGL 1.14(a)(ii); 2011 PGL 1.16(a)(ii)
YICHANG GEZHOUBA LANDSCAPING COMPANY.(宜昌市葛洲坝风景园林公司) Registration No.420500000054925 *263	1 YANJIANG AVENUE, YICHANG, HUBEI PROVINCE, CHINA 443000	China	26-MAY-2015	Ongoing	2010 PGL 1.14(a)(ii); 2011 PGL 1.16(a)(ii)
YICHANG ZHENGXIN ARCHITECTURAL ENGINEERING TEST COMPANY LTD.(宜昌正信建筑工程试验检测有限公司) Registration No.420500000131007 *263	54 DONGSHAN AVENUE, YICHANG, HUBEI PROVINCE, CHINA 443000	China	26-MAY-2015	Ongoing	2010 PGL 1.14a)(ii); 2011 PGL 1.16(a)(ii)
SHANDONG HUALONG LANDSCAPING ENGINEERING CO., LTD. (山东华龙园林工程有限公司)*261	ROOM #2312, 23RD FLOOR, TOWER 2, 61 HAIER ROAD, QINGDAO, SHANDONG PROVINCE	China	21-APR-2015	20-APR-2018	Procurement Guidelines, 1.14(a)(ii)
CHINA HUASHI HYDROPOWER DEVELOPMENT CORP.*227	230A CAIHUYING, GENGTAI DISTRICT, BEIJING	China	24-SEP-2014	24-SEP-2017	2006 PGL, 1.14(a)(ii); 1999 PGL 1.15(a)(ii)
CHINA INTERNATIONAL WATER & ELECTRIC CORP.*227	CWE MANSION, 3 LIUPUKANG STREET, XICHENG DISTRICT, BEIJING 100120	China	24-SEP-2014	24-SEP-2017	2006 PGL, 1.14(a)(ii); 1999 PGL 1.15(a)(ii)
CWE POWER DEVELOPMENT CO., LTD.*227	ROOM 603, BUILDING B, NEW MOER BUSINESS CENTER, 209 WUJING ROAD, YUNAN PROVINCE, KUNMING	China	24-SEP-2014	24-SEP-2017	2006 PGL, 1.14(a)(ii); 1999 PGL 1.15(a)(ii)
CWE SOUTH AMERICA LIMITED*227	230A CAIHUYING, FENGTAI DISTRICT, BEIJING	China	24-SEP-2014	24-SEP-2017	2006 PGL, 1.14(a)(ii); 1999 PGL 1.15(a)(ii)
WATER AND POWER PRESS PRINTING CO., LTD.*227	FLOOR 6, AIDE BUILDING, 20B CHEGONGZHUAGXI ROAD, BEIJING	China	24-SEP-2014	24-SEP-2017	2006 PGL, 1.14(a)(ii); 1999 PGL 1.15(a)(ii)
MR. PETER LEE (AKA MR. LI YI)*192	NO. 88 ERQI NORTH ROAD, NANCHANG, 330046	China	18-APR-2014	17-APR-2017	Procurement Guidelines, 1.14(a)(ii)

MR. ZHU HONGFENG*191	NO. 88 ERQI NORTH ROAD, NANCHANG, 330046	China	18-APR-2014	Ongoing	Procurement Guidelines, 1.14(a)(ii)
CHINA JIANGSU INTERNATIONAL ECONOMIC AND TECHNICAL COOPERATION GROUP LTD.*180	5 WEST BEIJING ROAD, NANJING 210008	China	14-FEB-2014	Ongoing	Procurement Guidelines, 1.14(a)(ii)
CHINA HUNAN CONSTRUCTION ENGINEERING GROUP CORPORATION (CHCEGC)*165	HEADQUARTERS ADDRESS: 788 SECTION 1, SOUTH FUROUNG AVENUE, CHANGSHA, HUNAN	China	01-OCT-2013	Ongoing	Procurement Guidelines, 1.14(a)(ii)
CECEP NEW HOPE & TARLROAD (BEIJING) ENVIRONMENTAL TECHNOLOGY CO., LTD.*157	FLOOR 6, BLOCK A, JIENENG BUILDING, 42 XIZHIMEN NORTH ST., HAIDIAN DISTRICT, 100082, BEIJING	China	28-JUN-2013	Ongoing	2006 Procurement Guidelines, para. 1.14(a)(ii)
SNC-LAVALIN (CHINA) ENGINEERING AND MANAGEMENT INC.*150	888 SHENDA ROAD, SHENYANG ECONOMIC & TECHNOLOGICAL DEVELOPMENT ZONE, SHENYANG	China	17-APR-2013	17-APR-2023	Consult. Guidelines 1.22(a)(i)-(ii); Proc. Guidelines 1.15(a) (i)-(ii)
SNC-LAVALIN (SHANGHAI) INTERNATIONAL TRADING CO. LTD.*150	401-405 HUA WEN PLAZA, 999 ZHONGSHAN ROAD (WEST), 20051, SHANGHAI	China	17-APR-2013	17-APR-2023	Consult. Guidelines 1.22(a)(i)-(ii); Proc. Guidelines 1.15(a) (i)-(ii)
ZHONGKE LIFE SCIENCE & TECHNOLOGY CO., LTD. *40	NO. 88, ZHIYUAN ROAD, WUKANG TOWN, DEQING COUNTY, ZHEJIANG 313200	China	26-JUL-2011	Ongoing	Procurement Guidelines 1.14(a)(ii)
HEFEI HIGHWAY & BRIDGE PROJECT CO. LTD. *37	NO. 199, BLOCK B, HAOZHOU ROAD, HEFEI CITY, ANHUI PROVINCE,	China	28-JUN-2011	Ongoing	Procurement Guidelines 1.14(a)(ii)
MR. YANG LIN * 30	C/O SUITE 617 EAST PLAZA, NO. 15 NORTH ROAD, WEST 4TH RING ROAD, HAI DIAN DISTRICT, 100195, BEIJING	China	11-MAY-2011	Ongoing	Procurement Guidelines 1.14(a)(ii)
DAQING OILFIELD HIGHWAY & BRIDGE ENGINEERING CO., LTD.	NO. 19, XIJING ROAD, RANGHULU DISTRICT, DAQING CITY	China	07-MAR-2011	19-NOV-2017	Cross Debarment: ADB

Cross-debarred Entities

It reveals that approximately thirty Chinese companies have been sanctioned by the MDBs, with a significant portion of those being SOEs, including several centrally controlled SOEs.

To the extent that trends are visible with the behaviour of Chinese companies, the following can be noted.

In some cases, the debarment was imposed as a default judgment, because the Chinese party did not respond.[29] This reflects the type of behaviour and company

---

[29] World Bank, 'Notice of Uncontested Sanctions Proceedings' (5 August 2016) Sanctions Case No 418 http://siteresources.worldbank.org/EXTOFFEVASUS/Resources/3601045-1371577728750/Notice_of_Uncontested_Sanctions_Proceedings_Case_418(8.5.2016).pdf; and Notice of Uncontested Sanctions Proceedings (2 July 2015) Sanctions Case No 268 http://siteresources.worldbank.org/EXTOFFEVASUS/Resources/3601045-1371577728750/Notice_of_Uncontested_Sanctions_Proceedings_Case_268.pdf, and Sanctions Case No 369 http://siteresources.worldbank.org/EXTOFFEVASUS/Resources/3601045-1371577728750/Notice_of_Uncontested_Sanctions_Proceedings_Case_369.pdf.

management thinking found in other situations when a Chinese company is involved in dispute resolution abroad, such as arbitration.[30]

Posing a challenge for the MDBs is that some SOEs have subsequently changed their name or have been incorporated into larger groups, as part of the reorganization of that group.[31]

Some trends are visible from sanctioning decisions in the last several years:

First, is that Chinese companies are beginning to cooperate more with MDB sanctioning procedures. One example of that is the Sinohydro Corporation case.[32] That case involved findings that the company had engaged in a fraudulent practice in its bid and the bidding letter by misrepresenting commissions paid or to be paid to an agent in relation to the contract. In that case[33] a reprimand letter was ultimately imposed. According to the sanctioning board decision, 'Respondent was represented by two of its officers and by outside counsel, all attending in person'.[34]

In some cases, the Chinese company negotiates a settlement with the MDB in question, such as the World Bank. Among the companies that have concluded negotiated resolution agreements with the World Bank are: China International Water and Electric Corp. China Gezhouba Nos 1, 5, and 6 Engineering Company Limited.[35] Chinese companies increasingly engage outside counsel, both Chinese and foreign, to assist them in the sanctioning procedures, including in the negotiated settlement process. For example, a team of twenty lawyers from Jun He Law Firm worked with China First Highway Engineering Co Ltd (CFHEC) and its parent company on the settlement process. In 2014, the African Development Bank concluded a negotiated settlement agreement in which CFHEC admitted to fraudulent and collusive practices in tendering for an African Development Bank-financed contract in the Democratic Republic of Congo. The agreement debarred CFHEC for a period of three years with conditional release and imposed a financial penalty of US$18.86 million. According to the law firm, negotiation led by the firm led to a significantly reduced penalty and debarment period.[36]

VII. Chinese Government Views of the MDB Sanctioning System

From 2018 press reports and activities organized by trade associations, it is clear that the MDB sanctioning system has now become a concern for SOEs, although the Chinese regulatory framework is not yet entirely in place. Therefore, it is difficult to trace Chinese government responses to follow up on cases referred by the MDBs.

---

[30] Supreme People's Court Monitor (29 October 2015) https://supremepeoplescourtmonitor.com/2015/10/29/result-of-the-3-nos-policy-when-chinese-companies-arbitrate-abroad/.
[31] Discussion with MDB staff (November 2016).
[32] World Bank, Sanctions Case No372: Letter of Reprimand (June 29, 2016) http://siteresources.worldbank.org/INTOFFEVASUS/Resources/3601037-1346795612671/SanctionsCaseNo372-LetterofReprimand.pdf.
[33] ibid.
[34] World Bank, Sanctions Board Decision No 88 (Sanctions Case No 372) (29 June 2016) http://siteresources.worldbank.org/INTOFFEVASUS/Resources/3601037-1346795612671/SanctionsBoardDecisionNo88.pdf.
[35] World Bank, Notes on Debarred Firms and Individuals (31 March 2017) http://pubdocs.worldbank.org/en/387181466627871302/World-Bank-Notes-on-Debarred-Firms-and-Individuals.pdf.
[36] Junhe Law Office, client note (in Chinese) http://mp.weixin.qq.com/s?__biz=MzA5MzYzMzYyNQ==&mid=2650644947&idx=1&sn=4473e43acc609c7ab4743adda1f896ad&chksm=8853ece5bf2465f30f91ca498bb83f4da9b8b8048b4012b0238835d8d65a0889772369afccaf&scene=0#rd.

According to the 2016 World Bank Integrity Vice President's report,[37] references by the World Bank group to Chinese authorities apparently have had no follow up, although it is unclear whether follow up had been in ways not reported, such as Party sanctions of senior personnel.

Since 2014, a slow evolution of official or semi-official awareness of the MDB sanctioning system can be noted. In 2014, two senior Supreme People's Procuratorate officials wrote on this issue.[38] They admitted that Chinese legislation in the area of the area of cross-border anti-corruption is inadequate and that China should cooperate more in this area with the international community. Issues that they discovered included: serious problems in SOEs with duty crimes, particularly corruption, bribery, and embezzlement of public funds, in increasingly large amounts. The persons tending to commit these crimes were mid- or senior management of SOEs. Issues for Chinese companies, particularly SOEs were that internal controls or compliance functions were inadequate, with management focused on business and profits, not anti-corruption, and any Party oversight merely for show. SOE management often does not take legal risk seriously. An important factor in preventing better integration of Chinese anti-corruption efforts with international efforts is the gap between crimes defined under Chinese law and the United Nations Convention against Corruption. However, the gap between Chinese legislation and the international framework remains. In 2018, the National Reform and Development Commission issued draft guidelines on compliance systems for Chinese companies operating overseas, aimed at preventing behaviour that could be sanctioned.[39] Professional associations and major Chinese law firms have been holding events to make the MDB sanctioning systems known to SOE executives.

VIII. AIIBB and the MDBs' Fraud and Corruption Regulatory System

Although it is not generally known, AIIB has already taken steps towards becoming a party to the Mutual Debarment Agreement. As part of those steps, it has taken action aimed at coordinating its rules and procedures with those of the MDBs. Most importantly, in March 2017, the AIIB announced that it was voluntarily adopting the MDBs' debarment list and that it would actively be engaging with the MDBs in an effort to join them as a signatory to the AMEDD.[40] Whether the AIIB would become party to the Mutual Debarment Agreement had been a concern among foreign commentators for some time, including, most recently a January 2017 article[41] with commentary by a current ADB Integrity official and several former senior MDB lawyers.[42] This author

[37] World Bank, 'Annual Update Integrity Vice Presidency' (n 22).

[38] Song Hansong and others, 'Establish an Anti-corruption Prevention System when our Enterprises "Go Out"' *People's Procuracy* (2014) 91–12.

[39] Announcement on Public Consultation on 'Guidelines for Corporate Overseas Compliance Management (Draft for Comment)' (5 July 2018) http://www.ndrc.gov.cn/yjzx/yjzx_add.jsp?SiteId=150.

[40] AIIB Says No to Doing Business with Corrupt Bidders (March 2017) https://www.aiib.org/en/news-events/news/2017/20170307_001.html.

[41] FINANCIER Worldwide, 'FORUM: Fraud and Corruption Investigations in Multilateral Development Banks' (n 9).

[42] 'Chinese Companies on World BANK's Name & Shame List' *Supreme People's Court Monitor* (4 November 2016) https://supremepeoplescourtmonitor.com/2016/11/04/chinese-companies-on-world-banks-name-shame-list/.

had previously written that given the profile of senior AIIB officials, it was likely that AIIB would seek to join the Mutual Debarment Agreement.[43]

On 8 December 2016, the AIIB adopted its Policy on Prohibited Practices. Prohibited Practices are defined in section 3.2. The AIIB definition overlaps with and is broader than the MDB consensus sanctionable practices. Section 3.2 sets out definitions of the MDB consensus sanctionable practices, coercive, collusive, corrupt, and fraudulent practices. Those definitions are similar to those of the MDBs:

3.2.1 *Coercive Practice*: impairing or harming, or threatening to impair or harm, directly or indirectly, any party or the property of a party to influence improperly the actions of a party.

3.2.2 *Collusive Practice*: an arrangement between two or more parties designed to achieve an improper purpose, including to influence improperly the actions of another party.

3.2.3 *Corrupt Practice*: the offering, giving, receiving or soliciting, directly or indirectly, of anything of value to influence improperly the actions of another party.

3.2.4 *Fraudulent Practice*: any act or omission that knowingly or recklessly misleads, or attempts to mislead, a party to obtain a financial or other benefit or to avoid an obligation.

In addition to those four practices, section 3.2 also defines four other practices as prohibited: misuse of resources, obstructive practice, and theft. Several of the MDBs, including the World Bank Group and the ADB also define obstruction as a sanctionable offense. These definitions lay the groundwork for AIIB's possible signing of the Mutual Debarment Agreement.

3.2.5 *Misuse of Resources*: improper use of the Bank's resources, carried out either intentionally or through reckless disregard.

3.2.6 *Obstructive Practice*: any of the following practices:
   (a) deliberately destroying, falsifying, altering or concealing of evidence material to a Bank investigation;
   (b) making false statements to investigators in order to materially impede a Bank investigation into allegations of a Prohibited Practice;
   (c) failing to comply with requests to provide information, documents or records in connection with a Bank investigation;
   (d) threatening, harassing or intimidating any party to prevent it from disclosing its knowledge of matters relevant to a Bank investigation or from pursuing the investigation; or
   (e) materially impeding the exercise of the Bank's contractual rights of audit or inspection or access to information.

3.2.7 *Theft*: the misappropriation of property belonging to another party.

Article 12 of the Policy on Prohibited Practices addresses three important issues related to the MDB's fraud and corruption regulatory systems: unilateral observance by AIIB of MDB debarment by AIIB; debarment procedures in co-financing projects; and intent to become a party to the Mutual Debarment Agreement.

---

[43] Susan Finder, 'Chinese Companies and the World Bank's Procurement Blacklists' (28 October 2016) Wong MNC Center http://mnccenter.org/blog/chinese-companies-and-world-bank%E2%80%99s-procurement-blacklists.

Section 12.1, on unilateral observance by AIIB of MDB debarment provides that AIIB will on a unilateral basis (given that it is not yet a party to the Debarment Agreement) debar all entities debarred under the Debarment Agreement if conditions set out in 12.2 are met. 'Prohibited practices' appears to be equivalent to 'sanctionable practices' as used by the MDBs. As part of that, the AIIB will provide a link to the relevant MDB's debarment. Section 12.1 states:

> All entities debarred under the Agreement for the Mutual Enforcement of Debarment Decisions between some MDBs (Comparator Institutions) shall be unilaterally debarred by the bank as external debarment decisions if conditions noted in section 12.2 are met. The bank's website shall provide a link to the MDB cross-debarment website. The bank shall not notify affected subjects of a debarment resulting from the application of cross-debarment unless the subject requests the bank [AIIB] for comments or clarification.[44]

The conditions set out in section 12.2 are multifold, and include determinations by AIIB officers that the MDB debarment decision was based on the commission of practices that are prohibited by the AIIB itself, the finding has been made public, the debarment has an initial period exceeding one year, relates to the commission of an act that was committed no longer than ten years ago, and is consistent with AIIB legal and other institutional considerations.

> [The] Investigations Officer has determined, and the Sanctions Officer has agreed, that such External Debarment Decision:
>
> (a) is based, in whole or in part, on a finding of a commission of one or more prohibited practices defined in sections 3.2.1 to 3.2.4;
> (b) has been made public by the institution that has issued that external debarment decision;
> (c) has an initial period of debarment exceeding one (1) year;
> (d) has been made within a period not exceeding ten (10) years of the commission of the last constituent act of the most recent Prohibited Practice to which such decision relates;
> (e) has not been made in recognition of a decision made in a national or other international forum; and
> (f) is not inconsistent with the Bank's legal and other institutional considerations.[45]

On debarment in co-financing projects, section 12.3 provides that AIIB may agree to the application of the prohibited practices or similar policy and investigations and sanctions processes of that co-financier for that project, provided that the AIIB is satisfied that the policy and processes are consistent with the bank's articles of agreement and the AIIB's prohibited practices policy. The AIIB also may agree that the co-financier will be responsible for the investigations and sanctions processes and the AIIB may agree to give full force and effect to the co-financier's sanctions decisions.

Finally, section 12.4 expresses the AIIB's intention to become a party to the Mutual Debarment Agreement: 'As soon as reasonably possible, the Bank will engage with the Comparator Institutions [MDBs that are party to the Mutual Debarment Agreement] with a view to becoming a party to the AMEDD'.

Additionally, section 9.2 of the Prohibited Practices policy permits the AIIB to refer to national authorities a matter involving prohibited practices that may violate local

---

[44] AIIB, Policy on Prohibited Practice (May 2016) https://www.aiib.org/en/policies-strategies/operational-policies/prohibited-practices.html.
[45] ibid.

law. More specifically, section 9.2 provides that the investigations officer in charge of the matter shall refer it to the matter to the Director General of the Compliance, Effectiveness, and Integrity Unit who, if he determines that it is in the best interest of the bank, may at any time recommend, in consultation with the general counsel, to the AIIB president that a matter be referred to appropriate governmental authorities.

This is an important indication of the seriousness of the AIIB to adhere to the shared practices of the other MDBs.

IX. Conclusion

The robust AIIB Prohibited Practices policy and its expressed intent for the AIIB to become party to the AMEDD is useful in encouraging the Chinese government to engage more seriously with the MDB sanctioning system. It is likely to be a long-term process for Chinese legislation to be integrated with the MDB's sanctioning system. It is clear that first steps have been taken to make SOE management aware of the possible impact of the system on their operations. Additionally, the Supervision Commission has only recently gone into operation and it will require some time to focus its efforts on sanctionable practices committed by SOEs abroad. In the near future, this disconnect is likely to remain, while the anti-corruption focus remains primarily domestic, with the exception of pursuing the return of Chinese officials accused of corruption-related offences from overseas.

22

He Who Makes the Rules Owns the Gold

The Potential Ramifications of the New International Law Architects

Joel Slawotsky*

I. Introduction

In the virtual world of Disney, the character Jafar states the 'Golden Rule' as 'He who owns the gold makes the rules'.[1] Yet in the real world of geo-political strategy, economic rivalry, cross-border investment and intense trade competition, the Golden Rule is: 'He who makes the rules owns the gold'. For seventy years the United States led order—the IMF, World Bank, WTO, ICSID, and the reign of the United States dollar—has governed the mechanics of the global legal and financial architecture. The architects of the existing order have wielded significant power[2] since the financial and legal orders are inextricably linked to the formation, context, interpretation, application, and enforcement of international law.[3] Indeed, arguments have been made that UN sanctions have been used as a lever against 'non-compliant' nations in a subjective fashion[4] and some have opined that the present-day architects have rewarded friends and punished enemies via IMF loans.[5] As chief architect, the United States has reaped

* Radzyner Law School, Interdisciplinary Center (IDC) Herzliya, Israel. He can be reached at jslawotsky@idc.ac.il.

[1] Quotes from Jafar (Character) from Aladdin (1992) www.imdb.com/character/ch0000672/quotes.
[2] Owning the global financial and legal orders and writing the rules of finance and trade has vested the United States with enormous power and leverage. In advocating for the Trans-Pacific Partnership (TPP), former President Obama openly conceded this fact. See Andrew Hammond, 'The TPP Gives the U.S.—Rather than China—the Power to Influence Global Trade' http://news.nationalpost.com/full-comment/andrew-hammond-the-tpp-gives-the-u-s-rather-than-china-the-power-to-influence-global-trade (last accessed 6 October 2015). ('[T]he TPP has an important rules-setting component: U.S. President Barack Obama has asserted that the treaty will enable Washington, *rather than Beijing*, to create the foundation for "21st-century trade rules," including standards on trade, investment, data flows and intellectual property') (emphasis added).
[3] See Teemu Ruskola, 'Canton Is Not Boston: The Invention of American Imperial Sovereignty' (2005) 57 American Quarterly 859, 861: ('[T]he vocabulary for analyzing U.S. power overseas is largely military and economic, as evidenced by terms such as "gunboat diplomacy" and "dollar diplomacy." This essay analyzes law as an important currency in its own right in American overseas imperialism. The exercise of American power has been rarely based merely on the assertion of sheer economic and military might. From the beginning, it has been mediated through the language of law, as a matter of right.').
[4] See http://faculty.georgetown.edu/jrv24/research.html. See also Anne Orford, 'Muscular Humanitarianism: Reading the Narratives of the New Interventionism' (1999) 10 Eur Journal Int'l Law 706 (arguing that these interventions are often imposed by the leading nations as a 'form of imperialism').
[5] See Helen Milner, 'Globalization, Development, and International Institutions: Normative and Positive Perspectives' (2005) 3 Perspectives on Politics 839:('in lending to the transition countries the IMF gave more and imposed lighter conditions on those states with stronger political ties to the United States') http://faculty.georgetown.edu/jrv24/milner_05.pdf.

great benefit and has become 'exceptional'[6] as exemplified by the fact that only the United States was able to eviscerate hundreds of years of Swiss banking secrecy.[7]

The current architects of the global economic and legal orders are the 'civilized' or 'advanced' nations of the world[8]—the Western Anglo powers[9] led by the United States[10]—'the indispensable nation'.[11] Unquestionably, the status of the United States as the indispensable nation is inextricably linked with the fact that global finance and trade are encapsulated in the rules and institutions dominated by the United States which has proximately caused 'the spread of [United States] values, both in Asia and beyond'.[12]

For example, China recognizes that the international law architects are vested with the privilege to dominate the world:

Western States try to impose their system, whether political or economic, on other societies. They do this through direct means such as trade and aid, or indirect means such as the monetary and economic policies imposed through the financial arms of the West-the World Bank and the International Monetary Fund.[13]

---

[6] See www.whitehouse.gov/the-press-office/2014/05/28/remarks-president-united-states-military-academy-commencement-ceremony (noting the US is the sole exceptional nation and will continue to be exceptional in the next century).

[7] See www.reuters.com/article/uk-ubs-idUKTRE76E3RH20110715 'Swiss court says was right to give US bank data July 15, 2011' ('Since FINMA had compelling reasons to believe that not relinquishing the customer data to the U.S. Department of Justice would have seriously impaired Switzerland's financial markets and have led to serious repercussions for the Swiss economy, the action taken by it was shown to be lawful').

[8] The term 'civilized nations' connotes a modern state which conducts itself 'civilly'. See Proclamation of President Sun Yat-sen on the Establishment of the Republic of China on 1 January 1912: www.njmuseum.com/zh/book/cqgc_big5/zhmg.htm ('With the establishment of Provisional Government we will try our best to carry out the duties of a civilized nation so as to obtain the rights of a civilized state'). See also the preamble to the 1907 Hague Convention referring to the term, 'civilized nations'. Gustavo Gozzi, 'History of International Law and Western Civilization' (2007) 9 Int'l Comm L Rev 353, 365.

[9] Japan also plays a substantial role as a US ally bringing great influence through the Asian Development Bank. The United States and Japan both hold 30% of the voting power of this institution. See www.adb.org/about/members (noting that the United States and Japan have a majority of the shares).

[10] Critics contend that the United States has imposed its will on others. See Jack Donnelly, 'The Relative Universality of Human Rights' (2007) 29 Human Rights Quarterly 281, 305: ('The dangers of such arrogant and abusive "universalism" are especially striking in international relations, where normative disputes that cannot be resolved by rational persuasion or appeal to agree upon international norms tend to be settled by (political, economic, and cultural) power—of which United States today has more than anyone else'). See also Putin's Prepared Remarks at the 43rd Munich Conference on Security Policy ('We are seeing a greater and greater disdain for the basic principles of international law. And independent legal norms are, as a matter of fact, coming increasingly closer to one state's legal system. One state and, of course, first and foremost the United States, has overstepped its national borders in every way. This is visible in the economic, political, cultural and educational policies it imposes on other nations. Well, who likes this? Who is happy about this?') www.washingtonpost.com/wp-dyn/content/article/2007/02/12/AR2007021200555.html (last accessed 12 February 2007).

[11] President Obama has referred to the United States as 'the indispensable nation'. See Remarks by the President at the United States Military Academy Commencement Ceremony ('In fact, by most measures, America has rarely been stronger relative to the rest of the world ... Our military has no peer ... Meanwhile, our economy remains the most dynamic on Earth; our businesses the most innovative. Each year, we grow more energy independent. From Europe to Asia, we are the hub of alliances unrivaled in the history of nations. America continues to attract striving immigrants ... So the United States is and remains the one indispensable nation. That has been true for the century passed and it will be true for the century to come') www.whitehouse.gov/the-press-office/2014/05/28/remarks-president-united-states-military-academy-commencement-ceremony.

[12] Former US NSA and Secretary of State, Condaleezza Rice, 'The New American Realism' (2008) 87 Foreign Affairs 7 https://www.foreignaffairs.com/articles/2008-06-01/rethinking-national-interest.

[13] www.fmprc.gov.cn/mfa_eng/xwfw_665399/s2510_665401/t1269971.shtml.

Indeed, as the White House readily admits, American exceptionality is proximately caused by the ability to make the rules of the international financial and legal architectures: 'That's why we have to make sure the United States—*and not countries like China*—is the one writing this century's rules for the world's economy'.[14]

However, new builders are positioning for a significant role in shaping international law and the incipient development of an alternative or supplemental governance architecture is underway.[15]

Alternative international financial institutions such as the Asian Infrastructure Investment Bank ('AIIB') and New Development Bank ('NDB') offer a replacement to the existing mechanics of lending and development: 'Reflect[ing] a *fundamental change in global economic and political power*'.[16]

The possibility exists that 'revisionist' states infused with strong motivations and global ambitions, strong religious, political or cultural personalities, and empowered with increasing economic and military abilities, will attempt to impose a very different architecture of economics and law:[17]

As in Europe, the Cold War had a military dimension, but the larger competition was over ideas of how governments, societies and individuals would work together. America championed a model where governments were subject to rule of law, as were private citizens. Governments were accountable to citizens, transparency was essential and international disputes were handled diplomatically, in a climate free of intimidation. That was a huge success.[18]

The rise of new architects raises serious implications for international law—a definitional moment as several of the new architects' customs and norms conflict inherently with current Western ideals. Ramifications of the new landscape will offer striking opportunities and immense challenges in the realms of the definition and applicability of international law, treaty negotiation, global power balances, global trade, international monetary institutions, and finance. This chapter raises the questions of how the rising prominence of 'competitor' and 'revisionist' states will collide—in the long-term—with current notions and values in international law.

---

[14] White House, 'President Obama: "Writing Rules for 21st Century Trade"' (18 February 2015) (emphasis added) https://obamawhitehouse.archives.gov/blog/2015/02/18/president-obama-writing-rules-21st-century-trade (last accessed 27 June 2016).

[15] Defense Technical Information Center (DTIC) www.dtic.mil/doctrine/concepts/joe/joe_2035_july16.pdf [2016] page 8 ('Rising powers including for example, China, Russia, India, Iran, or Brazil have increasingly expressed dissatisfaction with their roles, access, and authorities within the current international system. The inability or unwillingness to accommodate the aspirations of these powers in the future may increasingly cause some states to challenge or even reject current rules and norms').

[16] Joseph Stiglitz, Former World Bank Economist and Nobel Prize Winner for Economics www.washingtontimes.com/news/2014/aug/5/emerging-economic-powers-to-challenge-us-imf-with-/ (emphasis added).

[17] Indeed, the Pentagon's Think Tank has expressly stated that the states described as 'revisionist' nations—(ie the new architects) will significantly affect the global military and economic balance and will change the current international order. See generally Defense Technical Information Center (DTIC) www.dtic.mil/doctrine/concepts/joe/joe_2035_july16.pdf.

[18] Samuel Locklear and John Hamre, 'Don't Forget the National-Security Case for TPP Trade Deal' http://blogs.wsj.com/washwire/2015/10/23/dont-forget-the-national-security-case-for-tpp-trade-deal/ (last accessed 23 October 2015).

II. Post Second World War Exceptionality of the United States in the Global Economic and Legal Governance Architecture

The 'creators' or 'architects' of international law are those nations which constitute the 'civilized' nations of the world[19] or whose states generate the general principles common to the 'major' legal systems of the world.[20] The architects are therefore the 'leading' nations who possess the economic strength, technological prowess, cultural power and military means to enforce *their* values and norms. Over the last seventy years, the financial and legal orders of international law have been shaped by the advanced developed nations: the US and Western European nations and several key Asian allies.[21] Large swathes of 'other nations' located elsewhere have traditionally been considered 'uncivilized' and have thus been 'outcasted' as sources of international law.

The backdrop to American supremacy lies in the Bretton Woods agreement, which effectively conferred the prize of global economic leadership on the United States. The agreement served as the backdrop to the development of an institutional framework which was created, shaped, and influenced by the United States. For example, international financial institutions (IFIs)—the IMF and World Bank—confer loans and credit, facilitate global commerce, trade, and development and essentially enable nations either to prosper or to fail economically.[22] The institutional frameworks were

---

[19] See Article 38 of the ICJ www.icj-cij.org/documents/?p1=4&p2=2. According to the International Court of Justice, a major source of international law are the laws rooted in the laws of sovereigns belonging to the group of 'civilized nations of the world'; *Sosa v Alvarez-Machain*, 542 US 692 at 725. The United States Supreme Court directed federal courts to 'require any claim based on the present-day law of nations to rest on a norm of international character accepted *by the civilized world* and defined with a specificity comparable to the features of the 18th-century paradigms' (emphasis added). See also *Sosa v Alvarez-Machain*, 542 US 692 at 732 ('[F]ederal courts should not recognize private claims under federal common law for violations of any international law norm with less definite content and acceptance *among civilized nations* than the historical paradigms familiar when § 1350 was enacted') (emphasis added). See also *The Paquete Habana*, 175 US 677, 700 (1900) ('*customs and usages of civilized nations*; and, as evidence of these, to the works of jurists and commentators, who by years of labor, research and experience, have made themselves peculiarly well acquainted with the subjects').

[20] See Restatement (Third) of Foreign Relations Law of the United States § 102 1987. See also Rene David and J E C Brierley, *Major Legal Systems in the World Today: An Introduction to Comparative Law* (2nd edn, Stevens & Sons Ltd 1978) (noting that the Western common law and civil law systems are the 'major' legal systems).

[21] See Francis Fukuyama, *The End of History? The National Interest* (1989) https://ps321.community.uaf.edu/files/2012/10/Fukuyama-End-of-history-article.pdf (noting that by the end of the 1980s, China, the former Soviet Union, and the countries of Eastern Europe had all realized that the Western 'advanced' nations were successful and, to integrate with the world, they would need to become Westernized).

[22] This power cannot be under estimated and both the IMF and World Bank are literally 'close by' the White House—a mere two blocks away. See Serge F Kovaleski and Spencer Hsu, *Police Plan Traffic Stops Near IMF and World Bank* www.washingtonpost.com/wp-dyn/articles/A32878-2004Aug1.html (last accessed 2 August 2004) ('D.C. police said they have activated surveillance cameras trained on areas near the IMF and World Bank headquarters in Northwest Washington, just off Pennsylvania Avenue about two blocks from the White House'). Of course, 'Throughout the history of the International Bank for Reconstruction and Development (the World Bank), the United States has been the largest shareholder and the most influential member country. U.S. support for, pressure on, and criticisms of the Bank have been central to its growth and the evolution of its policies, programs, and practices' (emphasis added). See Catherine Gwin, 'U.S. Relations with the World Bank, 1945-1992' in Devesh Kapur and others, *The World Bank, Its First Half Century* (Brookings Institution Press 1997) 195.

developed by the United States and the UK with relatively little or no subsequent input and influence from 'less civilized/less advanced' states (and potential competitors) such as China, India, and Russia.[23] Moreover, the vast majority of trade disputes have been resolved through the World Bank's ICSID and the US dominated WTO. Furthermore, the United States dollar is the premier reserve currency and has dominated international business transactions.

In the arts—music, cinema, sports—American culture is sought after internationally.[24] The United States is the home of the world's most innovative and influential companies such as Amazon, Apple, Facebook, Google, Intel, Microsoft, and Twitter, which have transformed the global marketplace.[25] Dozens of United States land, sea, and air military bases are embedded strategically in a large number of nations and powerful American warships and aircraft carriers sail throughout the strategic waterways of the globe.[26] No other nation's taxing authority mandates disclosure from another sovereign's financial institutions.[27] No other sovereign's courts wield such power and influence.[28] Only the United States wielded the sole power to eviscerate hundreds of years of Swiss banking secrecy.[29] Indeed, as with its military,

---

[23] *China's Yuan Replacing US Dollar As Global Currency: A Not So Distant Prospect—Analysis* www.eurasiareview.com/04052016-chinas-yuan-replacing-us-dollar-as-global-currency-a-not-so-distant-prospect-analysis/ (last accessed 4 May 2016) ('During World War II, only the US and UK deliberated about the future of global economy, culminating into the 1944 Bretton Woods Accord. At that time, entire Europe was under Hitler and countries like India and China did not have any economy to have a say in the Accord'). See also Simon Chesterman, 'Asia's Ambivalence about International Law: Past, Present and Futures', https://academic.oup.com/ejil/article/27/4/945/2962207/Asia-s-Ambivalence-about-International-Law-and (2016) ('the vast majority of Asian states literally did not participate in the negotiation of most of the agreements that define the modern international order ... These observations are not unique to Asia, of course. Indeed, one could make a compelling case that the disenfranchisement of African states during these formative periods of international law was far greater').

[24] See Christina Larson, *The Humbling of American Tech Giants in China* www.bloomberg.com/news/articles/2016-08-02/the-humbling-of-american-tech-giants-in-china (last accessed 2 August 2016) (noting that China has 'an affinity for American pop culture from *Titanic* and *Friends* to Michael Jackson')

[25] See U.S. Extends Lead in International Patent and Trademark Filings www.wipo.int/pressroom/en/articles/2016/article_0002.html (last accessed 16 March 2016) ('The United States of America (U.S.) extended its long-standing position as the top source of international patent applications via WIPO amid another strong year of worldwide intellectual property (IP) filing growth, as an electronics manufacturer displaced a watch maker as the leading depositor of international industrial design applications').

[26] Vijay Prashad, *End of Exceptionalism* www.frontline.in/world-affairs/end-of-exceptionalism/article8811042.ece ('U.S. military bases litter the continents of the world, and U.S. warships move from ocean to ocean, bearing terrifying arsenals'). The United States maintains a large number of air, land, and sea bases in the UK, Germany, Italy, Turkey, South Korea, Saudi Arabia, Bahrain, Qatar, Japan, Australia, etc. See List of US military bases worldwide www.google.com/maps/d/viewer?mid=zOzzuQ7-jtRM.k7KCFP1zgCAw&hl=en_US.

[27] See Robert Wood www.forbes.com/sites/robertwood/2014/08/19/ten-facts-about-fatca-americas-manifest-destiny-law-changing-banking-worldwide/#300593551961 (noting the pervasive and onerous reach of the US IRS and its ability to force foreign banking institutions to comply with US directives).

[28] See Nadelle Grossman, 'Director Compliance with Elusive Fiduciary Duties in a Climate of Corporate Governance Reform' (2007) 12 Fordham J Corp & Fin L 393, 397 (Delaware USA law is a global authority, often providing guidance 'to courts in other jurisdictions in establishing their own [] law').

[29] See Robert E McKenzie www.forbes.com/sites/irswatch/2014/02/03/swiss-bank-secrecy-succumbs-to-u-s-tax-enforcers/#6f424c261bb ('It is worthwhile noting that if the Justice Department can overcome 400 years of Swiss bank secrecy it is unlikely that banks located in other tax havens could prevail in a battle against our tax cops').

the reach of US justice is global.[30] Even rivals admit that the United States is 'the' superpower[31] and send their children to US educational institutions.[32]

Notwithstanding these superlative indicia of leadership, an incipient adjustment is well-underway that poses potentially serious challenges to the US led Western-Anglo hegemony,[33] and thus to the intellectual construct of international law being created and enforced through the vantage point of the *present-day* architects.[34] The precipitating factor fostering these developments is the rise of 'competitor states' and/or 'revisionist states'—i.e., the new potential architects of international law.[35] The transformation, currently well-underway, is enabled primarily by remarkable rising economic power.[36]

Until recently, the United States had enjoyed the number one economic power position with close US ally Japan being number two. However, while the US remains number one, China has moved into second place with India now in the top four.[37] In the context of standards of living, per capita GDP and per capita wealth, a large concentration of the richest nations are located in the Middle East. For example, out of the

---

[30] See Russia accuses US of illegal overreach with FIFA corruption indictments www.theguardian.com/football/2015/may/27/russia-accuses-us-overreaching-fifa-corruption-indictments (according to the Russian Foreign Ministry, '[o]nce again we are calling on Washington to stop attempts to make justice far beyond its borders using its legal norms and to follow the generally accepted international legal procedures').

[31] Ilya Arkhipov and Olga Tanas, 'Putin Accepts U.S. as Sole Superpower while Grumbling over NATO' www.bloomberg.com/news/articles/2016-06-17/putin-says-russia-wants-to-mend-ties-with-west-bears-no-grudge ('President Vladimir Putin said he accepts the U.S. as the world's only superpower, dialing back years of Kremlin accusations that Russia's former Cold War adversary is seeking to impose its will on weaker nations').

[32] See Miriam Jordan, 'International Students Stream into U.S. Colleges' www.wsj.com/articles/international-students-stream-into-u-s-colleges-1427248801 (last accessed 24 March 2015) ('American universities are enrolling unprecedented numbers of foreign students, prompted by the rise of an affluent class in China and generous scholarships offered by oil-rich Gulf states such as Saudi Arabia').

[33] Indeed, China has become so important it affects US monetary policy. See Enda Curran and Christopher Condon, 'It's a New World: How China Growth Concerns Kept the Fed on Hold' www.bloomberg.com/news/articles/2015-09-18/it-s-a-new-world-how-china-growth-concerns-kept-the-fed-on-hold (last accessed 18 September 2015) ('Here's the latest sign of China's arrival as a global economic power: It's roiled financial markets enough to nudge the Federal Reserve away from raising interest rates').

[34] In an important strategic forward –looking document, the US Department of Defense's elite research unit—the Department of Technical Information Center www.dtic.mil/dtic/ produced a document titled: *The Joint Force in a Contested and Disordered World* (2016) www.dtic.mil/doctrine/concepts/joe/joe_2035_july16.pdf (articulating deep concerns regarding new rising powers and their effects on the United States); 8 ('Rising powers including for example, China, Russia, India, Iran, or Brazil have increasingly expressed dissatisfaction with their roles, access, and authorities within the current international system').

[35] Referring to these rising powers as 'competitors' and 'revisionist' openly concedes these rising powers as potential new architects. See Defense Technical Information Center (DTIC) www.dtic.mil/doctrine/concepts/joe/joe_2035_july16.pdf ('A range of *competitors* will confront the United States and its global partners and interests. Contested norms will feature adversaries that credibly challenge the rules and agreements that define the international order') at page ii (emphasis added); ('The first is contested norms, in which increasingly powerful *revisionist* states and select non-state actors will use any and all elements of power to establish their own sets of rules in ways unfavorable to the United States and its interests') at page 4 (emphasis added).

[36] Malcolm Scott, 'Here's the $17 Trillion Reason Why the BRICS Summit This Week Is a Big Deal' www.bloomberg.com/news/articles/2015-07-06/here-s-the-17-trillion-reason-why-the-brics-summit-this-week-is-a-big-deal (last accessed 7 July 2015) ('The combined economic output last year of Brazil, Russia, India, China and South Africa almost matched the U.S's gross domestic product. Back in 2007, the U.S. economy was double the BRICS').

[37] Joel Slawotsky, 'The Virtues of Shareholder Value Driven Activism: Avoiding Governance Pitfalls' (2016) 12 Hastings Business Law Journal 521, 555 ('By some measures India has already taken the number three position from Japan').

top richest states on the basis of the percentage of per capita millionaires, the oil and gas rich Middle East dominates.[38]

Moreover, the previously 'less civilized/advanced' nations are increasingly becoming players in the military,[39] financial,[40] technological,[41] and scientific research spheres[42] and are now positioned to become the 'leading nations'. The incipient shift from strict adherence to institutional frameworks and dominance of the IMF and World Bank, the weakening of the unchallenged premier status of the United States dollar[43] and other geo-political shifts such as the OBOR initiative,[44] all herald potentially significant changes to the existing international legal and economic architecture.[45] Therefore, international law models will become increasingly shaped by nations once considered 'developing' and/or 'less civilized'. Thus, it is timely to examine the implications on international law and the international governance architecture.

[38] See www.bcgperspectives.com/content/articles/financial_institutions_business_unit_strategy_global_wealth_2014_riding_wave_growth/?chapter=2#chapter2_section3 (ranking Qatar No 1, Kuwait No 5, Bahrain No 6, Israel No 8, Oman No 10, UAE No 12, and Saudi Arabia No 13).

[39] See Ben Blanchard and Benjamin Kang Lim, 'Give them a bloody nose: Xi pressed for stronger South China Sea response' www.reuters.com/article/us-southchinasea-ruling-china-insight-idUSKCN10B10G (last accessed 31 July 2016) ('China's leadership is resisting pressure from elements within the military for a more forceful response to an international court ruling against Beijing's claims in the South China Sea, sources said, wary of provoking a clash with the United States'); www.foxnews.com/politics/2016/05/18/navy-releases-video-russian-fighter-jets-buzzing-destroyer.html (last accessed 18 May 2016) ('The U.S. Navy on Wednesday released new footage of two Russian fighter jets and a host of helicopters buzzing a U.S. missile destroyer in April, the latest example in a recent series of provocative encounters between Russian aircraft and U.S. war ships').

[40] See Divya Lulla and others, 'Largest 100 Banks in the World' www.snl.com/InteractiveX/Article.aspx?cdid=A-33361429-13866 (last accessed 3 August 2015) (Chinese banks are among the world's largest).

[41] See Larson (n 24) (noting that Chinese technology companies are beginning to produce rival products and services that match or are superior to US companies).

[42] See Yingying Zhou, 'The Rapid Rise of a Research Nation' www.nature.com/nature/journal/v528/n7582_supp_ni/full/528S170a.html (last accessed 17 December 2015) (noting the tremendous growth in Chinese research and scientific achievement). See also China envisions becoming the hegemon in AI and plans to utilize AI for military purposes (as the United States plans to do). See Elsa Kania https://lawfareblog.com/dual-use-dilemma-chinas-new-ai-plan-leveraging-foreign-innovation-resources-and-military-civil, 'The Dual-Use Dilemma in China's New AI Plan: Leveraging Foreign Innovation Resources and Military-Civil Fusion' (28 July 2017) ('The Chinese leadership thus hopes to "occupy the commanding heights" of AI science and technology, leapfrogging the U.S. in the process ... The implementation of military-civil fusion will support China's effort to ensure that AI technology can be quickly leveraged to support national defense innovation through the "sharing and common use" (共享共用) of technologies').

[43] See www.bloomberg.com/news/articles/2015-11-30/imf-backs-yuan-in-reserve-currency-club-after-rejection-in-2010 (noting the Yuan had been rejected as a reserve currency in 2010 but the IMF accepted it in 2015).

[44] Navigate the new Silk Road www.bloomberg.com/professional/blog/navigate-the-new-silk-road/ (last accessed 29 September 2015) (overview of the project).

[45] For example, the concept of human rights is essentially a Western concept whose acceptance by the new architects is far from certain. See Jack Donnelly, 'Human Rights and Human Dignity: An Analytical Critique of Non Western Conceptions of Human Rights' (1982) 76 Am Pol Sci Rev 303, 303 ('most non-Western cultural and political traditions lack not only the practice of human rights but the very concept. As a matter of historical fact, the concept of human rights is an artifact of modern Western civilization'). But see Surya P Subedi, 'Are the Principles of Human Rights "Western" Ideas? An Analysis of the Claim of the "Asian" Concept of Human Rights from the Perspectives of Hinduism' [1999] 30 Cal W Int'l LJ 45, 49 ('The absence of sufficient literature unearthing and analyzing the practices of ancient States of Asia, Africa, and other parts of the world does not signify that human rights have their origin only in Christian Western civilization').

III. The Rise of the New Architects

Sensing a weakening of the unrivalled economic, political, and military status of an 'American Empire'[46] allegedly exhausted by wars, burdened by debt and less able to marshal the instruments of state power to protect its vital interests, other nations are stepping in, filling the power gaps and vacuums.[47] As the official statement of the BRICS conference in 2014 noted:

International governance structures designed within a different power configuration show increasingly evident signs of losing legitimacy and effectiveness.[48]

As a counter-balance to the IMF, World Bank, and ADB, China has launched the AIIB.[49] While both the United States and Japan 'have stayed out of the China-led institution, seen as a rival to the US-dominated World Bank and Japan-led Asian Development Bank',[50] many nations have embraced the AIIB:

The United States and Japan were caught off guard when a total of 57 countries, including Group of Seven members Britain, Germany and France jumped on board the AIIB bandwagon by March.[51]

Former US Treasury Secretary Summers has called 2015 as constituting 'the moment the United States lost its role as the underwriter of the global economic system',[52] referring to China's move to establish a rival development bank as a 'Bretton Woods' moment.[53] China has already utilized its leverage by imposing

---

[46] Many in the United States share this sense of decline and Presidential candidate Donald Trump's campaign theme of 'Make America Great Again' reflects this perception. See Prashad (n 26) ('The Republican nominee for President, Donald Trump, not known for his political sobriety, is running on a campaign slogan that admits to today's reality. "Make America Great Again!" says the slogan, which acknowledges the weaknesses of the U.S. at this present time').

[47] See Kurt Campbell and Brian Andrews, *'Explaining the US "Pivot" to Asia'* www.chathamhouse. org/sites/files/chathamhouse/public/Research/Americas/0813pp_pivottoasia.pdf ('The global financial crisis not only caused severe hardship at home, but it also raised profound questions about the long-term viability of the US economic model and the international liberal order the United States has championed since the Second World War, particularly when juxtaposed with the perceived success of China's economy').

[48] See Sixth Brics Summit—Fortaleza Declaration http://pib.nic.in/newsite/PrintRelease. aspx?relid=106712. See also Zakir Hussain, 'Indonesian President Jokowi Calls for New, More Equal Global Economic Order' www.straitstimes.com/asia/se-asia/indonesian-president-jokowi-calls-for-new-more-equal-global-economic-order (last accessed 23 April 2015) ('The view that the world's economic problems can be solved only by the World Bank, the International Monetary Fund (IMF) and the Asian Development Bank (ADB) is an obsolete one').

[49] See S.R., 'Why China Is Creating a New "World Bank" for Asia' www.economist.com/blogs/economist-explains/2014/11/economist-explains-6 (last accessed 11 November 2014). ('[T]he AIIB has stoked controversy because Asia already has a multilateral lender, the Asian Development Bank (ADB). Why is China creating a new development bank for Asia?').

[50] See Leika Kihara and Linda Sieg, 'Japan Unveils $110 Billion Plan to Fund Asia Infrastructure, Eye on AIIB' www.reuters.com/article/2015/05/21/us-japan-asia-investment-idUSKBN0O617G20150521 (last accessed 21 May 2015).

[51] ibid.

[52] 'Time US Leadership Woke Up to New Economic Era' http://larrysummers.com/2015/04/05/time-us-leadership-woke-up-to-new-economic-era/ (last accessed 5 April 2015).

[53] See www.project-syndicate.org/commentary/china-united-states-global-governance-by-paola-subacchi-2015-04 ('Bretton Woods system, the rules-based order—underpinned by the IMF and the World Bank, with the US dollar at its heart—that emerged after World War II. The Bretton Woods system institutionalized America's geopolitical supremacy').

conditions deemed unacceptable with respect to Taiwan's request to join the AIIB.[54]

An important manifestation of China's rise is the OBOR initiative; a broad based ambitious plan to empower Asian economies and expand the global influence of Asia.[55] The programme was founded in 2013 by China[56] and envisions a prosperous and profitable trade infrastructure to facilitate inter and intra-Asian trade:[57] 'The Silk Road Economic Belt focuses on bringing together China, Central Asia, Russia and Europe (the Baltic); linking China with the Persian Gulf and the Mediterranean Sea through Central Asia and the Indian Ocean'.[58] OBOR constitutes an important component of China's long-term strategic plan to regain dominance in Asia and prestige in the world.[59] As principle architect and leader, China stands to gain immensely.[60]

The potential dilution of the US dollar's status as global reserve currency is not merely a prestigious talking point; a nation whose currency is the world's reserve currency reaps substantial benefits: 'reserve status permits discounted borrowing of loans. And, central banks of other countries must hold [the reserve currency] in reserve to facilitate trade, in turn appreciating the [reserve currency] ... aid[ing] the reserve country with running a trade deficit in perpetuity'.[61] For example, the fact that the energy rich nations of the Middle East and Persian Gulf nations price their oil and gas in US dollars boosts the dollar's importance and is a significant lever of strategic power for the US.[62] If the US dollar loses its luster as the premier reserve currency the US will

[54] See 'Taiwan says it will not join Beijing-led AIIB after rejecting condition that 'violates dignity' XVII www.scmp.com/news/china/policies-politics/article/1935492/taiwan-says-it-will-not-join-beijing-led-aiib-after (last accessed 12 April 2016) ('Taiwan said on Tuesday it would not join the Beijing-led Asian Infrastructure Investment Bank (AIIB) because the condition it was set violates the island's dignity and the principal of equality').

[55] http://blogs.wsj.com/chinarealtime/tag/silk-road-economic-belt/.

[56] Chronology of China's Belt and Road Initiative http://news.xinhuanet.com/english/2015-03/28/c_134105435.htm (last accessed 28 March 2015) (discussing the Silk Road's timeline of development).

[57] ibid ('The Belt and Road routes run through the continents of Asia, Europe and Africa, connecting the vibrant East Asia economic circle at one end and developed European economic circle at the other').

[58] ibid. See also Julien Chaisse and Mitsuo Matsushita, 'China's "Belt and Road" Initiative: Mapping the World Trade Normative and Strategic Implications' (2018) 52(1) Journal of World Trade 163.

[59] John Kemp, 'China's Silk Road Challenges U.S. Dominance in Asia' www.japantoday.com/category/opinions/view/chinas-silk-road-challenges-u-s-dominance-in-asia (last accessed 14 November 2014): ('The New Silk Road Economic Belt: from China across Central Asia and Russia to Europe: and the 21st Century Maritime Silk Road: through the Malacca Strait to India, the Middle East and East Africa: have become the centrepiece of China's economic diplomacy').

[60] See Isabel Reynolds, 'Abe Pitches Japan's Infrastructure on China's Silk-Road Patch' www.bloomberg.com/news/articles/2015-10-22/abe-pitches-japan-s-infrastructure-on-china-s-silk-road-patch (last accessed 23 October 2015) ('China is increasingly dominating the economic landscape in the resource-rich region, seeking to deepen investments with its neighbours and bolster slowing growth through its Silk Road plan to revive an ancient trade link to Europe')

[61] Jordan Totten, 'BRICS New Development Bank Threatens Hegemony of U.S. Dollar' www.forbes.com/sites/realspin/2014/12/22/brics-new-development-bank-threatens-hegemony-of-u-s-dollar/ (last accessed 22 December 2014).

[62] China signs currency swap deal with Qatar in the heart of petro-dollar system www.examiner.com/article/china-signs-currency-swap-deal-with-qatar-the-heart-of-petro-dollar-system (last accessed 4 November 2014) ('The petro-dollar system is the heart and soul of America's domination over the global reserve currency, and their right to make all nations have to purchase U.S. dollars to be able to buy oil in the open market. Bound through an agreement with Saudi Arabia and OPEC in 1973, this de facto standard has lasted for over 41 years and has been the driving force behind America's economic, political, and military power').

suffer and would constitute a serious challenge to the United States' economy[63] severely constraining US policy-makers.[64]

China clearly has a major interest in promoting the yuan and the biggest rival to the US dollar is the yuan. 'The No. 1 status of the greenback leaves China's wealth and economic health reliant on US policy—a predicament Beijing desperately wishes to change'.[65] Russia, subject to sanctions in a US dollar denominated financial system would like to develop an alternative to the US dollar[66] and strongly supports the yuan's rising importance.[67]

Russia and China intend to use their national currencies to settle more energy deals to guard against instability in a world energy market dominated by the US dollar, Russian President Vladimir Putin said …[68]

The signing of deals using the yuan instead of the dollar is slowly increasing[69] and Brazil, India, and Russia are entering into non-dollar deals.[70] While the pro-yuan users are primarily the new architects as well as allied developing nations such as Indonesia,[71] surprisingly many US allies are also pursuing this venue.[72] Canada has embraced the yuan and has signed a deal that 'will allow direct business between the

---

[63] Bill Conerly, 'Future of the Dollar as World Reserve Currency' *Businomics Blog* (2013) www.forbes.com/sites/billconerly/2013/10/25/future-of-the-dollar-as-world-reserve-currency/#ef794f61517a (last accessed 25 October 2013) ('The dollar's role as the world's primary reserve currency helps all of us Americans by keeping interest rates low. Foreign countries buy United States Treasury debt not just as an investment, but because dollar-denominated assets are the best way to hold foreign exchange reserves').

[64] Joel Slawotsky, 'Sovereign Wealth Funds as Emerging Financial Superstars' (2009) 40 Georgetown Journal of International Law 1 ('Nations whose money does not enjoy the status of reserve currency cannot create staggering amounts of new currency without shouldering increased risk of inflationary currency debasement. If the dollar were no longer the world's reserve currency, the U.S. would be forced to assume similar risk, severely constraining the flexibility of American policy makers').

[65] Michael Schuman, 'Whose Money Will the World Follow?' www.bloomberg.com/news/articles/2015-05-14/u-s-china-rivalry-whose-money-will-the-world-follow- (last accessed 14 May 2015).

[66] 'Putin says China, Russia to settle more trade in yuan' www.reuters.com/article/2014/11/10/us-russia-economy-idUSKCN0IU0HV20141110 (last accessed 10 November 2014) ('Russia and China intend to increase the amount of trade settled in the yuan, President Vladimir Putin said on Monday in remarks that would be welcomed by Chinese authorities who want the currency to be used more widely around the world').

[67] See Kenneth Rapoza, 'Russia's Sberbank Lending In Chinese Currency' www.forbes.com/sites/kenrapoza/2015/06/07/russias-sberbank-lending-in-chinese-currency/#76e2341427da (last accessed 7 June 2015) ('Russia's biggest commercial lender is issuing letters of credit in the Chinese yuan').

[68] Li Xiang China, 'Russia to Use Yuan, Rouble in More Energy Deals' http://usa.chinadaily.com.cn/business/2014-11/11/content_18897132.htm (last accessed 11 November 2014).

[69] See Totten (n 61) ('Recent dollar-less BRICS energy deals, currency swaps and foreign direct investment indicate that trend is taking place').

[70] See www.telegraph.co.uk/finance/comment/liamhalligan/10978178/The-dollars-70-year-dominance-is-coming-to-an-end.html. See also Jack Farchy, 'Gazprom Neft Sells Oil to China in Renminbi Rather Than Dollars' https://next.ft.com/content/8e88d464-0870-11e5-85de-00144feabdc0 (last accessed 1 June 2015) ('Beijing has struck numerous agreements with Brazil and India that bypass the dollar. China and Russia have also set up rouble-yuan swaps pushing America's currency out of the picture').

[71] 'Indonesia to Use Yuan in Trade With China from 2016' www.plenglish.com/index.php?option=com_content&task=view&id=4366281&Itemid=1 ('Indonesia will use the yuan instead of US dollars in its trade with China starting next year, in a bid to save foreign exchange reserves and reduce dependency on the dollar').

[72] See News Release—People's Bank of China swap line www.bankofengland.co.uk/publications/Pages/news/2013/033.aspx (last accessed 22 February 2013) ('The establishment of a sterling-renminbi swap line will support UK domestic financial stability').

Canadian dollar and the Chinese yuan, *cutting out the middle man* —in most cases, the U.S. dollar'.[73]

The NDB is another alternative IFI to the Western IFIs[74] and should be viewed in the context of the other initiatives.[75] The objective of the NDB is to embrace a new financial order[76] and is a project of several nations all seeking a viable substitute to the current global governance architecture: '[T]he NDB remains important as a reminder that China is not alone in seeking alternatives to the Western financial system'.[77] According to the NDB's website:

The New Development Bank [] is multilateral development bank operated by the BRICS states (Brazil, Russia, India, China and South Africa) *as an alternative to the existing US-dominated World Bank and International Monetary Fund.*[78]

In an early indication of using the NDB to advance political interests, Russia has given incentive to Greece to obtain NDB funding in response to the EU–Greek debt crisis[79] and Russia is blunt that for Greece this is a 'political decision'.[80]

IV. Ramifications of the Current Framework Challenged

Given the rise of these new architects, it would be an historical anomaly if the current legal and financial orders would not be significantly altered to comport with the advancement and furtherance of the beliefs and goals of the rising power(s):

In particular, there does not appear to be a comparable example of a great power (or multiple powers) rising within a normative framework not of its own making, where that normative framework has not undergone substantial change or revolution as a result of the new power's values and interests.[81]

As rising powers (i.e., 'revisionists' and 'competitors') become increasingly influential international law norms will likely be challenged:

[73] Canada, 'China Sign Currency Deal Aimed at Boosting Trade' www.cbc.ca/news/politics/canada-china-sign-currency-deal-aimed-at-boosting-trade-1.2828707 (last accessed 8 November 2014) (emphasis added).
[74] Shannon Tiezzi, 'Don't Forget About the New BRICS Bank' http://thediplomat.com/2015/07/dont-forget-about-the-new-brics-bank/ (last accessed 22 July 2015)(last accessed 22 July 2015) ('The bank was—and is—envisioned as an answer to the current international financial system, which is dominated by the West').
[75] Scott (n 36) ('Additional glue for the BRICS leaders is a $100 billion currency-exchange reserve program discussed at last year's summit. Then there's the planned BRICS bank, which will be a big part of the agenda this year, along with China's "One Belt One Road" strategy and ways to deepen economic links').
[76] See www.telegraph.co.uk/finance/comment/liamhalligan/10978178/The-dollars-70-year-dominance-is-coming-to-an-end.html ('[T]he governments of Brazil, Russia, India and China led a conference in the Brazilian city of Fortaleza to mark the establishment of a new development bank that, whatever diplomatic niceties are put on it, is intent on competing with the IMF and World Bank')
[77] Tiezzi (n 74).
[78] New Development Bank BRICS http://ndbbrics.org/ (emphasis added).
[79] See Seema Mody, 'Russia May Win Politically if a Greek Deal Falls Through' www.cnbc.com/2015/07/13/russia-may-win-politically-if-a-greek-deal-falls-through.html (last accessed 15 July 2015) (discussing the debt crisis).
[80] Sounak Mukhopadhyay 'Greece Can Easily Get Funding from BRICS Bank: Russia' www.ibtimes.com/greece-can-easily-get-funding-brics-bank-russia-1998515 (last accessed 7 July 2015) ('Russia said Greece could get financing from the New Development Bank operated by Brazil, Russia, India, China and South Africa (BRICS) if it buys a few shares of the institution to become a member. The bank, which is set to begin operations next April, is seen an alternative to Western financing. Deputy Russian Finance Minister Sergey Storchak said becoming a part of the bank would require Greek officials to make a political decision').
[81] Chesterman (n 23).

The first [upcoming challenge] is contested norms, in which increasingly powerful revisionist states and select non-state actors will use any and all elements of power to establish their own sets of rules in ways unfavorable to the United States and its interests.[82]

One of the major ramifications of the rise of the new architects is with respect to the very definition and contours of international law norms. Shifting notions of acceptable conduct is hardly surprising as international law can and does change over time.[83]

All major civilizations have for long periods treated a significant portion of the human race as 'outsiders' not entitled to guarantees that could be taken for granted by 'insiders'.[84]

Corroborating the cyclical nature of international law, some argue that the current Western conceptualization of international law is itself a successor to a previous value system.:[85] 'The absence of sufficient literature unearthing and analyzing the practices of ancient States of Asia, Africa, and other parts of the world does not signify that human rights have their origin only in Christian Western civilization'.[86] International law may thus be viewed as a cyclical circle of architects, where dominant powers of centuries ago may reassert themselves depending upon new geo-political and economic conditions.

Global litigation against individuals and businesses for international law violations will likely be affected.[87] In the United States, the Alien Tort Statute (ATS)[88] permits aliens to file suits against defendants for violations of international law.[89] However, only misconduct defined as violating international law through the lens of 'civilized nations' is subject to suit.[90]

What if the benchmarks change as international law evolves?[91] Ironically, liability for state sponsored torture which was greenlighted in *Filartiga* contains the inherent means of its own 'reversal'. In *Filartiga*, the court had to decide whether state sponsored

---

[82] U.S. Department of Defense Report, *The Joint Force in a Contested and Disordered World* (2016) www.dtic.mil/doctrine/concepts/joe/joe_2035_july16.pdf

[83] See *Filartiga*, 630 F.2d at 881 (noting international law does not remain static).

[84] Donnelly, 'The Relative Universality of Human Rights' (n 10) 291 www.brandeis.edu/ethics/pdfs/internationaljustice/biij/BIIJ2013/donnelly.pdf.

[85] Subedi (n 45) 45, 58 ('These writers argue that modern international law is a creation of Western Christian civilization. The conclusion one arrives at depends on how far back in history one goes in unearthing the practices of States. If the examination is limited to the nineteenth century and onwards, then the conclusion would be based on a rather narrow Euro-centric perception of international law. However, if the inquiry goes farther back in history, taking into account all evidence available in writing since the days of thriving ancient civilizations of other regions of the world, then the conclusion is a broader global one based on a universal outlook of the history of international law').

[86] ibid.

[87] See Andrew Sanger, 'Corporations and Transnational Litigation: Comparing Kiobel with the Jurisprudence of English Courts' www.asil.org/sites/default/files/AGORA/201401/Sanger%20AJIL%20Unbound%20e-23%20(2014).pdf (noting UK litigation against multinationals); http://ohrh.law.ox.ac.uk/nigerian-farmers-can-sue-shell-in-dutch-court-precedent-for-transnational-cases-against-multinationals/ ('The case of the Nigerian farmers against Shell is the first in which a Dutch multinational has been brought before a Dutch court to account for environmental damage caused abroad'). See also Nevson v www.biv.com/article/2016/10/court-allows-eritrean-mine-workers-sue-nevsun/ (Canadian ruling allowing an action claiming a Canadian corporation violated international law in Eritera).

[88] 28 USC 1350.

[89] For a discussion of the Alien Tort Statute—corporate liability and litigation see Joel Slawotsky, Qatar University International Review of Law www.qscience.com/doi/pdf/10.5339/irl.2013.6 (2013).

[90] See *Sosa v Alvarez-Machain*, 542 US 692, 731 (2004).

[91] *Filartiga*, 630 F.2d at 881. See also Paul C Szasz, 'General Law-Making Processes' in Chris C Joyner (ed), *The United Nations and International Law* (Cambridge University Press 1997) 2, 31 (noting customary international law is increasingly changing due to the 'general acceleration of international interactions').

torture was cognizable as a violation of international law.[92] After examining the *current* state of international law, the court found that state sponsored torture should now be considered as an accepted violation of customary international law because the majority of *civilized* nations held such conduct to be wrong.[93] However, the rationale provides for the possibility that the opposite is also true; if the majority of civilized nations[94] find state sponsored torture acceptable (or acceptable under 'exigent' circumstances)—such conduct would not constitute an international law violation.

The historical underpinning of the *current* conceptualization of modern international law is based upon the creation of international law by the *civilized* nations of the world[95] or the general principles common to the *major* legal systems of the world.[96] For example, in *The Paquete Habana*,[97] the United States Supreme Court held that the prohibition against seizing an enemy's fishing vessels during wartime had grown over time to become established by the 'general assent of *civilized nations*, into a settled rule of international law'.[98]

The term 'civilized nations' served to distinguish 'superior' European[99] nations from the 'inferior' uncivilized nations[100] and invoked to impose various legal and economic initiatives onto the 'uncivilized nations'.[101] In this narrative, international law, 'does not exist for all states of the globe....it developed only within the circle of certain states and was rooted in the conscience of Christian Europe and European-originated states'.[102] Buddhist, Islamic, and Hindu nations were excluded since Western civilization was considered superior:[103] 'Semi-barbarous States like China, Turkey and Japan, whose municipal law and the judgments of whose courts are not recognised by civilised nations' were excluded from full participation in international law'.[104]

While the *present-day* 'civilized nations' and 'major' nations are those USA–Euro centric states that are rich and militarily powerful, the rising powers, i.e., the 'revisionist

---

[92] At the time of the ATS's enactment, torture was not one of the three violations of international law. The key is whether the 'new' tort, here torture, could be defined with the same 'definite content and acceptance among *civilized nations* than the historical paradigms familiar when § 1350 was enacted' See *Sosa v Alvarez-Machain*, 542 US at 731.

[93] See *Filartiga v Pena-Irala*, 630 F.2d 876 (2d Cir 1980).

[94] Moreover, what constitutes the *majority* of civilized nations—the majority of population or the number of states? If majority is a function of population, the two most populous nations are China and India whose combined populations dwarf the population of the United States and have very different norms.

[95] See J L Brierly, *The Law of Nations: An Introduction to the International Law of Peace* (6th edn, OUP 1963) (emphasis added).

[96] See Restatement (Third) of Foreign Relations Law Of The United States § 102 1987. See also David and Brierley (n 20) (noting that the Western common law and civil law systems are the 'major' legal systems).

[97] 175 US 677 (1900).   [98] 175 US 677, 694 (1900) (emphasis added).

[99] 175 US at 317 ('The idea that international law had a specifically European character was most actively and fully developed in and around the 19th century. It became conventional wisdom that international law developed through European treaties and customs, and that non-European countries did not participate in its development').

[100] See Alexander Orakhelashvili, 'The Idea of European International Law' (2006) 16 Eur J Int'l Law 318.

[101] ibid.   [102] ibid.

[103] See Amber Philips, 'Steve King: The idea that every culture is equal is "not objectively true"' www.washingtonpost.com/news/the-fix/wp/2016/07/20/steve-king-the-idea-that-every-culture-is-equal-is-not-objectively-true/ (last accessed 20 July 2016) ('The idea of multiculturalism, that every culture is equal — that's not objectively true ... Western civilization is the most successful civilization the world has ever seen').

[104] ibid 319 (citing Lorimer).

nations', are becoming affluent and strong. The currently outcasted 'barbarians'[105] are in fact on track to become international law architects. What happens when states that employ torture become international law architects? What if peaceful political dissent is considered by a majority of the civilized nations as an emergency circumstance justifying torture? What would happen if a majority of the civilized nations of the world found that discrimination against certain groups based upon ethnic, gender, or religious criteria was not merely permissible but obligatory? Perhaps child labour is not abuse but acceptable, educational, or even mandatory to a majority of the new architects? Are honour killings a legitimate exception to the rule against extra-judicial executions? Is torture a legitimate method to enforce social order and the public good?

In China, pro-Western reformers are accused of 'worshipping Western ways', 'glorifying Western models', or 'caving in to Western pressures'.[106] The CCP views Western democracy as flawed, proclaiming the 'ultimate defeat of capitalism would enable Communism to emerge victorious'.[107] Privacy rights and the ability to access the internet freely may be understood differently by the new architects. China has restricted the ability of VPNs to operate, claiming the right to cyber-sovereignty. Again, this demonstrates different notions of rights and values from Western ideals:

Data privacy is also an issue. If users are compelled to browse overseas sites using VPNs provided by official internet service providers, what assurances do they have that China's formidable security apparatus will not harvest their business secrets and other confidential material?[108]

Moreover, an important corollary is also true—certain rights currently entrenched in Western nations may in fact constitute outrageous misconduct in other cultures.[109] For instance, the EU nations[110] and the United States[111] may very well recognize same-sex marriages but this practice is considered illegal, abhorrent, and sacrilegious in other nations.[112] Similarly, freedoms of speech, to assembly, to protest, to drive, or to

---

[105] Jeffrey Kahn www.vjil.org/assets/pdfs/vol56/VJIL_56.1_Kahn_FINAL.pdf (2016) 32 ('There was, of course, racism present in the way some privileged (mainly European) civilization over the barbarism perceived in others'). See also Chesterman (n 23) ('The exclusion of non-European states from full participation in international law was justified variously by reference to culture, religion and biology. Much of this history can be explained by racism or realpolitik').

[106] Robert Lawrence Kuhn, 'Xi Jinping's Chinese Dream' http://www.nytimes.com/2013/06/05/opinion/global/xi-jinpings-chinese-dream.html (last accessed 4 June 2013).

[107] See https://www.bloomberg.com/politics/articles/2017-01-22/china-slams-western-democracy-as-flawed-as-trump-takes-office, stating that democracy has reached its limits, and deterioration is the inevitable future of capitalism, according to the People's Daily, the flagship paper of China's Communist Party.

[108] See 'The Dangers in Beijing's Bid for Cyber Sovereignty' https://www.ft.com/content/52d5880c-7607-11e7-a3e8-60495fe6ca71 (last accessed 31 July 2017) ('"Cyber sovereignty" has been a buzzword among China's political elite for more than 18 months').

[109] 'Sisi says "Western" human rights values don't apply in Egypt' *Al Arabiya English* (4 May 2016) http://english.alarabiya.net/en/News/middle-east/2016/05/04/Sisi-says-Western-human-rights-values-don-t-apply-in-Egypt.html (last accessed 27 June 2015).

[110] See 'Gay Marriage around the World' www.bbc.com/news/world-21321731 ('Since the Netherlands became the first country to allow same-sex marriage 12 years ago, many countries have followed suit').

[111] See US Supreme Court rules gay marriage is legal nationwide www.bbc.com/news/world-us-canada-33290341 (last accessed 27 June 2015) ('The US Supreme Court has ruled that same-sex marriage is a legal right across the United States').

[112] See Lora Mofta, ' "Gay Parties" Raided in Saudi Arabia; Religious Police Arrest Several People on Suspicion of Homosexuality' www.ibtimes.com/gay-parties-raided-saudi-arabia-religious-police-arrest-several-people-suspicion-1968038 ('Homosexuality is illegal under Saudi Arabia's strict interpretation of Islamic Shariah law, which holds that any married man found engaging in homosexual acts can be stoned to death. Other punishments for those found guilty of homosexuality include imprisonment, flogging, chemical castration and execution').

worship, may be denied in certain states based upon criteria that would be considered the most severe violations of human dignity in Western states but considered as important values in these other nations.[113] According to the norms of some of the new architects, it is perfectly acceptable and perhaps obligatory to deny these rights to certain groups based upon a religious, ethnic, gender, or political basis.[114]

Some of the new architects' norms and values may conflict with present-day architects' views on sustainable development, environmental concerns, labour rights, and climate change. Indeed, these values may vary among the new architects depending upon self-interest.[115] Moreover, relatively few of the potential new architects have taken meaningful or substantial remedial enforcement and/or preventative action on environmental crime;[116] and several of the new architects are prominent actors in perpetrating, and/or aiders and abettors of, environmental crime.[117]

As the new architects rise in influence, their divergent interests and values will likely make international enforcement and agreements on environmental and sustainability more difficult and/or reflective of a different set of values. With respect to labour rights, the rights of employees, including migrants and children, are not extensively recognized in the domestic legal systems of several new architects.[118] Will Western nations with a vested economic self-interest in the new architects pull-back from CSR initiatives?

Important rules affecting IFIs such as transparency, accountability and fairness have been shaped from the prism of the present-day architects, particularly the significant and influential role exerted by the United States.[119] For example, IFIs exert substantial influence with respect to 'the broad governance themes of climate change, corporate

---

[113] In the United States, using religious, ethnic, gender, or racial criteria is strictly forbidden. See eg Title VII of the Civil Rights Act 1964 (prohibiting employers from discriminating against employees on the basis of colour, race, sex, national origin, or religion).

[114] See Amulya Gopalakrishnan, 'Housing: We Need a Law against Discrimination' http://timesofindia.indiatimes.com/home/sunday-times/all-that-matters/Housing-We-need-a-law-against-discrimination/articleshow/47749962.cms (last accessed 21 June 2015) (noting open discrimination in the Indian housing market); Lu-Hai Liang, 'Discrimination Based on Ethnic Origin Can Be Blunt in China' www.telegraph.co.uk/expat/expatlife/11500033/Discrimination-based-on-ethnic-origin-can-be-blunt-in-China.html (last accessed 31 March 2015) (noting widespread ethnic discrimination in China).

[115] 'The Rise of Environmental Crime' (2016) https://wedocs.unep.org/bitstream/handle/20.500.11822/7662/-The_rise_of_environmental_crime_A_growing_threat_to_natural_resources_peace,_development_and_security-2016environmental_crimes.pdf.pdf?sequence=3&isAllowed=y at page 25 ('What may constitute a crime in one country, is not in another'). Indeed, even among the new architects the self-interest varies significantly. See Eduardo Porter, 'India Is Caught in a Climate Change Quandary' www.nytimes.com/2015/11/11/business/economy/india-is-caught-in-a-climate-change-quandary.html (last accessed 10 November 2015) (noting the conflict between pro-growth in a developing nation and climate change advocacy).

[116] John Aglionby, 'Agencies Detect Sharp Increase in Environmental Crime' https://next.ft.com/content/ae6a9af0-294a-11e6-8ba3-cdd781d02d89 (last accessed 4 June 2016).

[117] See generally 'The Rise of Environmental Crime' (n 115) (containing numerous references to Brazil, China, and India).

[118] See David Barboza, 'In Chinese Factories, Lost Fingers and Low Pay' www.nytimes.com/2008/01/05/business/worldbusiness/05sweatshop.html (last accessed 5 January 2008) (noting that in China, 'worker abuse is still commonplace'); see also 'Ending Child Labor in India' www.nytimes.com/2015/06/27/opinion/ending-child-labor-in-india.html (last accessed 26 June 2015) ('millions of India's children are denied an education, forced to toil on farms, in small-scale industries and as domestic help').

[119] See Larry Backer, 'International Financial Institutions (IFIs) and Sovereign Wealth Funds (SWFs) as Instruments to Combat Corruption and Enhance Fiscal Discipline in Developing States' http://www.qscience.com/doi/full/10.5339/irl.2015.swf.5 at note 23 ('That institutional architecture, the International Working Group of Sovereign Wealth Funds, "met at IMF Headquarters in Washington, D.C."').

governance of portfolio companies, environmental protection, ethical investing, global financial regulation, human rights, regulation of SWFs, renewable energy, and sustainable development'.[120] Thus, the future impact of the alternative IFIs, whose promoters and main shareholders have different interests and values than the existing architects, cannot be under-estimated.

Another aspect of the governance architecture likely to be modified relates to the emerging financial superstars—government funded sovereign wealth funds (SWFs). During the OECD discussions with regard to regulating SWFs, the US and EU nations established 'an informal group of member states' officials who meet in Washington, D.C. This system, driven by the United States and the EU, strives to draw up a code of best practice that includes a renunciation of political motives; however, it has stirred resentment among some countries with SWFs, particularly in China and some Gulf countries'.[121] Again, this corroborates the substantial influence wielded by international law architects and strongly suggests that the new architects will—if enabled—make rules that will serve the interests of the new architects thus potentially modifying the existing regulatory architecture of SWFs.

Self-interest drives law and economics—international trade agreements may encompass broader, geopolitical concerns and global governance contexts have always played a role in investment treaty law.[122] Indeed, the impetus for the TPP was the drive to retain the US lead in rule-making so that Washington, *rather than Beijing*, to create the foundation for '21st-century trade rules', including standards on trade, investment, data flows, and intellectual property.[123]

But power is shifting and the new architects—the 'non-civilized nations'—have become economic powerhouses and will be increasingly impacting this important pillar of global governance:[124]

More specifically, China, India, Brazil, Russia, and South Africa have emerged as great trading powers and they have formed a group representing developing countries to assert their position vis-à-vis developed countries as represented by the USA and the European Union (EU). A 'Green Room' style of negotiation in which a few developed countries decide the basic trade policies and persuade other countries, including developing countries,

---

[120] ibid 4, 6–7.

[121] See Julien Chaisse, 'Demystifying Public Security Exception and Limitations on Capital Movement: Hard Law, Soft Law and Sovereign Investments in the EU Internal Market' (2015) 37 U Pa J Int'l L 583, 626–7 http://scholarship.law.upenn.edu/cgi/viewcontent.cgi?article=1912&context=jil pages.

[122] See Locknie Hsu, 'Regulatory Flexibilities and Tensions in Public Health and Trade—An Asian Perspective' (2015) 10 Asian Journal of WTO & International Health Law and Policy 180. As Singaporean Ambassador Koh noted: 'Singapore wishes to entrench the presence of the U.S. in the region because it underpins the security of the whole Asia-Pacific region. Singapore regards the U.S.-Singapore FTA as a symbol of continued U.S. commitment to the region. Therefore, for Singapore, the USSFTA is not just about securing tariff-free entry for Singapore's exports to the U.S. market. It is not just about attracting more Foreign Direct Investment (FDI) to Singapore. It is also about enhancing the prospects of peace and stability in the region'. See also K Gordon and J Pohl, 'Investment Treaties over Time: Treaty Practice and Interpretation in a Changing World' *OECD Working Papers on International Investment* (OECD Publishing 2015) 9 http://dx.doi.org/10.1787/5js7rhd8sq7h-en ('countries adopting investment treaties had multiple reasons for signing BITs—reasons that related to both domestic and international politics').

[123] Hammond (n 2).

[124] See J: 'Gordon and Pohl, (n 122) 9 ('As the distinction between capital-exporting and capital-importing countries continues to fade——many countries are now "a bit of both"—countries' perceived self-interests in relation to investment treaties may have evolved').

to accept is no longer working anymore and, thus, a new decision-making process in WTO is needed.[125]

Significantly, investment treaty law decisions are impacted by and reference international law[126] and claims as well as defences are impacted by international law.[127] The definition, contours, and application of treaty obligations will have different outcomes depending upon interpretations of international law.[128]

For example, issues of sustainability and corporate social responsibility have steadily increased in importance[129] and arbitrators have increasingly incorporated these factors into rulings.[130] Concepts such as 'due process', 'necessity', and 'national emergency' have been understood through the perspective of Western inspired norms. However, such concepts may be understood and interpreted differently by the new competitor states. The new architects will have their own interests to advance and may result in different arbitral outcomes reflecting the international law norms of the new architects.[131]

V. Conclusion

New infrastructure and development banks, a growing usage of the yuan, the potential transformative role of OBOR and other incipient developments, herald an upcoming era of new international law architects. By using the mechanics of the current architecture to assume a leadership role, rising competitor powers will likely further entrench themselves in the governance architecture. Longer-term, these nations will likely exert substantial, if not dominating influence, on the legal and financial orders. While new institutions will initially work in conjunction within the existing framework, it is probable that the new architects' alternatives will reach a critical mass and achieve an independent role in the international economic and legal orders.[132] This transformation

---

[125] See Julien Chaisse and Mitsuo Matsushita, 'Maintaining the WTO's Supremacy in the International Trade Order: A Proposal to Refine and Revise the Role of the Trade Policy Review Mechanism' (2013) 16 Journal of International Economic Law 9, doi:10.1093/jiel/jgs043.

[126] See K Gordon, J Pohl, and M Bouchard, 'Investment Treaty Law, Sustainable Development and Responsible Business Conduct: A Fact Finding Survey' (OECD Publishing 2014) 21 http://dx.doi.org/10.1787/5jz0xvgx1zlt-en ('reference to other rules of international law in the course of interpreting a treaty is an everyday, often unconscious, part of the interpretation process').

[127] See Christoph Schreuer, 'The Development of International Law by ICSID Tribunals' (2016) 31(3) *ICSID Review* 728 doi:10.1093/icsidreview/siw017 ('Apart from contract claims, the claimant may pursue claims based on sources of international law beyond the treaty that provides for jurisdiction. These may be other treaties, bilateral as well as multilateral and customary international law. Examples for pertinent treaties would be double taxation agreements or human rights treaties').

[128] See Gordon, Pohl and Bouchard (n 126) 22 ('adjudicative bodies in international law increasingly seek to apply international law (including investment treaty law) in its general context—that is, interpreting treaties while also integrating, where relevant and applicable, other components of international law (both customary and conventional) and of domestic law').

[129] ibid 5 ('Inclusion of SD/RBC issues has become a dominant treaty practice in recent years. More than three-quarters of recently concluded IIAs (i.e. between 2008 and 2013) contain language on SD/RBC [] and virtually all of the investment treaties concluded in 2012 and 2013 include such language').

[130] ibid 6 ('Arbitrators frequently refer to issues and international agreements relating to SD/RBC').

[131] See R Zachary Torres-Fowler, 'Undermining ICSID: How The Global Antibribery Regime Impairs Investor-State Arbitration' (2012) 52(4) Virginia Journal of International Law 1009 www.vjil.org/assets/pdfs/vol52/issue4/Torres-Fowler_Post_Production.pdf (noting that in Brazil, China, India, and Russia 'between 47-75% of respondents reported multiple bribe solicitations per year with 7-20% stating they received over 100 requests' and is materially more common and socially acceptable).

[132] US Joint Chiefs of Staff, 'The Joint Force in a Contested and Disordered World' 52 www.dtic.mil/doctrine/concepts/joe/joe_2035_july16.pdf ('Moreover, anticipated scientific and technical

will likely lead to rewriting the international law writ and will serve to devalue the institutions which have enforced the global governance architecture over the previous seventy years.

At a minimum, the replacement of the present architects will present a definitional, let alone enforcement problem with respect to international law. It would be an historical anomaly for the new architects not to change the existing architecture substantially. A different code of conduct may conflict with current norms and international law will need to focus on this potential dichotomy between former and new standards and customs. The failure to address this impending clash of customs may lead to a fracture of global cooperation and enforcement of international law, reduced prosperity, and heightened economic and military conflict.

advances will likely lead to greater parity among a range of international actors thus allowing potential adversaries to more effectively challenge U.S. global interests').

23

Investment Treaty Arbitration in Asia
The China Factor

Matthew Hodgson* and Adam Bryan**

I. Introduction

The pace with which China has grown its bilateral and multi-lateral investment treaty networks over the past three decades is remarkable. As late as 1982, China was not party to a single investment treaty, a consequence of the closed economic system that it had pursued since the founding of the communist state in 1949. By comparison, Germany—the current world leader in terms of the scope of its bilateral investment treaty network—had already concluded forty-nine at that stage. Following Deng Xiaoping's 'opening up' of the Chinese economy in the late 1970s, however, China rapidly pursued investment treaties as a means to attract foreign investment and to protect the assets of its own investors overseas. As of the end of 2016, China has executed 145 bilateral investment treaties (of which 110 are currently in force).[1] This figure stands second only to Germany's 155.

This chapter seeks to explore China's historical and current approaches towards investment treaties and in turn analyse its possible future strategy. In particular, the chapter considers how the growth and nature of China's inward- and outward-bound foreign direct investment (FDI) interact with the protections provided in the bilateral investment treaties and the identity of counterparty states. As enthusiasm for investment treaties in the West stands at a crossroads—in the face of public antipathy in Europe to the draft Transatlantic Trade and Investment Partnership (TTIP) treaty, and hostility from the Trump administration to investment treaties in general[2]—there is maybe an opportunity for China to demonstrate leadership and cooperation to regional and global economic partners.[3]

Section II of this chapter maps the evolution of the protections provided in China's investment treaties, from the rudimentary protections in the early generation investment treaties to the wider-scale coverage in the more recent investment treaties.

* Partner, Allen & Overy, Hong Kong.
** Former Registered Foreign Lawyer, Allen & Overy, Hong Kong.

[1] 'International Investment Agreements Navigator' (United Nations Conference on Trade and development (UNCTAD), undated) http://investmentpolicyhub.unctad.org/IIA/CountryBits/42 (last accessed 18 January 2017).

[2] Since the Trump administration took office on 20 January 2017, it has pulled out of the Trans-Pacific Partnership. On 30 September 2018, negotiations for the new United States–Mexico–Canada Agreement (USMCA) were concluded. The USMCA will replace NAFTA after ratification by the three countries.

[3] See Julien Chaisse, 'The Shifting Tectonics of International Investment Law: Structure and Dynamics of Rules and Arbitration on Foreign Investment in the Asia-Pacific Region' (2015) 47 George Washington International Law Review 563, 615–16; Julien Chaisse and Rahul Donde, 'The State of Investor-State Arbitration: A Reality Check of the Issues, Trends, and Directions in Asia-Pacific' (2018) 51(1) The International Lawyer 47.

Section III reflects upon the extent to which China has succeeded in protecting its outbound investment, and the counter-balance of the protections granted to inbound investment. It considers (the relatively few) cases that have been brought under Chinese investment treaties and performs a statistical analysis of the protection of Chinese FDI stocks by reference to competitor economies. Finally, section IV looks at where China may focus its attention next, particularly in the context of the Trump administration in the US and China's upcoming investment priorities.

One of the authors first delivered the substance of this chapter at the excellent Asia FDI Forum II at the Chinese University of Hong Kong.

II. China's Development of its Investment Treaty Network

The map in Figure 23.1 categorizes China's investment treaties as broadly falling into three generations: a first generation spanning from 1982 to 1988; a second generation from 1989 to 1997; and a third generation since 1998. As this section goes on to explore, the investment treaties in each generation share certain characteristics both as a matter of substance and the identity of the partner state.

In 1982, China signed its first investment treaty with Sweden, heralding a new era in which China actively sought to attract inward investment. Across the course of the next six years, China executed a further twenty-three investment treaties. These twenty-four investment treaties constitute China's first generation of investment treaties. Figure 23.1 shows in stripes the location of the first generation investment treaty counterparties.[4]

The first generation treaty network is largely concentrated in the capital exporting states of Western Europe (together with the wealthy economies of Japan, Kuwait, Australia, and New Zealand). Indeed, in the 1982–1988 period, China only executed investment treaties with Sri Lanka, Thailand, and Malaysia from the developing world, and concluded no treaties with states from Africa or South America (or, for that matter, from North America). This reflected China's priority at that time of attracting inward investment rather than seeking to protect outward investment by Chinese investors in developing jurisdictions.

The first generation investment treaties also displayed common substantive characteristics. The protections granted to investors were rudimentary by modern standards, mainly limited to providing redress for breach of the fair and equitable treaty standard and for cases of expropriation. Table 23.1, set out in Appendix 1, compares the substantive protections and the investor–state dispute settlement mechanisms contained in the 1982 Sweden–China investment treaty, the 1984 Belgium/Luxembourg Economic Union–China investment treaty and the 1986 UK–China investment treaty. In addition to the relatively light substantive protections, Table 23.1 shows that the investor–state dispute settlement mechanisms in first generation treaties were either extremely limited, for example, to the resolution of questions of quantum of expropriation, or non-existent. This may have reflected China's then caution towards entering the new world of investment treaties as well as its bargaining power and ability to attract inward investment without conceding adjudication to an external authority.

China's second generation investment treaties are shown dotted on the map and date from 1989 to 1997. It is again possible to discern patterns in China's second

---

[4] As in n 2, China also executed first generation investment treaties with Germany, France, Belgium–Luxembourg, Finland, the Netherlands, and Switzerland in this period. These have all subsequently been superseded by third generation treaties.

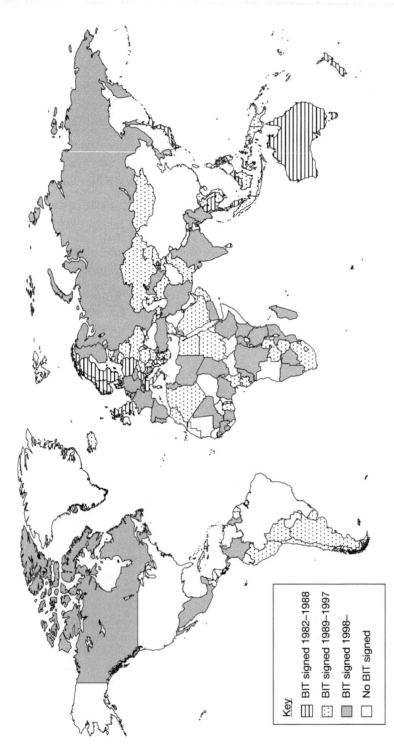

Figure 23.1 *Map of China's Bilateral Investment Treaty Network by Generation*[a]

[a]'International Investment Agreements Navigator' (United Nations Conference on Trade and development (*UNCTAD*), updated) http://investmentpolicyhub.unctad.org/IIA/CountryBits/42 (last accessed 18 January 2017). For simplicity, the map shows only the most recent bilateral treaty between China and the relevant counterparty. For instance, France signed a first generation treaty with China in 1984 and a third generation treaty in 2007. France is therefore coloured green on the map, showing that it is party to a third generation treaty; the map does not indicate that there was also a first generation treaty.

generation of investment treaties. Geographically, China clearly targeted the conclusion of treaties with members of the developing world. In stark contrast to the first generation, it only concluded treaties with Spain, Portugal, Iceland, and Greece from Western Europe within this period, and entered into treaties for the first time with states from Africa, South America, and the Caribbean. Central and South-East Asia was another fertile area for treaties in this era. China's second generation of investment treaties clearly reflected its desire to promote and protect outward investments by its nationals.

A significant development during this period was China's execution of the ICSID Convention in February 1990, which came some three years after it had entered into the New York Convention. China's reticence in respect of the International Centre for Settlement of Investment Disputes (ICSID) may have been partially motivated by concerns over the potential erosion of its political and judicial sovereignty, most notably through the investor–state dispute settlement provisions that the ICSID Convention would impose on China.[5] This concern was evident in China's instrument of ratification—which came some three years after signature, in 1993—pursuant to which China relied upon Article 25(4) of the ICSID Convention to declare a unilateral restriction on the cases that it was prepared to submit to ICSID. Specifically, China declared:

Pursuant to Article 25(4) of the Convention, the Chinese Government would only consider submitting to the jurisdiction of the International Centre for Settlement of Investment Disputes disputes over compensation resulting from expropriation and nationalization.[6]

Following China's ratification of the ICSID Convention in 1993, it began to include references to ICSID dispute resolution in its bilateral investment treaties, albeit in a limited fashion initially. For example, the China–Oman investment treaty of 1995 allows for the appointment of a tribunal by the Secretary General of ICSID,[7] and for a tribunal to adopt the ICSID Arbitration Rules as guidance when formulating its own rules of procedure.[8]

In terms of substantive protections, the contents of the second generation treaties vary considerably. At a high level, however, this generation of investment treaties did see the widespread introduction of some form of national treatment protection. So, for instance, the China–Iceland investment treaty provided that each state 'shall, to the extent possible, accord treatment in accordance with the stipulations of its laws and regulations, to the investments of the investors of the other Contracting Party the same as that accorded to its own investor',[9] while other second generation investment treaties included a full scope national treatment provision.[10]

China's third generation of investment treaties is shown shaded on the map at the start of this section. This generation is comprised of treaties concluded after 1997. Geographically, China continued to expand its spread of treaties across Europe, Asia,

---

[5] See A Chen, *The Voice From China: An Chen on International Economic Law (Understanding China)*, Section 11.4.2.

[6] Chinese Government Notification (7 January 1993) https://icsid.worldbank.org/en/Pages/about/MembershipStateDetails.aspx?state=ST30.

[7] Agreement between the Government of the People's Republic of China and the Government of the Sultanate of Oman for the Promotion and Protection of Investments (signed 18 March 1995, entered into force 1 August 1995) (China–Oman BIT) art 9(4).

[8] ibid art 9(5).

[9] Agreement between the Government of the People's Republic of China and the Government of the Republic of Iceland Concerning the Promotion and Reciprocal Protection of Investments (signed 31 March 1994, entered into force 1 March 1997) art 3(3).

[10] See eg Agreement on the Encouragement and Reciprocal Protection of Investments between the Government of the Republic of Korea and the Government of the People's Republic of China (signed 30 September 1992, entered into force 4 December 1992) art 3(2).

Africa, and the Americas, but also updated several of its earlier generation treaties with European states. As of October 2018, China has only extended its investment treaty network in the third generation era to one Western economy (the China–Canada investment treaty of 2012).[11]

Substantively, the third generation treaties display relatively fewer common traits than the earlier generations. They tend to offer fuller protections than the earlier generations, typically including full national treatment protection and most-favoured-nation clauses.[12] Perhaps more significantly, China began to offer full ICSID arbitration to investors (i.e., not merely for expropriation claims), despite its earlier reservation when acceding to the ICSID Convention.[13] The extent to which this has resulted in publicly available ICSID claims being brought against China, or by Chinese investors, is explored in the following section.

III. The Extent to which China's FDI Stock Benefits from BIT Protections

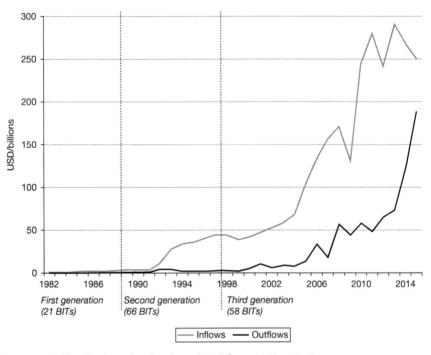

Figure 23.2 China's inbound and outbound FDI flows, 1982–2015

[11] As of October 2018, the European Union and China have been actively engaging in negotiations for a China–EU bilateral investment treaty.

[12] See eg Agreement between the Swiss Federal Council and the Government of the People's Republic of China on the Promotion and Reciprocal Protection of Investments (signed 27 January 2009, entered into force 13 April 2010) art 4(2); Agreement between the Government of the Russian Federation and the Government of the People's Republic of China on the Promotion and Reciprocal Protection of Investments (signed 9 November 2006, 1 May 2009) art 3(2); Agreement between the People's Republic of China and the Kingdom of Spain on the Promotion and Reciprocal Protection of Investments (signed 14 November 2005, entered into force 1 July 2008) (China–Spain BIT) art 3(2).

[13] See eg China–Spain BIT art 9(b); Agreement between the Government of Barbados and the Government of the People's Republic of China for the Promotion and Protection of Investments (signed 22 July 1999, entered into force 1 October 1999) art 9(2)(a).

Investment treaties essentially serve two purposes for a contracting state: (i) to attract foreign investment by offering established legal standards and protections within its domestic jurisdiction to overseas investors; and (ii) to ensure equivalent protections for that state's investors overseas. No analysis of a state's investment treaty strategy can therefore be complete without considering its impact on FDI flows and stocks.

Figure 23.2 shows the history of China's FDI inflows and outflows since the date of its first investment treaty in 1982. As one would expect given the closed economic system pursued by China until the late 1970s, FDI flows in both directions were practically non-existent in 1982, and remained negligible through 1990 (by which time China was moving on to its second generation of investment treaties). Around 1993, China began to attract significant inbound FDI. This may have resulted from a combination of China's ratification of the ICSID Convention—perceived as a very public commitment to the protection of inward investment—and a delayed effect from the suite of investment treaties concluded with capital exporting nations in the first generation.

China's second generation of investment treaties—targeted at developing countries—may have caused a similarly delayed effect in terms of outbound investment. This lagged significantly behind inbound investment and only really began to pick up in the mid-2000s. More recently, 2011 saw a significant upturn in Chinese investment overseas, to the extent that the two lines almost converged such that it appeared that Chinese investment overseas may surpass foreign investment in China for the first time in decades.[14]

Figure 23.2, however, only tells half the story. It is also necessary to examine whether there is correlation between China's investment treaties and its investment partners. Table 23.2 below considers China's top ten FDI instock and outstock partners and the extent to which these are protected by investment treaties.

Table 23.2 Treaty protection of China's FDI stock[a]

China's FDI Instock		China's FDI Outstock	
Investing Country	**Treaty Protection/ BIT Generation**	**Recipient Country**	**Treaty Protection/ BIT Generation**
British Virgin Islands	No[b]	US	No
Japan	1G	Australia	1G
US	No	Luxembourg	3G
South Korea	3G	UK	1G
Cayman Islands[52]	No	Canada	3G
Samoa	No	France	3G
Germany	3G	Bermuda	No
UK	1G	Germany	3G
Netherlands	3G	Sweden	1G
France	3G	Japan	1G

[a]Ministry of Commerce of the Government of China (via UNCTAD). The table excludes investments to/from Taiwan, Hong Kong, and Macau.
[b]The Agreement between the Government of the United Kingdom of Great Britain and Northern Ireland and the Government of the People's Republic of China Concerning the Promotion and Reciprocal Protection of Investments (signed 15 May 1986, entered into force 15 May 1986) (China-UK BIT) only extends to the territory of the United Kingdom and therefore does not cover crown dependencies and or other sub-State territories in respect of whom the United Kingdom is responsible for foreign relations (see n 12).

---

[14] However, since this chapter was first drafted, the level of Chinese outbound investment, specifically non-financial direct investment, has dropped by 29.4 per cent in 2017 owing to tightening government restrictions.

Although Table 23.2 provides a useful basis for analysis, it is first important to note its limitations. In particular, it only accounts for *direct* investments; accordingly, investments (inward and outward) that have been structured through offshore jurisdictions for tax purposes (or otherwise) are recorded to that jurisdiction rather than the ultimate destination/source. This may account for the presence of the BVI, Cayman Islands, Bermuda, and possibly Luxembourg on the list. Where these territories lack investment treaties with China, the investment may still be protected if there is a treaty between the ultimate destination/source and China.[15]

It is notable that China scores better in protecting its overseas investments than it does in offering protections to inbound investment: every major destination for Chinese investment is protected by an investment treaty other than Bermuda and the United States. Of these, four benefit from the greater protections offered by third generation treaties. By comparison, China only has investment treaties with six of its largest investors (of which again four are third generation). This suggests that some investors in China are not put off by the absence of investment treaty protections, despite the potential of political interference in the economy,[16] although of course investments may still be protected more generally through robust planning and structuring, even in the absence of investment treaties.

The second key conclusion from the data is that the significant exception to China's investment treaty coverage is the United States, which features as the largest recipient of Chinese outward investment, and is the third largest investor in China. This point is examined in further detail in section IV.

Despite China's enthusiasm for concluding investment treaties since 1982, it has faced—and its investors have brought—comparatively few investment treaty disputes. In total, China has faced only three cases and its investors have brought only six cases.[17] The three cases faced by China are *Ekran Berhad*,[18] *Ansung Housing*,[19] and *Hela Schwarz*.[20] Relatively few details of *Ekran Berhad* are in the public domain, and the case itself was withdrawn only a few months after filing. The *Ansung Housing* claim was brought by a Korean investor under the third generation China–Korea investment treaty and concerned the development of a golf and country club in Jiangsu. Ansung alleges that it was forced to dispose of its investment to a Chinese purchaser at a loss that it quantifies at US$80 million.[21] The Tribunal rendered its award on 9 March 2017, dismissing the claim and finding that it was time-barred under the China–Korea BIT. The third case *Hela Schwarz* was brought against China by a German investor on 21 June 2017 under the third generation China–Germany BIT and concerned the

---

[15] A further limitation is that the table makes no account for the temporal application of investment treaties.

[16] The Organization for Economic Cooperation and Development (OECD), for instance, ranks China as having the most restrictive FDI rules of the 58 countries that it examined (including every OECD and G20 states). 'FDI Regulatory Restrictiveness Index' (OECD, undated) www.oecd.org/investment/fdiindex.htm (last accessed 18 January 2017).

[17] The figures here include cases brought by Hong Kong or Macanese investors.

[18] *Ekran Berhad v People's Republic of China* (ICSID Case No ARB/11/15). Unusually, this case appears to have been brought under the Israeli and Malaysian investment treaties, neither of which allow for ICSID arbitration.

[19] *Ansung Housing v People's Republic of China* (ICSID Case No ARB/14/25).

[20] *Hela Schwarz GmbH v People's Republic of China* (ICSID Case No ARB/17/19).

[21] Alison Ross and Lacey Yong, 'China Faces Second ICSID Claim' (2014) *Global Arbitration Review* 1 https://globalarbitrationreview.com/article/1033850/china-faces-second-icsid-claim (last accessed 18 October 2018).

Jinan Municipal Government's expropriation of Hela's land and buildings in Shandong Province, China. It is understood as of October 2018 that China requested its objections to jurisdiction be addressed as a preliminary question.

There has been some speculation as to why China has yet to face a significant number of investment treaty cases. In part, this may be explained by China's refusal to accept ICSID arbitration (whose decisions are amongst the few arbitral awards that are publicly available) in investment treaties signed prior to the late 1990s. As discussed in section II, some of China's first generation investment treaties did not allow for investor–state dispute settlement at all, while others provided for fora that would not necessarily result in a public award. Other reasons that have been proffered include China's preference to resolve disputes amicably rather than have grievances publicly aired in an arbitral forum, and a concern on the part of investors that bringing a claim against China would compromise its ability to operate in the country in the future.[22] Whatever the explanation, the arbitration community is closely following the implications of the *Ansung Housing* award to see whether it will spur or deter further claims against China.

Chinese investors (including those from Hong Kong and Macau) have also been relatively slow to bring ICSID claims, having only brought six cases publicly. These include the well-known *Philip Morris* case, in which the American tobacco giant sought to restructure its investments in Australia through Hong Kong in order to benefit from the protection of the 1993 Hong Kong–Australia investment treaty.[23] This case was dismissed for lack of jurisdiction on the basis that Philip Morris had restructured its investment specifically to avail itself of treaty protection at a time that the dispute was foreseeable.[24] In terms of the other cases, one resulted in an award of US$786,306.24 for the investor,[25] two were dismissed for lack of jurisdiction,[26] and two were settled after strongly contested jurisdiction phases.[27]

A comparison of the use of Chinese investment treaties with that of competitor economies demonstrates how few cases have resulted. Of the G20, only Australia, Saudi Arabia, South Africa, France, and the UK have faced fewer investment treaty claims than China—and the first three have fewer than ninety investment treaties between them. Equally, the six claims brought by Chinese investors pale in comparison to the G7 average of over fifty cases each (only Japanese investors—who have brought two cases—are comparable to the Chinese). Again, the reason for this may be attributed to China's late arrival to the ICSID Convention, but it will be interesting to see whether the inclusion of ICSID dispute settlement in its third generation investment treaties, coupled with the increase in Chinese overseas investment since 1998, would lead to an increase in Chinese ICSID claims.

---

[22] ibid.

[23] *Philip Morris Asia Limited v The Commonwealth of Australia* (PCA Case No 2012-12) .

[24] ibid Award on Jurisdiction and Admissibility (17 December 2015).

[25] *Senor Tza Yap Shum v Peru* (ICSID Case No ARB/07/6), Award (7 July 2011). Peru applied for, among other things, annulment of the Award on 3 November 2011 but the application was subsequently dismissed in its entirety; see Decision on Annulment (12 February 2015).

[26] *Ping An Life Insurance Company Limited et al v Belgium* (ICSID Case No ARB/12/29), Award (30 April 2015); *China Heilongjiang v Mongolia* (PCA Case No 2010-20), Award (30 June 2017).

[27] *Sanum Investments v Laos* (PCA Case No2013-13), Award on Jurisdiction (13 December 2013); *Beijing Urban Construction v Yemen* (ICSID Case No ARB/14/30), Decision on Jurisdiction (31 May 2017).

IV. China's Future Investment Treaty Strategy

A significant gap in China's investment treaty network is the absence of a treaty with the United States. Although cross-investment between the world's two largest economies is not as great as might be expected, the figures in section III show that the United States is still one of the top ten investors in China, and the biggest recipient of Chinese investment. Although there is a clear incentive for the United States to obtain an investment treaty for American investors looking to access the vast Chinese market, Chinese investors have also shown a great appetite for procuring American assets in recent years. Chinese investors have made bids for Syngenta, Starwood, Ingram Micro, and General Electric's white goods division, amongst others.

China and the United States initially launched negotiations towards a bilateral investment treaty in 2008, under the administrations of George W Bush and Hu Jintao. The Obama administration intensified efforts to conclude the investment treaty, with over twenty rounds of negotiations since 2008. By 2016—the last full year of Obama's presidency—expectations were high that the treaty would be concluded. It is understood that the draft treaty includes full investor–state dispute settlement provisions, as well as a negative list, exempting certain industry sectors from the application of the treaty. In March 2016, the former Commerce Minister of China, Chen Deming, was reported as saying that most of the 'core issues' had been resolved, with the identity of industries on the negative list the main sticking point.[28]

The election of Donald Trump as US President in November 2016, however, casts uncertainty on the possibility of the conclusion of a successful US–China bilateral investment treaty, at least in the short term. Trump has repeatedly criticized China, both pre- and post-election.[29] In these circumstances, the prospects of a US–China bilateral investment treaty being concluded under the Trump administration do not appear high.[30]

A further consequence of the election of Donald Trump has been the failure of the Trans-Pacific Partnership, at least in its original form. This regional treaty sought to promote investment between the United States and eleven Pacific Rim states, including Japan, Canada, Australia, and New Zealand.[31] Although the Trans-Pacific Partnership was signed by all twelve countries on 4 February 2016, Trump signed an executive order on the third day of his presidency in January 2017, announcing the US withdrawal from the Trans-Pacific Partnership. The remaining

---

[28] See eg Avaneesh Pandey, 'US-China Investment Treaty: Core Issues Resolved, But Disagreements Over "Negative List" Persist' *International Business Times* (2016).

[29] Inter alia, Trump has (i) doubted the One China policy (see Liu Zhen, 'For Trump, One China, Like Everything Is Negotiable' *South China Morning Post* (2017)); (ii) pledged to impose a trade tariff of 45% on Chinese goods and accused China of being a currency manipulator (see Sara Hsu, 'How Far Can Trump Go On Chinese Trade Policy?' *Forbes* (2016)). He also described the Trans-Pacific Partnership as 'a terrible deal' that would allow China to 'come in, as they always do, through the back door and totally take advantage of everyone'; see *Fox Business/Wall Street Journal* Republican debate (10 November 2015) reported at '2016 presidential candidates on the Trans-Pacific Partnership trade deal' (Ballotpedia, undated) https://ballotpedia.org/2016_presidential_candidates_on_the_Trans-Pacific_Partnership_trade_deal (last accessed 18 January 2017).

[30] Since this chapter was first drafted, little progress has been made in the negotiations of the US–China BIT. US Treasury Secretary Steven Mnuchin said in June 2017 that a BIT was still 'on the docket, despite not being a top priority'. However, as of October 2018, there have been no signs of any revival of talks for a US–China BIT.

[31] The full list of signatories is: Australia, Brunei, Canada, Chile, Japan, Malaysia, Mexico, New Zealand, Peru, Singapore, the United States, and Vietnam.

eleven signatories decided to continue with the partnership in May 2017 and signed the Comprehensive and Progressive Agreement for Trans-Pacific Partnership on 8 March 2018.[32]

Significantly, China was not party to the Trans-Pacific Partnership or the Comprehensive and Progressive Agreement for Trans-Pacific Partnership, despite being the second largest economy in the Pacific Rim region. American policy analysts expressed hope that the establishment of a free trade area excluding China would at once (i) reduce the participants' reliance on Chinese trade; and (ii) force China to conform to the rules and norms set by the Trans-Pacific Partnership (i.e., as a prelude to accession) rather than use its economic power and influence to establish its own rules for the region.[33]

The US withdrawal from the Trans-Pacific Partnership may, conversely, leave a vacuum for a regional economic treaty in which China can assume the role of leader. The likely vehicle for this is the Regional Comprehensive Economic Partnership (RCEP), a proposed free trade agreement between China, Japan, Australia, New Zealand, India, South Korea, and the ten member states of ASEAN.[34] The RCEP was introduced in 2011 and has undergone twenty-four rounds of negotiations as of October 2018.[35] Prime Minister Abe of Japan foreshadowed a 'pivot' towards the RCEP if the United States were to withdraw from the Trans-Pacific Partnership.[36] The degree of overlap with the Trans-Pacific Partnership is significant. Apart from states from North and South America (i.e. the US, Mexico, Canada, Chile, and Peru), every state party to the Trans-Pacific Partnership is also party to the RCEP (which also extends to the large economies of India and South Korea).

An alternative to the RCEP may be for China to implement investment protections into its One Belt One Road scheme. Chinese President Xi Jinping launched the One Belt One Road project in late 2013 as a development initiative to promote Chinese initiatives along the Silk Road Economic Belt and the Maritime Silk Road.[37] The essence of the scheme is for China to lead the development of infrastructure across Belt and Road economies to ensure access for Chinese goods in Eurasian markets.[38] *The Economist* reports Chinese expectations of investing up to US$4 trillion in Belt and Road countries.[39]

Drawing lessons from the past—particularly the way in which China sought to protect its outward investment spree in the 1990s with a suite of treaties with developing states (i.e., the second generation of China's investment treaties)—it would be unsurprising to see China attempt to protect its One Belt One Road infrastructure projects

---

[32] The Comprehensive and Progressive Agreement for Trans-Pacific Partnership will enter into force sixty days after six of its signatories ratified the agreement. As of 19 October 2018, four countries have completed their domestic ratification processes and Canada's House of Commons has passed the ratification bill.

[33] See eg Barry Naughton and others, 'What Will the TPP Mean for China?' *Foreign Policy Magazine* (2015).

[34] Specifically: Brunei, Cambodia, Indonesia, Laos, Malaysia, Myanmar, the Philippines, Singapore, Thailand, and Vietnam.

[35] India's Minister of Commerce & Industry and Civil Aviation Suresh Prabhu expressed in September 2018 that the negotiations of the RCEP would likely continue in 2019.

[36] See Nicky Woolf and others, 'Trump to Withdraw from Trans-Pacific Partnership on First Day in Office' *The Guardian* (2016).

[37] See Julien Chaisse and Mitsuo Matsushita, 'China's "Belt and Road" Initiative: Mapping the World Trade Normative and Strategic Implications' (2018) 52(1) Journal of World Trade 163.

[38] Since this chapter was first drafted, there has been more visibility on the shape and form of the Belt and Road Initiative. The developments that have occurred thus far are recorded in the official website of the Belt and Road Initiative hosted by the Chinese State Information Centre https://eng.yidaiyilu.gov.cn/index.htm.

[39] 'Our Bulldozers, Our Rules' *The Economist* (2016).

with Investment treaties. Although, as noted above, the identity of One Belt One Road participants is currently uncertain, China only has investment treaties with around half of the sixty or so likely candidates.[40]

Rather than going to the effort of negotiating scores of individual investment treaties, or seeking a consensus on a new multi-lateral investment treaty (both of which are likely to take many years to come to fruition), China could significantly shorten the process of protecting its One Belt One Road investments by acceding to the Energy Charter Treaty, which would at least protect investments in the energy sector. The Energy Charter Treaty has a robust investment chapter, including provisions on expropriation,[41] fair and equitable treatment,[42] national treatment,[43] and investor–state dispute settlement pursuant to the ICSID or UNCITRAL rules.[44] There are currently fifty-three states that are party to the Energy Charter Treaty (all of whom have ratified it, with the exception of Australia, Belarus, and Norway),[45] including many along the Belt and Road. In May 2015, China signed the International Energy Charter Declaration along with over seventy other states. Although not legally-binding, the International Energy Charter Declaration manifested China's political will to engage with the Energy Charter regime and may yet prove to be the first step on the path to accession.

V. Conclusions

While the data show that China has one of the largest investment treaty networks in the world, they also reveal weaknesses in its coverage, both in terms of breadth and depth. Significantly, despite almost a decade of negotiations, China has failed to conclude a bilateral treaty with the United States and there appears to be little prospect of agreement being reached under the Trump administration. This leaves Chinese investors without the benefit of treaty protection in the single largest destination for Chinese FDI. Equally, China is yet to conclude investment treaties with a significant number of countries expected to benefit from its One Belt One Road initiative. In terms of depth, China still only has outdated first generation investment treaties with significant FDI partners such as the UK, Sweden, Japan, and Australia. The analysis shows that these treaties, signed when China was taking its initial tentative steps towards opening up its economy, provide relatively few protections and, crucially, limited investor–state dispute settlement rights.

There are relatively few Chinese-related investment treaty cases in the public domain (i.e., those brought by Chinese nationals or by foreign nationals against China). These first cases—together with the increasing availability of ICSID arbitration in China's recent investment treaties—may yet lead to more China-related investment disputes in

---

[40] The official website of the Belt and Road Initiative hosted by the Chinese State Information Centre lists eighty-four states as participants to the Belt and Road Initiative as of 19 October 2018 https://eng.yidaiyilu.gov.cn/info/iList.jsp?cat_id=10076&cur_page=1.
[41] Energy Charter Treaty (signed 17 December 1991) art 13.   [42] ibid art 10(1).
[43] ibid art 10(7).   [44] ibid art 26(4).
[45] A full list of members can be found on the Energy Charter Treaty website http://www.energycharter.org/who-we-are/members-observers/. On 17 April 2018, the Russian Federation officially confirmed its intention of withdrawal from the Energy Charter Treaty.

the coming years. In terms of China's future strategy, it appears well-placed to take advantage of American and European malaise and scepticism towards investment treaties to position itself as a regional and global economic leader.

Whether China does this through the implementation of investment treaties at a bilateral or multi-lateral (i.e., regional, or even global) level remains to be seen. On the one hand, China's network of investment treaties has historically been predominantly on a bilateral level. This preference may have been a function of its negotiating power at each stage of the three generations identified above, coupled with a desire to customize the terms of each investment treaty. On the other hand, China's economic and political influence has grown considerably in the past decade and seems likely to continue to do so in the future. As China's leverage at the negotiating table grows, and it becomes more experienced with investment treaties, there may be a shift towards multi-lateral investment treaties albeit that this is unlikely to replace bilateral treaties entirely. Indeed, we have already seen signs of this, such as the RCEP negotiations and China's 2015 signing of the International Energy Charter Declaration.

Appendix 1

TABLE 23.1 Comparison of Provisions of China's First Generation Investment Treaties

Provision	Sweden Treaty (1982)[a]	Belgium/Luxembourg Economic Union Treaty (1984)[b]	UK Treaty (1986)[c]
Fair and equitable treatment	Article 2 1. *Each Contracting State shall at all times ensure fair and equitable treatment to the investments by investors of the other Contracting State.* 2. *Investments by investors of either Contracting State in the territory of the other Contracting State shall not be subjected to a treatment less favourable than that accorded to investments by investors of third States.*	Article 3 1. *Direct or indirect investment made by investors of one Contracting Party in the territory of the other Contracting Party shall enjoy equitable treatment.* 2. *Protection and equitable treatment shall be accorded as regards management, operation, use or liquidation of the above said investment unless necessary measures should be taken for the maintenance of public order and in defence of the State law.*	Article 2 2. *Investments of nationals or companies of either Contracting Party shall at all times be accorded fair and equitable treatment and shall enjoy the most constant protection and security in the territory of the other Contracting Party. Each Contracting Party agrees that without prejudice to its laws and regulations it shall not take any unreasonable or discriminatory measures against the management, maintenance, use, enjoyment or disposal of investments in its territory of nationals or companies of the other Contracting Party. Each Contracting Party shall observe any obligation it may have entered into with regard to investments of nationals or companies of the other Contracting Party.*

TABLE 23.1 Continued

Provision	Sweden Treaty (1982)[a]	Belgium/Luxembourg Economic Union Treaty (1984)[b]	UK Treaty (1986)[c]
Expropriation	<u>Article 3</u>	<u>Article 4</u>	<u>Article 5</u>
	1. *Neither Contracting State shall expropriate or nationalize, or take any other similar measure in regard to, an investment made in its territory by an investor of the other Contracting State, except in the public interest, under due process of law and against compensation, the purpose of which shall be to place the investor in the same financial position as that in which the investor would have been if the expropriation or nationalization had not taken place. The expropriation or nationalization shall not be discriminatory and the compensation shall be paid without unreasonable delay and shall be convertible and freely transferable between the territories of the Contracting States.*	1. *Neither Contracting Party shall in its territory take the measure of expropriation, nationalization or other similar measures on the investment of the investor of the other Contracting Party except for the necessity of security and public interest under the following conditions ...*	1. *Investments of nationals or companies of either Contracting Party shall not be expropriated, nationalised or subjected to measures having effect equivalent to expropriation or nationalisation (hereinafter referred to as "expropriation") in the territory of the other Contracting Party except for a public purpose related to the internal needs of that Contracting Party and against reasonable compensation. ...*
Other substantive protections	• Free transfer of property (Article 4).	• Free transfer of property (Article 5). • Umbrella clause (Article 9). • Most-favoured nation clause (Article 11).	• Umbrella clause (Article 2(2), see above). • Most-favoured nation (Article 3(1)). • Free transfer of property (Article 6).

TABLE 23.1 Continued

Provision	Sweden Treaty (1982)[a]	Belgium/Luxembourg Economic Union Treaty (1984)[b]	UK Treaty (1986)[c]
Investor–state Dispute Settlement	None.[d]	Article 10[e] 3. *As an exception of Paragraph 2 above a dispute which arises from an amount of compensation for expropriation, nationalization or other similar measures and has not been settled within six months from the date of notification may, as the investor prefers referred for settlement either to: (1) a judicial body of the Contracting Party accepting the investment, or, (2) an international arbitration without resort to any other means.*	Article 7 1. *A dispute between a national or company of one Contracting Party and the other Contracting Party concerning an amount of compensation which has not been amicably settled after a period of six months from written notification of that dispute shall be submitted to international arbitration.* ...

[a]Agreement on the Mutual Protection of Investments (People's Republic of China–Sweden) (signed 29 March 1982, entered into force 29 March 1982).

[b]Agreement between the Government of the People's Republic of China and the Belgian–Luxembourg Economic Union on the Reciprocal Promotion and Protection of Investments (signed 4 June 1984, entered into force 5 October 1986).

[c]China–UK BIT (n 12).

[d]Sweden noted in a letter that it had not been possible to include an investor-state dispute settlement provision. It further noted that China was not party to the 1965 ICSID Convention and provided for investor-state dispute settlement to be revisited should China become party. It is unclear whether the contracting parties ever carried out this exercise after China acceded to the ICSID Convention in the early 1990s.

[e]Subsequently supplemented by Protocol on the Agreement between the Government of the People's Republic of China and the Belgian–Luxembourg Economic Union on the Reciprocal Promotion and Protection of Investments, 4 June 1984 art 6(1) ('[a] dispute on an amount of compensation for expropriation, nationalization or other similar measures may, under Paragraph 3 of Article 10 of the Agreement, be submitted to an arbitral tribunal').

24

Investment Disputes under China's BITs

Jurisdiction with Chinese Characteristics?

Jane Willems*

I. Introduction

The *Tza v Peru* (decision rendered under the auspices of the International Centre for the Settlement of Investment Disputes (ICSID),[1] confirmed by the ICSID ad hoc committee, PRC–Peru BIT) and the *Sanum v Laos* (ad hoc award, challenged before the High Court of Singapore, PRC–Laos BIT)[2] cases were the first decisions on jurisdiction by arbitral tribunals rendered in investor–state disputes involving Chinese bilateral investment treaties (BITs). These decisions which involve Chinese BITs of the second generation have raised different jurisdictional questions. First, they have with other decisions, contributed to the debate over the interpretation by arbitral tribunals and courts of restricted consent arbitration clauses, where the subject matter of the arbitration is limited to *quantum* on expropriation.

Additionally, and more specifically to China, these cases, which involved investors respectively from the Hong Kong and Macau special administrative regions (SARs) seeking the protection of Chinese BITs concluded before the retrocessions of these territories to China, have raised specific jurisdiction tests. First, in *Sanum v Laos*, the territorial scope of a Chinese BIT was examined for the first time. This case considered whether Chinese BITs entered into before the retrocession of Macau to China automatically applied to Macau after the retrocession and, secondly, whether the nationality requirement of the investor was complied with, and to what extent residents and legal entities from these Chinese SARs qualified as Chinese investors protected by the BIT.

This chapter will first examine and compare the decisions rendered by arbitral tribunals and state courts, on the scope of the consent clauses contained in the Chinese BITs of the first generation, with decisions rendered under other BITs with similar wordings. The decisions relating to Chinese BITs have contributed to the debate on the interpretation of treaties contained in arbitral awards that have extended the subject matter of the arbitral jurisdiction and the subsequent state court decisions that

---

* PhD in Law, Associate Professor, Tsinghua University, School of Law, China. Associate Director, International Arbitration and Dispute Settlement LL.M, Tsinghua University School of Law. Attorney at Law, California, *Avocat à la Cour*, Paris (France); Advisor, Asian Academy of International Law.

[1] *Tza Yap Shum v Republic of Peru*, ICSID Case No ARB/07/6, Decision on Jurisdiction and Competence (12 February 2007) (*Tza* decision on jurisdiction). *Tza Yap Shum v Republic of Peru*, ICSID *ad hoc* committee decision on annulment (25 February 2015).

[2] *Sanum Investments Ltd v Government of the Lao People's Democratic Republic*, ad hoc Tribunal, Award on jurisdiction (13 December 2013) (*Sanum* award on jurisdiction); *Government of the Lao People's Democratic Republic v Sanum Investments Ltd* [2015] SGHC 15; *Sanum Investments Ltd v Government of the Lao People's Democratic Republic* [2016] SGCA 57. Jane Willems acted as counsel for Laos.

Investment Disputes under China's BITs: Jurisdiction with Chinese Characteristics? Jane Willems. © Jane Willems, 2019. Published 2019 by Oxford University Press.

have reviewed, and on notable occasions have sanctioned these awards. These decisions contain more particulars pertaining to BITs emanating from socialists countries than characteristics specific to China's BITs (section 1).

The situation is different for other jurisdictional issues. The territorial jurisdiction of arbitral tribunals under the Chinese BITs—and whether they apply to an SAR—was examined under the interpretation of the territorial scope of treaties and under the moving frontier rule and the exceptions to these principles, in particular the intent expressed by China (section 2). The question of the nationality of the investor seeking the protection of a Chinese BITs also raised Chinese characteristics as it allowed for the first time arbitral tribunals to apply, at an international level, the nationality test for both individuals and corporations established in the SARs contained in the municipal law (section 3).

II. Subject Matter Jurisdiction with Chinese Characteristics?

The consent to arbitrate made under a BIT by the state contracting party constitutes a binding offer made by that host state to an investor of the other contracting state to arbitrate legal disputes which may arise against it—an offer limited, however, to arbitrate the legal disputes contemplated in the arbitration clause. Many BITs are broadly drafted so as to cover any class of investment disputes: 'any dispute concerning an investment'.[3] Other BITs limit the scope of the subject matter of the dispute resolution clause to investors' claims arising out of the breach of a substantive obligation under the BIT.[4]

Chinese BITs of the first and the second generation contained narrowly worded dispute resolution clauses. In these Chinese BITs, while the consent clause provided for international ad hoc arbitration or later to ICSID arbitration, the scope of the subject matter jurisdiction clause is narrower than the substantive obligations under the BIT. The consent clause is drafted to limit the subject matter of the arbitral jurisdiction to an issue(s) pertaining to expropriation, using the phrasing: 'a dispute involving the amount of compensation for expropriation',[5] leaving 'any disputes … in connection with an investment' to the jurisdiction of the courts of the host state.[6] This practice is consistent with the 'notification of intent concerning classes of dispute' made by China, under Article 25(4) of the Convention on the Settlement of Investment Disputes between States and Nationals of Other States ('ICSID Convention'), where

---

[3] France 2006 Model BIT art 7: 'any dispute concerning the investments occurring between one Contracting Party and a national or company of the other Contracting Party'; German 2008 Model BIT art 10(1) 'disputes concerning investments …'.

[4] Canadian FIPA Model art 22(1): 'a claim that the other Party has breached an obligation under Section B [Substantive Obligations], and that the investor has incurred loss or damage by reason of, or arising out of, that breach'. See also 2012 US model BIT art 24.

[5] See 1993 China–Laos BIT art 8(3) providing for ad hoc arbitration: 'If a dispute involving the amount of compensation for expropriation cannot be settled though negotiation within six months as specified in paragraph 1 of this Article 1, it may be submitted at the request of either party to an ad hoc arbitral tribunal …'; 1994 China–Peru BIT art 8(3) providing for ICSID arbitration: 'If a dispute involving the amount of compensation for expropriation cannot be settled within six months after resort to negotiations as specified in Paragraph 1 of this Article, it may be submitted at the request of either party to the international arbitration of ICSID'.

[6] See 1993 China–Laos BIT and 1994 China–Peru BIT art 8(2): 'If the dispute cannot be settled through negotiations within six months, either party to the dispute shall be entitled to submit this dispute to the competent court of the Contracting Party accepting the investment'.

China made known it would 'only consider submitting to the jurisdiction of disputes over compensation resulting from expropriation and nationalization'.[7]

The limited subject matter jurisdiction adopted by China is similar to the then contemporary treaty drafting practice of other socialist countries, including Russia, Hungary, and the Czech Republic, which provided for arbitral jurisdiction to cover only disputes involving the amount of compensation for expropriation.[8]

This narrow scope was abandoned in the third generation of Chinese BITs in the late 1990s[9] and in the renegotiated BITs with Germany and with the Netherlands.[10]

Notwithstanding the similarities in the identification of the disputes arbitrable under the narrow consent clauses, the case law resulting from the treaty interpretation of very similar clauses has been in conflict.[11] The arbitral decisions rendered upon the objection to jurisdiction raised by the defending state—and the decisions rendered on the basis of the challenges filed against these awards—have not been consistent. The decision reached depends in each case on the interpretation of each treaty, of course, but more than in any other area of investment arbitration—there is no general consensus on the interpretation of the scope of the subject matter jurisdiction of the arbitrators.

The consent clauses in the PRC–Peru BIT involved in *Tza v Peru* (*Tza*) and in the China–Laos BIT involved in *Sanum v Laos* (*Sanum*), were identical and provided for '[a] dispute involving the amount of compensation for expropriation ...'.[12] In each

---

[7] Notification dated 7 January 1993. See *Contracting States and Measures Taken by them for the Purpose of the Convention*, ICSID/8-D (May 2016).

[8] For Russian BITs see Belgium/Lux—Soviet BIT 1989, 'disputes concerning the amount or mode of compensation to be paid under Article 5 [expropriation, nationalization or other measures having a similar effect] of the present' in *Berschader v Russian Federation* ('*Berschader*'), Arb. Inst of Stockholm Chamber of Commerce, Award, Case No V 080/2004, para 129 (21 April 2006); UK–Soviet BIT/ IPPA 1988 art 8(1): 'disputes ... concerning the amount of payment or compensation under Article 4 or 5 [expropriation] of this Agreement or concerning any other matter consequential upon an act of expropriation in accordance with Article 5 of this Agreement' in *RosInvest Co UK Ltd v Russian Federation* (*RosInvest*), Arb. Inst of Stockholm Chamber of Commerce, Award on Jurisdiction, Case No V 079/2005, para 57; Spain–Russian Federation BIT 1989 art 10: 'relating to the amount or method of payment of the compensation due under Article 6 [nationalization, expropriation] of this Agreement' in *Quasar* (formerly *Renta 4 SVSA et al v Russian Federation* (*Quasar*)), Arb Inst of Stockholm Chamber of Commerce, Award on Preliminary Objections, Case No V 024/2007 (20 March 2009); Svea Court of appeal, judgment 18 January 2016. For Czech BITs see Belgian/ Luxembourg–Czech BIT 1989 providing for disputes 'concerning compensation due by virtue of article 3 paragraphs (1) and (3) [expropriation]', in *Czech Republic v European Media Ventures* [2007] EWHC (Comm) 2851, [2007] 2 CLC 908 (Eng) (*European Media Ventures*); Austria–Czech BIT 1990 art 8: '[c]oncerning the amount or the conditions of payment of a compensation' in *Austrian Airlines v Slovak Republic* (*Austrian Airlines*), UNCITRAL, Final Award, para 95 (9 October 2009).

[9] 1998 China–Barbados BIT, 1999 China–Bahrain BIT, 2000 China–Botswana BIT, 'Any dispute ... in connection with an investment'; 2000 China–Iran BIT: 'Any dispute with respect to an investment' 2001 Jordan–China BIT: 'any legal dispute'.

[10] China–Netherlands BIT 2001: 'Dispute which may arise ... concerning an investment'; China–Germany BIT 2003 art 9(1) 'Any dispute concerning investments ...'.

[11] See Jane Willems, 'The Settlement of Investor State Disputes and China: New Developments on ICSID Jurisdiction' (2011) 8 *SCJIL&B* 1.

[12] Article 8:

1. Any dispute between an investor of one Contracting Party and the other Contracting Party in connection with an investment in the territory of the other Contracting Party shall, as far as possible, be settled amicably through negotiations between the parties to the dispute.
2. If the dispute cannot be settled through negotiations within six months, either party to the dispute shall be entitled to submit this dispute to the competent court of the Contracting Party accepting the investment.
3. If a dispute involving the amount of compensation for expropriation cannot be settled within six months after resort to negotiations as specified in Paragraph 1 of this Article, it may be submitted at the request of either party to the international arbitration of ICSID.

case, the tribunal found that the interpretation of the consent clause required it to accept jurisdiction of the dispute including both the liability for and the quantum of the expropriation claim.

The *Tza* ICSID tribunal was tasked with deciding whether Article 8(3) of the PRC–Peru BIT required the tribunal to limit its jurisdiction to the issue of quantum after the claimant had established in a local court that there had been an expropriation. The *Tza* tribunal approached the issue and decided the issue solely on the basis that Article 8(2), which states the investor should submit its dispute to the court of the state of the contracting party, posed a barrier to any international arbitration at all. This reasoning, calling the interplay between Article 8(2) and Article 8(3) a 'fork in the road' clause, an either or choice, according to the *Tza* tribunal meant that ICSID arbitration to settle compensation could never be available.

In contrast, the *Sanum* tribunal made a more sophisticated analysis, yet coming to a similar conclusion. First, this tribunal adopted a broad understanding of the word 'involving' in Article 8(3)[13] as meaning to 'include' or to 'wrap' and considered it to be inclusionary rather than exclusionary. It reasoned that if the parties had intended to limit the jurisdiction of the tribunal exclusively to disputes on the amount of compensation, other terms such as 'limited to' would have been used.[14] Secondly, when read in the context of Article 4 of the PRC–Laos BIT (expropriation clause), it rejected an interpretation that would allow a split between jurisdiction on liability and on quantum for a claim for expropriation because the tribunal said it did not match the provisions of Article 4(1) and (2), since the last condition under Article 4(1) was an 'appropriate and effective compensation'. Finally, the tribunal applied the principle of *effet utile*,[15] which it said leaves 'without effect a clause of the Treaty on the basis of the purpose of the Treaty'.[16] Finally, the *Sanum* tribunal also found a fork-in-the-road clause in the underlying treaty was a significant factor: 'Indeed, in none of the BITs underlying the cases relied upon by the Respondent is there a fork-in-the-road clause that would limit the investor's access to arbitration if the investor had recourse first to the local courts to determine whether an expropriation had actually occurred'.

> Any disputes concerning other matters between an investor of either Contracting Party and the other Contracting Party may be submitted to the Centre if the parties to the disputes so agree. The provisions of this Paragraph shall not apply if the investor concerned has resorted to the procedure specified in Paragraph 2 of this Article.

[13] *Sanum* award on jurisdiction, para 329: 'As a first impression the text of this provision would seem to restrict the jurisdiction of the Tribunal to matters related to the amount of compensation due in instances of expropriation. However, other readings are possible. The term "involving" has a wider meaning than other possible terms such as "limited to" which could have been used if the intention of the State Parties had been to limit the jurisdiction of the Tribunal exclusively to disputes on the amount of compensation'.

[14] ibid para 329: 'This wider reading of Article 8(3) would seem more consistent with the other provisions of the Treaty as we will see shortly. It is also consistent with how a similar provision was interpreted by the Tza Yap Shum tribunal'.

[15] The *effet utile* principle requires international courts and tribunals to interpret international rules 'so as to give them their fullest weight and effect consistent with the normal sense of the words and with other parts of the text and in such a way that a reason and a meaning can be attributed to every part of the text'. *Sanum* award on jurisdiction, para 333.

[16] *Sanum* award on jurisdiction, para 339: 'The purpose and object of the Treaty covers two distinct aspects: the protection of investments and the development of economic cooperation between both States. The balance between these two aspects must be borne in mind by the Tribunal in the analysis of the text of the Treaty, but it does not mean that the Tribunal needs to give preponderance to one aspect over the meaning of a particular clause of the Treaty or leave a clause without effect. The purpose of a treaty as set forth in its preamble may be useful to resolve doubts in its interpretation but it would not justify leaving without effect a clause of the treaty'.

In both cases, the defending state challenged the arbitral decision on jurisdiction with different outcomes. In *Sanum*, the Singapore High Court examined the interpretation of the arbitration agreement (Article 8(3)) under the *de novo* review standard. It decided that Article 8(3) limited the arbitral jurisdiction to issues of quantum and annulled the arbitral award. It decided that the consent clause applied to the quantum of expropriation claims only:

On balance, I am of the view that the phrase, 'a dispute involving the amount of compensation' in Art 8(3) of the PRC–Laos BIT should be given a restrictive meaning, viz, disputes limited to the amount of compensation for expropriation. First, the word 'involve' is also capable of being interpreted restrictively to mean imply, entail or make necessary. The specific wording of the phrase, 'amount of compensation for expropriation' in Art 8(3), when compared with the broad wording of the phrase 'any dispute in connection with an investment' in Art 8(1), suggests that a more restrictive meaning was intended for the phrase in Art 8(3). Put another way, the PRC and Laos could have used the phrase, 'a dispute in connection with an investment' for consistency with the phrasing in Art 8(1) if they had truly intended for an arbitral tribunal to have a broad jurisdiction on all aspects of an expropriation dispute and it is of some significance that they chose not to do so.

   . . .

While the scope for submitting a dispute to arbitration under the PRC–Laos BIT may seem limited, this limited scope for the submission of a dispute to arbitration is understandable in the light of the observation made in Tza Yap Shum that communist regimes possessed a certain degree of distrust regarding investment of private capital and were concerned about the decisions of international tribunals on matters over which they have no control. I had no doubt that these concerns were also present when the PRC–Laos BIT was concluded between the two communist states and this in my judgment formed an important part of the context in which Article 8 of the PRC–Laos BIT should be interpreted (see Article 31(1) of the VCLT).

On appeal, The Court of Appeal of Singapore reversed the decision of the Singapore High Court and adopted the same reasoning as in *Tza*, holding that the judge was not correct to hold that the *Sanum* tribunal did not have jurisdiction under the PRC–Laos BIT to hear the claims brought by Sanum:

The words of the provision do not seem to us to be capable of accommodating the segregation of an expropriation claim in the way it was suggested such that the question of liability may be determined by the national courts leaving the issue of the quantum of compensation to be heard by an arbitral tribunal. In our judgment, the words '[t]he provisions of this paragraph shall not apply if the investor concerned has resorted to the procedure specified in paragraph 2' means that if any dispute is brought to the national court, the claimant will no longer be entitled to refer any aspect of that dispute to arbitration. Hence once an expropriation claim is referred to the national court, no aspect of that claim can then be brought to arbitration. It should be noted that this does not mean that any and every dispute relating to expropriation may be referred to arbitration. As provided in Art 8(3), this only avails if the dispute does involve a question as to the amount of compensation.[17]

The *Tza* ICSID ad hoc committee[18] confirmed the *Tza* decision on jurisdiction, but on the ground that the standard of the review under Article 52(1)(b) ICSID (manifest excess of powers) did not allow it to review the factual and legal findings of the arbitral

---

[17] [2016] SGCA 57, para 130.
[18] Peru filed an application before the ad hoc committee of ICSID for annulment of the *Tza* decision on jurisdiction and competence under art 52(1)(b) ICSID for manifest excess of powers, (d) serious departure from a fundamental rule of procedure and (e) failure to state reasons. Laos filed a request for annulment before the Singapore High Court of the *Sanum* award on jurisdiction, under s 10 of the Singapore International Arbitration Act (Cap 143A, 2002 Rev Ed).

tribunal.[19] Therefore it found that a misinterpretation by the tribunal of the arbitration agreement under Article 8(3) did not amount to a manifest, i.e. self-evident, excess of powers, and held:

On their face, the words of the first sentence of Article 8(3) of the Peru-China BIT which read '[i]f a dispute involving the amount of compensation for expropriation …' do not include the question of the legality of expropriation, but equally do not refer to disputes exclusively limited to the amount of compensation. Out of context, the meaning of the phrase is not textually obvious. The Arbitral Tribunal interpreted the expression 'dispute involving the amount of compensation for expropriation' in the overall context of Article 8.

The arbitral tribunal went through an interpretative process mandated by the VCLT. It looked at the ordinary meaning of the word 'involving', considered the context of Article 8(3), and then looked at subsidiary sources. It is not for the Committee to replace the arbitral tribunal's judgment by its own. A body that had appellate jurisdiction might well find fault as a matter of law with some aspects of the arbitral tribunal's application of the VCLT, but an ad hoc committee does not have such powers.

In one well cited case, the *Quasar* tribunal interpreted the phrase, 'disputes relating to the amount or method of payment of the compensation due under Article … [nationalization, expropriation]', and found it also included jurisdiction over the liability issue. However, in 2016, the Svea court of Appeal annulled the *Quasar* award on jurisdiction upon the recourse brought by the Russian Federation. It found that the wording 'Any dispute … relating to the amount or method of payment of the compensation due under Article 6 … [expropriation]' in Article 10 of the Spain–Russia BIT was clear insofar as it contains, unlike the state to state arbitration clause of the same treaty, a 'restriction regarding the material issues that an arbitral tribunal is authorized to examine':

In other words, article 10 does not amount to general authorisation for an arbitral tribunal to examine all the questions that could arise between an investor and a host state from the Treaty. The restriction on what could be included in jurisdiction follows from the reference in article 10 to article 6. This reference makes clear that it is only aimed at part of the content of article 6, namely the 'amount or method of payment of the compensation due under article 6.[20]

There are similar cases where arbitral tribunals' decisions are in harmony with the decision of the High Court of Singapore and the Svenska Court of Appeals. The *Berschader* tribunal found that the wording 'disputes … concerning the amount of payment or compensation under … [expropriation] … or concerning any other matter consequential upon an act of expropriation …' limited the arbitral jurisdiction to the quantum aspect of a claim for expropriation and declined its jurisdiction to examine the state's liability for expropriation. The *RosInvest* tribunal reached the same conclusion deciding that 'disputes concerning the amount or mode of compensation to be paid under Article 5 [expropriation]' did not allow arbitrators to examine the question of the entitlement to expropriation. The *Austrian Airlines* tribunal also considered that '[c]oncerning the amount or the conditions of payment of a compensation' excluded its jurisdiction at the liability phase of the examination of a claim for expropriation.

The only 'outlier' consistent with *Tza* is the decision of the *European Media Ventures* tribunal which considered that the wording 'concerning compensation due by virtue of article … [expropriation]' allowed not only for the tribunal to hear the dispute over the compensation, ie the quantum of the claim for expropriation, but also to hear the

---

[19] *Tza ad hoc* Committee, Decision on annulment, 12 February 2015, paras 79–80.
[20] *Svea* Court of appeal, judgment 18 January 2016, p 6.

entire claim for expropriation, including the liability phase. The supervisory English court confirmed the interpretation of the *European Media Ventures* tribunal.[21]

In summary, there is diversity in the findings of the courts and arbitral tribunals as to whether that the first and second generation of socialist BITs contain narrow jurisdiction clauses. Some have required an investor to establish the fact of expropriation in a court proceeding in a state court and only then may the investor bring a claim for quantum in an investor-state arbitration.

III. Territorial Jurisdiction: The Relevance of the Chinese Characteristics?

The next issues, relating to the territorial jurisdiction and to the personal jurisdiction of the arbitral tribunal, allow an examination of questions more specifically pertaining to Chinese BITs as they involve investors established in Macau and Hong Kong.

The binding force of a BIT with respect to the territory of the contracting parties determines the territorial jurisdiction of the arbitral tribunal. The principle applicable to the territorial scope of treaties is found in Article 29 of the VCLT: 'unless a different intentional appears from the treaty or is otherwise established, a treaty is binding upon each party in respect of its entire territory'. This provision is twofold. It first sets the freedom of states to determine the territorial scope of their treaty.[22] In addition, if no intention appears from the treaty or is otherwise established, it provides that the treaty will apply to the entire territory of each contracting state, as a general default rule.

Treaties rarely contain territorial clauses for the exclusion of territories for their application.[23] Almost none of the Chinese BITs contains any provision as to the scope of the territorial upon which it is binding. Are the Chinese BITs applicable to the entire territory of the PRC? The territorial jurisdiction of arbitral tribunals operating under the Chinese BITs raises a specific issue with respect to its two SARs, Hong Kong, a British colony until 1997, and Macau, a Portuguese colony until 1999. On 19 December 1984, China signed a joint declaration with the UK (Sino-British Joint Declaration). On 4 April 1990, the National Assembly of the PRC (NPC) adopted the Basic Law of the Hong Kong SAR, which went into effect on 1 July 1997. On 20 June 1997, China filed a unilateral declaration with the depository of the Secretary-General of the United Nations (1997 Declaration). It resumed sovereignty over Hong Kong on 1 July 1997.

As for Macau, on 13 April 1987, China signed a joint declaration with Portugal ('Sino-Portuguese Joint Declaration'). On 31 March 1993, the NPC adopted the Basic Law of the Macau SAR. On 13 December 1999, China filed a unilateral declaration with the depository of the Secretary-General of the United Nations ('1999 Declaration'). China resumed sovereignty over Macau on 20 December 1999. As

---

[21] Investors have also attempted to expand the scope of the narrow consent clauses contained in the first and second generation of Chinese BITS by others means that interpretation by having recourse to wider consent clauses under the mechanism of the MFN clause (eg *Tza* and *Sanum*), or to wider consent clauses contained in BITs of the third generation as renegotiated and concluded between the same contracting states (eg *Ping An Life Insurance Company of China Limited and Ping An Insurance (Group) Company of China Limited v Kingdom of Belgium*, ICSID Case No ARB/12/29, Award (30 April 2015)). These cases do not contain particulars pertaining to China.

[22] See Oliver Dörr and Kirsten Schmalenbach (eds), *Vienna Convention on the Law of Treaties: A Commentary* (Springer 2012) 492.

[23] ibid 490.

noted above the PRC had entered into first and second generation of BITs, before the recovery of Hong Kong and Macau.

Upon resumption by China of its sovereignty over the territories of Hong Kong and Macau, has the territorial scope of the prior investment international conventions signed by the PRC central government automatically extended to these SARs? Do the Chinese BITs entered after the resumption apply in the SARs? In this respect, the 'moving treaty frontiers' rule provides that a treaty of the successor state is in force in the territory to which the succession applies as from the date of the succession. This recognized principle of international customary law is embodied in Article 15 of the Vienna Convention on State Succession in Treaties (VCST).[24] Article 15(b) further provides for exceptions similar to Article 29 of the VCLT: where it appears from the treaty or is otherwise established that the application of the treaty of that territory (i) would be incompatible with the object and purpose of the treaty or (ii) would radically change the conditions for its operation.

The territorial application of a Chinese BIT under Article 29 of the VCLT and Article 15 of the VCST was examined for the first time in *Sanum v Laos*, where the territorial jurisdiction of the arbitral tribunal was raised by the defending state.

A. The default situation

In *Sanum*, the defending state objected to the tribunal's territorial jurisdiction over Macau, alleging that Macau was not part of the PRC territory in 1993 at the time the BIT was signed, and that upon the PRC recovery of sovereignty over Macau in 1999, the BIT had not been automatically extended to Macau. To determine the applicability the PRC BIT over Macau, the *Sanum* tribunal found that the rules under Article 29 of the VCLT and Article 15(b) of the VCST existed side-by-side and should be applied together:

Article 15 explains and regulates what happens at the moment of transition from one sovereign state to another whereas Article 29 prescribes what the general situation is outside of a transitional period, whether a territory has undergone a transition or not.

In other words, the rule of Article 15 can correctly be described as the 'moving treaty frontiers' rule.

The rule of Article 29 does not deal with a situation of change, but only states the general principle of international law related to the territorial extension of a state's sovereignty, which can be described as the principle of the territorial application of a state's legal order.

In other words, the two rules exist side-by-side, Article 15 being the corollary of Article 29 and Article 29 being a consequence of Article 15.

The *Sanum* tribunal first analysed that, in order to ascertain whether or not the PRC–Laos BIT applies to the Macao SAR, both Article 15 of the VCST, with its exceptions, and Article 29 of the VCLT, with its exceptions, were relevant and were the two faces of the same coin.[25] Therefore, it considered the general default rule on the territorial application of treaties regulated either 'the extension of the treaty to the whole territory, at the moment of a transfer of sovereignty or at any time' or the 'extension of the treaty to the new part of the territory, or in the case there is no succession, to

---

[24] 1978 Vienna Convention on Succession of States in respect of Treaties (VCST) art 15(b). The PRC and Laos are not parties to the VCST.
[25] *Sanum* award on jurisdiction, para 231.

the whole territory'.[26] In order to ascertain when the general default rule applied, the tribunal adopted a negative approach whereby it had to (i) verify whether any of the exceptions apply, and (ii) if the answer was negative, the general default rule of extension of the treaty applied.

B. Exceptions to the default rule

Article 29 of the VCLT and Article 15(b) of the VCST provide for exceptions to the default rule. The treaty does not apply automatically to the entire territory in two series of instances. The first exception arises where the 'expression of a different intention appears from the treaty'. The second exception arises where a different intention 'is otherwise established'. While these exceptions to the non-application of a treaty are both found in the two articles, the exceptions under Article 15 are more 'specific' or more 'limited' than the exceptions under Article 29 of the VCLT:

Indeed, automatic succession applies unless it appears from the treaty itself or is otherwise established that such a result would not be appropriate for one of two reasons: either because such succession would be incompatible with the object and the purpose of the treaty or because it would radically change the conditions of its operation.

As far as the non-application of a treaty to the whole territory is concerned, it is sufficient that such non-application results from the treaty or, for whatever reason, the State sees fit to decide such non-application: for example, the PRC and the Russian Federation decided that the PRC/Russia BIT would not apply to the Macao SAR, for no stated reason.[27]

The expression of a different intention appearing from the treaty

The expression of an intention of the contracting states may first be found in a provision of the treaty. Most Chinese BITs do not contain provisions on their territorial scope.[28] A rare exception is the China–Russia BIT 2006, which excludes the two SARs from its application.[29] Does the absence of express provision in a treaty imply that the treaty applies to the entire territory of each state? The High Court of Singapore which reviewed the *Sanum* arbitral award on jurisdiction held that no definitive conclusions could be drawn from the silence of an express provision in the China–Laos BIT but held the BIT was prima facie applicable to Macau.[30]

The term 'unless a different intention appears from the treaty' covers both the wording of the treaty itself and includes the interpretation of the treaty under the VCLT as well.[31] The rules of interpretation of a treaty are found in Articles 31 and 32 of the VCLT. Under Article 31 of the VCLT, the expression of intent found in other agreements of the contracting States constitutes, as a general rule of interpretation, the

---

[26] ibid para 230.

[27] ibid para 230. See also *Government of the Lao People's Democratic Republic v Sanum Investments Ltd* [2015] SGHC 15, para 61: 'The effect of Art 29 of the VCLT and Art 15 of the VCST is that a treaty is binding on the entire territory of each contracting state unless it appears from the treaty; or is otherwise established that the contracting states had intended otherwise. I note that Art 15 of the VCST is more specific in that the object and purpose of the treaty would also be considered'.

[28] BITs may provide for a definition of the territory, but it is irrelevant to the territorial scope, eg Canada–China FIPA 2012 art 1: 'In respect of China: the territory of China, including land territory, internal waters, territorial sea, territorial air space, and any maritime areas beyond the territorial sea over which, in accordance with international law and its domestic law, China exercises sovereign rights or jurisdiction with respect to the waters, seabed and subsoil and natural resources thereof'.

[29] Protocol accompanying the 2006 China–Russia BIT '[u]nless otherwise agreed by both Contracting Parties, the Agreement does not apply to [the Hong Kong and the Macao SARs]'.

[30] *Laos v Sanum* [2015] SGHC 15, para 62.   [31] See Dörr (2012) 491.

context of the treaty for the purpose of interpreting it or a provision thereof. Under this rule of interpretation, the context of the treaty shall comprise an agreement relating to the treaty made between all the parties in connexion with the conclusion of the treaty and an instrument made by one party and accepted by the other on (Article 31(2) of the VCLT). In addition, the VCLT requires that an arbitral tribunal take into consideration, together with the context, a subsequent agreement of the parties regarding the interpretation of the treaty or the application of its provisions (Article 31(3) of the VCLT).[32]

Absent a provision as to the territorial application of the treaty, the *Sanum* tribunal expressed concerns about the absence of factual evidence:

A first remark to be made by the Tribunal is the difficulty it faced in ascertaining the application or non-application of the PRC/Laos BIT to the Macao SAR due to the paucity of factual elements presented by the Parties: there were no affidavits from the PRC, Laos or the Macao SAR, which could probably have been obtained from the respective authorities.[33]

After the entry of the *Sanum* award, the contracting States reached an agreement as to the application of the BIT through an exchange of letters (the 'Diplomatic Notes') as the 'culmination of communications and meetings between the contracting States which undoubtedly took some time'.[34] On 9 January 2014, the Chinese Embassy in Laos sent to the Ministry of Foreign Affairs of Laos a letter, whereby China stated that the 1993 BIT was not applicable to the Macau SAR. It stated:

According to the Basic Law of the Macao SAR of the PRC, with the authorization of the Central People's Government, the Government of the Macao SAR may conclude and implement investment agreements with foreign states and regions on its own. *In principle, any bilateral investment agreement concluded by the Central People's Government is not applicable to the Macao SAR*, unless otherwise decided by the Central People's Government, after seeking the views of the government of the Macao SR and consulting with the other contracting party to the agreement.[35]

The Singapore High Court, which examined *de novo* the territorial jurisdiction of the *Sanum* tribunal, found that the first Embassy Letter—which was not available before the *Sanum* tribunal[36]—as a whole constituted an agreement between the PRC and Laos

---

[32] See Commentary to the ILC Draft Articles: 'A question of fact may sometimes arise as to whether an understanding reached during the negotiations concerning the meaning of a provision was or was not intended to constitute an agreed basis for its interpretation. But it is well settled that when an agreement as to the interpretation of a provision is established as having been reached before or at the time of the conclusion of the treaty, it is to be regarded as forming part of the treaty. [. . .] Similarly, an agreement as to the interpretation of a provision reached after the conclusion of the treaty represents an authentic interpretation by the parties which must be read into the treaty for purposes of its interpretation' (1966) 2 Yearbook of the ILC 122, para 14.

[33] *Sanum* award on jurisdiction, para 232.

[34] *Laos v Sanum* [2015] SGHC 15, para 48.

[35] Emphasis added. See 7 January 2014, Ministry of Foreign Affairs of Laos to the PRC Embassy in Laos: 'The Ministry of Foreign Affairs has the further honour to inform the Embassy that the Laos Government is of the view that the Agreement does not extend to [Macau] for the reasons based on the People's Republic of China's policy of one country, two systems, its constitutional and legal framework, the Basic Law of [Macau] as well as the fact that the Agreement itself is silent on its extension to [Macau], which returned to the sovereignty of the People's Republic of China in 1999, six years after the signing of the Agreement. It would be highly appreciated if the Embassy would communicate this request to the agencies concerned of the People's Republic of China and could provide a response in due course'.

[36] Sanum challenged the provenance of the Embassy letter in the High Court proceeding, calling it 'suspicious'. Later, the authenticity and provenance of the Embassy letter was confirmed by a second letter dated November 2015, issued by the PRC Ministry of Foreign Affairs, which was submitted to the Singapore Court of Appeals. It stated: 'With the authorization of the Ministry of Foreign Affairs

regarding the interpretation of the BIT under Article 31(3)(a) of the VCLT, and therefore expressed an intention which appeared from the Treaty 'that the PRC–Laos BIT does not apply to Macau' (Article 29 of the VCLT).[37] In particular the court found that the grounds relied upon by the investor for the non-application of the BIT to Macau SAR were irrelevant to the determination of the existence of an agreement between the two states:

74 ... The Laos Letter states that the Basic Law of Macau is *one* of the reasons for the non-applicability of the PRC–Laos BIT to Macau. The other reasons include the policy of one country, two systems and the constitutional and legal framework of the PRC.

In response, the PRC Letter refers to the Laos Letter and states that bilateral investment agreements concluded by PRC are not applicable to Macau. In other words, Mr Yeo [Sanum's counsel] has conflated the agreement reached between the contracting states with the *reasons* furnished for that agreement. Reading the Two Letters as a whole, it is clear that there is an agreement between the PRC and Laos that the PRC–Laos BIT does not apply to Macau.

This conclusion should be approved and the subsequent agreement should be regarded as an element of treaty interpretation binding upon the arbitral tribunal or the supervisory court. Indeed, the agreement relevant to the interpretation of the BIT has a strong normative force since it was reached between the two contracting States, a contracting state, defendant to the investor–state arbitration and a contracting state, which is a non-disputing party to the case. In addition, such an agreement is consistent with the modern practice that the contracting States' joint interpretation of a provision of a BIT is binding on an arbitral tribunal.[38]

The expression of an intention otherwise established

Absent an intention expressly stated in a provision of the BIT or resulting from its interpretation, the expression of intention needs to be 'otherwise established'. There is not a unanimous approach of what is an intention otherwise established. Gardiner proposes to refer to an intention which 'emanates from the nature of the treaty'.[39] One part of the evidence the defending State relied upon for the intention of the non-applicability of the BIT to Macao was the provision under Clause VIII of Annexe I to the 1987 PRC–Portugal Joint Declaration on the Macau's treaty making powers and the applicability to Macau of the PRC's international agreements:

Subject to the principle that foreign affairs are the responsibility of the Central People's Government, the Macao [SAR] may on its own, using the name 'Macao, China', maintain and develop relations and conclude and implement agreements with states, regions and relevant international or regional organizations in the appropriate fields, such as the economy, trade, finance, shipping, communications, tourism, culture, science and technology and sports....

The application to the Macao [SAR] of international agreements to which the [PRC] is a member or becomes a party shall be decided by the Central People's Government, in accordance with the circumstances and needs of the [SAR], and after seeking the views of the government of the [SAR].[40]

---

of the People's Republic of China, the Note of the Embassy of the People's Republic of China dated 9 January 2014 ... ' has stated the correct position of the PRC Government.

[37] *Laos v Sanum* [2015] SGHC 15, paras 70 and 74.

[38] See the authority of the NAFTA Free Trade Commission to issue decisions on interpretation that are binding on NAFTA-based tribunals art 1131(2) NAFTA; art 30(3) of the US Model BIT.

[39] Richard K Gardiner, *Treaty Interpretation* (Oxford University Press 2008) 492.

[40] *Sanum* award on jurisdiction, para 254. This provision is reproduced in Article 108 of the Macau Basic Law.

The defending State claimed the PRC–Portugal Joint Declaration sets the principle that the PRC Central government may at a future date decide whether a BIT should apply to Macau and to confirm that the process for extending the PRC–Laos BIT to Macau has not taken place. This position was supported by authors who have found that there was not automatic application of the PRC BITs to the SAR.[41] The Singapore court approved and accepted that the PRC–Portugal Joint Declaration constituted evidence of China's intention that the PRC–Laos BIT does not apply to Macau: 'In my opinion, [Laos] is entitled to do so. There was also no evidence before me to suggest that the PRC had taken measures to extend the scope of the PRC–Laos BIT to Macau. All this pointed towards the conclusion that the PRC–Laos BIT does not extend to Macau'.[42]

The defending State also relied on the SARs treaty making powers asserted in the Joint Declaration. Indeed, before and after the resumption of sovereignty of the PRC, Hong Kong and Macau entered into international agreements for the promotion and protection of investment with third states.[43] The Court adopted an analogy with the implementation in Hong Kong of the identical provision contained in the UK Joint Declaration (clause IX of Annex I).[44] The Court referred to the work of the Hong Kong Joint Liaison Group (JLG) in negotiating and concluding bilateral agreements on behalf of Hong Kong during the period leading up to the 1997 handover, which suggested that:

the PRC's treaties would not automatically apply to Hong Kong. If the converse were true, *ie*, if the PRC's treaties had automatically applied to Hong Kong, it would not have been necessary for the JLG to negotiate and conclude bilateral agreements for Hong Kong in a number of areas, including that of investment.

105.... the identical wording found in the two joint declarations and the approach taken by the Hong Kong Joint Liaison Group suggest that the PRC is likely to have adopted the same approach towards Hong Kong and Macau.

106. Consequently, the PRC was likely to have been of the view that their treaties would not automatically apply to Macau after the 1997 handover and the Hong Kong experience is to that extent relevant to the determination of the central question in the present case.[45]

---

[41] Andreas Zimmermann, *Staatennachfolge in völkerrechtliche Verträge: zugleich ein Beitrag zu den Möglichkeiten und Grenzen völkerrechtlicher Kodifikation* (Springer 2000) 445–6.

[42] *Laos v Sanum* [2015] SGHC 15, para 92. The *Sanum* tribunal also accepted this interpretation of the Joint Declaration. However, it rejected this argument in concluding that the legal nature of the Joint Declaration was that of a 'devolution treaty' and such treaty which could only bind third parties [ie, Laos], 'if they apply the customary principles of international law' and no element has been submitted to the tribunal to indicate that Laos was informed of the internal procedure or whether such procedure was ever enforced. *Sanum* award on jurisdiction, paras 263–5.

[43] For Hong Kong see the Agreement between the Government of Hong Kong and the Government of Japan for the Promotion and Protection of Investment, entered into force 18 June 1997; the Agreement between the Government of the Hong Kong SAR of the PRC and the Government of the United Kingdom of Great Britain and Northern Ireland for the Promotion and Protection of Investments, entered into force 12 April 1999; the Agreement between the Government of the Kingdom of Thailand and the Government of the Hong Kong SAR of the PRC for the Promotion and Protection of Investments, entered into force 18 April 2006. For Macau, Agreement between the Government of Macau and the Government of Portugal for the Promotion and Protection of Investment, entered into force 17 May 1997; Agreement between the Government of the Macau SAR of the PRC and the Netherlands for the Promotion and Protection of Investments, entered into force 22 May 2008.

[44] 1984 PRC–UK Joint Declaration Clause IX of Annex I: 'The application to [Hong Kong] of international agreements to which [the PRC] is or becomes a party shall be decided by the [the PRC government], in accordance with the circumstances and needs of [Hong Kong], and after seeking the views of the [Hong Kong government]'.

[45] *Laos v Sanum* [2015] SGHC 15, paras 104–6.

Finally, the Singapore High Court found the 2001 WTO Trade Report of Macau relevant to whether the PRC–Laos BIT applied to Macau, 'although the report is by no way conclusive'.[46] The 2001 WTO Trade Report provided: 'In 1999, [Macau] signed a double taxation agreement with Portugal … [Macau] also signed a bilateral agreement on investment protection with Portugal … [Macau] has no other bilateral investment treaties or bilateral tax treaties'.[47] The court held that the 2001 WTO Trade Report suggested to a limited extend that the PRC–Laos BIT did not apply to Macau:

> If the PRC–Laos BIT has indeed applied to Macau, it is unlikely that an unequivocal statement to the contrary [2001 WTO Trade Report] would have found its way into a report issued by a reputable organisation such as the WTO. Having said that, I am aware that the 2001 report explored a wide range of issues and was probably not intended to express a conclusive view on the *legal* issue of whether the PRC–Laos BIT applies to Macau.[48]

The Court of Appeals of Singapore disagreed with the judge's decision and decided to categorize the evidence relating to whether it has been 'otherwise established' that the PRC–Laos BIT is not to apply to Macau after the PRC had resumed sovereignty into three chronological periods and consider them accordingly: (a) the period before the handover of Macau in 1999; (b) the period between the handover and the Critical Date [the date the dispute had crystallized]; and (c) the period subsequent to the Critical Date.[49] As to the pre-Critical Date evidence, the court of appeals considered that there was insufficient evidence to find that it had been 'otherwise established' that the moving treaty frontier rule would not apply in respect of the PRC–Laos BIT.

The court held that the critical date doctrine acts as a time constraint in the context of determining the relevance or weight of evidence in cases concerning issues of public international law: 'the doctrine or principle renders evidence, which comes into being after the critical date and is self-serving and intended by the party putting it forward to improve its position in the arbitration, as being of little, if any, weight'.[50] The Court therefore found that since it had found that there was insufficient evidence to find that it had been 'otherwise established' on the facts, in its judgment the Diplomatic Notes should not bear any weight because they are post-Critical Date evidence adduced to contradict the pre-Critical Date position. Therefore, the most recent decision does not accept the view that the China–Laos BIT does not apply to Macau pursuant to the intention of the contracting state. This territorial issue is closely linked to the issue as to whether an investor from the Hong Kong or Macau SAR is a qualified investor under a Chinese BIT.

IV. The Qualified Chinese Investor: A Chinese Characteristic?

The first issue raised by Peru in defence of the *Tza* claim related to Mr Tza's nationality. Peru argued that Mr Tza's residence in Hong Kong made his reliance on the China–Peru BIT improper. Peru said Mr Tza must rely upon the separate Hong Kong–Peru BIT. This issue was a threshold issue for the arbitral tribunal in considering its jurisdiction over the claim because foreign nationality for an investor is crucial to ICSID jurisdiction. The issue is also very important to China investment dispute analysis because it involves the relationship between the PRC and Hong Kong SAR BITs.

---

[46] ibid para 109.   [47] ibid para 107.   [48] ibid para 109.
[49] [2016] SGCA 57, para 70.   [50] ibid para 104.

The nationality requirement in investor–state arbitration is derived from the idea that disputes between a local investor and its own state should naturally be resolved before local state courts.[51] Therefore, jurisdiction in investor–state arbitration is confined to international investments disputes, ie investment disputes between a foreign investor and the host state. ICSID jurisdiction requires a qualified foreign investor (personal jurisdiction or *rationae personae*).[52] Article 25(1) of the ICSID Convention provides as follows:

The jurisdiction of the Centre shall extend to any legal dispute arising directly out of an investment between a Contracting State (or any constituent subdivision or agency of a Contracting State designated to the Centre by that State) and a national of another Contracting State …[53]

Investors, individuals, or corporations allowed to bring an ICSID claim against the host state must meet a twofold nationality requirement: (i) a positive nationality requirement--the investor must have the nationality of a contracting state, and (ii) a negative nationality requirement--the investor must not be a national of the host state.[54] The *Tza* and the *Sanum* cases involved a determination of the positive nationality requirement of Chinese investors with the caveat that, in both cases, the investor was established in the SARs.

A. Qualification of a Chinese investor as a natural person residing in the SAR

The ICSID Convention provides that the foreign 'natural person' shall be a national of the contracting state but not a national of the host state, which excludes persons with a dual nationality in the state party to the dispute.[55] This nationality requirement is also a continuous requirement, and must be met on the date the parties consented to arbitration and on the date the foreign national files his request for arbitration. This dual requirement is guided by two principles.

First, the ICSID Convention itself does not set terms for the determination of the nationality of an individual. According to international law, the issue of nationality is usually dealt with by reference to the law of the state whose nationality is claimed.[56] The law governing the dispute, under Article 42 of the ICSID Convention, does not apply to the nationality of the individual claimant.[57] Chinese BITs provide that a

---

[51] See Nathalie Bernasconi-Osterwalder, State–State Dispute Settlement in Investment Treaties, International Institute for Sustainable Development (IISD) Best Practices Series, Winnipeg October 2014. See also Julien Chaisse and Lisa Li, 'Shareholder Protection Reloaded—Redesigning the Matrix of Shareholder Claims for Reflective Loss' (2016) 52(1) Stanford Journal of International Law 51–94.

[52] See Christoph H Schreuer, *The ICSID Convention: A Commentary* (2nd edn, Cambridge University Press 2009) 71–341; David A Williams, 'Jurisdiction and Admissibility' in Christoph Schreuer (ed), *The Oxford Handbook of International Investment Law* (Oxford University Press 2008) 884–5; *accord* Devashishm Krishan, 'Nationality of Physical Persons' in Andrea K Bjorkland, Ian A Laird, and Sergey Ripinsky (eds), *Investment Treaty Law: Current Issues, vol 2* (British Institute of International and Comparative Law 2007) 57–66; Roberto Aguirre Luzi and Ben Love, 'Individual Nationality in Investment Treaty Arbitration: The Tension between Customary International Law and Lex Specialis' in Andrea K Bjorkland, Ian A Laird, and Sergey Ripinsky (eds), *Investment Treaty Law: Current Issues, vol 3* (British Institute of International and Comparative Law 2009) 183–208.

[53] ICSID Convention art 25(1).   [54] ibid art 25(3).

[55] ibid art 25(2): '[A]ny natural person who had the nationality of a Contracting State other than the State party to the dispute on the date on which the parties consented to submit such dispute to conciliation or arbitration as well as on the date on which the request was registered pursuant to paragraph (3) of Article 28 or paragraph (3) of Article 36, but does not include any person who on either date also had the nationality of the Contracting State party to the dispute'. See Williams (n 52) 884–5.

[56] *Tza*, para 54: 'There is no question that according to international law it is for each State to determine who their nationals are under its law'.

[57] ICSID Convention art 42.

natural person qualifies as a Chinese investor when such person has the nationality of the PRC in accordance with its laws.[58] Questions of nationality are determined by reference to the municipal law, subject to the applicable rules of international law.[59] The same principle is found in international customary law embodied in the International Law Commission Draft Articles of Diplomatic Protection: 'State of nationality means a State whose nationality that person has acquired, in accordance with the law of that state, by birth, descent, naturalization, succession of States or in any other manner, not inconsistent with international law'.[60]

Secondly, since the nationality of the individual claimant is a jurisdictional requirement, tribunals also apply the conditions set out under the relevant municipal law in the frame of Article 41 of the ICSID Convention, which grants tribunals the power to be the judge of their own competence.[61] Therefore, a tribunal is empowered finally to decide for itself and make its own ruling on the nationality of the claimant, giving weight to the facts and municipal law before it.

The *Tza* case involved a Chinese national resident in Hong Kong. Under the China–Peru BIT (1994), Chinese law was the applicable law for the determination of Tza's nationality.[62] The *Tza* tribunal had to determine whether under Article 25(2) and the relevant provisions of the applicable BIT, (a) the Chinese investor had met his burden to prove his nationality under Chinese law, and (b) even if the burden was satisfied, his residence in Hong Kong prevented him from having recourse to the China–Peru BIT.[63]

The determination of the Chinese nationality

The first question before the *Tza* tribunal was whether the claimant had met his burden of proof with the evidence provided to the tribunal that he was a Chinese national. The issue the tribunal dealt with is not particular to China or to the law applicable, the Nationality Law of the PRC.[64] Chinese nationality is acquired by birth, and conferred upon any person born in China whose parents are both Chinese nationals or one of whose parents is a Chinese national (Article 4). Upon the resumption of sovereignty in Hong Kong in 1997, the Nationality Law of the PRC directly applied to the Hong Kong SAR by way of promulgation, in the same way as it applies in Mainland

---

[58] Agreement between the Government of the United Kingdom of Great Britain and Northern Ireland and the Government of the People's Republic of China Concerning the Promotion and Reciprocal Protection of Investments done at London on 15 May 1986, entered into force on 15 May 1986, 1462 UNTS 255 art 1(c)(ii); Peru–China BIT art 1(2)(a); Agreement on Encouragement and Reciprocal Protection of Investments between the Government of the Kingdom of the Netherlands and the Government of the People's Republic of China done at Beijing on 26 November 2011, 2369 UNTS 219 (Netherlands–PRC BIT) art 1(2)(a): 'The term "investor" means, (a) natural person who have the nationality of either Contracting Party in accordance with the laws of that Contracting Party'. The recent FTAs signed respectively between China and ASEAN (art 1(1)(i)) and New Zealand (art 135) provide for a unified definition and extend the protection to permanent residents: ' "natural person of a Party" means any natural person possessing the nationality or citizenship of, or right of permanent residence in the Party in accordance with its laws and regulations'. It is, however, to be noted that China does not have any domestic law for the treatment of permanent residents of foreign countries. Treaties *available at* http://www.unctadxi.org/templates/docsearch____779.aspx.
[59] Schreuer (n 52) para 641.
[60] Article 4 of the Draft Articles on Diplomatic Protection, UN Doc A/61/10 art 4, 61st Sess Supp No 10 (2006) http://untreaty.un.org/ilc/texts/instruments/english/draft%20articles/9_8_2006.pdf.
[61] ICSID Convention art 41.   [62] Peru–China BIT art 1(2)(a).
[63] *Tza Yap Shum v Republic of Peru*, ICSID Case No ARB/07/6, Decision on Jurisdiction and Competence, para 42 (12 February 2007).
[64] The Nationality Law (*Zhonghua Renmin Gongheguo guoji fa*) was adopted at the Third Session of the Fifth Chinese People's National Assembly (NPA) and effective as of 10 September 1980.

China.[65] In *Tza*, the claimant held a Hong Kong SAR ID and passport, stating he was born in the Fujian province of China in 1948. He was, however, not able to provide a birth certificate to establish the Chinese nationality, as required under the Nationality Law. The examination of the evidence by the *Tza* tribunal followed the consensus that an official document issued by the relevant competent national authority on the nationality of the party should be regarded as prima facie evidence of nationality only,[66] and that the issue was for the decision of the tribunal on all the evidence. The *Tza* tribunal referred to and adopted the solution found in *Micula v Romania*.[67] It balanced the burden of proof and determined that the claimant's evidence created a presumption that could be questioned, but the burden of proof then shifted to the respondent to invalidate such presumption and prove that the nationality was acquired in a manner that is inconsistent with international law.

Therefore, according to the Nationality Act as interpreted by the Permanent Committee of the People's National Assembly for its application to Hong Kong, it seems to be clear, prima facie, that 'the Claimant validly holds the Chinese nationality ... In the opinion of the Tribunal, the nationality conferred by a state to a person under its law has a strong presumption of validity'.[68]

The consequences of residence in the SARs

The territorial application of the Chinese BITs to the Hong Kong SAR had not been raised directly in *Tza*. The defending state objected to the jurisdiction *ratione materiae* of the *Tza* tribunal arguing that the scope of the Sino–Peru BIT did not apply to Chinese nationals with a residence in Hong Kong, since the UK-China Joint Declaration and the HK Basic Law, which listed the international conventions that were applicable to Hong Kong, had not listed the BIT at stake. Peru also referred to the numbers of investment agreements signed by Hong Kong with others states, among which was a Peru–Hong Kong investment agreement. The *Tza* tribunal did not examine the provisions of the UK–China Joint Declaration, the HK Basic Law and took the view that the standard of its duty resided in the terms of Article 25 of the ICSID Convention: to verifying whether claimant had the nationality of a 'Contracting State'. The tribunal found that the claimant had met his burden, proving that all Chinese nationals, including those residing in Hong Kong, were included in the scope Article 25 of the ICSID Convention.[69]

The *Tza* tribunal interpreted the intention of the contracting states under the Chinese investor nationality requirement under the China–Peru BIT primarily under the general rules of interpretation of treaties of Article 31 of the VCLT. It noted that the terms of the BIT merely provided 'natural persons who have nationality of the PRC in accordance with its laws' and held therefore that it considered the intention of the contracting parties as expressly provided for in the terms of the BIT in accordance with Article 31 of the VCLT, and that the defending state had not proven that the

---

[65] Pricilla Leung Mei-Fun, *The Hong Kong Basic Law, Hybrid of Common Law and Chinese Law* (LexisNexis 2007) 93. Pursuant to art 18 and Annex III of the Basic Law of the Hong Kong SAR, the Nationality Law applied in the Hong Kong SAR from 1 July 1997. It was implemented through the 'Explanations of Some Questions Concerning the Implementation of the Nationality Law of the PRC in the Hong Kong SAR' adopted by the Standing Committee of the NPA on 15 May 1996, a year prior to the Hong Kong handover that came into effect on 1 July 1997.
[66] Zachary Douglas, *The Investment Law of Investment Claims* (Cambridge University Press 2009) 537.
[67] ibid.   [68] *Tza* Decision on Jurisdiction, paras 62–3.   [69] ibid para 70.

contracting parties had the intention to exclude Hong Kong residents from the scope of the China–Peru BIT.[70]

The *Tza* tribunal refused to draw any consequence as to the fact Hong Kong had concluded its own investment agreements with countries with which the central government of China had also entered into BITs. It held that Hong Kong has historically been home to people with multiple nationalities. For that reason, it said, the Hong Kong SAR government had 'deployed a policy that seeks the promotion and protection of investments in other countries for the benefit of all of its residents, regardless of their nationalities'.[71]

B. Nationality of the Chinese Investor as a corporation

The *Ping An*[72] and the *Sanum* cases involved claims made by legal entities seeking the protection of a Chinese BIT. Juridical persons constitute the second category of investors (Article 25(2)(b) ICSID Convention) and are of two types: corporations that have a nationality different from the one of the host state or corporations that have the nationality of the host state but are under foreign control. Different from natural persons, the nationality requirement for juridical persons is not continuous and must be met only at the time the parties agreed to arbitrate. The ICSID convention does not define the term juridical person, but it is understood the entity must have legal personality. Nor does the ICSID Convention define the juridical person's nationality. It is left to BITs to define it.

In order to determine the nationality of the corporation, traditional private international law uses the test of the place of incorporation (or registered office) or the effective seat (*siege social*) and the control test. Chinese BITs show use of these tests and have often combined them. The place of incorporation is often used.[73] The place of incorporation and the seat criteria are combined to narrow the scope of application.[74] The control test does not seem to have been used as the sole test but only as an alternative to the other tests.[75]

In *Sanum*, the claimant was registered in Macao. This raises the issue as to whether a legal entity registered in the SARs is a qualified investor under a BIT concluded by the PRC central government. Two principles may support the position that legal entities registered in the SARs are not qualified Chinese investors under Chinese BITs. First, a legal entity established in any of the SARs is not a qualified investor if the Chinese BIT is found not to apply to the SAR. This is a direct consequence of the absence of territorial jurisdiction: if the BIT does not apply in the SAR, the company registered

---

[70] ibid para 74. [71] ibid para 76. [72] *Ping An* (n 21).

[73] UK–China BIT art 1(d)(ii) ('in respect of the People's Republic of China: corporations, firms or associations incorporated or constituted under the law in force in any part of the People's Republic of China').

[74] Peru–China BIT art 1(2)(b) ('in respect of the People's Republic of China: economic entities established in accordance with the laws of the People's Republic of China and domiciled in the territory of the People's Republic of China').

[75] China–Peru Free Trade Agreement, China–Peru, done at Beijing on 28 April 2009, ch 10 art 126(a), definition of Investors: '(ii) economic entities established in accordance with the laws of the People's Republic of China and domiciled in the territory of the People's Republic of China; or (iii) legal entities not established under the law of the People's Republic of China but effectively controlled, by natural persons, as defined in subparagraph (a)(i) [Chinese nationals] or by economic entities as defined in subparagraph (a)(ii), that have made an investment in the territory of the other Party' http://fta.mofcom.gov.cn/english/index.shtml.

in the SAR would not become a qualified investor. This principle is found *a contrario* in the *Sanum* award:

[T]he Tribunal has already decided that the Treaty applies to all the territory over which the PRC is sovereign. It is consequent with that decision that an economic entity established under the laws applicable in any part of the territory of the PRC is to be considered to have been established under the laws and regulations of the PRC.

304. The Respondent has placed particular emphasis on the mutual respect of the sovereignty of the parties recorded in the Preamble of the Treaty. There is no doubt that the PRC has sovereignty over the Macao SAR and the Hong Kong SAR; it would not be respectful of that sovereignty for the Tribunal to consider that laws enacted in either of the two SARs are not enacted in the PRC.[76]

Secondly, the definition of Chinese companies in Chinese BITs by the double requirement, 'economic entities established in accordance with the laws of the PRC and domiciled in the territory of the PRC', leaves the situation unresolved for companies incorporated in the SARs. Each SAR has been granted legislative powers under Article 2 of the two Basic Laws. Hong Kong has conserved its pre-1997 common law system.[77] Hong Kong companies and Macau companies are subject to a corpus of statutes enacted by each SAR, while Mainland companies are subject to the Company Law of the PRC of 1993 as revised in 2005. Article 18(3) of each Basic Law provides for the application of 'national laws' in the SAR limited to a list of laws specifically identified. While the Nationality Law is identified and has been expressly extended to the SARs, the Company Law of the PRC is not one of them.[78]

V. Conclusion

In conclusion, the unique international and constitutional legal framework created by the PRC for the Hong Kong and Macau SARs has been tested in the first decade after China's resumption of sovereignty, by international tribunals and courts. The fact that these SARs have entered into their own international agreements and have both vibrant economies and long-term inward and outward investments will no doubt give rise to further investor–state disputes where further Chinese characteristics of these BITs will be tested.

---

[76] *Sanum* award on jurisdiction, paras 303–4.

[77] The Basic Law of the Hong Kong Special Administrative Region of the People's Republic of China [Constitution] 19 December 1984, ch I, art 2 ('The National People's Congress authorizes the Hong Kong Special Administrative Region to exercise a high degree of autonomy and enjoy executive, legislative and independent judicial power, including that of final adjudication, in accordance with the provisions of this Law'), ch II, art 17 ('The Hong Kong Special Administrative Region shall be vested with legislative power') http://www.basiclaw.gov.hk/en/basiclawtext/index.html.

[78] See Annex III of the Hong Kong Basic Law which expressly includes the Nationality Law of the PRC. The *Sanum* tribunal, however, rejected that position: 'The language of the Treaty does not differentiate between economic entities in accordance with the legal regime under which they were established. There is no difference of treatment between the two States. The Preamble affirms the desire "to encourage, protect and create favorable conditions for investment by investors of one Contracting State in the territory of the other Contracting State …" '. See *Sanum* Award on jurisdiction, para 303.

25

Protecting Chinese Investment Under the Investor–state Dispute Settlement Regime

A Review in Light of *Ping An v Belgium*

*Claire Wilson**

I. Introduction

The decision in *Ping An v Kingdom of Belgium*[1] provides insight into a number of previously unexplored aspects of investor–state dispute settlement. It concerns the first mainland Chinese company to file a claim with the International Centre for the Settlement of Investment Disputes (ICSID)[2] and is the first known ICSID case involving the Kingdom of Belgium as a respondent.[3] The *Ping An* dispute arises from actions that were taken during the 2008 global financial crisis and concerns matters of considerable public importance. It seeks to address the level of protection afforded to existing Chinese investments where China has entered into successive treaties. Ping An alleged that Belgium's financial restructuring measures undertaken in 2008 resulted in a violation of the 1986 China–Belgium bilateral investment treaty.[4] Although Ping An invoked the 1986 bilateral investment treaty for the substance of its claim they relied upon a later 2009 bilateral investment treaty[5] in an attempt to establish jurisdiction.

Until recently, only a few bilateral investment treaty (BIT) claims related to measures taken during financial crisis have been filed against Member States of the European Union (EU). These are mostly limited to claims emanating from measures implemented in Cyprus[6] and Greece.[7] The position in Europe, however, lies in stark

---

* Head of Department, Associate Professor at Hong Kong Shue Yan University.

[1] *Ping An Life Insurance Company of China Limited and Ping An Insurance (Group) Company of China Limited v Kingdom of Belgium* (ICSID Case No ARB/12/29).

[2] *Señor Tza Yap Shum v. The Republic of Peru*, ICSID Case No. ARB/07/6, Award 7 July 2011.

[3] Research is based on the information provided on the ICSID case database available online at http//icsid.worldbank.org last viewed on 22 September 2015 and the UNCTAD database of Investor-State Dispute Settlement (reduced version) available online at http://unctad.org/en/Pages/DIAE/ISDS.aspx (last accessed 1 February 2016).

[4] Agreement between the Government of the People's Republic of China and the Belgian-Luxembourg Economic Union on the Reciprocal Promotion and Protection of Investments dated 4 June 1984 and entered into force on 5 October 1986 (China–Belgium BIT 1986).

[5] Agreement between the Government of the People's Republic of China and the Belgian-Luxembourg Economic Union on the Reciprocal Promotion and Protection of Investments dated 6 June 2005 and entered into force on 1 December 2009 (China–Belgium BIT 2009).

[6] *Marfin Investment Group Holdings SA, Alexandros Bakatselos and Others v Republic of Cyprus* (ICSID Case No ARB/13/27).

[7] *Poštová banka as and ISTROKAPITAL SE v Hellenic Republic*, ICSID Case No ARB/13/8; and *Cyprus Popular Bank Public Co Ltd v Hellenic Republic* (ICSID Case No ARB/14/16). For further discussion on the potential of an influx of claims against Greece from bondholders see Julien Chaisse,

contrast to the Argentine situation. Argentina has responded to numerous BIT claims and still faces more as a result of emergency legislation introduced in response to its own 2001 economic crisis.[8] The more recent Argentine bond cases involve novel types of BIT claims connected with bail-outs and forced restructurings undertaken during the 2001 Argentine crisis.[9]

Unlike many successful claimants against Argentina, Ping An was not able to achieve a favourable result against Belgium. On 30 April 2015, the award rendered by the ICSID tribunal dismissed Ping An's claim for lack of jurisdiction. Consequently, the decision in *Ping An v Belgium* has started to attract lively critique.[10]

The overarching theme of this book is to analyse China's international investment policy through consideration of its bilateral, regional, and global 'tracks'. Each chapter discretely addresses issues concerning one of the three tracks. This chapter is mainly concerned with how China manages its investment policy through the bilateral track. However, in practice, the three tracts no longer operate in isolation. Over the past decade China has become recognized as a major outward investor and has sought to protect its investments not only via a bilateral channel. China has become an active promoter of multi-lateral and global protections. In light of the furtherance of China's investment protections under the multi-lateral track this chapter also briefly considers the future prospects of the proposed China–EU treaty.

II. Investment Protection

States are not obliged to admit foreign investors. According to the principle of state sovereignty the right to control the entry of foreign investors is a right that belongs exclusively to the state. However, once a state accepts foreign investors it must treat them in accordance with the principles established under customary international law. Since the 1990s, states have zealously accepted foreign investors recognizing the economic advantages that foreign direct investment brings. At the same time, states also recognized the need to provide protections to its foreign investors. As a result, the modern foreign investment boom of the 1990s was accompanied by the proliferation of bilateral investment treaties between trading partners.[11]

'Greek Debt Restructuring, *Abaclat v Argentina* and Investment Treaty Commitments: The Impact of International Investment Agreements on the Greek Default' in C L Lim and Bryan Mercurio (eds), *International Economic Law After the Global Crisis: A Tale of Fragmented Disciplines* (Cambridge University Press 2015) 306–28.

[8] Over 40 BIT claims have been filed against Argentina with regard to measures introduced in response to the financial crisis: see eg *CMS Transmission Co v Argentine Republic* (ICSID Case No ARB/01/8); *LG&E Energy Corp v Argentine Republic* (ICSID Case No ARB/02/1); *Enron Corp Ponderosa Assets LP v Argentine Republic* (ICSID Case No ARB/01/3); *Sempra Energy Int'l v Argentine Republic* (ICSID Case No ARB/02/16); *Abaclat v Argentina Case* (ICSID Case No ARB/07/05). For further discussion of claims against Argentina see Stephan W Schill, 'International Investment Law and the Host State's Power to Handle Economic Crises: Comment on the ICSID Decision in LG&E v. Argentina' (2007) 24(3) Journal of International Arbitration 265–86; José E Alvarez and Kathryn Khamsi, 'The Argentine Crisis and Foreign Investors: A Glimpse into the Heart of the Investment Regime' in Karl P Sauvant (ed), *The Yearbook on International Investment Law and Policy 2008/2009* (Oxford University Press 2009) 379–478.

[9] See eg *Abaclat v Republic of Argentina* (ICSID Case No ARB/07/05) and *Ambiente Ufficio SpA v Republic of Argentina* (ICSID Case No ARB/ 08/9).

[10] See Qing Ren, 'Case Comment: Ping An v Belgium: Temporal Jurisdiction of Successive BITs' (2016) 31 ICSID Review 129; and Sebastián Green Martínez, 'Case Comment: Ping An Life Insurance Company of China Limited and Ping An Insurance (Group) Company of China Limited v Kingdom of Belgium: A Jurisdictional Black Hole between Two BITs?' *TDM* (December 2015).

[11] See UNCTAD, 'World Investment Report' (2001) 6.

In concluding BITs, states strive to stimulate inbound foreign investment, whilst also reducing risk to their own nationals who engage in direct investment in foreign states. There has been a great deal of discussion as to whether or not BITs significantly stimulate foreign direct investment. The results of such research are contradictory and inconclusive.[12] It is, however, widely recognized that the prime intended purpose of a BIT is to protect investments against illegitimate measures in a foreign state. BITs are entitled agreements for the 'reciprocal promotion and protection of investments' which clearly reflects this intention.

The preambles of the China–Belgium 1986 and 2009 BITs explicitly provides that their object is to strengthen economic co-operation between the parties by creating favourable conditions for the protection of investments of either party in the territory of the other party. The content of the 1986 and 2009 preambles are typical of preambles in other BITs concluded in the same era and there are no unique levels of protection offered between Belgium and China.

III. Structure of Discussion

This chapter seeks to highlight the key issues arising from the *Ping An* dispute and briefly contemplates whether the determination of the tribunal is reliable. More specifically, it aims to consider Ping An's options in light of the award and the ramifications of the decision.

Following this introductory section, the systemic importance of Ping An is explained in section III.A to provide a wider picture of the dispute. A brief account of the key events leading to the dispute between Ping An and Belgium, along with a summary of the award and brief commentary on the accuracy of the award are presented in section III.B. Thereafter, section III.C considers the immediate legal ramifications of the decision and explores whether Ping An has the right to challenge the award, or alternatively whether other proceedings can be initiated. Section III.D analyses whether the decision is likely to deter or encourage Chinese entities from pursuing claims under the Investor–state Dispute Settlement (ISDS) mechanism in the future. Finally, the impact of the decision on the future continuation of the ISDS mechanism, with specific reference to China and the European Union, is explored in section III.E.

---

[12] For literature supporting BITs as a significant driver in stimulating foreign direct investment see Eric Neumayer and Laura Spess, 'Do Bilateral Investment Treaties Increase Foreign Direct Investment to Developing Countries?' (2006) 33(10) World Development 1567; UNCTAD, 'The Impact on Foreign Direct Investment' in UNCTAD, *Bilateral Investment Treaties in the Mid-1990s* (UNCTAD 1998) 105–36. Literature advocating that BITs are not a significant driver in stimulating foreign direct investment. See Kevin P Gallagher and Melissa B L Birch, 'Do Investment Agreements Attract Investment? Evidence from Latin America' (2006) 7(6) Journal of World Investment and Trade 961; Jason W Yackee, 'Do Bilateral Investment Treaties Promote Foreign Direct Investment? Some Hints from Alternative Evidence' *University of Wisconsin Legal Studies Research Paper No 1114* (22 March 2010). For diverse views see Karl P Sauvant and Lisa E Sachs, *The Effect of Treaties on Foreign Direct Investment: Bilateral Investment Treaties, Double Taxation Treaties, and Investment Flows* (Oxford University Press 2009). More recently, an extensive amount of research on this area has been conducted by Julien Chaisse and Christian Bellak. See Julien Chaisse and Christian Bellak, 'Do Bilateral Investment Treaties Promote Foreign Direct Investment? Preliminary Reflections on a New Methodology' (2011) 3(4) Transnational Corporations Review 3; Julien Chaisse and Christian Bellak, 'Navigating the Expanding Universe of International Treaties on Foreign Investment - Creation and Use of a Critical Index' (2015) 18 Journal of International Economic Law 79 and a BITsel index masterminded by Chaisse and Bellak, BITSel (2015) Bilateral Investment Treaties Selection Index, Version 4.20 www.cuhk.edu.hk/proj/BITSel (last accessed 1 February 2016).

A. Systemic importance

A systemically important entity is one which may activate a financial crisis if it encounters financial distress or failure. The discussion in this section briefly digresses from the analysis of the award to assess the systemic importance of the claimants. An account of how Ping An dealt with the financial losses incurred in 2008 is set out in sub-section III.D 'Systemic risk'. The purpose of this discussion is to provide a more detailed picture of the dispute and to explore the economic-realities behind why the irrecoverable losses incurred by Ping An did not trigger a national or global crisis.

B. Who are the claimants?

The two claimants in the dispute are Ping An Life Insurance Company of China Limited and Ping An Insurance (Group) of China Limited.

The first named claimant, Ping An Life Insurance Company of China Limited (Ping An Life), is a limited company established in 2002 by the China Insurance Regulatory Commission under PRC Insurance Law with headquarters in Shenzhen, a major city in Guangdong Province, southern China.[13] Ping An Life operates as a subsidiary of Ping An Insurance (Group) Company of China Limited.

Ping An Insurance (Group) Company of China Limited (Ping An Group) was incorporated in Shenzhen, on 21 March 1988. The business was initially engaged primarily in the underwriting of property and casualty insurance in Shenzhen. However, the company was reorganized due to the expansion of business outside of Shenzhen, and growth of the business into the underwriting of life insurance. Its business scope now includes investing in financial and insurance enterprises, supervising and managing domestic and overseas businesses of subsidiaries, and utilizing funds.

Ping An Group is the holding company of Ping An Life and currently has several other subsidiaries.[14] The business of life insurance and property and casualty insurance is conducted through 99.0 per cent ownership in each of Ping An Life, and Ping An Property and Casualty, respectively. Ping An Group also operates the trust business through Ping An Trust, which in turn holds a 64.1 per cent equity interest in Ping An Securities.

The shares of Ping An Group are listed both on the Hong Kong Stock Exchange (HKEx)[15] and on the Shanghai Stock Exchange.[16]

C. National and global importance

Together, the Ping An Group and its subsidiary, Ping An Life, are of major systemic importance both within mainland China and on a global level.

---

[13] Initially the business was founded in 1988 under the name of Shenzhen Ping An Insurance Company with a registered capital of RMB 53 million. Full details of the establishment are available in a Listing Report published by HKEC http://www.hkexnews.hk/listedco/listconews/sehk/2004/0614/2318/F114_e.pdf (last accessed 28 October 2015).

[14] The subsidiaries of Ping An Group are as follows: Ping An Life Insurance Company of China Limited; Ping An Property and Casualty Insurance Company of China Ltd; Ping An Annuity Insurance Company; Ping An Health Insurance Co Ltd; Ping An Bank Co Ltd; Ping An Securities Limited; Ping An Trust Co Ltd; Ping An Futures Brokerage Co Ltd; Ping An Asset Management Co Ltd; Ping An of China Asset Management (Hong Kong) Co Ltd.

[15] Hong Kong Stock Exchange listing Ping An (2318).

[16] Shanghai Stock Exchange listing Ping An (601318).

Ping An Life is the second largest insurer in mainland China by premium size (market value).[17] It provides a wide-range of insurance products and services in China, in addition to telemarketing. The intention of Ping An Life is to provide a one-stop-shop of all round insurance and financial services. Currently, Ping An Life has forty-one branches and more than 2,800 outlets across mainland China. It engages more than 600,000 salespersons that provide a nationwide service. In addition to traditional counter services, Ping offers a range of multi-channel services to the Chinese public. Such services include telephone, internet, mobile phone WAP, mobile phone APP, and mobile counter facilities, to provide customers with simple, swift, and highly techno-logical financial services.[18]

The Ping An Group is a major personal financial services provider in China that engages in a wide range of business services within the three core businesses of insur-ance, banking, and investment. It has established a sales and services network covering almost the entirety of mainland China. By the end of 2008 the Ping An Group pro-vided more than 42 million individual and institutional clients with services.[19] The Ping An Group also provides employment opportunities to a large number of people, and currently engages approximately 798,000 life insurance sales agents and 246,000 full-time employees.

In 2009, the Financial Stability Board developed a policy framework to address the systemic and moral hazard risks associated with systemically important financial insti-tutions, and initially focussed on specific global systemically important financial insti-tutions.[20] The framework was subsequently endorsed by the G20 in November 2010.[21] A set of policy measures was published in November 2011 to address the systemic and moral hazard risks associated with global systemically important banks. On 18 July 2014, the International Association of Insurance Supervisors published a set of policy measures to apply to global systemically important insurers.[22]

Subsequently, on July 2013, the Financial Stability Board, in consultation with the International Association of Insurance Supervisors and national authorities, identified an initial list of nine globally systemically important financial institutions to which the policy measures should apply. Ping An was identified as one of the nine insurers along-side other internationally renowned companies such as AIA, Prudential, MetLife, and AXA.[23] Incidentally, Ping An is the only Chinese insurer on the list. Therefore, not only is Ping An systemically important on a national level in China, but the corporate group

---

[17] See official website of the Ping An group http://about.pingan.com/en/pinganrenshou.shtml (last accessed 1 February 2016).

[18] Information available from the official website of Ping An http://about.pingan.com/en/pinganrenshou.shtml (last accessed 1 February 2016).

[19] ibid.

[20] Financial Stability Board, Report to G20 Finance Ministers and Governors, Guidance to Assess the Systemic Importance of Financial Institutions, Markets and Instruments: Initial Considerations (28 October 2009).

[21] SIFI Framework, Financial Stability Board (11 November 2010).

[22] Global Systemically Important Insurers: Initial Assessment Methodology, IAIS (July 2013); Global Systemically Important Insurers: Policy Measures, IAIS (July 2013).

[23] Financial Stability Board, 'Global systemically important insurers (G-SIIs) and the policy measures that will apply to them' (18 July 2013), 'Annex I: G-SIIs in Alphabetical Order as of July 2013' Allianz SE, American International Group, Inc., Assicurazioni Generali SpA, Aviva plc, Axa SA, MetLife, Inc., Ping An Insurance (Group) Company of China Ltd, Prudential Financial, Inc., Prudential plc. The initial list is based on the methodology set out in the IAIS document Global sys-temically important insurers: initial assessment methodology, using data as of end-2011. The updated list in 2014 confirms the same nine companies http://www.financialstabilityboard.org/wp-content/uploads/r_130718.pdf?page_moved=1 (last accessed 1 February 2016).

is also systemically important on a global level. This means that Ping An is considered to be an institution of 'such size, market importance, and global interconnectedness that its distress or failure would cause dislocation in the global financial system and adverse economic consequences across a range of countries'.

D. Systemic risk

Establishing what constitutes systemic risk was not a simple task and up until 2009 most G20 members did not have a formal definition.[24] Systemic risk involves three major aspects: First, the threat of a triggering event; secondly, the threat of financial propagation; and, thirdly, a threat to the macro economy.[25] This means that the triggering event must be of such magnitude so as to pose 'a risk of disruption to financial services that are (i) caused by an impairment of all or parts of the financial system and (ii) has the potential to have serious negative consequences for the real economy'.[26]

In 2008, Ping An reported significant losses in Fortis shares of RMB22,790 million associated with overseas investments in Fortis shares. The group also declared a significant decrease in net profits in comparison with 2007 amounting to a shortfall of RMB19,219 million.[27] The insurance business, Ping An Life, suffered significantly reporting a loss of RMB 2,956 million in 2008 despite its premium income exceeding RMB100 billion for the first time.[28]

Ordinarily, the financial damage suffered in 2008 to Ping An Life and the Ping An group would have resulted financial distress. In 2008, other similar companies were not so abundantly capitalized. Fortunately, liquid assets that were held by the Ping An Group together with net cash generated from future operations and the availability of short-term borrowings were sufficient to meet the expected liquidity and capital adequacy requirements of the group. Under the circumstances, the loss was contained within the group without causing financial distress or propagation to other financial institutions.[29]

The measures that were taken by Ping An in response to the loss are commendable. For example, Ping An proactively took stringent cost control measures and embarked on a strategy to enhance sales channels so as to cope with the negative impacts of disasters on expenses in other insurance business operations.[30]

At the time when the loss was incurred Ping An operated on the developing and emerging insurance markets in mainland China—an economy that was not embroiled in the 2008 crisis. This position proved to be advantageous to Ping An. However, the position is completely different today since mainland Chinese institutions are now

---

[24] Guidance to Assess the Systemic Importance of Financial Institutions, Markets and Instruments: Initial Considerations, Report to the G-20 Finance Ministers and Central Bank Governors, Prepared by Staff of the International Monetary Fund and the Bank for International Settlements, and the Secretariat of the Financial Stability Board (October 2009) 5.

[25] John Taylor, 'Defining Systemic Risk Operationally' in Kenneth E Scott, George P Shultz, and John B Taylor, *Ending Government Bailouts as We Know Them* (Hoover Institution Press Publication 2010) 33–58.

[26] Guidance to Assess the Systemic Importance of Financial Institutions, Markets and Instruments: Initial Considerations, Report to the G-20 Finance Ministers and Central Bank Governors, Prepared by Staff of the International Monetary Fund and the Bank for International Settlements, and the Secretariat of the Financial Stability Board (October 2009) 5–6.

[27] In 2008, Ping An declared a net profit of RMB477 million. In 2007, the net profit declared was RMB19,219 million. See Ping An, Annual Report 2008, 'Key Figures' (2008) 4.

[28] In 2008, Ping An Life reported a loss of RMB2,956 million. In 2007, the net profit declared was RMB10,883 million. See Ping An, Annual Report 2008, 'Key Figures' (2008) 4.

[29] See Ping An, Annual Report 2008 54.   [30] ibid 30.

more interconnected with global markets. If these events were repeated today they would have a detrimental effect on both the national and global economy. For this reason, all states must seriously assess the inherent risks posed by systemically important entities investing in foreign states to ensure that adequate safeguards are put in place to avert financial catastrophes on both a national and global level.

IV. *Ping An* Dispute

Ping An's request for arbitration against Belgium was acknowledged by ICSID on 7 September 2012 and Belgium was informed of the claim by ICSID on 10 September 2012. This section strives to provide a simple overview of the dispute between *Ping An v Belgium* as a foundation to the main discussions concerning Ping An's options after the award was rendered (section C), and ramifications of the determination of the tribunal (sections D and E). The events leading to the dispute are summarized first before dealing with the allegations and claims. Belgium's response is dealt with next. The award is summarized in the final part of this section and is thereafter followed by a brief commentary on whether or not the determination of the tribunal is reliable.

A. Events leading to the claim

Ping An became the single largest shareholder of Fortis following a series of investments made between October and July 2008.[31] At that time Fortis was the twentieth largest business in the world by revenue with listings on the Euronext Brussels, Euronext Amsterdam, and Luxembourg stock exchange. In July 2008, Ping An held approximately 4.81 per cent of shares issued by Fortis in return for an investment of €2billion.[32]

On 15 September 2008, Lehman Brothers filed for bankruptcy, triggering the 2008 global financial crisis. After the failure of Lehman Brothers, banks feared that their counterparts in the interbank market would default, and this had a significant impact upon the decline of the interbank market. Other lending banks lost confidence in the banking division of Fortis[33] as a result of rumours that Fortis may attempt to raise extra capital by launching a new rights issue. This situation posed substantial risks to the funding liquidity position of Fortis. By 26 September 2008, Fortis was not able to access the interbank market. Institutional clients had started to make large withdrawals of capital, and Fortis was forced to adopt the marginal lending facility offered by the Belgian National Bank (BNB) at increased interest rates.[34]

---

[31] The two companies responsible for heading the Fortis Group were Fortis SA/NV, a Belgian company, and Fortis NV, a Dutch company. Fortis was subdivided into banking and insurance. The Belgian company Fortis Bank SA/NV, and its subsidiaries Fortis Banque Luxembourg SA and Fortis Bank Nederland (Holding NV carried out the banking operations. This meant that Fortis was subject to banking regulatory supervision in Belgium, the Netherlands, and Luxembourg. For further information see Fortis Financial Statement (2008)16–18 https://bib.kuleuven.be/files/ebib/jaarverslagen/Fortis_2008(2)eng.pdf (last accessed 1 February 2016).

[32] *Ping An v Belgium*, Award (30 April 2015), paras 52–7. For further information regarding the corporate structure and rearrangement of Fortis Group see Fortis Bank Nederland, Annual Review 2008 (23 March 2009) and Fortis Financial Statement (2008) 16–18 https://bib.kuleuven.be/files/ebib/jaarverslagen/Fortis_2008(2)eng.pdf (last accessed 1 February 2016).

[33] Fortis Bank SA/NV and its subsidiaries.

[34] *Ping An v Belgium*, Award (30 April 2015), paras 58–9.

On 28 September 2008, a series of measures to intervene in the Fortis Group were agreed by the Belgian, Dutch, and Luxembourg states. Two relevant phases of intervention are summarized below.

The first phase of measures, implemented on 29 September 2008, resulted in the following: Belgium acquired a 49.93 per cent share in the Belgian banking division of Fortis[35] in return for a capital injection of €4.7 billion; the Netherlands acquired a 49.9 per cent share in the Dutch banking division of Fortis[36] in return for €4 billion; and, Luxembourg acquired a 49.9 per cent share in the Luxembourg banking subsidiary for the provision of a mandatorily convertible loan of €2.5 billion. An additional €14.8 billion was provided to increase the capital of the Belgian banking division.[37]

The second phase of measures occurred between 3 October 2008 and 10 October 2008 to address further liquidity problems. On 3 October 2008, Fortis was informed by Belgium of the following arrangements: the Netherlands would acquire Fortis Netherlands for €16.8 billion;[38] the Netherlands would guarantee the immediate repayment of a short term debt of €34 billion owed by the Netherlands banking division to the Belgium banking division; and, within one month, to convert a €16 billion long term debt owed by the Netherlands banking division to the Belgian banking division into negotiable financial instruments that the Netherlands would guarantee; and Luxembourg would increase its share in the Belgian banking division from 49 per cent to 51 per cent; Belgium would acquire the remainder of the Belgian banking division for a nominal amount.

Further measures implemented in the second phase include the following: On 10 October 2008, Belgium purchased the remainder of the shares in the Belgian banking division for €4.7 billion and then transferred, back-to-back, 75 per cent of the shares to BNP Paribas in exchange for the issuance of new shares valued at €8.25 billion.[39]

There were many other important events that occurred prior to, during, and after the period discussed above.[40] The concise account of events in this section strives to provide the most relevant facts to the arbitral decision. Indeed, the award explicitly states that the material facts reported only serve as background to the issue of jurisdiction and do not deal with the specific merits of the claim.[41]

---

[35] Fortis Banque Luxembourg SA.   [36] Fortis Bank Nederland (Holding) NV.

[37] *Ping An v Belgium*, Award (30 April 2015), para 60. Also see a report published on the Belgian Government webpage Portal belgium.be official information and services 'Fortis: additional measures' (5 October 2008) http://www.belgium.be/en/news/2008/news_fortis_paribas.jsp (last accessed 1 February 2016).

[38] Subject to agreement between Belgium and the Netherlands. *Ping An v Belgium*, Award (30 April 2015), para 61.

[39] *Ping An v Belgium*, Award (30 April 2015), para 62.

[40] For example, in 2007 Fortis acquired ABN Amro in consortium with Banco Santander and the Royal Bank of Scotland in the collective name of RSF Holdings. The offer was made unconditional on 17 October 2007 and the division of business began shortly afterwards. This transaction is reputed to have weakened Fortis (and RBS). See Dimitris N Chorafas, *Banks, Bankers, and Bankruptcies under Crisis: Understanding Failure and Mergers during the Great Recession* (Palgrave Macmillan 2014) 179–84; Dirk Schoenmaker, *Governance of International Banking: The Financial Trilemma* (Oxford University Press 2013) 79–83; Mathias Dewatripont and Jean Charles Rochet, 'The Treatment of Distressed Banks' in Mathias Dewatripont, Xavier Freixas, and Richard Portes (eds), *Macroeconomic Stability and Financial Regulation: Key issues for the G20* (Centre for Economic Policy Research 2011) 159–64. *OECD Economic Surveys: Belgium 2009*, Volume 2009/12 (OECD, July 2009) 25–9.
There were also issues with regard to the Dutch government's sale of the Fortis banking division to BNP Paribas. In December 2008, the Brussels court suspended the sale to allow for further shareholder approval to be sought. This decision was later overturned by the Belgium Court of Appeal.

[41] *Ping An v Belgium*, Award (30 April 2015), para 51.

B. Allegations and claims

The claimants relied on the 1986 China–Belgium BIT with regard to the substance of their claim.[42] According to Ping An, Belgium had violated four discrete substantive provisions: (1) fair and equitable treatment,[43] (2) full protection and security,[44] (3) duty to provide full compensation for expropriation,[45] (4) protections equal to those 'enjoyed by investors of third countries' and, no less favourable treatment than afforded to investors of other nations.[46]

Ping An alleged that their indirect interest in the Belgian banking division was halved from 4.81 per cent to approximately 2.41 per cent as a result of the first interventions on 29 September. Ping An further alleged that this first intervention was 'unnecessary, unfair, unreasonable, inequitable and ineffective' since there were alternative measures that could have been adopted.[47] Accordingly, the claimants submitted that Belgium failed to afford their investments fair, just, and equitable treatment and constant protection and security accorded under the 1986 BIT. Ping An claimed damages arising from Belgium's treaty breaches.

Fortis' remaining share in the Belgian banking division was transferred to Belgium by a series of transactions occurring from 3 October 2008 to 10 October 2008. Ping An alleged that these second interventions resulted in the complete expropriation of the Belgian banking division of Fortis. As a result Ping An claimed full compensation 'in an amount equal to the fair market value of the claimants' expropriated investment at the date immediately preceding the expropriation, or the date on which the expropriation was made public'.[48]

Ping An submitted further alternative claims also applying general principles of law stating that the first interventions, whereby Belgium acquired Fortis' entire interest in the Belgium banking division for €4.7 billion which was significantly undervalued, resulted in Belgium unjustly enriching itself. Additionally, Ping An claimed that Belgium had failed to fairly provide compensation for the remaining 50 + 1 share stake in Fortis acquired in the second intervention, and in the process had unjustly enriched itself. According to the claimants when Belgium sold its 75 per cent stake in the Belgian banking division it made an immediate profit.[49] Ping An therefore sought restitution as a *pro rata* share equivalent to the value of Belgium's unjust enrichments.

Briefly stated, Ping An submitted the dispute to ICSID on the basis of the jurisdictional provisions set out in the 2009 China–Belgium BIT. The settlement of investment disputes clause in Article 8 of the 2009 BIT provided Ping An with the choice of submitting the dispute either to a competent Belgian court or to ICSID. The claimants also relied on Article 10, which deals with 'transition' from the 1986 BIT to the 2009 BIT and provides the following:

[42] In accordance with the principle of non-retroactivity (of substantive provisions): Vienna Convention on the Law of Treaties art 28; ILC Articles on State Responsibility art 13.
[43] 1986 BIT art 3(1).   [44] ibid art 3(2).   [45] ibid art 4 and art 2 of the Protocol.
[46] ibid art 3(3) and art 11. With regard to treatment afforded to investors of other states Ping An relied on BITs concluded between the Belgium–Luxembourg Economic Union and the following States: People's Republic of Bangladesh (1981), Republic of Albania (1999), Republic of Algeria (1991), Republic of Croatia (2001), and Republic of Burundi (1989).
[47] *Ping An v Belgium*, Award (30 April 2015), paras 69–73.
[48] This is referred to in the Award at para 87: but need to use provisions of 1986 BIT: art 4, and Protocol art 2.
[49] *Ping An v Belgium*, Award (30 April 2015), paras 66, 74–8, 85.

(1) This Agreement substitutes and replaces the Agreement between the Government of the People's Republic of China and the Belgium-Luxembourg Economic Union on the Reciprocal Promotion and Protection of investments, signed on 4th June, 1984 in Brussels.

(2) The present Agreement shall apply to all investments made by investors of either Contracting Party in the territory of the other Contracting Party, whether made before or after the entry into force of this Agreement, but shall not apply to any dispute or any claim concerning an investment which was already under judicial or arbitral process before its entry into force. Such disputes and claims shall continue to be settled according to the provisions of the Agreement of 1984 mentioned in paragraph 1 of this Article.

Ping An interpreted Article 10 to mean that the 2009 BIT could be used to establish jurisdiction for disputes related to investments made prior to the entry into force of the 2009 BIT because the dispute was not already under 'judicial or arbitral process' before the date of entry into force.

It is material at this point to note that the provisions of the 1986 BIT are less favourable than those set out in the 2009 BIT and only allow disputes 'relating to the amount of compensation payable in cases of expropriation, nationalisation or any other measure similarly affecting investments'[50] to be submitted to international arbitration.[51]

C. Belgium's response

Belgium did not submit a formal response to the merits of the claim. Alternatively, Belgium merely presented its own account of the facts[52] and raised five objections to the jurisdiction of the tribunal under the 2009 BIT which are summarized as follows:

(1) The dispute had arisen prior to the entry into force of the 2009 BIT[53] and accordingly the tribunal lacked jurisdiction *ratione temporis*. Jurisdiction under Article 8 of the 2009 BIT was limited to disputes arising after the 2009 BIT had entered into force.[54]

(2) The tribunal only had jurisdiction over claims arising in the substantive provisions of the 2009 BIT and therefore the tribunal lacked jurisdiction *ratione materiae*.[55]

---

[50] China–Belgium BIT 1986 art 10(3). For further discussion related to the scope of such clauses see J Romesh Weeramantry and Claire Wilson, 'The Scope of "Amount of Compensation" Dispute-Resolution Clauses in Investment Treaties' in Chester Brown and Kate Miles (eds), *Evolution in Investment Treaty Law and Arbitration* (Cambridge University Press 2011) 409–28; 422–7.

[51] Further clarification as to the meaning of 'international arbitration' is set out in The Protocol art 6. Accordingly, the tribunal shall consist of three persons and be presided by the Chairman of the Arbitration Institute of the Stockholm Chamber of Commerce. The tribunal may determine its own procedure but may take as guidance the Rules of the Arbitration Institute of the Stockholm Chamber of Commerce or the ICSID Arbitrational Rules.

[52] Belgium added that the first intervention consisted of capital increase pursuant to Belgian corporate law and the second intervention consisted of share purchase contracts. It was further stated that if Fortis had only limited choice but to accept the two interventions it was because 'it was facing extraordinary and dramatic circumstances, coupled with extreme urgency'. *Ping An v Belgium*, Award (30 April 2015), paras 99–103.

[53] It was commonly agreed by the parties that the dispute arose before the 2009 BIT came into force. *Ping An v Belgium*, Award (30 April 2015), para 105.

[54] *Ping An v Belgium*, Award (30 April 2015), paras 113–14.

[55] Relying on the China–Belgium 2009 BIT, Articles 7 and 8(1). *Ping An v Belgium*, Award (30 April 2015), paras 115–16.

(3) Ping An had failed to give the proper notice required under the 2009 treaty and therefore the tribunal lacked jurisdiction *ratione voluntatis*.[56] This objection arose from the correspondence dated 14 October 2009 that Ping An sent notifying Belgium of the dispute. In this correspondence reference was made to Article 10(1) of the 1986 BIT but not to Article 8 of the 2009 BIT.[57]

(4) The claims did not fall under the tribunal's jurisdiction in accordance with the 2009 BIT, and therefore Ping An failed to demonstrate a prima facie case. Ping An's claims under Articles 3(1), 3(2) and 4 of the 1986 BIT and the alternative claim of unjust enrichment were manifestly without merit.

(5) The *Monetary Gold* principles[58] provide that an international tribunal should not exercise its jurisdiction over a dispute if the resolution of such a dispute involves the determination of the rights and obligations of a third party which is not a party to the proceedings. To avoid determining the rights and obligations of a third party the tribunal should not exercise its jurisdiction since the Netherlands was not and could not be a party to the proceedings.[59]

D. Determination of the tribunal

On 30 April 2015, the tribunal comprising Lord Collins, Philippe Sands QC, and David Williams QC dismissed Ping An's claim due to lack of jurisdiction.[60]

Previous cases involving successive BITs were considered by the tribunal to assist with the interpretation of the temporal application of jurisdictional provisions. It was noted that in *ABCI Investments v Tunisia*[61] and *Jan de Nul v Egypt*[62] express provisions were included into the BITs to determine the applicable BIT. In the *ABCI* case the term 'arisen' has been used for disputes which were governed by an earlier BIT. The tribunal also considered the case of *Walter Bau v Thailand*[63] in which there was no express provision in the later BIT. In the *Walter Bau* case the tribunal concluded that it had no jurisdiction under the later BIT over disputes which had come into existence before that treaty came into force.[64] In reviewing the UNCITRAL case of *Nordzucker AG v Poland*,[65] the tribunal acknowledged that there was authority to support the

---

[56] In accordance with the China–Belgium 2009 BIT art 8. *Ping An v Belgium*, Award (30 April 2015), paras 117–21.

[57] *Ping An v Belgium*, Award (30 April 2015), paras 105–11. Ping An sent a letter to Belgium on 3 July 2012 'to confirm that Ping An's letter of 14 October 2009 constituted a notice of dispute in satisfaction of Article 8.1' of the 2009 BIT.

[58] *Case of the Monetary Gold Removed from Rome in 1943 (Italy v France, and Others)* [1954] ICJ Rep 19.

[59] Belgium argued that the Dutch and Belgian regulators have a long-standing history of cooperation with regard to the supervision and intervention of the Fortis Group. The claims against Belgium also implicate the Netherlands, which was not present. It was further argued that the absence of the Netherlands could impair the due process rights of Belgium. *Ping An v Belgium*, Award (30 April 2015), paras 127–8.

[60] David A R Williams QC was appointed by the claimants, Professor Philippe Sands QC by the respondents, and Lord Collins of Mapesbury presided over the tribunal.

[61] *ABCI Investments Ltd v Republic of Tunisia*, ICSID Case No ARB/04/12, Decision on Jurisdiction (18 February 2011).

[62] *Jan de Nul NV and Dredging International NV v Arab Republic of Egypt*, ICSID Case No ARB/04/13, Award (6 November 2008).

[63] *Walter Bau AG (in liquidation) v Kingdom of Thailand*, UNCITRAL, Award (1 July 2009).

[64] *Walter Bau v Thailand*, Award (1 July 2009), paras 9.67–9.68, 9.72–9.73.

[65] *Ping An v Belgium*, Award (30 April 2015), para 201 referring to *Nordzucker AG v Poland* (UNCITRAL), Partial Award, 10 December 2008.

position that the application of a new treaty jurisdiction clause to pre-existing substantive breaches was possible unless it was explicitly excluded, however, those decisions depended upon an analysis of the individual provisions.

The *Ping An* tribunal proceeded to analyse the individual provisions of the 2009 BIT adopting the principles of treaty interpretation as codified in the Vienna Convention of the Law of Treaties 'in good faith in accordance with the ordinary meaning to be given to their terms in the context of the 1986 BIT and the 2009 BIT (including its preamble), in the light of the object and purpose of the 2009 BIT and against the background of the 1986 BIT'.[66]

Six reasons were deployed by the tribunal to support the determination of lack of jurisdiction *ratione temporis*.[67] First, it was found that the plain meaning of Article 8(1), read together with Article 8(2) and Article 10(2), referred only to disputes which *arise* after the 2009 BIT comes into force. The first sentence of Article 8(1) provides: 'When a dispute *arises* between an investor of one Contracting Party and the other Contracting Party, either party to the dispute *shall notify* the other party to the dispute in writing'.[68] Adopting the rationale previously applied by the *ABCI Investments v Tunisia* tribunal[69] the *Ping An* tribunal took the view that that the word 'arises' referred to disputes that *arise* in the present and future but not those that *arose* in the past. The *Ping An* tribunal was therefore unable to extend the scope of Article 8(1) to include Ping An's disputes with Belgium that *had arisen* prior to the entry into force of the 2009 BIT.[70]

Secondly, the preamble to the 2009 BIT was not considered to be of assistance by the tribunal for the reason that preambles generally only have 'limited interpretive effects' and did not lead to an inference of deploying 'creative interpretation'.[71]

The tribunal relied on Article 10(2) to support the remaining four reasons.[72]

Referring to the common provision in Article 10(2) that the 'Agreement shall apply to all investments made by investors of either Contracting Party in the territory of the other Contracting Party, whether made before or after the entry into force' of the 2009 BIT, the tribunal was not willing to accept that it assisted in any way 'on the question of the effect of a dispute arising before entry into force'.[73]

The fourth reason that the tribunal deployed was that Article 10(2) was 'silent on the disposition' of disputes which were notified under the earlier 1986 BIT but were not under judicial or arbitral process.[74]

Imparting its fifth reason, the *Ping An* tribunal asserted that just because Article 10 clearly states that the intention was to substitute and replace the 1986 BIT it does not 'justify an inference' that disputes which had been notified but not developed into judicial or arbitral proceedings under the 1986 BIT could be processed under the 2009 BIT.[75]

The sixth reason that the tribunal put forward was that an expansive interpretation would have the effect of allowing the claimants to invoke the wider dispute resolution provisions provided in the 2009 BIT.[76]

---

[66] *Ping An v Belgium*, Award (30 April 2015), para 164.
[67] *Ping An v Belgium*, Award (30 April 2015), paras 223–31.
[68] In interpreting the plain meaning of Article 8(1) it was read together with Articles 8(2) and 10(2). See *Ping An v Belgium*, Award (30 April 2015), para 224.
[69] *Ping An v Belgium*, Award (30 April 2015), para 215, referring to *ABCI Investments v Tunisia*, Decision on Jurisdiction (18 February 2011), paras 162–3, 169–70.
[70] Emphasis by way of *italic font* is added by the author.
[71] *Ping An v Belgium*, Award (30 April 2015), para 225.   [72] ibid paras 226–32.
[73] *Ping An v Belgium*, Award (30 April 2015), para 226. The third reason of the Tribunal.
[74] *Ping An v Belgium*, Award (30 April 2015), para 227.   [75] ibid para 228.
[76] ibid para 229.

In light of the afore-stated six reasons, the tribunal accepted Belgium's objection to jurisdiction *ratione temporis* and determined that it was not necessary to address Belgium's alternative objections. The tribunal did, however, explicitly state that it did not adopt a position as to whether 'remedies may remain available to the Claimants either under the 1986 BIT or through Belgium's domestic courts'.[77]

E. Analysis of determination

The discussion below offers a brief analysis of the determination of the tribunal. It is difficult to support the reasoning of the tribunal for three main reasons. First, the tribunal appears to have overlooked important issues that are fundamental to the interpretation of Article 8 and Article 10 of the 2009 BIT. Secondly, the tribunal offers no further discussion on the circumstances when an expansive approach is justifiable and did not provide adequate reasoning to support its findings that Article 10(2) does not justify an expansive interpretation so as to provide for disputes that were notified before the promulgation of the 2009 BIT to be included within the scope of the 2009 BIT. Finally, the first, fourth, and sixth reasons deployed by the tribunal in its Overall Conclusion are controversial.

The relevant starting point of the *Ping An* dispute is that Article 10(2) provides clear direction that it is possible for the 2009 treaty to apply to disputes that were initiated before the 2009 BIT was brought into force. The next step is to ascertain what disputes are excluded. The final stage is to ascertain whether the disputes in question are excluded from the scope of the 2009 BIT. The tribunal appears to have placed overreliance on Article 8(1) of the 2009 BIT. The ordinary object and purpose of Article 8(1) is to provide a general delineation of the settlement of investment disputes under the ordinary circumstances whereby a dispute arises after the conclusion of the 2009 BIT. It is Article 10 and not Article 8 that provide rules for 'transition'—i.e. the application of the 2009 BIT to disputes arising prior to 2009.

The fourth reason deployed by the *Ping An* tribunal is not reliable. The tribunal noted that Article 10(2) was 'silent' on the treatment of disputes that were not under judicial or arbitral process but had been notified under the 1986 BIT. However, it regarded such silence as being conclusive evidence that the parties had not intended such disputes to be included in the 2009 BIT. This reasoning is incorrect. Adopting the alternative approach, *if* the parties had intended for such disputes to be excluded then Article 10(2) would have explicitly stated this point. The purpose of the relevant sentence in Article 10(2) is to explicitly state what disputes are excluded and the use of the words 'but shall not apply' is explicit reference that such exclusions are limited to 'any dispute or any claim concerning an investment which was already under judicial or arbitral process before its entry into force'. Rather, the silence of Article 10(2) on this matter demonstrates that Ping An's disputes *are* included under the 'transition' arrangements since they are not explicitly excluded.

The sixth reason that the tribunal put forward was that an expansive interpretation would result in the expansion of the dispute resolution from issues relating to the amount of compensation for expropriation to any legal dispute. This factor should not be regarded as a mitigating factor when interpreting the provision. Rather, this fact should be regarded simply as an outcome of interpreting the treaty expansively.

---

[77] ibid para 240.

For the reasons stated above it is concluded that the determination of the tribunal is not reliable and the decision to deny Ping An the opportunity to a hearing on the merits of the case due to grounds of lack of jurisdiction *ratione temporis* is not supported.

V. Alternative Remedies

The impact of the determination of the tribunal is clear—the case was regarded as concluded and the substantive merits were not considered. Counsel for the claimants issued a statement after the publication of the award pointing out that the case was decided on 'technical legal arguments relating to the tribunal's jurisdiction under the two successive bilateral investment treaties between Belgium and China and in no way reflects on the underlying merits of Ping An's substantive claims against Belgium'.[78]

From the limited facts that were presented in the award it would appear that Ping An has legitimate claims worthy of consideration. It is apparent from the discussion in section II.E above that the determination of the *Ping An* tribunal on jurisdiction is unduly restrictive. This section therefore examines whether there are any other remedies that remain available to Ping An to allow the underlying merits of the substantive claims to be heard.

A. Finality of decision

An appellate mechanism is not available under the ICSID system and therefore the claimants are not entitled to appeal the award. The principle of finality is a major feature of ICSID arbitration,[79] which is in line with two principles of customary international law: *pacta sunt servanda* and *res judicata*. According to Article 53(1) of the ICSID Convention 'The award shall be binding on the parties and shall not be subject to any appeal or any other remedy except those provided for in this Convention'.

The effect of Article 53(1) is that it limits investor–state arbitration to an 'autonomous and self-contained' system. Aron Broches further succinctly elaborates the principle of finality as follows: 'In fact, the self-contained nature of the Convention limits the role of national courts to recognition and enforcement of awards. Each Contracting State, whether or not it or any of its nationals have been parties to the proceeding, must recognize an ICSID award as binding and enforce the pecuniary obligations imposed by the award as if it were a final judgment of a court of that State ...'.[80]

The principle of finality serves the purposes of certainty and efficiency. However, the system has been criticized for favouring the importance of expediency rather than the principle of correctness.[81]

[78] 'Belgium Prevails against Chinese Investor' *Global Arbitration Review* (September 2015), quoting Chris Colbridge, partner at Kirkland Ellis International LLP, as counsel acting for Ping An.
[79] For further discussion see Aron Broches, 'Awards Rendered Pursuant to the ICSID Convention: Binding Force, Finality, Recognition, Enforcement, Execution' (1987) 2 ICSID Rev-FILJ 289.
[80] Aron Broches, 'Observations on the Finality of ICSID Awards' (1991) 6(2) ICSID Review 321.
[81] See R Doak Bishop and Silvia M Marchili, *Annulment under the ICSID Convention* (Oxford University Press 2012) 20–2.

B. Annulment

A limited exception to the principle of finality under the ICSID Convention is the annulment mechanism.[82] The annulment mechanism is designed to foster the 'integrity, not the outcome'[83] of arbitration proceedings under the ICSID Convention to protect the parties from procedural injustice. The annulment mechanism allows a party to invalidate the entire award, or part of the award. A three party ad hoc annulment committee is constituted for the sole purpose of making a decision on whether or not to annul the decision.[84] If the decision of the ad hoc committee is to annul the decision the consequence of such a result is that the investor may reinstate the claim to ICSID and a new tribunal will be constituted.

According to Article 52(2) of the ICSID Convention, there are five grounds upon which an ICSID award may be annulled; namely, the tribunal was not properly constituted, has manifestly exceeded its powers; there was corruption on the part of a member of the tribunal; there has been a serious departure from a fundamental rule of procedure; or that the award has failed to state the reasons on which it is based.[85]

Annulment is only available where a final award has been issued. Ping An would have been entitled to exercise the annulment mechanism since the tribunal has disposed of the dispute by making a conclusive decision that it lacks jurisdiction.[86] The option of annulment was not pursued by Ping An. An application for the annulment of an award must be made within 120 days after the date on which the award was rendered if the annulment is based on the grounds that the tribunal was not properly constituted; the tribunal has manifestly exceeded its powers; there has been a serious departure from a fundamental rule of procedure; or, the award has failed to state the reasons on which it is based.[87] The date of 28 August 2015 marked the expiry of the 120 day deadline and no annulment proceedings are known to have been filed by Ping An.

C. Recourse to domestic courts

1. *Before dispute submitted to ICSID*

Investors may seek to redress injury allegedly caused by host states in domestic courts on the basis of BITs. However, to avoid parallel proceedings in domestic courts and investor–state arbitration forums it is common for BITs to include a 'fork in the road' provision. A 'fork in the road' provision typically allows the parties, or on occasions the investor alone, to make a choice between submitting the dispute either to the domestic

---

[82] Final awards may also be subject to Interpretation under Article 50 or Review under Article 51 of the ICSID Convention. Interpretation does not compromise the finality of the award. Review of the award allows the award to be revised or amended upon the 'discovery of some fact of such a nature as decisively to affect the award'.

[83] Lucy Reed, Jan Paulson, and Nigel Blackaby, *Guide to ICSID Arbitration* (2nd edn, Wolters Kluwer 2011) 162.

[84] The annulment process has been severely criticized. See Hamid Gharavi, 'ICSID Annulment Committees: The Elephant in the Room' *GAR* (24 November 2014).

[85] Article 52(1) states that an application should be made in writing addressed to the Secretary-General on one or more of the grounds stated in art 52(2).

[86] The ICSID Convention art 48(3) states: 'The award shall deal with every question submitted to the Tribunal, and shall state the reasons upon which it is based'.

[87] ICSID Convention, Regulations and Rules (effective 10 April 2006), Rules of Procedure for Arbitration Proceedings, Rule 50(3)(b)(i). Note, however, that Rule 50(3)(b)(ii) provides that 'in the case of corruption on the part of a member of the Tribunal, within 120 days after discovery thereof, and in any event within three years after the date on which the award was rendered (or any subsequent decision or correction)'.

courts of the host state; or, alternatively to investor–state arbitration.[88] In the absence of such provisions the state would be at risk of multiple liability.

Additionally, the reputation of both international and national dispute settlement mechanisms could be adversely affected in the event that conflicting decisions were rendered on the same foreign investment case.

The option to pursue domestic dispute resolution through the national courts of Belgium was available to Ping An under the 2009 BIT. Article 10(2) clearly allows the dispute, at the sole discretion of the investor, to be submitted to (a) 'the competent court of the Contracting Party that is a party to the dispute; or, (b) ICSID'. The 1986 BIT similarly allows for disputes to be referred to a 'judicial body of the Contracting Party accepting the investment'.[89]

2. After dispute submitted to ICSID

Article 10(2) of the 2009 BIT provides that 'Once the investor has submitted the dispute to the competent court of the Contracting Party concerned or to ICSID, the choice of one of the two procedures shall be final'. Ping An would only be precluded from taking the matter to the local Belgian courts if the merits of the case were considered by the tribunal. Since the tribunal have determined that they lacked jurisdiction to consider the dispute the fork in the road provision is not triggered and the initial referral to ICSID would not preclude Ping An from submitting their claim to the Belgian courts.

On a practical level, whether Ping An would be eligible to pursue the dispute in the Belgian courts must be reviewed by taking into account the laws of limitation. A lapse of seven years has now passed since the second intervention of the Belgian government. Under the Belgian Civil Code, the general rule is that contractual claims must be brought within ten years from the date of the act, which gave rise to the claim.[90] All non-contractual civil claims, including tort, on the other hand are subject to a shorter limitation period of five years, which commences from the time that the plaintiff discovered the harm.[91] The total period is limited to no longer than 20 years from the time the harm actually occurred.

Ping An's initial decision to pursue its claim under ICSID as opposed to the domestic courts was reasonable. Disputes submitted to domestic courts are subject to laws of the host state, which may place a foreign party at a disadvantage with regard to knowledge of the local law. More pertinent, however, is the risk of bias and adverse treatment by the judiciary of the host state.

[88] For further discussion of the operation of 'fork in the road clauses' see Christoph Schreuer, 'Travelling the BIT Route: Of Waiting Periods, Umbrella Clauses, and Forks in the Road' (2004) 5(2) Journal of World Investment & Trade 231, 247. With regard to fork in the road provisions in Chinese BITs see Guiguo Wang, *International Investment Law: A Chinese Perspective* (Routledge 2014) 235–51.

The scope of the 'fork in the road' provision has been considered in a number of Tribunals constituted under the ICSID Convention: see *Compañía de Aguas del Aconquija SA & Compagnie Générale des Eaux (Vivendi I) v Argentine Republic*, ICSID Case No ARB/97/3 (Award, 21 November 2001); *Compañía de Aguas del Aconquija SA & Vivendi Universal (formerly Compagnie Générale des Eaux) v Argentine Republic*, ICSID Case No ARB/97/3 (Decision on Annulment, 3 July 2002); *Pantechniki SA Contractors & Engineers (Greece) v Republic of Albania*, ICSID Case No ARB/07/21, *Toto Costruzioni Generali SpA v Republic of Lebanon* (Decision on Jurisdiction) ICSID Case No ARB/07/12.

[89] Belgium–China 1986 BIT art 10.3(2). [90] Code Civil (Belge) art 2262bis.
[91] ibid.

D. Remedy under 1986 BIT?

The tribunal declined to comment on whether 'remedies may remain available' under the 1986 BIT.[92] So far, the answer to this question remains unresolved.

1. Scope of jurisdiction under 1986 BIT

The substance of the claim under the 1986 BIT is not in dispute since it is common ground that the dispute crystallized under the 1986 BIT. Ping An, however, relied on the 2009 BIT to establish jurisdiction since they believed that they had no jurisdictional right to bring their claims under the 1986 BIT.

The scope of jurisdiction with regard to the peculiar position of Ping An is uncertain under the 1986 BIT following the conclusion of the 2009 BIT, which purports to 'substitute' and 'replace' the 1986 BIT.[93] Accordingly, Ping An's position is that the 1986 BIT is redundant with regard to jurisdiction. The 2009 BIT has substituted and replaced the 1986 BIT and applies to investments made before it came into force. They further argued that only disputes that are excluded from Article 10, the transition clause of the 2009 BIT, are those already under judicial or arbitral process before 1 December 2009.

It is, however, possible for Ping An to demonstrate that notice has been served pursuant to the 1986 BIT. Ping An asserted that notice of the dispute pursuant to Article 10(2) of the 1986 BIT was first served to the Belgium Government, via a letter to the Belgian Embassy in Beijing, on 14 October 2008. Following a meeting with the Belgian ambassador in September 2009, Ping An sent a further letter dated 14 October 2009 to confirm and explicitly refer to the fact that notice of the dispute had been served on 14 November. Irrespective of the further notice that was served on 3 July 2012 it is likely that notice would be deemed as served either on 14 October 2008 or at the latest on 14 October 2009 as reflected in the request for arbitration. What is relevant is that it can be established that notice was served prior to the entry into force of the 2009 BIT.

One of the key issues with regard to establishing jurisdiction under the 1986 BIT is to ascertain whether the sunset clause of the 1986 extends relief to Ping An. Ping An argued that the sunset clause set out in Article 14(1) of the 1986 BIT does not provide relief. According to Pin An, Article 14(1) only provides for the continuation of the 1986 BIT for ten years after its expiration or unilateral termination. Since it is confirmed in Article 10(1) that the 2009 BIT has 'substituted' and 'replaced' the 1986 BIT they argue that the sunset clause is no longer operable.[94]

2. Amount of compensation

Even if Ping An were able to establish jurisdiction under the 1986 BIT international arbitration is only available for 'a dispute which arises from an amount of compensation for expropriation ...'. All other disputes must be submitted to the local courts. Accordingly, Ping An face the hurdle of delineating the scope of the 'amount of

---

[92] *Ping An v Belgium*, Award (30 April 2015), para 232.
[93] Belgium–China 2009 BIT art 14.
[94] *Ping An v Belgium*, Award (30 April 2015), para 160. The case of *Walter Bau AG (in liquidation) v Thailand* (Award on Jurisdiction, 1 July 2009) UNCITRAL was distinguished by Ping An since it concerned a sunset clause operating on the termination of a BIT.

compensation' clause to ascertain whether it allows Ping An (i) to bring a claim to determine entitlement to compensation or, (ii) limits the claim to merely quantifying the amount of compensation.[95] Tribunals have previously determined that 'amount of compensation' clauses within both a Chinese BIT, and separately, in a Belgian-Luxembourg BIT do provide the tribunal with jurisdiction to resolve both the issue of whether expropriation has occurred in the first place and the quantum of compensation.[96] However, there have been a number of awards, dealing with BITs concluded between states other than China and Belgium, which limit jurisdiction to quantum only.[97]

3. No suitable remedy?

The Ping An tribunal noted that 'it would, of course, be regrettable, if the claimants had valid claims (on which there is a sharp difference of view between the parties) for which they had no effective remedy'. It would, however, appear that the 'regrettable' has occurred. It is highly likely that Ping An do not have further suitable legal recourse under the 2009 BIT, 1986 BIT, or any other forum. The irony of the situation, noted by Matthew Weiniger QC, is that the limited scope of dispute resolution imposed by the PRC has penalized its own Chinese investor thus allowing Belgium, a state encompassing a more liberal scope to arbitrate, to evade culpability.[98]

VI. Future Claims by Chinese Entities

This section explores whether Chinese entities are likely to continue to pursue investor–state arbitration in the future when seeking to protect their growing investments outside of China. More specifically, the discussion focuses on whether the decision of Ping An is likely to deter or encourage Chinese investors to claim under a BIT.

A. Global ISDS trends

The creation of the ISDS mechanism, enabling foreign investors to sue host states, is widely regarded as a progressive turning point in international law.[99] According to the United Nations Conference on Trade and Development (UNCTAD) a total of 2,927 bilateral investment treaties have been agreed and signed with 2,280 in force.[100] Since

---

[95] For further discussion see Weeramantry and Wilson (n 50) 409–28; 422–7.

[96] *Tza Yap Shum v Republic of Peru*, ICSID Case No ARB/07/6, para 188 (Peru–China BIT 1995); *European Media Ventures v Czech Republic* (Award of 15 May 2007) (Belgio–Luxembourg BIT 1992), which is not published; however, the decision of the tribunal is cited in an action to set aside, which was heard in the High Court in England *Czech Republic v European Media Ventures SA* [2007] EWHC 2851 (Comm) (5 December 2007).

[97] *Plama Consortium Limited v Republic of Bulgaria*, ICSID Case No ARB/03/24 (Decision on Jurisdiction); *Vladimir and Moise Berschader v The Russian Federation*, SCC Case No 080/2004, Award, 21 April 2006); *RosInvestCo UK Ltd v The Russian Federation*, SCC Case No Arb V079/2005 (Award on Jurisdiction, October 2007); *Austrian Airlines v Slovak Republic* UNCITRAL (Final Award, 20 November 2009).

[98] Matthew Weiniger, 'Ping An v Belgium: A Tale of Two Treaties' (2015) 10(4) *GAR* 42.

[99] See Julien Chaisse and Christian Bellak, 'Navigating the Expanding Universe of Investment Treaties—Creation and Use of Critical Index' (2015) 18(1) Journal of International Economic Law 79.

[100] United Nations Conference on Trade and Development, official web page available at http://investmentpolicyhub.unctad.org/IIA last viewed on 29 October 2015. In stark comparison, 349 other international investment agreements have been agreed, of which 280 are in force. For a more detailed

concluding its first investment treaty with Sweden in 1982,[101] China has now concluded 131 BITs (108 of which are in force)[102] only to be surpassed by Germany, which has concluded 134 (131 of which are in force).[103]

The number and diversity of claimants involved in investment arbitration has increased. In 2014, forty-two known treaty-based claims were initiated—raising the total number of known claims to 608.[104] The total number of concluded cases is 405. Of these, 36 per cent of cases were decided in favour of states, and 27 per cent in favour of investors. The remaining 63 per cent of cases were either settled or discontinued.[105] With regard to the diversity of claims, 40 per cent of new cases filed in 2014 were initiated against developed economies.[106]

A. Chinese involvement in ISDS

China's participation in ISDS has been low both in terms of Chinese investors as claimants and China acting as state respondents. Recourse to ISDS by Chinese investors has however increased over the past ten years.[107]

Based on information that is publicly available China was not exposed to its first investor–state dispute as a respondent until 24 May 2011 when the Malaysian company Ekran Berhad filed its claim on the basis of the China–Israel BIT 1995 and the Malaysia-China BIT 1988.[108] On 4 November 2014, China was subject to its second case as respondent involving a South Korean investor.[109]

At the time of writing, five claims are reported as filed by Chinese investors against foreign states pursuant to a Chinese BIT. The first claim to be brought under a Chinese BIT against a foreign state was by *Tza Yap Shum* in 2007, relying on a BIT concluded between Peru and China.[110] The ICSID tribunal in Tza Yap Shum decided in favour of the claimant on the grounds that Peru had expropriated Mr Tza's investment. The case

---

statistical analysis of treaty development see United Nations Conference on Trade and Development, 'IIA Issue Notes: Recent Trends in IIAs and ISDs' No 1, February 2015.

[101] 'Agreement on the Mutual Protection of Investments' between The Government of the Kingdom of Sweden and the Government of the People's Republic of China', signed on 29 March 1982.

[102] The most recent BIT to be concluded is a second BIT with Turkey, which was signed on 29 August 2015 but has not yet been brought into force. For further discussion regarding Chinese BIT trends see Norah Gallagher and Wenhua Shan, *Chinese Investment Treaties: Policies and Practices* (Oxford University Press 2009); J Romesh Weeramantry, 'Investor-State Dispute Settlement Provisions in China's Investment Treaties' (2012) 27 ICSID Review 192; Wang Guiguo, *International Investment Law: A Chinese Perspective* (Routledge 2015).

[103] According to data provided by United Nations on Trade and Development see http://investmentpolicyhub.unctad.org/IIA/IiasByCountry (last accessed 1 February 2016).

[104] Investor–State Dispute Settlement: Review of Developments in 2014, IIA Issue Note, No 2, 2015, UNCTAD (15 July 2015) 1.

[105] UNCTAD, 'World Investment Report 2015: Reforming International Investment Governance' (July 2015) 146.

[106] ibid.

[107] Julien Chaisse and Rahul Donde, 'The State of Investor-State Arbitration: A Reality Check of the Issues, Trends, and Directions in Asia-Pacific' (2018) 51(1) The International Lawyer 47.

[108] *Ekran Berhad v People's Republic of China*, ICSID Case No ARB/11/15. The claim has however been discontinued and a procedural order has been issued pursuant to ICSID Arbitration Rule 43(1) on 16 May 2013.

[109] *Ansung Housing Co Ltd v People's Republic of China*, ICSID Case No ARB/14/25. China–Republic of Korea BIT 2007 (Status: pending).

[110] *Tza Yap Shum v Republic of Peru*, ICSID Case No ARB/07/6 (Award). Filed on 12 February 2007 on basis of Peru–China 1994.

was further subject to annulment proceedings; however, Peru's application for annulment was dismissed on 12 February 2015.[111]

A further claim was brought by a Chinese investor, and filed with ICSID on 3 December 2014, pursuant to a China–Yemen BIT concluded in 1998.[112] The dispute between Beijing Urban Construction Group and the Republic of Yemen is related to the construction of an airport terminal. The project was agreed to be completed within two years but suffered substantial delays. The arbitral tribunal was constituted on 10 July 2015 and comprised Ian Binnie (President), John Townsend, and Zachary Douglas.[113]

With regard to other arbitral forums, two investor–state disputes were filed with UNICITRAL in 2010 [114] and 2013[115] respectively under Chinese BITs.

In comparison, Belgium has been more actively engaged in ISDS than China via its nationals acting as claimants, although not to a significantly higher degree. Belgium had not previously had a claim filed against it with ICSID until the Ping An dispute. However, a Belgian party has made a claim under ICSID on the basis of a BIT on nine occasions.[116] There is only one other known claim that has been brought by a Belgian claimant relying on a Belgium BIT, and that claim was brought under the Arbitration Institute of the Stockholm Chamber of Commerce (SCC) rules in 2004.[117]

B. Effect on prospective Chinese claimants

The negative impact of the *Ping An* case on future claims by Chinese investors is limited to rare cases. Rather, it is likely that greater awareness of the utility of ISDS and arbitration strategy as a result of reporting the case will assist rather than deter future treaty claims by Chinese investors.

The *Ping An* decision could deter potential Chinese claimants from pursuing investor–state arbitration in rare cases when faced with restrictive dispute resolution provisions in earlier generation BITs that remain in force.[118] The issue in the instant case is unique and concerns jurisdictional issues as a result of the overlapping effect of

---

[111] *Tza Yap Shum v Republic of Peru*, ICSID Case No ARB/07/6 (Decision on Annulment) 12 February 2015.

[112] *Beijing Urban Construction Group Co Ltd v Republic of Yemen*, ICSID Case No ARB/14/30 (Status: pending).

[113] John Townsend (appointed by claimant), and Zachary Douglas (appointed by respondent).

[114] *China Heilongjiang International Economic & Technical Cooperative Corp, Beijing Shougang Mining Investment Company Ltd, Qinhuangdaoshi Qinlong International Industrial Co Ltd v Mongolia*, UNCITRAL, PCA (2010) (China–Mongolia BIT1991) (Status—pending—not public).

[115] *Sanum Investments Limited v Lao People's Democratic Republic*, UNCITRAL, PCA Case No 2013-13 (China–Laos BIT 1993) (Settled on 15 June 2014).

[116] According to information provided on the ICSID case database http//icsid.worldbank.org (last accessed 18 September 2015), the cases are as follows: *Blusun SA, Jean-Pierre Lecorcier and Michael Stein v Italian Republic*, ICSID Case No ARB/14/3; *Lieven J van Riet, Chantal C. van Riet and Christopher van Riet v Republic of Croatia*, ICSID Case No ARB/13/12; *Joseph Houben v Republic of Burundi*, ICSID Case No ARB/13/7; *LSF-KEB Holdings SCA and Others v Republic of Korea*, ICSID Case No ARB/12/37; *Baggerwerken Decloedt En Zoon NV v Republic of the Philippines*, ICSID Case No ARB/11/27; *Electrabel SA v Hungary*, ICSID Case No ARB/07/19; *Jan de Nul NV and Dredging International NV v Arab Republic of Egypt*, ICSID Case No ARB/04/13; *Antoine Goetz and Others v Republic of Burundi*, ICSID Case No ARB/01/2; *Antoine Goetz and Others v Republic of Burundi*, ICSID Case No ARB/01/2.

[117] *Vladimir Berschader and Michael Berschader v Russian Federation* (SCC Case No 080/2004) (Belgium and Luxembourg–USSR BIT).

[118] For further discussion see Gallagher and Shan (n 102); Weeramantry (n 102) 192; Wang Guiguo, *International Investment Law: A Chinese Perspective* (Routledge 2015).

treaties. It would be quite rare, although not impossible, for a Chinese investor to come across the same issue again. As a result of the jurisdictional idiosyncrasies, the decision of *Ping An* may not pose a significant deterrent for investors seeking to file claims.

Most investment treaties signed by China since the late 1990s provide far wider dispute resolution provisions and allow all investment disputes to be submitted to ISDS. It is therefore expected that China and Chinese investors would elect the ISDS mechanism as opposed to pursuing a claim through domestic courts.

The trends discussed in section IV.B above demonstrate that China has become a more active participator in ISDS over the past decade. The claim filed by Beijing Urban against Yemen in December 2014[119] demonstrates that Chinese entities are willing to pursue investor–state dispute settlement; however, it is noted that there have been no cases filed since the *Ping An* decision.

Owing to the fact that over 130 BITs have been concluded by China, and that China is the world leader in outbound foreign investment increases the probability of future disputes arising is high. It is therefore reasonable to assume that Chinese entities will continue to rely on investor–state dispute settlement mechanisms in the future.[120] Pursuing the matter before the courts of the host state is the only other option that is currently available. Given the choice of these two options, investors are more likely to pursue investor–state arbitration so as to avoid issues such as bias and unfamiliarity with a foreign legal system that would be encountered in the domestic courts of a host state.[121]

There is no evidence available to suggest that the *Ping An* decision will adversely affect the filing of potential Chinese investor's claims in the future. The determination of the *Ping An* tribunal does not establish binding rules on the interpretation of such provisions since the principle of stare decisis does not apply to awards and decisions rendered by investor–state tribunals. The possibility that the provisions may be interpreted differently by a tribunal comprising different arbitrators remains.

It is possible that the *Ping An* dispute may even have a positive effect upon the continued or increased use of the ISDS mechanism in the future by Chinese investors. The dispute and decision of the tribunal will no doubt generate a great deal of discussion and commentary, which will in turn raise the awareness of the use of the ISDS mechanism among the Chinese business and legal community.

The dispute and the decision also serve as an aid to inform strategy. China's limited involvement in the ISDS mechanism means that substantive provisions in Chinese treaties such as expropriation have only rarely been 'tested'. Whilst there have been seven disputes in total filed pursuant to a Chinese BIT only two of those disputes, namely *Tza Yap Shum* and *Ping An*, have reached conclusion by a tribunal. The other five cases have either been discontinued, settled, or are pending.[122] Commentary regarding the published decision may assist strategy by contemplating other potential ways in which the case could have been presented.[123]

[119] *Beijing Urban Construction Group Co Ltd v Republic of Yemen*, ICSID Case No ARB/14/30.

[120] For further discussion on the parameters of International Investment Arbitration within the Asia-Pacific region see Julien Chaisse, 'The Shifting Tectonics of International Investment Law: Structure and Dynamics of Rules and Arbitration on Foreign Investment in the Asia-Pacific Region', *The George Washington International Law Review* Vol. 47:3 (2015) 611–12.

[121] For an account of the advantages and disadvantages of investor-state arbitration see Julien Chaisse, 'Investor-State Arbitration in International Tax Dispute Resolution: A Cut above Dedicated Tax Dispute Resolution?' (2016) 41(2) Virginia Tax Review 149–222.

[122] See Annex 1: Table of disputes pursuant to Chinese BITs.

[123] Matthew Weiniger QC raises the point that other claimants had sought to rely on the MFN clause to gain more favourable jurisdiction. See Weiniger (n 98). The claimants presumably did not

There is no way to forecast accurately whether the outcome of the *Ping An* case will impede or assist the decision-making of potential claimants. It is, however, contemplated that the *Ping An* decision will not be significantly detrimental to the number of future treaty claims by Chinese investors. Investors may be wary of resorting to investment arbitration only in the rare event of encountering overlapping treaty provisions. Such a predicament will only affect a limited number of potential disputes since most treaties concluded by China now contain wider dispute resolution clauses that are more favourable to Chinese investors.

VII. Future of ISDS Regime—China–EU Context

The International Centre for the Settlement of Investment Disputes (ICSID) was established in 1966 by the Convention on the Settlement of Investment Disputes as an autonomous international organization for the purpose of providing a dispute settlement forum between states and nationals of other states. China joined the ICSID Convention some time later in February 1990 and ratified it three years later in February 1993 after a long period of negotiations.[124] It was not until the past decade that China has sought to rely on the dispute resolution provisions. It is predicted that given China's current extensive level of outward foreign direct investment alongside the vast number of BITs that China has concluded, the opportunity for Chinese investors to exercise their treaty rights will increase. This means that China is now a major stakeholder in investor–state arbitration.

In February 2012, China and the European Union (EU) agreed to initiate talks to further the negotiation of a single investment treaty.[125] The initiation of negotiations between China and the EU towards concluding a new BIT was later announced at the Sixteenth China–EU Summit held in Beijing on 21 November 2013.

A. China–EU BIT

The new China–EU BIT is intended to replace the 26 BITs that are already in place between China and individual Member States of the European Union. Of the 28 European Member States, Ireland is the only Member State that has not concluded a BIT with China. Belgium and Luxembourg have joined forces to conclude a BIT with China under the auspices of the Belgian-Luxembourg Economic Union.

Both parties expect that the conclusion of a new BIT will enhance FDI in each respective state. China only attracts a small percentage of inbound European FDI. Currently, this is below 5 per cent. Outbound FDI from China represents less than 3 per cent of the total FDI inflows into the EU.[126] Both the EU and China are hopeful that the conclusion of a comprehensive BIT will alleviate the clear discrepancy between

seek to rely on the 1986 MFN clause because they believed that jurisdiction was not available to them as the result of the 'substitution' and 'replacement' of the 2009 BIT.

[124] For further discussion see C A I Congyan, 'China' in Wenhua Shan, *The Legal Protection of Foreign Investment: A Comparative Study* (Hart Publishing 2012) 248–9.

[125] European Commission, 'Commission Proposes to Open Negotiations for an Investment Agreement with China' Press Release (23 May 2013) http://europa.eu/rapid/press-release_IP-13-458_en.htm (last accessed 20 October 2015).

[126] European Commission, Trade, 'China' http://ec.europa.eu/trade/policy/countries-and-regions/countries/china/ (last accessed 1 February 2016).

the levels of trade and investment and will give a new impetus to the cooperation that currently exists on a Member State level.

China will be keen to ensure adequate overseas protection of Chinese investments since in recent times 'FDI outflows from China [have] reached $116 billion. They continued to grow faster than inflows. FDI outflows from China grew by 15 per cent to a record-high $116 billion'.[127] It is anticipated that once the BIT is in place with China, Europe may begin to see an increase of outflows directed towards European Member States.

B. Criticism of the ISDS mechanism

The current state of ISDS has received scathing attacks over the past few years as a result of inconsistent decisions and other shortfalls within the current mechanism. UNCTAD has recently reported that: 'The IIA regime is going through a period of reflection, review and revision. Investment dispute settlement is at the heart of this debate, with a number of countries reassessing their positions. There is a strong case for a systematic reform of ISDS'.[128] A number of states including, Bolivia,[129] Ecuador,[130] and Venezuela have already withdrawn from the ICSID Convention.[131]

The issue has reached such magnitude that the UNCTAD has declared that reform is imminent: 'The question is not about whether or not to reform, but about the what, how and extent of such reform'.[132]

The European Parliament has identified dispute resolution as a concern and the preliminary discussions have indicated the need for 'investors to have access to a fair trial'.[133]

C. Issues arising from the *Ping An* dispute

The *Ping An* award has raised eyebrows among both professional and academic circles. Although the majority of critique available at the time of writing is merely anecdotal it is worth a mention. One senior arbitrator referred to the outcome of the dispute as 'unfortunate' and a senior practitioner has described it as 'troublesome to the ISDS'. Counsel representing the claimants described the award as 'a disappointing outcome, which comes at a time of unprecedented public scrutiny and criticisms of investment arbitration in the European and global public discourse'.[134]

---

[127] UNCTAD, 'World Investment Report 2015 (n 105) 42.

[128] UNCTAD, Investor-State Dispute Settlement: Review of Developments in 2014 IIA Issue Notes (No 2 May 2015) 1.

[129] Bolivia's notification of its withdrawal from the ICSID Convention was received by ICSID on 2 May 2007 and took effect on 3 November 2007.

[130] Ecuador's denunciation notification was received on 6 July 2009 and took effect on 7 January 2010.

[131] A Mezgravis and C González, 'Denunciation of the ICSID Convention: Two Problems, One Seen and One Overlooked' (2012) 9(7) *TDM* 1. See also Chaisse and Donde (n 107) 47.

[132] UNCTAD, 'World Investment Report 2015 (n 105) 120.

[133] European Parliament resolution of 9 October 2013 on the EU–China negotiations for a bilateral investment agreement (2013/2674(RSP), paras 42–3: para 42 considers that the agreement should include, as a key priority, effective state-to-state and investor-to-state dispute settlement mechanisms in order, on the one hand, to prevent frivolous claims from leading to unjustified arbitration, and, on the other, to ensure that all investors have access to a fair trial, followed by enforcement of all arbitration awards without delay; para 43 takes the view that the agreement should provide for state-to-state dispute settlement procedures and for investor-state dispute settlement mechanisms that are set within a suitable legal framework and subject to strict transparency criteria.

[134] See n 78 at 20.

The award is particularly important to China and Chinese investors since there is only one other investor–state dispute involving a Chinese party that has reached conclusion.[135] In light of this, the award will certainly be an important reference for both the EU and China in informing the future negotiations of the new China–EU BIT.

The fact that the determination of the *Ping An* tribunal was based on a technicality relating to the tribunal's jurisdiction under the 1986 BIT and the 2009 successor BIT will serve to encourage more thorough negotiations between China and the EU. The future BIT must clearly communicate the intention of the parties and such intentions must be capable of a strict application in accordance with Article 28 of the Vienna Convention on the Law of Treaties. The provisions of treaties only apply to acts or events that have occurred on or after the date of entry into force. Contracting States must explicitly provide for any derogation from this rule. Inferences to the intention of the states cannot replace explicit provision within the BIT. Taking the *Ping An* dispute into account, it is anticipated that the China–EU BIT will make clear representations regarding the temporal application of the new treaty.

With the above considerations in mind, the new BIT is expected to be far more detailed than the current BITs between China and individual member states. It is therefore likely that the negotiation time phase of the BIT will be lengthy due to the complexity of the issues involved in negotiations.

The dispute resolution methods that will be available to investors are expected to be clearly outlined in the new BIT. Dispute resolution has been raised as an issue of major concern to the EU and China. Considering the unfavourable decision rendered by the ICSID tribunal in the *Ping An* dispute it is highly likely that China may be willing to consider alternative methods of dispute resolution and forums. On 5 May 2015, Cecilia Malmström, EU Trade Commissioner, released a 'concept paper', which detailed plans to move the dispute forum from arbitration to an investment court.[136] It was proposed by Malmström that a specialized international investment court, with an appellate mechanism and tenured judges should replace the bilateral mechanism.

The investment court is presented by Malmström as an operational solution that has the capacity to apply to multiple agreements with multiple partners. Malmström points out that '… ISDS tribunals can get their decisions wrong, and there is no corrective mechanism via an appeal, as is found in almost all legal systems.'[137] Promoting consistency, Malmström continues to argue that: 'This lack of appellate mechanism also makes the system less predictable for governments and investors alike'. These are strong arguments put forward by Malmström and the proposal to include an appellate system within the dispute resolution mechanism is highly justifiable when contemplating the undesirable outcome of the *Ping An* award.

Recent negotiations among other jurisdictions reveal that the investment court proposal is gaining momentum in terms of international consensus. In addition to the proposed texts of the CETA and TTIP, the EU–Vietnam FTA (negotiations concluded, but not yet signed as of the time of writing) includes the investment tribunal (Court) mechanism.

---

[135] *Tza Yap Shum v Republic of Peru*, ICSID Case No ARB/07/6. See Annex 1: Table of disputes pursuant to Chinese BITs.
[136] Cecilia Malmström, 'Investment in TTIP and beyond—The Path for Reform' (15 May 2015) http://trade.ec.europa.eu/doclib/docs/2015/may/tradoc_153408.PDF (last accessed 1 February 2016).
[137] ibid 8.

Expropriation was one of the main substantive claims raised by Ping An. All of the BITs currently in force between China and Member States of the European Union contain a clause on expropriation. It is widely recognized that direct expropriation—the mandatory legal transfer of title to property or the outright physical seizure—is not commonly undertaken. It is therefore highly likely that the agreement between China and the EU will focus on ensuring that indirect expropriation is explicitly included.

On this point, it is anticipated that the China–EU BIT will include an Annex enclosing a definition of 'indirect expropriation', similar to the US Model BIT 2012, which involves total or near-total deprivation of the investor's fundamental attributes of property in its investment, including the right to use, enjoy and dispose of it, without formal transfer of title or outright seizure. It is also expected that there will be further guiding principles that explicitly define the boundaries of indirect expropriation.[138]

The root of the *Ping An* dispute, namely the government measures imposed in the aftermath of a financial crisis, is a significant cause for concern that both China and the EU will seek to address in the new BIT. China will be conscious of protecting its investments from similar repercussions, however, the negotiation of provisions to protect investments from loss in the event of a recurring financial crisis are unlikely. Europe, will forcefully seek to protect the right to implement any measures that are necessary in the event of future financial crisis. Given the precarious nature of the global economy, particularly within Europe, it is highly likely that the EU will successfully negotiate a carve-out excluding any measures taken in response to economic exigencies or financial crisis. On this point, it is worth noting that some Chinese BITs do provide for 'prudential measures' exceptions (for example, Article 20 of the China–China–Japan–Korea investment treaty), which appear to address this type of situation. The above example supports the proposition that Europe is highly likely to succeed in getting its way in obtaining such a carve-out.

The proposed China–EU BIT will contain a number of significant revisions.[139] Some commentators opine that, 'the shift of both the EU and China towards a new generation BIT is likely to significantly influence the BIT practice of other States and exhibit global implications'.[140] An exhaustive discussion of all of the provisions that may be included in the China–EU BIT is outside of the scope of this research. It is however evident from the discussion in section V of this chapter that the *Ping An* dispute will be influential in shaping the temporal application of the new treaty and dispute resolution provisions.

VIII. Conclusion

The discussion analysing the determination of the *Ping An* award in section III reveals that the decision is not reliable. It is concluded that the tribunal has taken an overly restrictive approach in interpreting Article 8 and Article 10 of the 2009 BIT. The tribunal does not provide further discussion to explain when an expansive approach

---

[138] Also see August Reinisch, 'The Future Shape of EU Investment Agreements' (2013) 28(2) ICSID Review 179, 192.

[139] On reforming ISDS see UNCTAD, 'World Investment Report 2015' (n 105) 147; Stephan W Schill, 'Reforming Investor-State Dispute Settlement (ISDS): Conceptual Framework and Options for the Way Forward' E15 Initiative *International Centre for Trade and Sustainable Development (ICTSD) and World Economic Forum* (2015) www.e15initiative.org/.

[140] Wenhua Shan and Lu Wang, 'The China–EU BIT and the Emerging "Global BIT 2.0"' (2015) 30 ICSID Review 267.

would be justifiable and does not provide adequate reasoning to support its findings that Article 10(2) does not justify an expansive interpretation. Furthermore, the analysis finds that the reasoning deployed by the tribunal is also doubtful.

The determination of the tribunal has significant ramifications—most notably denying Ping An access to a fair hearing.

It is apparent from the discussion in section III of this Chapter that Ping An's options to bring its substantive claims before a legal forum are severely limited. Practically, this means that the losses suffered by Ping An are irrecoverable. The *Ping An* tribunal has determined that jurisdiction is not available under the 2009 BIT. There is no prospect of an appeal or an annulment of that award. If redress under the 1986 BIT is still available to Ping An (and Ping An have remonstrated that it is not) further obstacles await. International arbitration is only available under the 1986 BIT for a dispute arising from an amount of compensation for expropriation. Ping An must therefore navigate the scope of the 'amount of compensation' clause to ascertain whether it allows Ping An to bring a claim to determine entitlement to compensation or simply limits the claim to only quantifying the amount of compensation.

Redress via the local courts is of limited assistance. Some claims may be time barred under the Belgian Civil Code. In the event that other civil claims are not yet limited by prescription the courts of the host state remain insufficiently impartial to settle investment disputes from foreign claimants. The Belgian courts would be bound to apply Belgian law even in the event that such laws failed to protect the rights of the claimants under international law. A further factor against pursuing action in the Belgian courts is that the dispute is complex and few domestic courts are equipped to handle such highly specialized legal principles.

Ping An Group and its subsidiary, Ping An Life, are both systemically significant players in the Chinese and global markets. This means that their failure would be highly likely to have a severe impact upon the Chinese and global economies. Although it was indeed fortunate that Ping An's irrecoverable losses did not trigger a systemic catastrophe such aversion would be unlikely to occur again in the future since Chinese entities of such size are now far more interconnected with international markets. The investment strategies of systemically important entities in foreign states must however be considered carefully to ensure future financial crises are not triggered.

From a practical business perspective, there is no doubt that the impact of the Belgian government's interventions has led to the reticence of Ping An to further invest in overseas financial institutions. The Chairman and CEO of Ping An, Mr Ma Mingzhe, made this point clear stating that 'The 2008 global financial crisis prompted us to rethink the development path of the global economy and financial industries'.[141] Ping An's investment in Fortis was the first offshore investment by a Chinese insurance company. It is therefore highly likely the catastrophic result has made the Central People's Government even more reserved about permitting its financial institutions to invest in such overseas markets in the future. As for future investment trends, current evidence suggests that China is focussing more on directing foreign direct investment into power and infrastructure sectors as opposed to the finance industry.[142]

Nonetheless, it is not the case that the *Ping An* decision will deter prospective Chinese claimants from claiming under Chinese BITs in the future. To the contrary, the discussion in section IV concludes that the outcome of the *Ping An* decision will not lead to

---

[141] See Ping An, Annual Report 2008, 'Chairman's Statement' (2008) 6.
[142] UNCTAD, 'World Investment Report 2015: Reforming International Investment Governance, 44 (n 105).

a decline in the number of future treaty claims by Chinese investors. Alternatively, it is postulated that the award will have a positive effect on the number of claims brought under Chinese BITs on the premise that the publication of the award will serve to raise the awareness of ISDS within the legal and business community.

On a final note, China has concluded over 130 BITs and is the world leader in outbound foreign investment. Such a high frequency of concluded agreements and high level of foreign direct investment activity increases the probability of future disputes arising. Dispute resolution has been earmarked as an issue of major concern by a number of stakeholders, notably UNCTAD.[143] Early negotiations between China and the EU have already revealed that the EU is opposed to retaining the current dispute resolution system. At the time of writing, it is not clear whether China would agree to an alternative model to the current ISDS model. However, the unsatisfactory outcome of the *Ping An* case is likely to be an influential factor when China is considering its options. Although it is not certain whether the future China–EU BIT will include provisions to refer disputes to a new ISDS mechanism, such as the investment court, this prospect should not be ruled out.

[143] UNCTAD, 'World Investment Report 2015 (n 105) 120.

26

Use of Investor–state against China's Enforcement of the Anti-Monopoly Law

Belling the Panda?

Sungjin Kang*

I. Introduction

Since China introduced the Anti-Monopoly Law (AML) in 2008, the Chinese government has been active to formulate competition policy, and enforce the AML.[1] However, since the adoption of the AML, foreign companies operating in China showed concern that the AML would be a new tool to 'control' them and 'favour' the domestic companies, and their concern is partly true. For example, since the AML took effect, the Ministry of Commerce (MOFCOM) reviewed over 1,300 merger cases, twenty-seven of which were approved with conditions.[2] Among those twenty-seven cases approved with conditions, twenty-three cases involved offshore transactions between foreign parties, while the other four transactions involved foreign companies merging/acquiring Chinese companies.[3] In addition, the only two cases rejected by the MOFCOM involve at least one foreign company as a party.[4] In addition, foreign companies complained that the National Development and Reform Commission (NDRC) and State Administration for Industry and Commerce (SAIC)'s enforcement in price-related and non-price related cartel and abuse of dominance cases for selective targeting on foreign companies, lack transparency and motivation behind those enforcement activities.[5] Despite improvements in recent years, foreign companies are still concerned that they may be subject to 'unfair' enforcement of the AML. As China signs more bilateral investment treaties (BITs) and free trade agreements (FTA) with ISDS its

---

* Advisor, Kim & Chang; PhD, Korea University; LL.M, University of Michigan. The views in this paper do not reflect the views of Kim & Chang. All arguments are strictly personal.

[1] As of March 2018, China consolidated the competition authorities into one single authority: State Administration for Market Regulation (SAMR). However, as most of the cases cited in this chapter occurred before the SAMR's inauguration, the author has retained the names of the relevant competition authorities.

[2] US Department of State, Investment Climate Statements—China (2016) www.state.gov/e/eb/rls/othr/ics/2016/eap/254271.htm (last accessed 29 October 2016).

[3] ibid.

[4] For example, MOFCOM rejected Coca-Cola's proposed acquisition of Huiyuan's beverage business in 2009, and rejected the plans by three leading European shipping companies' to form a shipping alliance. The US-China Business Council (USCBC), *Update: Competition Policy & Enforcement in China* (2015) 10 and 17.

[5] See US Department of State (n 2) 2 www.state.gov/e/eb/rls/othr/ics/2016/eap/254271.htm (last accessed 29 October 2016). Article 1 of the AML describes its purpose as 'of preventing and restraining monopolistic conducts, protecting fair competition in the market, enhancing economic efficiency, safeguarding the interests of consumers and the public interest and promoting the healthy development of the socialist market economy'.

---

trading partners, the investors, are increasingly using the ISDS as a means to recover their damages.[6] For example, there is an ongoing case before the International Center for Settlement of Investment Disputes (ICSID) where a medium-sized enterprise in South Korea filed a case against China.[7] In this regard, it is time for foreign investors in China to consider the possibility of bringing China's competition law enforcement before the ICSID, instead of appealing to the Chinese courts.

In this chapter, the author will briefly explain the possibility of using ISDS against competition law enforcement activities in general (section II). Then the author will discuss how this general rule may apply to the context of the Korea–China Free Trade Agreement (Korea–China FTA) (section III), and the practical considerations in filing a case against China (section IV). Then the author will conclude with brief remarks on how the existence of ISDS may be used to trigger changes in the enforcement of the AML.

II. Possibility of Filing an Investor–state Dispute Settlement System (ISDS) against Competition Law Enforcement

In international law, when a state breaches a treaty, the conduct of the state must be attributable to that state to pursue its responsibility.[8] ISDS practice also generally follows this principle, and the ICSID tribunals regularly apply the International Law Commission (ILC)'s Draft Article on State Responsibility (ILC Draft Articles) to find out attributability of a conduct of the respondent state. Article 4(1) of the ILC Articles makes it clear that

[t]he conduct of any State organ shall be considered an act of that State under international law, whether the organ exercises legislative, executive, judicial or any other functions, whatever position it holds in the organization of the State, and whatever its character as an organ of the central Government or of a territorial unit of the State.

Then, Article 4(2) of the ILC Articles defines an organ of a state would include 'any person or entity which has that status in accordance with the internal law of the State'.

A governmental organ established under the domestic law of the state is an 'organ' under the ILC Draft Articles, and it is generally accepted by the ICSID tribunals as well.[9] Many investment tribunals held that actions by state organs were attributable to the host states including local governments, even if they are contrary to the law or ultra vires acts.[10]

---

[6] See Julien Chaisse and Rahul Donde, 'The State of Investor-State Arbitration: A Reality Check of the Issues, Trends, and Directions in Asia-Pacific' (2018) 51(1) The International Lawyer 47.

[7] *Ansung Housing Co Ltd v People's Republic of China* (ICSID Case No ARB/14/25), filed on 4 November 2014.

[8] James Crawford and Paul Mertenskoetter, 'The Use of the ILC's Attribution Rules in International Arbitration' in Meg Kinnear and others (eds), *Building International Investment Law—The First 50 Years of ICSID* (Wolters Kluwer 2016) 27.

[9] ibid 28–9.

[10] Rudolf Dolzer and Christophe Schreuer, *Principles of International Investment Law* (1st edn, Oxford University Press 2008) 196–8. See also Julien Chaisse and Christian Bellak, 'Navigating the Expanding Universe of Investment Treaties: Creation and Use of Critical Index' (2015) 18(1) Journal of International Economic Law 79; Julien Chaisse, 'The Shifting Tectonics of International Investment Law: Structure and Dynamics of Rules and Arbitration on Foreign Investment in the Asia-Pacific Region' (2015) 47(3) George Washington International Law Review 563.

In this regard, if a competition authority is established within the executive branch under the domestic law of a state to enforce the competition law, there is no problem to attribute the conduct of the competition authority to that state. The same holds true with regard to the courts of the state, as the judicial function is clearly included in the scope of Article 4(1) of the ILC Draft Articles.[11] However, even if the ILC Draft Articles provide for the rules of attribution of a conduct, a foreign investor must also look into a BIT or an FTA to find out whether it is really possible to use the ISDS if the foreign investor suffers damages.

If a Korean investor makes an investment in a form defined in the Korea–China FTA,[12] and if the Chinese government fails to accord treatment under the Korea–China FTA which results in loss or damages of the Korean investor,[13] that Korean investor may request a court case or an arbitration.[14] In addition, the Korea–China FTA provides that each Party enforces its competition law 'consistent with the principles of the principles of transparency, non-discrimination, and procedural fairness'.[15] Korea–China FTA also provides that 'a person subject to an investigation to determine whether conduct violates its competition laws or what administrative sanctions or remedies should be ordered for violation of such laws is afforded the opportunity to present opinion or evidence in its defense in the investigation process'; and 'persons subject to the imposition of a sanction or remedy for violation of its competition laws should be given the opportunity to seek review of the sanction or remedy through administrative reconsideration and/or administrative lawsuit in accordance with each Party's laws'.[16]

In this regard, if the Chinese competition authority, the MOFCOM, the NDRC or the SAIC, fails to comply with the rules under the Korea–China FTA in its competition law enforcement activity, which incurs loss or damages of a Korean investor in China, it is possible for the Korean investor to consider the ISDS as an option to compensate their damages, as those authorities are clearly governmental 'organs' under the ILC Draft Articles, and the measures of those institutions affect the 'investment' under

---

[11] *Loewen v United States*, Decision on Jurisdiction, 9 January 2001, 7 ICSID Reports 425, paras 47–60.

[12] Korea–China FTA art 12.1:

> 'investments' means every kind of asset that an investor owns or controls, directly or indirectly, which has the characteristics of an investment, such as the commitment of capital or other resources, the expectation of gain or profit, or the assumption of risk. Forms that investments may take include:
>   (i)   an enterprise and a branch of an enterprise;
>   (ii) shares, stocks or other forms of equity participation in an enterprise, including rights derived therefrom;
>   (iii) bonds, debentures, loans and other forms of debt, including rights derived therefrom;
>   (iv) rights under contracts, including turnkey, construction, management, production or revenue-sharing contracts;
>   (v)   claims to money and claims to any performance under contract having a financial value associated with investment;
>   (vi) intellectual property rights, including copyrights and related rights, patent rights and rights relating to utility models, trademarks, industrial designs, layout-designs of integrated circuits, new varieties of plants, trade names, indications of source or geographical indications and undisclosed information;
>   (vii) rights conferred pursuant to laws and regulations or contracts such as concessions, licenses, authorizations and permits; and
>   (viii) any other tangible and intangible, movable and immovable property, and any related property rights, such as leases, mortgages, liens and pledges.

[13] Korea–China FTA art 12.12(1).   [14] ibid art 12.12(3).   [15] ibid art 14.3(1).

[16] ibid art 14.3(3).

the Korea–China FTA in principle. We will discuss the issue of 'measures affecting investment' in the later section.

III. The Reasons for Considering the ISDS against Competition Law Enforcement

First, we need to review how the discussion regarding arbitration and competition law issues has evolved over time. First, arbitrability of an antitrust claim was confirmed by the United States Supreme Court in the *Mitsubishi* case.[17] In that case, the US Supreme Court held that in an international arbitration, an arbitration is acceptable on grounds of 'international comity, respect of the capacities of foreign and transnational tribunals, and has sensitivity to the need of the International Commercial System for predictability in the resolution of disputes'.[18] European countries also accepted arbitrability of 'civil consequences of competition law breach' as well.[19] However, there has not been much debate regarding the use of ISDS in the competition law enforcement issues. This is because most cases were private contractual cases where a party invoked competition law as a part of their claims for contractual damages, and they did not discuss much about the arbitrability of competition law enforcement activities in an international arbitration, including an ISDS.[20]

However, it is time for a company/investor subject to a competition law enforcement activity to consider an ISD. The reasons are as follows.

First, as we considered in the preceding section, the antitrust enforcement activities are attributable to the home state as they seriously affect the investment. In most cases, a local subsidiary's anticompetitive conduct may constitute the liability of the headquarter in the home states due to various theories including 'single economic entity doctrine (EU)'.[21]

Secondly, an award under a BIT/FTA may not include 'remand' of the competition authority's decision. For example, Article 1135 of the North American Free Trade Agreement (NAFTA) and Article 11.26 of the Korea–US Free Trade Agreement provide that a tribunal may award only 'monetary damages and any applicable interest' and 'restitution of property'.[22] In this regard, an investor may not have to pursue the cancellation or annulment of a competition authority's decision in an ISD, but point out the breach of the host state's treaty obligation in an ISD proceeding and receive the monetary damage.

Thirdly, despite the existence of a functioning legal system in the host state, an appeal of the competition authority's decision before a court may take several years without guarantee to receive the desired outcome for the investor. Of course, the exhaustion of local remedies forces an aggrieved investor to use the locally available remedies including the appeal to the court.[23] However, the ILC is clear that:

[17] *Mitsubishi v Soler Chrysler-Plymouth*, 473 US 614 (1985).
[18] OECD, *Hearings—Arbitration and Competition*, DAF/COMP(2010) 40, 55.
[19] ibid 56.
[20] *Mitsubishi v Soler Chrysler-Plymouth*, 473 US 614 (1985); Case C-126/97 *Eco Swiss China Time Ltd v Benetton International NV*. Reference for a preliminary ruling: Hoge Raad—Netherlands Judgment of the Court of 1 June 1999. Opinion of the AG Saggio, delivered on 25 February 1999, para 52.
[21] Richard Whish and David Bailey, *Competition Law* (8th edn, Oxford University Press 2015) 95–101.
[22] NAFTA art 1135; Korea–US FTA art 11.26(1).   [23] ILC Draft Articles art 44(b).

Only those local remedies which are 'available and effective' have to be exhausted before invoking the responsibility of a State … there is no requirement to use a remedy which offers no possibility of redressing the situation, for instance, where it is clear from the outset that the law which the local court would have to apply can lead only to the rejection of any appeal.[24]

In addition, if the dispute arises directly from a violation of the treaty, the local remedy rule may be bypassed, and the case may be directly submitted to an arbitration under the BIT/FTA at issue.[25] In this regard, if an investor considers that a competition authority's decision may constitute a breach of the BIT/FTA to which its home state is a party, the investor may consider directly bringing the dispute before an ISD, instead of going to the court.

IV. Using ISDS in Chinese Anti-Monopoly Law (AML) Enforcement under the Korea–China FTA

We just found that it is possible for a Korean investor to use an ISDS under the Korea–China FTA against the measures by the Chinese competition authorities in principle. In this part, we will review more about the possibility of using an ISDS to the Chinese AML enforcement. The author uses the example of the Korea–China FTA, as it is one of the few FTAs by China with rather comprehensive coverage, and China is the largest trading partner of Korea, so that many Korean companies may face issues under the Korea–China FTA, including competition law enforcement. In addition, there is an ongoing ICSID case between a Korean investor and China.

Article 1 of the Chinese AML provides that the purpose of the AML is 'preventing and restraining monopolistic conducts, protecting fair competition in the market, enhancing economic efficiency, safeguarding the interests of consumers and the public interest and promoting the healthy development of the socialist market economy'.

The purpose of the Chinese AML is quite different from competition laws of other countries, as it explicitly states that the purpose of the law includes economic development of the country. For example, Article 1 of the Monopoly Regulation and Fair Trade Act (MRFTA) of Korea provides that the purpose of the act is to 'promote fair and free competition, to encourage thereby creative enterprising activities, to protect consumers and to strive for balanced development of the national economy, by preventing any abuse of market-dominating positions by enterprisers and any excessive concentration of economic power, and by regulating undue collaborative acts and unfair trade practices'. Also, Article 24(2) of the German Antitrust Act provides that:

Competition rules are provisions which regulate the conduct of undertakings in competition for counteracting conduct in competition which violates the principles of fair competition or effective competition based on performance, and of encouraging conduct in competition which is in line with these principles.[26]

These laws provide that the main purpose of the competition laws is to promote fair and effective competition, and protect consumers. In addition, Neelie Kroes, the

---

[24] ILC Commentary on the Draft articles on Responsibility of States for Internationally Wrongful Acts (2001), 121; Malcolm N Shaw, *International Law* (7th edn, Cambridge University Press 2014) 596.

[25] M Sornarajah, *The International Law on Foreign Investment* (3rd edn, Cambridge University Press 2010) 221.

[26] www.gesetze-im-internet.de/englisch_gwb/englisch_gwb.html.

former European Commissioner for competition policy, mentioned that the aim of competition law was 'to protect competition in the market as a means of enhancing consumer welfare and ensuring an efficient allocation of resources'.[27]

Based on the purpose under Article 1, Article 4 of the AML provides that the state shall 'formulate and implement competition rules which in accordance with the socialist market economy and improve macroeconomic and advance a unified, open, competitive and orderly market system'. Article 27 of the AML also provides that in addition to the competition-related factors, the MOFCOM may consider 'the influence over national economic development',[28] as well as 'other factors that affect the competition being considered by the antimonopoly authorities'.[29]

In addition, the functions of the Chinese competition authorities also present similar motivation to use the AML for economic development in addition to the 'normal' purpose of competition laws, i.e. promotion of fair and effective competition and consumer protection. First, the National Development and Reform Commission (NDRC), which is responsible for enforcing the AML on the price-related conducts, its main functions include macroeconomic planning, economic restructuring, monitoring the macroeconomic and social development trend, and providing forecasts and planning key construction projects and national investment policy.[30] Secondly, the mission of the State Administration for Industry and Commerce (SAIC), which is responsible for enforcing the AML on non-price-related conducts, includes regulation of the market, small and medium-sized enterprises (SMEs), and administrative supervision over contracts and auctions, etc.[31] Thirdly, the function of the Ministry of Commerce (MOFCOM), which is responsible for reviewing mergers, including trade policy formulation, trade defence measures, and trade negotiation, etc.

The purpose of the AML as well as the main missions of the Chinese competition authorities suggest that they serve the economic development, industrial policy formulation, and enforcement of such policies. As a result, foreign companies may suspect that the enforcement of competition policy would favour Chinese domestic companies. Their suspicion is partly supported by the records of the enforcement activities by the three competition authorities described above.[32] In this regard, the Chinese competition authorities may be vulnerable to challenge under ISD for setting up discrimination against foreign investors.

The Korea–China FTA provides for the definition of 'investment' very broadly, and the term 'investment' does not matter much in the Korea–China FTA and the Chinese AML context, since an investor subject to the AML enforcement who seeks remedies under the Korea–China FTA is likely to have a form of 'investment' under Article 12.1 of the Korea–China FTA in China. In addition, an investment dispute arises in the case of a 'dispute between a Party and an investor of the other Party that has incurred loss or damage by reason of, or arising out of, an alleged breach of any obligation of the

[27] SPPECH/05/12 of 15 September 2005 www.ec.europa.eu/competition/speeches/, Cited from Whish and Bailey (n 21) 19.
[28] AML art 27(5).   [29] ibid art 27(6).   [30] http://en.ndrc.gov.cn/mfndrc/.
[31] www.saic.gov.cn/english/aboutus/Mission/index.html.
[32] For example, MOFCOM rejected Coca-Cola's proposed acquisition of Huiyuan's beverage business in 2009, and rejected the plans by three leading European shipping companies to form a shipping alliance. The US–China Business Council (USCBC), Update (n 4) 10 and 17 and US Department of State (n 2) www.state.gov/e/eb/rls/othr/ics/2016/eap/254271.htm (last accessed 29 October 2016). Article 1 of the AML describes its purpose as 'of preventing and restraining monopolistic conducts, protecting fair competition in the market, enhancing economic efficiency, safeguarding the interests of consumers and the public interest and promoting the healthy development of the socialist market economy'.

former Party under this Chapter with respect to the investor or its covered investments in the territory of the former Party'.[33] In this regard, only governmental measures in breach of the Korea–China FTA which affect the investor or its covered investments in China or Korea are subject to the investment disputes under the Korea–China FTA. In this regard, an important question to find whether the Chinese AML enforcement measures are 'measures affecting investment' in breach of the Korea–China FTA.

As we reviewed in the previous section, Article 4 of the ILC Draft Articles and investment tribunals have found that actions by a variety of state organs are attributable to the state itself.[34] Such actions include actions by 'a government minister,[35] armed forces and police,[36] the state treasury,[37] the legislature[38] and courts'.[39] In this regard, the attribution of the conducts of the competition authorities in China and the courts can easily be attributed to China, as they are administrative and judicial institutions.

In addition, investors may argue that their acts seriously affect their investment in China. The Korea–China FTA's competition chapter defines 'anti-competitive business practices' as (1) cartels; (2) abuse of dominant positions; and (3) anti-competitive economic concentration.[40] The parties to the Korea–China FTA recognize that competition law enforcements 'contribute to preventing the benefits of trade liberalization from being undermined and to promoting economic efficiency and consumer welfare'.[41]

At the same time, competition law enforcement measures result in significant impacts in business. For companies subject to the measure, the impacts may include significant tangible and intangible resources to cooperate with the investigations, huge fines,[42] confiscation of illegal gains,[43] prevention of concentration,[44] possibility of private enforcement,[45] and huge reputational risks, which may ultimately make the investor reconsider whether to maintain business in China.[46] Also, the impact of the

---

[33] Korea–China FTA art 12.12(1).

[34] R Dolzer and C Schreuer, *Principles of International Investment Law* (2nd edn, Oxford University Press 2012) 217. See also Julien Chaisse, 'Investor-State Arbitration in International Tax Dispute Resolution: A Cut above Dedicated Tax Dispute Resolution?' (2016) 41(2) Virginia Tax Review 149.

[35] *Texaco v Libya*, Preliminary Award, 27 November 1975, para 23.

[36] *Amco v Indonesia*, Award, 20 November 1984, paras 155, 170–2; *AAPL v Sri Lanka*, Award, 27 June 1990.

[37] *Eureko v Poland*, Partial Award, 19 August 2005, paras 115–34.

[38] *Nycomb v Latvia*, Award, 16 December 2003, Stockholm Int'l Arb. Rev. 2005:1, s 4.2 at p 93.

[39] *Amco v Indonesia*, Award, 20 November 1984, para 150; *RosInvestCo v Russia*, Final Award, 12 September 2010, paras 602–3, cited from Dolzer and Schreuer (n 34) 217.

[40] Korea–China FTA art 14.13:

'anti-competitive business practices' means business conduct or transactions that adversely affect competition in the territory of a Party, such as:

(a) agreements between enterprises, decisions by associations of enterprises and concerted practices, which have as their object or effect the prevention, restriction or distortion of competition in the territory of either Party as a whole or in a substantial part thereof;

(b) any abuse by one or more enterprises of a dominant position in the territory of either Party as a whole or in a substantial part thereof; or

(c) concentrations between enterprises, which significantly impede effective competition, in particular as a result of the creation or strengthening of a dominant position in the territory of either Party as a whole or in a substantial part thereof; ...

[41] Korea–China FTA art 14.1.

[42] Articles 46 and 47 of the Chinese AML provide that the authorities may impose 'a fine between 1% and 10% of the turnover from the previous year' for monopolistic conducts and abuse of dominance.

[43] Chinese AML arts 46 and 47.   [44] ibid art 48.   [45] ibid art 50.

[46] Of course, even if a company pays a high fine, the investor may not leave the market considering the long-term benefit to maintain the status in the market. For example, Qualcomm had to pay US$975 million to resolve the antitrust case in China, but it did not contest the decision and

enforcement of the AML to third parties may include significant economic impacts through change in pricing, and opportunity to sue the infringers to recover their damages, etc.

Of course, scholars and international organizations argue that well-functioning competition law results in 'freer competition' leading to enhanced efficiency and higher consumer welfare.[47] Article 1 of the Chinese AML also expresses that the purpose of the AML is 'preventing and restraining monopolistic conducts, protecting fair competition in the market, enhancing economic efficiency, safeguarding the interests of consumers and the public interest'. In addition, the economic impact of the enforcement of the AML to the subject companies must be balanced with the positive effect in the overall economy. However, considering the records of the AML enforcement by the authorities, foreign enterprises cannot help wondering whether all these measures purely serve the 'protectionist' motivation, and they may raise procedural issues they face during the investigation.

In May 2015, the US–China Business Council (USCBC) released an annual report summarizing the updates and trends of Chinese AML enforcement.[48] The report first pointed out that despite the small number of monopolistic conduct investigation and merger cases involving foreign companies, there is more likelihood that foreign companies are subject to the sanctions for violations of the AML or commitment decisions/prohibition in merger cases.[49] In addition, the report pointed out the issues in the AML enforcement practices as follows:

Unclear provisions in the AML: Articles 46 and 47 of the AML provides that the competition authorities would impose 'fines between 1% and 10% of the previous year' as well we confiscation of illegal gains. However, it does not provide further basis of fine calculation. The USCBC report pointed out that even if the Chinese authorities argued that they applied the same fine calculation method based on the sales in Chinese market, publicly available information regarding the completed cases do not always provide definition of relevant markets.[50] Of course, the SAIC have implemented the internal fine calculation rules, and NDRC issued the draft penalty guidelines.[51] However, there are still large rooms of discretion for the SAIC and NDRC to define the relevant market, and the risk of double jeopardy still remains.[52]

Higher percentage of fines against foreign companies than domestic companies: The USCBC stated that the publicly available decisions by the NDRC indicated the average fine at 2.5 per cent of the relevant sales. However, the USCBC further argued that rate of fines on foreign companies was 3.3 per cent, while the rate of fines on

---

still tried to maintain the relationship with cell phone-makers and mobile network carriers in China. 'Qualcomm to pay $975 million to resolve China antitrust dispute' (Reuters 2015) www.reuters.com/article/us-china-qualcomm-idUSKBN0LD2EL20150210.

[47] United Nations Conference on Trade and Development (UNCTAD), *The role of competition policy in promoting economic development: The appropriate design and effectiveness of competition law and policy*—Note by the UNCTAD Secretariat, TD/RBP/CONF.7/3 (2010) 12.

[48] The US–China Business Council (USCBC), Update (n 4) 10 and 17.   [49] ibid.

[50] *See Texaco v Libya*, Preliminary Award, 27 November 1975, para 23.

[51] Global Compliance News, *China Antitrust: consultation on new and clearer penalty guidelines* https://globalcompliancenews.com/china-antitrust-consultation-new-and-clearer-penalty-guidelines-20160727/ (last accessed 31 December 2016.)

[52] Global Compliance News, *China Antitrust: consultation on new and clearer penalty guidelines* https://globalcompliancenews.com/china-antitrust-consultation-new-and-clearer-penalty-guidelines-20160727/ (last accessed 31 December 2016).

domestic companies was 1.9 per cent, which led to a significant difference in overall fine amount.[53] However, the simple fact that foreign companies paid higher fines itself does not support that there are issues with the AML enforcement, and therefore, one must look at other factors to make sure whether the AML enforcement activities were 'fair' to foreign companies.

Fair Treatment/Non-discrimination issues: The USCBC report also pointed out that despite the Chinese authorities' assurance that the AML enforcement activities did not target foreign companies, and they would treat all companies equally based on principles of fairness, objectivity, transparency and non-discrimination.[54] However, the USCBC argued that there are still concerns about fair treatment/non-discrimination in the AML enforcement activities. Such concerns would include:

Merger reviews: (1) MOFCOM's merger reviews allow rooms for non-competition factors including industrial policy objectives; (2) MOFCOM is required to consult with industry regulators and domestic interest which may open ways for domestic industrial policy influences; (3) Security reviews under the Article 31 of the AML could be used to promote economic protectionism.

NDRC/SAIC enforcement activities: The USCBC pointed out that there are little transparency on selection of targets and the decisions may have been influenced by broader Chinese policy concerns including intellectual property or protection of domestic industries.

Competition investigations do not fully value market considerations or make price comparisons between China and overseas markets without considering local market conditions.

Due process and Transparency: China has made commitments to enhance transparency in the AML investigation. However, the USCBC member companies and other foreign companies continue to raise issues such as (1) inability during enforcement proceedings to inquire about the complaints; (2) pressure to 'admit guilt' ability to respond to evidence; (3) inability to have legal counsel present during investigation and enforcement proceedings; (4) lack of transparency in publishing case decisions.[55]

Protracted time periods for merger reviews: Article 25 and 26 of the AML provides for a 2-stage merger review process: preliminary review (phase I) for up to 30 days and more detailed review (phase II) for up to 90 days, with the possibility to extend up to 60 days. However, in practice, the timelines often get stretched due to the increasing number of transactions for MOFCOM reviews, which MOFCOM may order 'withdraw and refile' of the notification. In addition, the so-called 'pre-notification consultation' process, which does not appear in the official timeline under the AML, is often used by MOFCOM to appear that it did not violate the AML timeline. In addition, even if more companies use the 'simplified case review system', there has been little evidence showing that such 'simplified review' resulted in shorter timelines in merger review cases. In this regard, MOFCOM's discretion to extend the time periods for merger reviews beyond the AML timeline remains

[53] See *Texaco v Libya*, Preliminary Award, 27 November 1975, para 23.
[54] ibid para 6.   [55] *Texaco v Libya*, Preliminary Award, 27 November 1975, paras 6–7.

intact, and they often cause significant costs for the parties by not closing the transactions in time.[56]

Role of non-competition factors in AML enforcement: Articles 4 and 27 provide that competition authorities may consider competitive factors and non-competitive factors in the competition policy formulation as well as enforcement.[57] As discussed in the previous section, since the purpose of the AML under Article 1 clearly includes 'promoting the healthy development of the socialist market economy', it is unavoidable that such non-competition factors may significantly influence the decision-making of the Chinese competition authorities.

The USCBC's report highlights the common concerns of the foreign companies operating in China. These issues were raised since the adoption of the AML, but there has not been much progress, and this may render the Chinese government somewhat vulnerable to the challenges under ISDS under the Korea–China FTA and other BITs signed by China. The next sections will discuss causes of action by Korean investors under the Korea–China FTA.

Article 12.3(1) of Korea–China FTA provides, 'Each Party shall in its territory accord to investors of the other Party and to covered investment treatment no less favourable than that it accords in like circumstances to its own investors and their investments with respect to investment activities'. Based on this, can a Korean investor challenge the fines imposed by NDRC or the SAIC before an investment tribunal in comparison with a Chinese company in the same case? The answer may not be simple. However, one may apply a three-step test applied by the ICSID in the *Bayindir v Pakistan* case[58] to determine whether the NDRC or the SAIC violated the national treatment principle.

First, the investment tribunal must determine whether the aggrieved Korean investor and the Chinese company were in 'like circumstances'; secondly, they must determine whether the Korean investor received less favourable treatment than the domestic company; and, thirdly, they must assess whether such different treatment may be justified by 'legitimate reasons'.[59] In a cartel case, as the companies are subject to the same investigation, it is likely that the companies are in 'like circumstances', i.e., the same cartel investigation. However, the fact that the Korean investor received heavier fines than the Chinese co-cartelist may not pass the second and the third test.

In a cartel investigation, there are many factors which legitimize cartel fines: relevant sales in the market, order of leniency application, degree of cooperation with the authority, recidivism, etc. In particular, the size of relevant sales is the key factor to determine the basic amount of the fine, and this is more an issue of equity than equality. Also, the NDRC/SAIC may justify the size of the fine against a Korean investor arguing that the Chinese company was the 'first to report' to receive fine immunity and the Chinese company cooperated with the authorities closer than the Korean investor. In this regard, it may be difficult for a Korean investor to challenge

---

[56] *Texaco v Libya*, Preliminary Award, 27 November 1975, para 7. Pre-notification consultations between the parties and the competition authorities became common practice in the EU as well. In the pre-notification phase, the parties submit draft notifications to the European Commission for preliminary review and they have face-to-face meetings to discuss the transaction. The EU's pre-notification consultations are used to make sure that the European Commission conducts the formal review process efficiently, while the parties may avoid risk of rejection of formal notification as incomplete. Porter Elliot, *Merger Control: Jurisdictional Comparisons* (Sweet & Maxwell 2011) 214.

[57] Elliot (n 56) 7.

[58] *Bayindir Insaat Turizm Ticaret Ve Sanayi AS v Islamic Republic of Pakistan*, ICSID Case No ARB/03/29, Award (27 August 2009).

[59] August Reinisch, 'National Treatment' in Meg Kinnear and others (eds), *Building International Investment law—The First 50 Years of ICSID* (Wolters Kluwer 2016) 395.

the amount of fine in a cartel investigation. However, if the Korean investor can prove that the Chinese competition authority did not treat the Korean investor as fairly as the Chinese co-cartelist by not providing them equal opportunity to present their case and not granting access to key documents, such national treatment claim may be accepted by the investment tribunal, based on the three-step test. This may also apply in a multi-party dominance case.

On the other hand, national treatment claims may not work in merger review cases, each and every case is considered to be 'unique', as each case involves different market definition and the resulting assessment of market power, so that it is very difficult to establish 'like circumstances' which may invoke national treatment claims.

Article 12.5(1) of the Korea–China FTA provides, 'Each Party shall accord to covered investments treatment in accordance with customary international law, including fair and equitable treatment and full protection and security'. In order to provide further clarification, the Korea–China FTA provides as follows:

2. For greater certainty, paragraph 1 prescribes the customary international law minimum standard of treatment of aliens as the minimum standard of treatment to be afforded to covered investments. The concepts of "fair and equitable treatment" and "full protection and security" do not require treatment in addition to or beyond that which is required by that standard, and do not create additional substantive rights. The obligation in paragraph 1 to provide:

   (a) 'fair and equitable treatment' includes the obligation not to deny justice in criminal, civil, or administrative adjudicatory proceedings in accordance with the principle of due process of law; and
   (b) 'full protection and security' requires each Party to provide the level of police protection required under customary international law.

In light of this provision, the due process issues pointed out by the USCBC may require scrutiny under the FET. As described above, the USCBC member companies and other foreign companies raised issues such as (1) inability during enforcement proceedings to inquire about the complaints; (2) pressure to 'admit guilt' ability to respond to evidence; (3) inability to have legal counsel present during investigation and enforcement proceedings; (4) lack of transparency in publishing case decisions.[60] In addition, the role of non-competition factors in the AML enforcement activities may put the Chinese competition authorities' actions under the FET scrutiny.

The author considers that the procedural issues pointed out by the USCBC may lead to 'denial of justice' claim under the Articles 12.5(1) and (2) of the Korea–China FTA. First, the procedural fairness and due process attained customary international law standard through many human rights treaties.[61] Secondly, the Korea Fair Trade Commission (KFTC) also amended its rules to allow more rooms for lawyers to present the cases for defendant companies more effectively.[62] In addition, the International Competition Network also recommends to improve procedural fairness and due process in the competition investigation process, so that Korean investors may use this as evidence of customary international law as well.

---

[60] See *Texaco v Libya*, Preliminary Award, 27 November 1975, paras 6–7.
[61] See eg art 14 of the International Covenant on Civil and Political Rights, adopted and opened for signature, ratification and accession by the UN General Assembly resolution 2200A (XXI) of 16 December 1966, entry into force 23 March 1976; European Convention on the Human Rights Article 6.
[62] See art 13 of the KFTC Rules of Investigation Procedures (KFTC Notice 2016-1), adopted on 4 February 2016.

In this regard, the abovementioned procedural issues as well as consideration of non-competition factors in the AML enforcement may expose the Chinese competition authorities to the denial of justice claims. In addition, the Chinese judiciary is not as 'independent' as other judicial systems, and the exhaustion of local remedies argument under the *ELSI* case[63] may help Korean investors to choose the ISDS under the Korea–China FTA rather than appeal to the Chinese People's Courts.

There may be a case where a foreign investor finds itself to be subject to a huge fine for violation of the AML, so that it may argue that the measure constitutes an 'expropriation' under the Korea–China FTA. The Korea–China FTA defines 'expropriation' as (1) direct expropriation; and (2) indirect expropriation.[64] The definition of the 'indirect expropriation' under Annex 12-B of Korea–China FTA is as follows:

The second situation is indirect expropriation, where an action or a series of actions by a Party has an effect equivalent to direct expropriation without formal transfer of title or outright seizure.

(a) The determination of whether an action or a series of actions by a Party, in a specific fact situation, constitutes an indirect expropriation, requires a case-by-case, fact-based inquiry that considers, among other factors:
  (i) the economic impact of the action or series of actions, although the fact that such action or series of actions has an adverse effect on the economic value of investments, standing alone, does not establish that an indirect expropriation has occurred;
  (ii) the extent to which the action or series of actions interferes with distinct and reasonable expectations arising out of investments; and
  (iii) the character and objectives of the action or series of actions, including whether such action is proportionate to its objectives.
(b) Except in rare circumstances, such as when an action or a series of actions by a Party is extremely severe or disproportionate in light of its purpose, non-discriminatory regulatory actions adopted by the Party for the purpose of legitimate public welfare do not constitute indirect expropriation.

In the AML enforcement context, if an AML investigation by the SAIC or NDRC results in a 'disproportionate' amount of fine comparing to the activities concerned, and the investigation itself was conducted in a clear violation of due process, the defendant investor may argue for the indirect expropriation under the Korea–China FTA.[65] In addition, the investment tribunals continued to find that the 'intent to expropriate' of the measure would not matter.[66]

However, it must be noted that an AML investigation is in its nature 'non-discriminatory regulatory actions' targeted at both domestic and foreign companies operating or affecting the Chinese domestic market. In addition, the purpose of the AML under the Article 1 is clear in that it is designed to 'protect fair competition in the market, enhance economic efficiency and protect consumer interests as well as public interest'. Also, the SAIC and the NDRC use their fining guidelines to make sure and prove that their fine calculations have a legal basis, and their fines are not 'extremely severe or disproportionate' under Annex 12-B of the Korea–China FTA. In this regard, China may argue that these measures fall within the 'the reasonable governmental

---

[63] *Elettronica Sicula S.p.A. (ELSI)* (United States of America v Italy), ICJ Judgment of 20 July 1989, para 59.
[64] Korea–China FTA, Annex 12-B.   [65] See Dolzer and Schreuer (n 34) 112–13.
[66] *Siemens v Argentina*, Award, 6 February 2007, para 98, cited from Dolzer and Schreuer (n 34) 114.

regulation' serving a general public purpose.[67] Therefore, it may be very difficult to argue that 'excessive' fines under the AML would constitute an 'indirect expropriation' under the Korea–China FTA.

One of the controversies in the international investment arbitration system is the practice of 'Treaty Shopping', whereby investors incorporate in a foreign jurisdiction to gain access to favourable investment protection treaties. There is also some concern that multinational companies would use Korea to benefit from the Korea–China FTA's ISDS provisions.

This may be a legitimate concern considering the recent *Philip Morris v Australia* case,[68] where Philip Morris took a series of corporate restructuring measures to qualify as an investor under the Hong Kong–Australia BIT.[69] However, unlike the Hong Kong–Australia BIT, the Korea–China FTA does have a provision on 'Denial of Benefits' under Article 12.15 as follows:

Article 12.15: Denial of Benefits

1. A Party may deny the benefits of this Chapter to an investor of the other Party that is an enterprise of the latter Party and to its investments if the enterprise is owned or controlled by an investor of a non-Party and the denying Party:
   (a) does not maintain normal economic relations with the non-Party; or
   (b) adopts or maintains measures with respect to the non-Party that prohibit transactions with the enterprise or that would be violated or circumvented if the benefits of this Chapter were accorded to the enterprise or to its investments.
2. A Party may deny the benefits of this Chapter to an investor of the other Party that is an enterprise of the latter Party and to its investments if the enterprise is owned or controlled by an investor of a non-Party or of the denying Party, and the enterprise has no substantial business activities in the territory of the latter Party.

The term 'substantial business activities' may not mean 'large' business activities. However, it requires that an investor wishing to benefit from the Korea–China FTA must maintain legal presence and investment-related activities conducted in Korea, including employment of a small but permanent staff.[70] In this regard, the provision may not provide a perfect protection from the 'treaty shopping'. However, by having such a provision, the degree of risk of 'treaty shopping' considerably decreases.

V. Practical Considerations—Can Anyone 'Dare' to 'Bell' the Panda?

So far, we have reviewed the Korea–China FTA's investment (Chapter 12) and competition (Chapter 14) chapters and found that it is possible to challenge the enforcement of the AML under the Korea–China FTA's ISDS. However, even if it is theoretically possible to do so, there are practical considerations for the aggrieved investors to 'think twice' before doing so. First, the Chinese competition enforcers are themselves pretty

[67] *Feldman v Mexico*, Award, 16 December 2002, para 103, cited from Dolzer and Schreuer (n 34) 120.

[68] *Philip Morris Asia Limited v The Commonwealth of Australia*, UNCITRAL, PCA Case No 2012–12, Award on Jurisdiction and Admissibility, 17 December 2015.

[69] *Philip Morris Asia Limited v The Commonwealth of Australia*, UNCITRAL, PCA Case No 2012–12, Award on Jurisdiction and Admissibility, 17 December 2015, paras 141–64.

[70] *AMTO v Ukraine*, Award, 26 March 2008, paras 67–70, cited from Dolzer and Schreuer (n 43) 55–6).

'powerful' institutions. As discussed in the previous sections, all three competition
authorities have broad powers to influence the market, and they consider competition law enforcement as a means to exert their power to 'lead' the country's economy.
Because of their powers, it is important for the foreign investors to maintain good
relationship to do business in China, instead of challenging them. In this regard, an
aggrieved investor suffered by challengeable AML enforcement measures may choose
to comply with the decision, rather than using an ISDS.

Secondly, the Chinese market is too large and attractive to leave. Considering that
most ISD cases are filed as an 'exit strategy' for the aggrieved investor, this is another
factor to discourage the investors against filing an ISD case against China for violation
of the Korea–China FTA in the AML enforcement. There are two cases supporting
this. First, when the NDRC imposed US$975 million fines on Qualcomm, it was
clear that Qualcomm did not challenge the measure as the fines could have been
higher if they confronted the NDRC, and the Chinese mobile phone market was too
attractive for Qualcomm to leave.[71] Secondly, the background of the ongoing dispute
between Ansung Housing and China[72] for claims arising out of the Jiangsu provincial
government's actions in relation to Ansung's investment in the construction shows
that the investor decided to file the case against China only when it was clear that
it could no longer sustain the business and decided to recoup at least a part of its
monetary damages. In this regard, it may not be practical for investors to file an ISD
case for Chinese competition enforcement measures under the Korea–China FTA.
However, the understanding the possibility of the ISD may work as an advantage
for both sides. First, an investor may use an ISD as a means to raise issues on 'unfair'
procedural elements of Chinese AML enforcement and ask the Chinese competition
authorities to consider their behaviours. At the same time, the Chinese competition
authorities may use this possibility as a reason to 'sit back and think' about their
current practice and improve the procedural aspects of its AML enforcement activities, along with the recommendations by other multilateral and regional bodies concerning competition policy.

VI. Conclusion

Since the adoption of the AML in 2008, Chinese AML enforcement has been very
active for the last few years, and it helped improve the culture of competition compliance for domestic and foreign companies in the Chinese market. However, as pointed
out in this chapter, there are still procedural issues which raise questions of 'fairness'
of the system, and there is a need for some calls for further reform of the competition
enforcement system in China.

In this regard, the author is of the view that the Investment and the competition
chapters of the Korea–China FTA provide a relatively comprehensive framework and
basis for challenging Chinese AML enforcement before the ISDS. In addition, the
Korea–China FTA may provide a model for the competition and investment chapters

[71] Reuters (n 46); On the other hand, when the KFTC imposed US$853 million of fines against
Qualcomm for abuse of dominant positions, Qualcomm explicitly said that it would appeal the decision before the court www.bloomberg.com/news/articles/2016-12-28/qualcomm-fined-853-million-
by-south-korea-s-antitrust-agency-ix8csvth (last accessed 15 January 2017).
[72] *Ansung Housing Co Ltd v People's Republic of China* (ICSID Case No ARB/14/25), filed on 4
November 2014.

of the China-led Regional Comprehensive Economic Partnership (RCEP) agreement. In this regard, both the investors benefiting from the Korea–China FTA and China must understand the possibility of using the ISD against Chinese AML enforcement activities.

On the other hand, it is true that the chance of challenges of the Chinese AML by an ISD is small, as China is one of the largest markets for companies to operate. However, the mere existence of the chance for Chinese AML enforcement to be challenged by an ISD may provide foreign investors and home state a momentum to induce the Chinese government to review the procedural issues raising concerns for foreign investors, and the Chinese competition authorities may use this possibility as an external force to drive procedural reform of the AML enforcement.

27

Implementing Investor–state Mediation in China's Next Generation Investment Treaties

Shu Shang*

Introduction

The remarks made by the chief executive officer (CEO) of Metalclad after the company was awarded US$4 million by an investment tribunal have been constantly mentioned as a representative voice from the community that the investor–state arbitration mechanism may not be an optimal way of settling treaty disputes.[1] Investors complain about the cost and slow pace of the process; states complain that the process favours investors and has produced an expansive application of international investment agreements (IIAs); scholars lament the lack of consistency and legal coherency of the jurisprudence; and NGOs criticize the process for lacking transparency and premising the rights of the investor over other important interests.[2] Investor–state arbitration has been criticized as being an anomaly of international arbitration because states have to waive their sovereign immunity in order to participate in a dispute resolution proceeding initiated by a private party. The political nature of investor–state claims usually implicates third parties, often citizens of the host state demanding more transparency in the process, or civic interest groups voluntarily involved by submitting *amicus* briefs.[3] In addition, investor–state arbitration is notoriously unpredictable. This sense of unfairness often gives rise to assumptions that better alternatives might be available to resolve the kind of disputes. Mediation, on the other hand, employs a much more flexible method and does not result in any form of precedent, and is therefore suggested by scholars to be adopted to resolve treaty disputes to supplement the uses of investor–state arbitrations.

I. The Rise of Mediation and its Applications in Resolving Investor–state Claims

Investor–state arbitration has faced criticism since the first day of its birth, which has become more intensive over the last decade probably due to the surge in the number of

* PhD Candidate, Faculty of Law, Chinese University of Hong Kong and Executive Director, Free Trade and ADR Research and Development Center, Shanghai University of Finance and Economics.

[1] Grant Kesler, in remarks at a panel organized by the ABA Section of International Law and Practice, mentioned that political methods might have been better. He made further comments that the process was too slow, too costly, and too indeterminate.

[2] Jack J Coe, 'Towards a Complementary Use of Conciliation in Investor-State Disputes: A Preliminary Sketch' (2005) 12 UC Davis Journal of International Law and Policy 7.

[3] See Julien Chaisse and Rahul Donde, 'The State of Investor-State Arbitration: A Reality Check of the Issues, Trends, and Directions in Asia-Pacific' (2018) 51(1) The International Lawyer 47.

Implementing Investor-state Mediation in China's Next Generation Investment Treaties. Shu Shang.
© Shu Shang, 2019. Published 2019 by Oxford University Press.

investors attempting to access investment treaty arbitration, and the increasing value of their claims.[4] For example, in *Abaclat v Argentina*, the claimant asked for an award of US$1.35 billon;[5] before Venezuela withdrew from the ICSID Convention, its cumulative debt in ICSID cases had reached approximately US$4.6 million,[6] which has been largely seen as one major reason for the country to drop out from the system. With the values going up in investors' claims, both investors and countries have also been spending significant amounts of money and time on their claims. A 2014 survey conducted by the British law firm Allen & Overy based on cases their lawyers have participated in shows that average time spent on resolving a treaty claim was about 3.8 years, and average costs are US$4 million dollars for the claimant, without adding additional time caused by uncertainties of enforcing awards.[7]

In the meantime, mediation has been proposed as a method to supplement the current arbitration-dominated scheme, in order to remedy some of the deficiencies in the system.[8] Since mediation need not be procedurally difficult and mediators charge considerably lower fees, it is considered that it should be possible to produce results with greater speed and less expense. In fact, ICSID statistics already suggest that about 40 per cent of investor–state disputes settle, a figure which could be higher in reality.[9] Therefore, the potential of mediating investor–state claims may seem greater than it is.

A. Mediation in Resolving Business Disputes

In this paper, we are not trying to differentiate mediation and conciliation as the two terms have been used interchangeably in a variety of different contexts. Although conciliation can imply more fact-finding roles of the neutral and to some extent 'more dynamic efforts',[10] in an investor–state context, the difference between conciliation and mediation is minor.

A revival of studies of resolving commercial and business disputes through the mediation mechanism started in the 1990s, which was usually inspired by original studies in less developed jurisdictions.[11] With costs and party autonomy issues raised, mediation could offer some certain advantages that litigation and arbitration could not. A number of arbitral institutions responded to the increasing needs by adding mediation to their institutional rules. For example, the International Chamber of Commerce (ICC) made conciliation available under its rules to facilitate the amicable settlement of disputes, and reference to such rules in the event of a contractual dispute between parties can

---

[4] See Jeswald W Salacuse, 'Is There a Better Way? Alternative Methods of Treaty Based Investor-State Dispute Resolution' (2007) 31 Fordham International Law Journal 138, 168; see also Nancy A Welsh and Andrea K Schneider, 'Becoming Investor-State Mediation' (2012) 1 Penn State Journal of Law & International Affairs 86.

[5] *Ablacat and Others v Argentine Republic*, ICSID Case No ARB/07/5.

[6] Javier Ferrero, 'Venezuela versus the ICSID Convention' *Global Arbitration News* (24 February 2015) https://globalarbitrationnews.com/venezuela-versus-icsid-convention-20120422/(last accessed 16 June 2017).

[7] Mathew Hodgson, 'Investment Treaty Arbitration: How Much Does it Cost? How Long Does it Take?' (*Allen & Overy Publication* 2015) http://www.allenovery.com/publications/en-gb/Pages/Investment-Treaty-Arbitration-How-much-does-it-cost-How-long-does-it-take-.aspx (last accessed 16 June 2017).

[8] Coe (n 2).   [9] ibid, supplemented by independent analysis based on ICSID data.

[10] Ibid.

[11] See M L Marasinghe, 'The Use of Conciliation for Dispute Settlement: The Sri Lanka Experience' (1980) 29 International Comparative Law Quarterly 389.

be established by the inclusion of a mediation clause or reference to the rules.[12] The
conciliator is given the broad power to conduct the conciliation process in the way that
he deems fit. The ICC Conciliation Rules were then replaced by the 2001 Amicable
Dispute Resolution Rules (ADR rules), and, eventually, by the 2014 Mediation Rules,
which reflected modern day practices by providing users with clear instructions for the
conduct of the proceedings while maintaining necessary flexibilities. The UNCITRAL
Conciliation Rules are more detailed, which can be initiated if there is acceptance by
one party of an invitation to conciliate, without needing a specific contract before
the dispute arises. In the Asia-Pacific region, Hong Kong's judiciary has, since 2004,
in its report on the civil justice reform, treated the promotion of a mediation scheme
as an important legislative agenda, and the cross-sector working group headed by the
Secretary for Justice promulgated the Hong Kong Mediation Code as the professional
standard for mediators.[13] As the region's leading dispute resolution provider, the Hong
Kong International Arbitration Center (HKIAC) has accommodated parties' needs
to mediate as early as the 1990s and the institution's statistics show that its Rule of
Mediation is invoked at least a couple of times per year, usually referred to by domestic
parties to settle disputes involving small claims, but sometimes also international ones.
Recently, mediation played a successful role in resolving the disputes over the 'Lehman
mini-bonds' in Hong Kong, in which process 105 requests for mediation have been
made.[14] In Singapore and China, parties can seek to convert settlements reached during
the arbitration proceedings into a consent award that is as enforceable as an arbitration
award.[15] These collective efforts demonstrate that commercial parties' interests to settle
disputes through mediation have always existed, and have been supported by legislators in many regions.[16]

B. Mediation in resolving investor–state disputes

ICSID has had its Conciliation Rule since its inception and negotiation may be conducted before or after the investor begun arbitration.[17] Therefore, scholars have proposed ways to make ADR a more attractive option to investors. In order to make
investor–state mediation happen when a conflict arises, it is usually necessary for treaty
negotiators to incorporate certain mediation clauses into the proper dispute resolution
process. This could be as simple as mentioning the possibility of mediation in the
context of a 'cooling-off period', or as complex as creating a system which contains
compulsory mediation. Overall, investment treaties or domestic laws that already contemplated alternative dispute resolution methods by disposing resources for parties
to mediate could be broadly classified into three categories: those casually refer to
informal amicable settlement methods; those that designate an arbitral institution to

[12] International Chamber of Commerce Conciliation Rules: 'all disputes arising in connection with
the present contract shall be finally settled under the Rules of Conciliation and Arbitration of the ICC
by one or more mediators'.
[13] *Mediation and Dispute Resolution Handbook* (2nd edn, Joint Mediation Helpline Office
2015) xi–xii.
[14] See Bonnie Chen, 'Minibond Investors Urged to Try Mediation' *The Standard* (26 March 2009).
[15] *Mediation and Dispute Resolution Handbook* (n 13) xi–xii.
[16] Linda C Reif, 'Conciliation as a Mechanism for the Resolution of International Economic and
Business Disputes' (1990) 14 Fordham International Law Journal 578.
[17] 'Overview of Conciliation under the ICSID Convention' (*International Centre for Settlement of
Investment Disputes*) https://icsid.worldbank.org/en/Pages/process/ICSID-Convention-Conciliation.
aspx (last accessed 16 June 2017).

handle formal mediation claims; or those that created special responding authorities solely for the purposes of mediation.

1. Informal mediation methods

The first type of treaties usually refers to treaties containing a 'cooling-off' period that allows for amicable settlement between parties, and it is common for investment treaties to allow for a time period for the parties to seek amicable settlement of the dispute before an arbitration may be commenced. These include languages such as 'the parties to the dispute shall initially seek to resolve the dispute by consultations and negotiations', like in the US–Argentina BIT.[18] Because these treaties do not specifically mention mediation nor specify how negotiations and consultations shall be conducted, the cooling-off period has been subject to inconsistent interpretations by different enforcement tribunals. But according to a former official of the US Department of Commerce, requests of investors during this period to negotiate or mediate will usually be granted by the US government.[19]

The latest generation of BITs goes beyond traditional cooling-off periods to express needs and wishes for a stand-alone mediation option, as a fully-fledged alternative mechanism to which disputing parties may resort. For example, the US–Poland BIT states that 'in the event of an investment dispute … the parties to the dispute shall initially seek to resolve the dispute by consultation and negotiation, which may include the use of non-binding, third party procedures'.[20] Article 23 of the 2012 United States Model BIT also provides that: 'In the event of an investment dispute, the claimant and the respondent shall initially seek to resolve the dispute through consultation and negotiation, which may include the use of non-binding, third party procedures', which engages informal uses of mediation methods.

2. Formal mediation

Formal types of investor–state mediation as seen in investment treaties usually involve the appointment of an arbitral institution to administer the dispute. ICSID is the most frequently referred to institution that handles mediation based on its prominent status in administering investor–state disputes, and conciliation has always been treated as an optional form of ICSID dispute and can be structured as either an alternative or preliminary to arbitration. There are treaties that have referred to ICISID mediation and the recommendation of adoption of the ICSID Conciliation Rules. For example, the Netherlands–Uganda BIT in its Article 9 has mentioned that 'Each Contracting Party hereby consents to submit any legal dispute arising between the Contracting Party concerning an investment of that investor in the territory of the former Contracting Party to the ICSID for settlement by conciliation or arbitration under the ICSID Convention'. Generally, in institutional conciliation, the investor submits a request for conciliation to the institution offering conciliation services, subject to the parties' objection, the institution will also appoint a conciliator. Since ICSID provides its

---

[18] US–Argentina Bilateral Investment Treaty (adopted 14 November 1991, entered into force 20 October 1994) Article VII.
[19] Interview with a former official of the US Department of Commerce who refused to disclose identity.
[20] US–Poland Bilateral Investment Treaty (adopted 21 March 1990, entered into force 6 August 1994) Article IX.

own list of conciliators, it is presumed to be referred to at times, and one can choose a sole conciliator or any odd number of conciliators appointed by party agreement, which is closely associated with the ICSID arbitration.[21] In history, the ICSID Rule of Conciliation has been invoked six times in total, and one of the few published accounts concerns the first conciliation conducted under the ICSID between Tesoro Petroleum Corporation and the State of Trinidad and Tobago was conducted by Lord Wilberforce, a retired English judge, who successfully acted as a conciliator to help resolve a dispute involving the distribution of US$143 million in profits.[22] However, it has been criticized that this process is not usually preferred by parties in the event of disputes and that parties go directly to arbitration after amicable efforts had proven futile.

3. Domestic law responding mechanisms

Domestic law has also played some part in promoting investor–state mediation, oftentimes as a preventive mechanism. Some states have created processes in their domestic laws that allow for such experimenting for the encouragement of early termination of cases. For example, Peru passed Law No 28,933, which has the object of creating a 'coordinated response system' to investment disputes and to attempt to resolve such disputes by negotiation and mediation wherever possible.[23] The Response System Law created a Special Commission to represent the state in international investment dispute settlement proceedings, which analyses each case, determines the feasibility of an amicable resolution, and conducts negotiations for resolution. The Responsive System was thought to be a preventive mechanism of Peru's ISDS mechanism and the Special Commission was assigned to the MEF to represent Peru in any pending ISDS or ADR procedure, which is empowered to negotiate and mediate.[24] Columbia has also adopted a very similar system in its law, by having appointed a domestic authority.[25]

II. Applying the Investor–state Mediation Mechanism to China

China has shown a growing interest in the work of ICSID, and has more frequently included investor–state arbitration proceedings in its treaties.[26] Although legal representatives of the Chinese state were able to successfully get the government out of an investor–state claim by disputing the tribunal's jurisdiction based on a 'statutory limitation' defence in the recent case of *Ansung Housing Co Ltd v People's Republic of China*,[27]

---

[21] 'ICSID Panels of Arbitrators and Conciliators' (*International Centre for Settlement of Investment Disputes*) https://icsid.worldbank.org/en/Pages/about/Database-of-Panel-Members.aspx (last accessed 16 June 2017).

[22] See 'List of Concluded Cases' (*International Centre for Settlement of Investment Disputes*) https://icsid.worldbank.org/en/Pages/cases/ConcludedCases.aspx?status=c (last accessed 16 June 2017).

[23] 'Best Practice in Investment for Development: How to Prevent and Manage Investor-States Disputes: Lessons from Peru' (United Nations Conference on Trade and Development (UNCTD): Investment Advisory Series B No 10, 19–33, Geneva, November 2011).

[24] ibid.

[25] Magrete Stevens and Ben Love, 'Investor-State Mediation: Observations on the Role of Institutions' (2009) 3 Contemporary Issues in International Arbitration and Mediation: The Fordham Papers 389.

[26] Leon E Trakman, 'China and Investor-State Arbitration' (2012) UNSW Law Research Paper No 2012-48 1 SSRN: https://ssrn.com/abstract=2157387 (last accessed 16 June 2017).

[27] *Ansung Housing Co Ltd v People's Republic of China*, ICSID Case No ARB/14/25.

the country's experiences with treaty arbitration are still quite limited. Early concerns that China will unilaterally withdraw from the current ISDS mechanism have faded away as this is very unlikely. Unlike some other BRICS countries such as Brazil and India, both the Chinese state and its investors seem to possess an open-minded mentality towards the use of investor–state arbitration mechanisms. Despite that, the country's distrust of the ISDS system remained.[28] The negotiation of an appropriate dispute resolution clause still takes up a huge amount of time and has caused serious media attention as the government is constantly seeking alternative methods to tackle this problem.[29] Mediation, on the other hand, may offer a buffer for the Chinese state to try to settle some claims before they become full-blown, without losing the country's growing friendly appeal to foreign investors.

A. The development of mediation practice in China

Mediation has always been a major form of dispute resolution in China, which was often associated with the value of harmony that is not only central to the Chinese Confucian philosophy, but also to the controlling methods that the Communist Chinese government has employed after the establishment of the People's Republic of China. China has a very long history of favouring mediation, based on its cultural heritages. As a means of dispute settlement, mediation survived from the Pre-Qin period to the Ming and Qing periods.[30] Although the court reform in many parts of urban China has reduced the volume of mediation cases, there has been a revival of interests in developing ADR in recent years, probably as a result of the explosion of the courts' caseloads in many parts of China.[31] To Chinese parties, mediation is less disruptive, better for saving face because the result of any mediation proceeding does not simply label one party as 'right' or 'wrong', and sometimes can lead to better results for both parties.

Mediation carried out in arbitration proceedings is also commonly accepted by the Chinese people. It has long been the practice of the China International Economic and Trade Commission (CIETAC), one of the most prominent arbitral institutions in China which has the capacity to deal with cross-border disputes, to combine mediation with arbitration. Although CIETAC can independently handle mediation cases, it is more common to see mediation occurring as part of the arbitration process, a process called 'med-arb'.[32] Article 45 of the Rules of Arbitration of China International Economic and Trade Commission of People's Republic of China 2012 makes general provisions covering practices and outcomes, along with a few other institutions.[33]

[28] Julien Chaisse, 'The Shifting Tectonics of International Investment Law—Structure and Dynamics of Rules and Arbitration on Foreign Investment in the Asia-Pacific Region' (2015) 47 George Washington International Law Review 563, 615–16 (2015).

[29] See 'Towards a US-China Investment Treaty' (Peterson Institute for International Economics, February 2015) https://www.goldmansachs.com/insights/pages/us-china-bilateral-investment-dialogue/multimedia/papers/toward-a-us-china-investment-treaty.pdf (last accessed 31 October 2018).

[30] Lian Hong, 'Harmonious Concept of Confucianism and Chinese Traditional Mediation System' (2005) 18 Chang Chun University of Science and Technology (Social Sciences) 89.

[31] See eg Randall Peerenhoom and Xin He, 'Dispute Resolution in China: Patterns, Causes and Prognosis' (2009) 4 East Asia Law Review 1. *Contra*, it is also mentioned in other literature that the outburst of litigation is not one of the reasons that ADR has been developing rapidly in China.

[32] Wang Guiguo and He Xiaoli, 'Mediation and International Investment: A Chinese Perspective' (2012) 65 Maine Law Review 216.

[33] China International Economic and Trade Arbitration Commission (CIETAC) Arbitration Rules 2012, Article 45.

In foreign investment settings, treaties and agreements that China entered into also encouraged amicable ways of settling disputes. In China's earlier BIT practices, state–state consultation has already been adopted as a method to resolve disputes arising between parties, an example of such a treaty is the BIT concluded between China and Botswana in the year 2000.[34] The evolution of such practice also continued in some of the recently signed treaties. For example, the China–New Zealand FTA asked investors to give three months' advance notice to the state party, and the purpose of this provision is to allow the host country to require the use of its domestic administrative review procedures. Under this administrative reconsideration process, the applicant can initiate an application by applying to the same level of government or higher level of government, or an administrative body that has failed to act. The applicant may also claim for administrative compensation while asking for administrative reconsideration. Different levels of government have also established complaint centres, mediation panels, and other forms of working panels to facilitate non-judicial means of resolving disputes with foreign investors, without the need of invoking external mechanisms such as treaty arbitration.

This practice has undergone some further development following the recent wave of responses to the deepening of the 'open door' policy and simplifying administrative procedures for foreign investors in order to improve foreign investment facilitation.[35] China's Ministry of Commerce (MOFCOM) has encouraged the use of mediation by having promulgated a special interim measure in 2006, the Interim Measures on Complaints from Foreign-Related Enterprises (Interim Measures).[36] Although the National Complaint Center and local Coordination Office do not seem to have established it successfully, the MOFCOM's determination was reinforced by the 2014 Draft of the Foreign Investment Law, which was supposed to be made into law within the next year or two. Regarding investor–state mediation, in the recent draft of the Foreign Investment Law, there is actually a provision dedicated to exploring means that help to resolve disputes between investors and government agencies. Although a literal reading of the law may suggest that the drafters have been contemplating disputes between foreign investors and local governments, it does not preclude the possibility that governments are interested in further exploring ways to avoid more intensive ISDS.

- Article 119. The State builds a *mechanism for coordinating* the handling and resolving foreign investment complaints, which shall be responsible for coordinating and handling of and resolving investment disputes between foreign investors and/or foreign invested enterprises and administrative organs.
- Article 120. The international investment promotion institution shall establish a national foreign investment complaints coordination and resolution center to coordinate the handling of and resolve major foreign investment complaints with a national influence.

---

[34] Agreement between the Government of the Republic of Botswana and the Government of the People's Republic of China on Promotion and Protection of Investments (adopted 12 June 2000) Article 8, Settlement of Disputes Between Contracting Parties, 'any dispute between the Contracting Parties concerning the interpretation or application of this Agreement Shall, as far as possible, be settled with consultation through diplomatic channels'.

[35] See Chapter 3, 'Recent Policy Developments and Key Issues' (United Nations Conference on Trade and Development (UNCTAD) World Investment Report 2016)

[36] Interim Provisions on Mergers and Acquisitions of Domestic Enterprises by Foreign Investors *(Ministry of Commerce People's Republic of China)* http://english.mofcom.gov.cn/article/policyrelease/Businessregulations/201303/20130300045825.shtml (last accessed 16 June 2017).

Therefore, mediation has its special appeal to both Chinese states and investors, and its practices are quite prevalent in China compared to many other forms of more judicialized ADR.

B. Proposals for incorporating investor–state mediation mechanism in China's next generation BITs

By proposing for an incorporation of investor–state mediation mechanism in China's next generation of BITs, the author of this chapter considers that a such mechanism should encompass a mediation model that is facilitative, compulsory, and institution assisted. Some detailed suggestions and analysis are discussed below:

1. Facilitative mediation

The debate between facilitative and evaluative mediation is a very old one. From a variety of sources, one usually gets the impression that, unlike its Western counterparts, evaluative mediation that is centred around a legal authority (usually a judge) is the golden standard in China.[37] It is true that alternative dispute resolution has not departed very far from traditional judicial means in many parts of China; however, many Westerners have had a wrong conception of the function of the judicial umpires, who have evolved to have more of a facilitative rather than an evaluative role.[38] Although it is true that in many Asian countries like China, where a particular aversion to adversarial procedures is still prevalent, arbitrators can be more energetic than their European and American counterparts in seeking to facilitate agreement among litigants, it is nowadays becoming much less common for them to try to impose solutions on parties to a dispute.[39] Recent literature also suggests that there is a functional switch of third party neutrals in mediation proceedings taking place in China, although many mediators are appointed to perform their roles due to their senior status in the professional communities, their methods of resolving disputes between parties have become far more amicable. Therefore, facilitative mediation is not only not unknown in China, but has also developed at a rapid pace and is seen as gradually being accepted by parties.[40]

In essence, facilitative mediation more resembles the mediation in the minds of dispute resolution designers, because a non-rights approach is often used here. For example, a long-time proponent of mediating investor–state disputes and mediation scholar Nancy Welsh suggested that the default mediation model should be presumptively facilitative and interests-based, thus allowing a third party neutral facilitating the parties' communication, information sharing and negotiation, which provides a more explicit opportunity to identify and focus on the discussion of interests rather than rights.[41] According to Professor Welsh, a process that begins facilitatively should enable the parties' mutual consideration of each other's perspectives and underlying needs,

---

[37] See Jarome Cohen, 'Chinese Mediation on the Eve of Modernization' (1996) 54 California Law Review 1201; Peerenhoom and He (n 31).

[38] Xin Xu, *Mediation in Comparative Perspective* (China University of Political Science and Law Press 2003) chs 15–21.

[39] Salacuse (n 4) 138, 168.

[40] Interim Provisions on Mergers and Acquisitions of Domestic Enterprises by Foreign Investors (n 36).

[41] Nancy Welsh and Andrea Kupfer Schneider, 'The Thoughtful Integration of Mediation into Bilateral Investment Treaty Arbitration' (2013) 18 Harvard Negotiation Law Review 71.

which offers investors and state ample opportunities to speak to each other, while being
able to listen to each other and make meaningful steps towards resolution.[42] Because of
the readily available option of arbitration, the facilitative model of mediation can offer
something presumptively interests-based and more novel and meaningful. It provides
a neutral third party to assist parties' negotiations rather than to impose a solution that
shows the parties' rights and wrongs. Importantly, this model of mediation should be
supplemented by some form of evaluative or interventionist measures that consider
the parties' legal rights.[43] Since the entire investor–state arbitration process has been
criticized as overly abused by lawyers and arbitrators who are increasingly 'judicializing'
the process, a facilitative method that improves trust-building between parties and information exchange regarding important underlying interests, but which 'also permits
both evaluative interventions by the mediator' and discussion of relevant legal authorities and principles is more likely to work in this investor–state context involving the
Chinese state.

2. Compulsory mediation

People have questioned why in the past mediation has not been frequently used in
the investor–state context. The very limited numbers of investor–state conciliations
that have been invoked probably suggests that, among other resources, mediation is
not going to work for investor–state cases if it is not made compulsory. On the other
hand, studies have shown that lawyers who are experienced in mediation are very likely
to recommend the use of mediation on a voluntary basis: it is not the case for parties
that do not possess similar skills in mediation settings. Therefore, the current low inci-
dence rate of voluntary usage of conciliation and mediation should probably be seen as
parties lacking familiarity with the mediation process, rather than parties' perceptions
of success rates of mediation proceedings or their willingness to do so. Research based
on the United States ADR system has shown that, in a typical mediation proceeding,
if judges utilize *referrals* frequently enough, repeat players are likely to perceive these
discretionary referrals as de facto categorical referrals to mediation, and are therefore
more likely to initiate the mechanism.[44] As in the United States, in China mediation
is frequently ordered by the courts and it is often perceived as mandatory, especially
in family matters and other matters involving small claims.[45] Therefore, in order to
promote more frequent uses of the investor–state mediation, it should be made compulsory in treaties.

One difficulty of making mediation compulsory is to ensure that sufficient time (but
not too much time) is allowed for mediation, before another proceeding (such as arbitration) is commenced. Experienced arbitral institutions can assist to fulfil this part of
the analysis. As pointed out by Professor Welsh, if an investor has worked with a lead
agency or pursued administrative review in compliance with a BIT's pre-arbitration requirements, and the investor then requests mediation with an independent third party
mediator (or requests a case conference or initial mediation session as described below),

[42] ibid.   [43] ibid.
[44] See Bobbi McAdoo and Nancy Welsh, 'Court-Connected General Civil ADR Programs: Aiming
for Institutionalization, Efficient Resolution, and the Experience of Justice' in Donna Stienstra
and Susan M Yates (eds), *ADR Handbook for Judges* (American Bar Association Section of Dispute
Resolution 2004).
[45] Interim Provisions on Mergers and Acquisitions of Domestic Enterprises by Foreign Investors
(n 36).

the BIT could compel the state or affected agency to comply with such a request. To balance the concerns that parties will walk away from mediation without accepting a binding written settlement requiring the parties to enter into an official settlement by providing guidelines of the process would be helpful.

3. *Institutional assistance*

Although China's recent BITs have shown a preference for ICSID, it might not be the most ideal forum for China to designate for its investor–state mediation provision. Some past proposals for reforming ICSID procedures to incorporate and promote mediation have been discussed, including having ICSID adding mediation procedures to its current dispute resolution process and having it informally suggest that users consider mediation at an early stage.[46] It is suggested that, although ICSID has tried to promote its conciliation procedures informally but that it has not had much success with its current alternatives to arbitration, some obstacles might be encountered were it to attempt to promote the use of conciliation procedures even further, just because its leadership and staff might misguidedly believe that mediation would be unpopular even if it were actively implemented.[47]

These challenges and criticisms that the institutions already administering investor–state arbitrations may face in providing alternatives to investor–state arbitration are very similar. Institutions like ICSID, the ICC, and the SCC—all well-known for their prominence in investor–state arbitration—already have mechanisms for resolving disputes by means other than arbitration, although there are few reports of parties using such mechanisms in investor–state disputes. However, one big difficulty faced by these institutions, for example, the ICSID, is that their panels of arbitrators and conciliators for the most part consist of individuals known for their arbitration skills instead of mediation skills, and it is very widely recognized that skills required by conciliators and arbitrators are very different.[48]

What about the possibility of having a state agency to lead this process by employing their own procedures and recommending third party neutrals? Although the Chinese state might have some preference for this method, as Professor Welsh mentioned in her article with the particular reference to Colombia's responsive agency, where a government agency responsible for the relationship between the investor and the government has already been set up, state officials leading these kinds of efforts have the potential to serve as 'quasi-mediators', making this format of mediation more of an integrated process resembling an administrative process.[49] If investors perceive these quasi-mediators as biased against the government (more likely) or themselves (less likely), these investors are less likely to agree to participate in this kind of process in the future. Since the state-led process is more subject to political and social pressure and therefore abuse, for obvious reasons, investors are more likely to perceive a mediation process involving an outside and neutral mediator as trustworthy.

Responding to the mediation trend, a couple of prominent Chinese arbitral institutions are also revolutionizing their rules to embrace mediation more. Important dispute resolution bodies, such as the China Council for the Promotion of International Trade (CCPIT) Mediation Centre in Beijing have started to conduct training programmes

---

[46] ibid.
[47] 'Mediation of Investor-State Conflicts' (2014) 127 Harvard Law Review 2543.
[48] Stevens and Love (n 25) 389.   [49] Welsh and Schneider (n 41) 71.

in modern commercial mediation processes as well as professionalizing its group of qualified mediators.[50] The Shanghai Commercial Mediation Centre(SCMC) was also established in the year of 2012 and the centre tries to focus solely on resolving business and investment disputes, especially those that are concerning foreign investors.[51]

At the same time, the Hong Kong SAR government and its Department of Justice (DOJ) have also a keen interest in making Hong Kong an important hub in China's foreign investment related One Belt One Road (OBOR) initiatives, by attracting more investment related claims to be settled in Hong Kong.[52] The SAR does have its traditional advantages in acting as a proper venue for resolving such disputes. Primarily, Hong Kong's judicial system remains relatively intact and strong even after the handover, which makes the place attractive both to Chinese and foreign states in the negotiation process. Recently, this status has only been reinforced by the *TNB Fuel Services SDN BHD v China National Coal Group Corporation* case (HKCFI 1016), in which the court held that a Chinese state-owned enterprise does not enjoy crown immunity in a relevant enforcement proceeding pursued by a Malaysian investor, further confirming Hong Kong's judicial independence principles.[53] Secondly, Hong Kong already has a well-balanced mediation tradition with mixed elements of the East and the West, and the SAR's Arbitration Ordinance leaves some important provisions out for different alternative dispute resolution methods to be tried out; thirdly, Hong Kong already hosts some of the most leading dispute resolution institutions including the Hong Kong International Arbitration Centre (HKIAC), which has the institutional knowledge and experiences of assisting parties in investor–state mediation proceedings, while being able to offer the safe pair of hands of the Secretariat as the appointing authority. The institution's appointment capacity is extremely important for parties who are new to investor–state processes, since for many years, a small group of people served as international arbitrators and an even smaller group served as mediators; they have earned their reputation and prestige by performing their roles extremely well. Generally, institutions are in the best position to bring this valuable group of people together, while constantly monitoring their performances to keep them up to standard. Therefore, with the effective assistance of institutions, the mediator selection process will become so much easier.

C. Obstacles of implementations

Here we have discussed possibilities of incorporating investor–state mediation mechanisms in China's future BIT talks, especially for investor–state disputes that are initiated against the Chinese state. However, a major obstacle to investor–state mediation arises from the incapacity of the state to make settlement decisions because of complicated internal governance structures. In response to Jack Coe's seminal article on investor–state mediation, Bart Legum placed particular emphasis on the multiplicity

---

[50] 'Inauguration Ceremony of Mainland' *(Hong Kong Joint Mediation Center)* http://www.mediationcentre.org.hk/en/CCPIT/CCPIT.php (last accessed 16 June 2017).

[51] Danny McFadden, 'Resolving Disputes in China Using Mediation' (2011) Business Disputes in China http://www.cedr-asia-pacific.com/cedr/uploads/articles/pdf/ARTICLE-20120116100514.pdf (last accessed 16 June 2017).

[52] See eg Kevin Sneader, 'China's One Belt One Road is the Perfect Stage for Hong Kong to Showcase its Strength', *South China Morning Post* (Hong Kong, 17 May 2016) http://www.scmp.com/comment/insight-opinion/article/1946161/chinas-one-belt-one-road-perfect-stage-hong-kong-showcase (last accessed 16 June 2017)

[53] *TNB Fuel Services SDN BHD v China National Coal Group Corporation Case*, HCCT 23/2015.

of government agencies often needed to agree to a mediated settlement in an investor–state mediation.[54] For example, the government agencies involved in the dispute often require a legislative act or approval from another government agency to either enter into a settlement or make a payment on a settlement. Where an agency has the authority to enter into the settlement, internal struggles over which agency is responsible for the settlement could arise. This obstacle also exists in China. Right now, the Ministry of Commerce is the government authority responsible for negotiating treaties on behalf of the Chinese state. Similarly, the same department within the MOFCOM is also the responsive authority when an investor from another state files a claim against China. Currently, the MOFCOM started to engage in a bidding process to select the best law firms to represent the Chinese state in investment-related claims, and maintains a list of foreign and domestic law firms that serve as its 'legal consultants'.[55] Although it is possible for the MOFCOM to continue to take the lead in mediation, the facilitative manner of the dispute resolution resolving process usually means that the Ministry will need to take a more active approach during the dispute resolution proceeding by directly participating in dealings and bargaining with the investors, and will therefore be less successful in relocating the blame if mediation efforts fail. With the current government hierarchy structure in China, the MOFCOM might need some additional momentum to agree to develop this method.

Another obstacle of investor–state mediation that many commentators have surmised is that it will lack an enforcement mechanism akin to that provided for in the New York or Washington Conventions accounts for the infrequent use of alternatives to investor–state arbitration. As Eric van Ginkel remarked, if the settlement were to provide for monetary consideration in favour of the investor, the investor would have no better assurance that the state will recognize and fulfil its obligations under the settlement agreement than it had when the state entered into the investment agreement.[56] This concern remains valid and has inspired at least one prominent practitioner to remark in confidence about the 'pointlessness' of formal investor–state conciliation processes. However, even with the Washington Convention in place the ICSID enforcement procedure is no better relief for parties, resulting in some cases taking more than ten years in the enforcement proceedings.[57]

In addition to those, there are surely many other perceived deficiencies to investor–state mediation proceedings. Fortunately, more and more states have recognized the benefits of early settlement of investor–state claims and have thought of using some forms of third party intervention to serve as a cure. However, we must also recognize that, as a whole, the investor–state mediation mechanism is not often invoked by parties, whatever the reasons offered to explain such a phenomenon. In general, interest-based approaches like mediation seem to have presented a less predictable way of settling disputes, at least in the eyes of states. Therefore, investor–state mediation has never been considered as a sole method of resolving investment disputes, and is

---

[54] Stevens and Love (n 25) 389.

[55] See Ministry of Commerce's Candidate list of Law Firms Sub List for International Investment Foreign Law Firms Bid Winning Announcement (*Ministry of Commerce People's Republic of China*) http://www.mofcom.gov.cn/article/cwgongzuo/jingmaoluntan/zhongbiao/201510/20151001151161.shtml (last accessed 16 June 2017).

[56] Stevens and Love (n 25) 389.

[57] Ben Knowles, Khaled Moyeed, and Nefeli Lamprou, 'The US $50 Billion Yukus Enforcement Award Overturned – Enforcement Becomes a Game of Russian Roulette' (*Kluwer Arbitration Blog*, 13 May 2016) http://kluwerarbitrationblog.com/2016/05/13/the-us50-billion-yukos-award-overturned-enforcement-becomes-a-game-of-russian-roulette/ (last accessed 16 June 2017).

recommended to be used in conjunction with other more rights based approaches to be more effective.

III. A Preliminary Conclusion: A Return to Political Dispute Resolution Means to the International Legal System or Improved Dispute Resolution Design?

Investment disputes concerning China are on the rise. Given China's formidable growth in inbound and outbound investment, it certainly has the economic potential to influence the development of international investment law's practice now and in future. At the same time, the world of international investment law is full of unpredictability caused by changing political and economic leadership. It is investment rights ought to be determined by established principle of investment law operating prospectively, rather than by geopolitical and economic interests that circumscribe those principles and their application. From the beginning, investment law issues are never purely legal issues and are unlikely to be resolved solely by professionals who only apply legal principles. This is especially difficult for existing ICSID tribunals, which are mostly composed of people with little Asian experience, in order to apply common norms of investment law to different kinds of expropriation in investment contexts that are complicated by cultural and ideological differences as they relate to China.[58]

A more balanced approach of resolving investor–state dispute has long been called for. Traditional diplomatic approaches of resolving international disputes have their advantages; however, at least two issues need to be addressed to rectify procedural deficiencies of traditional investor–state disputes, intervention of third parties to facilitate two sides in settling, and effective enforcement of awards. Old theories hold that parties with different bargaining powers are unlikely to reach settlement in international disputes, which has led to the shape of today's ISDS mechanism. The political nature of the dispute, public interests at stake, etc, have not been properly contemplated by the drafters. However, with the parties' intentions to continue to conduct economic and trade activities across the globe, dispute resolution design theories have been compelling us to think further of some hybrid method of diplomatic methods and judicialized methods, and investor–state mediation seems to offer us some thoughts to consider. Applying traditional dispute system design theory to the field of investor–state disputes reveals that the currently dominant system for resolving investor–state disputes relies explicitly on one method in the 'imposed category'—'binding arbitration'. Owing to currently existing problems within the present system, the next generation of dispute system design features more of the preventive measures, which describes a system that consists of: (1) multiple process options for parties; (2) ability for the parties to 'loop back' and 'look forward' among these options; (3) substantial stakeholder involvement in the system design; (4) voluntary participation; (5) system transparency and accountability; and (6) education and training of stakeholders on the use of available process options.[59] Compared to arbitration, a very strong advantage

[58] Trakman (n 26).
[59] See eg Stephanie Smith and Jan Martinez, 'An Analytical Framework for Dispute System Design' (2009) 14 Harvard Negotiation Law Review 123, 128; Carrie Menkel-Meadow, 'Peace and Justice: Notes on the Evolution and Purposes of Legal Process' (2006) 94 Georgetown Law Review 553, 554–6; John Lande, 'Getting the Faith: Why Business Lawyers and Executives Believe in Mediation' (2000) 5 Harvard Negotiation Law Review, 137, 147–50.

of mediation is that in mediation disputing parties retain almost complete autonomy of the dispute resolution process, which represents a movement from power-based to rights-based and eventually to interest-based approaches, not vice versa. Recent dispute resolution theory suggests that, rather than solely focusing on rights, the best dispute system simply includes an interest-based process, and parties may begin with that process while looping forward or backward among that available process.[60] Therefore, integrating mediation into the investment treaty context would provide investors and states with the opportunity to resolve their disputes through a process that provides for explicit consideration of their interests, rather than eliminating the consideration of their rights.[61] Because parties directly participate in the communication and negotiation during mediation, for the investor–state process this method has the potential of resolving the disputes more fairly and efficiently as less legal issues are at the core of the discussion. To take a step further, it also does not run counter to the recent transparency call in reforming ISDS mechanisms. The call for transparency arises in investor–state proceedings from inherent failures of the process itself, and is not exactly relevant in investor–state mediation when more parties can easily participate in the process by participating in the co-conciliation process. Therefore, it might be of less concern in investor–state mediation proceedings.

As Professor Welsh has suggested, although the current investment treaty arbitration has definitely improved 'gunboat diplomacy' used at times to address disputes between investors and sovereign states, mediation has been called upon as a supplementary mechanism to investor–state arbitration, rather than to replace it. Owing to the recent rise of China's economic position and its stated ambition of further leading the global investment order, the recommendation that the integration of a compulsory mediation mechanism in the facilitative measure and is administered by an existing institution is feasible, and can be required by a mandatory clause in China's next generation BITs.

---

[60] Welsh and Schneider (n 4) 86, 94.   [61] ibid.

Index

Tables and figures are indicated by an italic t and f following the page number